P9-CAO-314

How to Use This Book

Teach Yourself Mac C++ Programming in 21 Days has two major goals: to teach you how to program in C++ and to teach you how to create Macintosh applications using Symantec C++. It uses some special features to guide you on your journey.

This book contains 21 chapters, one for each study day. Each day ends with a Q&A section containing answers to common questions related to the day's material. There is also a workshop at the end of each day which contains a quiz and exercises. The quiz tests your knowledge of the concepts presented that day, and the exercises put your new skills to use.

Syntax sections help you master a specific Symantec C++ topic. Note, Warning, and DO/DON'T boxes point out special considerations on the current subject, and new terms are highlighted and collected in a glossary at the end of the book.

The listings in this book are available from the author for those readers who want to save the time of typing them (see the order form in the back of the book).

This book will enable you to step boldly into the world of programming. It's an exciting world that gives you more control over what your machine does. Happy programming!

Conventions Used in This Book

This book uses various typefaces to help you differentiate between Symantec C++ code and regular English, and also to help you identify important concepts. Actual Symantec C++ code is typeset in a special monospace font. Placeholders—terms used to represent what you actually type within the code—are typeset in an *italic monospace* font. New or important terms are typeset in *italic*.

There are three flavors of listings in this book, and each type is denoted by a special icon next to the listing's heading.

Type This icon indicates that you are to type all the code in the listing.

VArc This icon indicates that the Visual Architect utility automatically generates the code for you, and you don't type any of the code in the listing.

VArc Type This icon indicates that the listing contains code generated automatically by the Visual Architect utility *and* code that you need to type. The lines of code you are to type are presented in a **bold monospace** font.

Teach Yourself
Mac C++
Programming

in 21 Days

Teach Yourself
Mac C++
Programming
in 21 Days

Namir Clement Shammas

PUBLISHING

201 West 103rd Street, Indianapolis, Indiana 46290

To my dear friend Ponnam,
whose soul never stops growing.

Copyright © 1994 by Sams Publishing

FIRST EDITION

All rights reserved. No part of this book shall be reproduced, stored in a retrieval system, or transmitted by any means, electronic, mechanical, photocopying, recording, or otherwise, without written permission from the publisher. No patent liability is assumed with respect to the use of the information contained herein. Although every precaution has been taken in the preparation of this book, the publisher and author assume no responsibility for errors or omissions. Neither is any liability assumed for damages resulting from the use of the information contained herein. For information, address Sams Publishing, 201 W. 103rd St., Indianapolis, IN 46290.

International Standard Book Number: 0-672-30610-7

Library of Congress Catalog Card Number: 94-67504

97 96 95 94   4 3 2 1

Interpretation of the printing code: the rightmost double-digit number is the year of the book's printing; the rightmost single-digit, the number of the book's printing. For example, a printing code of 94-1 shows that the first printing of the book occurred in 1994.

Composed in AGaramond and MCPdigital by Macmillan Computer Publishing

Printed in the United States of America

Trademarks

All terms mentioned in this book that are known to be trademarks or service marks have been appropriately capitalized. Sams Publishing cannot attest to the accuracy of this information. Use of a term in this book should not be regarded as affecting the validity of any trademark or service mark.

Publisher
Richard K. Swadley

Associate Publisher
Jordan Gold

Acquisitions Manager
Stacy Hiquet

Managing Editor
Cindy Morrow

Acquisitions Editor
Grace Buechlein

Development Editor
Stacy Hiquet

**Production and
Copy Editor**
Kristi Hart

Editorial Coordinator
Bill Whitmer

Editorial Assistants
Carol Ackerman
Sharon Cox
Lynette Quinn

Technical Reviewer
Bob Zigon

Marketing Manager
Gregg Bushyeager

Cover Designer
Dan Armstrong

Book Designer
Alyssa Yesh

**Director of
Production and
Manufacturing**
Jeff Valler

Imprint Manager
Juli Cook

**Manufacturing
Coordinator**
Paul Gilchrist

Production Analysts
Dennis Clay Hager
Mary Beth Wakefield

**Graphics Image
Specialists**
Stacey Beheler
Teresa Forrester
Clint Lahnen
Tim Montgomery
Dennis Sheehan
Greg Simsic
Susan Vande Walle

Page Layout
Elaine Brush
Steph Davis
Rob Falco
Angela P. Judy
Ayanna Lacey
Chad Poore
Casey Price
Kim Scott
Marc Shecter
Susan Shepard
Scott Tullis

Proofreading
Mona Brown
Ayrika Bryant
Amanda Byus
Cheryl Cameron
Kimberly K. Hannel
Greg Kemp
Brian-Kent Proffitt
Sharon Provart
Linda Quigley
Beth Rago
S A Springer

Indexer
Jeanne Clark

Overview

Appendixes

Contents

Day	2	**C++ Program Components**	**35**

Day   16   The Static Text Control   449

Day   17   The Edit Box and Button Controls   495

Acknowledgments

I would like to thank many people at Sams for encouraging me and working with me on this project. First, I would like to thank Publisher Richard Swadley and Associate Publisher Jordan Gold for their support. Many thanks also to Acquisitions Editor Grace Buechlein, Development Editor Stacy Hiquet, Production and Copy Editor Kristi Hart, and Technical Editor Bob Zigon for their first-class work. Thanks to all who participated in producing this book.

About the Author

Namir Clement Shammas is a software engineer and an expert in object-oriented programming. He has written many articles for leading computer magazines and is responsible for many books on computer programming, including *Turbo Pascal 6 Object-Oriented Programming*, *Windows Programmer's Guide to ObjectWindows Library*, and *Teach Yourself QBasic in 21 Days*.

Introduction

Teach Yourself Mac C++ Programming in 21 Days has two major goals: to teach you how to program in C++ and to teach you how to create Macintosh applications using Symantec C++. No prior programming experience is required. However, knowing how to program in other languages, such as BASIC or Pascal, certainly helps. This book is not for the faint-hearted, because learning to program in C++ and to write Macintosh applications in C++ are two non-trivial tasks.

This book relies on the new Visual Architect utility to create Macintosh programs that support the graphical user interface (GUI). Through visual programming techniques, this utility empowers you to create Macintosh programs with much ease. By using the Visual Architect utility and the new version of the THINK Class Library, you can write Macintosh programs quickly and efficiently.

This book contains 21 chapters, one for each study day. The material is somewhat fast-paced because of the goals of the book. Each chapter concludes with a Q&A section, a quiz section, and an exercise section. Appendix B contains the answers to the quizzes and some of the exercises.

Day 1 gives you a brief tour of the Symantec C++ THINK Project Manager, the environment you'll use to develop C++ programs. You also write your first C++ program, which demonstrates the basic components of a non-GUI C++ program for the Macintosh.

Day 2 examines C++ program components in more detail and discusses naming and declaring variables, constants, and functions. It also focuses on C++ functions because they are important program building blocks.

Day 3 presents the various C++ operators and expressions. Operators enable you to manipulate data and to form expressions that support more complex data manipulation.

Day 4 discusses formatted stream input and output. You also learn about the famous printf function, which supports versatile formatted output.

Day 5 covers C++ decision-making constructs. These constructs include the various kinds of if statements as well as the switch statement.

Day 6 discusses C++ loops which include the for, do-while, and while loops. In addition, you learn how to use the for loop as an open loop as well as how to skip loop iterations, exit loops, and nest loops.

Day 7 presents arrays in C++. You learn about both single-dimensional and multidimensional arrays as well as how to declare them and initialize them. In addition, you learn about sorting and searching single-dimensional arrays.

Day 8 discusses user-defined types and pointers. You learn about enumerated data types, structures, unions, reference variables, and pointers. You also learn how to declare and use pointers with simple variables, arrays, structures, and dynamic memory.

Day 9 focuses on strings and the STRING.H library that is inherited from C. You learn about topics that include assigning, concatenating, comparing, converting, and reversing strings. You also learn how to search for characters and substrings in strings.

Day 10 presents advanced function parameters and focuses mainly on parameters that are arrays, strings, structures, and pointers to functions. You also learn about the various ways to pass structures as parameters and about recursive functions.

Day 11 introduces you to the world of object-oriented programming (OOP). You learn about the basics of OOP and about C++ classes. You also learn what the basic components of a C++ class are, as well as the rules related to using these components.

Day 12 discusses the basic stream file I/O that is supported by the C++ stream library. You learn about the common stream functions, sequential text stream I/O, sequential binary stream I/O, and random-access stream I/O.

Day 13 introduces you to programming Macintosh applications using the THINK Class Library (TCL). The chapter includes a brief overview of TCL classes as well as coverage of popular data types, Macintosh messages, and managing Macintosh commands.

Day 14 presents the Visual Architect utility. This utility plays a vital role in simplifying the process of creating Macintosh programs. In this chapter, you learn how to use the Visual Architect utility to create new commands, menus, menu items, controls, and dialog boxes.

Day 15 presents very simple TCL-based Macintosh applications. You begin the day by creating a minimal TCL program and then enhance it to include menus and responses to mouse clicks.

Day 16 focuses on creating text in a window using static text controls. You learn how to alter the font style, size, and alignment of static text controls at runtime.

Day 17 presents the TCL classes that support the edit controls and pushbutton controls. The chapter also presents examples that use the above controls and demonstrate some of their basic operations.

Day 18 presents the TCL classes that model the check box and radio controls. You learn how to use these controls and how to group the radio controls.

Day 19 covers the TCL class that models list box controls. The chapter discusses single-selection list boxes. An example teaches you how to create list boxes that display strings.

Day 20 presents the TCL library classes that model the scroll bar and the pop-up menu pane. A simple timer example illustrates using the scroll bar and includes a simple menu-item selection that uses the pop-up menu pane.

Day 21 focuses on creating and using dialog boxes. You learn how to define dialog boxes using the Visual Architect utility. An example illustrates creating and using your own message dialog box and creating and using an interactive dialog box. With the interactive dialog box, you learn how to support a two-way data transfer between the controls of the dialog box and the data members of the supporting class.

Appendix A introduces you to the resource statements used to create menus, windows, controls, and dialog boxes.

In the back of the book, you'll find an offer for the companion disk that includes the source code and the project files for all the days' lessons.

I hope that this book empowers you to boldly step into the world of programming the Macintosh.

1

M T W R F S

AT A GLANCE

1

2

3

4

5

6

7

The first week of your journey into learning to write Macintosh applications starts with an introduction to the THINK Project Manager in Day 1. The remaining days in this week present the basic components of the C++ language itself. You learn about predefined data types; naming constants, variables, and functions; C++ operators and expressions; managing basic input and output; making decisions; writing loops; and declaring and using arrays.

Getting Started

Welcome to the world of C++ and Macintosh programming. Your journey into this exciting venture begins today! Most of the information in today's lesson familiarizes you with the Symantec THINK Project Manager. You learn about the following topics:

☐ The basics and history of C++ programs

☐ Loading and using the THINK Project Manager

☐ The various menus in the THINK Project Manager

☐ Typing and running your first C++ program

The Basics of C++ Programs

You don't need any previous experience in programming to learn Symantec C++ with this book, but if you have programmed before, things will be easier. As with other languages, C++ is made up of declarations and statements that specify exact instructions to be executed when the program runs.

C++ was developed by Bjarn Stroustrup at Bell Labs. The language is meant to supersede and build on the popular C language, mainly by adding object-oriented language extensions.

NEW TERM An *object-oriented language* represents the attributes and operations of objects.

In addition, C++ offers a number of enhancements to C that are not object-oriented. Thus, learning C++ gives you the bonus of becoming very familiar with C. However, unlike C, which has been standardized, C++ is still undergoing the standardization process.

Programming in C++ requires you to learn about the supporting libraries, which perform various tasks such as input/output, text manipulation, math operations, file I/O (input/output), and so on. In languages such as BASIC, support for such operations is transparent to programs, meaning that it is automatically available to these programs. As a result, many programs come across as single components that are independent of any other programming components. By contrast, programming in C++ makes you more aware of a program's dependency on various libraries. The advantage of this language feature is that you are able to select between similar libraries, including ones that you develop. Thus, C++ programs are modular. C++ compilers, including Symantec C++, use project files and program files. The Symantec C++ THINK Project Manager uses project files to manage the creation and updating of a program.

NEW ☞ *Project files* specify the library. *Program files* create an application.
TERM

Loading the THINK Project Manager

The THINK Project Manager is the visual interface for the C++ compiler, linker, debugger, and other tools that are used to create, manage, and maintain C++ programs. You can load the THINK Project Manager by clicking the THINK Project Manager icon in the Development folder.

An Overview of the THINK Project Manager

The THINK Project Manager contains a menu bar, shown in Figure 1.1, which enables you to manage the various aspects of a C or C++ program project.

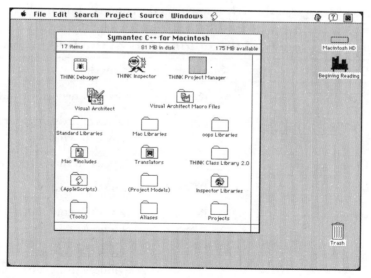

Figure 1.1. *The THINK Project Manager's menu bar.*

Note: Because the THINK Project Manager is meant to accommodate software developers, many of the options will seem advanced to you if you are a novice programmer. However, you need only a basic familiarity with the options and their related terms. As you become more experienced, these options and terms will become a routine part of your knowledge as a Symantec C++ programmer.

The Apple Menu

The Apple menu contains the About THINK Project Manager command (as well as other menus that may vary from one system to another) which tells you the version of the THINK Project Manager.

The File Menu

The File menu provides commands to manage files, to print text, and to exit the THINK Project Manager. Table 1.1 summarizes the commands in the File menu.

Table 1.1. Summary of the commands in the File menu.

Command	Shortcut Key	Function
New	⌘N	Opens a new edit window.
Open...	⌘O	Loads an existing source-code file into a new edit window.
Open Selection	⌘D	Opens an included header file.
Close	⌘W	Closes a window.
Save	⌘S	Saves the contents of the active edit window.
Save As...		Saves the contents of the active edit window using a new filename.
Save A Copy As...		Saves all the opened source-code windows in their respective files.

Command	Shortcut Key	Function
Revert		Restores the last saved version of the current file.
Page Setup...		Sets up the printed page.
Print...	⌘P	Prints the contents of a source code window.
Modify Read-Only		Enables you to modify a file marked as read-only by the SourceServer or the MPW Projector.
Quit	⌘Q	Exits the THINK Project Manager.

The New Command

The New command opens a new untitled edit window. The newly opened window is initially empty. Although you can save this file using any valid Macintosh name, you need to use a filename with an extension defined on the Extensions page (in the THINK Project Manager Options dialog box; see the section titled "The Options Command" later in this chapter) in order to compile the file in a project.

> **Note:** It is important to point out that the THINK Project Manager shows the New Project... command instead of the New command when you first load the THINK Project Manager or when there is no project loaded. This command enables you to open a new project and specify its type.

The Open... Command

The Open... command enables you to load the contents of an existing source code file into a new edit window. In fact, the THINK Project Manager can load multiple files. The option invokes the Open File dialog box, shown in Figure 1.2. The dialog box enables you to locate the source-code file and then select it. The dialog box permits you to browse through the existing drives and folders to locate the source-code file you seek.

> **Note:** It is important to point out that the THINK Project Manager shows the Open Project... command instead of the Open... command when you first load the THINK Project Manager or when there is no project loaded. This command enables you to open an existing project.

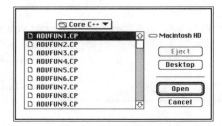

Figure 1.2. *The Open File dialog box.*

The Open Selection Command

The Open Selection command enables you to open an included header file (header files that contain special declarations are typically incorporated in implementation files using special include directives).

The Close Command

The Close command enables you to close the active window. The THINK Project Manager prompts you, with a dialog box, to save any modified edit window that has not yet been saved.

The Save Command

The Save command assists you in saving the contents of the active edit window to its associated file. If you invoke this command while editing an existing file, the file automatically is saved with its current name. If you invoke this command with a new edit window, the Save command invokes the Save File As dialog box, where you can specify the filename as well as the destination drive and folder.

The Save As... Command

The Save As... command enables you to save the contents of the active edit window in a file that is different from the currently associated file. In fact, the new filename becomes the new associated file for the active edit window. The Save As... command invokes the Save File As dialog box, shown in Figure 1.3. If you select an existing file, the option brings up a message dialog box to ask you if you wish to overwrite the contents of the existing file with those of the active edit window.

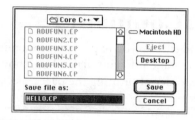

Figure 1.3. *The Save File As dialog box.*

The Save Copy As... Command

The Save Copy As... command writes the current contents of the active window to a separate file. This command does not change the filename associated with the currently active window.

The Revert Command

The Revert command restores the last version of the file that you saved. This command also discards the recent updates you made to the files since the last time you saved its contents.

The Page Setup... Command

The Page Setup... command displays the Page Setup dialog box, shown in Figure 1.4, where you can specify the size of the printed paper and the output orientation (tall or wide orientation).

Figure 1.4. *The Page Setup dialog box.*

The Print... Command

The Print... command enables you to print the contents of the active edit window. This command invokes the standard Print dialog box, shown in Figure 1.5, where you can select the page range, order of printing the pages, as well as other options.

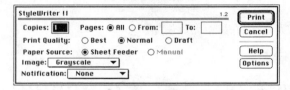

Figure 1.5. *The Print dialog box.*

The Modify Read-Only Command

The Modify Read-Only command empowers you to modify a file that has been marked as read-only by the SourceServer or the MPW Projector. The THINK Project Manager makes this command available only when you turn on the Project-Aware option in the Editor page of the THINK Project Manager Options dialog box (see the section titled "The Options Command" later in this chapter).

The Quit Command

The Quit command exits the C++ THINK Project Manager altogether. The THINK Project Manager prompts you for any modified edit window that has not been saved.

The Edit Menu

The Edit menu contains commands that enable you to edit the text in the edit windows. Table 1.2 summarizes the commands in the Edit menu.

Table 1.2. Summary of the commands in the Edit menu.

Command	Shortcut Key	Function
Undo	⌘Z	Undoes the last editing action.
Cut	⌘X	Deletes the selected text and copies it to the clipboard. The previous contents of the clipboard are lost.
Copy	⌘C	Copies the selected text to the clipboard. The previous contents of the clipboard are lost.
Paste	⌘V	Inserts the contents of the clipboard at the current cursor location.
Clear		Deletes selected text, but does not write it to the clipboard.
Select All	⌘A	Selects all the text in the active window.
Options		Controls the options for the THINK Project Manager, object code, C++ compiler, C compiler, and resource editor.
Set Tabs & Fonts...		Sets the tab stops and selects the fonts.
Shift Left	⌘[	Moves the selected text block to the left, deleting leading spaces and tab characters.
Shift Right	⌘]	Moves the selected text block to the right, inserting tab characters.
Balance	⌘B	Balance parentheses, brackets, and braces by finding their counterpart character in the source code.

The Undo Command

The Undo command enables you to reverse the effect of the last editing task and restore the contents of the active edit window. The shortcut for this command is ⌘Z. This command enables you to quickly and efficiently deal with editing errors—especially after working long hours.

The Cut Command

The Cut command deletes selected text and places it in the clipboard. The previous contents of the clipboard are lost. The shortcut for the Cut command is ⌘X.

The Copy Command

The Copy command copies the selected text into the clipboard. The previous contents of the clipboard are lost. The shortcut for the Copy command is ⌘C.

The Paste Command

The Paste command inserts the contents of the clipboard at the current insertion point. The contents of the clipboard remain unaffected. Thus you can use the Cut and Paste commands to move text in the same edit window or across different edit windows. You can use the Copy and Paste commands also to duplicate blocks of text in the same edit window or across different edit windows. The shortcut for the Paste command is ⌘V.

The Clear Command

The Clear command clears the selected text without copying it to the clipboard. This does not mean that the deleted text is irreversibly lost, because you can use the Undo command to undelete that text.

The Select All Command

The Select All command selects all the lines in the currently active window. The shortcut for this command is ⌘A.

The Options Command

The Options command enables you to control the behavior of the THINK Project Manager, including how its translator compiles your code. The command displays a nested menu that contains the following commands:

Command	Function
THINK Project Manager...	Invokes a versatile dialog box that enables you to set the options for preferences, editor, debugging, extensions, and project window. Consult the *THINK C User's Guide*, which is part of the Symantec C++ package, for more details regarding the paged dialog box displayed by this command.
.o Convert...	Controls the object code options.
Symantec C++...	Controls the C++ compiler options.
THINK C...	Controls the C compiler options.
THINK Rez...	Controls the C++ resource editor options.

The Set Tabs & Font... Command

The Set Tabs & Font... command enables you to set and alter the tab stops and the font of the source code. Figure 1.6 shows a sample session with the Font/Tabs dialog box.

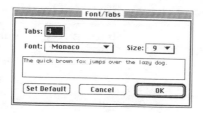

Figure 1.6. *The Font/Tabs dialog box.*

The Shift Left Command

The Shift Left command shifts a group of selected lines to the left. The command also deletes the first character in each line if that character is a tab. The shortcut for the Paste command is ⌘[.

The Shift Right Command

The Shift Right command shifts a group of selected lines to the right. The command also inserts a tab at the beginning of each shifted line. The shortcut for the Paste command is ⌘].

The Balance Command

The Balance command enables you to match text enclosed in parentheses ( ), brackets [ ], and braces { }. C and C++ programs use these characters in declaring various kinds of components. The Balance command enables you to find the matching closure character—a feature that is very convenient in a long listing. The shortcut for this command is ⌘B.

The Search Menu

The Search menu contains commands that enable you to locate various kinds of information, such as text, bookmarks, and program-building errors. Table 1.3 summarizes the commands in the Search menu.

Table 1.3. Summary of the commands in the Search menu.

Command	Shortcut Key	Function
Find...	⌘F	Searches for text in the active edit window.
Enter Selection	⌘E	Repeats the last Find or Replace operation.
Find Again	⌘G	Finds the next occurrence of the search string.

Command	Shortcut Key	Function
Replace...	⌘=	Replaces text in the active source-code window.
Replace & Find Again		Replaces the next match of the search string, and then finds another match of the search string.
Replace All		Replaces all matching search string occurrences with the replacement string.
Find In Next File		Finds the search string in the next file.
Find In THINK Reference	⌘-	Finds the topic in the THINK Reference that matches the symbol containing the cursor.
Go to Line...	⌘,	Goes to a line number.
Mark...	⌘M	Places a marker in a file.
Remove Marker...		Removes markers from a file.
Go To Next Error	⌘´	Selects the next program-building message and places the cursor at the offending line in an edit window.
Go To Previous Error	⌘`	Selects the previous program-building message and places the cursor at the offending line in an edit window.

The Find... Command

The Find... command supports searches for text in the active edit window as well as other project source files. This command, which has the shortcut ⌘F, brings up the Find dialog box, shown in Figure 1.7. This dialog box has the following controls:

Search for	This edit box enables you either to type in the search text or to recall text recently used for a search.
Replace with	This edit box enables you either to type in the replacement text or to recall text recently used for a replacement.
Entire Word	This check box enables you to choose between matching entire words or matching any text. The default setting for this command is off.
Wrap Around	This check box enables you to search/replace in the entire file, instead of limiting the search/replace from the current cursor location. The default setting for this command is off.
Ignore Case	This check box enables you to select case-sensitive or case-insensitive text search. The default setting for this command is on.
Grep	This check box turns on or off the use of the regular expressions feature. Such expressions result in using the text in the Search for control as the text pattern. The default setting for this command is off.
Multi-File Search	This check box turns on or off searching and replacing text in multiple files. The default setting for this command is off.
Batch Search	This check box enables you to find and display all the matching occurrences of the search text pattern. This command is disabled if the Multi-File Search check box is unchecked. The default setting for this command is off.
Exclude <System> Files	This check box determines whether or not to search through the files that are in the THINK Project Manager tree. This command is disabled if the Multi-File Search check box is unchecked. The default setting for this command is off.

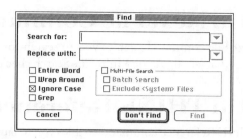

Figure 1.7. *The Find dialog box.*

The Enter Selection Command

The Enter Selection command assigns a new search string to the current selection, and it also clears the Grep and Multi-File Search check boxes. Use the Find Again command to resume searching. The shortcut for the Enter command is ⌘E.

The Find Again Command

The Find Again command searches for the next occurrence of the currently specified search string. The shortcut for the Find Again command is ⌘G.

The Replace Command

The Replace command supports replacing text in the active edit window. The Replace command uses the settings of the Find dialog box (invoked with the Find command). The shortcut for this command is ⌘=.

The Replace & Find Again Command

The Replace & Find Again command enables you to replace the current selection with the replacement string, and then it finds the next occurrence of the search string. The shortcut for this command is ⌘H.

The Replace All Command

The Replace All command enables you to replace all strings that match the search string with the replacement string. The check boxes of the Find dialog box determine the extent of the text replacement, which can include the contents of the entire file or multiple files.

The Find in Next File Command

The Find in Next File command enables you to search for text in multiple files. This command requires that you mark the Multi-File Search check box in the Find dialog box.

The Find in THINK Reference Command

The Find in THINK Reference command enables you to launch the THINK Reference (if it isn't already open) or to select it (if it is already open). You can obtain information related to the symbol that contains the cursor location when you invoked the command.

The Go to Line... Command

The Go to Line command brings up the simple Go To dialog box, where you can enter a line number. The shortcut for this command is ⌘,.

The Mark... Command

The Mark... command enables you to insert a marker (or bookmark, if you prefer) in a file. This command brings up the simple Mark dialog box, shown in Figure 1.8, where you can enter the marker name. The THINK Project Manager associates the marker with the current line or with the selected text (if such text exists). The shortcut for this command is ⌘M. To jump to the marker, hold down the Command key (⌘) and click the title bar of the edit window. This action brings up a pop-up menu of the file's markers.

Figure 1.8. *The Mark dialog box.*

The Remove Marker... Command

The Remove Marker... command enables you to remove markers from a file. This command brings up the Remove Markers dialog box, shown in Figure 1.9, which lists the current markers. You can remove one or more selected markers by clicking on the Remove button.

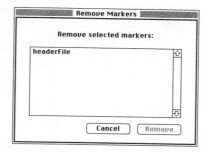

1

Figure 1.9. *The Remove Markers dialog box.*

The Go To Next Error Command

The Go To Next Error command enables you to zoom in on the offending source-code line that is associated with the next error message. The THINK Project Manager responds to this command by displaying the edit window that contains the offending source-code line. The shortcut for this command is ⌘´.

The Go To Previous Error Command

The Go To Previous error command enables you to zoom in on the offending source-code line that is associated with the previous error message. The THINK Project Manager responds to this command by displaying the edit window that contains the offending source-code line. The shortcut for this command is ⌘`.

The Project Menu

The Project menu provides commands to run your program and to start the Symantec Debugger for Macintosh applications. Table 1.4 summarizes the commands in the Project menu.

Table 1.4. Summary of the commands in the Project menu.

Command	Shortcut Key	Function
Close Project		Closes the current project and prompts you to open a new one.
Close & Compact		Same as Close Project, except it also compacts the source code.
Switch To Project		Selects another project that you previously opened in the current session with the THINK Project Manager.
Set Project Type...		Enables you to create an application, desk accessory, device driver, or code resource.
Remove Objects		Purges binary files generated by the compiler and the linker.
Bring Up To Date	⌘U	Updates the compiled files and loads libraries to update the project.
Check Link	⌘L	Similar to the Run command except it does not run the application.
Build Application...		Builds the current project as an application.
Use Debugger		Toggles using the debugger when running the application.
Run	⌘R	Runs the application.

The Close Project Command

The Close Project command closes the current project and enables you to open either a new or an existing project. The THINK Project Manager prompts you to save any updated project files what have not yet been saved.

The Close & Compact Command

The Close & Compact command closes the current project, like the Close Project command, using as little storage space as possible.

DO	**DON'T**

DO use the Close & Compact command to shrink the size of your project files before distributing them on disk or before sending them to an electronic bulletin board or a computer network.

DON'T forget to back up your project files.

The Switch To Project Command

The Switch To Project command invokes a dynamic pop-up menu that contains the names of existing projects. This menu holds the names of the projects you opened with the THINK Project Manager in the current session.

The Set Project Type... Command

The Set Project Type... command enables you to set the kind of programming project by invoking the Application dialog box, shown in Figure 1.10. The default kind of project is Application. You can select Desk Accessory, Device Driver, or Code Resource. Most of this book's programs use the default setting. The dialog box contains controls that enable you to fine-tune the creation of the program's executable code. These options might be a bit advanced for you, so you can just use the default settings for this book.

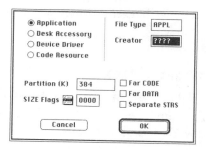

Figure 1.10. *The Application dialog box.*

The Remove Objects Command

The Remove Objects command eliminates the object code (the code generated by the compiler) from the current project. As a result of using this command, you need to recompile and relink the project files.

The Bring Up To Date Command

The Bring Up To Date command compiles any updated files and reloads any libraries that have not yet been loaded. The shortcut for this command is ⌘U.

The Check Link Command

The Check Link command performs the same tasks as the Run and Build Application commands, except that it doesn't run the program. This command compiles and links the project files as needed. If a linking error results, the command displays the Link Errors window, which contains the link error messages. The shortcut for this command is ⌘L.

The Build Application... Command

The Build Application... command builds the current project as an application. The THINK Project Manager displays different captions for this menu depending on whether you are building a library, desk accessory, device driver, or code resources. These menus perform somewhat similar tasks—each is oriented towards a specific kind of code.

The Use Debugger Command

The Use Debugger command toggles the source debugger. The THINK Project Manager displays a bug column in the project window when the source debugger is on. When you run the project, a debugger's window appears on the screen, enabling you to single-step through the code.

The Run Command

The Run command runs the current project. If needed, this command compiles and links source code files. If the compiler or linker detect errors, the THINK Project Manager displays an error window that lists these errors.

The Source Menu

The Source menu provides commands that enable you to manage the source code in the current project. Table 1.5 summarizes the commands in the Source menu.

Note: I'd like to remind you that most of the Source menu commands are advanced.

Table 1.5. Summary of the commands in the Source menu.

Command	Shortcut Key	Function
Add Window		Adds a file in the front-most edit window to the current project.
Add Files...		Adds source code files or libraries to the current project.
Remove		Deletes a source code file or a library from the current project.
Get Info		Displays the sizes of various project components.
Debug	⌘I	Selects the front-most source-code window for debugging.
SourceServer		Invokes the SourceServer utility, which provides advanced source management features.
Check Syntax	⌘Y	Verifies the syntax of the source code in the front-most window.
Preprocess		Runs the translator's preprocessor and shows the result in a new window.

continues

Table 1.5. continued

Command	Shortcut Key	Function
Disassemble		Converts the source code of the front-most window into the equivalent assembly language code, which appears in a new window.
Precompile		Compiles the header files (that contain the various kinds of declarations) for the front-most window.
Compile Load Library	⌘K	Compiles a single source file or loads an individual library without compiling the entire project.
Make...	⌘\	Updates the project's files.
Browser	⌘J	Invokes the class browser, which is a tool used to show you all the classes defined in your project.

The Add Window Command

The Add Window command adds the file in the front-most edit window to the current project. The added file must end with one of the extensions defined in the Extensions page of the THINK Project Manager Options dialog box (see the section titled "The Options Command" earlier in this chapter).

The Add Files Command

The Add Files command permits you to add source code files or libraries to the current project. This command brings up the Add Files dialog box, as shown in Figure 1.11. The two list box controls in the dialog box display a list of available files and a list of the added files (which is initially empty). The Add button adds the file that is currently selected in the list of available files to the list of files to be added for the current project. The Add All button adds all the files in the current folder to the list of files to be added. The Remove button removes the currently selected file from the list of files to be added.

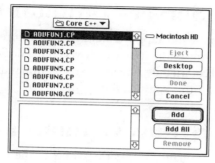

Figure 1.11. *The Add Files dialog box.*

The Remove Command

The Remove command deletes the currently selected source code file or library from the project.

The Get Info Command

The Get Info command brings up the Get Info dialog box, as shown in Figure 1.12. This dialog box displays the sizes of the various project components. The information that appears in the dialog box is more meaningful after you compile the files of the current project.

HELLO.CP				
	CODE	DATA	STRS	JUMP
File	16	18	0	8
Segment 2	30516	3804	0	2112
Project	61366	6942	0	4032

[Next] [Prev] File
[Next] [Prev] Segment   [OK]

Figure 1.12. *The Get Info dialog box.*

The Debug Command

The Debug command works with the source-level debugger. Invoking this command sends the front-most edit window (or the selected file in the project window) to the source window of the debugger.

The SourceServer Command

The SourceServer command supports an advanced feature that enables you to manage the source code and control the source code version. The SourceServer pops up a menu that offers additional commands; however, these commands are beyond the scope of this book. The shortcut for this command is ⌘I.

The Check Syntax Command

The Check Syntax command verifies the syntax of the source code in the front-most window, but it does not add the file associated with that window to the project window. You can use the Check Syntax command to verify on the fly the syntax of files. The shortcut for this command is ⌘Y.

The Preprocess Command

The Preprocess command works with the source code in the front-most window. This command runs the translator's preprocessor and shows the result in a new window. Use this command to detect bugs in `#define`, `#include`, and `#ifndef` macros.

The Disassemble Command

The Disassemble command works with the front-most window. The command converts the source code of the front-most window into the equivalent assembly language code, which appears in a new window. This option is definitely for the advanced programmer who is familiar with assembly language.

The Precompile Command

The Precompile command compiles the header files (that contain the various kinds of declarations) for the front-most window. Precompiled code enables you to speed up the overall process of recompiling the header files of a project.

The Compile Load Library Command

The Compile Load Library command enables you to compile a single source file or to load an individual library without compiling the entire project. The shortcut for this command is ⌘K.

The Make... Command

The Make... command brings up the Make dialog box, as shown in Figure 1.13. This dialog shows the files in the current project. The dialog box places a check mark to the left of the files or libraries to be recompiled or reloaded, respectively. Using the Check All, Check Sources, and Check None buttons, you can specify which files to recompile. Click the Make button to recompile and link the project's files. The shortcut for this command is ⌘\.

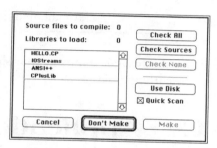

Figure 1.13. *The Make dialog box.*

The Browser Command

The Browser command invokes the class browser which is a tool used to show you all the classes defined in your project. The THINK Project Manager displays these classes as a tree. You can use the class browser to inspect the declaration of a class. The shortcut for this command is ⌘J.

The Windows Menu

The Windows menu offers commands to manage windows. These options, which are summarized in Table 1.6, enable you to arrange, zoom, and close all windows. In addition to the standard options, the Windows menu also lists the current windows.

Table 1.6. Summary of the options in the Windows menu.

Command	Shortcut Key	Function
Arrange...		Arranges the windows.
Zoom	⌘/	Zooms in on the front-most window.
Full Titles		Displays the full titles of each edit window.
Close All		Closes all edit windows.
Save All		Saves all modified edit windows.

The Windows menu includes dynamic commands that show the name of the project and the edit windows for the current project.

The Core C++ Applications

The THINK Project Manager enables you to build generic C++ programs that do not use the controls of the Macintosh GUI, such as buttons and list boxes. These applications are a cross between generic C++ programs and GUI programs. The programs in Days 1 through 12 of this book are generic applications that enable you to focus on learning C++ using a simple input/output interface.

Before I describe the steps involved in creating an application, I recommend that you first create a folder for this book's program. Open the Development folder, which contains the Symantec C++ nested folders and files, and then create a new folder. Name the new folder MAC21DAY, or something comparable. Open the MAC21DAY folder and create another new folder inside it. Call that new folder "Core C++." I recommend that this folder contain the source code files for Day 1 through Day 12.

The first C++ program presented in this book displays a one-line greeting message. This simple program enables you to see the very basic components of a C++ program.

Listing 1.1 contains the source code for the program HELLO.CP with numbered lines. Do *not* enter the line numbers when you type in the program. These line numbers serve as reference only. This simple program displays the string Hello Programmer!. Carry out the following steps to create and run this first C++ program:

1. Use the generic text editor to type in the source code (leave out the line number and the colon that follows that number), and then save it as file HELLO.CP in the Core C++ folder.

2. Load the Symantec C++ THINK Project Manager if it isn't already loaded.

3. Invoke the File | New Project command to create a new project.

4. The THINK Project Manager displays the New Project manager, which lists the types of projects. Select the Empty Project from the list of project types. Also, uncheck the Create folder check box.

5. Type in the project name CoreCpp.

6. Select the Core C++ folder as the repertoire for the CoreCpp project.

7. Click the Save button to create the new project. The THINK Project Manager displays the CoreCpp.p project window, which shows an empty list project.

8. Select the Source | Add Files command to add the required files.

9. The THINK Project Manager displays the Add Files dialog box. Select the Development folder, then the Symantec C++ for Macintosh folder, and finally the Standard Libraries folder.

10. Select the IOStreams, ANSI++, and CPlusLib library files, and then the click the Add button.

11. Select the Core C++ folder, and then add the HELLO.CP file.

12. Close the Add Files dialog box by clicking the Done button.

To compile, link, and run the HELLO.CP program, use the ⌘R shortcut. The program displays its single-line message. When the program ends, the runtime system alters the title of the program's window to read press <<return>> to exit. To close the program's window, press the Return key.

 Listing 1.1. Source code for the program HELLO.CP.

```
1: // a trivial C++ program that says hello
2:
3: #include <iostream.h>
4:
5: main()
6: {
7:   cout << "Hello Programmer!";
8:   return 0;
9: }
```

The output of the program is shown in Figure 1.14. Notice that the title of the output window is press <<return>> to exit, indicating that the program has terminated.

Figure 1.14. *The output of the compiled HELLO.CP program.*

Examine the short code of the C++ program and notice the following characteristics:

☐ C++ uses the / / characters for comments that run to the end of the line. C++ also supports the C-style comments that begin with the /* characters and end with the */ characters. Line 1 contains a comment that briefly describes the program.

NEW *Comments* are remarks that you put in the program to explain or clarify certain **TERM** parts of the program. The compiler ignores comments.

☐ The C++ program has no reserved keywords that declare the end of a program. In fact, C++ uses a rather simple scheme for organizing a program. This scheme supports two levels of code: global and single-level functions. In addition, the function main, which starts in line 5, plays a very special role because runtime execution begins with this function. Therefore, there can be only one function main in a C++ program. You can place the function main anywhere in the code.

☐ The C++ strings and characters are enclosed in double and single quotes, respectively. Thus, "A" is a single-character string, whereas 'A' is a single character. Mixing C++ single-character strings and single characters is not allowed.

NEW TERM Strings can have any number of characters, including no characters. A string without any characters is called the *empty string*.

☐ C++ defines blocks using the { and } characters. See examples in lines 6 and 9, respectively.

☐ Every statement in a C++ program must end with a semicolon (;).

☐ C++ contains the `#include` compiler directive. An example of this is in line 3, which instructs the Symantec C++ compiler to include the IOSTREAM.H header file. C++ extends the notion of streams, which already exists in C. IOSTREAM.H provides the operations that support basic stream input and output. The C++ language does not include built-in I/O routines. Instead, the language relies on libraries specializing in various types of I/O.

NEW TERM A *compiler directive* is a special instruction for the compiler. A *header file* contains the declarations of constants, data types, variables, and forward (early) declarations of functions. A *stream* is a sequence of data flowing from one part of a computer to another.

☐ The C++ program outputs the string `Hello Programmer!` to a special window that displays the output to the standard output stream, `cout`. In addition, the program uses the extractor operator, `<<`, to send the emitted string to the output stream.

☐ The function `main` must return a value that reflects the error status of the C++ program. Returning the value 0 signals to the operating system that the program terminated normally.

I'd like to point out that the programs in the next 11 chapters use the CoreCpp project to reduce storage space. Because each project cannot have more than one file with the function `main`, you'll use the Project | Remove command to remove a source file, and the Project | Add Files command to insert a new source code file.

Exiting the THINK Project Manager

To exit the THINK Project Manager, choose the Quit command in the File menu. The shortcut for this command is ⌘Q.

Summary

Today's lesson introduced you to the THINK Project Manager and presented you with the first C++ program. You learned these basics:

- ☐ C++ programs are modular and rely on standard and custom libraries.

- ☐ You load the THINK Project Manager by clicking the THINK Project Manager icon in the Development folder.

- ☐ The THINK Project Manager is a versatile environment for developing, maintaining, and debugging C and C++ programs and libraries for Macintosh applications.

- ☐ The File menu manages the tasks of creating new files, opening files, saving files, printing files, and exiting the THINK Project Manager.

- ☐ The Edit menu offers commands for performing popular editing operations (such as undo, cut, copy, paste, and delete).

- ☐ The Search menu enables you to find and replace text, as well as to jump to lines, manage markers, and visit the offending source-code lines.

- ☐ The Project menu provides commands to manage a project. These commands enable you to close the current project, switch to another project, build applications, maintain compiled code, use the debugger, and run the current project.

- ☐ The Source menu offers commands to manage the source code, including ones that add and remove files from the current project, as well as compile, make, and precompile project files.

- ☐ The Windows menu provides you with commands to manage, zoom in, arrange, select, and close all the windows related to the current project.

- ☐ The generic C++ applications are Macintosh applications that provide special windows which act as standard input and output devices. These applications enable you to write character input/output programs.

- ☐ The first C++ program in this book is a simple greeting program that illustrates the basic components of a C++ program. These components include comments, the #include directive, and the main function.

- ☐ You exit the THINK Project Manager by choosing the Quit command in the File menu.

Q&A

Q Does C++ use line numbers?

A No. I use line numbers in the listings in this book only for the sake of reference.

Q What happens if I forget to type the second double quote in the first program?

A The compiler tells you that there is an error in the program. You need to add the second double quote and build the project.

Q How do I delete text in the currently edited window?

A Use the Replace command in the Edit menu, and then specify nothing for the replacement string. Alternatively, you can use the Edit menu's Cut and Clear commands.

Workshop

The Workshop provides quiz questions to help you solidify your understanding of the material covered and exercises to provide you with experience in using what you've learned. Try to understand the quiz and exercise answers before continuing on to the next day's lesson. (Answers are provided in Appendix B, "Answers.")

Quiz

1. What is the output of the following program?

```
1: // quiz program #1
2:
3: #include <iostream.h>
4:
5: main()
6: {
7:   cout << "C++ in 21 Days?";
8:   return 0;
9: }
```

2. What is the output of the following program?

```
1: // quiz program #2
2:
3: #include <iostream.h>
4:
5: main()
6: {
7:    // cout << "C++ in 21 Days?";
8:    return 0;
9: }
```

3. What is wrong with the following program?

```
1: // quiz program #3
2:
3: #include <iostream.h>
4:
5: main()
6: {
7:    cout << "C++ in 21 Days?"
8:    return 0;
9: }
```

Exercise

Write a program that displays the message I am a C++ Programmer.

C++ Program Components

Day 1 presented the Symantec development environment and a simple C++ program. Today's lesson focuses on the basic components of C++ programs, including data types, variables, constants, and functions. You learn about the following topics:

☐ The predefined data types in Symantec C++

☐ Naming items in Symantec C++

☐ The `#include` directive

☐ Declaring variables

☐ Declaring constants

☐ Declaring and prototyping functions

☐ Local variables in functions

☐ Static variables in functions

☐ Inline functions

☐ Exiting functions

☐ Default arguments

☐ Function overloading

Predefined Data Types in Symantec C++

Symantec C++ offers the `int`, `char`, `float`, `double`, and `void` data types to represent integers, characters, single-precision floating-point numbers, double-precision floating point numbers, and valueless data, respectively. C++ uses the `void` type with a function's returned values to indicate that the function acts as a procedure.

C++ adds more flexibility to data types by supporting data type modifiers. The type modifiers are: `signed`, `unsigned`, `short`, and `long`. Table 2.1 shows the predefined data types in C++ (and includes the type modifiers) along with their sizes and ranges. Notice that the `int` and `unsigned int` are system-dependent. The table shows the 16-bit values for these data types.

 NEW TERM *Data type modifiers* alter the precision and the range of values.

Table 2.1. Predefined data types in C++.

Data Type	Byte Size	Range	Examples
char	1	−128 to 127	'A', '!'
signed char	1	−128 to 127	23
unsigned char	1	0 to 255	200, 0x1a
int	4	−2147483648 to 2147483647	3000
unsigned int	4	0 to 4294967295	0xffff, 65535
short int	2	−32768 to 32767	100
unsigned short int	2	0 to 65535	0xff, 40000
long int	4	−2147483648 to 2147483647	0xfffff, −123456
unsigned long int	4	0 to 4294967295	123456
float	4	3.4E−38 to 3.4E+38 and −3.4E−38 to −3.4E+38	2.35, −52.354, 1.3e+10
double	8	1.7E−308 to 1.7E+308 and −1.7E−308 to −1.7E+308	12.354, 2.5e+100, 2.5e+100, 78.32544
long double	10	3.4E−4932 to 1.1E+4932 and −1.1E−4932 to −3.4E+4932	8.5e−3000

 C++ supports *hexadecimal numbers*. Such numbers begin with the characters 0x followed by the hexadecimal value. For example, the number 0xff is the hexadecimal equivalent of the decimal number 255.

Naming Items in Symantec C++

Symantec C++ requires you to observe the following rules with identifiers:

1. The first character must be a letter or an underscore (_).

2. Subsequent characters can be letters, digits, or underscores.

3. The maximum length of an identifier is 256 characters.

4. Identifiers are case-sensitive in C++. Thus, the names `rate`, `RATE`, and `Rate` refer to three different identifiers.

5. Identifiers cannot be reserved words such as `int`, `double`, or `static` (to name just a few).

Here are some examples of valid identifiers:

```
X
x
aString
DAYS_IN_WEEK
BinNumber0
bin_number_0
bin0Number2
_length
```

DO	DON'T
DO use descriptive names that have a reasonable length. **DON'T** use identifier names that are too short or too long. Short names yield poor readability, and long names are prone to typos.	

The *#include* Directive

Recall that a directive is a special instruction for C and C++ compilers. A directive begins with the # character and is followed by the directive name. Directives usually are placed in the first column of a line. They can be preceded only by spaces or tab characters. The C++ program in Day 1 contains the `#include` directive. This directive tells the compiler to include the text of a file as if you have typed that text yourself. Thus, the `#include` directive is a better alternative than cutting text from one file and pasting it in another file. Recall from Day 1 that programs use the `#include` directive to include header files.

SAMS PUBLISHING

Sams Learning Center

Syntax

The #include Directive

The general syntax for the #include directive is

```
#include <filename>
#include "filename"
```

Example:

```
#include <iostream.h>
#include "string.h"
```

The `filename` represents the name of the included file. The two forms differ in how the #include directive searches for the included file. The first form searches for the file in the special directory for included files. The second form extends the search to involve the current directory.

Declaring Variables

Declaring variables requires you to state the data type of the variable and the name of the variable. The word *variable* indicates that you can alter the data of these data containers.

NEW TERM *Variables* are identifiers used to store and recall information. You can regard a variable as a labeled data container.

Syntax

Declaring Variables

The general syntax for declaring variables is

```
type variableName;
type variableName = initialValue;
type var1 [= initVal1], var2 [= initVal2], ...;
```

Example:

```
int j;
double z = 32.314;
long fileSize, diskSize, totalFileSize = 0;
```

C++ allows you to declare a list of variables (that have the same types) in a declarative statement. For example:

```
int j, i = 2, k = 3;
double x = 3.12;
double y = 2 * x, z = 4.5, a = 45.7;
```

The initializing values may contain other variables defined earlier.

DO	DON'T

DO resist using global variables.

DON'T declare variables, within the same program unit, with names that are different in character case (such as `rate` and `Rate`).

Listing 2.1 presents a simple example that uses variables. It shows the source code for the program VAR1.CP. The program declares four variables, two of which are initialized during their declarations. The program then assigns values to the uninitialized variables and displays the contents of all four variables. Replace the current HELLO.CP file with the VAR1.CP file in the CORECPP project. Compile and run the VAR1.CP program.

Listing 2.1. Source code for the program VAR1.CP.

```
1: // C++ program that illustrates simple variables
2:
3: #include <iostream.h>
4:
5: main()
6: {
7:    int i, j = 2;
8:    double x, y = 355.0 / 113;
9:
10:   i = 3 * j;
11:   cout << "i = " << i << "\n"
12:        << "j = " << j << "\n";
13:
14:   x = 2 * y;
15:   x = x * x;
16:   cout << "y = " << y << "\n"
17:        << "x = " << x << "\n";
18:   return 0;
19:
20: }
```

Here is a sample session with the program in Listing 2.1:

```
i = 6
j = 2
y = 3.14159
x = 39.478424
```

Analysis The program uses the `#include` directive in line 3 to include the stream I/O header file IOSTREAM.H. The function `main` appears in line 5. The function contains the declarations of the `int`-typed variables `i` and `j` in line 7, and the `double`-typed

variables x and y in line 8. The declarations initialize the variables j and y. The statement in line 10 multiplies the value in variable j (which is 2) by 3 and stores the result in variable x. The stream output statement in lines 11 and 12 displays the values of variables i and j. The statement includes strings that label the output.

The statement in line 14 doubles the value in variable y and stores it in variable x. The statement in line 15 squares the value in variable x and assigns the result back to variable x. This statement uses the variable x on both sides of the equal sign. The stream output statement in lines 16 and 17 displays the values in variables x and y. The statement in line 18 returns 0 as the result of function main.

Declaring Constants

Many languages such as BASIC (the more recent implementations), Modula-2, Ada, C, Pascal, and C++ support constants. No one can deny that constants enhance the readability of a program by replacing numeric constants with identifiers that are more descriptive. Moreover, using constants enables you to change the value of a program parameter by merely changing the value of that parameter in one location. This capability is certainly easier and less prone to generate errors that may occur when you employ your text editor to replace certain numbers with other numbers.

NEW TERM *Constants* are identifiers that are associated with fixed values. C++ offers constants in two flavors: *macro-based* and *formal.* The macro-based constants are inherited from C and use the #define compiler directive.

The #define Directive

The general syntax for the #define directive is

```
#define constantName constantValue
```

The #define directive causes the compiler to invoke the preprocessor and perform text substitution to replace the macro-based constants with their values. This text replacement step occurs before the compiler processes the statements in the source file. Consequently, the compiler never sees the macro-based constants themselves—only what they expand to.

Examples:

```
#define ASCII_A 65
#define DAYS_IN_WEEK 7
```

Formal Constants

The second type of constant in C++ is the formal constant. The general syntax for the formal constant is

```
const dataType constantName = constantValue;
```

The *dataType* item is an optional item that specifies the data type of the constant values. If you omit the data type, the C++ compiler assumes the int type.

Examples:

```
const unsigned char ASCII_A = 65;
const DAYS_IN_WEEK = 7;
const char FIRST_DISK_DRIVE = 'A';
```

DO	DON'T

DO use uppercase names for constants. This naming style enables you to quickly determine if an identifier is a constant.

DON'T assume that other people who read your code will know what embedded numbers mean. Use declared constants to enhance the readability of your programs.

Using Macro-Based Constants

Here is an example that uses macro-based constants. Listing 2.2 shows the source code for program CONST1.CP. The program prompts you to enter the number of hours, minutes, and seconds since midnight. The program then calculates and displays the total number of seconds since midnight. Replace the VAR1.CP file with the CONST1.CP file in the C++ core project. Compile and run the CONST1.CP program.

Listing 2.2. Source code for the program CONST1.CP.

```
1: // C++ program that illustrates constants
2:
3: #include <iostream.h>
4:
5: #define SEC_IN_MIN 60
6: #define MIN_IN_HOUR 60
7:
8: main()
```

```
 9: {
10:   long hours, minutes, seconds;
11:   long totalSec;
12:
13:   cout << "Enter hours: ";
14:   cin >> hours;
15:   cout << "Enter minutes: ";
16:   cin >> minutes;
17:   cout << "Enter seconds: ";
18:   cin >> seconds;
19:
20:   totalSec = ((hours * MIN_IN_HOUR + minutes) *
21:              SEC_IN_MIN) + seconds;
22:
23:   cout <<"\n\n" << totalSec << " seconds since midnight";
24:   return 0;
25: }
```

Here is a sample session with the program in Listing 2.2:

```
Enter hours: 10
Enter minutes: 0
Enter seconds: 0


36000 seconds since midnight
```

The program uses the #include directive in line 3 to include the header file IOSTREAM.H. Lines 5 and 6 contain the #define directive that declares the macro-based constants SEC_IN_MIN and MIN_IN_HOUR. Both constants have the value 60, but each value has a different meaning. The function main which starts at line 8 declares four long-typed variables: hours, minutes, seconds, and totalSec.

The function uses pairs of statements to output the prompting messages and receive input. Line 13 contains the stream output statement that prompts you for the number of hours. Line 14 contains the stream input statement. The identifier cin is the name of the standard input stream and uses the *insertion operator* >> to read data from the keyboard and to store it in the variable hours. The input and output statements in lines 15 through 18 perform a similar task of prompting for input and obtaining keyboard input.

Line 20 contains a statement that calculates the total number of seconds since midnight and stores the result in variable totalSec. The statement uses the macro-based constants MIN_IN_HOUR and SEC_IN_MIN. As you can see, using these constants enhances the readability of the statement compared to using the number 60 in place of both constants. Line 23 contains a stream output statement that displays the total number of seconds since midnight (stored in variable totalSec), followed by qualifying text to clarify the output.

Using Formal Constants

Now let's look at a new version of the program, one that uses the formal C++ constants. Listing 2.3 shows the source code for program CONST2.CP. This program works like the CONST1.CP program. Replace the CONST1.CP file with CONST2.CP file in the CORECPP project. Compile and run the CONST2.CP program.

Note: At this point I assume that you are familiar with the process of creating the .CP source file and replacing the current .CP file with the new one in the CORECPP project file. From now on I will not mention creating these files, unless there is a special set of source files in a project.

Listing 2.3. Source code for the program CONST2.CP.

```
1: // C++ program that illustrates constants
2:
3: #include <iostream.h>
4:
5: const SEC_IN_MIN = 60; // global constant
6:
7: main()
8: {
9:   const MIN_IN_HOUR = 60; // local constant
10:
11:   long hours, minutes, seconds;
12:   long totalSec;
13:
14:   cout << "Enter hours: ";
15:   cin >> hours;
16:   cout << "Enter minutes: ";
17:   cin >> minutes;
18:   cout << "Enter seconds: ";
19:   cin >> seconds;
20:
21:   totalSec = ((hours * MIN_IN_HOUR + minutes) *
22:              SEC_IN_MIN) + seconds;
23:
24:   cout <<"\n\n" << totalSec << " seconds since midnight";
25:   return 0;
26: }
```

Here is a sample session with the program in Listing 2.3:

```
Enter hours: 1
Enter minutes: 10
Enter seconds: 20


4220 seconds since midnight
```

The programs in Listings 2.2 and 2.3 are similar. The difference between them is in how they declare their constants. In Listing 2.3 I use the formal C++ constant syntax to declare the constants. In addition, I declare constant SEC_IN_MIN in line 5, outside the function main. This kind of declaration makes the constant global. That is, if there were another function in the program, it would be able to use the constant SEC_IN_MIN. By contrast, I declare the constant MIN_IN_HOUR inside the function main. Thus, the constant MIN_IN_HOUR is local to the function main.

Declaring and Prototyping Functions

Most programming languages use functions and procedures. C++ does not support formal procedures. Instead, all C++ routines are functions!

 Functions are the primary building blocks that conceptually extend the C++ language to fit your custom programs.

Syntax

Declaring Functions

The general form for the ANSI C style of declaring functions (which is maintained by C++) is

```
returnType functionName(typedParameterList)
```

Examples:

```
double sqr(double y)
{ return y * y; }

char prevChar(char c)
{ return c - 1; }
```

Remember the following rules when declaring C++ functions:

- ☐ The return type of the C++ function appears before the function's name.

- ☐ If the parameter list is empty, you still use empty parentheses. C++ also allows you the option of using the `void` keyword to explicitly state that the parameter list is void.

- ☐ The typed parameter list consists of a list of typed parameters that use the following general format:

```
[const] type1 parameter1, [const] type2 parameter2, ...
```

  This format shows that the individual parameter is declared like a variable—you state the type first and then the parameter's identifier. The list of parameters in C++ is comma-delimited. In addition, you cannot group a sequence of parameters that have the exact same data type. You must declare each parameter explicitly. If a parameter has the `const` clause, the compiler makes sure that the function does *not* alter the arguments of that parameter.

- ☐ The body of a C++ function is enclosed in braces ({}). There is no semicolon after the closing brace.

- ☐ C++ supports passing arguments either by value or by reference. By default, parameters pass their arguments by value. Consequently, the functions work with a copy of the data, preserving the original data. To declare a reference parameter, insert the & character after the data type of the parameter. A reference parameter becomes an alias to its arguments. Any changes made to the reference parameter also affect the argument. The general form for reference parameters is

```
[const] type1& parameter1, [const] type2& parameter2, ...
```

  If a parameter has the `const` clause, the compiler makes sure that the function does not alter the arguments of that parameter.

- ☐ C++ supports local constants, data types, and variables. Although these data items can appear in nested block statements, C++ does not support nested functions.

- ☐ The `return` keyword returns the function's value.

- ☐ If the function's return type is `void`, you do not have to use the `return` keyword unless you need to provide an exit route in the middle of the function.

NEW☞ TERM C++ dictates that you either declare or define a function before you use it. Declaring a function, which is commonly called *prototyping*, lists the function name, return type, and the number and type of its parameters. Including the name of the parameter is optional. You also need to place a semicolon after the closing parenthesis. C++ requires that you declare a function if you call it before you define it.

The following is a simple example of prototyping:

```
// prototype the function square
double sqr(double);

main()
{
  cout << "5^2 = " << sqr(5) << "\n";
  return 0;
}

double sqr(double z)
{ return z * z; }
```

Notice that the declaration of function sqr contains only the type of its single parameter.

Typically, the declaration of a function is global. You may still prototype a function within its client function. This technique conceals the prototype from other functions.

Calling a function requires that you supply its parameter with arguments. The arguments are mapped onto the parameter by the sequence in which the parameters are declared. The arguments must be data types that match or are compatible with those of the parameters. For example, you may have a function volume that is defined as follows:

```
double volume(double length, double width, double height)
{
  return length * width * height;
}
```

To call the function volume you need to supply double-typed arguments or arguments with compatible types (which in this case are all numeric data types). Here are a number of sample calls to function volume:

```
double len = 34, width = 55, ht = 100;
int i = 3;
long j = 44;
unsigned k = 33;

cout << volume(len, width, ht) << "\n";
cout << volume(1, 2, 3) << "\n";
cout << volume(i, j, k) << "\n";
cout << volume(len, j, 22.3) << "\n";
```

> **Note:** C++ allows you to discard the result of a function. This kind of function call is used when the focus is on what the function does rather than on its return value.

Local Variables in Functions

Sound structured-programming techniques foster the notion that functions should be as independent and as reusable as possible. Consequently, functions can have their own data types, constants, and variables to give them this independence.

 NEW TERM The *local variable* in a function exists only when the host function is called. Once the function terminates, the runtime system removes the local variables. Consequently, local variables lose their data between function calls. In addition, the runtime system applies any initialization to local variables every time the host function is called.

DO	DON'T

DO use local variables to store and alter the values of parameters that are declared with the const clause.

DON'T declare a local variable to have the same name of a global variable you need to access in the function.

Let's look at an example. Listing 2.4 displays the value of the following mathematical function:

```
f(X) = X2 - 5 X + 10
```

and its slope at the argument 3.5 (assigned to variable x in line 20). The program calculates the slope using the following approximation, where h is a small increment:

```
f'(X) = (f(X + h) - f(X - h)) / 2h
```

Listing 2.4. Source code for the program VAR2.CP.

```
1: // C++ program that illustrates local variables in a function
2:
3: #include <iostream.h>
4:
5: double f(double x)
6: {
7:    return x * x - 5 * x + 10;
8: }
9:
10: double slope(double x)
11: {
12:    double f1, f2, incrim = 0.01 * x;
13:    f1 = f(x + incrim);
14:    f2 = f(x - incrim);
15:    return (f1 - f2) / 2 / incrim;
16: }
17:
18: main()
19: {
20:   double x = 3.5;
21:
22:    cout << "f("  << x << ") = " << f(x) << "\n"
23:         << "f'(" << x << ") = " << slope(x) << "\n";
24:
25:    return 0;
26: }
```

 Here is a sample session with the program in Listing 2.4:

```
f(3.5) = 4.75
f'(3.5) = 2
```

 The program in Listing 2.4 declares three functions, namely f (in line 5), slope (in line 10), and main (in line 18). The function f is simple and returns the value of the mathematical function. The function f is void of local variables. By contrast, the function slope declares the local variables f1, f2, and incrim. This function also initializes the latter variable. Line 13 assigns the value of f(x + incrim) to the local variable f1. Line 14 assigns the value of f(x - incrim) to the local variable f2. Line 15 returns the value for function slope using the local variables f1, f2, and incrim. The function main simply displays the values of the mathematical function and its slope when x = 3.5.

Static Variables in Functions

In Listing 2.4, the local variables in function `slope` lose their values once the function terminates. C++ allows you to declare a local variable as static by simply placing the `static` keyword to the left of its data type. Static variables are usually initialized. This initialization is performed once, when the host function is called the first time.

NEW TERM   There are a number of programming techniques that require maintaining the values of local variables between function calls. These special local variables are called *static variables*.

When the host function terminates, the static variables maintain their values. The compiler supports this language feature by storing static variables in a separate memory location that is maintained while the program is running. You can use the same names for static variables in different functions. This duplication does not confuse the compiler because it keeps track of which function owns which static variables.

Let's look at a simple program. Listing 2.5 uses a function with static variables to maintain a moving average. The program supplies its own data and calls that function several times to obtain and display the current value of the moving average.

Type   **Listing 2.5. Source code for the program STATIC1.CP.**

```
 1: // C++ program that illustrates static local variables
 2:
 3: #include <iostream.h>
 4:
 5: double mean(double x)
 6: {
 7:   static double sum = 0;
 8:   static double sumx = 0;
 9:
10:   sum = sum + 1;
11:   sumx = sumx + x;
12:   return sumx / sum;
13: }
14:
15: main()
16: {
17:   cout << "mean = " << mean(1) << "\n";
18:   cout << "mean = " << mean(2) << "\n";
19:   cout << "mean = " << mean(4) << "\n";
20:   cout << "mean = " << mean(10) << "\n";
21:   cout << "mean = " << mean(11) << "\n";
22:   return 0;
23: }
```

Here is a sample session with the program in Listing 2.5:

```
mean = 1
mean = 1.5
mean = 2.333333
mean = 4.25
mean = 5.6
```

The program in Listing 2.5 declares the function mean that contains static local variables. Lines 7 and 8 declare the static variables sum and sumx, respectively. The function initializes both static variables with 0. The statement in line 10 increments the variable sum by 1. The statement in line 11 increments the variable sumx by the value of parameter x. Line 12 returns the updated moving average, obtained by dividing sumx by sum.

The function main issues a series of calls to function mean. The stream output statements in lines 17 through 21 display the updated moving average. These results are possible thanks to the static local variables sum and sumx in function mean. If static variables are not supported by C++, you must resort to using global variables—a highly questionable programming choice!

Inline Functions

Using functions requires the overhead of calling them, passing their arguments, and returning their results. C++ allows you to use inline functions that expand into their statements. Thus, inline functions offer faster execution speed—especially where speed is critical—at the cost of expanding the code.

The *inline* Function

The general syntax for the inline function is

```
inline returnType functionName(typedParameterList)
```

Examples:

```
inline double cube(double x)
{ return x * x * x; }

inline char nextChar(char c)
{ return c + 1; }
```

The alternative to using inline functions is the use of the #define directive to create macro-based pseudofunctions. Many C++ programmers (including me) strongly recommend abandoning this method in favor of inline functions. The justification for this inclination is that inline functions provide type checking. Macros created with the #define directive do not.

DO   **DON'T**

DO start by declaring inline functions as ordinary functions when you develop your programs. Non-inline functions are easier to debug. Once your program is working, insert the inline keyword where needed.

DON'T declare inline functions with too many statements. The increase in program size may not be acceptable.

Here is a simple example of a program that uses inline functions. Listing 2.6 contains the source code for program INLINE1.CP. The program prompts you for a number. Then the program calculates and displays the square and cube values for your input.

 Listing 2.6. Source code for the program INLINE1.CP.

```
1: // C++ program that illustrates inline functions
2:
3: #include <iostream.h>
4:
5: inline double sqr(double x)
6: {
7:   return x * x;
8: }
9:
10: inline double cube(double x)
11: {
12:   return x * x * x;
13: }
14:
15: main()
16: {
17:   double x;
18:
19:   cout << "Enter a number: ";
20:   cin >> x;
21:
22:   cout << "square of "  << x << " = " << sqr(x) << "\n"
23:        << "cube of " << x << " = " << cube(x) << "\n";
24:
25:   return 0;
26: }
```

Here is a sample session with the program in Listing 2.6:

```
Enter a number: 2.5
square of 2.5 = 6.25
cube of 2.5 = 15.625
```

The program in Listing 2.6 declares the inline functions `sqr` and `cube`. Each function heading starts with the keyword `inline`. The other aspects of the inline functions resemble short normal functions. The function `main` calls the functions `sqr` and `cube` to display the square and cube values, respectively.

Exiting Functions

Usually you make an early exit from a function because particular conditions do not allow you to proceed with executing the statements in that function. C++ provides the `return` statement to exit from a function. If the function has the `void` type, you employ the statement `return` and include no expression after the return. By contrast, if you exit a non-void function, the return statement should produce a value that indicates the purpose for exiting the function.

Default Arguments

Default arguments are a language feature that is quite simple and yet very powerful. When you omit the argument of a parameter that has a default argument, the default argument is used automatically.

C++ permits you to assign *default arguments* to the parameters of a function.

Using default arguments requires that you follow these rules:

☐ Once you assign a default argument to a parameter, you must do so for all subsequent parameters in the same parameter list. You cannot randomly assign default arguments to parameters. This rule means the parameter list can be divided into two sublists: the leading parameters that do not have default arguments, and the trailing parameters that do.

☐ You must provide an argument for every parameter that has no default argument.

☐ You may omit the argument for a parameter that has a default argument.

☐ Once you omit the argument for a parameter with a default argument, the arguments for all subsequent parameters must also be omitted.

 Note: The best way to list the parameters with default arguments is to locate them according to the likelihood of using their default arguments. Place the least likely used arguments first and the most likely used arguments last.

Here is a simple example that uses a function with default arguments. Listing 2.7 shows the source code for program DEFARGS1.CP. The program prompts you to enter the x and y coordinates of two points. Then the program calculates and displays the distance between the two points and between each point and the origin (0,0).

 Listing 2.7. Source code for the program DEFARGS1.CP.

```
1: // C++ program that illustrates default arguments
2:
3: #include <iostream.h>
4: #include <math.h>
5:
6: inline double sqr(double x)
7: { return x * x; }
8:
9: double distance(double x2, double y2,
10:                 double x1 = 0, double y1 = 0)
11: {
12:   return sqrt(sqr(x2 - x1) + sqr(y2 - y1));
13: }
14:
15: main()
16: {
17:   double x1, y1, x2, y2;
18:
19:   cout << "Enter x coordinate for point 1: ";
20:   cin >> x1;
21:   cout << "Enter y coordinate for point 1: ";
22:   cin >> y1;
23:   cout << "Enter x coordinate for point 2: ";
24:   cin >> x2;
25:   cout << "Enter y coordinate for point 2: ";
26:   cin >> y2;
27:
28:   cout << "distance between points = "
29:        << distance(x1, y1, x2, y2) << "\n";
30:   cout << "distance between point 1 and (0,0) = "
31:        << distance(x1, y1, 0) << "\n";
32:   cout << "distance between point 2 and (0,0) = "
33:        << distance(x2, y2) << "\n";
34:
35:   return 0;
36: }
```

Here is a sample session with the program in Listing 2.7:

```
Enter x coordinate for point 1: 1
Enter y coordinate for point 1: 1
Enter x coordinate for point 2: -1
Enter y coordinate for point 2: 1
distance between points = 2
distance between point 1 and (0,0) = 1.414214
distance between point 2 and (0,0) = 1.414214
```

The program in Listing 2.7 includes not one but two header files. Line 4 uses the #include directive to include the MATH.H header file that declares the square root math function, sqrt. Line 6 declares the inline sqr function. This function returns the square value of the arguments for parameter x. The program also declares the function distance with four double-typed parameters. The parameters x2 and y2 represent the x and y coordinates, respectively, for the second point, whereas the parameters x1 and y1 represent the x and y coordinates, respectively, for the first point. Both parameters x1 and y1 have the default argument of 0. The function returns the distance between the two points. If you omit the arguments for x1 and y1, the function returns the distance between the point (x2,y2) and the origin (0,0). If you omit the argument only for the last parameter, the function yields the distance between the points (x2,y2) and (x1,0).

The function main prompts you to enter the X and Y coordinates for two points, using the statements in lines 19 through 26. The output statement in lines 28 and 29 calls the function distance, providing it with four arguments, namely, x1, y1, x2, and y2. Therefore, this call to function distance uses no default arguments. By contrast, the statement in lines 30 and 31 calls function distance, supplying it with only three arguments. This call to function distance uses the default argument for the last parameter. The statement in lines 32 and 33 calls function distance, providing it with only two arguments. This call to function distance uses the two default arguments for the third and fourth parameters. I can omit the third argument in the second call to function distance and still compile and run the program.

Function Overloading

Function overloading is a language feature in C++ that has no parallel in C, Pascal, or BASIC. This new feature enables you to declare multiple functions that have the same name but different parameter lists. The function's return type is not part of the function signature because C++ allows you to discard the result type. Consequently, the compiler is not able to distinguish between two functions with the same parameters and different return types when the return types are omitted.

 NEW☞ TERM A parameter list is also called the *function signature*.

Warning: Using default arguments with overloaded functions may duplicate the signature for some of the functions (when the default arguments are used). The C++ compiler is able to detect this ambiguity and generate a compile-time error.

DO   DON'T

DO use default arguments to reduce the number of overloaded functions.

DON'T use overloaded functions to implement different operations.

Listing 2.8 is a simple program that uses overloaded functions. It contains the source code for program OVERLOAD.CP. The program performs the following tasks:

☐ Declares variables that have the char, int, and double types, and initializes them with values

☐ Displays the initial values

☐ Invokes overloaded functions that increment the variables

☐ Displays the updated values stored in the variables

 Listing 2.8. Source code for the program OVERLOAD.CP.

```
1: // C++ program that illustrates function overloading
2:
3: #include <iostream.h>
4:
5: // inc version for int types
6: void inc(int& i)
7: {
8:    i = i + 1;
9: }
10:
11: // inc version for double types
12: void inc(double& x)
13: {
14:    x = x + 1;
```

```
15: }
16:
17: // inc version for char types
18: void inc(char& c)
19: {
20:    c = c + 1;
21: }
22:
23: main()
24: {
25:    char c = 'A';
26:    int i = 10;
27:    double x = 10.2;
28:
29:    // display initial values
30:    cout << "c = " << c << "\n"
31:         << "i = " << i << "\n"
32:         << "x = " << x << "\n";
33:    // invoke the inc functions
34:    inc(c);
35:    inc(i);
36:    inc(x);
37:    // display updated values
38:    cout << "After using the overloaded inc function\n";
39:    cout << "c = " << c << "\n"
40:         << "i = " << i << "\n"
41:         << "x = " << x << "\n";
42:
43:    return 0;
44: }
```

Here is a sample session with the program in Listing 2.8:

```
c = A
i = 10
x = 10.2
After using the overloaded inc function
c = B
i = 11
x = 11.2
```

The program in Listing 2.8 declares three versions of the overloaded void function inc. The first version of function inc has an int-typed reference parameter, i. The function increments the parameter i by 1. Because the parameter i is a reference to its arguments, the action of function inc(int&) affects the argument outside the scope of the function. The second version of function inc has a double-typed reference parameter, x. The function increments the parameter x by 1. Because the parameter x is a reference to its arguments, the action of function inc(double&) affects the argument beyond the scope of the function. The second version of function inc has a char-typed reference parameter, c. The function increments the parameter c by 1. The reference parameter affects its arguments outside the scope of the function.

The function `main` declares the variables `c`, `i`, and `x` to have the `char`, `int`, and `double` types, respectively. The function also initializes the variables `c`, `i`, and `x` using the values `'A'`, `10`, and `10.2`, respectively. The statement in lines 30 through 32 displays the initial values in variables `c`, `i`, and `x`. The function `main` invokes the overloaded function `inc` in lines 34 through 36. The call to function `inc` in line 34 ends up calling the function `inc(char&)` because the argument used is a char-typed variable. The call to function `inc` in line 35 results in calling the function `inc(int&)` because the argument used is an int-typed variable. The call to function `inc` in line 36 invokes the function `inc(double&)` because the argument used is a double-typed variable. The output statement in lines 39 through 41 displays the updated values in variable `c`, `i`, and `x`.

Summary

Today's lesson presented the basic components of C++ programs. These components include data types, variables, constants, and functions. You learned these basics:

☐ The predefined data types in Symantec C++ include the `int`, `char`, `float`, `double`, and `void` data types. C++ adds more flexibility to data types by supporting data type modifiers. These modifiers alter the precision and the range of values. The type modifiers are: `signed`, `unsigned`, `short`, and `long`.

☐ Symantec C++ identifiers can be up to 256 characters long and must begin with a letter or an underscore. The subsequent characters of an identifier may be a letter, digit, or underscore. C++ identifiers are case-sensitive.

☐ The `#include` directive is a special instruction to the compiler. The directive tells the compiler to include the contents of the specified file as though you typed it in the currently scanned source file.

☐ Declaring variables requires you to state the data type of the variable and the name of the variable. C++ allows you to initialize a variable when you declare it. You can declare multiple variables in a single declarative statement.

☐ Declaring constants involves using the `#define` directive to declare macro-based constants, or using the `const` keyword to declare formal constants. The formal constants require that you specify the constant's type (the default is `int`, when the type is omitted), the name of the constants, and the associated value.

☐ The general form for defining functions is

```
                    returnType functionName(parameterList)
{
    <declarations of data items>

    <function body>
    return returnValue;
}
```

You need to prototype a function if it is used by a client function before the prototyped function is defined. The general form for prototyping functions is

```
returnType functionName(parameterList);
```

You can omit the names of the parameters from the parameter list.

☐ Local variables in a function support the implementation of highly independent functions. Declaring local variables is similar to declaring global variables.

☐ Static variables in functions are declared by placing the keyword `static` before the data type of the variables. Static variables retain their values between function calls. In most cases, you need to initialize static variables. These initial values are assigned to the static variables the first time the program calls the host function.

☐ Inline functions enable you to expand their statements in place, like macro-based pseudofunctions. However, unlike these pseudofunctions, inline functions perform type checking.

☐ You exit functions with the `return` statement. Void functions do not need to include an expression after the `return` keyword.

☐ Default arguments enable you to assign default values to the parameters of a function. When you omit the argument of a parameter that has a default argument, the default argument is automatically used.

☐ Function overloading enables you to declare multiple functions that have the same name but different parameter lists (also called the function signature). The function's return type is not part of the function signature because C++ allows you to discard the result type.

Q&A

Q Is there a specific style for naming identifiers?

A There are a few styles that have become popular in recent years. The one I use has the identifier begin with a lowercase character. If the identifier contains multiple words, such as `numberOfElements`, make the first character of each subsequent word an uppercase letter.

Q Can C++ functions declare nested functions?

A No. Nested functions actually add a lot of overhead at runtime.

Q When can I use static global variables?

A Never! Global variables need not be declared static because they exist for the entire program's lifetime.

Workshop

The Workshop provides quiz questions to help you solidify your understanding of the material covered and exercises to provide you with experience in using what you've learned. Try to understand the quiz and exercise answers before continuing on to the next day's lesson. Answers are provided in Appendix B, "Answers."

Quiz

1. Which of the following variables is valid, and which is not (and why)?

```
numFiles
n0Distance_02_Line
0Weight
Bin Number
static
Static
```

2. What is the output of the following program? What can you say about the function swap?

```cpp
#include <iostream.h>

void swap(int i, int j)
{
  int temp = i;
  i = j;
  j = temp;
}

main()
{
  int a = 10, b = 3;
  swap(a, b);
  cout << "a = " << a << " and b = " << b;
  return 0;
}
```

3. What is the output of the following program? What can you say about the function swap?

```cpp
#include <iostream.h>

void swap(int& i, int& j)
{
  int temp = i;
  i = j;
  j = temp;
}

main()
{
  int a = 10, b = 3;
  swap(a, b);
  cout << "a = " << a << " and b = " << b;
  return 0;
}
```

4. What is the problem with the following overloaded functions?

```
void inc(int& i)
{
  i = i + 1;
}

void inc(int& i, int diff = 1)
{
  i = i + diff;
}
```

5. Where is the error in the following function?

```
double volume(double length, double width = 1, double
height)
{
  return length * width * height
}
```

6. Where is the error in the following function?

```
void inc(int& i, int diff = 1)
{
  i = I + diff;
}
```

7. What is the error in the following program, and how can you correct it?

```
#include <iostream.h>

main()
{
  double x = 5.2;

  cout << x << "^2 = " << sqr(x);
  return 0;
}

double sqr(double x)
{ return x * x ; }
```

Exercise

Create the program OVERLOD2.CP by adding a second parameter with default arguments to the overloaded inc functions in program OVERLOAD.CP. The new parameter should represent the increment value with a default argument of 1.

Operators and Expressions

The manipulation of data involves expressions that are made up of operands and operators. C++ supports several kinds of operators and expressions.

NEW☞ TERM *Operators* are special symbols that take the values of *operands* and produce a new value.

Each category of operators manipulates data in a specific way. Today you learn about the following topics:

☐ Arithmetic operators and expressions

☐ Increment operators

☐ Arithmetic assignment operators

☐ Typecasting and data conversion

☐ Relational operators and conditional expressions

☐ Bit-manipulating operators

☐ The comma operator

Arithmetic Operators

Table 3.1 presents the C++ arithmetic operators. The compiler carries out floating-point or integer division depending on the operands. If both operands are integer expressions, the compiler yields the code for an integer division. If either or both operands are floating-point expressions, the compiler generates code for floating-point division.

Table 3.1. C++ arithmetic operators.

C++ Operator	Purpose	Data Type	Example
+	Unary plus	Numeric	x = +y + 3;
-	Unary minus	Numeric	x = -y;
+	Add	Numeric	z = y + x;
-	Subtract	Numeric	z = y - x;

C++ Operator	Purpose	Data Type	Example
*	Multiply	Numeric	z = y * x;
/	Divide	Numeric	z = y / x;
%	Modulus	Integers	z = y % x;

Let's look at an example that uses the mathematical operators with integers and floating-point numbers. Listing 3.1 shows the source code for program OPER1.CP. The program performs the following tasks:

- ☐ Prompts you to enter two integers (one integer per prompt)
- ☐ Applies the +, -, *, /, and % operators to the two integers, storing the results in separate variables
- ☐ Displays the result of the integer operations
- ☐ Prompts you to enter two floating-point numbers (one number per prompt)
- ☐ Applies the +, -, *, and / operators to the two numbers, storing the results in separate variables
- ☐ Displays the result of the floating-point operations

 Listing 3.1. Source code for the program OPER1.CP.

```
1: // simple C++ program to illustrate simple math operations
2:
3: #include <iostream.h>
4:
5: main()
6: {
7:
8:     int int1, int2;
9:     long long1, long2, long3, long4, long5;
10:    float x, y, real1, real2, real3, real4;
11:
12:    cout << "\nType first  integer : ";
13:    cin >> int1;
14:    cout << "Type second integer : ";
15:    cin >> int2;
16:    cout << "\n";
17:    long1 = int1 + int2;
18:    long2 = int1 - int2;
19:    long3 = int1 * int2;
```

continues

Listing 3.1. continued

```
20:      long4 = int1 / int2;
21:      long5 = int1 % int2;
22:      cout << int1 << " + " << int2 << " = " << long1 << '\n';
23:      cout << int1 << " - " << int2 << " = " << long2 << '\n';
24:      cout << int1 << " * " << int2 << " = " << long3 << '\n';
25:      cout << int1 << " / " << int2 << " = " << long4 << '\n';
26:      cout << int1 << " mod " << int2 << " = " << long5 << '\n';
27:      cout << "\n\n";
28:      cout << "Type first  real number : ";
29:      cin >> x;
30:      cout << "Type second real number : ";
31:      cin >> y;
32:      cout << "\n";
33:      real1 = x + y;
34:      real2 = x - y;
35:      real3 = x * y;
36:      real4 = x / y;
37:      cout << x << " + " << y << " = " << real1 << '\n';
38:      cout << x << " - " << y << " = " << real2 << '\n';
39:      cout << x << " * " << y << " = " << real3 << '\n';
40:      cout << x << " / " << y << " = " << real4 << '\n';
41:      cout << "\n\n";
42:      return 0;
43: }
```

Here is a sample session with the program in Listing 3.1:

```
Type first  integer : 10
Type second integer : 5

10 + 5 = 15
10 - 5 = 5
10 * 5 = 50
10 / 5 = 2
10 mod 5 = 0


Type first  real number : 1.25
Type second real number : 2.58

1.25 + 2.58 = 3.83
1.25 - 2.58 = -1.33
1.25 * 2.58 = 3.225
1.25 / 2.58 = 0.484496
```

The program in Listing 3.1 declares a set of int-typed, long-typed, and float-typed variables in the function main. Some of these variables store your input, and others store the results of the mathematical operations. The output statement in line 12 prompts you to enter the first integer. The input statement in line 13 obtains your input and stores it in the variable int1. Lines 14 and 15 perform a similar operation to prompt you for the second integer and to store it in variable int2.

The program performs the integer math operation in lines 17 through 21 and stores the results of these operations in variables long1 though long5. I declared these variables as long-typed to guard against possible numeric overflow. The output statements in lines 22 through 26 display the integer operands, the operators used, and the results.

The output statement in line 28 prompts you to enter the first floating-point number. The input statement in line 29 obtains your input and stores it in the variable x. Lines 30 and 31 perform a similar operation to prompt you for the second floating-point number and to store it in variable y.

NEW☞ A floating-point number is also known as a *real number*.
TERM

The program performs the floating-point math operation in lines 33 through 36 and stores the results of these operations in variables real1 through real4. The output statements in lines 37 through 40 display the operands, the operators used, and the results.

Arithmetic Expressions

The simplest kinds of expressions are the ones that contain literals, such as

```
-12
34.45
'A'
"Hello"
```

NEW☞ In general terms, an *arithmetic expression* is part of a program statement that
TERM contains a value.

The literal constants -12 and 35.45 are the simplest arithmetic expressions. The next level of arithmetic expressions includes single variables or constants, such as

```
DAYS_IN_WEEK // a constant
i
x
```

The next level of arithmetic expressions contains a single operator with numbers, constants, and variables as operands. Here are a few examples:

```
355 / 113
4 * i
45.67 + x
```

More advanced arithmetic expressions contain multiple operators and parentheses, as well as functions, such as

```
(355 / 113) * square(radius)
PIE * square(radius)
(((2 * x - 3) * x + 2) * x - 5
(1 + x) / (3 - x)
```

I discuss the order of executing the operators at the end of today's lesson, after introducing the other types of operators.

Increment Operators

C++ supports the special increment and decrement operators.

NEW TERM

Increment (++) and *decrement* (--) *operators* enable you to increment and decrement, respectively, by one the value stored in a variable.

Increment Operators

The general syntax for the increment operators is

```
variable++  // post-increment
++variable  // pre-increment
```

Examples:

```
lineNumber++;
++index;
```

Decrement Operators

The general syntax for the decrement operators is

```
variable--  // post-decrement
--variable  // pre-decrement
```

Examples:

```
lineNumber--;
--index;
```

This general syntax demonstrates that there are two ways to apply the ++ and -- operators. Placing these operators to the left of their operand changes the value of the operand *before* the operand contributes its value in an expression. Likewise, placing these operators to

the right of their operands alters the value of the operand *after* the operand contributes its value in an expression. If the ++ or -- operators are the only operators in a statement, there is no practical distinction between using the pre- or post- forms.

Here are a few simple examples:

```
int n, m, t = 5;

t++; // t is now 6, same effect as ++t
--t; // t is now 5, same effect as t--
t = 5;
n = 4 * t++; // t is now 6 and n is 20
t = 5;
m = 4 * ++m; // m is now 6 and n is 24
```

The first statement uses the post-increment ++ operator to increment the value of variable t. If you write ++t instead, you get the same result once the statement finishes executing. The second statement uses the pre-decrement -- operator. Again, if I write t-- instead, I get the same result. The next two statements assign 5 to variable t and then use the post-increment ++ operator in a simple math expression. This statement multiplies 4 by the current value of t (that is, 5), assigns the result of 20 to the variable n, and then increments the values in variable t to 6. The last two statements show a different outcome. The statement first increments the value in variable t (the value in variable t becomes 6), then performs the multiplication, and finally assigns the result of 24 to the variable n.

Let's look at a simple program that illustrates the feature of the increment operator. Listing 3.2 shows the source code for program OPER2.CP. The program requires no input from you. It simply displays two integers whose values were obtained using the increment operator.

 Listing 3.2. Source code for the program OPER2.CP.

```
1: /*
2:    C++ program to illustrate the feature of the increment operator.
3:    The ++ or -- may be included in an expression.  The value
4:    of the associated variable is altered after the expression
5:    is evaluated if the var++ (or var--) is used, or before
6:    when ++var (or --var) is used.
7: */
8:
9: #include <iostream.h>
10:
11: main()
12: {
13:    int i, k = 5;
14:
15:    // use post-incrementing
```

continues

Listing 3.2. continued

```
16:    i = 10 * (k++); // k contributes 5 to the expression
17:    cout << "i = " << i << "\n\n"; // displays 50 (= 10 * 5)
18:
19:    k--; // restores the value of k to 5
20:
21:    // use pre-incrementing
22:    i = 10 * (++k); // k contributes 6 to the expression
23:    cout << "i = " << i << "\n\n"; // displays 60 (= 10 * 6)
24:    return 0;
25: }
```

 Here is a sample session with the program in Listing 3.2:

```
i = 50

i = 60
```

 The program in Listing 3.2 has the function main which declares two int-typed variables, i and k. The function initializes the variable k by assigning it the value 5. Line 16 contains a statement that applies the post-increment operator to the variable k. Consequently, the statement multiplies 10 by the initial value in k, 5, and assigns the product, 50, to variable i. After assigning the result to variable i, the program increments the value in variable k. The output statement in line 17 displays the value in variable i. The statement in line 19 decrements the value in variable k back to 5. The statement in line 22 applies the pre-increment operator to the variable k. Therefore, the program first increments the value in variable k (from 5 to 6) and then multiplies 10 by the updated value in k. The program assigns the result of the multiplication, 60, to the variable i. The output statement in line 23 displays the current value of variable i.

Assignment Operators

As a programmer, you often come across statements that look like this:

```
IndexOfFirstElement = IndexOfFirstElement + 4;
GraphicsScaleRatio = GraphicsScaleRatio * 3;
CurrentRateOfReturn = CurrentRateOfReturn / 4;
DOSfileListSize = DOSfileListSize - 10;
```

The variable that receives the result of an expression is also the first operand. (Of course, the addition and multiplication are communicative operations; therefore, the assigned

variable can be either operand with these operations.) Notice that I chose relatively long names to remind you of your need to shorten the expression without making the names of the variables shorter.

NEW☞ TERM C++ offers *assignment operators* that merge with simple math operators.

You also can construct statements like these:

```
IndexOfFirstElement += 4;
GraphicsScaleRatio *= 3;
CurrentRateOfReturn /= 4;
DOSfileListSize -= 10;
```

Notice that the name of the variable appears only once and that the statements use the operators +=, *=, /=, and -=. Table 3.2 shows the arithmetic assignment operators. C++ supports other types of assignment operators associated with bit-manipulating operators.

Table 3.2. Arithmetic assignment operators.

Assignment Operator	Long Form	Example
x += y	x = x + y	x += 12;
x -= y	x = x - y	x -= 34 + y;
x *= y	x = x * y	scale *= 10;
x /= y	x = x / y	z /= 34 * y;
x %= y	x = x % y	z %= 2;

Let's look at a program that applies the assignment operators to integers and floating-point numbers. Listing 3.3 shows the source code for program OPER3.CP. The program performs the following tasks:

☐ Prompts you to enter two integers (one integer per prompt)

☐ Applies a set of assignment and increment operators to the two integers

☐ Displays the new values of the integers

☐ Prompts you to enter two floating-point numbers (one number per prompt)

☐ Applies a set of assignment and increment operators to the two numbers

☐ Displays the new values of the floating-point numbers

Listing 3.3. Source code for the program OPER3.CP.

```
1: // C++ program to illustrate math assignment operators
2:
3: #include <iostream.h>
4:
5: main()
6: {
7:     int i, j;
8:     double x, y;
9:
10:     cout << "Type first  integer : ";
11:     cin >> i;
12:     cout << "Type second integer : ";
13:     cin >> j;
14:     i += j;
15:     j -= 6;
16:     i *= 4;
17:     j /= 3;
18:     i++;
19:     j--;
20:     cout << "i = " << i << "\n";
21:     cout << "j = " << j << "\n";
22:
23:     cout << "Type first  real number : ";
24:     cin >> x;
25:     cout << "Type second real number : ";
26:     cin >> y;
27:     // abbreviated assignments also work with doubles in C++
28:     x += y;
29:     y -= 4.0;
30:     x *= 4.0;
31:     y /=  3.0;
32:     x++;
33:     y--;
34:     cout << "x = " << x << "\n";
35:     cout << "y = " << y << "\n";
36:     return 0;
37: }
```

Here is a sample session with the program in Listing 3.3:

```
Type first  integer : 55
Type second integer : 66
i = 485
j = 19
Type first  real number : 2.5
Type second real number : 4.58
x = 29.32
y = -0.806667
```

Analysis   The program in Listing 3.3 contains the function `main` which declares two `int`-typed variables (`i` and `j`) and two `double`-typed variables (`x` and `y`) in lines 7 and 8, respectively. The output statement in line 10 prompts you to enter the first integer. The input statement in line 11 receives your input and stores it in the variable `i`. Lines 12 and 13 are similar to lines 10 and 11—they prompt you for the second integer and store it in variable `j`.

The program manipulates the values in variables `i` and `j` using the statements in lines 14 through 19. In line 14, the program uses the `+=` operator to increment the value in variable `i` by the value in variable `j`. Line 15 uses the `-=` operator to decrement the value in variable `j` by 6. Line 16 applies the `*=` operator to multiply the value in variable `i` by 4 and to assign the result back to variable `i`. Line 17 utilizes the `/=` operator to divide the value in variable `j` by 3 and to store the result in `j`. Lines 18 and 19 apply the increment and decrement operators to variables `i` and `j`, respectively. The output statements in lines 20 and 21 display the contents of variables `i` and `j`, respectively.

The output statement in line 23 prompts you to enter the first floating-point number. The input statement in line 24 receives your input and saves it in the variable `x`. Lines 25 and 26 are similar to lines 23 and 24—they prompt you for the second floating-point number and store it in variable `y`.

The program manipulates the values in variables `x` and `y` using the statements in lines 28 through 33. In line 28, the program uses the `+=` operator to increment the value in variable `x` by the value in variable `y`. Line 29 uses the `-=` operator to decrement the value in variable `y` by 4. Line 30 applies the `*=` operator to multiply the value in variable `x` by 4 and to save the result back to `x`. Line 31 utilizes the `/=` operator to divide the value in variable `y` by 3 and to store the result in `y`. Lines 32 and 33 apply the increment and decrement operators to variables `x` and `y`, respectively. The output statements in lines 34 and 35 display the contents of variables `x` and `y`, respectively.

The *sizeof* Operator

Frequently your programs need to know the byte size of a data type or a variable. C++ provides the `sizeof` operator which takes for an argument either a data type or the name of a variable (`scalar`, `array`, `record`, and so on).

The *sizeof* Operator

The general syntax for the `sizeof` operator is

```
sizeof({variable_name ¦ data_type})
sizeof {variable_name ¦ data_type}
```

Examples:

```
int sizeDifference = sizeof(double) - sizeof(float);
int intSize = sizeof int;
```

DO	DON'T

DO use `sizeof` with the name of the variable instead of its data type. This approach is the safest because if you alter the data type of the variable, the `sizeof` operator still returns the correct answer. By contrast, if you use the `sizeof` operator with the data type of the variable and later alter the variable's type, you create a bug if you do not update the argument of the `sizeof` operator.

DON'T use numbers to represent the size of a variable. This approach often causes errors.

Let's look at an example that uses the `sizeof` operator with variables and data types. Listing 3.4 contains the source code for program SIZEOF1.CP. The program displays two similar tables that indicate the sizes of the `short int`, `int`, `long int`, `char`, and `float` data types. The program displays the first table by applying the `sizeof` operators to variables of the above types. The program displays the second table by directly applying the `sizeof` operator to the data types.

Listing 3.4. Source code for the program SIZEOF1.CP.

```
1: /*
2:    simple program that returns the data sizes using the sizeof()
3:    operator with variables and data types.
4: */
5:
6: #include <iostream.h>
7:
8: main()
9:
10: {
11:    short int aShort;
12:    int anInt;
```

```
13:      long aLong;
14:      char aChar;
15:      float aReal;
16:
17:      cout << "Table 1. Data sizes using sizeof(variable)\n\n";
18:      cout << "     Data type          Memory used\n";
19:      cout << "                           (bytes)\n";
20:      cout << "------------------     ----------";
21:      cout << "\n    short int              " << sizeof(aShort);
22:      cout << "\n     integer               " << sizeof(anInt);
23:      cout << "\n   long integer            " << sizeof(aLong);
24:      cout << "\n     character             " << sizeof(aChar);
25:      cout << "\n       float               " << sizeof(aReal);
26:      cout << "\n\n\n\n";
27:
28:      cout << "Table 2. Data sizes using sizeof(dataType)\n\n";
29:      cout << "     Data type          Memory used\n";
30:      cout << "                           (bytes)\n";
31:      cout << "------------------     ----------";
32:      cout << "\n    short int              " << sizeof(short int);
33:      cout << "\n     integer               " << sizeof(int);
34:      cout << "\n   long integer            " << sizeof(long);
35:      cout << "\n     character             " << sizeof(char);
36:      cout << "\n       float               " << sizeof(float);
37:      cout << "\n\n\n\n";
38:
39:      return 0;
40: }
```

 Here is a sample session with the program in Listing 3.4:

```
Table 1. Data sizes using sizeof(variable)

     Data type          Memory used
                          (bytes)
------------------     ----------
    short int              2
     integer               4
   long integer            4
     character             1
       float               4



Table 2. Data sizes using sizeof(dataType)

     Data type          Memory used
                          (bytes)
------------------     ----------
    short int              2
     integer               4
   long integer            4
     character             1
       float               4
```

 The program in Listing 3.4 declares five variables in function `main`. Each variable has a different data type and derives its name from its data type. For example, the variable `anInt` is an `int`-typed variable, the variable `aLong` is a `long`-typed variable, and so on.

The statements in lines 17 through 25 display the table of data sizes. The output statements in lines 21 through 25 use the `sizeof` operator with the variables.

The statements in lines 28 through 36 also display the table of data sizes. The output statements in lines 32 through 36 use the `sizeof` operator with the data type identifiers.

Typecasting

Automatic data conversion of a value from one data type to another compatible data type is one of the duties of a compiler. This data conversion simplifies expressions and eases the frustration of both novice and veteran programmers. With behind-the-scenes data conversion, you do not need to examine every expression that mixes compatible data types in your program. For example, the compiler handles most expressions that mix various types of integers or that mix integers and floating-point types. You get a compile-time error if you attempt to do something illegal!

NEW *Typecasting* is a language feature that enables you to specify explicitly how to
TERM convert a value from its original data type into a compatible data type. Thus, typecasting instructs the compiler to perform the conversion you want and not the one the compiler thinks is needed!

Typecasting

C++ supports the following forms of typecasting:

```
type_cast(expression)
(type_cast) expression
```

Examples:

```
int i = 2;
float a, b;
a = float(i);
b = (float) i;
```

Let's look at an example that illustrates implicit data conversion and typecasting. Listing 3.5 shows the source code for program TYPCAST1.CP. The program declares variables that have the character, integer, and floating-point data types. Then the program

performs two sets of similar mathematical operations. The first set relies on the automatic conversions of data types performed by the compiler. The second set of operations uses typecasting to explicitly instruct the compiler on how to convert the data types. The program requires no input—it provides its own data—and displays the output values for both sets of operations. The program illustrates that the compiler succeeds in generating the same output for both sets of operations.

 Listing 3.5. Source code for the program TYPCAST1.CP.

```
 1:  // simple C++ program that demonstrates typecasting
 2:
 3:  #include <iostream.h>
 4:
 5:  main()
 6:  {
 7:      short shortInt1, shortInt2;
 8:      unsigned short aByte;
 9:      int anInt;
10:      long aLong;
11:      char aChar;
12:      float aReal;
13:
14:      // assign values
15:      shortInt1 = 10;
16:      shortInt2 = 6;
17:      // perform operations without typecasting
18:      aByte = shortInt1 + shortInt2;
19:      anInt = shortInt1 - shortInt2;
20:      aLong = shortInt1 * shortInt2;
21:      aChar = aLong + 5; // conversion is automatic to character
22:      aReal = shortInt1 * shortInt2 + 0.5;
23:
24:      cout << "shortInt1 = " << shortInt1 << '\n'
25:           << "shortInt2 = " << shortInt2 << '\n'
26:           << "aByte = " << aByte << '\n'
27:           << "anInt = " << anInt << '\n'
28:           << "aLong = " << aLong << '\n'
29:           << "aChar is " << aChar << '\n'
30:           << "aReal = " << aReal << "\n\n\n";
31:
32:      // perform operations with typecasting
33:      aByte = (unsigned short) (shortInt1 + shortInt2);
34:      anInt = (int) (shortInt1 - shortInt2);
35:      aLong = (long) (shortInt1 * shortInt2);
36:      aChar = (unsigned char) (aLong + 5);
37:      aReal = (float) (shortInt1 * shortInt2 + 0.5);
38:
39:      cout << "shortInt1 = " << shortInt1 << '\n'
40:           << "shortInt2 = " << shortInt2 << '\n'
41:           << "aByte = " << aByte << '\n'
42:           << "anInt = " << anInt << '\n'
43:           << "aLong = " << aLong << '\n'
```

continues

Listing 3.5. continued

```
44:          << "aChar is " << aChar << '\n'
45:          << "aReal = " << aReal << "\n\n\n";
46:     return 0;
47: }
```

Here is a sample session with the program in Listing 3.5:

```
shortInt1 = 10
shortInt2 = 6
aByte = 16
anInt = 4
aLong = 60
aChar is A
aReal = 60.5


shortInt1 = 10
shortInt2 = 6
aByte = 16
anInt = 4
aLong = 60
aChar is A
aReal = 60.5
```

The program in Listing 3.5 declares the following variables in the function main:

☐ The short-typed variables shortInt1 and shortInt2

☐ The unsigned short-typed variable aByte

☐ The int-typed variable anInt

☐ The long-typed variable aLong

☐ The char-typed variable aChar

☐ The float-typed variable aReal

Lines 15 and 16 assign the integers 10 and 6 to variables shortInt1 and shortIn2, respectively. Lines 18 through 22 perform various mathematical operations and assign the results to variables aByte, anInt, aLong, aChar, and aReal.

> **Note:** C and C++ treat the char type as a special integer. Each char-typed literal (such as 'A'), constant, or variable has an integer value that is equal to its ASCII representation. This language feature enables you to store an integer in a char-typed variable and treat a char-type data item as an integer. The statement in line 21 adds the integer 5 to the value of the variable aLong and assigns the result, an integer, to variable aChar. The value of the assigned integer, 65, represents the ASCII code for the letter *A*.

The output statement in lines 24 through 30 displays the values stored in the variables. Notice that the output for variable aChar is the letter A. If I write the output term for variable aChar as << (int) aChar, I get 65, the ASCII code of the character stored in aChar.

The statements in lines 32 through 37 perform similar operations to the statements in lines 18 through 22. The main difference is that the statements in lines 32 through 37 use typecasting to explicitly instruct the compiler on how to convert the result. The output statement in lines 39 through 45 displays the contents of the variables.

Relational and Logical Operators

Table 3.3 shows the C++ relational and logical operators. Notice that C++ does not spell out the operators AND, OR, and NOT. Rather, it utilizes single- and dual-character symbols. Also notice that C++ does not support the relational XOR operator. You can use the following #define macro directives to define the AND, OR, and NOT identifiers as macros:

```
#define AND &&
#define OR ||
#define NOT !
```

NEW TERM The *relational operators* (less than, greater than, and equal to) and *logical operators* (AND, OR, and NOT) are the basic building blocks of decision-making constructs in any programming language.

Table 3.3. C++ relational and logical operators.

C++ Operator	Meaning	Example
&&	Logical AND	if (i > 1 && i < 10)
¦¦	Logical OR	if (c==0 ¦¦ c==9)
!	Logical NOT	if (!(c>1 && c<9))
<	Less than	if (i < 0)
<=	Less than or equal to	if (i <= 0)
>	Greater than	if (j > 10)
>=	Greater than or equal to	if (x >= 8.2)
==	Equal to	if (c == '\0')
!=	Not equal to	if (c != '\n')
? :	Conditional assignment	k = (i<1) ? 1 : i;

Although these macros are permissible in C++, you might get a negative reaction from veteran C++ programmers who read your code. Who said that programming is always objective?

Warning: Do *not* use the = operator as the equality relational operator. This common error is a source of logical bugs in a C++ program. You may be accustomed to using the = operator in other languages to test the equality of two data items. *In C++, you must use the == operator.*

What happens if you employ the = operator in C++? Do you get a compiler error? The answer is that you may get a compiler warning. Other than that, your C++ program should run. When the program reaches the expression that is supposed to test for equality, it actually attempts to assign the operand on the right of the = sign to the operand on the left of the = sign. Of course, a session with such a program most likely leads to weird program behavior, or even a system hang!

Note: C++ does not support predefined Boolean identifiers. Instead, the language regards 0 as false and a nonzero value as true. To add clarity to your programs I suggest that you declare global constants TRUE and FALSE and assign them 1 and 0, respectively.

Notice that the last operator in Table 3.3 is the ?:. This special operator supports what is known as the conditional expression.

NEW TERM The *conditional expression* is a shorthand for a dual-alternative, simple if-else statement (see Day 5 for more information about the if statement).

For example, the following is an if-else statement:

```
if (condition)
    variable = expression1;
else
    variable = expression2;
```

The equivalent conditional expression is

```
variable = (condition) ? expression1 : expression2;
```

The conditional expression tests the condition. If that condition is true, it assigns *expression1* to the target variable. Otherwise, it assigns *expression2* to the target variable.

Boolean Expressions

Often, you need to use a collection of relational and logical operators to formulate a nontrivial condition. Here are examples of such conditions:

```
x < 0 || x > 11
(i != 0 || i > 100) && (j != i || j > 0)
x != 0 && x != 10 && x != 100
```

NEW TERM *Boolean* (also called *logical*) *expressions* are expressions that involve logical operators and/or relational operators.

DO   **DON'T**

DO double-check to avoid Boolean expressions that are either always true or always false. For example, the expression (x < 0 && x > 10) is always false, because no value of x can be negative and greater than 10 at the same time.

DON'T use the = operator to test for equality.

Let's look at an example that uses relational and logical operators and expressions. Listing 3.6 shows the source code for program RELOP1.CP. The program prompts you to enter three integers and then proceeds to perform a battery of tests. The program displays the relational and logical operations, their operands, and their results.

 Listing 3.6. Source code for the program RELOP1.CP.

```
 1: /*
 2:    simple C++ program that uses logical expressions
 3:    this program uses the conditional expression to display
 4:    TRUE or FALSE messages, since C++ does not support the
 5:    BOOLEAN data type.
 6: */
 7:
 8: #include <iostream.h>
 9:
10: const MIN_NUM = 30;
11: const MAX_NUM = 199;
12: // const int TRUE = 1;
13: // const int FALSE = 0;
14:
15: main()
16: {
17:     int i, j, k;
18:     int flag1, flag2, in_range,
19:         same_int, xor_flag;
20:
21:     cout << "Type first  integer : "; cin >> i;
22:     cout << "Type second integer : "; cin >> j;
23:     cout << "Type third  integer : "; cin >> k;
24:
25:     // test for range [MIN_NUM..MAX_NUM]
26:     flag1 = i >= MIN_NUM;
27:     flag2 = i <= MAX_NUM;
28:     in_range = flag1 && flag2;
29:     cout << "\n" << i << " is in the range "
30:         << MIN_NUM << " to " << MAX_NUM << " : "
31:         << ((in_range) ? "TRUE" : "FALSE");
32:
33:     // test if two or more entered numbers are equal
34:     same_int = i == j || i == k || j == k;
35:     cout << "\nat least two integers you typed are equal : "
```

```
36:              << ((same_int) ? "TRUE" : "FALSE");
37:
38:      // miscellaneous tests
39:      cout << "\n" << i << " != " << j << " : "
40:              << ((i != j) ? "TRUE" : "FALSE");
41:      cout << "\nNOT (" << i << " < " << j << ") : "
42:              << ((!(i < j)) ? "TRUE" : "FALSE");
43:      cout << "\n" << i << " <= " << j << " : "
44:              << ((i <= j) ? "TRUE" : "FALSE");
45:      cout << "\n" << k << " > " << j << " : "
46:              << ((k > j) ? "TRUE" : "FALSE");
47:      cout << "\n(" << k << " = " << i << ") AND ("
48:              << j << " != " << k << ") : "
49:              << ((k == i && j != k) ? "TRUE" : "FALSE");
50:
51:      // NOTE: C++ does NOT support the logical XOR operator for
52:      // boolean expressions.
53:      // add numeric results of logical tests.  Value is in 0..2
54:      xor_flag = (k <= i) + (j >= k);
55:      // if xor_flag is either 0 or 2 (i.e. not = 1), it is
56:      // FALSE therefore interpret 0 or 2 as false.
57:      xor_flag = (xor_flag == 1) ? TRUE : FALSE;
58:      cout << "\n(" << k << " <= " << i << ") XOR ("
59:              << j << " >= " << k << ") : "
60:              << ((xor_flag) ? "TRUE" : "FALSE");
61:      cout << "\n(" << k << " > " << i << ") AND("
62:              << j << " <= " << k << ") : "
63:              << ((k > i && j <= k) ? "TRUE" : "FALSE");
64:      cout << "\n\n";
65:      return 0;
66: }
```

Here is a sample session with the program in Listing 3.6:

```
Type first  integer : 55
Type second integer : 64
Type third  integer : 87

55 is in the range 30 to 199 : TRUE
at least two integers you typed are equal : FALSE
55 != 64 : TRUE
NOT (55 < 64) : FALSE
55 <= 64 : TRUE
87 > 64 : TRUE
(87 = 55) AND (64 != 87) : FALSE
(87 <= 55) XOR (64 >= 87) : FALSE
(87 > 55) AND(64 <= 87) : TRUE
```

The program in Listing 3.6 declares two global constants. The constants MIN_NUM and MAX_NUM define a range of numbers used in the logical tests. The commented constants TRUE and FALSE represent the Boolean values and are predefined in the Symantec C++ libraries. Typically, these constants are not predefined in C++, which is why I inserted the commented declaration to remind you that you need these

declarations if you port the program to other C++ compilers. The function main declares a number of int variables that are used for input and various testing. The statements in lines 21 through 23 prompt you for three integers and store them in the variables i, j, and k, respectively.

The statements in lines 26 through 31 deal with testing whether the value in variable i lies in the range of MIN_NUM and MAX_NUM. The statement in line 26 tests if the value in i is greater than or equal to the constant MIN_NUM. The program assigns the Boolean result to the variable flag1. The statement in line 27 tests whether the value in i is less than or equal to the constant MAX_NUM. The program assigns the Boolean result to the variable flag2. The statement in line 28 applies the && operator to the variables flag1 and flag2, and assigns the Boolean result to the variable in_range. The output statement in lines 29 through 31 states what the test is and displays TRUE or FALSE depending on the value in variable in_range. The statement uses the conditional operator ?: to display the string TRUE if in_range has a nonzero value and to display the string FALSE if otherwise.

The statements in lines 34 through 36 determine whether at least two of the three integers you entered are equal. The statement in line 34 uses a Boolean expression that applies the == relational operators and the ¦¦ logical operators. The statement assigns the Boolean result to the variable same_int. The output statement in lines 35 and 36 states the test and displays the TRUE/FALSE outcome. The output statement uses the conditional operator to display the strings TRUE or FALSE depending on the value in variable same_int.

The statements in lines 39 through 49 perform miscellaneous tests that involve the input values and display both the test and the results. Feel free to alter these statements to conduct different tests.

> **Note:** The statements in lines 54 through 60 perform an XOR test and display the outcome. The program uses a simple programming trick to implement the XOR operator. The statement in line 54 adds the Boolean value of the sub-expressions (k <= i) and (j >= k). The result is 0 if both sub-expressions are false, 1 if only one of the sub-expressions is true, and 2 if both sub-expressions are true. Because the XOR operator is true only if either sub-expression is true, the statement in line 57 assigns TRUE to the variable xor_flag if the previous value is 1. Otherwise, the statement assigns FALSE to xor_flag. The statements in lines 61 through 63 perform another miscellaneous test.

Bit-Manipulation Operators

C++ is a programming language that is suitable for system development. System development requires bit-manipulating operators.

NEW☞ *Bit-manipulation operators* toggle, set, query, and shift the bits of a byte or a word.
TERM

Table 3.4 shows the bit-manipulating operators. Notice that C++ uses the symbols & and ¦ to represent the bitwise AND and OR operators, respectively. Recall that the && and ¦¦ characters represent the logical AND and OR operators, respectively. In addition to the bit-manipulating operators, C++ supports the bit-manipulating assignment operators, shown in Table 3.5. (Using bit-manipulating operators is part of advanced programming, which involves fiddling with single bits. As a novice C++ programmer you will most likely not use these operators in the near future.)

Table 3.4. C++ bit-manipulating operators.

C++ Operator	Meaning	Example
&	Bitwise AND	i & 128
¦	Bitwise OR	j ¦ 64
^	Bitwise XOR	j ^ 12
~	Bitwise NOT	~j
<<	Bitwise shift left	i << 2
>>	Bitwise shift right	j >> 3

Table 3.5. C++ bit-manipulating assignment operators.

C++ Operator	Long Form	Example
x &= y	x = x & y	i &= 128
x ¦= y	x = x ¦ y	j ¦= 64
x ^= y	x = x ^ y	k ^= 15
x <<= y	x = x << y	j <<= 2
x >>= y	x = x >> y	k >>= 3

Let's look at a C++ program that performs simple bit manipulation. Listing 3.7 contains the source code for program BITS1.CP. The program requires no input because it uses internal data. The program applies the ¦, &, ^, >>, and << bitwise operators and displays the results of the bitwise manipulation.

 Listing 3.7. Source code for the program BITS1.CP.

```
1: // C++ program to perform bit manipulations
2:
3: #include <iostream.h>
4:
5: main()
6: {
7:
8:     int i, j, k;
9:
10:     // assign values to i and j
11:     i = 0xF0;
12:     j = 0x1A;
13:
14:     k = j & i;
15:     cout << j << " AND " << i << " = " << k << "\n";
16:
17:     k = j ¦ i;
18:     cout << j << " OR " << i << " = " << k << "\n";
19:
20:     k = j ^ 0x1C;
21:     cout << j << " XOR " << 0x1C << " = " << k << "\n";
22:
23:     k = i << 2;
24:     cout << i << " shifted left by 2 bits = " << k << "\n";
25:
26:     k = i >> 2;
27:     cout << i << " shifted right by 2 bits = " << k << "\n";
28:     return 0;
29: }
```

 Here is a sample session with the program in Listing 3.7:

```
26 AND 240 = 16
26 OR 240 = 250
26 XOR 28 = 6
240 shifted left by 2 bits = 960
240 shifted right by 2 bits = 60
```

 The program in Listing 3.7 declares three int-typed variables, i, j, and k. The statements in lines 11 and 12 assign hexadecimal numbers to the variables i and j, respectively. The statement in line 14 applies the bitwise AND operator

to the variables i and j then stores the result in variable k. The output statement in line 15 displays the operands, the bitwise operator, and the results. The statement in line 17 applies the bitwise OR operator to the variables i and j then saves the result to variable k. The output statement in line 18 displays the operands, the bitwise operator, and the results. The statement in line 20 applies the bitwise XOR operator using the variable j and the hexadecimal integer 0x1C. The output statement in line 21 displays the operands, the bitwise operator, and the results.

The statements in lines 23 through 27 apply the shift left and shift right operators to variable i. These operators shift the bits of variable i by two bits and assign the result to variable k. The effect of the left shift operator is the same as multiplying the value in variable i by four. Similarly, the effect of the right shift operator is the same as dividing the value in variable i by four.

The Comma Operator

The comma operator requires that the program completely evaluate the first expression before evaluating the second expression. Both expressions are located in the same C++ statement! What does *located in the same C++ statement* mean exactly? Why utilize this rather unusual operator in the first place? Because the comma operator, with its peculiar role, does serve a specific and very important purpose in the for loop.

**NEW
TERM**   *Loops* are powerful language constructs that enable computers to excel in performing repetitive tasks. The *comma operator* enables you to create multiple expressions that initialize multiple loop-related variables.

Syntax

The Comma Operator

The general syntax for the comma operator is

```
expression1, expression2
```

Example:

```
for (i = 0, j = 0; i < 10; i++, j++)
```

You learn more about the for loop in Day 6. For now, this example shows you how to apply the comma operator.

Operator Precedence and Evaluation Direction

Now that you are familiar with most of the C++ operators (there are a few more operators that deal with pointers and addresses), there are two related aspects you need to know: first, the precedence of the C++ operators, and second, the direction (or sequence) of evaluation. Table 3.6 shows the C++ precedence of the C++ operators that I have covered so far and also indicates the evaluation direction.

Table 3.6. C++ operators and their precedence.

Category	Name	Symbol	Evaluation Direction	Precedence
Monadic				
	Post-increment	++	Left to right	2
	Post-decrement	--	Left to right	2
	Address	&	Right to left	2
	Bitwise NOT	~	Right to left	2
	Typecast	(`type`)	Right to left	2
	Logical NOT	!	Right to left	2
	Negation	-	Right to left	2
	Plus sign	+	Right to left	2
	Pre-increment	++	Right to left	2
	Pre-decrement	--	Right to left	2
	Size of data	`sizeof`	Right to left	2
Multiplicative				
	Modulus	%	Left to right	3
	Multiply	*	Left to right	3
	Divide	/	Left to right	3

Category	Name	Symbol	Evaluation Direction	Precedence
Additive				
	Add	+	Left to right	4
	Subtract	-	Left to right	4
Bitwise Shift				
	Shift left	<<	Left to right	5
	Shift right	>>	Left to right	5
Relational				
	Less than	<	Left to right	6
	Less or equal	<=	Left to right	6
	Greater than	>	Left to right	6
	Greater or equal	>=	Left to right	6
	Equal	==	Left to right	7
	Not equal	!=	Left to right	7
Bitwise				
	AND	&	Left to right	8
	XOR	^	Left to right	9
	OR	¦	Left to right	10
Logical				
	AND	&&	Left to right	11
	OR	¦¦	Left to right	12
Ternary				
	Cond. express.	?:	Right to left	13
Assignment				
	Arithmetic	=	Right to left	14

continues

Table 3.6. continued

Category	Name	Symbol	Evaluation Direction	Precedence
		+=	Right to left	14
		-=	Right to left	14
		*=	Right to left	14
		/=	Right to left	14
		%=	Right to left	14
	Shift	>>=	Right to left	14
		<<=	Right to left	14
	Bitwise	&=	Right to left	14
		¦=	Right to left	14
		^=	Right to left	14
	Comma	,	Left to right	15

Summary

Today's lesson presented the various C++ operators and discussed how to use these operators to manipulate data. You learned the following:

☐ The arithmetic operators include +, -, *, /, and % (modulus).

☐ The arithmetic expressions vary in complexity. The simplest expression contains a single data item (literal, constant, or variable). Complex expressions include multiple operators, functions, literals, constants, and variables.

☐ The increment and decrement operators come in the pre- and post- forms. C++ enables you to apply these operators to variables that store characters, integers, and even floating-point numbers.

☐ The arithmetic assignment operators enable you to write shorter arithmetic expressions in which the primary operand is also the variable receiving the result of the expression.

- The `sizeof` operator returns the byte size of either a data type or a variable.

- Typecasting enables you to force the type conversion of an expression.

- Relational and logical operators permit you to build logical expressions. C++ does not support a predefined Boolean type but instead considers 0 as false and any nonzero value as true.

- Boolean expressions combine relational and logical operators to formulate nontrivial conditions. These expressions enable a program to make sophisticated decisions.

- The conditional expression offers you a short form for the simple dual-alternative `if-else` statement.

- The bit-manipulation operators perform bitwise AND, OR, XOR, and NOT operations. In addition, C++ supports the << and >> bitwise shift operators.

- The bit-manipulation assignment operators offer short forms for simple bit-manipulation statements.

Q&A

Q How does the compiler react when you declare a variable but never assign a value to it?

A The compiler issues a warning that the variable is unreferenced.

Q What is the Boolean expression for checking that the value of a variable, call it `i`, is in the range of values (for example, defined by variables `loVal` and `hiVal`)?

A The expression that determines whether the value in variable `i` is located in a range is

```
(i >= lowVal && i <= hiVal)
```

Q What is the Boolean expression for checking that the value of a variable, call it `i`, is *inside* the range of values (for example, defined by variables `loVal` and `hiVal`)?

A The expression that determines whether the value in variable `i` is located inside a range is

```
(i > lowVal && i < hiVal)
```

Workshop

The Workshop provides quiz questions to help you solidify your understanding of the material covered and exercises to provide you with experience in using what you've learned. Try to understand the quiz and exercise answers before continuing on to the next day's lesson. Answers are provided in Appendix B, "Answers."

Quiz

1. What is the output of the following program?

```
#include <iostream.h>

main()
{
  int i = 3;
  int j = 5;
  double x = 33.5;
  double y = 10.0;

  cout << 10 + j % i << "\n";
  cout << i * i - 2 * i + 5 << "\n";
  cout << (19 + i + j) / (2 * j + 2) << "\n";
  cout << x / y + y / x << "\n";
  cout << i * x + j * y << "\n";
  return 0;
}
```

2. What is the output of the following program?

```
#include <iostream.h>

main()
{
  int i = 3;
 int j = 5;

  cout << 10 + j % i++ << "\n";
  cout << --i * i - 2 * i + 5 << "\n";
```

```
    cout << (19 + ++i + ++j) / (2 * j + 2) << "\n";
    return 0;
}
```

3. What is the output of the following program?

```
#include <iostream.h>

main()
{
  int i = 3;
  int j = 5;

  i += j;
  j *= 2;
  cout << 10 + j % i << "\n";
  i -= 2;
  j /= 3;
  cout << i * i - 2 * i + j << "\n";
  return 0;
}
```

4. What is the output of the following program?

```
#include <iostream.h>

main()
{
  int i = 5;
  int j = 10;

  cout << ((i <= j) ? "TRUE" : "FALSE") << "\n";
  cout << ((i > 0 && j < 100) ?  "TRUE" : "FALSE") << "\n";
  cout << ((i > 0 && i < 10) ? "TRUE" : "FALSE") << "\n";
  cout << ((i == 5 && i == j) ? "TRUE" : "FALSE") << "\n";
  return 0;
}
```

Exercises

1. Use the conditional operator to write the function max, which returns the greater of two integers.

2. Use the conditional operator to write the function min, which returns the smaller of two integers.

3. Use the conditional operator to write the function abs, which returns the absolute value of an integer.

4. Use the conditional operator to write the function isOdd, which returns 0 if its integer argument is an odd number and returns 1 if otherwise.

Managing I/O

C++, like its parent language C, does not define I/O operations that are part of the core language. Instead, C++ and C rely on I/O libraries to provide the needed I/O support. Such libraries are mainly aimed at non-GUI (graphical user interface) environments such as MS-DOS. These libraries usually work with generic non-GUI applications, which is why they are of interest in this book. However, because my primary goal is to teach you how to write Macintosh programs, I keep the discussion of these I/O libraries to a minimum. Today's short lesson looks at a small selection of input and output operations and functions that are supported by the STDIO.H and IOSTREAM.H header files. You learn about the following topics:

- ☐ Formatted stream output
- ☐ Stream input
- ☐ The `printf` function

Formatted Stream Output

C++ brought with it a family of extendable I/O libraries. The language designers recognized that the I/O functions in STDIO.H, inherited from C, have their limitations when dealing with classes (you learn more about classes in Day 11). Consequently, C++ extends the notion of streams. Recall that streams, which already exist in C, are a sequence of data flowing from one part of a computer to another. In the programs that I have presented so far, you have seen the extractor operator << working with the standard output stream, `cout`. You also saw the inserter operator >> and the standard input stream, `cin`. In this section I introduce you to the stream functions `width` and `precision` which help in formatting the output. The C++ stream libraries have many more functions to further fine-tune the output. However, as I stated earlier, because these functions work for non-GUI interfaces, I don't want to overwhelm you with information that is relevant to Macintosh programming. The `width` function specifies the width of the output. The general form for using this function with the `cout` stream is

```
cout.width(widthOfOutput);
```

The `precision` function specifies the number of digits for floating-point numbers. The general form for using this function with the `cout` stream is

```
cout.precision(numberOfDigits);
```

Let's look at an example. Listing 4.1 contains the source code for program OUT1.CP. The program, which requires no input, displays formatted integers, floating-point numbers, and characters using the `width` and `precision` stream functions.

Listing 4.1. Source code for the program OUT1.CP.

```
1: // Program that illustrates C++ formatted stream output
2: // using the width and precision functions
3:
4: #include <iostream.h>
5:
6: main()
7: {
8:    short     aShort     = 4;
9:    int       anInt      = 67;
10:   unsigned char aByte   = 128;
11:   char      aChar      = '@';
12:   float     aSingle    = 355.0;
13:   double    aDouble    = 1.130e+002;
14:   // display sample expressions
15:   cout.width(3); cout << int(aByte) << " + ";
16:   cout.width(2); cout << anInt << " = ";
17:   cout.width(3); cout << (aByte + anInt) << '\n';
18:
19:   cout.precision(4); cout << aSingle << " / ";
20:   cout.precision(4); cout << aDouble << " = ";
21:   cout.precision(5); cout << (aSingle / aDouble) << '\n';
22:
23:   cout << "The character in variable aChar is "
24:        << aChar << '\n';
25:   return 0;
26: }
```

4

Here is a sample session with the program in Listing 4.1:

```
128 + 67 = 195
355 / 113 = 3.14159
The character in variable aChar is @
```

The program in Listing 4.1 declares a set of variables that have different data types. The statements in lines 15 through 17 use the stream function width to specify the output width for the next item displayed by a cout statement. Notice that it takes six statements to display three integers. In addition, notice that in line 15 the program uses the expression int(aByte) to typecast the unsigned char type into an int. Without this type conversion, the contents of variable aByte appear as a character instead of a number. If I use the stream output to display integers that have default widths, I can replace the six stream output statements with a single one.

Lines 19 through 21 contain the second set of stream output statements for the floating-point numbers. The statements in these lines contain the stream function precision to specify the total number of digits to display. Again, it takes six C++ statements to output three floating-point numbers. However, if I use the stream output to display numbers that have default widths, I can replace the six stream output statements with a single one.

Stream Input

Like the standard output stream, C++ offers the standard input stream, `cin`. This input stream can read predefined data types such as `int`, `unsigned`, `long`, and `char`. Typically, you use the inserter operator `>>` to obtain input for the predefined data types. The programs that I have presented so far use the `>>` operator to enter a single item. C++ streams enable you to chain the `>>` operator to enter multiple items. In the case of multiple items, you need to observe the following rules:

☐ Enter a space between two consecutive numbers to separate them.

☐ Entering a space between two consecutive characters is optional.

☐ Entering a space between a character and a number (and vice versa) is necessary only if the character is a digit.

☐ The input stream ignores spaces.

☐ You can enter multiple items on different lines. The stream input statements are not fully executed until they obtain all the specified input.

Note: I postpone discussing the input of character strings for now. Day 9 covers strings and includes the input of strings.

Let's look at a program that illustrates both the input of multiple items and different combinations of data types. Listing 4.2 shows the source code for program IN1.CP. The program performs the following tasks:

☐ Prompts you to enter three numbers

☐ Calculates the sum of the three numbers

☐ Displays the sum and the average of the three numbers you entered

☐ Prompts you to type in three characters

☐ Displays your input

☐ Prompts you to enter a number, a character, and a number

☐ Displays your input

☐ Prompts you to enter a character, a number, and a character

☐ Displays your input

Listing 4.2. Source code for the program IN1.CP.

```
1: // Program that illustrates standard stream input
2:
3: #include <iostream.h>
4:
5: main()
6: {
7:    double x, y, z, sum;
8:    char c1, c2, c3;
9:
10:    cout << "Enter three numbers separated by a space : ";
11:    cin >> x >> y >> z;
12:    sum = x + y + z;
13:    cout << "Sum of numbers = " << sum
14:         << "\nAverage of numbers = " << sum / 2 << "\n";
15:    cout << "Enter three characters : ";
16:    cin >> c1 >> c2 >> c3;
17:    cout << "You entered characters '" << c1
18:         << "', '" << c2 << "', and '"
19:         << c3 << "'\n";
20:    cout << "Enter a number, a character, and a number : ";
21:    cin >> x >> c1 >> y;
22:    cout << "You entered " << x << " " << c1 << " " << y << "\n";
23:    cout << "Enter a character, a number, and a character : ";
24:    cin >> c1 >> x >> c2;
25:    cout << "You entered " << c1 << " " << x << " " << c2 << "\n";
26:
27:    return 0;
28: }
```

Here is a sample session with the program in Listing 4.2:

```
Enter three numbers separated by a space : 1 2 3
Sum of numbers = 6
Average of numbers = 3
Enter three characters : ABC
You entered characters 'A', 'B', and 'C'
Enter a number, a character, and a number : 12A34.4
You entered 12 A 34.4
Enter a character, a number, and a character : A3.14Z
You entered A 3.14 Z
```

The program in Listing 4.2 declares four double-typed variables and three char-typed variables. The output statement in line 10 prompts you to enter three numbers. The input statement in line 11 obtains your input and stores the numbers in variables x, y, and z. You need to enter a space character between any two numbers. You can also enter each number on a separate line. The statement stores the first number you enter in variable x, the second number in variable y, and the third one in variable z. This sequence is determined by the sequence in which these variables appear in line 11.

The statement in line 12 calculates the sum of the values in variables x, y, and z. The output statement in lines 13 and 14 displays the sum and average of the numbers you entered.

The output statement in line 15 prompts you to enter three characters. The input statement in line 16 obtains your input and sequentially stores the characters in variables c1, c2, and c3. Your input need not separate the characters with a space. Thus, you can type in characters such as 1A2, Bob, and 1 D d. The output statement in lines 17 through 19 displays the characters you typed, separated by spaces.

The output statement in line 20 prompts you to enter a number, a character, and a number. The input statement in line 21 sequentially stores your input in variables x, c1, and y. You need to type in a space between the character and either number only if the character can be interpreted as part of either number. For example, if you want to enter the number 12, the dot character, and the number 55, type in 12 . 55. The spaces around the dot ensure that the input stream does not consider it as a decimal part of either floating-point number. The output statement in line 22 displays the values you entered separated by spaces.

The output statement in line 23 prompts you to enter a character, a number, and a character. The input statement in line 24 sequentially stores your input in variables c1, x, and c2. You need to enter a space between the characters and the number only if the characters can be interpreted as part of the number. For example, if you want to enter the character -, the number 12, and the digit 0, type in - 12 0. The output statement in line 25 displays the values you entered separated by spaces.

The *printf* Function

As a novice C++ programmer, you have a wealth of I/O functions to choose from. In this section I discuss the formatting features of function printf, which is part of the standard I/O of C. The function is prototyped in the header file STDIO.H.

The printf function offers much power and presents formatted controls. The general syntax for the individual formatting instruction is

```
% [flags] [width] [.precision] [F ¦ N ¦ h ¦ l] <type character>
```

The *flags* options indicate the output justification, numeric signs, decimal points, and trailing zeros. In addition, these flags also specify the octal and hexadecimal prefixes. Table 4.1 shows the escape sequences for the format string of the printf function.

Table 4.1. The escape sequences for the format string of the printf function.

Escape Sequence	Decimal Value	Hex Value	Task
\a	7	0x07	Bell
\b	8	0x08	Backspace
\f	12	0x0C	Formfeed
\n	10	0x0A	New line
\r	13	0x0D	Carriage return
\t	9	0x09	Horizontal tab
\v	11	0x0B	Vertical tab
\\	92	0x5C	Backslash
\'	44	0x2C	Single quote
\"	34	0x22	Double quote
\?	63	0x3F	Question mark
\000			1 to 3 digits for octal value
\Xhhh and \xhhh		0xhhh	Hexadecimal value

The *width* option indicates the minimum number of displayed characters. The printf function uses zeros and blanks to pad the output if needed. When the width number begins with a 0, the printf function uses leading zeros, instead of spaces, for padding. When the * character appears instead of a width number, the printf function obtains the actual width number from the function's argument list. The argument that specifies the required width must come before the argument actually being formatted. The following example displays the integer 3 using 2 characters, as specified by the third argument of printf:

```
printf("%*d", 3, 2);
```

The *precision* option specifies the maximum number of displayed characters. If you include an integer, the precision option defines the minimum number of displayed digits. When the * character is used in place of a precision number, the printf function obtains the actual precision from the argument list. The argument that specifies the

required precision must come before the argument that is actually being formatted. The following example displays the floating-point number 3.3244 using 10 characters, as specified by the third argument of `printf`:

```
printf("%7.*f", 3.3244, 10);
```

The F, N, h, and l options are sized options used to overrule the argument's default size. The F and N options are used in conjunction with far and near pointers, respectively. The h and l options are used to indicate short int or long, respectively.

The `printf` function requires that you specify a data type character with each % format code. Table 4.2 presents the options for the flags in the format string of `printf`. Table 4.3 presents the data type characters used in the format string of `printf`.

Table 4.2. Options for the flags in the format string of the `printf` function.

Format Option	Outcome
-	Justifies to the left within the specified field
+	Displays the plus or minus sign of a value
blank	Displays a leading blank if the value is positive; displays a minus sign if the value is negative
#	No effect on decimal integers; displays a leading 0X or 0x for hexadecimal integers; displays a leading zero for octal integers; displays the decimal point for reals

Table 4.3. Data type characters used in the format string of `printf`.

Category	Type Character	Outcome
Character	c	Single character
	d	Signed decimal int
	i	Signed decimal int
	o	Unsigned octal int
	u	Unsigned decimal int

Category	Type Character	Outcome
	x	Unsigned hexadecimal int (the set of numeric characters used is 01234567890abcdef)
	X	Unsigned hexadecimal int (the set of numeric characters used is 01234567890abcdef)
Pointer	p	Displays only the offset for near pointers as OOOO; displays far pointers as SSSS:OOOO
Pointer to int	n	
real	f	Displays signed value in the format [-]dddd.dddd
	e	Displays signed scientific value in the format [-]d.dddde[+I-]ddd
	E	Displays signed scientific value in the format [-]d.ddddE[+I-]ddd
	g	Displays signed value using either the f or e formats, depending on the value and the specified precision
	G	Displays signed value using either the f or E formats, depending on the value and the specified precision
String pointer	s	Displays characters until the null terminator of the string is reached

Note: Although the function printf plays no role in the output of Macintosh applications, its sister function, sprintf, does. The latter function creates a string of characters which contains the formatted image of the output. I discuss the sprintf function in Day 9 and use it in the latter lessons of this book to create a dialog box that contains messages which include numbers.

Let's look at a simple example. Listing 4.3 shows the source code for program OUT2.CP. I created this program by editing the OUT1.CP in Listing 4.1. The new version displays formatted output using the `printf` function. The program displays the same floating-point numbers using three different sets of format code.

Listing 4.3. Source code for the program OUT2.CP.

```
 1: // C++ program that uses the printf function for formatted output
 2:
 3: #include <stdio.h>
 4:
 5: main()
 6: {
 7:    short     aShort    = 4;
 8:    int       anInt     = 67;
 9:    unsigned char aByte  = 128;
10:    char      aChar     = '@';
11:    float     aSingle   = 355.0;
12:    double    aDouble   = 1.130e+002;
13:    // display sample expressions
14:    printf("%3d %c %2d = %3d\n",
15:            aByte, '+', anInt, aByte + anInt);
16:
17:    printf("Output uses the %%lf format\n");
18:    printf("%6.4f / %6.4lf = %7.5lf\n", aSingle, aDouble,
19:                                aSingle / aDouble);
20:    printf("Output uses the %%le format\n");
21:    printf("%6.4e / %6.4le = %7.5le\n", aSingle, aDouble,
22:                                aSingle / aDouble);
23:    printf("Output uses the %%lg format\n");
24:    printf("%6.4g / %6.4lg = %7.5lg\n", aSingle, aDouble,
25:                                aSingle / aDouble);
26:
27:    printf("The character in variable aChar is %c\n", aChar);
28:    printf("The ASCII code of %c is %d\n", aChar, aChar);
29     return 0;
30: }
```

Here is a sample session with the program in Listing 4.3:

```
128 + 67 = 195
Output uses the %lf format
355.0000 / 113.0000 = 3.14159
Output uses the %le format
3.5500e+02 / 1.1300e+02 = 3.14159e+00
Output uses the %lg format
    355 / 113 = 3.1416
The character in variable aChar is @
The ASCII code of @ is 64
```

Analysis The program in Listing 4.3 declares a collection of variables with different data types. The output statement in lines 14 and 15 displays integers and characters using the %d and %c format controls. Table 4.4 shows the effect of the various format controls in the printf statement at line 14. Notice that the printf function converts the first item in output from an unsigned char to an int.

Table 4.4. Effects of the various format controls in the printf statement at line 16.

Format Control	Item	Data Type	Output
%3d	aByte	unsigned char	Integer
%c	'+'	char	Character
%2d	anInt	int	Integer
%3d	aByte + anInt	int	Integer

The output statement in line 18 displays the variable aSingle, the variable aDouble, and the expression aSingle / aDouble using the format controls %6.4f, %6.4lf, and %7.5lf. These controls specify precision values of 4, 4, and 5 digits, respectively, and minimum widths of 6, 6, and 7 characters, respectively. The last two format controls indicate that they display a double-typed value.

The output statement in line 21 is similar to that in line 18. The main difference is that the printf in line 21 uses the e format instead of the f format. Consequently, the three items in the printf statement appear in scientific notation.

The output statement in line 24 is similar to that in line 18. The main difference is that the printf in line 24 uses the g format instead of the f format. Consequently, the first two items in the printf statement appear with no decimal places because they are whole numbers.

The output statement in line 27 displays the contents in variable aChar using the %c format control. The output statement in line 28 displays the contents of variable aChar twice: once as a character and once as an integer (the ASCII code of a character, to be more exact). The printf function in line 28 performs this task by using the %c and %d format controls, respectively.

4

Summary

Today's lesson examined the basic input and output operations and functions that are supported by the IOSTREAM.H and STDIO.H header files. You learned the following:

☐ Formatted stream output uses the `precision` and `width` functions to provide some basic output formatting.

☐ Standard stream input supports the insert operator `>>` to obtain input for the predefined data types in C++.

☐ The format codes involved in the format string of the `printf` function empower the `printf` function to control the appearance of the output and even perform type conversion.

Q&A

Q How can I chain `>>` or `<<` operators?

A Each of these operators returns a special stream data type that can be the input for another similar stream operator.

Q Why can't I use the stream I/O operators in Macintosh applications?

A Windows applications have a fundamentally different way of interacting with you. When an EasyWin program (which emulates a non-GUI MS-DOS application) executes an input statement, it goes into a special mode where it monitors the keyboard input. By contrast, Windows programs (which are GUI applications) are always monitoring the mouse (its movements and its button clicks) and the keyboard and reporting the current status to the part of Windows which monitors events. The vast difference between GUI and non-GUI applications render non-GUI input functions useless in GUI applications.

Workshop

The Workshop provides quiz questions to help you solidify your understanding of the material covered and exercises to provide you with experience in using what you've learned. Try to understand the quiz and exercise answers before continuing on to the next day's lesson. Answers are provided in Appendix B, "Answers."

Quiz

1. What is wrong with the following statement?

   ```
   cout << "Enter a number " >> x;
   ```

2. What happens in the following statement?

   ```
   cout << "Enter three numbers : ";
   cin >> x >> y >> x;
   ```

Exercises

1. Write the program OUT3.CP that displays a table of square roots for whole numbers in the range of 2 to 10. Use the MATH.H header file to import the sqrt function which calculates the square root of a double-typed argument. Because I have not discussed C++ loops yet, use repetitive statements to display the various values. Employ the format controls %3.0lf and %3.4lf to display the number and its square root, respectively.

2. Write the program OUT4.CP that prompts you for an integer and displays the hexadecimal and octal equivalent forms. Use the printf format controls to perform the conversion between decimal, hexadecimal, and octal numbers.

Decision-Making Constructs

The support for decision-making in different programming languages varies depending on their decision-making constructs. Some languages offer more flexibility than others.

NEW TERM *Decision-making constructs* enable your applications to examine conditions and designate courses of action.

Today's lesson looks at the decision-making constructs in C++ and covers the following topics:

- ☐ The single-alternative `if` statement
- ☐ The dual-alternative `if-else` statement
- ☐ The multiple-alternative `if-else` statement
- ☐ The multiple-alternative `switch` statement
- ☐ Nested decision-making constructs

The Single-Alternative *if* Statement

Unlike many programming languages, C++ does not have the keyword `then` in any form of the `if` statement. This language feature may lead you to ask how the `if` statement separates the tested condition from the executable statements. The answer is that C++ requires you to enclose the tested condition in parentheses.

NEW TERM An `if` statement is a *single-alternative* statement.

Syntax

The Single-Alternative *if* Statement

The general syntax for the single-alternative `if` statement is

```
if (condition)
    statement;
```

for a single executable statement, and

```
if (tested_condition) {
    <sequence of statements>
}
```

for a sequence of executable statements.

Examples:

```
if (numberOfLines < 0)
    numberOfLines = 0;

if ((height - 54) < 3) {
    area = length * width;
    volume = area * height;
}
```

C++ uses the open and close braces ({}) to define a block of statements. Figure 5.1 shows the flow in a single-alternative if statement.

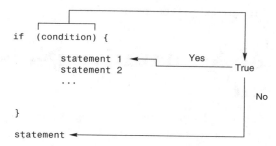

Figure 5.1. *The program flow in the single-alternative* if *statement.*

Let's look at an example. Listing 5.1 contains the source code for program IF1.CP, which demonstrates the single-alternative if statement. The program prompts you to enter a nonzero number and stores the input in the variable x. If the value in x is not zero, the program displays the reciprocal of x.

Type   **Listing 5.1. Source code for the program IF1.CP.**

```
 1: // Program that demonstrates the single-alternative if statement
 2:
 3: #include <iostream.h>
 4:
 5: main()
 6: {
 7:    double x;
 8:    cout << "Enter a non-zero number : ";
 9:    cin >> x;
10:    if (x != 0)
11:      cout << "The reciprocal of " << x
12:            << " is " << (1/x) << "\n";
13:    return 0;
14: }
```

Here is a sample session with the program in Listing 5.1:

```
Enter a non-zero number : 25
The reciprocal of 25 is 0.04
```

The program in Listing 5.1 declares the `double`-typed variable x in function `main`. The output statement in line 8 prompts you to enter a nonzero number. The input statement in line 9 stores your input in variable x. The `if` statement in line 10 determines whether x is not equal to zero. If this condition is true, the program executes the output statement in lines 11 and 12. This statement displays the value of x and its reciprocal, `1/x`. If the tested condition is false, the program skips the statement in lines 11 and 12 and resumes at the statement in line 13.

The Dual-Alternative *if-else* Statement

In the *dual-alternative* form of the `if` statement, the `else` keyword separates the statements used to execute each alternative.

NEW☞ TERM The *dual-alternative* `if-else` statement provides you with two alternate courses of action based on the Boolean value of the tested condition.

The Dual-Alternative *if-else* Statement

The general syntax for the dual-alternative `if-else` statement is

```
if (condition)
     statement1;
else
     statement2;
```

for a single executable statement in each clause, and

```
if (tested_condition) {
     <sequence #1 of statements>
}
else {
     <sequence #2 of statements>
}
```

for a sequence of executable statements in both clauses.

Example:

```
if (moneyInAccount > withdraw) {
  moneyInAccount -= withdraw;
  cout << "You withdrew $" << withdraw << "\n";
```

```
    cout << "Balance is $" << moneyInAccount << "\n";
}
else {
  cout << "Cannot withdraw $" << withdraw << "\n";
  cout << "Account has $" << moneyInAccount << "\n";
}
```

Figure 5.2. shows the program flow in the dual-alternative if-else statement.

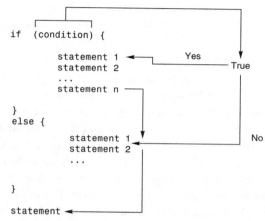

Figure 5.2. *The program flow in the dual-alternative if-else statement.*

Let's look at an example that uses the dual-alternative if-else statement. Listing 5.2 contains the source code for the program IF2.CP. The program prompts you to enter a character and then determines whether or not you entered a letter. The program output classifies your input as either a letter or a nonletter character.

 Listing 5.2. Source code for the program IF2.CP.

```
1: // Program that demonstrates the dual-alternative if statement
2:
3: #include <iostream.h>
4: #include <ctype.h>
5:
6: main()
7: {
8:    char c;
9:    cout << "Enter a letter : ";
10:   cin >> c;
11:   // convert to uppercase
12:   c = toupper(c);
```

Listing 5.2. continued

```
13:    if (c >= 'A' && c <= 'Z')
14:      cout << "You entered a letter\n";
15:    else
16:      cout << "Your input was not a letter\n";
17:    return 0;
18: }
```

Here is a sample session with the program in Listing 5.2:

```
Enter a character : g
You entered a letter
```

The program in listing 5.2 declares the `char`-typed variable c in line 8. The output statement in line 9 prompts you to enter a letter. The input statement in line 10 obtains your input and stores it in variable c. The statement in line 12 converts the value in the variable to uppercase by calling the function `toupper` (prototyped in the CTYPE.H header file). This character case conversion simplifies the tested condition in the `if-else` statement at line 13. The `if-else` statement determines whether the variable c contains a character in the range of A to Z. If this condition is true, the program executes the output statement in line 14. This statement displays a message stating that you have entered a letter. By contrast, if the tested condition is false, the program executes the `else` clause statement in line 16. This statement displays a message stating that your input was not a letter.

Potential Problems with the Dual-Alternative *if* Statement

There is a potential problem with the dual-alternative `if` statement. This problem occurs when the `if` clause also includes a single-alternative `if` statement. In this case, the compiler considers that the `else` clause pertains to the nested `if` statement. (A nested `if` statement is one that contains another `if` statement in the `if` and/or `else` clauses—more about nesting in the next section.) Here is an example:

```
if (i > 0)
    if (i == 10)
        cout << "You guessed the magic number";
else
    cout << "Number is out of range";
```

In this code fragment, when variable i is a positive number other than 10, the code displays the message `Number is out of range`. The compiler treats these statements as though the code fragment meant the following:

```
if (i > 0)
    if (i == 10)
        cout << "You guessed the magic number";
    else
        cout << "Number is out of range";
```

To correct this problem, enclose the nested `if` statement in a statement block:

```
if (i > 0) {
    if (i == 10)
        cout << "You guessed the magic number";
}
else
    cout << "Number is out of range";
```

The Multiple-Alternative *if-else* Statement

C++ enables you to nest if-else statements to create a multiple-alternative form. This alternative gives a lot of power and flexibility to your applications.

**NEW☞
TERM** The *multiple-alternative* `if-else` statement contains nested `if-else` statements.

5

Syntax

The Multiple-Alternative *if-else* Statement

The general syntax for the multiple-alternative `if-else` statement is

```
if (tested_condition1)
    statement1; ¦ { <sequence #1 of statement> }
else if (tested_condition2)
    statement2; ¦ { <sequence #2 of statement> }
...
else if (tested_conditionN)
    statementN; ¦ { <sequence #N of statement> }
[else
    statementN+1; ¦ { <sequence #N+1 of statement> }]
```

Example:

```
char op;

int opOk = 1;
double x, y, z;
cout << "Enter operand1 operator operand2: ";
cin >> x >> op >> y;
if (op == '+')
    z = x + y;
```

```
else if (op == '-')
    z = x - y;
else if (op == '*')
    z = x * y;
else if (op == '/' && y != 0)
    z = x / y;
else
    opOk = 0;
```

The multiple-alternative `if-else` statement performs a series of cascaded tests until one of the following occurs:

1. One of the conditions in the `if` clause or in the `else if` clauses is true. In this case, the accompanying statements are executed.

2. None of the tested conditions is true. The program executes the statements in the catch-all `else` clause (if there is an `else` clause).

Figure 5.3 shows the program flow in the multiple-alternative `if-else` statement.

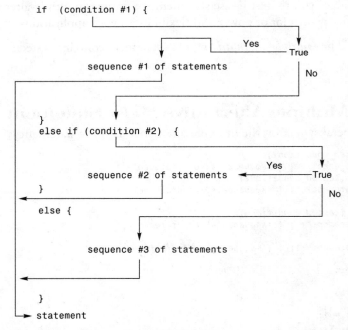

Figure 5.3. *The program flow in the multiple-alternative* `if-else` *statement.*

Let's look at an example. Listing 5.3 shows the source code for program IF3.CP. The program prompts you to enter a character and uses the multiple-alternative if-else statement to determine whether your input is one of the following:

☐ An uppercase letter

☐ A lowercase letter

☐ A digit

☐ A non-alphanumeric character

Listing 5.3. Source code for the IF3.CP program.

```
 1: // Program that demonstrates the multiple-alternative if statement
 2:
 3: #include <iostream.h>
 4:
 5: main()
 6: {
 7:   char c;
 8:   cout << "Enter a character : ";
 9:   cin >> c;
10:   if (c >= 'A' && c <= 'Z')
11:     cout << "You entered an uppercase letter\n";
12:   else if (c >= 'a' && c <= 'z')
13:     cout << "You entered a lowercase letter\n";
14:   else if (c >= '0' && c <= '9')
15:     cout << "You entered a digit\n";
16:   else
17:     cout << "You entered a non-alphanumeric character\n";
18:   return 0;
19: }
```

Here is a sample session with the program in Listing 5.3:

```
Enter a character : !
You entered a non-alphanumeric character
```

The program in Listing 5.3 declares the char-typed variable c in line 7. The output statement in line 8 prompts you to enter a letter. The input statement in line 9 obtains your input and stores it in variable c. The multi-alternative if-else statement tests the following conditions:

1. In line 10, the if statement determines whether the variable c contains a letter in the range of A to Z. If this condition is true, the program executes the output statement in line 11. This statement confirms that you entered an uppercase letter. The program then resumes at line 18.

119

2. If the condition in line 10 is false, the program jumps to the first else if clause in line 12. There the program determines whether the variable c contains a letter in the range of a to z. If this condition is true, the program executes the output statement in line 13. This statement confirms that you entered a lowercase letter. The program then resumes at line 18.

3. If the condition in line 12 is false, the program jumps to the second else if clause in line 14. There the program determines whether the variable c contains a digit. If this condition is true, the program executes the output statement in line 15. This statement confirms that you entered a digit. The program then resumes at line 18.

4. If the condition in line 14 is false, the program jumps to the catch-all else clause in line 16 and executes the output statement in line 17. This statement displays a message telling you that your input was neither a letter nor a digit.

The *switch* Statement

The switch statement offers a special form of multiple-alternative decision-making. It enables you to examine the various values of an integer-compatible expression and choose the appropriate course of action.

Syntax

The *switch* Statement

The general syntax for the switch statement is

```
switch (expression) {
    case constant1_1:
[   case constant1_2: ...]
        <one or more statements>
        break;
    case constant2_1:
[   case constant2_2: ...]
        <one or more statements>
        break;
...
    case constantN_1:
[   case constantN_2: ...]
        <one or more statements>
        break;
    default:
        <one or more statements>
}
```

Example:

```
OK = 1;
switch (op) {
    case '+':
        z = x + y;
        break;
    case '-':
        z = x - y;
        break;
    case '*':
        z = x * y;
        break;
    case '/':
        if (y != 0)
            z = x / y;
        else
            OK = 0;
        break;
    default:
        Ok = 0;
}
```

The rules for using a switch statement are

- The switch requires an integer-compatible value. This value may be a constant, variable, function call, or expression. The switch statement does not work with floating-point data types.

- The value after each case label *must be* a constant.

- C++ does not support case labels with ranges of values. Instead, *each* value must appear in a separate case label.

- You need to use a break statement after each set of executable statements. The break statement causes program execution to resume after the end of the current switch statement. If you do not use the break statement, the program execution resumes at the subsequent case label.

- The default clause is a catch-all clause.

- The set of statements in each case label or grouped case labels need not be enclosed in braces ({}).

Note: The lack of single case labels with ranges of values makes it more appealing to use a multiple-alternative if-else statement if you have a large, contiguous range of values.

Figure 5.4 shows the program flow in the multiple-alternative `switch` statement.

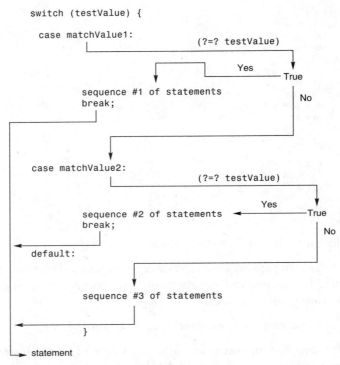

Figure 5.4. *The program flow in the multiple-alternative* `switch` *statement.*

Let's look at an example that uses the `switch` statement. Listing 5.4 contains the source code for program SWITCH1.CP that I obtained by editing Listing 5.3. The new program performs the same task of classifying your character input, this time using a `switch` statement.

 Listing 5.4. Source code for the SWITCH1.CP program.

```
1: // Program that demonstrates the multiple-alternative switch statement
2:
3: #include <iostream.h>
4:
5: main()
6: {
7:   char c;
8:   cout << "Enter a character : ";
9:   cin >> c;
10:   switch (c) {
```

```
11:     case 'A':
12:     case 'B':
13:     case 'C':
14:     case 'D':
15:     // other case labels
16:       cout << "You entered an uppercase letter\n";
17:       break;
18:     case 'a':
19:     case 'b':
20:     case 'c':
21:     case 'd':
22:     // other case labels
23:       cout << "You entered a lowercase letter\n";
24:       break;
25:     case '0':
26:     case '1':
27:     case '2':
28:     case '3':
29:     // other case labels
30:       cout << "You entered a digit\n";
31:       break;
32:     default:
33:       cout << "You entered a non-alphanumeric character\n";
34:    }
35:   return 0;
36: }
```

Here is a sample session with the program in Listing 5.4:

```
Enter a character : 2
You entered a digit
```

The program in Listing 5.4 declares the char-typed variable c. The output statement in line 8 prompts you to enter a character. The statement in line 9 stores your input in variable c. The switch statement starts at line 10. Lines 11 through 14 contain the case labels for the letters A through D. I omitted the case labels for the rest of the uppercase letters to keep the program short. If the character in variable c matches any value in lines 11 through 14, the program executes the output statement in line 16. This statement confirms that you entered an uppercase letter. (Because I reduced the number of case labels, the program executes the statement in line 16 only if you enter the letters A to D.) The break statement in line 17 causes the program flow to jump to line 35, past the end of the switch statement.

If the character in variable c does not match any of the case labels in lines 11 through 14, the program resumes at line 18 where it encounters another set of case labels. These labels are supposed to represent lowercase characters. As you can see, I reduced the number of labels to shorten the program. If the character in variable c matches any value in lines 18 through 21, the program executes the output statement in line 23. This statement confirms that you entered a lowercase letter. (Because I reduced the number

5

of `case` labels, the program executes the statement in line 23 only if you enter the letters a to d.) The `break` statement in line 24 causes the program flow to jump to line 35, past the end of the `switch` statement.

If the character in variable c does not match any of the `case` labels in lines 18 through 21, the program resumes at line 25 where it encounters another set of `case` labels. These labels are supposed to represent digits. Again, you can see that I reduced the number of labels to shorten the program. If the character in variable c matches any value in lines 25 through 28, the program executes the output statement in line 30. This statement confirms that you entered a digit. (Because I reduced the number of `case` labels, the program executes the statement in line 30 only if you enter the digits 0 to 3.) The `break` statement in line 31 causes the program flow to jump to line 35, past the end of the `switch` statement.

If the character in variable c does not match any `case` label in lines 25 through 28, the program jumps to the catch-all clause in line 32. The program executes the output statement in line 33. This statement tells you that you entered a non-alphanumeric character.

Nested Decision-Making Constructs

Often you need to use nested decision-making constructs to manage nontrivial conditions. Nesting decision-making constructs enables you to deal with complicated conditions using a divide-and-conquer approach. The outer-level constructs help you to test preliminary or more general conditions. The inner-level constructs help you deal with more specific conditions.

Let's look at an example. Listing 5.5 shows the source code for program IF4.CP. The program prompts you to enter a character. Then the program determines if your input is an uppercase letter, a lowercase letter, or a character that is not a letter. The program displays a message that classifies your input.

Listing 5.5. Source code for the program IF4.CP.

```
1: // Program that demonstrates the nested if statements
2:
3: #include <iostream.h>
4:
5: main()
6: {
7:   char c;
8:   cout << "Enter a character : ";
```

```
 9:    cin >> c;
10:    if ((c >= 'A' && c <= 'Z') || (c >= 'a' && c <= 'z'))
11:      if (c >= 'A' && c <= 'Z')
12:        cout << "You entered an uppercase letter\n";
13:      else
14:        cout << "You entered a lowercase letter\n";
15:    else
16:      cout << "You entered a non-letter character\n";
17:    return 0;
18: }
```

Here is a sample session with the program in Listing 5.5:

```
Enter a character : a
You entered a lowercase letter
```

The program in Listing 5.5 declares the char-typed variable c. The output statement in line 8 prompts you to enter a character. The statement in line 9 stores your input in variable c. The program uses nested if-else statements that begin at lines 10 and 11. The outer if-else statement determines whether or not the variable c contains a letter. If the tested condition is true, the program executes the inner if-else statement in line 11. Otherwise, the program resumes at the else clause of the outer if-else statement and executes the output statement in line 16. This statement tells you that your input was not a letter.

The program uses the inner if-else statement to further examine the condition of the outer if-else statement. The if-else statement in line 11 determines whether or not the variable c contains an uppercase letter. If this condition is true, the program executes the output statement in line 12. Otherwise, the program executes the else clause statement in line 14. These output statements tell you whether you entered an uppercase or a lowercase letter. After executing the inner if-else statement, the program jumps to line 17, past the end of the outer if-else statement.

5

Summary

Today's lesson presented the various decision-making constructs in C++, including the following:

☐ The single-alternative if statement, such as

```
if (tested_condition)
    statement; | {      <sequence of statements> }
```

☐ The dual-alternative `if`-`else` statement, such as

```
if (tested_condition)
    statement1; { <sequence #1 of statements> }
else
    statement1; { <sequence #1 of statements> }
```

☐ The multiple-alternative `if`-`else` statement, such as

```
if (tested_condition1)
    statement1; ¦ { <sequence #1 of statement> }
else if (tested_condition2)
    statement2; ¦ { <sequence #2 of statement> }
...
else if (tested_conditionN)
    statementN; ¦ { <sequence #N of statement> }
[else
    statementN+1; ¦ { <sequence #N+1 of statement> }]
```

☐ The multiple-alternative `switch` statement, such as

```
switch (caseVar) {
    case constant1_1:
    case constant1_2:
    <other case labels>
        <one or more statements>
        break;
    case constant2_1:
    case constant2_2:
    <other case labels>
        <one or more statements>
        break;
    ...
    case constantN_1:
    case constantN_2:
    <other case labels>
        <one or more statements>
        break;
```

```
    default:
        <one or more statements>
        break;
}
```

You also learned about the following topics:

☐ The `if` statements require you to observe two rules:

  ☐ The tested condition must be enclosed in parentheses.

  ☐ Blocks of statements are enclosed in pairs of open and close braces.

☐ Nested decision-making constructs empower you to deal with complex conditions using a divide-and-conquer approach. The outer-level constructs help you in testing preliminary or more general conditions. The inner-level constructs assist in handling more specific conditions.

Q&A

Q Does C++ impose any rules for indenting statements in the clauses of an `if` statement?

A No. The indentation is purely up to you. Typical indentations range from two to four spaces. Using indentations makes your listings much more readable. Here is the case of an `if` statement with unindented clause statements:

```
if (i > 0)
j = i * i;
else
j = 10 - i;
```

Compare the readability of that listing with the following indented version, which is much easier to read:

```
if (i > 0)
  j = i * i;
else
  j = 10 - i;
```

5

Q **What are the rules for writing the condition of an `if-else` statement?**

A There are two schools of thought. The first one recommends that you write the condition so that it is more often true than not. The second school recommends avoiding negative expressions (those that use the relational operator `!=` and the Boolean operator `!`). Programmers in this camp translate this `if` statement:

```
if (i != 0)
    j = 100 / i;
else
    j = 1;
```

into the following equivalent form, even though the likelihood of variable `i` storing 0 might be very low:

```
if (i == 0)
    j = 1;
else
    j = 100 \ i;
```

Q **How do I handle a condition such as the following, which divides by a variable that can possibly be zero?**

```
if (i != 0 && 1/i > 1)
    j = i * i;
```

A C++ does not always evaluate the entire tested condition. This partial evaluation occurs when a term in the Boolean expression renders the entire expression false or true, regardless of the values of the other terms. In this case, if variable `i` is 0, the runtime system does not evaluate the term `1/i > 1`. This is because the term `i != 0` is false and would render the entire expression false, regardless of what the second term yields.

Q **Is it really necessary to include an `else` or `default` clause in multi-alternative `if-else` and `switch` statements?**

A Programmers highly recommend the inclusion of these catch-all clauses to ensure that the multiple-alternative statements handle all conditions.

Workshop

The Workshop provides quiz questions to help you solidify your understanding of the material covered and exercises to provide you with experience in using what you've learned. Try to understand the quiz and exercise answers before continuing on to the next day's lesson. Answers are provided in Appendix B, "Answers."

Quiz

1. Simplify the following nested `if` statements by replacing them with a single `if` statement:

```
if (i > 0)
  if (i < 10)
    cout << "i = " << i << "\n";
```

2. Simplify the following `if` statements by replacing them with a single `if` statement:

```
if (i > 0) {
    j = i * i;
    cout << "j = " << j << "\n";
}
if (i < 0) {
    j = 4 * i;
    cout << "j = " << j << "\n";
}
if (i == 0) {
    j = 10 + i
    cout << "j = " << j << "\n";
}
```

3. True or false? The following `if` statements perform the same tasks as the `if-else` statement:

```
if (i < 0) {
    i = 10 + i;
    j = i * i;
    cout << "i = " << i << "\n";
    cout << "j = " << j << "\n";
```

```
    }
    if (i >= 0) {
        k = 4 * i + 1;
        cout << "k = " << k << "\n";

    }

    if (i < 0) {
        i = 10 - i;
        j = i * i;
        cout << "i = " << i << "\n";
        cout << "j = " << j << "\n";
    }
    else {
        k = 4 * i + 1;
        cout << "k = " << k << "\n";
    }
```

4. Simplify the following if-else statement:

```
if (i > 0 && i < 100)
  j = i * i;
else if (i > 10 && i < 50)
  j = 10 + i;
else if (i >= 100)
  j = i;
else
  j = 1;
```

5. What is wrong with the following if statement?

```
if (i > (1 + i * i)) {
  j = i * i;
  cout << "i = " << i << " and j = " << j << "\n";
}
```

Exercises

1. Write the program IF5.CP to solve for the roots of a quadratic equation. The quadratic equation is

   ```
   A X2 + B X + C = 0
   ```

   The roots of the quadratic equation are

   ```
   root1 = (-B + √(B2 - 4AC)) / (2A)
   root1 = (-B - √(B2 - 4AC)) / (2A)
   ```

   If the term in the square root is negative, the roots are complex. If the term in the square root term is zero, the two roots are the same and are equal to `-B/(2A)`.

2. Write the program SWITCH2.CP, which implements a simple four-function calculator. The program should prompt you for the operand and the operator, and then display both the input and the result. Include error-checking for bad operators and the attempt to divide by zero.

5

6

Loops

Recall from Day 3 that loops are powerful language constructs that enable computers to excel in performing repetitive tasks. Computers are able to repeat tasks quickly, accurately, and tirelessly—an area where computers seem to do a better job than humans. Today's lesson presents the following loops in C++:

☐ The `for` loop statement

☐ The `do-while` loop statement

☐ The `while` loop statement

☐ Skipping iterations

☐ Exiting loops

☐ Nested loops

The *for* Loop

The `for` loop in C++ is a versatile loop because it offers both fixed and conditional iterations. The latter feature of the `for` loop deviates from the typical use of the `for` loop in other programming languages, such as Pascal and BASIC.

Syntax

The *for* Loop

The general syntax for the `for` loop statement is

```
for (<initialization of loop control variables>;
     <loop continuation test>;
     <increment/decrement of loop control variables>)
```

Example:

```
for (i = 0; i < 10; i++)
    cout << "The cube of " << i << " = " << i * i * i << "\n";
```

The `for` loop statement has three components, all of which are optional. The first component initializes the loop control variables. (C++ permits you to use more than one loop control variable.) The second part of the loop is the condition that determines whether or not the loop makes another iteration. The last part of the `for` loop is the clause that increments or decrements the loop control variables.

Note: The C++ `for` loop enables you to declare the loop control variables. Such variables exist in the scope of the loop.

Let's look at an example. Listing 6.1 contains the source code for program FOR1.CP. The program prompts you to define a range of integers by specifying its lower and upper bounds. Then the program calculates the sum of integers in the range you specify as well as their average value.

Listing 6.1. Source code for the program FOR1.CP.

```
1: // Program that calculates a sum and average of a range of
2: // integers using a for loop
3:
4: #include <iostream.h>
5:
6: main()
7: {
8:     double sum = 0;
9:     double sumx = 0.0;
10:    int first, last, temp;
11:
12:    cout << "Enter the first integer : ";
13:    cin >> first;
14:    cout << "Enter the last integer : ";
15:    cin >> last;
16:    if (first > last) {
17:      temp= first;
18:      first = last;
19:      last = temp;
20:    }
21:    for (int i = first; i <= last; i++) {
22:      sum++;
23:      sumx += (double)i;
24:    }
25:    cout << "Sum of integers from "
26:         << first << " to " << last << " = "
27:         << sumx << "\n";
28:    cout << "Average value = " << sumx / sum;
29:    return 0;
30: }
```

6

Here is a sample session with the program in Listing 6.1:

```
Enter the first integer : 1
Enter the last integer : 100
Sum of integers from 1 to 100 = 5050
Average value = 50.5
```

The program in Listing 6.1 declares a collection of `int`-typed and `double`-typed variables in function `main`. The function initializes the summation variables, `sum` and `sumx`, to 0. The input and output statements in lines 12 through 15 prompt you to enter the integers that define a range of values. The program stores these integers in the variables `first` and `last`. The `if` statement in line 16 determines whether or not the value in variable `first` is greater than the value in variable `last`. If this condition is true,

the program executes the block of statements in lines 17 through 19. These statements swap the values in variables `first` and `last`, using the variable `temp` as a swap buffer. Thus, the `if` statement ensures that the integer in variable `first` is less than or equal to the integer in variable `last`.

The program carries out the summation using the `for` loop in line 21. The loop declares its own control variable, `i`, and initializes it with the value in variable `first`. The loop continuation condition is `i <= last`. This condition indicates that the loop iterates as long as `i` is less than or equal to the value in variable `last`. The loop increment component is `i++`, which increments the loop control variable by one for every iteration. The loop contains two statements. The first statement increments the value in variable `sum`. The second statement adds the value of `i` (after typecasting it to `double`) to the variable `sumx`.

Note: I can rewrite the `for` loop to move the first loop statement to the loop increment component:

```
for (int i = first; i <= last; i++, sum++)
    sumx += (double)i;
```

The output statement in lines 25 through 27 displays the sum and average of integers in the range you specified.

To illustrate the flexibility of the `for` loop, I created the program FOR2.CP, shown in Listing 6.2, by editing program FOR1.CP. The two programs perform the same tasks and interact identically with you. The changes I made are in line 10 and lines 21 through 25. Line 10 declares the loop control variable. In line 21 I initialize the variable `i` using the value in variable `first`. The `for` loop is located at line 22. The loop has no initialization part, because I took care of that in line 21. In addition, I removed the loop increment component and compensated for it by applying the post-increment operator to variable `i` in line 24.

 Listing 6.2. Source code for the program FOR2.CP.

```
1: // Program that calculates a sum and average of a range of
2: // integers using a for loop
3:
4: #include <iostream.h>
5:
6: main()
7: {
```

```
 8:      double sum = 0;
 9:      double sumx = 0.0;
10:      int first, last, temp, i;
11:
12:      cout << "Enter the first integer : ";
13:      cin >> first;
14:      cout << "Enter the last integer : ";
15:      cin >> last;
16:      if (first > last) {
17:        temp= first;
18:        first = last;
19:        last = temp;
20:      }
21:      i = first;
22:      for (; i <= last; ) {
23:        sum++;
24:        sumx += (double)i++;
25:      }
26:      cout << "Sum of integers from "
27:           << first << " to " << last << " = "
28:           << sumx << "\n";
29:      cout << "Average value = " << sumx / sum;
30:      return 0;
31: }
```

Here is a sample session with the program in Listing 6.2:

```
Enter the first integer : 10
Enter the last integer : 100
Sum of integers from 10 to 100 = 5005
Average value = 55
```

Open Loops Using the *for* Loop

When I introduced you to the C++ for loop, I stated that the three components of the for loop are optional. In fact, C++ permits you to leave these three components empty!

When you leave the three components of a loop empty, the result is an *open loop*.

It is worthwhile pointing out that other languages, such as Ada and Modula-2, do support formal open loops and provide mechanisms to exit these loops. C++ permits you to exit from a loop in one of the following two ways:

☐ The break statement causes the program execution to resume after the end of the current loop. Use the break statement when you wish to exit a for loop and resume with the remaining parts of the program.

☐ The exit function (declared in the STDLIB.H header file) enables you to exit the program. Use the exit function if you want to stop iterating and also exit the program.

Let's look at an example. Listing 6.3 contains the source code for program FOR3.CP. The program uses an open loop to repeatedly prompt you for a number. The program takes your input and displays it along with its reciprocal value. Then the program asks you whether or not you wish to calculate the reciprocal of another number. If you type in the letter *Y* or *y*, the program performs another iteration. Otherwise, the program ends. If you keep typing *Y* or *y* for the latter prompt, the program keeps running—at least until the computer breaks down!

Listing 6.3. Source code for the program FOR3.CP.

```
1: // Program that demonstrates using the
2: // for loop to emulate an infinite loop.
3:
4: #include <iostream.h>
5: #include <ctype.h>
6:
7: main()
8: {
9:     char ch;
10:    double x, y;
11:
12:    // for loop with empty parts
13:    for (;;) {
14:       cout << "\nEnter a number : ";
15:       cin >> x;
16:       // process number if non-zero
17:       if (x != 0) {
18:          y = 1/ x;
19:          cout << "1/(" << x << ") = " << y << "\n";
20:          cout << "More calculations? (Y/N) ";
21:          cin >> ch;
22:          ch = toupper(ch);
23:          if (ch != 'Y')
24:             break;
25:       }
26:       else
27:          // display error message
28:          cout << "Error: cannot accept 0\n";
29:    }
30:    return 0;
31: }
```

Here is a sample session with the program in Listing 6.3:

```
Enter a number : 5
1/(5) = 0.2
More calculations? (Y/N) y

Enter a number : 12
1/(12) = 0.083333
More calculations? (Y/N) y

Enter a number : 16
1/(16) = 0.0625
More calculations? (Y/N) n
```

The program in Listing 6.3 declares the char-typed variable ch and two double-typed variables, x and y. The function main uses the for loop in line 13 as an open loop by eliminating all three loop components. The output statement in line 14 prompts you to enter a number. The input statement in line 15 obtains your input and stores it in variable x. The if-else statement in line 17 determines whether the value in variable x is equal to zero. If this condition is true, the program executes the block of statements in lines 18 through 24. Otherwise, the program executes the statement in line 28 which is associated with the else clause. This statement displays an error message.

The statement in line 18 assigns the reciprocal of the value in variable x to variable y. The output statement in line 19 displays the values in variables x and y. The output statement in line 20 prompts you for more calculations and requires a *Y* or *N* (in either uppercase or lowercase) type of answer. The input statement in line 21 stores your single-character input in variable c. The statement in line 22 converts your input into uppercase using the function toupper (this function is prototyped in the CTYPE.H header file). The if statement in line 23 determines whether the character in variable c is not the letter *Y*. If this condition is true, the program executes the break statement in line 24. This statement causes the program execution to exit the open loop and to resume at line 30.

The *do-while* Loop

The do-while loop in C++ is a conditional loop. Therefore, the do-while loop iterates at least once.

A *conditional loop* iterates as long as a condition is true. This condition is tested at the end of the loop.

The *do-while* Loop

The general syntax for the do-while loop is

```
do {
    <sequence of statements>
} while (condition);
```

Example:

The following loop displays the squares of 2 to 10:

```
int i = 2;
do {
    cout << i << "^2 = " << i * i << "\n";
} while (++i < 11);
```

Let's look at an example. Listing 6.4 shows the source code for program DOWHILE1.CP which calculates square root values. The program performs the following tasks:

☐ Prompts you to enter a number (if you enter a negative number, the program reprompts you for a number)

☐ Calculates and displays the square root of the number you entered

☐ Asks you whether you wish to enter another number (if you enter the letter *Y* or *y*, the program resumes at step number 1; otherwise, the program ends)

Type

Listing 6.4. Source code for the program DOWHILE1.CP.

```
1: // Program that demonstrates the do-while loop
2:
3: #include <iostream.h>
4:
5: const double TOLERANCE = 1.0e-7;
6:
7: double abs(double x)
8: {
9:   return (x >= 0) ? x : -x;
10: }
11:
12: double sqroot(double x)
13: {
14:   double guess = x / 2;
15:   do {
16:     guess = (guess + x / guess) / 2;
17:   } while (abs(guess * guess - x) > TOLERANCE);
18:   return guess;
19: }
20:
21: double getNumber()
22: {
23:   double x;
```

```
24:    do {
25:      cout << "Enter a number: ";
26:      cin >> x;
27:    } while (x < 0);
28:    return x;
29: }
30:
31: main()
32: {
33:    char c;
34:    double x, y;
35:
36:    do {
37:      x = getNumber();
38:      y = sqroot(x);
39:      cout << "Sqrt(" << x << ") = " << y << "\n"
40:            << "Enter another number? (Y/N) ";
41:      cin >> c;
42:      cout << "\n";
43:    } while (c == 'Y' || c == 'y');
44:    return 0;
45: }
```

Here is a sample session with the program in Listing 6.4:

```
Enter a number: 25
Sqrt(25) = 5
Enter another number? (Y/N) y

Enter a number: 144
Sqrt(144) = 12
Enter another number? (Y/N) n
```

The program in Listing 6.4 declares the global constant TOLERANCE and the functions abs, sqroot, getNumber, and main. The function abs in line 7 returns the absolute value of double-typed arguments.

The function sqroot in line 12 returns the square root of the parameter x. The function sets the initial guess for the square root to x / 2 in line 14. Then the function uses a do-while loop to refine iteratively the guess for the square root. The condition in the while clause determines whether the absolute difference between the square of the current guess and the parameter x is greater than the allowable error (represented by the constant TOLERANCE). The loop iterates as long as this condition is true. The function returns the guess for the square root in line 18. The function sqroot implements Newton's method for iteratively obtaining the square root of a number.

The function getNumber in line 21 prompts you for a number and stores your input in the local variable x. The function uses a do-while loop to ensure that you enter a nonnegative number. The while clause in line 27 determines whether the value in

6

variable x is negative. As long as this condition is true, the do-while loop iterates. In line 28 the return statement yields the value of x.

The function main in line 31 uses a do-while loop to perform the following tasks:

☐ Prompts you for a number by calling function getNumber (the statement in line 37 contains the function call and assigns the result to the local variable x)

☐ Calculates the square root of x by calling function sqroot, and then assigns the result to variable y (the statement that contains this function call is in line 38)

☐ Displays the values in variables x and y

☐ Asks if you want to enter another number (the input statement in line 41 takes your single-character Y or N input and stores it in variable c)

The while clause in line 43 determines whether the variable c contains either the letter Y or y. The do-while loop iterates as long as this condition is true.

The program in Listing 6.4 illustrates the following uses for the do-while loop:

Iterative calculations	The loop in function sqroot shows this aspect.
Data validation	The loop in function getNumber illustrates this aspect.
Program continuation	The loop in function main shows this aspect.

The *while* Loop

The while loop in C++ is another conditional loop that iterates as long as a condition is true. Thus, the while loop may not iterate if the tested condition is initially false.

Syntax

The *while* Loop

The general syntax of the while loop is

```
while (condition)
    statement; ¦ { <sequence of statements> }
```

Example:

```
function power(double x, int n)
{
  double pwr = 1;
  while (n-- > 0)
    pwr *= x;
  return pwr;
}
```

Let's look at an example. Listing 6.5 shows the source code for program WHILE1.CP. This program performs the same operations as program FOR1.CP in Listing 6.1. The two programs interact in the same way and yield the same results.

Listing 6.5. Source code for the program WHILE1.CP.

```
 1: // Program that demonstrates the while loop
 2:
 3: #include <iostream.h>
 4:
 5: main()
 6: {
 7:     double sum = 0;
 8:     double sumx = 0.0;
 9:     int first, last, temp, i;
10:
11:     cout << "Enter the first integer : ";
12:     cin >> first;
13:     cout << "Enter the last integer : ";
14:     cin >> last;
15:     if (first > last) {
16:        temp= first;
17:        first = last;
18:        last = temp;
19:     }
20:     i = first;
21:     while (i <= last) {
22:        sum++;
23:        sumx += (double)i++;
24:     }
25:     cout << "Sum of integers from "
26:          << first << " to " << last << " = "
27:          << sumx << "\n";
28:     cout << "Average value = " << sumx / sum;
29:     return 0;
30: }
```

6

Here is a sample session with the program in Listing 6.5:

```
Enter the first integer : 1
Enter the last integer : 100
Sum of integers from 1 to 100 = 5050
Average value = 50.5
```

Because the programs in Listings 6.5 and 6.1 are similar, I focus on lines 20 through 24 where the main difference between the two programs lies. The statement in line 20 assigns the value of variable `first` to variable `i`. The `while` loop starts at line 21. The loop iterates as long as the value in variable `i` is less than or equal to the value in variable `last`. The variable `i` plays the role of the loop control variable. The statement

in line 22 increments the value in variable sum. The statement in line 23 adds the value in variable i to the variable sumx and also increments the variable i. The statement performs the latter task by applying the post-increment operator to the variable i.

Skipping Loop Iterations

C++ enables you to jump to the end of a loop and resume the next iteration using the continue statement. This programming feature permits your loop to skip iterations for special values that may cause runtime errors.

Syntax

The *continue* Statement

The general form for using the continue statement is

```
<loop-start clause> {
    // <sequence #1 of statements>
    if (skipCondition)
        continue;
    // <sequence #2 of statements>
} <loop-end clause>
```

Example (in a for loop):

```
double x, y;
for (int i = -10; i < 11; i++) {
  x = i;
  if (i == 1)
    continue;
  y = 1/sqrt(x * x - 1);
  cout << "1/sqrt(" << (x*x-1) << ") = " << y << "\n";
}
```

This form shows that the evaluation of the first sequence of statements in the for loop gives rise to a condition tested in the if statement. If that condition is true, the if statement invokes the continue statement to skip the second sequence of statements in the for loop.

Let's look at an example. Listing 6.6 shows the source code for program FOR4.CP. The program displays the table of values for the mathematical function $f(X) = \sqrt{(X^2 - 9)}$ at integer values between −10 and 10. Because the integers between −2 and 2 yield complex results, which the program avoids, the table does not display the complex values for f(X) between −2 and 2.

Listing 6.6. Source code for the program FOR4.CP.

```
1: // Program that demonstrates using the continue statement
2: // to skip iterations.
3:
4: #include <iostream.h>
5: #include <math.h>
6:
7:
8: double f(double x)
9: {
10:    return sqrt(x * x - 9);
11: }
12:
13: main()
14: {
15:     double x, y;
16:
17:     cout << "         X";
18:     cout << "           f(X)\n";
19:     cout << "_____\n\n";
20:     // for loop with empty parts
21:     for (int i = -10; i <= 10; i++) {
22:       if (i > -3 && i < 3)
23:          continue;
24:       x = (double)i;
25:       y = f(x);
26:       cout << "     ";
27:       cout.width(3);
28:       cout << x << "       ";
29:       cout.width(7);
30:       cout << y << "\n";
31:     }
32:     return 0;
33: }
```

Here is a sample session with the program in Listing 6.6:

```
        X          f(X)

    ---------------------------------

       -10       9.539392
        -9       8.485281
        -8       7.416198
        -7       6.324555
        -6       5.196152
        -5              4
        -4       2.645751
        -3              0
         3              0
         4       2.645751
         5              4
         6       5.196152
         7       6.324555
```

6

```
        8       7.416198
        9       8.485281
       10       9.539392
```

The program in Listing 6.6 declares the function f to represent the mathematical function f(X). The function main declares the double-typed variables x and y in line 15. The output statements in lines 17 through 19 display the table's heading. The for loop in line 21 declares its own control variable and iterates between −10 to 10 in increments of 1. The first statement inside the loop is the if statement located at line 22. This statement determines whether the value in variable i is greater than −3 and less than 3. If this condition is true, the program executes the continue statement in line 23. Thus, the if statement enables the for loop to skip error-generating iterations and resume with the next iteration. The statement in line 24 assigns the value in variable i to variable x. The statement in line 25 calls the function f and supplies it with the argument x. The statement then assigns the result to variable y. The output statements in lines 25 through 30 display the values of variables x and y. The statements use the function width for simple formatting.

Exiting Loops

C++ supports the break statement to exit a loop. The break statement causes the program to resume after the end of the current loop.

Syntax

The *break* Statement

The general form for using the break statement in a loop is

```
<start-loop clause> {
    // <sequence #1 of statements>
    if (exitLoopCondition)
        break;
    // <sequence #2 of statements>
} <end-loop clause>
// <sequence #3 of statements>
```

Example:

```
// calculate the factorial of n
factorial = 1;
for (int i = 1; ; i++) {
  if (i > n)
      break;
  factorial *= (double)i;
}
```

This form shows that the evaluation of the first sequence of statements in the for loop gives rise to a condition tested in the if statement. If that condition is true, the if statement invokes the break statement to exit the loop altogether. The program execution resumes at the third sequence of statements.

For a good example that uses the break statement, I recommend that you reexamine the FOR3.CP program in Listing 6.3.

Nested Loops

Nested loops enable you to perform repetitive tasks as part of other repetitive tasks. C++ enables you to nest any kind of loops to just about any level needed. Nested loops are frequently used to process arrays (covered in Day 7).

Let's look at an example that uses nested loops. Listing 6.7 shows the source code for the program NESTFOR1.CP. The program displays a table of square roots for whole numbers in the range of 1 to 10. The program uses an outer loop to iterate over the above range of numbers, and employs an inner loop to iteratively calculate the square root.

Listing 6.7. Source code for the program NESTFOR1.CP.

```
1: // Program that demonstrates nested loops
2:
3: #include <stdio.h>
4:
5: const double TOLERANCE = 1.0e-7;
6: const int MIN_NUM = 1;
7: const int MAX_NUM = 10;
8:
9: double abs(double x)
10: {
11:    return (x >= 0) ? x : -x;
12: }
13:
14: main()
15: {
16:    double x, sqrt;
17:
18:    printf("  X       Sqrt(X)\n");
19:    printf("_____\n\n");
20:    // outer loop
21:    for (int i = MIN_NUM; i <= MAX_NUM; i++) {
22:      x = (double)i;
23:      sqrt = x /2;
24:      // inner loop
25:      do {
26:        sqrt = (sqrt + x / sqrt) / 2;
```

continues

Listing 6.7. continued

```
27:        } while (abs(sqrt * sqrt - x) > TOLERANCE);
28:        printf("%4.1f     %8.6lf\n", x, sqrt);
29:    }
30:    return 0;
31: }
```

Here is a sample session with the program in Listing 6.7:

```
X       Sqrt(X)
--------------------
1.0      1.000000
2.0      1.414214
3.0      1.732051
4.0      2.000000
5.0      2.236068
6.0      2.449490
7.0      2.645751
8.0      2.828427
9.0      3.000000
10.0     3.162278
```

The program in Listing 6.7 includes the header file STDIO.H in order to use the printf output function with its powerful formatting capabilities. Lines 5 through 7 define the constants TOLERANCE, MIN_NUM, and MAX_NUM to represent the tolerance in square root values, the first number in the output table, and the last number in the output table, respectively. The program defines the function abs to return the absolute number of a double-typed number.

The function main declares the double-typed variables x and sqrt. The output statements in lines 18 and 19 display the table's heading. Line 21 contains the outer loop, a for loop. This loop declares its control variable, i, and iterates from MIN_NUM to MAX_NUM in increments of 1. Line 22 stores the typecast value of i in variable x. The statement in line 23 obtains the initial guess for the square root and stores it in variable sqrt. Line 25 contains the inner loop, a do-while loop that iterates to refine the guess for the square root. The statement in line 26 refines the guess for the square root. The while clause in line 27 determines whether or not the refined guess is adequate. The output statement in line 28 displays the formatted values for the variables x and sqrt.

Summary

Today's lesson covered the C++ loops and topics related to loops. You learned about the following:

☐ The `for` loop in C++ has the following general syntax. The `for` loop contains three components: the loop initialization, loop continuation condition, and the increment or decrement of the loop variables.

```
for (<initialization of loop control variables>;
     <loop continuation test>;
     <increment/decrement of loop control variables>)
```

☐ The conditional `do-while` loop has the following general syntax. The `do-while` loop iterates at least once.

```
do {
    <sequence of statements>
} while (condition);
```

☐ The conditional `while` loop has the following general syntax. The `while` loop may not iterate if its tested condition is initially false.

```
while (condition)
    statement; ¦ { <sequence of statements> }
```

☐ The `continue` statement enables you to jump to the end of the loop and resume with the next iteration. The advantage of the `continue` statement is that it uses no labels to direct the jump.

☐ Open loops are `for` loops with empty components. The `break` statement enables you to exit the current loop and resume program execution at the first statement that comes after the loop. The `exit` function (declared in STDLIB.H) enables you to make a critical loop exit by halting the C++ program altogether.

☐ Nested loops empower you to perform repetitive tasks as part of other repetitive tasks. C++ enables you to nest any kind of loops to just about any level needed.

6

Q&A

Q How can a `while` loop simulate a `for` loop?

A Here is a simple example:

```
                                        int i = 1;
for (int i = 1; i <= 10; i +=2) {       while (i <= 10) {
  cout << i << "\n";                       cout << i << "\n";
                                          i += 2;
                                        }
```

The `while` loop needs a leading statement that initializes the loop control variable. Also notice that the `while` loop uses a statement inside it to alter the value of the loop control variable.

Q How can a `while` loop simulate a `do-while` loop?

A Here is a simple example:

```
i = 1;                        i = 1;
do {                          while (i <= 10) {
  cout << i << "\n";            cout << i << "\n";
  i += 2;                       i += 2;
} while (i <= 10);            }
```

The two loops have the same condition in their `while` clauses.

Q How can the open `for` loop emulate the `while` and `do-while` loops?

A The open `for` loop is able to emulate the other C++ loops by placing the loop-escape `if` statement near the beginning or end of the loop. Here is how the open `for` loop emulates a sample `while` loop:

```
i = 1;                        i = 1;
while (i <= 10) {             for (;;) {
                               if(i > 10) break;
  cout << i << "\n"             cout << i << "\n"
  i += 2;                       i += 2;
}                             }
```

Notice that the open `for` loop uses a loop-escape `if` statement as the first statement inside the loop. The condition tested by the `if` statement is the logical reverse of the `while` loop condition.

Here is a simple example showing the emulation of the `do-while` loop:

```
i = 1;                          i = 1;
do {                            for (;;) {
  cout << i << "\n"               cout << i << "\n"
  i += 2;                         i += 2;
                                  if (i > 10) break;
} while (i <= 10);              }
```

The open `for` loop uses a loop-escape `if` statement right before the end of the loop. The condition tested by the `if` statement is the logical reverse of the `do-while` loop condition.

Q In nested `for` loops, can I use the loop control variable of the outer loops as part of the range of values for the inner loops?

A Yes. C++ does not object to such use. Here is a simple example:

```
for (int i = 1; i <= 100; i += 5)
    for (int j = i; j <= 100; j++)
        cout << i * j << "\n";
```

Q Does C++ restrict nesting of the various types of loops?

A No, you can nest any combination of loops in a C++ program.

Workshop

The Workshop provides quiz questions to help you solidify your understanding of the material covered and exercises to provide you with experience in using what you've learned. Try to understand the quiz and exercise answers before continuing on to the next day's lesson. Answers are provided in Appendix B, "Answers."

Quiz

1. What is wrong with the following loop?

```
i = 1;
while (i < 10) {
  j = i * i - 1;
  k = 2 * j - i;
```

```
    cout << "i = " << i << "\n";
    cout << "j = " <<  j << "\n";
    cout << "k = " << k << "\n";
}
```

2. What is the output of the following `for` loop?

```
for (int i = 5; i < 10; i + 2)
    cout << i - 2 << "\n";
```

3. What is the output of the following `for` loop?

```
for (int i = 5; i < 10; )
    cout << i - 2 << "\n";
```

4. What is wrong with the following code?

```
for (int i = 1; i <= 10; i++)
    for (i = 8; i <= 12; i++)
        cout << i << "\n";
```

5. Where is the error in the following nested loops?

```
for (int i = 1; i <= 10; i++) {
  cout << i * i << "\n";
  for (int i = 1; i <= 10; i++)
    cout << i * i * i << "\n";
}
```

6. Where is the error in the following loop?

```
i = 1;
while (1 > 0) {
  cout << i << "\n";
  i++;
}
```

7. The factorial of a number is the product of the sequence of integers from 1 to that number. The following general equation defines the factorial (which uses the symbol !):

```
n! = 1 * 2 * 3 * ... * n
```

Here is a C++ program that calculates the factorial of a number. The problem is that, for whatever positive value you enter, the program displays the value 0 for the factorial. Where is the error in the program?

```
int n;
double factorial;
cout << "Enter positive integer : ";
cin >> n;
for (int i = 1; i <= n; i++)
  factorial *= i;
cout << n << "!= " << factorial;
```

Exercises

1. Write the program FOR5.CP that uses a `for` loop to obtain and display the sum of odd integers in the range of 11 to 121.

2. Write the program WHILE2.CP that uses a `while` loop to obtain and display the sum of the squared odd integers in the range of 11 to 121.

3. Write the program DOWHILE2.CP that uses a `do-while` loop to obtain and display the sum of the squared odd integers in the range of 11 to 121.

6

Arrays

Arrays are among the most popular data structures. They enable programs to store data for processing later on. Most popular programming languages support static arrays. Many languages also support dynamic arrays.

NEW An *array* is a group of variables.
TERM

Today, you learn about the following topics related to static arrays:

- ☐ Declaring single-dimensional arrays
- ☐ Using single-dimensional arrays
- ☐ Initializing single-dimensional arrays
- ☐ Declaring single-dimensional arrays as function parameters
- ☐ Sorting arrays
- ☐ Searching arrays
- ☐ Declaring multidimensional arrays
- ☐ Using multidimensional arrays
- ☐ Initializing multidimensional arrays
- ☐ Declaring multidimensional arrays as function parameters

Declaring Single-Dimensional Arrays

The single-dimensional array is the simplest kind of array. In a single-dimensional array, each variable is individually accessed using a single index.

NEW A *single-dimensional array* is a group of variables that share the same name
TERM (which is the name of the array).

Syntax

A Single-Dimensional Array

The general syntax for declaring a single-dimensional array is

```
type arrayName[numberOfElements];
```

C++ requires you to observe the following rules in declaring single-dimensional arrays:

☐ The lower bound of a C++ array is set at 0. C++ does not allow you to override or alter this lower bound.

☐ Declaring a C++ array entails specifying the number of members. Keep in mind that the number of members is equal to the upper bound plus one.

The valid range of indices for this general form is between 0 and numberOfElements - 1.

Examples:

```
int intArray[10];
char name[31];
double x[100];
```

Using Single-Dimensional Arrays

Using a single-dimensional array involves stating both its name and the valid index to access one of its members. Depending on where the reference to an array element occurs, it can either store or recall a value. The simple rules to remember are

☐ Assign a value to an array element before accessing that element to recall data. Otherwise, you get garbage data.

☐ Use a valid index.

DO	DON'T
DO make reasonable checks for the indices that access the arrays.	
DON'T assume that indices are always valid.	

7

Arrays

Let's look at an example. Listing 7.1 shows the source code for the program ARRAY1.CP. The program uses a 30-element numeric array to calculate the average for the data in a numeric array. The program performs the following tasks:

- ☐ Prompts you to enter the number of actual data points (this value must lie in the range of valid numbers indicated by the prompting message)

- ☐ Prompts you to enter the data for the array elements

- ☐ Calculates the average of the data in the array

- ☐ Displays the average value

 Listing 7.1. Source code for the program ARRAY1.CP.

```
1: /*
2:    C++ program that demonstrates the use of one-dimension
3:    arrays.  The average value of the array is calculated.
4: */
5:
6: #include <iostream.h>
7:
8: const int MAX = 30;
9:
10: main()
11: {
12:
13:     double x[MAX];
14:     double sum, sumx = 0.0, mean;
15:     int i, n;
16:
17:     do { // obtain number of data points
18:         cout << "Enter number of data points [2 to "
19:             << MAX << "] : ";
20:         cin >> n;
21:         cout << "\n";
22:     } while (n < 2 || n > MAX);
23:
24:     // prompt user for data
25:     for (i = 0; i < n; i++) {
26:         cout << "X[" << i << "] : ";
27:         cin >> x[i];
28:     }
29:
30:     // initialize summations
31:     sum = n;
32:
33:     // calculate sum of observations
34:     for (i = 0; i < n; i++)
35:         sumx += x[i];
36:
```

```
37:      mean = sumx / sum; // calculate the mean value
38:      cout << "\nMean = " << mean << "\n\n";
39:      return 0;
40: }
```

Here is a sample session with the program in Listing 7.1:

```
Enter number of data points [2 to 30] : 5

X[0] : 12.5
X[1] : 45.7
X[2] : 25.6
X[3] : 14.1
X[4] : 68.4

Mean = 33.26
```

The program in Listing 7.1 declares the global constant MAX as the size of the array used in the program. The function main declares the double-typed array x, in line 13, to have MAX elements. The function also declares other nonarray variables in lines 14 and 15.

The do-while loop located in lines 17 through 22 obtains the number of data points you want to store in the array x. The output statement in lines 18 and 19 prompts you to enter the number of data points. The output indicates the range of valid numbers, which is 2 to MAX. The statement in line 20 obtains your input and stores it in variable n. The while clause validates your input. The clause determines whether the value in variable n is either less than 2 or greater than MAX. If this condition is true, the do-while loop iterates again to obtain a correct input value.

The for loop statement in lines 25 through 28 prompts you to enter the data. The loop uses the control variable i and iterates from 0 to n–1, in increments of 1. The output statement in line 26 prompts you to enter the value for the indicated array element. The input statement in line 27 obtains your input and stores it in the element x[i].

The statement in line 31 assigns the integer in variable n to the double-typed variable sum. The for loop in lines 34 and 35 adds the values in array x to the variable sumx. The loop uses the control variable i and iterates from 0 to n–1 in increments of 1. The statement in line 35 uses the increment assignment operator to add the value in element x[i] to the variable sumx.

The statement in line 37 calculates the mean value and stores it in variable mean. The output statement in line 38 displays the mean value.

7

Note: The program in Listing 7.1 shows how to use a `for` loop to process the elements of an array. The loop continuation test uses the < operator and the value beyond the last valid index. You can use the <= operator followed by the last index. For example, I can write the data input loop as

```
24:      // prompt user for data
25:      for (i = 0; i <= (n - 1); i++) {
26:          cout << "X[" << i << "] : ";
27:          cin >> x[i];
28:      }
```

However, this form is not popular because it requires an additional operator, whereas the condition `i < n` does not.

DO   DON'T

DO write the loop continuation expression so that it uses the minimum number of operators. This approach reduces the code size and speeds up loop execution.

DON'T use the <= operator in the loop continuation condition, unless using the operator helps you write an expression that minimizes the number of operations.

Initializing Single-Dimensional Arrays

C++ enables you to initialize arrays and is flexible about the initialization. You need to enclose the list of initializing values in a pair of open and close braces ({}). The list is comma-delimited and may continue on multiple lines. If there are fewer items in the initializing list than there are array elements, the compiler assigns 0 to balance the array elements. By contrast, if the list of initializing values has more items than the number of array elements, the compiler flags a compile-time error.

The next program, Listing 7.2, modifies Listing 7.1 to supply data internally. Consequently, I eliminate the steps that prompt you for the number of data points and the data

itself. The program simply displays the array elements (obtained from the initialization list) and the average value for the data. Although this program does not interact with the user, it offers a version that stores data in the source code. You can edit the program periodically to add, edit, and delete data before recalculating a new average value.

 Listing 7.2. Source code for the program ARRAY2.CP.

```
1: /*
2:    C++ program that demonstrates the use of single-dimensional
3:    arrays.  The average value of the array is calculated.
4:    The array has its values preassigned internally.
5: */
6:
7: #include <iostream.h>
8:
9: const int MAX = 10;
10:
11: main()
12: {
13:
14:     double x[MAX] = { 12.2, 45.4, 67.2, 12.2, 34.6, 87.4,
15:                       83.6, 12.3, 14.8, 55.5 };
16:     double sum = MAX, sumx = 0.0, mean;
17:     int n = MAX;
18:
19:     // calculate sum of observations
20:     cout << "Array is:\n";
21:     for (int i = 0; i < n; i++) {
22:         sumx += x[i];
23:         cout << "x[" << i << "] = " << x[i] << "\n";
24:     }
25:
26:     mean = sumx / sum; // calculate the mean value
27:     cout << "\nMean = " << mean << "\n\n";
28:     return 0;
29: }
```

 Here is a sample session with the program in Listing 7.2:

```
Array is:
x[0] = 12.2
x[1] = 45.4
x[2] = 67.2
x[3] = 12.2
x[4] = 34.6
x[5] = 87.4
x[6] = 83.6
x[7] = 12.3
x[8] = 14.8
x[9] = 55.5

Mean = 42.52
```

The initialization of the array x in Listing 7.2 requires some further examination. Line 14 contains the declaration of array x and its initialization. The initializing list, which runs to line 15, is enclosed in a pair of braces and has comma-delimited values. The statement in line 16 declares the variables sum and sumx and initializes these variables to MAX and 0, respectively. The statement in line 17 declares the int-typed variable n and initializes it with the value MAX. The rest of the program resembles parts of the program in Listing 7.1.

If you are somewhat dismayed by the fact that you have to count the exact number of initializing values, then I have some good news for you: C++ enables you to size an array automatically using the number of items in the corresponding initializing list. Consequently, you don't need to place a number in the square brackets of the array and can let the compiler do the work for you.

DO	DON'T
DO include dummy values in the initializing list, if the initialized array needs to expand later.	
DON'T rely on counting the number of items in the initializing list to provide the data for the number of array elements.	

Listing 7.3 shows the source code for the program ARRAY3.CP. This new version uses the feature of automatic array sizing.

Listing 7.3. Source code for the program ARRAY3.CP.

```
1: /*
2:    C++ program that demonstrates the use of single-dimensional
3:    arrays.  The average value of the array is calculated.
4:    The array has its values preassigned internally.
5: */
6:
7: #include <iostream.h>
8:
9: main()
10: {
11:
12:     double x[] = { 12.2, 45.4, 67.2, 12.2, 34.6, 87.4,
13:                    83.6, 12.3, 14.8, 55.5 };
14:     double sum,  sumx = 0.0, mean;
15:     int n;
16:
```

```
17:      n = sizeof(x) / sizeof(x[0]);
18:      sum = n;
19:
20:      // calculate sum of observations
21:      cout << "Array is:\n";
22:      for (int i = 0; i < n; i++) {
23:          sumx += x[i];
24:          cout << "x[" << i << "] = " << x[i] << "\n";
25:      }
26:
27:      mean = sumx / sum; // calculate the mean value
28:      cout << "\nNumber of data points = " << n << "\n"
29:           << "Mean = " << mean << "\n";
30:      return 0;
31: }
```

Here is a sample session with the program in Listing 7.3:

```
Array is:
x[0] = 12.2
x[1] = 45.4
x[2] = 67.2
x[3] = 12.2
x[4] = 34.6
x[5] = 87.4
x[6] = 83.6
x[7] = 12.3
x[8] = 14.8
x[9] = 55.5

Number of data points = 10
Mean = 42.52
```

Notice that the program in Listing 7.3 does not declare the constant MAX, which appears in the previous version shown in Listing 7.2. How does the program determine the number of array elements? Line 17 shows that the program calculates the number of elements in array x by dividing the size of the array x (obtained by using sizeof(x)) by the size of the first element (obtained by using sizeof(x[0])). You can use this method to obtain the size of any array of any data type.

Array Parameters in Functions

C++ enables you to declare function parameters that are arrays. In fact, C++ permits you to either be specific or general about the size of the array parameter. If you want an array parameter to accept arrays of a fixed size, you can specify the size of the array in the parameter declaration. By contrast, if you want the array parameter to accept arrays with the same basic type but have different sizes, use empty brackets with the array parameter.

Syntax

A Fixed-Array Parameter

The general syntax for declaring a fixed-array parameter is

```
type parameterName[arraySize]
```

Examples:

```
int minArray(int arr[100], int n);
void sort(unsigned dayNum[7]);
```

Syntax

An Open-Array Parameter

The general syntax for declaring an open-array parameter is

```
type parameterName[]
```

Examples:

```
int minArray(int arr[], int n);
void sort(unsigned dayNum[]);
```

DO   DON'T

DO use open-array parameters in functions.

DON'T forget to check the upper bound of an open-array parameter in general-purpose functions.

Let's look at a simple example. Listing 7.4 shows the source code for program ARRAY4.CP. The program performs the following tasks:

☐ Prompts you to enter the number of data points, which ranges from 2 to 10

☐ Prompts you to enter the integer values for the arrays

☐ Displays the smallest value in the array

☐ Displays the largest value in the array

Type   **Listing 7.4. Source code for the program ARRAY4.CP.**

```
1: // C++ program that passes arrays as arguments of functions
2:
3: #include <iostream.h>
4:
```

```
 5: const int MAX = 10;
 6:
 7: main()
 8: {
 9:    int arr[MAX];
10:    int n;
11:
12:    // declare prototypes of functions
13:    int getMin(int a[MAX], int size);
14:    int getMax(int a[], int size);
15:
16:    do { // obtain number of data points
17:      cout << "Enter number of data points [2 to "
18:           << MAX << "] : ";
19:      cin >> n;
20:      cout << "\n";
21:    } while (n < 2 || n > MAX);
22:
23:    // prompt user for data
24:    for (int i = 0; i < n; i++) {
25:      cout << "arr[" << i << "] : ";
26:      cin >> arr[i];
27:    }
28:
29:    cout << "Smallest value in array is "
30:         << getMin(arr, n) << "\n"
31:         << "Biggest value in array is "
32:         << getMax(arr, n) << "\n";
33:    return 0;
34: }
35:
36:
37: int getMin(int a[MAX], int size)
38: {
39:    int small = a[0];
40:    // search for the smallest value in the
41:    // remaining array elements
42:    for (int i = 1; i < size; i++)
43:      if (small > a[i])
44:        small = a[i];
45:    return small;
46: }
47:
48: int getMax(int a[], int size)
49: {
50:    int big = a[0];
51:    // search for the biggest value in the
52:    // remaining array elements
53:    for (int i = 1; i < size; i++)
54:      if (big < a[i])
55:        big = a[i];
56:    return big;
57: }
```

7

Here is a sample session with the program in Listing 7.4:

```
Enter number of data points [2 to 10] : 5

arr[0] : 55
arr[1] : 69
arr[2] : 47
arr[3] : 85
arr[4] : 14
Smallest value in array is 14
Biggest value in array is 85
```

The program in Listing 7.4 declares the global constant MAX in line 5 to size the array of data. The function main declares the int-typed array arr in line 9. Line 10 contains the declaration of the int-typed variable n. Lines 13 and 14 declare the prototypes for the functions getMin and getMax, which return the smallest and biggest values in an int-typed array, respectively. The prototype of function getMin indicates that it uses a fixed-array parameter. By contrast, the prototype of function getMax indicates that it uses an open-array parameter. I use both kinds of array parameters for the sake of demonstration.

The do-while loop in lines 16 through 21 obtains the number of data points you want to store in the array arr. The output statement in lines 17 and 18 prompts you to enter the number of data points. The output indicates the range of valid numbers, which runs between 2 and MAX. The statement in line 19 obtains your input and stores it in variable n. The while clause validates your input. The clause determines whether the value in variable n is either less than 2 or greater than MAX. If this condition is true, the do-while loop iterates again to obtain a correct input value.

The for loop statement in lines 24 through 27 prompts you to enter the data. The loop uses the control variable i and iterates from 0 to n−1 in increments of 1. The output statement in line 25 prompts you to enter the value for the indicated array element. The statement in line 26 obtains your input and stores it in the element arr[i].

The output statement in lines 29 through 32 displays the smallest and biggest integers in array arr. The statement invokes the functions getMin and getMax, supplying each one with the arguments arr and n.

The program defines function getMin in lines 37 through 46. The function has two parameters: the int-typed, fixed-array parameter a and the int-typed parameter size. The function declares the local variable small and initializes it with a[0], the first element of parameter a. The function searches for the smallest value in the parameter a using the for loop in line 42. This loop declares the control variable i and iterates from 1 to size−1 in increments of 1. The loop contains an if statement that assigns the value in element a[i] to variable small if the latter is greater than element a[i].

The function returns the value in variable `small`. The function `getMin` accepts only `int`-typed arrays that have `MAX` elements.

The program defines function `getMax` in lines 48 through 57. This function, which is similar to function `getMin`, has two parameters: the `int`-typed, open-array parameter `a` and the `int`-typed parameter `size`. The function declares the local variable `big` and initializes it with `a[0]`, the first element of parameter `a`. The function searches for the smallest value in the parameter `a` using the `for` loop in line 53. This loop declares the control variable `i` and iterates from 1 to `size`-1 in increments of 1. The loop contains an `if` statement that assigns the value in element `a[i]` to variable `big` if the latter is less than element `a[i]`. The function returns the value in variable `big`. The function `getMax` accepts `int`-typed arrays of any size.

Sorting Arrays

Sorting and searching arrays are the most common nonnumerical operations for arrays. Sorting an array typically arranges its elements in ascending order. The process uses part or all of the value in each element to determine the precedence of the elements in the array. Searching for data in sorted arrays is much easier than in unordered arrays.

Computer scientists have spent much time and effort studying and creating methods for sorting arrays. Discussing and comparing these methods is beyond the scope of this book. I only mention that my favorite array sorting methods include the QuickSort, Shell-Metzner sort, heap sort, and the new Comb sort. The QuickSort method is the fastest method, in general, but requires some operational overhead. The Shell-Metzner and Comb sort methods do not require similar overhead. The example in this section uses the new Comb sort method, which is more efficient than the Shell-Metzner method.

The Comb sort method uses the following steps, given an array `A` with `N` elements:

1. Initializes the `Offset` value, used in comparing elements, to `N`

2. Sets the `Offset` value to either `8*Offset/11` or `1`, whichever is bigger

3. Sets the `InOrder` flag to true

4. Loops for values 0 to `N`—`Offset`, using the loop control variable `i`:

    Assigns `I + Offset` to `J`

    If `A[I]` is greater than `A[J]`, swaps `A[I]` with `A[J]` and sets the `InOrder` flag to false

5. Resumes at step 2 if `Offset` is not 1 and `InOrder` is false

Let's look at a program that sorts an array of integers. Listing 7.5 shows the source code for program ARRAY5.CP. The program performs the following tasks:

☐ Prompts you to enter the number of data points

☐ Prompts you to enter the integer values for the array

☐ Displays the elements of the unordered array

☐ Displays the elements of the sorted array

 Listing 7.5. Source code for the program ARRAY5.CP.

```
1: // C++ program that sorts arrays using the Comb sort method
2:
3: #include <iostream.h>
4:
5: const int MAX = 10;
6: // const int TRUE = 1;
7: // const int FALSE = 0;
8:
9: int obtainNumData()
10: {
11:   int m;
12:   do { // obtain number of data points
13:     cout << "Enter number of data points [2 to "
14:          << MAX << "] : ";
15:     cin >> m;
16:     cout << "\n";
17:   } while (m < 2 || m > MAX);
18:   return m;
19: }
20:
21: void inputArray(int intArr[], int n)
22: {
23:   // prompt user for data
24:   for (int i = 0; i < n; i++) {
25:     cout << "arr[" << i << "] : ";
26:     cin >> intArr[i];
27:   }
28: }
29:
30: void showArray(int intArr[], int n)
31: {
32:   for (int i = 0; i < n; i++) {
33:     cout.width(5);
34:     cout << intArr[i] << " ";
35:   }
36:   cout << "\n";
37: }
38:
39: void sortArray(int intArr[], int n)
```

```
40: {
41:    int offset, temp, inOrder;
42:
43:    offset = n;
44:    do {
45:      offset = (8 * offset) / 11;
46:      offset = (offset == 0) ? 1 : offset;
47:      inOrder = TRUE;
48:      for (int i = 0, j = offset; i < (n - offset); i++, j++) {
49:        if (intArr[i] > intArr[j]) {
50:          inOrder = FALSE;
51:          temp = intArr[i];
52:          intArr[i] = intArr[j];
53:          intArr[j] = temp;
54:        }
55:      }
56:    } while (!(offset == 1 && inOrder == TRUE));
57: }
58:
59: main()
60: {
61:    int arr[MAX];
62:    int n;
63:
64:    n = obtainNumData();
65:    inputArray(arr, n);
66:    cout << "Unordered array is:\n";
67:    showArray(arr, n);
68:    sortArray(arr, n);
69:    cout << "\nSorted array is:\n";
70:    showArray(arr, n);
71:    return 0;
72: }
```

Here is a sample session with the program in Listing 7.5:

```
Enter number of data points [2 to 10] : 10
arr[0] : 55
arr[1] : 68
arr[2] : 74
arr[3] : 15
arr[4] : 28
arr[5] : 23
arr[6] : 69
arr[7] : 95
arr[8] : 22
arr[9] : 33
Unordered array is:
    55    68    74    15    28    23    69    95    22    33

Sorted array is:
    15    22    23    28    33    55    68    69    74    95
```

The program in Listing 7.5 declares the constant MAX, in line 5, which defines the size of the array used in the program. The commented constants TRUE and FALSE define the Boolean values for other C++ compilers because these constants are defined in the Symantec libraries. The program also defines the functions obtainNumData, inputArray, showArray, sortArray, and main.

The parameterless function obtainNumData defined in lines 9 through 19 prompts you to enter the number of values. The output statement in lines 13 and 14 also specifies the valid range for your input. The statement in line 15 stores your input in the local variable m. The function uses a do-while loop to ensure that it returns a valid number. The loop iterates as long as the value in variable m is less than 2 or greater than MAX. The function returns the value in variable m.

The function inputArray defined in lines 21 through 28 obtains the data for the tested array. The function has two parameters. The open-array parameter intArr passes the input values back to the caller of the function. The parameter n specifies how many values to obtain for parameter intArr. The function uses a for loop that iterates from 0 to n−1 in increments of 1. Each loop iteration prompts you for a value and stores that value in an element of array intArr.

Note: The function inputArray illustrates that C++ functions treat array parameters as if they are references to their arguments because these parameters affect the values in the arguments beyond the scope of the functions. In reality, the C++ compiler passes a copy of the address of the array argument to the function when dealing with an array parameter. Armed with the address of the array, C++ functions can then alter the values of the array beyond the scope of these functions. This feature is possible because the function is working with the original array and not a copy.

The function showArray defined in lines 30 through 37 displays the meaningful data in an array. The function has two parameters. The open-array parameter intArr passes the array values to be displayed by the function. The parameter n specifies how many elements of array intArr to display (remember that not all of the array elements are used to store your data). The function uses a for loop that iterates from 0 to n−1 in increments of 1. Each loop iteration displays the value in an array element. The array elements appear on the same line.

The function `sortArray` defined in lines 39 through 57 sorts the elements of an array using the Comb sort method. The function has two parameters. The open-array parameter `intArr` passes the array values to be sorted by the function. The parameter `n` specifies how many array elements to sort. The statements in the function `sortArray` implement the Comb sort method outlined earlier.

> **Note:** The function `sortArray` illustrates how array parameters can pass data to and from a function. The function `sortArray` receives an unordered array, sorts it, and passes the ordered array to the function's caller. The compiler supports this feature by passing a copy of the address of the array to the function. Thus, the function need not explicitly return the array because it is working with the original data and not a copy.

The function `main` performs the various program tasks by calling the functions mentioned earlier. The function declares the array `arr` and the simple variable `n` in lines 61 and 62, respectively. The statement in line 64 calls function `obtainNumData` to obtain the number of data you want to store in the array. The statement assigns the result of the function `obtainNumData` to variable `n`. The statement in line 65 calls the function `inputArray` to prompt you for the data. The function call passes the arguments `arr` and `n`. The output statement in line 66 displays a message which indicates that the program is about to display the elements of the unordered array. The statement in line 67 calls `showArray` and passes it the arguments `arr` and `n`. This function call displays the elements of the array `arr` on one line. The statement in line 68 calls the function `sortArray` to sort the first `n` elements in array `arr`. The output statement in line 69 displays a message which indicates that the program is about to display the elements of the sorted array. The statement in line 70 calls `showArray` and passes it the arguments `arr` and `n`. This function call displays the elements of the ordered array `arr` on one line.

Searching Arrays

Searching arrays is another important nonnumerical operation. Because arrays can be sorted or unordered, there is a general category of search methods for each. The simplest search method for unordered arrays is the linear search method. The simplest search method for sorted arrays is the versatile binary search method. The search methods for unordered arrays can also be applied to sorted arrays. However, they do not take advantage of the array order.

NEW ☞ The *linear search* method sequentially examines the array elements, looking for
TERM an element that matches the search value. If the sought value is not in the array,
the linear search method examines every element in the array.

NEW ☞ The *binary search* method takes advantage of the order in the array. The method
TERM searches for a matching value by using the shrinking-intervals approach. The
initial search interval includes all the array elements (which contain meaningful
data). The method compares the median element of the interval with the search value.
If the two match, the search stops. Otherwise, the method determines which subinterval
to use as the next search interval. Consequently, each search interval is half the size of the
previous one. If the search value has no match in the examined array, the binary method
makes far fewer examinations than the linear search method. The binary search method
is the most efficient general-purpose search method for sorted arrays.

DO	**DON'T**

DO use the unordered-array search method when you are not sure that the
array is sorted.

DON'T use sorted-array search methods with unordered arrays. The results of
such searches are not reliable.

Let's look at a program that sorts an array of integers. Listing 7.6 shows the source code
for program ARRAY6.CP. I created this program by adding functions and operations to
program ARRAY5.CP. The program performs the following tasks:

☐ Prompts you to enter the number of data points

☐ Prompts you to enter the integer values for the array

☐ Displays the elements of the unordered array

☐ Asks you if you want to search for data in the unordered array (if you type
characters other than *Y* or *y*, the program resumes at step 8)

☐ Prompts you for a search value

☐ Displays the search outcome (if the program finds a matching element, it
displays the index of that element; otherwise, the program tells you that it
found no match for the search value)

☐ Resumes at step 4

☐ Displays the elements of the sorted array

☐ Asks you if you want to search for data in the unordered array (if you type characters other than *Y* or *y*, the program ends)

☐ Prompts you for a search value

☐ Displays the search outcome (if the program finds a matching element, it displays the index of that element; otherwise, the program tells you that it found no match for the search value)

☐ Resumes at step 9

 Listing 7.6. Source code for the program ARRAY6.CP.

```
1: // C++ program that searches arrays using the linear
2: // and binary searches methods
3:
4: #include <iostream.h>
5:
6: const int MAX = 10;
7: // const int TRUE = 1;
8: // const int FALSE = 0;
9: const int NOT_FOUND = -1;
10:
11: int obtainNumData()
12: {
13:   int m;
14:   do { // obtain number of data points
15:     cout << "Enter number of data points [2 to "
16:          << MAX << "] : ";
17:     cin >> m;
18:     cout << "\n";
19:   } while (m < 2 || m > MAX);
20:   return m;
21: }
22:
23: void inputArray(int intArr[], int n)
24: {
25:   // prompt user for data
26:   for (int i = 0; i < n; i++) {
27:     cout << "arr[" << i << "] : ";
28:     cin >> intArr[i];
29:   }
30: }
31:
32: void showArray(int intArr[], int n)
33: {
34:   for (int i = 0; i < n; i++) {
35:     cout.width(5);
36:     cout << intArr[i] << " ";
37:   }
```

continues

Listing 7.6. continued

```
38:    cout << "\n";
39: }
40:
41: void sortArray(int intArr[], int n)
42: // sort the first n elements of array intArr
43: // using the Comb sort method
44: {
45:    int offset, temp, inOrder;
46:
47:    offset = n;
48:    do {
49:      offset = (8 * offset) / 11;
50:      offset = (offset == 0) ? 1 : offset;
51:      inOrder = TRUE;
52:      for (int i = 0, j = offset; i < (n - offset); i++, j++) {
53:        if (intArr[i] > intArr[j]) {
54:          inOrder = FALSE;
55:          temp = intArr[i];
56:          intArr[i] = intArr[j];
57:          intArr[j] = temp;
58:        }
59:      }
60:    } while (!(offset == 1 && inOrder == TRUE));
61: }
62:
63: int linearSearch(int searchVal, int intArr[], int n)
64: // perform linear search to locate the first
65: // element in array intArr that matches the value
66: // of searchVal
67: {
68:    int notFound = TRUE;
69:    int i = 0;
70:    // search through the array elements
71:    while (i < n && notFound)
72:      // no match?
73:      if (searchVal != intArr[i])
74:        i++; // increment index to compare the next element
75:      else
76:        notFound = FALSE; // found a match
77:    // return search outcome
78:    return (notFound == FALSE) ? i : NOT_FOUND;
79: }
80:
81: int binarySearch(int searchVal, int intArr[], int n)
82: // perform binary search to locate the first
83: // element in array intArr that matches the value
84: // of searchVal
85: {
86:    int median, low, high;
87:
88:    // initialize the search range
89:    low = 0;
90:    high = n - 1;
91:    // search in array
```

```
 92:    do {
 93:      // obtain the median index of the current search range
 94:      median = (low + high) / 2;
 95:      // update search range
 96:      if (searchVal > intArr[median])
 97:        low = median + 1;
 98:      else
 99:        high = median - 1;
100:    } while (!(searchVal == intArr[median] || low > high));
101:    // return search outcome
102:    return (searchVal == intArr[median]) ? median : NOT_FOUND;
103: }
104:
105: void searchInUnorderedArray(int intArr[], int n)
106: // manage the linear search test
107: {
108:    int x, i;
109:    char c;
110:    // perform linear search
111:    cout << "Search in unordered array? (Y/N) ";
112:    cin >> c;
113:    while (c == 'Y' || c == 'y') {
114:      cout << "Enter search value : ";
115:      cin >> x;
116:      i = linearSearch(x, intArr, n);
117:      if (i != NOT_FOUND)
118:        cout << "Found matching element at index " << i << "\n";
119:      else
120:        cout << "No match found\n";
121:      cout << "Search in unordered array? (Y/N) ";
122:      cin >> c;
123:    }
124: }
125:
126: void searchInSortedArray(int intArr[], int n)
127: // manage the binary search test
128: {
129:    int x, i;
130:    char c;
131:    // perform binary search
132:    cout << "Search in sorted array? (Y/N) ";
133:    cin >> c;
134:    while (c == 'Y' || c == 'y') {
135:      cout << "Enter search value : ";
136:      cin >> x;
137:      i = binarySearch(x, intArr, n);
138:      if (i != NOT_FOUND)
139:        cout << "Found matching element at index " << i << "\n";
140:      else
141:        cout << "No match found\n";
142:      cout << "Search in sorted array? (Y/N) ";
143:      cin >> c;
144:    }
145: }
```

continues

Listing 7.6. continued

```
146:
147: main()
148: {
149:    int arr[MAX];
150:    int n;
151:
152:    n = obtainNumData();
153:    inputArray(arr, n);
154:    cout << "Unordered array is:\n";
155:    showArray(arr, n);
156:    searchInUnorderedArray(arr, n);
157:    sortArray(arr, n);
158:    cout << "\nSorted array is:\n";
159:    showArray(arr, n);
160:    searchInSortedArray(arr, n);
161:    return 0;
162: }
```

Here is a sample session with the program in Listing 7.6:

```
Enter number of data points [2 to 10] : 5

arr[0] : 85
arr[1] : 41
arr[2] : 55
arr[3] : 67
arr[4] : 48
Unordered array is:
    85    41    55    67    48
Search in unordered array? (Y/N) y
Enter search value : 55
Found matching element at index 2
Search in unordered array? (Y/N) y
Enter search value : 41
Found matching element at index 1
Search in unordered array? (Y/N) n

Sorted array is:
    41    48    55    67    85
Search in sorted array? (Y/N) y
Enter search value : 55
Found matching element at index 2
Search in sorted array? (Y/N) y
Enter search value : 67
Found matching element at index 3
Search in sorted array? (Y/N) n
```

The program in Listing 7.6 declares the functions `obtainNumData`, `inputArray`, `sortArray`, `linearSearch`, `binarySearch`, `searchInUnorderedArray`, `searchInSortedArray`, and `main`. Because the first three functions are identical to those in Listing 7.5, I discuss only the remaining functions.

The linearSearch function (lines 63 through 79) performs a linear search to find the first element in array intArr with a value that matches the one in parameter searchVal. The function searches the first n elements in array intArr. The linearSearch function either returns the index of the matching element in array intArr or yields the value of the global constant NOT_FOUND if no match is found. The function uses a while loop to examine the elements in array intArr. The search loop iterates while the value in variable i is less than that in variable n and while the local variable notFound stores TRUE. The statement in line 78 returns the function result using the conditional operator.

The binarySearch function (lines 81 through 103) has the same parameters as the linearSearch function and returns the same kind of value. The function uses the local variables low and high to store the current search interval. The function initializes the variables low and high using the values 0 and n - 1, respectively. The do-while loop in lines 92 through 100 calculates the index of the median element and compares the median element with the search value. The if statement in line 96 performs this comparison, and its clauses update the value of either variable low or variable high, depending on the outcome of the comparison. The update in either variable shrinks the search interval. The return statement in line 102 yields the function's value based on one last comparison between the search value and the median element of the current search interval.

The function searchInUnorderedArray (lines 105 through 124) manages the search in the unordered array. The function accesses the unordered array using the open-array parameter intArr. The function declares local variables that are used to prompt you for and store the search value. The statement in line 116 calls the function linearSearch and passes the argument x (the local variable that stores the search value), intArr, and n. The statement assigns the result of function linearSearch to the local variable i. The if statement in line 117 determines whether the value in variable i is not NOT_FOUND. If this condition is true, the output statement in line 118 shows the index of the matching element. Otherwise, the output statement in line 120 displays a no-match-found message.

The function searchInSortedArray (lines 126 through 145) is very similar to the function searchInUnorderedArray. The main difference is that the function searchInSortedArray deals with ordered arrays and therefore calls the binarySearch function to conduct a binary search on the ordered array intArr.

The function main defined in lines 147 through 162 invokes these functions to support the program tasks that I described earlier.

7

Multidimensional Arrays

In a multidimensional array, each additional dimension provides you with an additional access attribute. Two-dimensional arrays (or matrices, if you prefer) are the most popular kind of multidimensional arrays. Three-dimensional arrays are used less frequently than matrices.

NEW☞ TERM   *Multidimensional* arrays are supersets of single-dimensional arrays.

Syntax

Two-Dimensional and Three-Dimensional Arrays

The general syntax for declaring two-dimensional and three-dimensional arrays is

```
type array [size1][size2];
type array [size1][size2][size3];
```

As with simple arrays, each dimension has a lower bound index of 0, and the declaration defines the number of elements in each dimension.

Examples:

```
double matrixA[100][10];
char table[41][22][3];
int index[7][12];
```

It is important to understand how C++ stores the elements of a multidimensional array. Most compilers store the elements of a multidimensional array in a contiguous fashion (that is, as one long array). The runtime code calculates where a sought element is located in that long array. To explain the storage scheme of multidimensional arrays, let me start by employing a convention for referencing the indices of the different dimensions. The following schema specifies the dimension numbering and the concept of high- and low-order dimensions. Here is a six-dimensional array—an extreme case that is a good example:

```
              1     2    3    4    5    6   ◄────── dimension
        M [20]  [7]  [5]  [3]  [2]  [2]           number
              └──────────────────────►
                 higher dimension order
```

The first element of the array M is M[0][0][0][0][0][0] and is stored at the first memory location of array M. The array M is stored in a contiguous block of 8,400 elements. The memory location in that contiguous block stores the element at index 1 in the highest dimension number, dimension 6 (that is, M[0][0][0][0][0][1]). The memory location of the next elements in the contiguous block stores the subsequent elements in dimension 6 until the upper limit of dimension 6 is reached. Reaching this limit bumps the index of dimension 5 by 1 and resets the index of dimension 6 to 0. This process is repeated

until every element in a multidimensional array is accessed. You can think of this storage scheme as you would a gasoline-pump meter when refueling your car: the right digits turn the fastest, the left digits turn the slowest.

Here is another example that uses a three-dimensional array, M[3][2][2]:

```
M[0][0][0]  ◄── the starting memory address
M[0][0][1]  ◄── 2nd dimension is filled
M[0][1][0]
M[0][1][1]  ◄── 2nd and 3rd dimensions are filled
M[1][0][0]
M[1][0][1]  ◄── 3rd dimension is filled
M[1][1][0]
M[1][1][1]  ◄── 2nd and 3rd dimensions are filled
M[2][0][0]
M[2][0][1]  ◄── 3rd dimension is filled
M[2][1][0]
M[2][1][1]  ◄── all dimensions are filled
```

Let's look at a program example that illustrates basic matrix manipulation. Listing 7.7 shows the source code for the MAT1.CP program. The program manages a matrix that contains up to 10 columns and 30 rows and performs the following tasks:

☐ Prompts you to enter the number of rows (the program validates your input)

☐ Prompts you to enter the number of columns (the program validates your input)

☐ Prompts you to enter the matrix elements

☐ Calculates and displays the average for each column in the matrix

 Listing 7.7. Source code for the program MAT1.CP.

```
1: /*
2:    C++ program that demonstrates the use of two-dimension arrays.
3:    The average value of each matrix column is calculated.
4: */
5:
6: #include <iostream.h>
7:
8: const int MAX_COL = 10;
9: const int MAX_ROW = 30;
10:
11: main()
12: {
13:     double x[MAX_ROW][MAX_COL];
14:     double sum, sumx, mean;
15:     int rows, columns;
16:
17:     // get the number of rows
```

continues

Listing 7.7. continued

```
18:      do {
19:        cout << "Enter number of rows [2 to "
20:             << MAX_ROW << "] : ";
21:        cin >> rows;
22:      } while (rows < 2 || rows > MAX_ROW);
23:
24:      // get the number of columns
25:      do {
26:        cout << "Enter number of columns [1 to "
27:             << MAX_COL << "] : ";
28:        cin >> columns;
29:      } while (columns < 1 || columns > MAX_COL);
30:
31:      // get the matrix elements
32:      for (int i = 0; i < rows; i++)  {
33:        for (int j = 0; j < columns; j++)  {
34:          cout << "X[" << i << "][" << j << "] : ";
35:          cin >> x[i][j];
36:        }
37:        cout << "\n";
38:      }
39:
40:      sum = rows;
41:      // obtain the sum of each column
42:      for (int j = 0; j < columns; j++)  {
43:        // initialize summations
44:        sumx = 0.0;
45:        for (i = 0; i < rows; i++)
46:          sumx += x[i][j];
47:        mean = sumx / sum;
48:        cout << "Mean for column " << j
49:             << " = " << mean << "\n";
50:      }
51:      return 0;
52: }
```

Here is a sample session with the program in Listing 7.7:

```
Enter number of rows [2 to 30] : 3
Enter number of columns [1 to 10] : 3
X[0][0] : 1
X[0][1] : 2
X[0][2] : 3

X[1][0] : 4
X[1][1] : 5
X[1][2] : 6

X[2][0] : 7
X[2][1] : 8
X[2][2] : 9
```

```
Mean for column 0 = 4
Mean for column 1 = 5
Mean for column 2 = 6
```

Analysis

The program in Listing 7.7 declares the global constants MAX_COL and MAX_ROW in lines 8 and 9, respectively. These constants define the dimensions of the matrix created in the program. The function main declares the matrix x to have MAX_ROW rows and MAX_COL columns. The function also declares other nonarray variables.

The do-while loop in lines 18 through 22 prompts you to enter the number of rows of matrix x that will contain your data. The output statement in lines 19 and 20 indicates the range of the valid number of rows. The statement in line 21 stores your input in the variable rows.

The second do-while loop, in lines 25 through 29, prompts you to enter the number of columns of matrix x that will contain your data. The output statement in lines 26 and 27 indicates the range of the valid number of columns. The statement in line 28 saves your input in the variable columns.

The nested for loops in lines 32 through 38 prompt you for the matrix elements. The outer for loop uses the control variable i and iterates from 0 to rows−1 in increments of 1. The inner for loop uses the control variable j and iterates from 0 to columns−1 in increments of 1. The output statement in line 34 displays the index of the matrix element that will receive your input. The statement in line 35 stores your input in the matrix element x[i][j].

The process of obtaining the average of each matrix column starts at line 40. The statement in that line assigns the integer in variable rows to the double-typed variable sum. The program uses another pair of nested for loops in lines 42 through 50. The outer for loop uses the control variable j and iterates from 0 to columns−1 in increments of 1. This loop processes each column. The first statement inside the outer for loop assigns 0 to the variable sumx. The inner for loop is located at line 45. This loop uses the control variable i and iterates from 0 to rows−1 in increments of 1. The inner loop uses the statement in line 46 to add the values of elements x[i][j] to the variable sumx. The statement in line 47 (which is outside the inner for loop) calculates the column average and assigns it to the variable mean. The output statement in lines 48 and 49 displays the column number and its average value.

7

Note: The `for` loop in line 42 redeclares its control variable `j` (not so with the `for` loop in line 45). Why? The `for` loop in line 33 also declares the control variable `j`. However, the scope of that loop is limited to the scope of the outer `for` loop. Once the first pair of nested loops finishes executing, the loop control variable `j` is removed by the runtime system.

Initializing Multidimensional Arrays

C++ enables you to initialize a multidimensional array in a manner similar to single-dimensional arrays. You need to use a list of values that appear in the same sequence in which the elements of the initialized multidimensional array are stored. Now you realize the importance of understanding how C++ stores the elements of a multidimensional array. I modified the previous C++ program (Listing 7.7) to use an initializing list that internally supplies the program with data. Consequently, the program does not prompt you for any data. Rather, the program displays the values of the matrix and the average for its columns.

Listing 7.8. Source code for the program MAT2.CP.

```
1: /*
2:    C++ program that demonstrates the use of two-dimension arrays.
3:    The average value of each matrix column is calculated.
4: */
5:
6: #include <iostream.h>
7:
8: const int MAX_COL = 3;
9: const int MAX_ROW = 3;
10:
11: main()
12: {
13:     double x[MAX_ROW][MAX_COL] = {
14:                                    1, 2, 3, // row # 1
15:                                    4, 5, 6, // row # 2
16:                                    7, 8, 9  // row # 3
17:                                    };
18:     double sum, sumx, mean;
19:     int rows = MAX_ROW, columns = MAX_COL;
20:
21:     cout << "Matrix is:\n";
22:     // display the matrix elements
23:     for (int i = 0; i < rows; i++)  {
```

```
24:        for (int j = 0; j < columns; j++)  {
25:            cout.width(4);
26:            cout.precision(1);
27:            cout << x[i][j] << " ";
28:        }
29:        cout << "\n";
30:    }
31:    cout << "\n";
32:
33:    sum = rows;
34:    // obtain the sum of each column
35:    for (int j = 0; j < columns; j++)  {
36:        // initialize summations
37:        sumx = 0.0;
38:        for (i = 0; i < rows; i++)
39:            sumx += x[i][j];
40:        mean = sumx / sum;
41:        cout << "Mean for column " << j
42:            << " = " << mean << "\n";
43:    }
44:    return 0;
45: }
```

Here is a sample session with the program in Listing 7.8:

```
Matrix is:
   1    2    3
   4    5    6
   7    8    9

Mean for column 0 = 4
Mean for column 1 = 5
Mean for column 2 = 6
```

The program in Listing 7.8 declares the matrix x and initializes it with a list of values. Notice that the program declares the constants MAX_COL and MAX_ROW with values that match the size of the initialized matrix. The declaration statement in lines 13 through 17 shows the elements assigned to each row. The function main also initializes the variables rows and columns with the constants MAX_ROW and MAX_COL, respectively. The function performs this initialization for two reasons: first, the program no longer prompts you to enter values for the variables rows and columns. Second, the program is working with a custom-fit size for matrix x.

The program uses the nested for loops in lines 21 through 30 to display the elements of the matrix x. The second pair of nested for loops calculates the average for each matrix column. This nested for loop is identical to the one in Listing 7.7.

Multidimensional Array Parameters

C++ enables you to declare function parameters that are multidimensional arrays. As with single-dimensional arrays, you can be either specific or general when specifying the size of the array parameter. However, in the latter case, you can generalize only the first dimension of the array. If you want an array parameter to accept arrays of a fixed dimension, you can specify the size of each dimension of the array in the parameter declaration. By contrast, if you want the array parameter to accept arrays of the same basic type but of different first-dimension sizes, use empty brackets ([ ]) for the first dimension in the array parameter.

A Fixed-Array Parameter

The general syntax for declaring a fixed-array parameter is

```
type parameterName[dim1Size][dim2Size]...
```

Examples:

```
int minMatrix(int intMat[100][20], int rows, int cols);
void sort(unsigned mat[23][55],
          int rows, int cols, int colIndex);
```

An Open-Array Parameter

The general syntax for declaring an open-array parameter is

```
type parameterName[][dim2Size]...
```

Examples:

```
int minMat(int intMat[][100], int rows, int cols);
void sort(unsigned mat[][55],
          int rows, int cols, int colIndex);
```

Let's look at an example. Listing 7.9 shows the source code for program MAT3.CP. The program performs the same tasks as program MAT1.CP in Listing 7.7. I created program MAT3.CP by editing program MAT1.CP and placing each program task in a separate function. Thus, program MAT3.CP is a highly structured version of program MAT1.CP.

Type

Listing 7.9. Source code for the program MAT3.CP.

```
1: /*
2:    C++ program that demonstrates the use of two-dimension arrays.
3:    The average value of each matrix column is calculated.
4: */
5:
```

```
 6: #include <iostream.h>
 7:
 8: const int MAX_COL = 10;
 9: const int MAX_ROW = 30;
10:
11: int getRows()
12: {
13:   int n;
14:   // get the number of rows
15:   do {
16:     cout << "Enter number of rows [2 to "
17:          << MAX_ROW << "] : ";
18:     cin >> n;
19:   } while (n < 2 || n > MAX_ROW);
20:   return n;
21: }
22:
23: int getColumns()
24: {
25:   int n;
26:   // get the number of columns
27:   do {
28:     cout << "Enter number of columns [1 to "
29:          << MAX_COL << "] : ";
30:     cin >> n;
31:   } while (n < 1 || n > MAX_COL);
32:   return n;
33: }
34:
35: void inputMatrix(double mat[][MAX_COL],
36:                  int rows, int columns)
37: {
38:   // get the matrix elements
39:   for (int i = 0; i < rows; i++)  {
40:     for (int j = 0; j < columns; j++)  {
41:       cout << "X[" << i << "][" << j << "] : ";
42:       cin >> mat[i][j];
43:     }
44:     cout << "\n";
45:   }
46: }
47:
48: void showColumnAverage(double mat[][MAX_COL],
49:                        int rows, int columns)
50: {
51:   double sum, sumx, mean;
52:   sum = rows;
53:   // obtain the sum of each column
54:   for (int j = 0; j < columns; j++)  {
55:     // initialize summations
56:     sumx = 0.0;
57:     for (int i = 0; i < rows; i++)
58:       sumx += mat[i][j];
59:     mean = sumx / sum;
```

continues

Listing 7.9. continued

```
60:     cout << "Mean for column " << j
61:          << " = " << mean << "\n";
62:   }
63: }
64:
65: main()
66: {
67:     double x[MAX_ROW][MAX_COL];
68:     int rows, columns;
69:     // get matrix dimensions
70:     rows = getRows();
71:     columns = getColumns();
72:     // get matrix data
73:     inputMatrix(x, rows, columns);
74:     // show results
75:     showColumnAverage(x, rows, columns);
76:     return 0;
77: }
```

Here is a sample session with the program in Listing 7.9:

```
Enter number of rows [2 to 30] : 3
Enter number of columns [1 to 10] : 3
X[0][0] : 10
X[0][1] : 20
X[0][2] : 30

X[1][0] : 40
X[1][1] : 50
X[1][2] : 60

X[2][0] : 70
X[2][1] : 80
X[2][2] : 90

Mean for column 0 = 40
Mean for column 1 = 50
Mean for column 2 = 60
```

The program in Listing 7.9 declares the functions getRows, getColumns, inputMatrix, showColumnAverage, and main. The function getRows defined in lines 11 through 21 prompts you for the number of matrix rows that you will be using and returns your validated input. Similarly, the function getColumns defined in lines 23 through 33 returns the validated number of matrix columns.

The function inputMatrix defined in lines 35 through 46 obtains the data for the matrix. It has three parameters. The parameter mat specifies the matrix parameter (with an open first dimension). The parameters rows and columns specify the number of rows and columns of matrix mat, respectively, that will receive input data.

The function showColumnAverage defined in lines 48 through 63 calculates and displays the column averages for the matrix parameter mat. The parameters rows and columns specify the number of rows and columns of matrix mat, respectively, that contain meaningful data.

This function contains the same statements that appeared in program MAT1.CP. Program MAT3.CP uses the functions getRows, getColumns, inputMatrix, and showColumnAverage as shells or wrappers for the statements that perform the various tasks. From a structured programming point of view, program MAT3.CP is superior to program MAT1.CP.

The function main defined in lines 65 through 77 declares the matrix x with MAX_ROW rows and MAX_COL columns. It calls the functions getRows and getColumns to obtain the number of working rows and columns, respectively. The statement in line 73 invokes the function inputMatrix and supplies it with the arguments x, rows, and columns. The statement in line 75 calls function showColumnAverage and passes it the arguments x, rows, and columns.

Summary

Today's lesson covered various topics that deal with arrays, including single-dimensional and multidimensional arrays. You learned about the following topics:

☐ Declaring single-dimensional arrays requires you to state the data type of the array elements, the name of the array, and the number of array elements (enclosed in square brackets). All C++ arrays have a 0 lower bound. The upper bound of an array is equal to the number of elements minus 1.

☐ Using single-dimensional arrays requires you to state the array's name and include a valid index. The index must be enclosed in square brackets.

☐ Initializing single-dimensional arrays can be carried out while declaring them. The initializing list of data is enclosed in braces and contains comma-delimited data. In C++, you can include fewer data than the size of the array. In this case, the compiler automatically assigns zeros to the elements that you do not explicitly initialize. In addition, you can omit the explicit size of the initialized array and instead use the number of initializing items as the number of array elements.

☐ Declaring single-dimensional arrays as function parameters takes two forms. The first one deals with fixed-array parameters, whereas the second one handles open-array parameters. Fixed-array parameters include the size of the array in the parameter. Arguments for this kind of parameter must match the type and size of the parameter. Open-array parameters use empty brackets to indicate that the arguments for the parameters can be of any size.

☐ Sorting arrays is an important nonnumerical array operation. Sorting arranges the elements of an array in either ascending or descending order. Sorted arrays are much easier to search. For sorting arrays, the new Comb sort method is very efficient.

☐ Searching arrays involves locating an array element that contains the same data as the search value. Searching methods are geared toward unordered or ordered arrays. The linear search method is used for unordered arrays, and the binary search method is used for sorted arrays.

☐ Declaring multidimensional arrays requires you to state the data type of the array elements, the name of the array, and the size of each dimension (enclosed in separate brackets). The lower index of each dimension is 0. The upper bound of each dimension in an array is equal to the dimension size minus 1.

☐ Using multidimensional arrays requires you to state the array's name and include valid indices. Each index must be enclosed in a separate set of brackets.

☐ Initializing multidimensional arrays can be carried out while declaring them. The initializing list of data is enclosed in braces and contains comma-delimited data. In C++, you can include fewer data than the total size of the array. In this case, the compiler automatically assigns zeros to the elements that you do not explicitly initialize.

☐ Declaring multidimensional arrays as function parameters takes two forms. The first one deals with fixed-array parameters, whereas the second one handles parameters with an open first dimension. Fixed-array parameters include the size of each dimension in the array parameter. Arguments for this kind of parameter must match the type and size of the parameter. Open-array parameters use empty brackets for only the first dimension to indicate that the arguments for the parameters have varying sizes for the first dimensions. The other dimensions of the arguments must match those of the array parameter.

Q&A

Q Does C++ permit me to alter the size of an array?

A No. C++ does not allow you to redimension arrays.

Q Can I declare arrays with the basic type void (for example, void array[81];) to create buffers?

A No. C++ does not allow you to use the void type with an array because the type void has no defined size. Use the char or unsigned char type to create an array that works as a buffer.

Q Does C++ allow me to redeclare an array?

A C++ allows you to redeclare an array to change its basic type, number of dimensions, and size if you declare these arrays in nested statement blocks. Here is an example:

```
#include <iostream.h>
const MAX = 100;
const MAX_ROWS = 100;
const MAX_COLS = 20;

main()
{
  // declare variables here?
  {
    double x[MAX];
    // declare other variables?
    // statements to manipulate the single-dimensional
       array x
  }
  {
    double x[MAX_ROWS][MAX_COLS];
    // declare other variables?
    // statements to manipulate the matrix x
  }
  return 0;
}
```

The function main declares the array x in the first nested statement block. When program execution reaches the end of that block, the runtime system removes the array x and all other variables declared in that block. Then the function redeclares x as a matrix in the second block. When program execution reaches the end of the second block, the runtime system removes the matrix x and all other variables declared in that block.

Q Are arrays limited to the predefined types?

A Not at all. C++ allows you to create arrays using user-defined types (see Day 8).

Workshop

The Workshop provides quiz questions to help you solidify your understanding of the material covered and exercises to provide you with experience in using what you've learned. Try to understand the quiz and exercise answers before continuing on to the next day's lesson. Answers are provided in Appendix B, "Answers."

Quiz

1. What is the output of the following program?

```
#include <iostream.h>
const int MAX = 5;
main()
{
  double x[MAX];
  x[0] = 1;
  for (int i = 1; i < MAX; i++)
    x[i] = i * x[i-1];
  for (i = 0; i < MAX; i++)
    cout << "x[" << i << "] = " << x[i] << "\n";
  return 0;
}
```

2. What is the output of the following program?

```cpp
#include <iostream.h>
#include <math.h>
const int MAX = 5;
main()
{
  double x[MAX];
  for (int i = 0; i < MAX; i++)
    x[i] = sqrt(double(i));
  for (i = 0; i < MAX; i++)
    cout << "x[" << i << "] = " << x[i] << "\n";
  return 0;
}
```

3. Where is the error in the following program?

```cpp
#include <iostream.h>
const int MAX = 5;
main()
{
  double x[MAX];
  x[0] = 1;
  for (int i = 0; i < MAX; i++)
    x[i] = i * x[i-1];
  for (i = 0; i < MAX; i++)
    cout << "x[" << i << "] = " << x[i] << "\n";
  return 0;
}
```

Exercise

Write the program ARRAY7.CP by editing program ARRAY6.CP and replacing the Comb sort method in function sortArray with an implementation of the Shell-Metzner method.

Before you proceed to the second week of learning about programming with Symantec C++, let's look at a special example that evolves by the end of the next two weeks. The example is a simple number-guessing game, shown in Listing R1.1. The program selects a number at random between 0 and 1,000, and it prompts you to enter a number in that range. If your input is greater than the secret number, the program tells you that your guess is higher. By contrast, if your input is less than the secret number, the program tells you that your guess is lower. If you guess the secret number, the game ends with your victory. The program gives you up to 11 guesses. You can end the game at any prompt by entering a negative integer. The program then stops the game and displays the secret number.

Listing R1.1. Source code for program GAME1.CP.

```
1:   #include <stdlib.h>
2:   #include <iostream.h>
3:   #include <time.h>
4:
5:   main()
6:   {
7:     int n, m;
8:     int MaxIter = 11;
9:     int iter = 0;
10:    int ok = 1;
11:
12:    // reseed random-number generator
13:    srand((unsigned int)clock());
14:    n = rand() % 1001;
15:    m = -1;
16:
17:    // loop to obtain the other guesses
18:    while (m != n && iter < MaxIter && ok == 1) {
19:      cout << "Enter a number between 0 and 1000 : ";
20:      cin >> m;
21:      ok = (m < 0) ? 0 : 1;
22:      iter++;
23:      // is the user's guess higher?
24:      if (m > n)
25:        cout << "Enter a lower guess\n\n";
26:      else if (m < n)
27:        cout << "Enter a higher guess\n\n";
28:      else
29:        cout << "You guessed it! Congratulations.";
30:    }
31:    // did the user guess the secret number
32:    if (iter >= MaxIter || ok == 0)
33:      cout << "The secret number is " << n << "\n";
34:
35:    return 0;
36:  }
```

 Here is a sample session with the program in Listing R1.1:

```
Enter a number between 0 and 1000 : 500
Enter a lower guess

Enter a number between 0 and 1000 : 250
Enter a higher guess

Enter a number between 0 and 1000 : -1
Enter a higher guess
The secret number is 399
```

 The program in Listing R1.1 declares the function `main` which conducts the guessing game. The function declares a number of local variables in lines 7 through 10. The statement in line 13 reseeds the random number generator. The statement in line 14 assigns the secret number to the variable n. The statement in line 15 assigns −1 to the variable m, which stores your guesses.

The `while` loop in lines 18 through 30 conducts the game. The `while` loop determines whether or not all the following conditions are true:

☐ Your guess (stored in variable m) does not match the secret number stored in variable n.

☐ The number of iterations (stored in variable `iter`) is less than the maximum number of iterations (stored in variable `MaxIter`).

☐ The variable `ok` stores 1.

The first statement in the loop prompts you to enter a number between 0 and 1,000. The statement in line 20 obtains your input and stores it in variable m. The statement in line 21 assigns 0 to the variable `ok` if you entered a negative integer. Otherwise, the statement assigns 1 to variable `ok`. The statement in line 22 increments the variable `iter`.

The multi-alternative `if` statement in lines 24 through 29 compares your input with the secret number and displays the appropriate message reflecting your guess.

The `if` statement in line 32 displays the secret number if you failed to guess it in `MaxIter` iterations or if you entered a negative integer.

2

This second week continues teaching you about the C++ language. The topics cover the more advanced side of C++. You learn about user-defined data types—especially structures—and about pointers. The week also covers advanced topics on functions and introduces you to object-oriented programming (OOP) in C++. You learn about classes, components, and the rules for using these components. In addition, you learn about basic file I/O using the C++ stream library. Day 13 introduces you to the basics of programming for the Macintosh using the THINK Class Library (TCL). Day 14 discusses using the Visual Architect utility to create Macintosh applications.

8

User-Defined
Types and Pointers

WEEK
2

Creating user-defined data types is one of the features that are expected of modern programming languages. Today's lesson looks at the enumerated data types and structures that enable you to better organize your data. In addition, this lesson discusses using pointers with simple variables, arrays, structures, and dynamic data. Today, you learn about the following topics:

- [ ] The type definition using `typedef`
- [ ] Enumerated data types
- [ ] Structures
- [ ] Unions
- [ ] Reference variables
- [ ] Pointers to existing variables
- [ ] Pointers to arrays
- [ ] Pointers to structures
- [ ] Using pointers to access and manage dynamic data

Type Definition in C++

C++ offers the `typedef` keyword that enables you to define new data type names as aliases of existing types.

Syntax

The *typedef* Keyword

The general syntax for using `typedef` is

```
typedef knownType newType;
```

Examples:

```
typedef unsigned word;
typedef unsigned char byte;
type unsigned char boolean;
```

The `typedef` keyword defines a new type from a known one. You can use `typedef` to create aliases that shorten the names of existing data types or define names of data types that are more familiar to you (see the previous second example which `typedef`s a byte type). In addition, the `typedef` statement can define a new type name that better describes how the data type is used. The previous third example illustrates this use of `typedef`. You can also use `typedef` to define the name of an array type.

SAMS PUBLISHING

Sams Learning Center

An Array Type Name

The general syntax for defining the name of an array type is

```
typedef baseType arrayTypeName[arraySize];
```

The typedef statement defines the *arrayTypeName* whose basic type and size are *baseType* and *arraySize*, respectively.

Examples:

```
typedef double vector[10];
typedef double matrix[10][30];
```

Thus, the identifiers vector and matrix are names of data types.

Enumerated Data Types

The rule to follow with enumerated data types is that although the enumerated identifiers must be unique, the values assigned to them are not.

NEW☞ TERM   An *enumerated type* defines a list of unique identifiers and associates values with these identifiers.

An Enumerated Type

The general syntax for declaring an enumerated type is

```
enum enumType { <list of enumerated identifiers> };
```

Example:

```
enum Boolean { false, true };
num YesNo { no, yes, dontCare, maybe };
enum weekday { Sunday, Monday, Tuesday,
               Wednesday, Thursday, Friday, Saturday };
```

Here is an example of declaring an enumerated type:

```
enum CPUtype { i8088, i80286, i80386DX, i80386SX,
               i80486DX, i80486SX };
```

C++ associates integer values with the enumerated identifiers. For example, in this type, the compiler assigns 0 to i8088, 1 to i80286, and so on.

C++ is very flexible in declaring an enumerated type. First, the language allows you to explicitly assign a value to an enumerated identifier. Here is an example:

```
enum weekday { Sunday = 1, Monday, Tuesday, Wednesday,
               Thursday, Friday, Saturday };
```

This declaration explicitly assigns 1 to the enumerated identifier Sunday. The compiler then assigns the next integer, 2, to the next identifier Monday, and so on. C++ allows you to explicitly assign a value to each member of the enumerated list. Moreover, these values need not be unique. Here are some examples of the flexibility in declaring enumerated types in C++:

```
// explicit value assignment for every list member
enum colors { black = 1, red = 2, blue = 3, green = 5,
              yellow = 7, white = 11 };

// intermittent value assignment
enum colors { black = 1, red, blue, green = 5,
              yellow = 7, white = 11 };

// duplicate values
enum CPUtype { i8088 = 1, i80286 = 2,
               i80386DX = 3, i80386SX = 3,
               i80486DX = 4, i80486SX = 4 };

enum choiceType { false, true, dontCare = 0 };
```

In the last example, the compiler associates the identifier false with 0 by default. However, the compiler also associates the value 0 with dontCare because of the explicit assignment.

C++ allows you to declare variables that have enumerated types in the following ways:

☐ The declaration of the enumerated type may include the declaration of the variables of that type. The general syntax is

```
enum enumType { <list of enumerated identifiers> }
              <list of variables>;
```

Here is an example:

```
enum weekDay { Sun = 1, Mon, Tue, Wed, Thu, Fri, Sat }
             recycleDay, payDay, movieDay;
```

☐ The separate declaration of the enumerated type and its variables includes multiple statements to declare the type and the associated variables separately. The general syntax is

```
enum enumType { <list of enumerated identifiers> };
enumType var1, var2, ..., varN;
```

Let's look at an example. Listing 8.1 shows the source code for program ENUM1.CP. The program implements a simple one-line, four-function calculator that performs the following tasks:

☐ Prompts you to enter a number, an operator (+, -, *, or /), and a number

☐ Performs the requested operation, if valid

☐ Displays the operands, the operator, and the result, if the operation was valid; otherwise, displays an error message that indicates the kind of error (either you entered a bad operator, or attempted to divide by 0)

 Listing 8.1. Source code for the program ENUM1.CP.

```
1: /*
2:   C++ program that demonstrates enumerated types
3: */
4:
5: #include <iostream.h>
6:
7: enum mathError { noError, badOperator, divideByZero };
8:
9: void sayError(mathError err)
10: {
11:   switch (err) {
12:     case noError:
13:       cout << "No error";
14:       break;
15:     case badOperator:
16:       cout << "Error: invalid operator";
17:       break;
18:     case divideByZero:
19:       cout << "Error: attempt to divide by zero";
20:   }
21: }
22:
23: main()
24: {
25:   double x, y, z;
26:   char op;
27:   mathError error = noError;
28:
29:   cout << "Enter a number, an operator, and a number : ";
30:   cin >> x >> op >> y;
31:
32:   switch (op) {
33:     case '+':
34:       z = x + y;
35:       break;
36:     case '-':
37:       z = x - y;
```

continues

Listing 8.1. continued

```
38:        break;
39:      case '*':
40:        z = x * y;
41:        break;
42:      case '/':
43:        if (y != 0)
44:          z = x / y;
45:        else
46:          error = divideByZero;
47:        break;
48:      default:
49:        error = badOperator;
50:    }
51:
52:    if (error == noError)
53:      cout << x << " " << op << " " << y << " = " << z;
54:    else
55:      sayError(error);
56:    return 0;
57: }
```

Here is a sample session with the program in Listing 8.1:

```
Enter a number, an operator, and a number : 355 / 113
355 / 113 = 3.141593
```

The program in Listing 8.1 declares the enumerated type mathError in line 7. This data type has three enumerated values: noError, badOperator, and divideByZero.

The program also defines the function sayError in lines 9 through 21 to display a message based on the value of the enumerated parameter err. The function uses the switch statement in line 11 to display messages that correspond to the various enumerated values.

The function main declares the double-typed variables x, y, and z to represent the operands and the result, respectively. In addition, the function declares the char-typed variable op to store the requested operation, and the enumerated variable error to store the error status. The function initializes the variable error with the enumerated value noError.

The output statement in line 29 prompts you to enter the operands and the operator. The statement in line 30 stores your input in variables x, op, and y, in that order. The function uses the switch statement in line 32 to examine the value in variable op and perform the requested operation. The case labels at lines 33, 36, 39, and 42 provide the values for the four supported math operations. The last case label contains an if statement that

detects the attempt to divide by zero. If this is true, the statement in the `else` clause assigns the enumerated value `divideByZero` to the variable `error`.

The catch-all `default` clause in line 48 handles invalid operators. The statement in line 49 assigns the enumerated value `badOperator` to the variable `error`.

The `if` statement in line 52 determines whether or not the variable `error` contains the enumerated value `noError`. If this condition is true, the program executes the output statement in line 53. This statement displays the operands, the operator, and the result. Otherwise, the program executes the statement in the `else` clause which calls the function `sayError` and passes it the argument `error`. This function call displays a message that identifies the error.

Structures

C++ supports structures, and these members can be predefined types or other structures.

 Structures enable you to define a new type that logically groups several fields or members.

A Structure

The general syntax for declaring a structure is

```
struct structTag {
    < list of members >
};
```

Example:

```
struct point {
    double x;
    double y;
};

struct rectangle {
    point upperLeftCorner;
    point lowerRightCorner;
    double area;
};

struct circle {
    point center;
    double radius;
    double area;
};
```

Syntax

Once you define a `struct` type, you can use that type to declare variables. Here is an example of declarations that use structures that I declared in the syntax box:

```
point p1, p2, p3;
```

You can also declare structured variables when you define the structure itself:

```
struct point {
    double x;
    double y;
} p1, p2, p3;
```

 Untagged structures enable you to declare structure variables without defining a name for their structures.

Note: Interestingly, C++ permits you to declare untagged structures. For example, the following structure definition declares the variables p1, p2, and p3 but omits the name of the structure:

```
struct {
    double x;
    double y;
} p1, p2, p3;
```

C++ allows you to declare and initialize a structured variable. Here is an example:

```
point pt = { 1.0, -8.3 };
```

Accessing the members of a structure uses the dot (.) operator. Here are a few examples:

```
p1.x = 12.45;
p1.y = 34.56;
p2.x = 23.4 / p1.x;
p2.y = 0.98 * p1.y;
```

Let's look at a program. Listing 8.2 shows the source code for program STRUCT1.CP. The program prompts you for four sets of coordinates that define four rectangles. Each rectangle is defined by the x and y coordinates of the upper-left and lower-right corners. The program calculates the areas of each rectangle, sorts the rectangles by area, and displays the rectangles in the ascending order of their areas.

Listing 8.2. Source code for the program STRUCT1.CP.

```
 1: /*
 2:    C++ program that demonstrates structured types
 3: */
 4:
 5: #include <iostream.h>
 6: #include <stdio.h>
 7: #include <math.h>
 8:
 9: const MAX_RECT = 4;
10:
11: struct point {
12:   double x;
13:   double y;
14: };
15:
16: struct rect {
17:   point ulc; // upper left corner
18:   point lrc; // lower right corner
19:   double area;
20:   int id;
21: };
22:
23: typedef rect rectArr[MAX_RECT];
24:
25: main()
26: {
27:   rectArr r;
28:   rect temp;
29:   double length, width;
30:
31:   for (int i = 0; i < MAX_RECT; i++) {
32:     cout << "Enter (X,Y) coord. for ULC of rect. # "
33:          << i << " : ";
34:     cin >> r[i].ulc.x >> r[i].ulc.y;
35:     cout << "Enter (X,Y) coord. for LRC of rect. # "
36:          << i << " : ";
37:     cin >> r[i].lrc.x >> r[i].lrc.y;
38:     r[i].id = i;
39:     length = fabs(r[i].ulc.x - r[i].lrc.x);
40:     width = fabs(r[i].ulc.y - r[i].lrc.y);
41:     r[i].area = length * width;
42:   }
43:
44:   // sort the rectangles by areas
45:   for (i = 0; i < (MAX_RECT - 1); i++)
46:     for (int j = i + 1; j < MAX_RECT; j++)
47:       if (r[i].area > r[j].area) {
48:         temp = r[i];
49:         r[i] = r[j];
50:         r[j] = temp;
```

continues

Listing 8.2. continued

```
51:       }
52:
53:    // display rectangles sorted by area
54:    for (i = 0; i < MAX_RECT; i++)
55:      printf("Rect # %d has area %5.4lf\n", r[i].id, r[i].area);
56:    return 0;
57: }
```

Here is a sample session with the program in Listing 8.2:

```
Enter (X,Y) coord. for ULC of rect. # 0 : 1 1
Enter (X,Y) coord. for LRC of rect. # 0 : 2 2
Enter (X,Y) coord. for ULC of rect. # 1 : 1.5 1.5
Enter (X,Y) coord. for LRC of rect. # 1 : 3 4
Enter (X,Y) coord. for ULC of rect. # 2 : 1 2
Enter (X,Y) coord. for LRC of rect. # 2 : 5 8
Enter (X,Y) coord. for ULC of rect. # 3 : 4 6
Enter (X,Y) coord. for LRC of rect. # 3 : 8 4
Rect # 0 has area 1.0000
Rect # 1 has area 3.7500
Rect # 3 has area 8.0000
Rect # 2 has area 24.0000
```

The program in Listing 8.2 includes the header files IOSTREAM.H, MATH.H, and STDIO.H. The program declares the global constant MAX_RECT to specify the maximum number of rectangles. Line 11 contains the declaration of structure point, which is made up of two double-typed members, x and y. This structure models a two-dimensional point. Line 16 contains the declaration of structure rect which models a rectangle. The structure contains two point-typed members, ulc and lrc, the double-typed member area, and the int-typed member id. The members ulc and lrc represent the coordinates for the upper-left and lower-right corners that define a rectangle. The member area stores the area of the rectangle. The member id stores a numeric identification number.

The typedef statement in line 23 defines the type recArr as an array of MAX_RECT elements of structure rect.

The function main declares the rectArr-typed array r, the rect-typed structure temp, and the double-typed variables length and width.

The function main uses the for loop in lines 31 through 42 to prompt you for the coordinates of the rectangles, calculate their areas, and assign their id numbers. The output statements in lines 32 and 33 and in lines 35 and 36 prompt you for the x and y coordinates of the upper-left and lower-right corners, respectively. The input statements in lines 34 and 37 store the coordinates you enter in members r[i].ulc.x, r[i].ulc.y, r[i].lrc.x, and r[i].lrc.y, respectively. The statement in line 38 stores the value of the loop control variable i in member r[i].id. The statement in line 39 calculates the length of a rectangle using the x members of the ulc and lrc members in the element r[i]. The statement in line 40 calculates the width of a rectangle using the y members of the ulc and lrc members in the element r[i]. The statement in line 41 calculates the area of the rectangle and stores it in member r[i].area.

The nested loops in lines 44 through 51 sort the elements of array r using the member area. The loops implement the simple bubble sort method (which is useful for very small arrays). The if statement in line 47 compares the areas of elements r[i] and r[j]. If the area of rectangle r[i] is larger than that of rectangle r[j], the statements in lines 48 through 50 swap all the members of r[i] and r[j]. The swap uses the structure temp. This task illustrates that you can assign all the members of a structure to another structure in one statement.

The for loop in lines 54 and 55 displays the rectangles sorted in ascending order according to their areas. The output statement in line 55 uses the printf function to display the rectangle ID numbers and areas.

Unions

The size of a union is equal to the size of its largest member.

NEW☞ TERM *Unions* are special structures that store members that are mutually exclusive.

Syntax

Unions

The general syntax for unions is

```
union unionTag {
    type1 member1;
    type2 member2;
    ...
    typeN memberN;
};
```

Example:

```
union Long {
    unsigned mWord[2];
    long mLong;
};
```

Unions offer an easy alternative for quick data conversion. Unions were more significant in past decades when the price of memory was much higher and consolidating memory using unions was feasible. Accessing union members involves the dot access operators, just as in structures.

Reference Variables

In Day 2, you learned that you declare reference parameters by placing the & symbol after the parameter's type. Recall that a reference parameter becomes an alias to its arguments. Also, any changes made to the reference parameter affect its argument. In addition to reference parameters, C++ supports reference variables. You can manipulate the referenced variable by using its alias. As a novice C++ programmer, you probably won't use reference variables very often. On the other hand, you probably are using reference parameters more frequently. As you advance in using C++, you discover how reference variables can implement programming tricks that deal with advanced class design. This book discusses only the basics of reference variables.

NEW TERM Like reference parameters, *reference variables* become aliases to the variables they access.

Syntax

A Reference Variable

The general syntax for declaring a reference variable is

```
type& refVar;
type& refVar = aVar;
```

The *refVar* is the reference variable that can be initialized when declared. You must ensure that a reference variable is initialized or assigned a referenced variable before using the reference variable.

Examples:

```
int x = 10, y = 3;
int& rx = x;
int& ry;
ry = y; // take the reference
```

Here is a simple example that shows a reference variable at work. Listing 8.3 shows the source code for program REFVAR1.CP. The program displays and alters the values of a variable using either the variable itself or its reference. The program requires no input.

 Listing 8.3. Source code for the program REFVAR1.CP.

```
1: /*
2:    C++ program that demonstrates reference variables
3: */
4:
5: #include <iostream.h>
6:
7: main()
8: {
9:    int x = 10;
10:   int& rx = x;
11:   // display x using x and rx
12:   cout << "x contains " << x << "\n";
13:   cout << "x contains (using the reference rx) "
14:        << rx << "\n";
15:   // alter x and display its value using rx
16:   x *= 2;
17:   cout << "x contains (using the reference rx) "
18:        << rx << "\n";
19:   // alter rx and display value using x
20:   rx *= 2;
21:   cout << "x contains " << x << "\n";
22:   return 0;
23: }
```

 Here is a sample session with the program in Listing 8.3:

```
x contains 10
x contains (using the reference rx) 10
x contains (using the reference rx) 20
x contains 40
```

 The program in Listing 8.3 declares the int-typed variable x and the int-typed reference variable rx. The program initializes the variable x with the value 10 and the reference variable rx with the variable x.

The output statement in line 12 displays the value in variable x using the variable x. By contrast, the output statement in lines 13 and 14 displays the value in variable x using the reference variable rx.

The statement in line 16 doubles the integer in variable x. The output statement in lines 17 and 18 displays the new value in variable x using the reference variable rx. As the output shows, the reference variable accurately displays the updated value in variable x.

The statement in line 20 doubles the value in variable x by using the reference variable rx. The output statement in line 21 displays the updated value in variable x using variable x. Again, the output shows that the variable x and reference variable rx are synchronized.

Overview of Pointers

Each piece of information, both program and data, in the computer's memory resides at a specific address and occupies a specific number of bytes. When you run a program, your variables reside at specific addresses. With a high-level language such as C++ you don't need to be concerned about the actual address of every variable. That task is handled transparently by the compiler and the runtime system. Conceptually, each variable in your program is a tag for a memory address. Manipulating the data using the tag is much easier than dealing with an actual numerical address.

**NEW☞
TERM**   An *address* is a memory location. A *tag* is the variable's name.

C++ and its parent C are programming languages that are also used for low-level systems programming. In fact, many regard C as a high-level assembler. Low-level systems programming requires that you frequently work with the address of data. This is where pointers, in general, come into play. Knowing the address of a piece of data enables you to set and query its value.

**NEW☞
TERM**   A *pointer* is a special variable that stores the address of another variable or information.

 Warning: Pointers are very powerful language components. They also can be dangerous if used carelessly because they may hang your system! This malfunction occurs when the pointer happens to have a low memory address of some critical data or function.

Pointers to Existing Variables

In this section you learn how to use pointers to access the values in existing variables. C++ requires that you associate a data type (including `void`) with a declared pointer. The associated data type can be a predefined type or a user-defined structure.

Syntax

A Pointer

The general syntax for declaring a pointer is

```
type* pointerName;
type* pointerName = &variable;
```

The `&` operator is the address-of operator and is used to take the address of a variable.

Examples:

```
int *intPtr; // pointer to an int
double *realPtr; // pointer to a double
char *aString; // pointer to a character
long lv;
long* lp = &lv;
```

You also can declare nonpointers in the same lines that declare pointers:

```
int *intPtr, anInt;
double *realPtr, x;
char *aString, aKey;
```

> **Note:** C++ permits you to place the asterisk character right after the associated data type. You should not interpret this kind of syntax to mean that every other identifier appearing in the same declaration is automatically a pointer:
>
> ```
> int* intPtr; // pointer to an int
> double* realPtr; // pointer to a double
> char* aString; // pointer to a character
> int *intP, j; // intP is a pointer to int, j is an int
> double *realPtr, *doublePtr;  // both identifiers
>                              // are pointers to a double
> ```

DO   DON'T

DO initialize a pointer before you use it, just as you do with ordinary variables. In fact, the need to initialize pointers is more pressing—using uninitialized pointers invites trouble that leads to unpredictable program behavior or even a system hang!

DON'T assume that uninitialized pointers are harmless!

Once a pointer contains the address of a variable, you can access the value in that variable using the * operator followed by the pointer's name. For example, if px is a pointer to the variable x, you can use *px to access the value in variable x.

DO	DON'T

DO include the * operator to the left of a pointer to access the variable whose address is stored in the pointer.

DON'T forget to use the * operator. Without it, a statement ends up manipulating the address in the pointer instead of the data at that address.

Here is a simple example that shows a pointer at work. Listing 8.4 shows the source code for program PTR1.CP. The program displays and alters the values of a variable using either the variable itself or its pointer. The program requires no input.

Type **Listing 8.4. Source code for the program PTR1.CP.**

```
 1: /*
 2:    C++ program that demonstrates pointers to existing variables
 3: */
 4:
 5: #include <iostream.h>
 6:
 7: main()
 8: {
 9:    int x = 10;
10:    int* px = &x;
11:    // display x using x and rx
12:    cout << "x contains " << x << "\n";
13:    cout << "x contains (using the pointer px) "
14:         << *px << "\n";
15:    // alter x and display its value using *px
16:    x *= 2;
17:    cout << "x contains (using the pointer px) "
18:         << *px << "\n";
19:    // alter *px and display value using x
20:    *px *= 2;
21:    cout << "x contains " << x << "\n";
22:    return 0;
23: }
```

Here is a sample session with the program in Listing 8.4:

```
x contains 10
x contains (using the pointer px) 10
x contains (using the pointer px) 20
x contains 40
```

The program in Listing 8.4 declares the int-typed variable x and the int-typed pointer px. The program initializes the variable x with 10 and the pointer px with the address of variable x.

The output statement in line 12 displays the value in variable x using the variable x. By contrast, the output statement in lines 13 and 14 displays the value in variable x using the pointer px. Notice that the statement uses *px to access the value in variable x.

The statement in line 16 doubles the integer in variable x. The output statement in lines 17 and 18 displays the new value in variable x using the pointer px. As the output shows, the pointer accurately displays the updated value in variable x.

The statement in line 20 doubles the value in variable x by using the pointer px. Notice that the assignment statement uses *px on the left side of the = operator to access the variable x. The output statement in line 21 displays the updated value in variable x using variable x. Again, the output shows that the variable x and the pointer px are synchronized.

Pointers to Arrays

C++ and its parent language C support a special use for the names of arrays. The compiler interprets the name of an array as the address of its first element. Thus, if x is an array, the expressions &x[0] and x are equivalent. In the case of a matrix—call it mat—the expressions &mat[0][0] and mat also are equivalent. This aspect of C++ and C make them work as high-level assembly languages. Once you have the address of a data item, you've got its number, so to speak. The knowledge of the memory address of a variable or array enables you to manipulate its contents using pointers.

 A *program variable* is a label that tags a memory address. Using a variable in a program means accessing the associated memory location by specifying its name (or tag, if you prefer). In this sense, a variable becomes a name that points to a memory location—a pointer.

C++ enables you to use a pointer to access the various elements of an array. When you access the element x[i] of an array x, the compiled code performs two tasks. First, it obtains the base address of the array x (that is, where the first array element is located). Second, it uses the index i to calculate the offset from the base address of the array. This offset equals i multiplied by the size of the basic array type:

```
<address of element x>[i] = <address of x> + i * sizeof(basicType)
```

215

Looking at the above equation, assume that I have a pointer ptr that takes the base address of array x:

```
ptr = x; // pointer ptr points to address of x[0]
```

I can now substitute x with ptr in the equation and come up with the following:

```
<address of element x>[i] = ptr + i * sizeof(basicType)
```

In order for C++ and C to become high-level assemblers, they simplify the use of this equation by absolving it from having to explicitly state the size of the basic array type. Thus, you can write the following:

```
<address of element x>[i] = p + i
```

This equation states that the address of element x[i] is the expression (p + i).

Let me illustrate the use of pointers to access one-dimensional arrays by presenting the next program, PTR2.CP (Listing 8.5). This program is a modified version of the program ARRAY1.CP that calculates the average value for data in an array. The program begins by prompting you to enter the number of data and the data itself. Then the program calculates the average of the data in the array. Next, the program displays the average value.

Type **Listing 8.5. Source code for the program PTR2.CP.**

```
 1: /*
 2:     C++ program that demonstrates the use of pointer with
 3:     one-dimension arrays.  Program calculates the average
 4:     value of the data found in the array.
 5: */
 6:
 7: #include <iostream.h>
 8:
 9: const int MAX = 30;
10:
11: main()
12: {
13:
14:     double x[MAX];
15:     // declare pointer and initialize with base
16:     // address of array x
17:     double *realPtr = x; // same as = &x[0]
18:     double sum, sumx = 0.0, mean;
19:     int n;
20:     // obtain the number of data points
21:     do {
```

```
22:            cout << "Enter number of data points [2 to "
23:                 << MAX << "] : ";
24:            cin >> n;
25:            cout << "\n";
26:        } while (n < 2 || n > MAX);
27:
28:        // prompt for the data
29:        for (int i = 0; i < n; i++) {
30:            cout << "X[" << i << "] : ";
31:            // use the form *(x+i) to store data in x[i]
32:            cin >> *(x + i);
33:        }
34:
35:        sum = n;
36:        for (i = 0; i < n; i++)
37:        // use the form *(realPtr + i) to access x[i]
38:            sumx += *(realPtr + i);
39:        mean = sumx / sum;
40:        cout << "\nMean = " << mean << "\n\n";
41:        return 0;
42: }
```

Here is a sample session with the program in Listing 8.5:

```
Enter number of data points [2 to 30] : 5

X[0] : 1
X[1] : 2
X[2] : 3
X[3] : 4
X[4] : 5

Mean = 3
```

The program in Listing 8.5 declares the double-typed array x to have MAX elements. In addition, the program declares the pointer realPtr and initializes it using the array x. Thus, the pointer realPtr stores the address of x[0], the first element in array x.

The program uses the pointer for *(x + i) in the input statement at line 32. Thus, the identifier x works as a pointer to the array x. Using the expression *(x + i) accesses the element number i of array x, just as using the expression x[i] does.

The program uses the pointer realPtr in the for loop at lines 37 and 38. The expression *(realPtr + i) is the equivalent of *(x + i), which in turn is equivalent to x[i]. Thus, the for loop uses the pointer realPtr with an offset value, i, to access the elements of array x.

The Pointer Increment/Decrement Method

The previous C++ program (Listing 8.5) maintains the same address in the pointer realPtr. Employing pointer arithmetic with the for loop index i, I can write a new program version that increments the offset to access the elements of array x. C++ provides you with another choice that enables you to access sequentially the elements of an array without the help of an explicit offset value. The method merely involves using the increment or decrement operator with a pointer. You still need to initialize the pointer to the base address of an array and then use the ++ operator to access the next array element.

Here is a modified version of the previous program that uses the pointer increment method. Listing 8.6 shows the source code for the PTR3.CP program.

 Listing 8.6. Source code for the program PTR3.CP.

```
 1: /*
 2:    C++ program that demonstrates the use of pointers with
 3:    one-dimension arrays.  The average value of the array
 4:    is calculated.  This program modifies the previous version
 5:    in the following way:  the realPtr is used to access the
 6:    array without any help from any loop control variable.
 7:    This is accomplished by 'incrementing' the pointer, and
 8:    consequently incrementing its address.  This program
 9:    illustrates pointer arithmetic that alters the pointer's
10:    address.
11:
12: */
13:
14: #include <iostream.h>
15:
16: const int MAX = 30;
17:
18: main()
19: {
20:
21:     double x[MAX];
22:     double *realPtr = x;
23:     double sum, sumx = 0.0, mean;
24:     int i, n;
25:
26:     do {
27:         cout << "Enter number of data points [2 to "
28:              << MAX << "] : ";
29:         cin >> n;
30:         cout << "\n";
31:     } while (n < 2 || n > MAX);
32:
33:     // loop variable i is not directly involved in accessing
34:     //   the elements of array x
```

```
35:     for (i = 0; i < n; i++) {
36:         cout << "X[" << i << "] : ";
37:         // increment pointer realPtr after taking its reference
38:         cin >> *realPtr++;
39:     }
40:
41:     // restore original address by using pointer arithmetic
42:     realPtr -= n;
43:     sum = n;
44:     // loop variable i serves as a simple counter
45:     for (i = 0; i < n; i++)
46:         // increment pointer realPtr after taking a reference
47:         sumx += *(realPtr++);
48:     mean = sumx / sum;
49:     cout << "\nMean = " << mean << "\n\n";
50:     return 0;
51:
52: }
```

Here is a sample session with the program in Listing 8.6:

```
Enter number of data points [2 to 30] : 5

X[0] : 10
X[1] : 20
X[2] : 30
X[3] : 40
X[4] : 50

Mean = 30
```

Analysis The program in Listing 8.6 initializes the realPtr pointer to the base address of array x, in line 22. The program uses the realPtr pointer in the keyboard input statement in line 38. This statement uses *realPtr++ to store your input in the currently accessed element of array x and then to increment the pointer to the next element of array x. When the input loop terminates, the pointer realPtr points past the tail of array x. To reset the pointer to the base address of array x, the program uses the assignment statement in line 42. This statement uses pointer arithmetic to decrease the current address in pointer realPtr by n times sizeof(real). The statement resets the address in the pointer realPtr to access the array element x[0]. The program uses the same incrementing method to calculate the sum of data in the second for loop in line 47.

Pointers to Structures

C++ supports declaring and using pointers to structures. Assigning the address of a structured variable to a pointer of the same type uses the same syntax as with simple variables. Once the pointer has the address of the structured variable, it needs to use the -> operator to access the members of the structure.

Syntax

Accessing Structure Members

The general syntax for accessing the members of a structure by a pointer is

```
structPtr->aMember
```

Example:

```
struct point {
  double x;
  double y;
};

point p;
point* ptr = &p;

ptr->x = 23.3;
ptr->y = ptr->x + 12.3;
```

Here is a sample program that uses pointers to structures. Listing 8.7 shows the source code for program PTR4.CP. This program is the version of program STRUCT1.CP that uses pointers. The program prompts you for four sets of coordinates that define four rectangles. Each rectangle is defined by the x and y coordinates of the upper-left and lower-right corners. The program calculates the areas of each rectangle, sorts the rectangles by area, and displays the rectangles in the order of their areas.

Listing 8.7. Source code for the program PTR4.CP.

```
1: /*
2:    C++ program that demonstrates pointers to structured types
3: */
4:
5: #include <iostream.h>
6: #include <stdio.h>
7: #include <math.h>
8:
9: const MAX_RECT = 4;
10:
11: struct point {
12:    double x;
13:    double y;
14: };
15:
16: struct rect {
17:    point ulc; // upper left corner
18:    point lrc; // lower right corner
19:    double area;
20:    int id;
21: };
22:
23: typedef rect rectArr[MAX_RECT];
```

```
24:
25: main()
26: {
27:   rectArr r;
28:   rect temp;
29:   rect* pr = r;
30:   rect* pr2;
31:   double length, width;
32:
33:   for (int i = 0; i < MAX_RECT; i++, pr++) {
34:     cout << "Enter (X,Y) coord. for ULC of rect. # "
35:          << i << " : ";
36:     cin >> pr->ulc.x >> pr->ulc.y;
37:     cout << "Enter (X,Y) coord. for LRC of rect. # "
38:          << i << " : ";
39:     cin >> pr->lrc.x >> pr->lrc.y;
40:     pr->id = i;
41:     length = fabs(pr->ulc.x - pr->lrc.x);
42:     width = fabs(pr->ulc.y - pr->lrc.y);
43:     pr->area = length * width;
44:   }
45:
46:   pr -= MAX_RECT; // reset pointer
47:   // sort the rectangles by areas
48:   for (i = 0; i < (MAX_RECT - 1); i++, pr++) {
49:     pr2 = pr + 1; // reset pointer pr2
50:     for (int j = i + 1; j < MAX_RECT; j++, pr2++)
51:       if (pr->area > pr2->area) {
52:         temp = *pr;
53:         *pr = *pr2;
54:         *pr2 = temp;
55:       }
56:   }
57:
58:   pr -= MAX_RECT - 1; // reset pointer
59:   // display rectangles sorted by area
60:   for (i = 0; i < MAX_RECT; i++, pr++)
61:     printf("Rect # %d has area %5.4lf\n", pr->id, pr->area);
62:   return 0;
63: }
```

Here is a sample session with the program in Listing 8.7:

```
Enter (X,Y) coord. for ULC of rect. # 0 : 1 1
Enter (X,Y) coord. for LRC of rect. # 0 : 2 2
Enter (X,Y) coord. for ULC of rect. # 1 : 1.5 1.5
Enter (X,Y) coord. for LRC of rect. # 1 : 3 4
Enter (X,Y) coord. for ULC of rect. # 2 : 1 2
Enter (X,Y) coord. for LRC of rect. # 2 : 5 8
Enter (X,Y) coord. for ULC of rect. # 3 : 4 6
Enter (X,Y) coord. for LRC of rect. # 3 : 8 4
Rect # 0 has area 1.0000
Rect # 1 has area 3.7500
Rect # 3 has area 8.0000
Rect # 2 has area 24.0000
```

The program in Listing 8.7 declares the pointers pr and pr2 in lines 29 and 30, respectively. These pointers access the structure of type rect. The program initializes the pointer pr with the base address of array r.

The first for loop, which begins at line 33, uses the pointer pr to access the elements of array r. The loop increment part contains the expression pr++, which uses pointer arithmetic to make the pointer pr access the next element in array r. The input statements in lines 36 and 39 use the pointer pr to access the members ulc and lrc. Notice that the statements use the pointer access operator -> to allow pointer pr to access the members ulc and lrc. The statements in lines 40 through 43 also use the pointer pr to access the members id, ulc, lrc, and area using the -> operator.

The statement in line 46 resets the address stored in pointer pr by MAX_RECT units (that is MAX_RECT * sizeof(double) bytes). The nested loops in lines 48 through 56 use the pointers pr and pr2. The outer for loop increments the address in pointer pr by one before the next iteration. The statement in line 49 assigns pr + 1 to the pointer pr2. This statement gives the pointer pr2 the initial access to the element i + 1 in array r. The inner for loop increments the pointer pr2 by 1 before the next iteration. Thus, the nested for loops use the pointers pr and pr2 to access the elements of array r. The if statement in line 51 uses the pointers pr and pr2 to access the area member in comparing the areas of various rectangles. The statements in lines 52 through 54 swap the elements of array r, which are accessed by pointers pr and pr2. Notice that the statements use *pr and *pr2 to access an entire element of array r.

The statement in line 58 resets the address in pointer pr by subtracting MAX_RECT - 1. The last for loop also uses the pointer pr to access and display the members id and area of the various elements in array r.

This program illustrates that you can completely manipulate an array using only pointers—they are powerful and versatile.

Pointers and Dynamic Memory

The programs presented so far create the space for their variables at compile time. When the programs start running, the variables have their memory spaces preassigned. There are many applications in which you need to create new variables during the program execution. You need to allocate the memory space dynamically for these new variables at runtime. The designers of C++ have chosen to introduce new operators, that are not found in C, to handle the dynamic allocation and deallocation of memory. These new

C++ operators are new and delete. Although the C-style dynamic memory functions malloc, calloc, and free are still available, you should use the operators new and delete. These operators are more aware of the type of dynamic data created than are functions malloc, calloc, and free.

The *new* and *delete* Operators

The general syntax for using the new and delete operators in creating dynamic scalar variables is

```
pointer = new type;
delete pointer;
```

The operator new returns the address of the dynamically allocated variable. The operator delete removes the dynamically allocated memory accessed by a pointer. If the dynamic allocation of operator new fails, it returns a NULL (equivalent to 0) pointer. Therefore, you need to test for a NULL pointer after using the new operator if you suspect trouble.

Example:

```
int *pint;
pint = new int;
*pint = 33;
cout << "Pointer pint stores " << *pint;
delete pint;
```

A Dynamic Array

To allocate and deallocate a dynamic array, use the following general syntax:

```
arrayPointer = new type[arraySize];
delete [] arrayPointer;
```

The operator new returns the address of the dynamically allocated array. If the allocation fails, the operator assigns NULL to the pointer. The operator delete removes the dynamically allocated array accessed by a pointer.

Example:

```
const int MAX = 10;
int* pint;
pint = new int[MAX];
for (int i = 0; i < MAX; i++)
    *pint[i] = i * i
for (i = 0; i < MAX; i++)
    cout << *(pint + i) << "\n";
delete [] pint;
```

DO	**DON'T**

DO maintain access to dynamic variables and arrays at all times. Such access does not need the original pointers used to create these dynamic variables and arrays. Here is an example:

```
int* p = new int;
int* q;
*p = 123;
q = p; // q now also points to 123
p = new int; // create another dynamic variable
*p = 345; // p points to 345 whereas q points to 123
cout << *p << " " << *q << " " << (*p + *q) << "\n";
delete p;
delete q;
```

DON'T forget to delete dynamic variables and arrays at the end of their scope.

Using pointers to create and access dynamic data can be illustrated with the next program, PTR5.CP (Listing 8.8). This program is a modified version of the program ARRAY1.CP that calculates the average value for data in an array. The program begins by prompting you to enter the actual number of data and validating your input. Then the program prompts you for the data and calculates the average of the data in the array. Next, the program displays the average value.

 Listing 8.8. Source code for the program PTR5.CP.

```
 1: /*
 2:    C++ program that demonstrates the pointers to manage
 3:    dynamic data
 4: */
 5:
 6: #include <iostream.h>
 7:
 8: const int MAX = 30;
 9:
10: main()
11: {
12:
13:     double* x;
14:     double sum, sumx = 0, mean;
15:     int *n;
16:
17:     n = new int;
18:     if (n == NULL)
```

```
19:        return 1;
20:
21:    do { // obtain number of data points
22:        cout << "Enter number of data points [2 to "
23:            << MAX << "] : ";
24:        cin >> *n;
25:        cout << "\n";
26:    } while (*n < 2 || *n > MAX);
27:    // create tailor-fit dynamic array
28:    x = new double[*n];
29:    if (!x) {
30:      delete n;
31:      return 1;
32:    }
33:    // prompt user for data
34:    for (int i = 0; i < *n; i++) {
35:        cout << "X[" << i << "] : ";
36:        cin >> x[i];
37:    }
38:
39:    // initialize summations
40:    sum = *n;
41:    // calculate sum of observations
42:    for (i = 0; i < *n; i++)
43:        sumx += *(x + i);
44:
45:    mean = sumx / sum; // calculate the mean value
46:    cout << "\nMean = " << mean << "\n\n";
47:    // deallocate dynamic memory
48:    delete n;
49:    delete [] x;
50:    return 0;
51: }
```

Here is a sample session with the program in Listing 8.8:

```
Enter number of data points [2 to 30] : 5

X[0] : 1
X[1] : 2
X[2] : 3
X[3] : 4
X[4] : 5

Mean = 3
```

The program in Listing 8.8 uses two pointers for dynamic allocations. Line 13 declares the first pointer, which is used to allocate and access the dynamic array. Line 15 declares the pointer to create a dynamic variable.

The statement in line 17 uses the operator new to allocate the space for a dynamic int variable. The statement returns the address of the dynamic data to the pointer n. The if statement in line 18 determines whether or not the dynamic allocation failed. If it failed, the function `main` exits and returns an exit code of 1 (to flag an error).

The `do-while` loop in lines 21 through 26 prompts you to enter the number of data points. The statement in line 24 stores your input in the dynamic variable accessed by pointer `n`. The statement uses the pointer reference `*n` for this access. The `while` clause also uses `*n` to access the value in the dynamic variable. In fact, all the statements in the program access the number of data using the pointer reference `*n`.

The statement in line 28 creates a dynamic array using the operator `new`. The statement creates a dynamic `double`-typed array with the number of elements that you specify. This feature shows the advantage of using dynamic allocation to create custom-fit arrays. The `if` statement in line 29 determines whether or not the allocation of the dynamic array was successful. If not, the statements in lines 30 and 31 deallocate the dynamic variable accessed by pointer `n` and exit the function with a return value of 1.

The `for` loop in lines 34 through 37 prompts you to enter values for the dynamic array. The statement in line 36 stores your input to the element `i` of the dynamic array. Notice that the statement uses the expression `x[i]` to access the targeted element. This form resembles that of static arrays. C++ treats the expression `x[i]` as equivalent to `*(x + i)`. In fact, the program uses the latter form in the second `for` loop in lines 42 and 43. The statement in line 43 accesses the elements in the dynamic array using the form `*(x + i)`.

The last statements in function `main` delete the dynamic variable and array. The statement in line 48 deallocates the space for the dynamic variable accessed by pointer `n`. The statement in line 49 deletes the dynamic array accessed by pointer `x`.

Summary

Today's lesson introduced you to user-defined data types and covered the following topics:

☐ You can use the `typedef` statements to create alias types of existing types and also to define array types. The general syntax for using `typedef` is

```
typedef knownType newType;
```

☐ Enumerated data types enable you to declare unique identifiers that represent a collection of logically related constants. The general syntax for declaring an enumerated type is

```
enum enumType { <list of enumerated identifiers> };
```

☐ Structures enable you to define a new type that logically groups several fields or members. These members can be predefined types or other structures. The general syntax for declaring a structure is

```
struct structTag {
    < list of members >
};
```

☐ Unions are a form of variant structures. The general syntax for unions is

```
union unionTag {
    type1 member1;
    type2 member2;
    ...
    typeN memberN;
};
```

☐ Reference variables are aliases of the variables that they reference. To declare a reference variable, place the & after the data type of the reference variable or to the left of the variable's name.

☐ Pointers are variables that store the addresses of other variables or data. C++ uses pointers to offer flexible and efficient manipulation of data and system resources.

☐ Pointers to existing variables use the & operator to obtain the addresses of these variables. Armed with these addresses, pointers offer access to the data in their associated variables. To access the value using a pointer, use the * operator followed by the name of the pointer.

☐ Pointers access the elements of arrays by being assigned the base address of a class. C++ considers the name of an array as equivalent to the pointer of the base address. For example, the name of the array X is treated as &X[0]. Pointers can be used to sequentially traverse the elements of an array to store and/or recall values from these elements.

☐ Pointers to structures manipulate structures and access their members. C++ provides the -> operator to allow a pointer access to the members of a structure.

☐ Pointers can create and access dynamic data using the operators new and delete. These operators enable you to create dynamic variables and arrays. The new operator assigns the address of the dynamic data to the pointer used in creating and accessing the data. The operator delete assists in recuperating the space of dynamic data when that information is no longer needed.

Q&A

Q Does C++ support pointers to the predefined type void?

A Yes, void* pointers are considered typeless pointers and can be used to copy data.

Q Because C++ pointers have types (even void* pointers), can I use typecasting to translate the data accessed by the general-purpose void* pointers to non-void* pointers?

A Yes, C++ allows you to typecast pointer references. For example:

```
void* p = data;
long *lp = (long*) p;
```

The pointer lp uses the typecast to translate the data it accesses.

Q What happens if I delete a dynamic array using the delete operator without following it with the empty brackets?

A The runtime system deletes only the first element of the dynamic array. The other elements remain in memory as inaccessible data.

Q Can a structure contain a pointer to itself?

A Yes. Many structures that model dynamic data structures use this kind of declaration. For example, the following structure models the nodes of a dynamic list with pointer-based links:

```
struct listNode {
  dataType data;
  listNode *next;
};
```

Q Does C++ allow the declaration of a pointer-to-structure type before declaring the structure?

A Yes, this feature makes declaring nodes of dynamic data structure possible.

Q Does C++ allow pointers that access the addresses of other pointers?

A Yes, C++ supports pointers to pointers (also called *double pointers*). To declare such pointers, use two * characters, as shown in the following example, which declares the double pointer p:

```
int x;
int *px = &x;
int **p = &px;
```

The expression *p accesses the pointer px and the expression **p accesses the variable x.

Workshop

The Workshop provides quiz questions to help you solidify your understanding of the material covered and exercises to provide you with experience in using what you've learned. Try to understand the quiz and exercise answers before continuing on to the next day's lesson. Answers are provided in Appendix B, "Answers."

Quiz

1. What is the error in the following statements?

```
enum Boolean { false, true };
enum State { on, off };
enum YesNo { yes, no };
enum DiskDriveStatus { on , off };
```

2. Is the declaration of the following enumerated type incorrect?

```
enum YesNo ( no = 0, No = 0, yes = 1, Yes = 1 };
```

3. What is the problem with the following program?

```
#include <iostream.h>
main()
{
  int *p = new int;
  cout << "Enter a number : ";
  cin >> *p;
  cout << "The square of " << *p << " = " << (*p * *p);
  return 0;
}
```

Exercises

1. Modify program PTR4.CP to create program PTR6.CP that uses the Comb sort method to sort the array of rectangles.

2. Define a structure that can be used to model a dynamic array of integers. The structure should have a member to access the dynamic data and a member to store the size of the dynamic array. Call the structure `intArrStruct`.

3. Define a structure that can be used to model a dynamic matrix. The structure should have one member to access the dynamic data and two members to store the number of rows and columns. Call the structure `matStruct`.

9

Strings

The examples presented from Day 1 through Day 8 are predominantly numeric, with a few aimed at character manipulation. You may have grown suspicious about the absence of strings in all of these examples. Today's lesson discusses C++ strings. You learn about the following topics:

- ☐ Strings in C++
- ☐ String input
- ☐ Using the standard string library
- ☐ Assigning strings
- ☐ Getting the length of strings
- ☐ Concatenating strings
- ☐ Comparing strings
- ☐ Converting strings
- ☐ Reversing the characters in a string
- ☐ Locating characters
- ☐ Locating substrings

C++ Strings

C++ (and its parent language C) has no predefined string type. Instead, C++, like C, regards strings as arrays of characters that end with the ASCII 0 null character (`'\0'`).

 The `'\0'` character is also called the *null terminator*. Strings that end with the null terminator are sometimes called *ASCIIZ strings*, with the letter *Z* standing for zero, the ASCII code of the null terminator.

The null terminator *must* be present in all strings and taken into account when dimensioning a string. When you declare a string variable as an array of characters, be sure to reserve an extra space for the null terminator. The advantage of using the null terminator is that you can create strings that are not restricted by any limit imposed by the C++ implementation. In addition, ASCIIZ strings have very simple structures.

Note: The lesson in Day 8 discusses how pointers can access and manipulate the elements of an array. C and C++ make extensive use of this programming feature in manipulating the characters of a string.

DO	DON'T

DO include an extra space for the null terminator when specifying the size of a string.

DON'T declare a string variable as a single-character array. Such a variable is useless!

String Input

The programs that I have presented so far display string literals in output stream statements. Thus, C++ supports stream output for strings as a special case for a non-predefined data type. (You can say the support came by popular demand!) String output using string variables uses the same operator and syntax. With string input, the inserter operator >> does not work well because strings often contain spaces, and spaces are ignored by the inserter operator. Instead of the inserter operator, you need to use the getline function. This function reads up to a specified number of characters.

The *getline* function

The general syntax for the overloaded getline function is

```
istream& getline(signed char* buffer,
                 int size,
                 char delimiter = '\n');

istream& getline(unsigned char* buffer,
                 int size,
                 char delimiter = '\n');
istream& getline(char* buffer,
                 int size,
                 char delimiter = '\n');
```

The parameter *buffer* is a pointer to the string receiving the characters from the stream. The parameter *size* specifies the maximum number of characters to read. The parameter `delimiter` specifies the delimiting character that causes the string input to stop before reaching the number of characters specified by parameter *size*. The parameter delimiter has the default argument of `'\n'`.

Example:

```
#include <iostream.h>
main()
{
  char name[80];
  cout << "Enter your name: ";
  cin.getline(name, sizeof(name)-1);
  cout << "Hello " << name << ", how are you";
  return 0;
}
```

Using the STRING.H Library

The community of C programmers has developed the standard string library STRING.H, which contains the most frequently used string-manipulation functions. The STDIO.H and IOSTREAM.H header file prototype functions also support string I/O. The different C++ compiler vendors also have developed C++-style string libraries. These libraries use classes to model strings (more about classes in Day 11). However, these string libraries *are not standard*, whereas the C-style string routines in STRING.H are part of the ANSI C standard. In the next subsections I present several, but not all, of the functions that are prototyped in the STRING.H header file.

Some of the string functions in STRING.H have more than one version. The extra versions, which append the characters _f, f, or _, work with strings that are accessed using far pointers.

Assigning Strings

C++ supports two methods for assigning strings. You can assign a string literal to a string variable when you initialize it. This method is simple and requires using the = operator and the assigning string.

Initializing a String

The general syntax for initializing a string is

```
char stringVar[stringSize] = stringLiteral;
```

Example:

```
char aString[81] = "Symantec C++ in 21 days";
char name[] = "Namir Shammas";
```

The second method for assigning one ASCIIZ string to another uses the function `strcpy`. This function assumes that the copied string ends with the null character.

The *strcpy* Function

The prototype for the function `strcpy` is

```
char* strcpy(char* target, const char* source)
```

This function copies the characters from string *source* to string *target*. The function *assumes* that the target string accesses enough space to contain the source string.

Example:

```
char name[41];
strcpy(name,"Symantec C++");
```

The variable `name` contains the string `"Symantec C++"`.

The string library also offers the function `strncpy` to support copying a specified number of characters from one string to another.

The *strncpy* Function

The prototype for the function `strncpy` is

```
char* strncpy(char* target, const char* source, size_t num);
```

This function copies *num* characters from the string *source* to the string *target*. The function performs character truncation or padding, if necessary.

Example:

```
char str1[] = "Pascal";
char str2[] = "Hello there";

strncpy(str1, str2, 6);
```

The variable `str1` now contains the string `"Hello "`.

Note: Using pointers to manipulate strings is new to many novice C++ programmers. In fact, you can use pointers to manipulate the trailing parts of a string by assigning the address of the first character to manipulate. For example, if I declare the string str1 as follows:

```
char str1[41] = "Hello World";
char str2[41];
char* p = str1;

p += 6; // p now points to substring "World" in str
strcpy(str2, p);
cout << str2 << "\n";
```

the output statement displays the string "World". This example shows how using pointers can incorporate an offset number of characters.

The Length of a String

Many string operations require the number of characters in a string. The STRING.H library offers the function strlen to return the number of characters, excluding the null terminator, in a string.

Syntax

The *strlen* Function

The prototype for the function strlen is

```
size_t strlen(const char* string)
```

This function strlen returns the number of characters in parameter *string*. The resulting type size_t represents a general integer type.

Example:

```
char str[] = "1234567890";
unsigned i;
i = strlen(str);
```

These statements assign the value 10 to the variable i.

Concatenating Strings

Often, you build a string by concatenating two or more strings. The function `strcat` enables you to concatenate one string to another.

NEW☞ TERM When you *concatenate* strings, you join or link them together.

The *strcat* Function

The prototype for the function `strcat` is

```
char* strcat(char* target, const char* source)
```

This function appends the contents of the string *source* to the string *target* and returns the pointer to the target string. The function *assumes* that the target string can accommodate the characters of the source string.

Example:

```
char string[81];
strcpy(string, "Symantec");
strcat(string," C++")
```

The variable `string` now contains `"Symantec C++"`.

The function `strncat` concatenates a specified number of characters from the source string to the target string.

The *strncat* Function

The prototype for the function `strncat` is

```
char* strncat(char* target, const char* source, size_t num)
```

This function appends *num* characters of the string *source* to the string *target* and returns the pointer to the target string.

Example:

```
char str1[81] = "Hello I am ";
char str2[41] = "Thomas Jones";

strncat(str1, str2, 6);
```

The variable `str1` now contains `"Hello I am Thomas"`.

DO	DON'T

DO use the function strncat to control the number of concatenated characters when you are unsure of the capacity of the target string.

DON'T assume that the target string is always adequate to store the characters of the source string.

Let's look at a program that uses the getline, strlen, and strcat functions. Listing 9.1 contains the source code for the program STRING1.CP. The program performs the following tasks:

- Prompts you to enter a string (your input should not exceed 40 characters)
- Prompts you to enter a second string (your input should not exceed 40 characters)
- Displays the number of characters in each of the strings you enter
- Concatenates the second string to the first one
- Displays the concatenated strings
- Displays the number of characters in the concatenated strings
- Prompts you to enter a search character
- Prompts you to enter a replacement character
- Displays the concatenated string after replacing all the occurrences of the search character with the replacement character

 Listing 9.1. Source code for the program STRING1.CP.

```
 1: /*
 2:    C++ program that demonstrates C-style strings
 3: */
 4:
 5: #include <iostream.h>
 6: #include <string.h>
 7:
 8: const unsigned MAX1 = 40;
 9: const unsigned MAX2 = 80;
10:
11: main()
12: {
13:
```

```
14:       char smallStr[MAX1+1];
15:       char bigStr[MAX2+1];
16:       char findChar, replChar;
17:
18:       cout << "Enter first string:\n";
19:       cin.getline(bigStr, MAX2);
20:       cout << "Enter second string:\n";
21:       cin.getline(smallStr, MAX1);
22:       cout << "String 1 has " << strlen(bigStr)
23:            << " characters\n";
24:       cout << "String 2 has " << strlen(smallStr)
25:            << " characters\n";
26:       // concatenate bigStr to smallStr
27:       strcat(bigStr, smallStr);
28:       cout << "Concatenated strings are:\n"
29:            << bigStr << "\n";
30:       cout << "New string has " << strlen(bigStr)
31:            << " characters\n";
32:       // get the search and replacement characters
33:       cout << "Enter search character : ";
34:       cin >> findChar;
35:       cout << "Enter replacement character : ";
36:       cin >> replChar;
37:       // replace characters in string bigStr
38:       for (unsigned i = 0; i < strlen(bigStr); i++)
39:         if (bigStr[i] == findChar)
40:           bigStr[i] = replChar;
41:       // display the updated string bigStr
42:       cout << "New string is:\n"
43:            << bigStr;
44:       return 0;
45: }
```

Here is a sample session with the program in Listing 9.1:

```
Enter first string:
The rain in Spain stays
Enter second string:
 mainly in the plain
String 1 has 23 characters
String 2 has 20 characters
Concatenated strings are:
The rain in Spain stays mainly in the plain
New string has 43 characters
Enter search character : a
Enter replacement character : A
New string is:
The rAin in SpAin stAys mAinly in the plAin
```

The program in Listing 9.1 includes the STRING.H header file for the string-manipulation functions. Lines 8 and 9 declare the global constants MAX1 and MAX2 used to size a small string and a big string, respectively. The function main declares two strings, smallStr and bigStr. Line 14 declares the variable smallStr to store MAX1+1

characters (the extra space is for the null character). Line 15 declares the variable `bigStr` to store `MAX2+1` characters. Line 16 declares the `char`-typed variables `findChar` and `replChar`.

The output statement in line 18 prompts you to enter the first string. The statement in line 19 uses the stream input function `getline` to obtain your input and store it in variable `bigStr`. The function call specifies that you can enter up to `MAX2` characters. The output statement in line 20 prompts you to enter the second string. The statement in line 21 uses the stream input function `getline` to obtain your input and store it in variable `smallStr`. The function call specifies that you can enter up to `MAX1` characters.

The output statements in lines 22 through 25 display the number of characters in variables `bigStr` and `smallStr`, respectively. Each output statement calls function `strlen` and passes it a string variable.

The statement in line 27 concatenates the string in variable `smallStr` to variable `bigStr`. The output statement in lines 28 and 29 displays the updated string `bigStr`. The output statement in lines 30 and 31 displays the number of characters in the updated string variable `bigStr`. This statement also uses the function `strlen` to obtain the number of characters.

The statement in line 33 prompts you to enter the search character. The statement in line 34 obtains your input and stores it in variable `findChar`. The statement in line 35 prompts you to enter the replacement character. The statement in line 36 obtains your input and stores it in variable `replChar`.

The `for` loop in lines 38 through 40 translates the characters in string `bigStr`. The loop uses the control variable `i` and iterates, in increments of 1, from 0 to `strlen(bigstr)-1`. The `if` statement in line 39 determines whether or not character number `i` in `bigStr` matches the character in variable `findChar`. If this condition is true, the program executes the statement in line 40, which assigns the character in variable `replChar` to character number `i` in variable `bigStr`. This loop shows how you can manipulate the contents of a string variable by accessing each character in that string.

The output statement in lines 42 and 43 displays the updated string `bigStr`.

String Comparison

Because strings are arrays of characters, the STRING.H library provides a set of functions to compare strings. These functions compare the characters of two strings using the ASCII value of each character. The functions are `strcmp` and `strncmp`.

The function strcmp performs a case-sensitive comparison of two strings, using every character possible.

The *strcmp* Function

The prototype for the function strcmp is

```
int strcmp(const char* str1, const char* str2);
```

This function compares strings *str1* and *str2*. The integer result indicates the outcome of the comparison:

    < 0   when *str1* is less than *str2*
    = 0   when *str1* is equal to *str2*
    > 0   when *str1* is greater than *str2*

Example:

```
char string1[] = "Symantec C++";
char string2[] = "SYMANTEC C++";
int i;

i = strcmp(string1, string2);
```

The last statement assigns a positive number to the variable i because the string in variable string1 is greater than the string in variable string2.

The function strncmp performs a case-sensitive comparison on specified leading characters in two strings.

The *strncmp* Function

The prototype for the function strncmp is

```
int strncmp(const char* str1, const char* str2, size_t num);
```

This function compares the *num* leading characters in two strings, *str1* and *str2*. The integer result indicates the outcome of the comparison:

    < 0   when *str1* is less than *str2*
    = 0   when *str1* is equal to *str2*
    > 0   when *str1* is greater than *str2*

Example:

```
char string1[] = "Symantec C++";
char string2[] = "Symantec Pascal";
int i;

i = strncmp(string1, string2, 7);
```

This assigns a negative number to the variable i because "Symantec C" is less than "Symantec P".

Let's look at an example that compares strings. Listing 9.2 creates an array of strings and initializes it with data. Then the program displays the unordered array of strings, sorts the array, and displays the sorted array.

Listing 9.2. Source code for the program STRING2.CP.

```
1: /*
2:    C++ program that demonstrates comparing strings
3: */
4:
5: #include <iostream.h>
6: #include <string.h>
7:
8: const unsigned STR_SIZE = 40;
9: const unsigned ARRAY_SIZE = 11;
10: // const int TRUE = 1;
11: // const int FALSE = 0;
12:
13: main()
14: {
15:
16:     char strArr[STR_SIZE][ARRAY_SIZE] =
17:        { "California", "Virginia", "Alaska", "New York",
18:          "Michigan", "Nevada", "Ohio", "Florida",
19:          "Washington", "Oregon", "Arizona" };
20:     char temp[STR_SIZE];
21:     unsigned n = ARRAY_SIZE;
22:     unsigned offset;
23:     int inOrder;
24:
25:     cout << "Unordered array of strings is:\n";
26:     for (unsigned i = 0; i < ARRAY_SIZE; i++)
27:       cout << strArr[i] << "\n";
28:
29:     cout << "\nEnter a non-space character and press Enter";
30:     cin >> temp[0];
31:     cout << "\n";
32:
33:     offset = n;
34:     do {
35:       offset = (8 * offset) / 11;
36:       offset = (offset == 0) ? 1 : offset;
37:       inOrder = TRUE;
```

```
38:      for (unsigned i = 0, j = offset;
39:           i < n - offset; i++, j++)
40:        if (strcmp(strArr[i], strArr[j]) > 0) {
41:          strcpy(temp, strArr[i]);
42:          strcpy(strArr[i], strArr[j]);
43:          strcpy(strArr[j], temp);
44:          inOrder = FALSE;
45:        }
46:    } while (!(offset == 1 && inOrder));
47:
48:    cout << "Sorted array of strings is:\n";
49:    for (i = 0; i < ARRAY_SIZE; i++)
50:      cout << strArr[i] << "\n";
51:    return 0;
52: }
```

9

Here is a sample session with the program in Listing 9.2:

```
Unordered array of strings is:
California
Virginia
Alaska
New York
Michigan
Nevada
Ohio
Florida
Washington
Oregon
Arizona
Enter a non-space character and press Enter
Sorted array of strings is:
Alaska
Arizona
California
Florida
Michigan
Nevada
New York
Ohio
Oregon
Virginia
Washington
```

The program in Listing 9.2 declares the global constants STR_SIZE and ARRAY_SIZE in lines 8 and 9. The constant STR_SIZE specifies the size of each string. The constant ARRAY_SIZE indicates the number of strings in the array used by the program. The commented constants TRUE and FALSE (in lines 10 and 11) represent the Boolean values employed when you run the program using other C++ compilers (after uncommenting the constants). The function main declares the array strArr (actually, the variable strArr is a matrix of characters) to have ARRAY_SIZE elements and STR_SIZE characters per

243

element. Notice that the declaration states the size of each string in the first dimension and the size of the array in the second dimension. The function also initializes the array strArr. The function also declares the variable temp as a swap buffer. Lines 21 through 23 declare miscellaneous variables.

The output statement in line 25 displays the title before showing the elements of the unordered array strArr. The for loop in lines 26 and 27 displays these elements. The loop uses the control variable i and iterates, in increments of 1, from 0 to ARRAY_SIZE-1. The output statement in line 27 displays the string at element i, using the expression strArr[i].

The output and input statements in lines 29 and 30 prompt you to enter a nonspace character. This input enables you to examine the unordered array before the program sorts the array and displays its ordered elements.

The statements in lines 33 through 46 implement the Comb sort method. Notice that the if statement in line 40 uses the function strcmp to compare elements i and j, which are accessed using the expressions strArr[i] and strArr[j], respectively. The statements in lines 41 through 43 swap the elements i and j using the function strcpy and the swap buffer temp.

The output statement in line 48 displays the title before showing the elements of the sorted array. The for loop in lines 49 and 50 displays these elements. The loop uses the control variable i and iterates, in increments of 1, from 0 to ARRAY_SIZE-1. The output statement in line 50 displays the string at element i using the expression strArr[i].

Converting Strings

String manipulation often involves converting the strings' characters into uppercase or lowercase, as well as reversing the order of these characters. Although the Symantec C++ STRING.H library does not support these functions (and other C++ compilers do), I feel compelled to present my own implementation of these functions. I present the functions strlwr and strupr to convert the characters of a string to lowercase and uppercase, respectively.

Syntax

The *strlwr* Function

The prototype for the function strlwr is

```
char* strlwr(char* source)
```

This function converts the uppercase characters in string *source* to lowercase. Other characters are not affected. The function also returns the pointer to the string *source*.

Example:

```
char str[] = "HELLO THERE";

strlwr(str);
```

The variable str now contains the string "hello there".

Syntax

The *strupr* Function

The prototype for the function strupr is

```
char* strupr(char* source)
```

This function converts the lowercase characters in string *source* to uppercase. Other characters are not affected. The function also returns the pointer to the string *source*.

Example:

```
char str[] = "Symantec C++";
strupr(str);
```

The variable str now contains the string "SYMANTEC C++".

DO   DON'T

DO make copies for the arguments of functions strlwr and strupr if you need the original arguments later in a program.

DON'T always assume that applying the function strlwr and then the function strupr (or vice versa) to the same variable will succeed in restoring the original characters in that variable.

Listing 9.3 presents the NCSSTR.H header file, which declares the functions strlwr, strupr, and strrev. Listing 9.4 shows the file NCSSTR.CP, which contains the implementation of these functions. (Function strrev is discussed in the next section, "Reversing Strings.")

 Listing 9.3. The source code for the NCSSTR.H header file.

```
 1:  /*
 2:    header file for supplimentary string functions
 3:  */
 4:
 5:  #ifndef _ncsstr_h_
 6:  #define _ncsstr_h_
 7:
 8:  char* strlwr(char* source);
 9:  char* strupr(char* source);
10:  char* strrev(char* str);
11:
12:  #endif
```

 Listing 9.4. The source code for the NCSSTR.CP implementation file.

```
 1:  #include <string.h>
 2:  #include <ctype.h>
 3:
 4:  char* strlwr(char* source)
 5:  {
 6:    int i;
 7:    for (i = 0; source[i] != '\0'; i++)
 8:      source[i] = tolower(source[i]);
 9:    return source;
10:  }
11:
12:
13:  char* strupr(char* source)
14:  {
15:    int i;
16:    for (i = 0; source[i] != '\0'; i++)
17:      source[i] = toupper(source[i]);
18:    return source;
19:  }
20:
21:
22:  char* strrev(char* str)
23:  {
24:    int n = strlen(str);
25:    int i, j;
26:    char c;
27:
28:    for (i = 0, j = n - 1; i <= (n / 2); i++, j--) {
```

```
29:      c = str[i];
30:      str[i] = str[j];
31:      str[j] = c;
32:    }
33:    return str;
34: }
```

Note: Remember to include the file NCSSTR.CP in the project file when using the `strlwr`, `strupr`, and `strrev` functions.

Reversing Strings

In this section I present the function `strrev`, which is defined in Listing 9.3 and implemented in Listing 9.4, to reverse the characters in a string.

The *strrev* Function

The prototype for the function `strrev` is

```
char* strrev(char* str)
```

This function reverses the order of the characters in string *str* and returns the pointer to the string *str*.

Example:

```
char string[] = "Hello";

strrev(string);
cout << string;
```

This example displays the string `"olleH"`.

Let's look at a program that manipulates the characters in a string. Listing 9.5 shows the source code for the program STRING3.CP. The program performs the following tasks:

☐ Prompts you to enter a string

☐ Displays your input

☐ Displays the lowercase version of your input

☐ Displays the uppercase version of your input

☐ Displays in reverse order the characters you typed

☐ Displays a message that your input has no uppercase letters, if this is true

☐ Displays a message that your input has no lowercase letters, if this is true

☐ Displays a message that your input has symmetrical characters, if this is true

Type   **Listing 9.5. Source code for the program STRING3.CP.**

```
1:  /*
2:     C++ program that demonstrates manipulating the
3:     characters in a string
4:  */
5:
6:  #include <iostream.h>
7:  #include <string.h>
8:  #include "ncsstr.h"
9:  const unsigned STR_SIZE = 40;
10: // const int TRUE = 1;
11: // const int FALSE = 0;
12:
13: main()
14: {
15:     char str1[STR_SIZE+1];
16:     char str2[STR_SIZE+1];
17:     int isLowerCase;
18:     int isUpperCase;
19:     int isSymmetrical;
20:
21:
22:     cout << "Enter a string : ";
23:     cin.getline(str1, STR_SIZE);
24:     cout << "Input: " << str1 << "\n";
25:     // copy str1 to str2
26:     strcpy(str2, str1);
27:     // convert to lowercase
28:     strlwr(str2);
29:     isLowerCase = (strcmp(str1, str2) == 0) ? TRUE : FALSE;
30:     cout << "Lowercase: " << str2 << "\n";
31:     // convert to uppercase
32:     strupr(str2);
33:     isUpperCase = (strcmp(str1, str2) == 0) ? TRUE : FALSE;
34:     cout << "Uppercase: " << str2 << "\n";
35:     // copy str1 to str2
36:     strcpy(str2, str1);
37:     // reverse characters
38:     strrev(str2);
39:     isSymmetrical = (strcmp(str1, str2) == 0) ? TRUE : FALSE;
40:     cout << "Reversed: " << str2 << "\n";
41:     if (isLowerCase)
42:       cout << "Your input has no uppercase letters\n";
43:     if (isUpperCase)
44:       cout << "Your input has no lowercase letters\n";
```

```
45:    if (isSymmetrical)
46:      cout << "Your input has symmetrical characters\n";
47:    return 0;
48: }
```

Here is a sample session with the program in Listing 9.3:

```
Enter a string : level
Input: level
Lowercase: level
Uppercase: LEVEL
Reversed: level
Your input has no uppercase letters
Your input has symmetrical characters
```

The program in Listing 9.5 declares the string variables str1 and str2 in function main, which is defined in lines 13 through 48. Each string stores STR_SIZE + 1 characters (including the null terminator). The function also declares the flags isLowerCase, isUpperCase, and isSymmetrical.

The output statement in line 22 prompts you to enter a string. The statement in line 23 uses the string input function getline to store your input in variable str1. The output statement in line 24 echoes your input.

The statement in line 26 copies the characters in variable str1 to variable str2. The statement in line 28 calls the function str1wr to convert the characters in variable str2. The program manipulates the characters of variable str2 while maintaining the original input in variable str1. The statement in line 29 calls the function strcmp to compare the characters in str1 and str2. The two strings can be equal only if your input has no uppercase characters. The statement uses the conditional operator to assign the constant TRUE to the flag isLowerCase if the above condition is true. Otherwise, the statement assigns FALSE to the flag isLowerCase. The output statement in line 30 displays the characters in variable str2.

The statement in line 32 calls the function strupr and supplies it the argument str2. This function call converts any lowercase character in variable str2 into uppercase. The statement in line 33 calls the function strcmp to compare the characters in str1 and str2. The two strings can be equal only if your input has no lowercase characters. The statement uses the conditional operator to assign the constant TRUE to the flag isUpperCase if that is true. Otherwise, the statement assigns FALSE to the flag isUpperCase. The output statement in line 34 displays the characters in variable str2.

To display the original input in reverse order, the program calls the function strcpy to copy the characters of variable str1 to variable str2 once more. The statement in line 38 calls the function strrev and passes it the argument str2. The statement in line 39 calls

the function strcmp to compare the characters in str1 and str2. The two strings can be equal only if your input has symmetrical characters. The statement uses the conditional operator to assign the constant TRUE to the flag isSymmetrical if the above condition is true. Otherwise, the statement assigns FALSE to the flag isSymmetrical. The output statement in line 40 displays the characters in variable str2.

The program uses the if statements in lines 41, 43, and 45 to indicate that your input has special characteristics. The if statement in line 41 tells you that your input has no uppercase letters when the value in variable isLowerCase is TRUE. The if statement in line 43 tells you that your input has no lowercase letters when the value in variable isUpperCase is TRUE. The if statement in line 45 tells you that your input has symmetrical characters when the value in variable isSymmetrical is TRUE.

Locating Characters

The STRING.H library offers a number of functions for locating characters in strings, including strchr, strrchr, strspn, strcspn, and strpbrk. These functions enable you to search for characters and simple character patterns in strings.

The function strchr locates the first occurrence of a character in a string.

Syntax

The *strchr* Function

The prototype for the function strchr is

```
char* strchr(const char* target, int c)
```

This function locates the first occurrence of pattern c in string target. The function returns the pointer to the character in string target that matches the specified pattern c. If the character c does not occur in the string target, the function yields a NULL.

Example:

```
char str[81] = "Symantec C++";
char* strPtr;

strPtr = strchr(str, '+');
```

The pointer strPtr points to the substring "++" in string str.

The function strrchr locates the last occurrence of a character in a string.

Syntax

The *strrchr* Function

The prototype for the function strrchr is

```
char* strrchr(const char* target, int c)
```

This function locates the last occurrence of pattern c in string *target*. The function returns the pointer to the character in string *target* that matches the specified pattern c. If the character c does not occur in the string *target*, the function yields a NULL.

Example:

```
char str[81] = "Symantec C++ is here";
char* strPtr;

strPtr = strrchr(str, '+');
```

The pointer strPtr points to the substring "+ is here" in string str.

The function strspn yields the number of characters in the leading part of a string that match any character in a pattern of characters.

Syntax

The *strspn* Function

The prototype for the function strspn is

```
size_t strspn(const char* target, const char* pattern)
```

This function returns the number of characters in the leading part of string *target* that matches any character in the string *pattern*.

Example:

```
char str[] = "Symantec C++";
char substr[] = "obruT ";
int index;

index = strspn(str, substr);
```

This statement assigns the value 6 to variable index because the characters in substr found a match in every one of the first six characters of str.

The function strcspn scans a string and yields the number of the leading characters in a string that is totally void of the characters in a substring.

Syntax

The *strcspn* Function

The prototype for the function strcspn is

```
size_t strcspn(const char* str1, const char* str2)
```

This function scans *str1* and returns the length of the leftmost substring that is totally void of the characters of the substring *str2*.

Example:

```
char strng[] = "The rain in Spain";
int i;

i = strcspn(strng," in");
```

This example assigns the value 8 (the length of "The rain") to the variable i.

The function strpbrk searches a string for the first occurrence of any character in a pattern of characters.

Syntax

The *strpbrk* Function

The prototype for the function strpbrk is

```
char* strpbrk(const char* target, const char* pattern)
```

This function searches the *target* string for the first occurrence of *any character* in the characters of string *pattern*. If the characters in the pattern do not occur in the string *target*, the function yields a NULL.

Example:

```
char* str = "Hello there how are you";
char* substr = "hr";
char* ptr;

ptr = strpbrk(str, substr);
cout << ptr << "\n";
```

This displays "here how are you" because the 'h' is encountered in the string before the 'r'.

Locating Strings

The STRING.H library offers the function strstr to locate a substring in a string.

Syntax

The *strstr* Function

The prototype for the function strstr is

```
char* strstr(const char* str, const char* substr);
```

This function scans the string *str* for the first occurrence of a string *substr*. The function yields the pointer to the first character in string *str* that matches the parameter *substr*. If the string *substr* does not occur in the string *str*, the function yields a NULL.

Example:

```
char str[] = "Hello there! how are you";
char substr[] = "how";
char* ptr;

ptr = strstr(str, substr);
cout << ptr << "\n";
```

This displays "how are you" because the string search matched "how". The pointer ptr points to the rest of the original string starting with "how".

DO   DON'T

DO use the function strrev before calling function strstr if you want to search for the last occurrence of a string.

DON'T forget to reverse both the main and the search strings when using the strrev function to locate the last occurrence of the search string.

The string library also provides the function strtok, which enables you to break down a string into substrings based on a specified set of delimiting characters.

NEW☞
TERM Substrings are sometimes called *tokens*.

Syntax

The *strtok* Function

The prototype for the function strtok is

```
char* strtok(char* target, const char* delimiters);
```

This function searches the string *target* for tokens. A string supplies the set of delimiter characters. The following example shows how this function works in returning the tokens in a string. The function strtok modifies the string *target* by inserting '\0' characters after each token. Make sure that you store a copy of the original target string in another string variable.

Example:

```
#include <stdio.h>
#include <string.h>

main()
{
   char* str = "(Base_Cost+Profit) * Margin";
   char* tkn = "+* ()";
   char* ptr = str;

   printf("%s\n", str);
   // the first call looks normal
   ptr = strtok(str, tkn);
   printf("\n\nThis is broken into: %s",ptr);
   while (ptr) {
       printf(" ,%s",ptr);
       // must make first argument a NULL character
       ptr = strtok(NULL, tkn);
   }
   printf("\n\n");
}
```

This example displays the following when the program is run:

```
(Base_Cost+Profit) * Margin
```

This is divided into Base_Cost, Profit, and Margin.

DO	DON'T
DO remember to supply NULL as the first argument to function strtok to locate the next token.	
DON'T forget to store a copy of the target string in the function strtok.	

Let's look at an example that searches for characters and strings. Listing 9.6 shows the source code for the program STRING4.CP. The program performs the following tasks:

☐ Prompts you to enter the main string

☐ Prompts you to enter the search string

☐ Prompts you to enter the search character

☐ Displays a character ruler and the main string

☐ Displays the indices where the search string occurs in the main string

☐ Displays the indices where the search character occurs in the main string

Listing 9.6. Source code for the program STRING4.CP.

```
1: /*
2:    C++ program that demonstrates searching for the
3:    characters and strings
4: */
5:
6: #include <iostream.h>
7: #include <string.h>
8:
9: const unsigned STR_SIZE = 40;
10:
11: main()
12: {
13:     char mainStr[STR_SIZE+1];
14:     char subStr[STR_SIZE+1];
15:     char findChar;
16:     char *p;
17:     int index;
18:     int count;
19:
20:     cout << "Enter a string : ";
21:     cin.getline(mainStr, STR_SIZE);
22:     cout << "Enter a search string : ";
23:     cin.getline(subStr, STR_SIZE);
24:     cout << "Enter a search character : ";
25:     cin >> findChar;
26:
27:     cout << "          1         2         3         4\n";
28:     cout << "0123456789012345678901234567890123456789\n";
29:     cout << mainStr << "\n";
30:     cout << "Searching for string " << subStr << "\n";
31:     p = strstr(mainStr, subStr);
32:     count = 0;
33:     while (p) {
34:       count++;
35:       index = p - mainStr;
```

continues

Listing 9.6. continued

```
36:            cout << "Match at index " << index << "\n";
37:            p = strstr(++p, subStr);
38:        }
39:        if (count == 0)
40:            cout << "No match for substring in main string\n";
41:
42:        cout << "Searching for character " << findChar << "\n";
43:        p = strchr(mainStr, findChar);
44:        count = 0;
45:        while (p) {
46:            count++;
47:            index = p - mainStr;
48:            cout << "Match at index " << index << "\n";
49:            p = strchr(++p, findChar);
50:        }
51:        if (count == 0)
52:            cout << "No match for search character in main string\n";
53:        return 0;
54: }
```

Here is a sample session with the program in Listing 9.6:

```
Enter a string : here, there, and everywhere
Enter a search string : here
Enter a search character : e
          1         2         3         4
0123456789012345678901234567890123456789 0
here, there, and everywhere
Searching for string here
Match at index 0
Match at index 7
Match at index 23
Searching for character e
Match at index 1
Match at index 3
Match at index 8
Match at index 10
Match at index 17
Match at index 19
Match at index 24
Match at index 26
```

The program in Listing 9.6 declares the strings mainStr and subStr to represent the main and search strings, respectively. The program also declares the variable findChar to store the search character. In addition, the program declares the character pointer p and the int-typed variables index and count.

The output statement in line 20 prompts you to enter a string. The statement in line 21 calls the stream input function `getline` and stores your input in variable `mainStr`. The output statement in line 22 prompts you to enter the search string. The statement in line 23 calls the stream input function `getline` and saves your input in variable `subStr`. The output statement in line 24 prompts you to enter the search character. The statement in line 25 obtains your input and stores it in variable `findChar`.

The output statements in lines 27 through 29 display a ruler and your input aligned under the ruler. The output statement in line 30 informs you that the program is searching for the substring you entered. The search begins at the statement in line 31. This statement calls function `strstr` to locate the first occurrence of string `subStr` in the string `mainStr`. The statement in line 32 assigns 0 to the variable `count`, which keeps track of the number of times the string `mainStr` contains the string `subStr`.

The program uses the `while` loop in lines 33 through 38 to locate all the occurrences of `subStr` in `mainStr`. The condition of the `while` loop examines the address of pointer `p`. If that pointer is not `NULL`, the loop iterates. The first statement inside the loop increments the variable `count`. The statement in line 35 calculates the index of string `mainStr` where the last match occurs. The statement obtains the sought index by subtracting the address of pointer `p` from the address of the first character in variable `mainStr` (remember that the expression `&mainStr[0]` is equivalent to the simpler expression `mainStr`). The statement assigns the result to variable `index`. The output statement in line 36 displays the value in variable `index`.

The statement in line 37 searches for the next occurrence of the string `subStr` in `mainStr`. Notice that this statement calls `strstr` and supplies it the pointer `p` as the first argument. The statement also applies the pre-increment operator to pointer `p` to store the address of the next character. This action ensures that the call to function `strstr` finds the next occurrence, if any, and is not stuck at the last occurrence. The `if` statement outside the `while` loop examines the value in variable `count`. If it contains zero, the program executes the output statement in line 40 to inform you that no match was found for the search string.

The output statement in line 42 informs you that the program is now searching for the character you specified in the main string. The process of searching for the character in `findChar` is very similar to searching for the string `subStr`. The main difference is that searching for a character involves the function `strchr`.

Summary

Today's lesson presented C++ strings and discussed string-manipulation functions that are exported by the STRING.H header file. You learned about the following topics:

- Strings in C++ are arrays of characters that end with the null character (the ASCII 0 character).

- String input requires the use of the `getline` stream input function. This function requires you to specify the input variable, the maximum number of input characters, and the optional line delimiter.

- The STRING.H header file contains the standard (for the C language) string library. This library contains many versatile functions that support copying, concatenating, and searching for strings. The chapter also presented the NCSSTR.H header file, which contains functions for converting and reversing characters.

- C++ supports two methods for assigning strings. The first method assigns a string to another string when you declare the latter string. The second method uses the function `strcpy` to assign one string to another at any stage in the program.

- The function `strlen` returns the length of a string.

- The `strcat` and `strncat` functions enable you to concatenate two strings. The function `strncat` enables you to specify the number of characters to concatenate.

- The functions `strcmp` and `strncmp` enable you to perform various types of string comparisons. The function `strcmp` performs a case-insensitive comparison of two strings using every character possible. The function `strncmp` is a variant of function `strcmp`, which uses a specified number of characters in comparing the strings.

- The functions `strlwr` and `strupr` convert the characters of a string into lowercase and uppercase, respectively.

- The function `strrev` reverses the order of characters in a string.

☐ The functions strchr, strrchr, strspn, strcspn, and strpbrk enable you to search for characters and simple character patterns in strings.

☐ The function strstr searches for a string in another string. The function strtok empowers you to break down a string into small strings that are delimited by a set of characters you specify.

Q&A

Q Can a statement initialize a pointer using a string literal?

A Yes, the compiler stores the characters of the string literal in memory and assigns its address to that pointer. Here is an example:

```
char* p = "I am a small string";
```

In addition, you can overwrite the characters of the string literal using their pointers. However, keep in mind that the pointer p accesses a string with a fixed number of characters.

Q Can a statement declare a constant pointer to a literal string?

A Yes, this kind of declaration resembles the one I mentioned previously. However, because the statement declares a constant pointer, you cannot overwrite the characters of the initializing string literal. Here is an example:

```
const char* p = "Version 1.0";
```

Use the const char pointer to store fixed messages and titles.

Q Can a statement declare an array of pointers to a set of string-literal strings?

A Yes, this is the easiest method to use an array of pointers to access a collection of messages, titles, or other kinds of fixed strings. Here is an example:

```
char* mainMenu[] = { "File", "Edit", "Search", "View",
                     "Debug", "Options", "Windows", "Help"};
```

Thus the element p[0] accesses the first string, p[1] the second string, and so on.

Q How can I use `strcmp` to compare strings, starting at a specific number of characters?

A Simply add the offset value to the arguments of the function `strcmp`. Here is an example:

```
char s1[41] = "Symantec C++";
char s2[41] = "SYMANTEC Pascal";
int offset = 9;
int i;
i = strcmp(str1 + offset, str2 + offset);
```

Q How can I use `strncmp` to compare a specific number of characters in two strings, starting at a specific character?

A Simply add the offset value to the arguments of the function `strcmp`. Here is an example:

```
char s1[41] = "Symantec C++";
char s2[41] = "SYMANTEC Pascal";
int offset = 9;
int num = 3;
int i;
i = strncmp(str1 + offset, str2 + offset, num);
```

Workshop

The Workshop provides quiz questions to help you solidify your understanding of the material covered and exercises to provide you with experience in using what you've learned. Try to understand the quiz and exercise answers before continuing on to the next day's lesson. Answers are provided in Appendix B, "Answers."

Quiz

1. Where is the error in the following program?

```
#include <iostream.h>
#include <string.h>
const int MAX = 10;
main()
{
  char s1[MAX+1];
  char s2[] = "12345678901234567890123456789";
  strcpy(s1, s2);
  cout << "String 1 is " << s1
       << "\nString 2 is " << s2;
  return 0;
}
```

2. How can you fix the program in the question 1 using the function strncpy instead of strcpy?

3. What is the value assigned to variable i in the following statements?

```
char s1[] = "Symantec C++";
char s2[] = "Symantec Pascal";
int i;
i = strcmp(s1, s2);
```

4. What is the value assigned to variable i in the following statements?

```
char s1[] = "Symantec C++";
char s2[] = "Symantec Pascal";
int offset = strlen("Symantec ");
int i;
i = strcmp(s1 + offset, s2 + offset);
```

5. True or false? The following function correctly returns 1 if a string does not contain lowercase characters, and yields 0 if otherwise:

```
int hasNoLowerCase(const char* s)
{
  char s2[strlen(s)+1];
  strcpy(s2, s);
  strupr(s2);
  return (strcmp(s, s2) == 0) ? 1 : 0);
}
```

261

Exercises

1. Write your own version of function strlen. Use a while loop and a character-counting variable to obtain the function result.

2. Write another version of function strlen. This time use a while loop and a local pointer to obtain the function result.

3. Write the program STRING5.CP, which uses the function strtok to break down the string "2*(X+Y)/(X+Z) - (X+10)/(Y-5)" into three sets of tokens, using the token delimiter strings "+-*/ ()", "( )", and "+-*/ ".

10

Advanced Parameters of Functions

Functions are the basic building blocks that conceptually extend the C++ language to fit your custom applications. C, the parent language of C++, is more function-oriented than C++. This difference is due to the support for classes, inheritance, and other object-oriented programming features (more about the latter in tomorrow's lesson). Nevertheless, functions still play an important role in C++. In today's lesson, you learn about the following advanced aspects of C++ functions:

- ☐ Passing arrays as function arguments
- ☐ Passing strings as function arguments
- ☐ Passing structures by value
- ☐ Passing structures by reference
- ☐ Passing structures by pointer
- ☐ Recursive functions
- ☐ Passing pointers to dynamic structures
- ☐ Pointers to functions

Passing Arrays as Arguments

When you write a C++ function that passes an array parameter, you can declare that parameter as a pointer to the basic type of the array.

A Pointer-to-Array Parameter

The general syntax for prototyping a function with a pointer-to-array parameter is

```
returnType function(basicType*, <other parameter types>);
```

The general syntax for defining this function is

```
returnType function(basicType *arrParam, <other parameters>)
```

Example:

```
// prototypes
void ShellSort(unsigned *doubleArray, unsigned arraySize);
void QuickSort(unsigned *intArray, unsigned arraySize);
```

In Day 7 I state that C++ enables you to declare open array parameters using a pair of empty brackets. This kind of declaration is equivalent to using a pointer parameter. C++ programmers use the open array form less frequently than the explicit pointer form, even though using the brackets shows the intent of the parameter more clearly.

DO	DON'T

DO use const parameters to prevent the host function from altering the arguments.

DON'T forget to include a parameter that specifies the number of array elements to manipulate, when the array-typed arguments are only partially filled with meaningful data.

Let's look at an example. Listing 10.1 shows the source code for the program ADVFUN1.CP. I created this program by performing minor edits to program ARRAY5.CP (Listing 7.5 of Day 7). The program performs the following tasks:

- Prompts you to enter the number of data points

- Prompts you to enter the integer values for the array

- Displays the elements of the unordered array

- Displays the elements of the sorted array

Listing 10.1. Source code for the program ADVFUN1.CP.

```
1: // C++ program that sorts arrays using the Comb sort method
2:
3: #include <iostream.h>
4:
5: const int MAX = 10;
6: const int TRUE = 1;
7: const int FALSE = 0;
8:
9: int obtainNumData()
10: {
11:   int m;
12:   do { // obtain number of data points
13:     cout << "Enter number of data points [2 to "
14:         << MAX << "] : ";
```

continues

Listing 10.1. continued

```
15:      cin >> m;
16:      cout << "\n";
17:   } while (m < 2 || m > MAX);
18:   return m;
19: }
20:
21: void inputArray(int *intArr, int n)
22: {
23:   // prompt user for data
24:   for (int i = 0; i < n; i++) {
25:     cout << "arr[" << i << "] : ";
26:     cin >> *(intArr + i);
27:   }
28: }
29:
30: void showArray(const int *intArr, int n)
31: {
32:   for (int i = 0; i < n; i++) {
33:     cout.width(5);
34:     cout << *(intArr + i) << " ";
35:   }
36:   cout << "\n";
37: }
38:
39: void sortArray(int *intArr, int n)
40: {
41:   int offset, temp, inOrder;
42:
43:   offset = n;
44:   do {
45:     offset = (8 * offset) / 11;
46:     offset = (offset == 0) ? 1 : offset;
47:     inOrder = TRUE;
48:     for (int i = 0, j = offset; i < (n - offset); i++, j++) {
49:       if (intArr[i] > intArr[j]) {
50:         inOrder = FALSE;
51:         temp = intArr[i];
52:         intArr[i] = intArr[j];
53:         intArr[j] = temp;
54:       }
55:     }
56:   } while (!(offset == 1 && inOrder == TRUE));
57: }
58:
59: main()
60: {
61:   int arr[MAX];
62:   int n;
63:
64:   n = obtainNumData();
65:   inputArray(arr, n);
```

```
66:    cout << "Unordered array is:\n";
67:    showArray(arr, n);
68:    sortArray(arr, n);
69:    cout << "\nSorted array is:\n";
70:    showArray(arr, n);
71:    return 0;
72: }
```

 Here is a sample session with the program in Listing 10.1:

```
Enter number of data points [2 to 10] : 5

arr[0] : 55
arr[1] : 22
arr[2] : 78
arr[3] : 35
arr[4] : 45
Unordered array is:
    55    22    78    35    45

Sorted array is:
    22    35    45    55    78
```

 The program in Listing 10.1 is almost identical to that in Listing 7.5 of Day 7. The
new program uses slightly different parameters in functions inputArray, showArray,
and sortArray. The first parameter in these functions is a pointer to the int type.
The function showArray prefixes the pointer type with const. Such a declaration tells the
compiler that the function showArray cannot alter the elements of the arguments for
parameter intArray.

Passing Strings as Arguments

Because C++ treats strings as arrays of characters, the rules for passing arrays as arguments
to functions also apply to strings. The next program contains functions that manipulate
strings. Listing 10.2 shows the source code for the program ADVFUN2.CP. The
program prompts you to enter a string. It then displays the number of characters you
typed (the size of the input string) and the uppercase version of your input.

 Listing 10.2. Source code for the program ADVFUN2.CP.

```
1: /*
2:    C++ program that declares functions with string parameters
3: */
4:
5: #include <iostream.h>
```

continues

Listing 10.2. continued

```
 6:
 7: const unsigned MAX = 40;
 8:
 9: char* upperCase(char* str)
10: {
11:    int ascii_shift = 'A' - 'a';
12:    char* p = str;
13:
14:    // loop to convert each character to uppercase
15:    while ( *p != '\0') {
16:        if ((*p  >= 'a' && *p <= 'z'))
17:            *p += ascii_shift;
18:        p++;
19:    }
20:    return str;
21: }
22:
23: int strlen(char* str)
24: {
25:   char *p = str;
26:   while (*p++ != '\0');
27:   return —p - str;
28: }
29:
30: main()
31: {
32:    char aString[MAX+1];
33:
34:    cout << "Enter a string: ";
35:    cin.getline(aString, MAX);
36:    cout << "Your string has " << strlen(aString)
37:        << " characters\n";
38:    // concatenate bigStr to aString
39:    upperCase(aString);
40:    cout << "The uppercase version of your input is: "
41:        << aString;
42:    return 0;
43: }
```

Here is a sample session with the program in Listing 10.2:

```
Enter a string: Symantec C++
Your string has 12 characters
The uppercase version of your input is: SYMANTEC C++
```

Analysis The program in Listing 10.2 declares its own string-manipulating functions: upperCase and strlen. The function upperCase, defined in lines 9 through 21, has a single parameter, str, which is a pointer to the char type. This parameter passes the address of an array of characters. The function converts the characters accessed by the pointer string to uppercase, and returns the pointer to the string. The function declares the local variable ascii_shift and the local char-pointer p. The function also initializes the variable ascii_shift with the difference between the ASCII values of the letters A and a. Thus, the ascii_shift variable contains the difference in ASCII codes needed to convert a lowercase character into an uppercase character. The function also initializes the local pointer p with the address in parameter str.

The upperCase function uses the while loop in line 15 to traverse the characters of the string argument. The while clause determines whether the pointer p does not access the null terminator. The if statement in line 16 determines whether the character accessed by pointer p is a lowercase letter. If this condition is true, the function executes the statement in line 17. This statement adds the value in variable ascii_shift to the character currently accessed by pointer p. This action converts a lowercase character into uppercase. The statement in line 18 increments the address of pointer p to access the next character. The function returns the address of pointer str.

The function strlen, defined in lines 23 through 28, returns the number of characters in the string accessed by the char-pointer parameter str. The function declares the local char-pointer p and initializes it with the address of parameter str. The function uses a while loop with an empty loop statement to locate the null terminator in the string accessed by pointer p. The return statement yields the sought value by taking the difference between the addresses of pointers p and str. The return statement first applies the pre-decrement operator to pointer p to adjust the address of that pointer.

The function main, defined in lines 30 through 43, declares the string variable aString. The output statement in line 34 prompts you to enter a string. The statement in line 35 calls the stream input function getline to obtain your input and to store it in variable aString. The output statement in line 36 displays the number of characters you typed. The statement calls the function strlen and passes it the argument aString. The statement in line 39 calls the function upperCase and also passes it the argument aString. The output statement in line 40 displays the uppercase version of your input, which is now stored in variable aString.

Passing Structures by Value

C++ enables you to pass structures either by value or by reference. In this section I demonstrate passing structures by value. In the next sections I show you how to pass structures by reference. The structure's type appears in the function prototype and heading in a manner similar to that of predefined types.

Listing 10.3 shows the source code for the program ADVFUN3.CP. The program performs the following tasks:

☐ Prompts you for the x and y coordinates of a first point

☐ Prompts you for the x and y coordinates of a second point

☐ Calculates coordinates of the median point between the two points that you entered

☐ Displays the coordinates of the median point

 Listing 10.3. Source code for the program ADVFUN3.CP.

```
1: // C++ program which uses a function that passes
2: // a structure by value
3:
4: #include <iostream.h>
5:
6: struct point {
7:    double x;
8:    double y;
9: };
10:
11: // declare the prototype of function getMedian
12: point getMedian(point, point);
13:
14: main()
15: {
16:    point pt1;
17:    point pt2;
18:    point median;
19:
20:    cout << "Enter the X and Y coordinates for point # 1 : ";
21:    cin >> pt1.x >> pt1.y;
22:    cout << "Enter the X and Y coordinates for point # 2 : ";
23:    cin >> pt2.x >> pt2.y;
24:    // get the coordinates for the median point
25:    median = getMedian(pt1, pt2);
26:    // get the median point
```

```
27:    cout << "Mid point is (" << median.x
28:        << ", " << median.y << ")\n";
29:    return 0;
30: }
31:
32: point getMedian(point p1, point p2)
33: {
34:    point result;
35:    result.x = (p1.x + p2.x) / 2;
36:    result.y = (p1.y + p2.y) / 2;
37:    return result;
38: };
```

Here is a sample session with the program in Listing 10.3:

```
Enter the X and Y coordinates for point # 1 : 1 1
Enter the X and Y coordinates for point # 2 : 5 5
Mid point is (3, 3)
```

The program in Listing 10.3 declares the structure point, which models a two-dimensional point. This structure has two double-typed members, x and y. Line 12 declares the prototype for the function getMedian. The function takes two point-typed parameters that are passed by value.

The function main declares the point-typed variables pt1, pt2, and median in lines 16 through 18, respectively. The output statement in line 20 prompts you to enter the x and y coordinates for the first point. The statement in line 21 obtains your input and stores the coordinates in the members pt1.x and pt1.y. Lines 22 and 23 repeat the same prompting and input process for the second point. The input statement in line 23 stores the values for the second point in members pt2.x and pt2.y. The statement in line 25 calls function getMedian and passes it the arguments pt1 and pt2. The function receives a copy of the arguments pt1 and pt2. The statement assigns the point-typed function result to the variable median. The output statement in lines 27 and 28 displays the x and y coordinates of the median point (by displaying the x and y members of the variable median).

The function getMedian declares two point-typed parameters, p1 and p2. In addition, the function declares the local point-typed variable result. The statement in line 35 assigns the average of members p1.x and p2.x to member result.x. The statement in line 36 assigns the average of members p1.y and p2.y to member result.y. Notice that these statements use the dot operator to access the members x and y of the structures p1, p2, and result. This syntax is used when the function passes a copy or a reference of a structure. The return statement yields the value in the local structure result.

Passing Arguments by Reference

C++ enables you to write functions with parameters that pass arguments by reference. This kind of parameter enables you to change the value of the argument beyond the scope of the function. C++ offers two ways to implement such parameters: with pointers and with formal reference parameters. The following section presents functions that pass various kinds of data types by reference.

Passing Structures by Reference

You can pass structures to functions either by using pointers or by using formal reference. Many C++ programmers consider either approach as more efficient than passing the structure parameters by copy—you save on the overhead of copying the structure-typed arguments.

Note: When you pass a structure by reference, you use the dot operator with the reference parameters (as with passing by value). The added advantage is that the reference parameters do not create copies of the original arguments. Thus, they are faster and save memory resources. The down side is that because reference parameters become aliases to their arguments, any changes made to the parameters inside the function affect their arguments. One method to prevent this change is to use const reference parameters. Such parameters tell the compiler that the function cannot assign new values to the reference parameters.

DO	DON'T

DO pass structures either by formal reference or by pointers when both of the following two circumstances apply: the host function does not alter the arguments, and the function returns values through these structures.

DON'T pass structures by value unless you need to supply the host function with a copy of the data that will be modified by the function.

Let's look at an example. Listing 10.4 shows the source code for the program ADVFUN4.CP. The program performs the same tasks as the previous program, ADVFUN3.CP. The new version differs only in its implementation.

Listing 10.4. Source code for the program ADVFUN4.CP.

```
1: // C++ program which uses a function that passes
2: // a structure by reference
3:
4: #include <iostream.h>
5:
6: struct point {
7:   double x;
8:   double y;
9: };
10:
11: // declare the prototype of function getMedian
12: point getMedian(const point&, const point&);
13:
14: main()
15: {
16:   point pt1;
17:   point pt2;
18:   point median;
19:
20:   cout << "Enter the X and Y coordinates for point # 1 : ";
21:   cin >> pt1.x >> pt1.y;
22:   cout << "Enter the X and Y coordinates for point # 2 : ";
23:   cin >> pt2.x >> pt2.y;
24:   // get the coordinates for the median point
25:   median = getMedian(pt1, pt2);
26:   // get the median point
27:   cout << "Mid point is (" << median.x
28:        << ", " << median.y << ")\n";
29:   return 0;
30: }
31:
32: point getMedian(const point& p1, const point& p2)
33: {
34:   point result;
35:   result.x = (p1.x + p2.x) / 2;
36:   result.y = (p1.y + p2.y) / 2;
37:   return result;
38: };
```

Here is a sample session with the program in Listing 10.4:

```
Enter the X and Y coordinates for point # 1 : 1 1
Enter the X and Y coordinates for point # 2 : 9 9
Mid point is (5, 5)
```

 The program in Listing 10.4 is very similar to Listing 10.3. The new program version uses reference parameters in function getMedian. Thus, the prototype and the function's declaration place the & character after the structure type point. Using reference parameters, the call to function getMedian looks very much like the call to the version in Listing 10.3. Likewise, the implementation of function getMedian is similar to the one in Listing 10.3—both versions use the dot operator to access the members x and y in the structure point.

Passing Structures by Pointers

Using pointers is another efficient way to pass structures. As with the reference parameter types, use the const declaration to prevent the implementation from changing the structured variables accessed by the pointer parameters.

The next example is, as you might expect, the version of program ADVFUN3.CP that uses pointer parameters. Listing 10.5 shows the source code for the new version, program ADVFUN5.CP.

Type **Listing 10.5. Source code for the program ADVFUN5.CP.**

```
1: // C++ program which uses a function that passes
2: // a structure by pointer
3:
4: #include <iostream.h>
5:
6: struct point {
7:    double x;
8:    double y;
9: };
10:
11: // declare the prototype of function getMedian
12: point getMedian(const point*, const point*);
13:
14: main()
15: {
16:    point pt1;
17:    point pt2;
18:    point median;
19:
20:    cout << "Enter the X and Y coordinates for point # 1 : ";
21:    cin >> pt1.x >> pt1.y;
22:    cout << "Enter the X and Y coordinates for point # 2 : ";
23:    cin >> pt2.x >> pt2.y;
24:    // get the coordinates for the median point
25:    median = getMedian(&pt1, &pt2);
26:    // get the median point
27:    cout << "Mid point is (" << median.x
28:         << ", " << median.y << ")\n";
```

```
29:    return 0;
30: }
31:
32: point getMedian(const point* p1, const point* p2)
33: {
34:    point result;
35:    result.x = (p1->x + p2->x) / 2;
36:    result.y = (p1->y + p2->y) / 2;
37:    return result;
38: };
```

Here is a sample session with the program in Listing 10.5:

```
Enter the X and Y coordinates for point # 1 : 2 2
Enter the X and Y coordinates for point # 2 : 8 8
Mid point is (5, 5)
```

10

The program in Listing 10.5 uses pointer parameters in function getMedian. The prototype and the implementation of the function use the const point* type for both parameters. The statement in line 25, which calls the function getMedian, passes the addresses of the variables pt1 and pt2, using the address-of operator &. The implementation of the function getMedian uses the -> operator to access the members x and y for the pointer parameters p1 and p2.

Recursive Functions

There are many problems that can be solved by breaking them down into simpler and similar problems. For example, the way the compiler parses an expression is simplified by using recursion—because an expression can contain smaller expressions. Such problems are solved using recursion.

Recursive functions are functions that obtain a result and/or perform a task by calling themselves. You should limit your use of recursive calls to avoid exhausting the memory resources of the computer. Consequently, every recursive function must examine a condition which determines the end of the recursion.

A common example of a recursive function is the factorial function. A factorial of a number N is the product of all the integers from 1 to N, with the exclamation point (!) as the mathematical symbol for the factorial function.

The mathematical equation for a factorial is

```
N! = 1 * 2 * 3 * ... * (N-2) * (N-1) * N
```

The recursive version of this equation is

```
N! = N * (N-1)!
(N-1)! = (N-1) * (N-2)!
(N-2)! = (N-2) * (N-3)!
...
2! = 2 * 1!
1! = 1
```

Recursion entails looping to obtain a result. Most recursive solutions have alternate nonrecursive solutions. In some cases, the recursive solutions are more elegant than the nonrecursive ones. The factorial function is an example of a mathematical function that can be implemented using either recursion or a nonrecursive straightforward loop.

DO   DON'T

DO include a decision-making statement in a recursive function to end the recursion.

DON'T use recursion unless its advantages significantly outweigh the alternate nonrecursive solution.

Here is an example that implements the recursive factorial function. Listing 10.6 shows the source code for the program ADVFUN6.CP. The program prompts you to enter two positive integers—the first one must be greater than or equal to the second one. The program displays the number of combinations and permutations obtained from the two integers. The number of combinations is given by the following equation:

```
mCn = m! / ((m - n)! * n!)
```

The number of permutations is given by the following equation:

```
mPn = m! / (m - n)!
```

Listing 10.6. Source code for the program ADVFUN6.CP.

```
1: // C++ program which uses a recursive function
2:
3: #include <iostream.h>
4:
```

```
 5: const int MIN = 4;
 6: const int MAX = 30;
 7:
 8: double factorial(int i)
 9: {
10:   if (i > 1)
11:     return double(i) * factorial(i - 1);
12:   else
13:     return 1;
14: }
15:
16: double permutation(int m, int n)
17: {
18:   return factorial(m) / factorial(m - n);
19: }
20:
21: double combination(int m, int n)
22: {
23:   return permutation(m, n) / factorial(n);
24: }
25:
26: main()
27: {
28:   int m, n;
29:
30:   do {
31:     cout << "Enter an integer between "
32:          << MIN << " and " << MAX << " : ";
33:     cin >> m;
34:   } while (m < MIN || m > MAX);
35:
36:   do {
37:     cout << "Enter an integer between "
38:          << MIN << " and " << m << ": ";
39:     cin >> n;
40:   } while (n < MIN || n > m);
41:
42:   cout << "Permutations(" << m << ", " << n
43:        << ") = " << permutation(m, n) << "\n";
44:   cout << "Combinations(" << m << ", " << n
45:        << ") = " << combination(m, n) << "\n";
46:
47:   return 0;
48: }
```

Here is a sample session with the program in Listing 10.6:

```
Enter an integer between 4 and 30 : 10
Enter an integer between 4 and 10 : 5
Permutations(10, 5) = 30240
Combinations(10, 5) = 252
```

The program in Listing 10.6 declares the recursive function `factorial`, and the functions `permutation`, `combination`, and `main`. The program also declares the global constants `MIN` and `MAX`, which specify the limits of the first integer you enter.

The function `factorial` has one parameter, the `int`-typed parameter `i`. The function returns a `double`-typed value. The `if` statement in line 10 compares the value of parameter `i` with 1. This comparison determines whether to make a recursive call, in line 11, or return the value 1, in line 13. The recursive call in line 11 invokes the function `factorial` with the argument `i - 1`. Thus, the recursive call supplies the function with a smaller (or simpler, if you prefer) argument.

The function `permutation` takes two `int`-typed parameters, `m` and `n`. The function calls the recursive function `factorial` twice: once with the argument `m` and once with the argument `m - n`. The function `permutation` returns the ratio of the two calls to function `factorial`.

The function `combination` also takes two `int`-typed parameters, `m` and `n`. It calls the function `permutation` and passes it the arguments `m` and `n`. It also calls the function `factorial` and passes it the argument `n`. The function `combination` returns the ratio of the values returned by functions `permutation` and `factorial`.

The function `main` declares the `int`-typed variables `m` and `n`. The function uses two `do-while` loops to prompt you for integer values. The output statement in the first loop prompts you to enter an integer between `MIN` and `MAX`. The statement in line 33 stores your input in variable `m`. The `while` clause of the `do-while` loop validates your input. The clause determines whether your input is either less than `MIN` or greater than `MAX`. If this condition is true, the loop iterates again.

The output statement in the second `do-while` loop prompts you to enter an integer between `m` and `MAX`. The statement in line 39 saves your input in variable `n`. The `while` clause validates your input. The clause determines whether your input is either less than `MIN` or greater than `m`. If this condition is true, the loop iterates again.

The output statement in lines 42 and 43 displays the permutations of the values in variables `m` and `n`. The statement calls function `permutation` and passes it the arguments `m` and `n`. The output statement in lines 44 and 45 displays the combinations of the values in variables `m` and `n`. The statement calls function `combination` and passes it the arguments `m` and `n`.

Passing Pointers to Dynamic Structures

Implementing a binary tree requires functions that—at least—insert, search, delete, and traverse the tree. All these functions access the binary tree through the pointer of its *root*. Interestingly, operations such as tree insertion and deletion may affect the root itself. In such cases, the address of the root node changes. Consequently, you need to pass a reference to the pointer of the root node. Using a reference to a pointer guarantees that you maintain an updated address of the tree root.

NEW☞ TERM The binary tree is among the popular dynamic data structures. These structures enable you to build ordered collections of data without prior knowledge of the number of data items. The basic building block for a binary tree is a node. Every node in a binary tree is the root of all subtrees below it. Terminal nodes are the roots of empty subtrees. The binary tree has a special node which is the root of all other nodes. Each node has a field (used as a sorting key), optional additional data (called non-key data), and two pointers to establish a link with other tree nodes. Dynamic memory allocation enables you to create space for each node and to set up the links between the various nodes dynamically. To learn more about binary tree structure, consult a data structure text book.

10

DO	DON'T

DO declare the parameters handling critical pointers to a data structure using the reference to these pointers. This declaration ensures that the addresses of these parameters are updated outside the scope of the function.

DON'T assume that when a function alters the address of a nonreference pointer parameter, the change also affects the address of the argument.

Let's look at an example that inserts and displays dynamic data in a binary tree. Listing 10.7 shows the source code for the program ADVFUN7.CP. The program supplies its own set of data (a list of names), inserts the data in a binary tree, and then displays the data in ascending order.

Listing 10.7. Source code for the program ADVFUN7.CP.

```cpp
1: // C++ program which passes parameter to dynamic data
2:
3: #include <iostream.h>
4: #include <string.h>
5:
6: const unsigned MAX = 30;
7:
8: typedef struct node* nodeptr;
9:
10: struct node {
11:    char value[MAX+1];
12:    nodeptr left;
13:    nodeptr right;
14: };
15:
16: void insert(nodeptr& root, const char* item)
17: // Recursively insert element in binary tree
18: {
19:   if (!root)  {
20:     root = new node;
21:     strncpy(root->value, item, MAX);
22:     root->left = NULL;
23:     root->right = NULL;
24:   }
25:   else {
26:     if (strcmp(item, root->value) < 0)
27:       insert(root->left, item);
28:     else
29:       insert(root->right, item);
30:   }
31: }
32:
33: void showTree(nodeptr& root)
34: {
35:   if (!root)
36:     return;
37:
38:   showTree(root->left);
39:   cout << root->value << "\n";
40:   showTree(root->right);
41: }
42:
43: main()
44: {
```

```
45:    char *names[] = { "Virginia", "California", "Maine", "Michigan",
46:                      "New York", "Florida", "Ohio", "Illinois",
47:                      "Alaska", "Arizona", "Oregon", "Vermont",
48:                      "Maryland", "Delaware", "NULL" };
49:    nodeptr treeRoot = NULL;
50:    int i = 0;
51:
52:    // insert the names in the binary tree
53:    while (strcmp(names[i], "NULL") != 0)
54:      insert(treeRoot, names[i++]);
55:
56:    showTree(treeRoot);
57:    return 0;
58: }
```

 Here is a sample session with the program in Listing 10.7:

```
Alaska
Arizona
California
Delaware
Florida
Illinois
Maine
Maryland
Michigan
New York
Ohio
Oregon
Vermont
Virginia
```

10

 The program in Listing 10.7 declares the global constant MAX to specify the maximum number of characters stored by each node in the binary tree. The declaration in line 8 defines the pointer-type nodeptr based on the structure node. The program defines the structure node in lines 10 through 14. The structure contains the member value (which stores a string), the pointer to the left node, left, and the pointer to the right node, right. Both pointers have the nodeptr type.

The program declares the recursive function insert to insert a string in the binary tree. The function has two parameters: root and item. The parameter root is a reference to a nodeptr-typed pointer. This parameter keeps track of the various nodes of the binary tree and updates their addresses as needed. This update occurs when the binary tree inserts a data item.

The if statement in line 19 determines whether or not the parameter root is NULL. If this condition is true, the function executes the statements in lines 20 through 23. The statement in line 20 allocates a new node using the operator new. The statement in line

21 uses the function strncpy to copy up to MAX characters from the parameter item to the member value. The statements in lines 22 and 23 assign NULLs to the left and right node pointers of the newly created node. The statements in lines 20 to 24 not only affect the actual root of the tree, but also alter the pointers to the various nodes. The condition in the if statement helps to end the recursive calls.

The else clause in line 25 handles the case when the parameter root is not NULL. The if statement in line 26 determines whether the string accessed by pointer item is less than the string in the value member of the currently accessed tree node. If this condition is true, the function makes a recursive call passing the arguments root->left and item. This call inserts the new string in the left subtree, whose root is the current node. Otherwise, the function makes a recursive call passing the arguments root->right and item. This call inserts the new string in the right subtree, whose root is the current node.

The recursive function showTree traverses, in order, the nodes of the tree and subtree whose root is the reference parameter root. The function quickly exits if the current value of the parameter root is NULL. This condition indicates that the argument for parameter root is a terminal node. Therefore, this condition ends the recursive call. If the argument for parameter root is not NULL, the function makes a recursive call passing the argument root->left. This call allows the function to visit the left subtree whose root is the current node. Once the left subtree of the current node is visited, the function displays the string stored in the member value of the current node. Then the function makes another recursive call, this time passing the argument root->right. This call allows the function to visit the right subtree whose root is the current node. Once the right subtree of the current node is visited, the function exits.

The function main declares an array of pointers to the internal data, shown in lines 45 through 48. The function also declares the variable treeRoot as the root of the binary tree. The declaration of this variable also initializes the variable to NULL. The function also declares the int-typed variable i and initializes it with 0.

The function main uses the while loop in line 53 to insert the strings in the list of state names. The loop iterates until the current name matches the string "NULL". This string is a special name that I use to track the end of the list. If you modify the program and add more state names, be sure to make the string "NULL" the last item in the list. The statement in line 54 calls the function insert to insert the element names[i] in the binary tree whose root is the pointer treeRoot.

The statement in line 56 calls the function showTree and supplies it the argument treeRoot. The call to this recursive function displays the names of the states in ascending order.

Pointers to Functions

The program compilation process translates the names of variables into memory addresses where data are stored and retrieved. Pointers to addresses also can access these addresses. This translation step holds true for variables and functions alike. The compiler translates the name of a function into the address of executable code. C++ extends the strategy of manipulating variables by using pointers to include functions.

A Pointer to a Function

The general syntax for declaring a pointer to a function is

```
returnType (*functionPointer)(<list of parameters>);
```

This form tells the compiler that the *functionPointer* is a pointer to a function that has the *returnType* return type and a list of parameters.

Examples:

```
double (*fx)(int n);
void (*sort)(int* intArray, unsigned n);
unsigned (*search)(int searchKey, int* intArray, unsigned n);
```

The first identifier, fx, points to a function that returns a double and has a single int-typed parameter. The second identifier, sort, is a pointer to a function that returns a void type and takes two parameters: a pointer to int and an unsigned. The third identifier, search, is a pointer to a function that returns an unsigned and has three parameters: an int, a pointer to an int, and an unsigned.

An Array of Function Pointers

C++ enables you to declare an array of function pointers. The general syntax is

```
returnType (*functionPointer[arraySize])(<list of parameters>);
```

Examples:

```
double (*fx[3])(int n);
void (*sort[MAX_SORT])(int* intArray, unsigned n);
```

```
unsigned (*search[MAX_SEARCH])(int searchKey,
                              int* intArray, unsigned n);
```

The first identifier, fx, points to an array of functions. Each member returns a double and has a single int-typed parameter. The second identifier, sort, is a pointer to an array of functions. Each member returns a void type and takes two parameters: a pointer to an int and an unsigned. The third identifier, search, is a pointer to an array of functions. Each member returns an unsigned and has three parameters: an int, a pointer to an int, and an unsigned.

As with any pointer, you need to initialize a function pointer before using it. This step is very simple. You merely assign the bare name of a function to the function pointer.

Initializing a Function Pointer

The general syntax for initializing a pointer to a function is

```
functionPointer = aFunction;
```

The assigned function must have the same return type and parameter list as the function pointer. Otherwise, the compiler flags an error.

Example:

```
void (*sort)(int* intArray, unsigned n);
sort = qsort;
```

Assigning a Function to an Element

The general syntax for assigning a function to an element in an array of function pointers is

```
functionPointer[index] = aFunction;
```

Once you assign a function name to a function pointer, you can use the pointer to invoke its associated function. Now it should be evident why the function pointer must have the same return type and parameter list as the accessed function.

Example:

```
void (*sort[2])(int* intArray, unsigned n);
sort[0] = shellSort;
sort[1] = CombSort;
```

The Function Pointer Expression

The general syntax for the expression that invokes function pointers is

```
(*functionPointer)(<argument list>);
(*functionPointer[index])(<argument list>);
```

Examples:

```
(*sort)(&intArray, n);
(*sort[0])(&intArray, n);
```

Let's look at an example. Listing 10.8 shows the source code for the program ADVFUN8.CP. The program performs linearized regression on two observed variables: the independent variable X, and the dependent variable Y. The model that relates these two variables is

```
f(Y) = intercept + slope * g(X)
```

The function f(Y) transforms the data for the Y variable. The function g(X) transforms the data for the X variable. The functions f(Y) and g(X) can be linear, logarithmic, exponential, square root, square, or any other mathematical function. When both f(Y) = Y and g(X) = X, the model becomes this linear regression model:

```
Y = intercept + slope * X
```

The linearized regression (back to the general model) calculates the best values for the slope and intercept for the values of f(Y) and g(X). The regression also provides the correlation coefficient statistic that represents the percent (as a fractional number) of the f(Y) data which is explained by the variation in g(X). A value of 1 represents a perfect fit, and 0 represents a total lack of any correlation between f(Y) and g(X) data.

Listing 10.8 performs linear regression and carries out the following tasks:

☐ Prompts you to enter the number of data (your input must be in the limit indicated by the program)

☐ Prompts you to enter the observed values of X and Y

☐ Prompts you to select the function that transforms the observations for variable X (the program displays a small itemized menu that shows your options, indicating the linear, logarithmic, square, square root, and reciprocal functions)

10

☐ Prompts you to select the function that transforms the observations for variable Y (the program displays a small itemized menu that shows your options, indicating the linear, logarithmic, square, square root, and reciprocal functions)

☐ Performs the regression calculations

☐ Displays the intercept, slope, and correlation coefficient for the linearized regression

☐ Prompts you to select another set of transformation functions (if you choose to use another set of functions, the program resumes at step 3)

Listing 10.8. Source code for the program ADVFUN8.CP.

```
1:  /*
2:      C++ program that uses pointers to functions to implement a
3:      a linear regression program that supports temporary
4:      mathematical transformations.
5:  */
6:
7:  #include <iostream.h>
8:  #include <math.h>
9:
10: const unsigned MAX_SIZE = 100;
11:
12: typedef double vector[MAX_SIZE];
13:
14: struct regression {
15:     double Rsqr;
16:     double slope;
17:     double intercept;
18: };
19:
20: // declare function pointer
21: double (*fx)(double);
22: double (*fy)(double);
23:
24: // declare function prototypes
25: void initArray(double*, double*, unsigned);
26: double linear(double);
27: double sqr(double);
28: double _sqrt(double);
29: double _log(double);
30: double reciprocal(double);
31: void calcRegression(double*, double*, unsigned, regression&,
32:                     double (*fx)(double), double (*fy)(double));
33: int select_transf(const char*);
34:
35: main()
36: {
37:     char ans;
38:     unsigned count;
39:     vector x, y;
```

```
40:        regression stat;
41:        int trnsfx, trnsfy;
42:
43:        do {
44:            cout << "Enter array size [2.."
45:                << MAX_SIZE << "] : ";
46:            cin >> count;
47:        } while (count <= 1 || count > MAX_SIZE);
48:
49:        // initialize array
50:        initArray(x, y, count);
51:        // transform data
52:        do {
53:            // set the transformation functions
54:            trnsfx = select_transf("X");
55:            trnsfy = select_transf("Y");
56:            // set function pointer fx
57:            switch (trnsfx) {
58:             case 0 :
59:                 fx = linear;
60:                 break;
61:             case 1 :
62:                 fx = _log;
63:                 break;
64:             case 2 :
65:                 fx = _sqrt;
66:                 break;
67:             case 3 :
68:                 fx = sqr;
69:                 break;
70:             case 4 :
71:                 fx = reciprocal;
72:                 break;
73:             default :
74:                 fx = linear;
75:                 break;
76:            }
77:            // set function pointer fy
78:            switch (trnsfy) {
79:             case 0 :
80:                 fy = linear;
81:                 break;
82:             case 1 :
83:                 fy = _log;
84:                 break;
85:             case 2 :
86:                 fy = _sqrt;
87:                 break;
88:             case 3 :
89:                 fy = sqr;
90:                 break;
91:             case 4 :
92:                 fy = reciprocal;
93:                 break;
94:             default :
```

continues

Listing 10.8. continued

```
 95:              fy = linear;
 96:              break;
 97:        }
 98:
 99:        /*  call function with functional arguments
100:                                              |     |
101:                                              V     V */
102:        calcRegression(x, y, count, stat, fx, fy);
103:
104:        cout << "\n\n"
105:            << "R-square = " << stat.Rsqr << "\n"
106:            << "Slope = " << stat.slope << "\n"
107:            << "Intercept = " << stat.intercept << "\n\n\n";
108:        cout << "Want to use other transformations? (Y/N) ";
109:        cin >> ans;
110:      } while (ans == 'Y' || ans == 'y');
111:    return 0;
112: }
113:
114: void initArray(double* x, double* y, unsigned count)
115: // read data for array from the keyboard
116: {
117:     for (unsigned i = 0; i < count; i++, x++, y++) {
118:         cout << "X[" << i << "] : ";
119:         cin >> *x;
120:         cout << "Y[" << i << "] : ";
121:         cin >> *y;
122:     }
123: }
124:
125: int select_transf(const char* var_name)
126: // select choice of transformation
127: {
128:
129:     int choice = -1;
130:     cout << "\n";
131:     cout << "select transformation for variable " << var_name
132:         << "\n"
133:         << "0) No transformation\n"
134:         << "1) Logarithmic transformation\n"
135:         << "2) Square root transformation\n"
136:         << "3) Square   transformation\n"
137:         << "4) Reciprocal transformation\n";
138:     while (choice < 0 || choice > 4) {
139:         cout << "\nSelect choice by number : ";
140:         cin >> choice;
141:     }
142:     return choice;
143: }
```

```
144:
145:    double linear(double x)
146:    { return x; }
147:
148:    double _log(double x)
149:    { return log(x); }
150:
151:    double _sqrt(double x)
152:    { return sqrt(x); }
153:
154:    double sqr(double x)
155:    { return x * x; }
156:
157:    double reciprocal(double x)
158:    { return 1.0 / x; }
159:
160:    void calcRegression(double* x,
161:                        double* y,
162:                        unsigned count,
163:                        regression &stat,
164:                        double (*fx)(double),
165:                        double (*fy)(double))
166:
167:    {
168:        double meanx, meany, sdevx, sdevy;
169:        double sum = (double) count, sumx = 0, sumy = 0;
170:        double sumxx = 0, sumyy = 0, sumxy = 0;
171:        double xdata, ydata;
172:
173:        for (unsigned i = 0; i < count; i++) {
174:            xdata = (*fx)(*(x+i));
175:            ydata = (*fy)(*(y+i));
176:            sumx += xdata;
177:            sumy += ydata;
178:            sumxx += sqr(xdata);
179:            sumyy += sqr(ydata);
180:            sumxy += xdata * ydata;
181:        }
182:
183:        meanx = sumx / sum;
184:        meany = sumy / sum;
185:        sdevx = sqrt((sumxx - sqr(sumx) / sum)/(sum-1.0));
186:        sdevy = sqrt((sumyy - sqr(sumy) / sum)/(sum-1.0));
187:        stat.slope = (sumxy - meanx * meany * sum) /
188:                        sqr(sdevx)/(sum-1);
189:        stat.intercept = meany - stat.slope * meanx;
190:        stat.Rsqr = sqr(sdevx / sdevy * stat.slope);
191:
192:    }
```

Here is a sample session with the program in Listing 10.8:

```
Enter array size [2..100] : 5
X[0] : 10
Y[0] : 50
X[1] : 25
Y[1] : 78
X[2] : 30
Y[2] : 85
X[3] : 35
Y[3] : 95
X[4] : 100
Y[4] : 212

select transformation for variable X
0) No transformation
1) Logarithmic transformation
2) Square root transformation
3) Square  transformation
4) Reciprocal transformation

Select choice by number : 1

select transformation for variable Y
0) No transformation
1) Logarithmic transformation
2) Square root transformation
3) Square  transformation
4) Reciprocal transformation

Select choice by number : 1


R-square = 0.977011
Slope = 0.63039
Intercept = 2.370556


Want to use other transformations? (Y/N) y

select transformation for variable X
0) No transformation
1) Logarithmic transformation
2) Square root transformation
3) Square  transformation
4) Reciprocal transformation

Select choice by number : 0

select transformation for variable Y

0) No transformation
1) Logarithmic transformation
2) Square root transformation
3) Square  transformation
4) Reciprocal transformation
```

```
Select choice by number : 0


R-square = 0.999873
Slope = 1.798969
Intercept = 32.041237


Want to use other transformations? (Y/N) n
```

The program in Listing 10.8 declares the global constant MAX_SIZE, which determines the maximum size of the arrays. The program also declares the type vector in line 12. In addition, the program defines the structure regression in lines 14 through 18. This structure stores the statistics of a regression. Lines 21 and 22 define the global function pointers fx and fy. Each pointer deals with a function that takes a double-typed argument and returns a double-typed value. The program uses these global pointers to store the mathematical transformations that you select.

The program also declares the functions initArray, linear, sqr, _sqrt, _log, reciprocal, calcRegression, select_transf, and main. The function initArray prompts you to enter the data for the arrays x and y. The functions linear, sqr, _sqrt, _log, and reciprocal are simple functions that provide the transformations for the data. Each one of these functions has the same parameter and return type as the function pointers fx and fy.

The function calcRegression calculates the regression statistics based on the arrays passed by its array parameters x and y. The function uses the function pointer parameters fx and fy to transform the data in arrays x and y. The statements in lines 174 and 175 use the pointers fx and fy to transform the elements of arrays x and y, respectively.

The function select_transf prompts with a simple itemized menu to select the transformation functions by number. The function returns the value for the transformation code number that you select.

The function main declares the arrays x and y using the type vector. The function also declares the structure stat which stores the regression statistics. The function main prompts you to enter the number of data points you want to process. Then, main calls function initArray to obtain the data for the arrays x and y. Next, the function main invokes the function select_trans twice, to select the transformation functions for the data in arrays x and y. The switch statement in line 57 examines the value in variable trnsfx, which contains the index of the transformation value for the array x. The various case labels assign the proper function to the pointer fx. The switch statement in line 78 performs a similar task to assign the proper function to pointer fy.

The function main then calls the function calcRegression and passes the arguments x, y, count, stat, the function pointer fx, and the function pointer fy. The output statement in lines 104 through 107 displays the regression statistics for the current set of transformation functions. The statement in line 108 asks you if you wish to select another set of transformation functions. The statement in line 109 stores your input in variable ans. The while clause in line 110 determines whether or not the program repeats the process of selecting the transformation functions and calculating the corresponding regression statistics.

Summary

Today's lesson presented simple C++ functions. You learned about the following topics:

☐ You can pass arrays as function arguments using pointers to the basic types. C++ enables you to declare array parameters using explicit pointer types or using the empty brackets. Such parameters enable you to write general-purpose functions that work with arrays of different sizes. In addition, these pointers access the array by using its address instead of making a copy of the entire array.

☐ Passing strings as function arguments follows the same rules as passing arrays because C++ strings are arrays of characters.

☐ Passing structures as function arguments enables you to shorten the parameter list by encapsulating various related information in C++ structures. C++ supports passing structures by value. Such parameters pass a copy of their arguments to the host function. Consequently, the changes made to the structure members do not affect the arguments outside the scope of the function.

☐ When passing reference parameters, you can use pointers or formal references. The formal references become aliases of their arguments. Any changes made to the parameters affect their arguments outside the function. You can declare a constant reference parameter to ensure that the function does not alter the arguments for the reference parameter. Accessing the members of a structured reference parameter uses the dot operator.

☐ Passing structures by pointer gives the host function the address of the structure. The pointer parameter needs to use the -> operator to access the various members of the structure. You can use the const prefix with the pointer parameter to prevent the function from changing the members of the structure, which is accessed by the pointer parameters.

☐ Recursive functions are functions that obtain a result and/or perform a task by calling themselves. You should limit your use of these recursive calls to avoid exhausting the memory resources of the computer. Consequently, every recursive function must examine a condition that determines the end of the recursion.

☐ Passing pointers to dynamic structures often requires passing the reference to the root or head pointers that manage such structures. Today's lesson illustrated how to create functions to insert data in a binary tree and display its data.

☐ Pointers to functions store the addresses of functions. Such pointers need to have the parameter list and return type defined in order to access functions with the same prototype. Pointers to functions enable you to select which function you wish to invoke at runtime.

Q&A

Q Compared to a value parameter, how does using a reference parameter impact the design of a function?

A The reference parameter also can update—unless it is declared as a const parameter—the argument. Thus, the function can use reference parameters as an input/output data conduit and also as an output data conduit.

Q How can I distinguish between a pointer that passes an array of value and one used to pass back a value through its argument?

A You need to read the declaration of the function in context. However, you can use a reference parameter to declare a parameter that passes a value back to the caller.

Q What is the memory resource used in managing calls to recursive functions?

A The runtime system uses the stack to store intermediate values, including the ones generated by calls to recursive functions. As with other memory resources, stacks have a limited space. Consequently, recursive calls with a long sequence of arguments or memory-consuming arguments drain the stack space and cause a runtime error.

NEW A *stack* is a memory location where information is inserted and removed on a
TERM Last-In-First-Out (LIFO) priority.

Workshop

The Workshop provides quiz questions to help you solidify your understanding of the material covered and exercises to provide you with experience in using what you've learned. Try to understand the quiz and exercise answers before continuing on to the next day's lesson. Answers are provided in Appendix B, "Answers."

Quiz

1. Can you use the conditional operator to write the recursive factorial function?

2. What is wrong with the following recursive function?

```
double factorial(int i)
{
  switch (i) {
    case 0:
    case 1:
        return 1;
        break;
    case 2:
        return 2;
        break;
    case 3:
        return 6;
        break;
    case 4:
        return 24;
        break;
    default:
        return double(i) * factorial(i-1);
  }
}
```

3. Convert the following recursive Fibonacci function (this function has the sequence Fib(0) = 0, Fib(1) = 1, Fib(2) = 1, Fib(3) = 2, Fib(4) = 3, and so on) into a nonrecursive version:

```
double Fibonacci(int n)
{
  if (n == 0)
    return 0;
  else if (n == 1 || n == 2)
    return 1;
  else
    return Fibonacci(n - 1) + Fibonacci(n - 2);
}
```

4. True or false? The two versions of the following functions are equivalent:

```
struct stringStruct {
    char source[MAX+1];
    char uprStr[MAX+1];
    char lwrStr[MAX+];
    char revStr[MAX+1];
};

void convertStr2(const char* str, stringStruct& s)
{
  strncpy(s.source, str, MAX);
  strncpy(s.uprStr, str, MAX);
  strncpy(s.lwrStr, str, MAX);
  strncpy(s.revStr, str, MAX);
  strlwr(s.lwrStr);
  strupr(s.uprStr);
  strrev(s.revStr);
}

void convertStr2(const char* str, stringStruct* s)
{
  strncpy(s->source, str, MAX);
  strncpy(s->uprStr, str, MAX);
  strncpy(s->lwrStr, str, MAX);
```

```
    strncpy(s->revStr, str, MAX);
    _strlwr(s->lwrStr);
    _strupr(s->uprStr);
    strrev(s->revStr);
}
```

Exercise

Create the program ADVFUN9.CP from ADVFUN8.CP by replacing the individual function pointers fx and fy with the array of function pointers f. In addition, replace the two function pointer parameters of function calcRegression with a parameter that is an array of function pointers.

Object-Oriented Programming and C++ Classes

Classes provide C++ with object-oriented programming (OOP) constructs. Today's lesson, which marks an important milestone for learning C++, introduces you to building individual classes as well as class hierarchy. You learn about the following topics:

☐ The basics of object-oriented programming

☐ Declaring base classes

☐ Constructors

☐ Destructors

☐ Declaring a class hierarchy

☐ Virtual functions

☐ Friend functions

☐ Operators and friend operators

Basics of Object-Oriented Programming

We live in a world of objects. Each object has its attributes and operations. Some objects are more animated than others. You can categorize objects into classes. For example, my CASIO Data Bank watch is an object that belongs to the class of the CASIO Data Bank watches.

NEW *Object-oriented programming (OOP)* uses the notions of real-world objects to
TERM develop applications.

You also can relate individual classes in a class hierarchy. The class of CASIO Data Bank watches is part of the watch class hierarchy. The basics of OOP include classes, objects, messages, methods, inheritance, and polymorphism.

NEW A class defines a category of objects. Each object is an instance of a class.
TERM

Classes and Objects

An object shares the same attributes and functionality with other objects in the same class. Typically, an object has a unique state, defined by the current values of its attributes. The

functionality of a class determines the operations that are possible for the class instances. C++ calls the attributes of a class *data members* and calls the operations of a class *member functions.* Classes encapsulate data members and member functions.

Going back to the CASIO watch example, the buttons in the watch represent the member functions of the class of CASIO watches, and the display represents a data member. I can press certain buttons to edit the date and/or time. In OOP terms, the member functions alter the state of the object by changing its data members.

Messages and Methods

Object-oriented programming models the interaction with objects as events where messages are sent to an object or between objects. The object receiving a message responds by invoking the appropriate method (that's the member function in C++). C++ does not explicitly foster the notion of messages and methods as other OOP languages such as SmallTalk do. However, I find it easier to discuss invoking member functions using the term "message." The terms "methods" and "member functions" are equivalent.

NEW TERM The *message* is *what* is done to an object. The *method* is *how* the object responds to the incoming message.

Inheritance

In object-oriented languages, you can derive a class from another one.

NEW TERM With *inheritance*, the derived class (also called the *descendant class*) inherits the data members and member functions of its *parent* and *ancestor classes*.

Deriving a class refines the parent class by appending new attributes and new operations. The derived class typically declares new data members and new member functions. In addition, the derived class also can override inherited member functions when the operations of these functions are not suitable for the derived class.

To apply the concept of inheritance to the CASIO Data Bank watch, consider the following scenario. Suppose that the watch manufacturer decides to create a CASIO Data Comm watch that offers the same features of the CASIO Data Bank plus a beeper! Rather than redesigning the new model (that is, the new class in OOP terms) from scratch, the CASIO engineers start with the existing design of the CASIO Data Bank and build on it. This process may well add new attributes and operations to the existing

design and alter some existing operations to fit the new design. Thus, the CASIO Data Comm model inherits the attributes and the operations of the CASIO Data Bank model. In OOP terms, the class of CASIO Data Comm watches is a descendant of the class of CASIO Data Bank watches.

Polymorphism

The OOP feature of polymorphism enables the instances of different classes to react in a particular way to a message (or function invocation, in C++ terms). For example, in a hierarchy of graphical shapes (point, line, square, rectangle, circle, ellipse, and so on), each shape has a *Draw* function that is responsible for properly responding to a request to draw that shape.

NEW TERM

Polymorphism enables the instances of different classes to respond to the same function in ways that are appropriate to each class.

Declaring Base Classes

C++ enables you to declare a class that encapsulates data members and member functions. These functions alter and/or retrieve the values of the data members as well as perform related tasks.

Syntax

A Base Class

The general syntax for declaring a base class is

```
class className
{
    private:
        <private data members>
        <private constructors>
        <private member functions>
    protected:
        <protected data members>
        <protected constructors>
        <protected member functions>
    public:
        <public data members>
        <public constructors>
        <public destructor>
        <public member functions>
};
```

Example:

```
class point
{
    protected:
        double x;
        double y;
    public:
        point(double xVal, double yVal);
        double getX();
        double getY();
        void assign(double xVal, double yVal);
        point& assign(point& pt);
};
```

The Sections of a Class

The previous syntax shows that the declaration involves the keyword `class`. C++ classes offer three levels of visibility for the various members (that is, both data members and member functions):

☐ The private section

☐ The protected section

☐ The public section

NEW☞ TERM In the *private section*, only the member functions of the class can access the private members. The class instances are denied access to private members.

NEW☞ TERM In the *protected section*, only the member functions of the class and its descendant classes can access protected members. The class instances are denied access to protected members.

NEW☞ TERM The *public section* specifies members that are visible to the member functions of the class, class instances, member functions of descendant classes, and their instances.

The following rules apply to the various class sections:

☐ The class sections can appear in any order.

☐ The class sections can appear more than once.

☐ If no class section is specified, the C++ compiler treats the members as protected.

☐ You should avoid placing data members in the public section, unless such a declaration significantly simplifies your design. Data members typically are placed in the protected section to enable member functions of descendant classes to access them.

☐ Use member functions to set and/or query the values of data members. The members that set the data members assist in performing validation and updating other data members, if need be.

☐ The class can have multiple constructors, which are typically located in the public section.

☐ The class can have only one destructor, which must be declared in the public section.

☐ The member functions (as well as the constructors and destructors) that have multiple statements are defined outside the class declaration. The definition can reside in the same file that declares the class.

NEW TERM *Constructors* are special members that must have the same name as the host class. *Destructors* automatically remove class instances.

In software libraries, the definition of the member functions referred to in rule 8 typically reside in a separate source file. When you define a member function, you must qualify the function name with the class name. The syntax of such a qualification involves using the class name followed by two colons (::) and then the name of a function. For example, consider the following class:

```
class point
{
    protected:
        double x;
        double y;
    public:
        point(double xVal, double yVal);
        double getX();
        // other member functions
};
```

The definitions of the constructor and member functions are

```
point::point(double xVal, double yVal)
{
  // statements
```

```
     }

double point::getX()
{
  // statements
}
```

Once you declare a class, you can use the class name as a type identifier to declare class instances. The syntax resembles declaring variables.

Let's look at an example. Listing 11.1 shows the source code for the program CLASS1.CP. The program prompts you to enter the length and width of a rectangle (which is an object). The program then displays the length, width, and area of the rectangle you specified.

 Listing 11.1. Source code for the program CLASS1.CP.

```
1: // C++ program that illustrates a class
2:
3: #include <iostream.h>
4:
5: class rectangle
6: {
7:   protected:
8:     double length;
9:     double width;
10:   public:
11:     rectangle() { assign(0, 0); }
12:     rectangle(double len, double wide) { assign(len, wide); }
13:     double getLength() { return length; }
14:     double getWidth() { return width; }
15:     double getArea() { return length * width; }
16:     void assign(double len, double wide);
17: };
18:
19: void rectangle::assign(double len, double wide)
20: {
21:   length = len;
22:   width = wide;
23: }
24:
25: main()
26: {
27:   rectangle rect;
28:   double len, wide;
29:
30:   cout << "Enter length of rectangle : ";
31:   cin >> len;
32:   cout << "Enter width of rectangle : ";
33:   cin >> wide;
34:   rect.assign(len, wide);
35:   cout << "Rectangle length = " << rect.getLength() << "\n"
36:        << "          width  = " << rect.getWidth() << "\n"
```

continues

Listing 11.1. continued

```
37:          << "         area   = " << rect.getArea() << "\n";
38:   return 0;
39: }
```

Here is a sample session with the program in Listing 11.1:

```
Enter length of rectangle : 10
Enter width of rectangle : 12
Rectangle length = 10
        width  = 12
        area   = 120
```

The program in Listing 11.1 declares the class rectangle, which models a rectangle. The class has two double-typed data members, length and width, which store the dimension of a rectangle. In addition, the class has two constructors: the default constructor and the nondefault constructor. The class also defines the member functions getLength, getWidth, getArea, and assign.

The *default constructor* creates an instance with 0 dimensions, and the *nondefault constructor* creates an instance with nonzero dimensions.

The function getLength, defined in the class declaration, simply returns the value in member length. The function getWidth, also defined in the class declaration, merely returns the value in member width. The function getArea, defined in the class declaration, simply returns the value of the result of multiplying the members length and width.

The member function assign, defined outside the class declaration, assigns the arguments for its parameters len and wide to the data members length and width, respectively. I simplify the implementation of this function by not checking for negative values.

The function main declares rect as the instance of class rectangle and declares the double-typed variables len and wide. The output statement in line 30 prompts you to enter the length of the rectangle. The statement in line 31 obtains your input and stores it in variable len. The output statement in line 32 prompts you to enter the width of the rectangle. The statement in line 33 obtains your input and stores it in variable wide.

The function main assigns the input values to the instance rect using the assign member function. In OOP terms, I can say that the function main sends the assign message to the object rect. The arguments of the message are variables len and wide. The object rect responds by invoking the method (the member function) rectangle::assign(double, double).

The output statement in lines 35 through 37 displays the length, width, and area of the object rect. This statement sends the messages getLength, getWidth, and getArea to the object rect. In turn, the object rect invokes the appropriate methods (or member functions, if you prefer) to respond to each one of these messages.

Constructors

C++ constructors and destructors work automatically to guarantee the appropriate creation and removal of class instances.

Syntax

Constructors

The general syntax for constructors is

```
class className
{
    public:
        className(); // default constructor
        className(className& c); // copy constructor
        className(<parameter list>); // another constructor
};
```

Example:

```
class point
{
    protected:
        double x;
        double y;
    public:
        point();
        point(double xVal, double yVal);
        point(point& pt);
        double getX();
        double getY();
        void assign(double xVal, double yVal);
        point& assign(point& pt);
};
```

 A *copy constructor* enables you to create class instances by copying the data from existing instances.

C++ has the following features and rules regarding constructors:

☐ The name of the constructor must be identical to the name of its class.

☐ You must not include any return type, not even void.

☐ A class can have any number of constructors, including none. In the latter case, the compiler automatically creates one for that class.

☐ The default constructor is the one that either has no parameters or possesses a parameter list where all the parameters use default arguments. Here are two examples:

```
// class use parameterless constructor
class point1
{
    protected:
        double x;
        double y;
    public:
        point1();
        // other member functions
};

// class use constructor with default arguments
class point2
{
    protected:
        double x;
        double y;
    public:
        point(double xVal = 0, double yVal = 0);
        // other member functions
};
```

☐ The copy constructor enables you to create a class instance using an existing instance. Here is an example:

```
class point
{
    protected:
        double x;
        double y;
    public:
        point();
        point(double xVal, double yVal);
        point(point& pt);
```

```
        // other member functions
};
```

☐ The declaration of a class instance (which includes function parameters and local instances) involves a constructor. Which constructor is called? The answer depends on how many constructors you have declared for the class and how you declared the class instance. For example, consider the following instances of the previous bullet item's class point:

```
point p1; // involves the default constructor
point p2(1.1, 1.3); // uses the second constructor
point p3(p2); // uses the copy constructor
```

Because instance p1 specifies no arguments, the compiler uses the default constructor. The instance p2 specifies two floating-point arguments. Consequently, the compiler uses the second constructor. The instance p3 has the instance p2 as an argument. Therefore, the compiler uses the copy constructor to create instance p3 from instance p2.

DO   DON'T

DO declare copy constructors, especially for classes that model dynamic data structures. These constructors perform what is called a *deep copy*, which includes the dynamic data. By default, the compiler creates what is called *shallow copy* constructors, which copy the data members only.

DON'T rely on the shallow copy constructor to copy instances for classes which have members that are pointers.

Destructors

C++ classes can contain destructors that automatically remove class instances.

Syntax

Destructors

The general syntax for destructors is

```
class className
{
    public:
```

```
        className(); // default constructor
        // other constructors
        ~className();
        // other member function
};
```

Example:

```
class String
{
    protected:
        char *str;
        int len;

    public:
        String();
        String(String& s);
        ~String();
        // other member functions
};
```

C++ has the following features and rules regarding destructors:

☐ The name of the destructor must begin with a tilde (~). The rest of the destructor name must be identical to the name of its class.

☐ You must not include any return type, not even void.

☐ A class can have no more than one destructor. In addition, if you omit the destructor, the compiler automatically creates one for you.

☐ The destructor cannot have any parameters.

☐ The runtime system automatically invokes a class destructor when the instance of that class is out of scope.

Examples of Constructors and Destructors

Let's look at a program that typifies the use of constructors and destructors. Listing 11.2 contains the source code for the CLASS2.CP program. The program performs the following tasks:

☐ Creates a dynamic array (the object)

☐ Assigns values to the elements of the dynamic array

☐ Displays the values in the dynamic array

☐ Removes the dynamic array

Type Listing 11.2. Source code for the CLASS2.CP program.

```
1: // Program demonstrates constructors and destructors
2:
3: #include <iostream.h>
4:
5: const unsigned MIN_SIZE = 4;
6:
7: class Array
8: {
9:    protected:
10:       double *dataPtr;
11:       unsigned size;
12:
13:    public:
14:       Array(unsigned Size = MIN_SIZE);
15:       ~Array()
16:         { delete [] dataPtr; }
17:       unsigned getSize() const
18:         { return size; }
19:       void store(double x, unsigned index)
20:         { dataPtr[index] = x; }
21:       double recall(unsigned index)
22:          { return dataPtr[index]; }
23: };
24:
25: Array::Array(unsigned Size)
26: {
27:    size = (Size < MIN_SIZE) ? MIN_SIZE : Size;
28:    dataPtr = new double[size];
29: }
30:
31: main()
32: {
33:    Array Arr(10);
34:    double x;
35:    // assign data to array elements
36:    for (unsigned i = 0; i < Arr.getSize(); i++) {
37:      x = double(i);
38:      x = x * x - 5 * x + 10;
39:      Arr.store(x, i);
40:    }
41:    // display data in the array element
42:    cout << "Array Arr has the following values:\n\n";
43:    for (i = 0; i < Arr.getSize(); i++)
44:      cout << "Arr[" << i << "] = " << Arr.recall(i) << "\n";
45:    return 0;
46: }
```

11

Here is a sample session with the program in Listing 11.2:

```
Array Arr has the following values:

Arr[0] = 10
Arr[1] = 6
Arr[2] = 4
Arr[3] = 4
Arr[4] = 6
Arr[5] = 10
Arr[6] = 16
Arr[7] = 24
Arr[8] = 34
Arr[9] = 46
```

The program in Listing 11.2 declares the global constant MIN_SIZE, in line 5, which specifies the minimum size of dynamic arrays. The program also declares the class Array in line 7. The class has two data members, dataPtr and size. The member dataPtr is the pointer to the elements' dynamically allocated array. The member size stores the number of elements in an instance of class Array.

The class declares a default constructor. (The constructor actually has a parameter with the default value MIN_SIZE.) The program defines the constructor in lines 25 through 29. The arguments for the parameter Size specify the number of array elements. The statement in line 27 assigns the greater value of parameter Size and the constant MIN_SIZE to the data member size. The statement in line 28 allocates the dynamic space for the array by using the operator new. The statement assigns the base address of the dynamic array to the member dataPtr.

The destructor ~Array removes the dynamic space of the array by applying the operator delete to the member dataPtr.

The member function getSize, defined in the class declaration, returns the value in data member size.

The function store, defined in the class declaration, stores the value passed by parameter x at the element number specified by the parameter index. I simplify the implementation of this function by eliminating the out-of-range index check.

The function recall, defined in the class declaration, returns the value in the element specified by the parameter index. I simplify the implementation of this function by eliminating the out-of-range index check.

The function main declares the object Arr as an instance of class Array. The declaration, located in line 33, specifies that the instance has 10 elements. The function also declares the double-typed variable x. The for loop in lines 36 through 40 stores values in the instance Arr. The loop uses the control variable i and iterates from 0 to Arr.getSize()-1 in increments of 1. The loop continuation condition sends the getSize message to instance Arr to obtain the number of elements in the array. The statements in lines 37 and 38 calculate the value to store in an element of instance Arr. The statement in line 39 sends the message store to instance Arr and passes the arguments x and i. The object Arr saves the value in variable x at the element number i.

The output statement in line 42 comments on the output of the for loop in lines 43 and 44. The loop uses the control variable i and iterates from 0 to Arr.getSize()-1 in increments of 1. The output statement in line 44 displays the element in instance Arr by sending the message recall to that instance. The message has the argument i.

Declaring a Class Hierarchy

The power of the OOP features of C++ comes from the fact that you can derive classes from existing ones. A descendant class inherits the members of its ancestor classes (that is, parent class, grandparent class, and so on) and also can override some of the inherited functions. Inheritance enables you to reuse code in descendant classes.

Syntax

A Derived Class

The general syntax for declaring a derived class is

```
class className : [public] parentClass
{
    <friend classes>

    private:
        <private data members>
        <private constructors>
        <private member functions>

    protected:
        <protected data members>
        <protected constructors>
        <protected member functions>

    public:
        <public data members>
        <public constructors>
        <public destructor>
        <public member functions>

        <friend functions and friend operators>
};
```

Example:

The following example shows the class cRectangle and its descendant, class cBox:

```
class cRectangle
{
    protected:
        double length;
        double width;
    public:
        cRectangle(double len, double wide);
        double getLength() const;
        double getWidth(); const;
        double assign(double len, double wide);
        double calcArea();
};

class cBox : public cRectangle
{
    protected:
        double height;

    public:
        cBox(double len, double wide, double height);
        double getHeight() const;
        assign(double len, double wide, double height);
        double calcVolume();
};
```

The class lineage is indicated by a colon followed by the optional keyword public and then the name of the parent class. When you include the keyword public, you allow the instances of the descendant class to access the public members of the parent and other ancestor classes. By contrast, when you omit the keyword public, you deprive the instance of the descendant class from accessing the members of the ancestor classes.

A descendant class inherits the data members of its ancestor classes. C++ has no mechanism for removing unwanted inherited data members—you are basically stuck with them. By contrast, you can override inherited member functions. More about this topic later in today's lesson. The descendant class declares new data members, new member functions, and overriding member functions. Again, you can place these members in the private, protected, or public sections in your class design as you see fit.

DO   DON'T

DO reduce the number of constructors by using default argument parameters.

DO use member functions to access the values in the data members. These member functions enable you to control and validate the values in the data members.

DON'T declare all the constructors of a class as protected unless you want to force the client programs (that is, those programs that use the class) to use the class by declaring its descendants with public constructors.

DON'T declare the data members in the public section.

Let's look at an example that declares a small class hierarchy. Listing 11.3 shows the source code for the CLASS3.CP program. This program declares classes that contain a hierarchy of two simple geometric shapes: a circle and a cylinder. The program requires no input. Instead, it uses internal data to create the geometric shapes and to display their dimensions, areas, and volume.

Type **Listing 11.3. Source code for the CLASS3.CP program.**

```
1: // Program that demonstrates a small hierarchy of classes
2:
3: #include <iostream.h>
4: #include <math.h>
5:
6: const double pi = 4 * atan(1);
7:
8: inline double sqr(double x)
9: { return x * x; }
10:
11: class cCircle
12: {
13:   protected:
14:     double radius;
15:
16:   public:
17:     cCircle(double radiusVal = 0) : radius(radiusVal) {}
18:     void setRadius(double radiusVal)
19:       { radius = radiusVal; }
20:     double getRadius() const
21:       { return radius; }
22:     double area() const
23:       { return pi * sqr(radius); }
24:     void showData();
25: };
26:
27: class cCylinder : public cCircle
28: {
29:   protected:
30:     double height;
31:
32:   public:
33:     cCylinder(double heightVal = 0, double radiusVal = 0)
34:       : height(heightVal), cCircle(radiusVal) {}
35:     void setHeight(double heightVal)
36:       { height = heightVal; }
37:     double getHeight() const
38:       { return height; }
39:     double area() const
40:         { return 2 * cCircle::area() +
```

continues

Listing 11.3. continued

```
41:                   2 * pi * radius * height; }
42:     void showData();
43: };
44:
45: void cCircle::showData()
46: {
47:    cout << "Circle radius       = " << getRadius() << "\n"
48:         << "Circle area         = " << area() << "\n\n";
49: }
50:
51: void cCylinder::showData()
52: {
53:    cout << "Cylinder radius     = " << getRadius() << "\n"
54:         << "Cylinder height     = " << getHeight() << "\n"
55:         << "Cylinder area       = " << area() << "\n\n";
56: }
57:
58: main()
59: {
60:    cCircle Circle(1);
61:    cCylinder Cylinder(10, 1);
62:
63:    Circle.showData();
64:    Cylinder.showData();
65:    return 0;
66: }
```

 Here is a sample session with the program in Listing 11.3:

```
Circle radius       = 1
Circle area         = 3.141593

Cylinder radius     = 1
Cylinder height     = 10
Cylinder area       = 69.115038
```

 The program in Listing 11.3 declares the classes cCircle and cCylinder. The class cCircle models a circle, whereas class cCylinder models a cylinder.

The cCircle class declares a single data member, radius, to store the radius of the circle. The class also declares a constructor and a number of member functions. The constructor assigns a value to the data member radius when you declare a class instance. Notice that the constructor uses a new syntax to initialize the member radius. The functions setRadius and getRadius serve to set and query the value in member radius, respectively. The function area returns the area of the circle. The function showData displays the radius and area of a class instance.

The class cCylinder, a descendant of cCircle, declares a single data member, height, to store the height of the cylinder. The class inherits the member radius needed to store the radius of the cylinder. The cCylinder class declares a constructor and a number of member functions. The constructor assigns values to the radius and height members when creating a class instance. Notice the use of a new syntax to initialize the members— member height is initialized, and member radius is initialized by invoking the constructor of class cCircle with the argument radiusVal. The functions getHeight and setHeight serve to set and query the value in member height, respectively. The class uses the inherited functions setRadius and getRadius to manipulate the inherited member radius. The function area, which overrides the inherited function cCircle::area(), returns the surface area of the cylinder. Notice that this function explicitly invokes the inherited function cCircle::area(). The function showData displays the radius, height, and area of a class instance.

The function main declares the instance Circle, of class cCircle, and assigns 1 to the circle's radius. In addition, the function declares the instance Cylinder, of class cCylinder, and assigns 10 and 1 to the circle's height and radius, respectively. The function then sends the showData message to the instances Circle and Cylinder. Each object responds to this message by invoking the appropriate member function.

Virtual Functions

As I mentioned previously, polymorphism is an important object-oriented programming feature. Consider the following simple classes and the function main:

```
#include <iostream.h>
class cA
{
    public:
        double A(double x) { return x * x; }
        double B(double x) { return A(x) / 2; }
};

class cB : public cA
{
    public:
        double A(double x) { return x * x * x; }
};

main()
{
    cB aB;
    cout << aB.B(3) << "\n";
    return 0;
}
```

Class cA contains functions A and B, where function B calls function A. Class cB, a descendant of class cA, inherits function B but overrides function A. The intent here is

to have the inherited function `cA::B` call function `cB::A` in order to support polymorphic behavior. What is the program output? The answer is 4.5 and not 13.5! Why? The answer lies in the fact that the compiler resolves the expression `aB.B(3)` by using the inherited function `cA::B`, which in turn calls function `cA::A`. Therefore, function `cB::A` is left out, and the program fails to support polymorphic behavior.

C++ supports polymorphic behavior by offering virtual functions.

Virtual functions, which are bound at runtime, are declared by placing the keyword virtual before the function's return type.

Once you declare a function `virtual`, you can override it only with virtual functions in descendant classes. These overriding functions must have the same parameter list. Virtual functions can override nonvirtual functions in descendant classes.

Virtual Functions

The general syntax for declaring virtual functions is

```
class className1
{
    // member functions
    virtual returnType functionName(<parameter list>);
};

class className2 : public className1
{
    // member functions
    virtual returnType functionName(<parameter list>);
};
```

Example:

This example shows how virtual functions can successfully implement polymorphic behavior in classes `cA` and `cB`:

```
#include <iostream.h>
class cA
{
    public:
        virtual double A(double x) { return x * x; }
        double B(double x) { return A(x) / 2; }
};

class cB : public cA
{
    public:
        virtual double A(double x) { return x * x * x; }
};
```

```
main()
{
    cB aB;
    cout << aB.B(3) << "\n";
    return 0;
}
```

This example displays 13.5, the correct result, because the call to the inherited function cA::B is resolved at runtime by calling cB::A.

DO   **DON'T**

DO use virtual functions when you have a callable function that implements a class-specific behavior. Declaring such a function as virtual ensures that it provides the correct response that is relevant to the associated class.

DON'T declare a member function as virtual by default. Virtual functions have some additional overhead.

Let's look at an example. Listing 11.4 shows the source code for the program CLASS4.CP. The program creates a square and a rectangle, and displays their dimensions and areas. No input is required.

Type

Listing 11.4. Source code for the program CLASS4.CP.

```
1: // Program that demonstrates virtual functions
2:
3: #include <iostream.h>
4:
5: class cSquare
6: {
7:   protected:
8:     double length;
9:
10:   public:
11:     cSquare(double len) { length = len; }
12:     double getLength() { return length; }
13:     virtual double getWidth() { return length; }
14:     double getArea() { return getLength() * getWidth(); }
15: };
16:
17: class cRectangle : public cSquare
18: {
19:   protected:
20:     double width;
21:
22:   public:
23:     cRectangle(double len, double wide) :
```

continues

11

Listing 11.4. continued

```
24:          cSquare(len), width(wide) {}
25:      virtual double getWidth() { return width; }
26: };
27:
28: main()
29: {
30:    cSquare square(10);
31:    cRectangle rectangle(10, 12);
32:
33:    cout << "Square has length = " << square.getLength() << "\n"
34:         << "         and area   = " << square.getArea() << "\n";
35:    cout << "Rectangle has length = "
36:         << rectangle.getLength() << "\n"
37:         << "            and width  = "
38:         << rectangle.getWidth() << "\n"
39:         << "            and area   = "
40:         << rectangle.getArea() << "\n";
41:    return 0;
42: }
```

Here is a sample session with the program in Listing 11.4:

```
Square has length = 10
        and area   = 100
Rectangle has length = 10
          and width  = 12
          and area   = 120
```

The program in Listing 11.4 declares the classes cSquare and cRectangle to model squares and rectangles, respectively. The class cSquare declares a single data member, length, to store the length (and width) of the square. The class declares a constructor with the parameter len, which passes arguments to the member length. The class also declares the functions getLength, getWidth, and getArea. Functions getLength and getWidth both return the value in member length. Notice that the class declares function getWidth as virtual. The function getArea returns the area of the rectangle, calculated by calling the functions getLength and getWidth. I choose to invoke these functions rather than use the data member length so that I can demonstrate how the virtual function getWidth works.

The program declares class cRectangle as a descendant of class cSquare. The class cRectangle declares the data member width and inherits the member length. These members enable the class to store the basic dimensions of a rectangle. The class constructor has the parameters len and wide which pass values to the members len and wide. Notice that the constructor invokes the constructor cSquare and supplies it with the argument len. The constructor initializes the data member width with the value of parameter wide.

The class cRectangle declares the virtual function getWidth. This version returns the value in data member width. The class inherits the member functions getLength and getArea because their implementation is adequate for the cRectangle.

The function main declares the object square as an instance of class cSquare. The instance square has a length of 10. The function main also declares the object rectangle as an instance of class cRectangle. The instance rectangle has the length of 10 and the width of 12.

The output statement in lines 33 and 34 displays the length and area of the instance square. The statement sends the messages getLength and getArea to the above instance in order to obtain the sought values. The instance square invokes the function getArea, which in turn calls the functions cSquare::getLength and cSquare::getWidth.

The output statement in lines 35 through 40 displays the length, width, and area of the instance rectangle. The statement sends the messages getLength, getWidth, and getArea to this instance. The instance responds by calling the inherited function cSquare::getLength, the virtual function cRectangle::getWidth, and the inherited function cSquare::getArea. The latter function calls the inherited function cSquare::getLength and the virtual function cRectange::getWidth to correctly calculate the area of the rectangle.

11

DO / DON'T

DO declare your destructor as virtual. This ensures polymorphic behavior in destroying class instances. In addition, it is highly recommended that you declare a copy constructor and an assignment operator for each class.

DON'T forget that you can inherit virtual functions and destructors for the descendant class, when appropriate. You need not declare shell functions and destructors that simply call the corresponding member of the parent class.

Rules for Virtual Functions

The rule for declaring a virtual function is "once virtual, always virtual." In other words, once you declare a function to be virtual in a class, any subclass that overrides the virtual function must do so using another virtual function (which has the same parameter list). The virtual declaration is mandatory for the descendant classes. At first this rule may seem to lock you in. This limitation is certainly true for object-oriented programming

languages that support virtual functions but not overloaded functions. In the case of C++, the work-around is interesting. You can declare nonvirtual and overloaded functions that have the same name as the virtual function but have a different parameter list. Moreover, you cannot inherit nonvirtual member functions that share the same name with a virtual function. Here is a simple example that illustrates the point:

```
#include <iostream.h>
class cA
{
  public:
    cA() {}
    virtual void foo(char c)
      { cout << "virtual cA::foo() returns " << c << '\n'; }
};

class cB : public cA
{
  public:
    cB() {}
    void foo(const char* s)
      { cout << "cB::foo() returns " << s << '\n'; }
    void foo(int i)
      { cout << "cB::foo() returns " << i << '\n'; }
    virtual void foo(char c)
      { cout << "virtual cB::foo() returns " << c << '\n'; }
};

class cC : public cB
{
  public:
    cC() {}
    void foo(const char* s)
      { cout << "cC::foo() returns " << s << '\n'; }
    void foo(double x)
      { cout << "cC::foo() returns " << x << '\n'; }
    virtual void foo(char c)
      { cout << "virtual cC::foo() returns " << c << '\n'; }
};

main()
{
  int n = 100;
  cA Aobj;
  cB Bobj;
  cC Cobj;

  Aobj.foo('A');
  Bobj.foo('B');
  Bobj.foo(10);
  Bobj.foo("Bobj");
  Cobj.foo('C');
  // if you uncomment the next statement,
  // program does not compile
  // Cobj.foo(n);
```

```
    Cobj.foo(144.123);
    Cobj.foo("Cobj");
    return 0;
}
```

This code declares three classes, cA, cB, and cC, to form a linear hierarchy of classes. Class cA declares function foo(char) as virtual. Class cB also declares its own version of the virtual function foo(char). In addition, class cB declares the nonvirtual overloaded functions foo(const char* s) and foo(int), respectively. Class cC, the descendant of class B, declares the virtual function foo(char) and the nonvirtual and overloaded functions foo(const char*) and foo(double), respectively. Notice that class cC must declare the foo(const char*) function if it needs the function, because it cannot inherit the member function cB::foo(const char*). C++ supports a different function inheritance scheme when there is an overloaded and virtual function involved. The function main creates an instance for each of the three classes and involves the various versions of the member function foo.

Friend Functions

C++ permits member functions to access all the data members of a class. In addition, C++ grants the same privileged access to friend functions. The declaration of friend functions appears in the class and begins with the keyword friend. Other than using the special keyword, friend functions look very much like member functions, except they cannot return a reference to the befriended class because this requires returning the self-reference *this. However, when you define friend functions outside the declaration of their befriended class, you need not qualify the function names with the name of the class.

NEW TERM *Friend functions* are ordinary functions that have access to all data members of one or more classes.

Syntax

Friend Functions

The general form of friend functions is

```
class className
{
    public:
        className();
        // other constructors

        friend returnType friendFunction(<parameter list>);
};
```

Example:

```
class String
{
    protected:
        char *str;
        int len;

    public:
        String();
        ~String();
        // other member functions
        friend String& append(String& str1, String& str2);
        friend String& append(const char* str1,
                              String& str2);
        friend String& append(String& str1,
                              const char* str2);
};
```

Friend classes are able to accomplish tasks that are awkward, difficult, and even impossible with member functions.

Let's look at a simple example for using friend functions. Listing 11.5 contains the source code for the CLASS5.CP program. This program internally creates two complex numbers, adds them, stores the result in another complex number, and then displays the operands and resulting complex numbers.

 Listing 11.5. Source code for the CLASS5.CP program.

```
1: // Program that demonstrates friend functions
2:
3: #include <iostream.h>
4:
5: class Complex
6: {
7:     protected:
8:       double x;
9:       double y;
10:
11:    public:
12:      Complex(double real = 0, double imag = 0);
13:      Complex(Complex& c) { assign(c); }
14:      void assign(Complex& c);
15:      double getReal() const { return x; }
16:      double getImag() const { return y; }
17:      friend Complex add(Complex& c1, Complex& c2);
18: };
19:
20: Complex::Complex(double real, double imag)
21: {
22:   x = real;
23:   y = imag;
24: }
```

```
25:
26: void Complex::assign(Complex& c)
27: {
28:    x = c.x;
29:    y = c.y;
30: }
31:
32: Complex add(Complex& c1, Complex& c2)
33: {
34:    Complex result(c1);
35:
36:    result.x += c2.x;
37:    result.y += c2.y;
38:    return result;
39: }
40:
41: main()
42: {
43:    Complex c1(2, 3);
44:    Complex c2(5, 7);
45:    Complex c3;
46:
47:    c3.assign(add(c1, c2));
48:    cout << "(" << c1.getReal() << " + i" << c1.getImag() << ")"
49:         << " + "
50:         << "(" << c2.getReal() << " + i" << c2.getImag() << ")"
51:         << " = "
52:         << "(" << c3.getReal() << " + i" << c3.getImag() << ")"
53:         << "\n\n";
54:    return 0;
55: }
```

Here is a sample session with the program in Listing 11.5:

```
(2 + i3) + (5 + i7) = (7 + i10)
```

The program in Listing 11.5 declares the class Complex, which models complex numbers. This class declares two data members, two constructors, a friend function (the highlight of this example), and a set of member functions. The data members x and y store the real and imaginary components of a complex number, respectively.

The class has two constructors. The first constructor has two parameters (with default arguments) that enable you to build a class instance using the real and imaginary components of a complex. Because the two parameters have default arguments, the constructor doubles up as the default constructor. The second constructor, complex(complex&), is the copy constructor.

The Complex class declares three member functions. The function assign copies a class instance into another one. The functions getReal and getImag return the value stored in the members real and imag, respectively.

The `Complex` class declares the friend function `add` to add two complex numbers. To make the program short, I do not implement complementary friend functions that subtract, multiply, and divide class instances. What is so special about the friend function `add`? Why not use an ordinary member function to add a class instance? The following declaration of the alternate `add` member function answers these questions:

```
complex& add(complex& c)
```

This declaration states that the function treats the parameter `c` as a second operand. Here is how the member function `add` works:

```
complex c1(3, 4), c2(1.2, 4.5);
c1.add(c2); // adds c2 to c1
```

First, the member function `add` works as an increment and not as an addition function. Second, the targeted class instance is always the first operand. This is not a problem for operations like addition and multiplication, but it is a problem for subtraction and division. That is why the friend function `add` works better by giving you the freedom of choosing how to add the class instances.

The friend function `add` returns a class instance. The function creates a local instance of class `Complex` and returns that instance.

The function `main` uses the member function `assign` and the friend function `add` to perform simple complex operations. In addition, the function `main` invokes the functions `getReal` and `getImag` with the various instances of class `Complex` to display the components of each instance.

Operators and Friend Operators

The program in Listing 11.5 uses a member function and a friend function to implement complex math operations. The approach is typical in C and Pascal, because these languages do not support user-defined operators. By contrast, C++ enables you to declare operators and friend operators. These operators include +, -, *, /, %, ==, !=, <=, <, >=, >, +=, -=, *=, /=, %=, [], (), <<, and >>. Consult a C++ language reference book for more details on the rules of using these operators. C++ treats operators and friend operators as special member functions and friend functions.

Operators and Friend Operators

The general syntax for declaring operators and friend operators is

```
class className
{
    public:
        // constructors and destructor
        // member functions

        // unary operator
        returnType operator operatorSymbol(operand);
        // binary operator
        returnType operator operatorSymbol(firstOperand,
                                                secondOperand);
        // unary friend operator
        friend returnType operator operatorSymbol(operand);
        // binary operator
        friend returnType operator
                        operatorSymbol(firstOperand,
                                                secondOperand);
};
```

Example:

```
class String
{
    protected:
        char *str;
        int len;

    public:
        String();
        ~String();
        // other member functions
        // assignment operator
        String& operator =(String& s);
        String& operator +=(String& s);
        // concatenation operators
        friend String& operator +(String& s1, String& s2);
        friend String& operator +(const char* s1, String& s2);
        friend String& operator +(String& s1, const char* s2);
        // relational operators
        friend int operator >(String& s1, String& s2);
        friend int operator =>(String& s1, String& s2);
        friend int operator <(String& s1, String& s2);
        friend int operator <=(String& s1, String& s2);
        friend int operator ==(String& s1, String& s2);
        friend int operator !=(String& s1, String& s2);
};
```

11

The functions you write use the operators and friend operators just like predefined operators. Therefore, you can create operators to support the operations of classes that model, for example, complex numbers, strings, arrays, and matrices. These operators enable you to write expressions that are far more readable than expressions that use named functions.

Let's look at an example. Listing 11.6 contains the source code for the CLASS6.CP program. I created this program by modifying and expanding Listing 11.5. The new program performs more additions and displays two sets of operands and results.

Type

Listing 11.6. Source code for the CLASS6.CP program.

```
1: // Program that demonstrates operators and friend operators
2:
3: #include <iostream.h>
4:
5: class Complex
6: {
7:    protected:
8:      double x;
9:      double y;
10:
11:   public:
12:     Complex(double real = 0, double imag = 0)
13:       { assign(real, imag); }
14:     Complex(Complex& c);
15:     void assign(double real = 0, double imag = 0);
16:     double getReal() const { return x; }
17:     double getImag() const { return y; }
18:     Complex& operator =(Complex& c);
19:     Complex& operator +=(Complex& c);
20:     friend Complex operator +(Complex& c1, Complex& c2);
21:     friend ostream& operator <<(ostream& os, Complex& c);
22: };
23:
24: Complex::Complex(Complex& c)
25: {
26:   x = c.x;
27:   y = c.y;
28: }
29:
30: void Complex::assign(double real, double imag)
31: {
32:   x = real;
33:   y = imag;
34: }
35:
36: Complex& Complex::operator =(Complex& c)
37: {
38:   x = c.x;
39:   y = c.y;
40:   return *this;
41: }
42:
43: Complex& Complex::operator +=(Complex& c)
44: {
45:   x += c.x;
```

```
46:    y += c.y;
47:    return *this;
48: }
49:
50: Complex operator +(Complex& c1, Complex& c2)
51: {
52:    Complex result(c1);
53:
54:    result.x += c2.x;
55:    result.y += c2.y;
56:    return result;
57: }
58:
59: ostream& operator <<(ostream& os, Complex& c)
60: {
61:    os << "(" << c.x << " + i" << c.y << ")";
62:    return os;
63: }
64:
65: main()
66: {
67:    Complex c1(3, 5);
68:    Complex c2(7, 5);
69:    Complex c3;
70:    Complex c4(2, 3);
71:
72:    c3 = c1 + c2;
73:    cout << c1 << " + " << c2 << " = " << c3 << "\n";
74:    cout << c3 << " + " << c4 << " = ";
75:    c3 += c4;
76:    cout << c3 << "\n";
77:    return 0;
78: }
```

11

 Here is a sample session with the program in Listing 11.6:

```
(3 + i5) + (7 + i5) = (10 + i10)
(10 + i10) + (2 + i3) = (12 + i13)
```

 The new class Complex replaces the assign(Complex&) member function with the operator =. The class also replaces the friend function add with the friend operator +:

```
Complex& operator =(Complex& c);
friend Complex operator +(Complex& c1, Complex& c2);
```

The operator = has one parameter, a reference to an instance of class Complex, and also returns a reference to the same class. The friend operator + has two parameters (both are references to instances of class Complex) and yields a complex class type.

I also took the opportunity to add two new operators:

```
complex& operator +=(complex& c);
friend ostream& operator <<(ostream& os, complex& c);
```

The operator += is a member of class Complex. It takes one parameter, a reference to an instance of class Complex, and yields a reference to the same class. The other new operator is the friend operator <<, which illustrates how to write a stream extractor operator for a class. The friend operator has two parameters: a reference to class ostream (the output stream class) and a reference to class Complex. The operator << returns a reference to class ostream. This type of value enables you to chain stream output with other predefined types or other classes (assuming that these classes have a friend operator <<). The definition of friend operator << has two statements. The first one outputs strings and the data members of class Complex to the output stream parameter os. The friendship status of operator << enables it to access the real and imag data members of its Complex-typed parameter c. The second statement in the operator definition returns the first parameter, os.

The function main declares four instances of class Complex: c1, c2, c3, and c4. The instances c1, c2, and c4 are created with nondefault values assigned to the data members real and imag. The function tests the use of the operators =, +, <<, +=. The program illustrates that you can use operators and friend operators to write code that is more readable and supports a higher level of abstraction.

Summary

Today's lesson introduced you to C++ classes and discussed the following topics:

☐ The basics of object-oriented programming include classes, objects, messages, methods, inheritance, and polymorphism.

☐ You declare base classes to specify the various private, protected, and public members. C++ classes contain data members and member functions. The data members store the state of a class instance, and the member functions query and manipulate that state.

☐ Constructors and destructors support the automatic creation and removal of class instances. Constructors are special members that must have the same name as the host class. You can declare any number of constructors, or none at all. In the latter case, the compiler creates one for you. Each constructor enables you to create a class instance in a different way. There are two special kinds of constructors: the default constructor and the copy constructor. In contrast with constructors, C++ enables you to declare only one parameterless destructor. Destructors automatically remove class instances. The runtime system automatically invokes the constructor and destructor when a class instance comes into and goes out of its scope.

☐ Declaring a class hierarchy enables you to derive classes from existing ones. The descendant classes inherit the members of their ancestor classes. C++ classes are able to override inherited member functions by defining their own versions. If you override a nonvirtual function, you can declare the new version using a different parameter list. By contrast, you cannot alter the parameter list of an inherited virtual function.

☐ Virtual member functions enable your classes to support polymorphic behavior. Such behavior offers a response that is suitable for each class in a hierarchy. Once you declare a function as virtual, you can override it only with a virtual function in a descendant class. All versions of a virtual function in a class hierarchy must have the same signature.

☐ Friend functions are special nonmember functions that can access protected and private data members. These functions enable you to implement operations that are more flexible than those offered by member functions.

☐ Operators and friend operators enable you to support various operations, such as addition, assignment, and indexing. These operators enable you to offer a level of abstraction for your classes. In addition, they assist in making the expressions that manipulate class instances more readable and more intuitive.

11

Q&A

Q What happens if I declare the default, copy, and other constructors as protected?

A Client programs are unable to create instances of that class. However, client programs can use that class by declaring descendant classes with public constructors.

Q Can I use the constructor for typecasting?

A Yes, you can incorporate this kind of typecasting in the creation of a class instance. For example, if the class Complex has the constructor Complex(double real, double imag), you can declare the instance c of class Complex as follows:

```
Complex c = Complex(1.7, 2.4);
```

Q Can I chain messages to an instance?

A Yes, as long as the chained messages invoke member functions that return a reference to the same class that receives the message. For example, if you have a class String with the following member functions:

```
String& upperCase();
string& reverse();
String& mapChars(char find, char replace);
```

you can write the following statement for the instance of class `String` s:

```
s.upperCase().reverse().mapChar(' ', '+');
```

Q **What happens if a class relies on the copy constructor, which is created by the compiler, to copy instances of a class that has pointers?**

A These constructors perform a bit-by-bit copy. Consequently, the corresponding pointer members in both instances end up with the address to the same dynamic data. This kind of duplication is a recipe for trouble!

Q **Can I create an array of instances?**

A Yes; however, the accompanying class must have a default constructor. The instantiation of the array uses the default constructor .

Q **Can I use a pointer to create an instance of class?**

A Yes, you need to use the operators `new` and `delete` to allocate and deallocate the dynamic space for the instance. Here are two examples of using the class `Complex`:

```
Complex* pC;
pC = new Complex;
// manipulate the instance accessed by pointer pC
delete pC;

Complex* pC = new Complex;
// manipulate the instance accessed by pointer pC
delete pC;
```

Workshop

The Workshop provides quiz questions to help you solidify your understanding of the material covered and exercises to provide you with experience in using what you've learned. Try to understand the quiz and exercise answers before continuing on to the next day's lesson. Answers are provided in Appendix B, "Answers."

Quiz

1. Where is the error in the following class declaration?

```
class String {
        char *str;
        unsigned len;
        String();
        String(String& s);
        String(unsigned size, char = ' ');
        String(unsigned size);
        String& assign(String& s);
        ~String();
        unsigned getLen() const;
        char* getString();
        // other member functions
};
```

2. Where is the error in the following class declaration?

```
class String {
    protected:
        char *str;
        unsigned len;
    public:
        String();
        String(const char* s);
        String(String& s);
        String(unsigned size, char = ' ');
        String(unsigned size);
        ~String();
        // other member functions
};
```

3. True or false? The following statement, which creates the instance s based on the above declaration of class String, is correct:

```
s = String("Hello Symantec C++");
```

4. In program CLASS6.CP (Listing 11.6), if you change the declarations of the instances in function main to the following, will the program still compile?

```
Complex c1 = Complex(3, 5);
```

```
Complex c2 = Complex(7, 5);
Complex c3 = c1;
Complex c4 = Complex(2, 3);
```

Exercise

Create program CLASS7.CP from CLASS6.CP by replacing the individual instances c1 through c4 with c, an array of instances.

12

Basic Stream
File I/O

Today's lesson introduces you to file I/O operations using the C++ stream library. Although the STDIO.H library in C has been standardized by the ANSI C committee, the C++ stream library has not. You have a choice of using file I/O functions in the STDIO.H file or those in the C++ stream library. Each of these two I/O libraries offers a lot of power and flexibility. Today's lesson presents basic and practical operations that enable you to read data from and write to files. You learn about the following topics:

☐ Common stream I/O functions

☐ Sequential stream I/O for text

☐ Sequential stream I/O for binary data

☐ Random-access stream I/O for binary data

To learn more about the C++ stream library, consult a C++ language reference book, such as *Tom Swan's C++ Primer* (Sams Publishing).

The C++ Stream Library

The C++ stream I/O library is comprised of a hierarchy of classes that are declared in several header files. The IOSTREAM.H header file that I have used so far is only one of these. Others include IO.H, ISTREAM.H, OSTREAM.H, IFSTREAM.H, OFSTREAM.H, and FSTREAM.H. The IO.H header file declares low-level classes and identifiers. The ISTREAM.H and OSTREAM.H files support the basic input and output stream classes. The IOSTREAM.H file combines the operations of the classes in the previous two header files. Similarly, the IFSTREAM.H and OFSTREAM.H files support the basic file input and output stream classes. The FSTREAM.H file combines the operations of the classes in the previous two header files. There are additional stream library files that offer even more specialized stream I/O.

Note: The C++ ANSI committee eventually will define the standard stream I/O library, and this will end any confusion regarding which classes and header files are part of the standard stream library and which ones are not.

Common Stream I/O Functions

In this section I present stream I/O functions that are common to both sequential and random-access I/O. These functions include open, close, good, and fail, in addition to the operator !.

The open function enables you to open a file stream for input, output, append, and both input and output. The function also enables you to specify whether the related I/O is binary or text.

The *open* Function

The prototype for the open function is

```
void open(const char* filename,
          int mode,
          int m = filebuf::openprot);
```

The parameter *filename* specifies the name of the file to open. The parameter *mode* indicates the I/O mode. Here is a list of arguments for parameter mode that are exported by the IO.H header file:

I/O Mode	Action
in	Open stream for input.
out	Open stream for output.
ate	Set stream pointer to the end of the file.
app	Open stream for append mode.
trunc	Truncate file size to 0 if the file already exists.
nocreate	Raise an error if the file does not already exist.
noreplace	Raise an error if the file already exists.
translated	Translate the character \r into \n for input and the character \n into \r for output.

Examples:

```
// open stream for input
fstream f;
f.open("mySource.dat", ios::in);

// open stream for output
fstream f;
f.open("myTarget.dat", ios:out);

// open stream for input and output
fstream f;
f.open("INCOME.DAT", ios::in | ios::out);
```

12

Note: The file stream classes offer constructors that include the action (and have the same parameters) of function `open`.

The `close` function closes the stream and recuperates the resources involved. These resources include the memory buffer used in the stream I/O operations.

The *close* Function

The prototype for the `close` function is

```
void close();
```

Example:

```
fstream f;
// open stream
f.open("mySource.date", ios::in);
// process file
// now close stream
f.close();
```

The C++ stream library includes a set of basic functions that check the error status of a stream operation. These functions include the following:

☐ The `good()` function returns a nonzero value if there is no error in a stream operation. The declaration of function `good` is

```
int good();
```

☐ The `fail()` function returns a nonzero value if there is an error in a stream operation. The declaration of function `fail` is

```
int fail();
```

☐ The overloaded operator `!` is applied to a stream instance to determine the error status.

The C++ stream libraries offer additional functions to set and query other aspects and types of stream errors.

Sequential Text Stream I/O

The functions and operators involved in sequential text I/O are simple—you have already been exposed to most of them in earlier lessons. The functions and operators include the following:

☐ The stream extractor operator << writes strings and characters to a stream.

☐ The stream inserter operator >> reads characters from a stream.

☐ The getline function reads strings from a stream.

Syntax

The *getline* Function

The prototype for the function getline is

```
istream& getline(char* buffer,
                 int size,
                 char delimiter = '\n');

istream& getline(signed char* buffer,
                 int size,
                 char delimiter = '\n');

istream& getline(unsigned char* buffer,
                 int size,
                 char delimiter = '\n');
```

The parameter *buffer* is a pointer to the string receiving the characters from the stream. The parameter *size* specifies the maximum number of characters to read. The parameter *delimiter* specifies the delimiting character which causes the string input to stop before reaching the number of characters specified by the parameter *size*. The parameter delimiter has the default argument of '\n'.

Example:

```
fstream f;
char textLine[MAX];
f.open("mySource.dat", ios::in);
while (!f.eof()) {
  f.getline(textLine, MAX);
  cout << textLine << "\n";
}
f.close();
```

12

Let's look at an example. Listing 12.1 shows the source code for the IO1.CP program. The program performs the following tasks:

☐ Prompts you to enter the name of an input text file

☐ Prompts you to enter the name of an output text file (the program detects whether the names of the input and output files are the same, and if so, prompts you again for a different output filename)

☐ Reads the lines from the input files and removes any trailing spaces in these lines

☐ Writes the lines to the output file and also to the standard output window

 Listing 12.1. Source code for the IO1.CP program.

```
1:  // C++ program that demonstrates sequential file I/O
2:
3:  #include <iostream.h>
4:  #include <fstream.h>
5:  #include <string.h>
6:
7:  enum boolean { false, true };
8:
9:  const unsigned LINE_SIZE = 128;
10: const unsigned NAME_SIZE = 64;
11:
12: void trimStr(char* s)
13: {
14:   int i = strlen(s) - 1;
15:   // locate the character where the trailing spaces begin
16:   while (i >= 0 && s[i] == ' ')
17:     i--;
18:   // truncate string
19:   s[i+1] = '\0';
20: }
21:
22: void getInputFilename(char* inFile, fstream& f)
23: {
24:   boolean ok;
25:
26:   do {
27:     ok = true;
28:     cout << "Enter input file : ";
29:     cin.getline(inFile, NAME_SIZE);
30:     f.open(inFile, ios::in | ios::translated);
31:     if (!f) {
32:       cout << "Cannot open file " << inFile << "\n\n";
33:       ok = false;
34:     }
35:   } while (!ok);
```

```
36:
37: }
38:
39: void getOutputFilename(char* outFile, const char* inFile,
40:                        fstream& f)
41: {
42:   boolean ok;
43:
44:   do {
45:     ok = true;
46:     cout << "Enter output file : ";
47:     cin.getline(outFile, NAME_SIZE);
48:     if (strcmp(inFile, outFile) != 0) {
49:       f.open(outFile, ios::out | ios::translated);
50:       if (!f) {
51:         cout << "File " << outFile << " is invalid\n\n";
52:         ok = false;
53:       }
54:     }
55:     else {
56:       cout << "Input and output files must be different!\n";
57:       ok = false;
58:     }
59:   } while (!ok);
60: }
61:
62: void processLines(fstream& fin, fstream& fout)
63: {
64:   char line[LINE_SIZE + 1];
65:
66:   // loop to trim trailing spaces
67:   while (fin.getline(line, LINE_SIZE)) {
68:     trimStr(line);
69:     // write line to the output file
70:     fout << line << "\n";
71:     // echo updated line to the output window
72:     cout << line << "\n";
73:   }
74:
75: }
76: main()
77: {
78:
79:   fstream fin, fout;
80:   char inFile[NAME_SIZE + 1], outFile[NAME_SIZE + 1];
81:
82:   getInputFilename(inFile, fin);
83:   getOutputFilename(outFile, inFile, fout);
84:   processLines(fin, fout);
85:   // close streams
86:   fin.close();
87:   fout.close();
88:   return 0;
89: }
```

12

Here is a sample session with the program in Listing 12.1:

```
Enter input file : sample.txt
Enter output file : sample.out
This is line 1
This is line 2
This is line 3
This is line 4
```

The program in Listing 12.1 declares no classes and instead focuses on using file streams to input and output text. The program declares the functions trimStr, getInputFilename, getOutputFilename, processLines, and main.

The function trimStr in lines 12 through 20 deletes the trailing spaces in the strings passed by parameter s. The function declares the local variable i and assigns it the index of the character just before the null terminator. The function uses the while loop in line 13 to perform a backward scan of the characters in string s for the first nonspace character. The statement at line 16 assigns the null-terminator character to the character located right after the last nonspace character in the string s.

The function getInputFilename in lines 22 through 37 obtains the input filename and opens its corresponding input file stream. The parameter inFile passes the name of the input file to the function caller. The reference parameter f passes the opened input stream to the function caller. The function getInputFilename declares the local flag ok. The function uses the do-while loop in lines 26 through 35 to obtain a valid filename and to open that file for input. Line 27 contains the first statement inside the loop that assigns the enumerated value true to the local variable ok. The output statement in line 28 prompts you for the input filename. The statement in line 29 calls the stream input function getline to obtain your input and to store it in the parameter inFile. The statement in line 30 opens the input file using the stream parameter f. The open statement uses the ios::in ¦ ios::translated value to indicate that the stream is opened for translated input. The if statement in line 31 determines whether or not the stream f is successfully opened. If not, the function executes the statements in lines 32 and 33. These statements display an error message and assign the enumerated value false to the local variable ok. The loop's while clause in line 35 examines the condition !ok. The loop iterates until you supply it a valid filename that successfully opens the file for input.

The function getOutputFilename in lines 39 through 60 complements the function getInputFilename and has three parameters. The parameter outFile passes the output filename of the function caller. The parameter inFile supplies the function with the input filename. The function uses this parameter to ensure that the input and output filenames are not the same. The parameter f passes the output stream to the function caller. The implementation of function `getOutputFilename` is very similar to that of function `getInputFilename`. The main difference is that the function `getOutputFilename` calls the function `stricmp` to compare the values in parameter `inFile` and `outFile`. The function uses the result of `stricmp` to determine whether the names of the input and output files are identical. If so, the function executes the statements in the `else` clause in lines 57 and 58. These statements display an error message and assign `false` to the local variable `ok`.

The function `processLines` in lines 62 through 75 reads the lines from the input file stream, trims them, and writes them to the output file stream. The parameters `fin` and `fout` pass the input and output file streams, respectively. The function declares the local string variable `line` and uses the `while` loop in lines 67 through 73 to process the text lines. The `while` clause contains the call to function `getline`, which reads the next line in the input stream `fin` and assigns the input line to variable `line`. The result of function `getline` causes the `while` loop to stop iterating when there are no more input lines. The first statement inside the loop, located at line 68, calls the function `trimStr` and passes it the argument `line`. This function call prunes any existing trailing spaces from the local variable `line`. The statement in line 70 writes the string in variable `line` to the output file stream. The statement in line 72 echoes the string in `line` to the standard output window. I placed this statement in the program so that you can monitor the progress of the program.

The function `main` in lines 76 through 89 declares the file streams `fin` and `fout`, and the string variables `inFile` and `outFile`. The statement in line 82 calls function `getInputFilename` and passes it the arguments `inFile` and `fin`. This call obtains the name of the input file and the input stream through the arguments `inFile` and `fin`, respectively. The statement in line 83 calls the function `getOutputFilename` and passes it the arguments `outFile`, `inFile`, and `fout`. This call obtains the name of the output file and the output stream through the arguments `outFile` and `fout`, respectively. The statement in line 84 calls function `processLines` and passes it the arguments `fin` and `fout`. This call processes the lines in the input file stream `fin` and writes the results to the output file stream `fout`. The statements in lines 86 and 87 close the input and output file streams, respectively.

Sequential Binary File Stream I/O

The C++ stream library offers the overloaded stream functions `write` and `read` for sequential binary file stream I/O. The function `write` sends multiple bytes to an output stream. This function can write any variable or instance to a stream.

Syntax

The *write* Function

The prototype for the overloaded function `write` is

```
ostream& write(const signed char* buff, int num);
ostream& write(const unsigned char* buff, int num);
```

The parameter *buff* is the pointer to the buffer that contains the data to be sent to the output stream. The parameter *num* indicates the number of bytes in the buffer that are sent to the stream.

Example:

```
const MAX = 80;
char buff[MAX+1] = "Hello World!";
int len = strlen(buffer) + 1;
fstream f;
f.open("CALC.DAT", ios::out);
f.write((const unsigned char*)*len, sizeof(len));
f.write((const unsigned char*)buff, len);
f.close();
```

The function read receives multiple bytes from an input stream. This function can read any variable or array from a stream.

Syntax

The *read* Function

The prototype for the overloaded function `read` is

```
istream& read(signed char* buff, int num);
istream& read(unsigned char* buff, int num);
```

The parameter *buff* is the pointer to the buffer that receives the data from the input stream. The parameter *num* indicates the number of bytes to read from the stream.

Example:

```
const MAX = 80;
char buff[MAX+1];
int len;
fstream f;
f.open("CALC.DAT", ios::in);
f.read((const unsigned char*)*len, sizeof(len));
f.read((const unsigned char*)buff, len);
f.close();
```

Let's look at an example that performs sequential binary stream I/O. Listing 12.2 shows the source code for the IO2.CP program. The program declares a class that models dynamic numerical arrays. The stream I/O operations enable the program to read and write both the individual array elements and an entire array in binary files. The program creates the arrays arr1, arr2, and arr3, and then performs the following tasks:

☐ Assigns values to the elements of array arr1 (this array has 10 elements)

☐ Assigns values to the elements of array arr2 (this array has 10 elements)

☐ Assigns values to the elements of array arr3 (this array has 20 elements)

☐ Displays the values in array arr1

☐ Writes the elements of array arr1 to the file ARR1.DAT, one element at a time

☐ Reads the elements of arr1 from the file into the array arr2 (the array arr2 has 10 elements—the same size as array arr1)

☐ Displays the values in array arr2

☐ Displays the values in array arr3

☐ Writes, in one swoop, the elements of array arr3 to file ARR3.DAT

☐ Reads, in one swoop, the data in file ARR3.DAT and stores them in array arr1

☐ Displays the values in array arr1 (the output shows that array arr1 has the same size and data as array arr3)

 Listing 12.2. Source code for the IO2.CP program.

12

```
1: /*
2:     C++ program that demonstrates sequential binary file I/O
3: */
4:
5: #include <iostream.h>
6: #include <fstream.h>
7:
8: const unsigned MIN_SIZE = 10;
9: const double BAD_VALUE = -1.0e+30;
10: enum boolean { false, true };
11:
12: class Array
13: {
14:    protected:
15:       double *dataPtr;
16:       unsigned size;
17:       double badIndex;
18:
19:    public:
20:       Array(unsigned Size = MIN_SIZE);
```

continues

Listing 12.2. continued

```
21:        ~Array()
22:          { delete [] dataPtr; }
23:        unsigned getSize() const { return size; }
24:        double& operator [](unsigned index)
25:          { return (index < size) ? *(dataPtr + index) : badIndex; }
26:        boolean writeElem(fstream& os, unsigned index);
27:        boolean readElem(fstream& is, unsigned index);
28:        boolean writeArray(const char* filename);
29:        boolean readArray(const char* filename);
30: };
31:
32: Array::Array(unsigned Size)
33: {
34:   size = (Size < MIN_SIZE) ? MIN_SIZE : Size;
35:   badIndex = BAD_VALUE;
36:   dataPtr = new double[size];
37: }
38:
39: boolean Array::writeElem(fstream& os, unsigned index)
40: {
41:    if (index < size) {
42:      os.write((unsigned char*)(dataPtr + index), sizeof(double));
43:      return (os.good()) ? true : false;
44:    }
45:    else
46:      return false;
47: }
48:
49: boolean Array::readElem(fstream& is, unsigned index)
50: {
51:    if (index < size) {
52:      is.read((unsigned char*)(dataPtr + index), sizeof(double));
53:      return (is.good()) ? true : false;
54:    }
55:    else
56:      return false;
57: }
58:
59: boolean Array::writeArray(const char* filename)
60: {
61:    fstream f(filename, ios::out);
62:
63:    if (f.fail())
64:       return false;
65:    f.write((unsigned char*) &size, sizeof(size));
66:    f.write((unsigned char*)dataPtr, size * sizeof(double));
67:    f.close();
68:    return (f.good()) ? true : false;
69: }
70:
71: boolean Array::readArray(const char* filename)
72: {
73:    fstream f(filename, ios::in);
74:    unsigned sz;
```

```
75:
76:      if (f.fail())
77:        return false;
78:      f.read((unsigned char*) &sz, sizeof(sz));
79:      // need to expand the array
80:      if (sz != size) {
81:        delete [] dataPtr;
82:        dataPtr = new double[sz];
83:        size = sz;
84:      }
85:      f.read((unsigned char*)dataPtr, size * sizeof(double));
86:      f.close();
87:      return (f.good()) ? true : false;
88: }
89:
90: main()
91: {
92:    const unsigned SIZE1 = 10;
93:    const unsigned SIZE2 = 20;
94:    char* filename1 = "array1.dat";
95:    char* filename2 = "array3.dat";
96:    Array arr1(SIZE1), arr2(SIZE1), arr3(SIZE2);
97:    fstream f(filename1, ios::out);
98:
99:    // assign values to array arr1
100:    for (unsigned i = 0; i < arr1.getSize(); i++)
101:      arr1[i] = 10 * i;
102:
103:    // assign values to array arr3
104:    for (i = 0; i < SIZE2; i++)
105:      arr3[i] = i;
106:
107:    cout << "Array arr1 has the following values:\n";
108:    for (i = 0; i < arr1.getSize(); i++)
109:      cout << arr1[i] << "   ";
110:    cout << "\n\n";
111:
112:    // write elements of array arr1 to the stream
113:    for (i = 0; i < arr1.getSize(); i++)
114:      arr1.writeElem(f, i);
115:    f.close();
116:
117:    // reopen the stream for input
118:    f.open(filename1, ios::in);
119:
120:    for (i = 0; i < arr1.getSize(); i++)
121:      arr2.readElem(f, i);
122:    f.close();
123:
124:    // display the elements of array arr2
125:    cout << "Array arr2 has the following values:\n";
126:    for (i = 0; i < arr2.getSize(); i++)
127:      cout << arr2[i] << "   ";
128:    cout << "\n\n";
```

continues

12

Listing 12.2. continued

```
129:
130:    // display the elements of array arr3
131:    cout << "Array arr3 has the following values:\n";
132:    for (i = 0; i < arr3.getSize(); i++)
133:      cout << arr3[i] << "  ";
134:    cout << "\n\n";
135:
136:    // write the array arr3 to file ARRAY3.DAT
137:    arr3.writeArray(filename2);
138:    // read the array arr1 from file ARRAY3.DAT
139:    arr1.readArray(filename2);
140:
141:      // display the elements of array arr1
142:    cout << "Array arr1 now has the following values:\n";
143:    for (i = 0; i < arr1.getSize(); i++)
144:      cout << arr1[i] << "  ";
145:    cout << "\n\n";
146:    return 0;
147: }
```

Here is a sample session with the program in Listing 12.2:

```
Array arr1 has the following values:
0   10   20   30   40   50   60   70   80   90

Array arr2 has the following values:
0   10   20   30   40   50   60   70   80   90

Array arr3 has the following values:
0   1   2   3   4   5   6   7   8   9   10   11   12   13   14   15   16   17   18   19

Array arr1 now has the following values:
0   1   2   3   4   5   6   7   8   9   10   11   12   13   14   15   16   17   18   19
```

The program in Listing 12.2 declares a version of class Array that resembles the one in Day 11, Listing 11.2. The main difference is that I used the operator [ ] to replace both the member functions store and recall. This operator checks for valid indices and returns the value in member badIndex if the argument is out of range. In addition to operator [ ], I added the member functions writeElem, readElem, writeArray, and readArray to perform sequential binary file stream I/O.

The function writeElem in lines 39 through 47 writes a single array element to an output stream. The parameter os represents the output stream. The parameter index specifies the array element to write. The function writeElem yields true if the argument for the index is valid and if the stream output proceeds without any error. After writeElem writes an array element, the internal stream pointer advances to the next location.

The function `readElem` in lines 49 through 57 reads a single array element from an input stream. The parameter `is` represents the input stream. The parameter `index` specifies the array element to read. The function `readElem` returns `true` if the argument for the index is valid and if the stream input proceeds without any error. After the `readElem` reads an array element, the internal stream pointer advances to the next location.

The functions `writeElem` and `readElem` permit the same class instance to write and read data elements, respectively, from multiple streams.

The function `writeArray` in lines 59 through 69 writes all elements of the array to a binary file. The parameter `filename` specifies the name of the output file. The function opens an output stream, writes the value of the data member `size`, and then writes the elements of the dynamic array. The `writeArray` function returns `true` if it successfully writes the array to the stream. Otherwise, the function yields `false`. The function opens a local output stream by using the stream function `open` and supplying it with the filename and I/O mode arguments. The I/O mode argument is the expression `ios::out`, which specifies that the stream is opened for binary output only. The function makes two calls to the stream function `write`: the first to write the data member `size`, and the second to write the elements of the dynamic array.

The function `readArray`, defined in lines 71 through 88, reads all the elements of the array from a binary file. The parameter `filename` specifies the name of the input file. The function opens an input stream and reads the value of the data member `size`, and then reads the elements of the dynamic array. The `readArray` function returns `true` if it successfully reads the array to the stream. Otherwise, the function yields `false`. The function opens a local input stream by using the stream function `open` and supplying it the filename and I/O mode arguments. The I/O mode argument is the expression `ios::in`, which specifies that the stream is opened for binary input only. The function makes two calls to the stream function `read`: the first to read the data member `size`, and the second to read the elements of the dynamic array. Another feature of function `readArray` is that it resizes the instance of class `Array` to accommodate the data from the binary file. This means that a dynamic array accessed by the class instance may either shrink or expand, depending on the size of the array stored on file.

The member functions in Listing 12.2 indicate that the program performs two types of sequential binary stream I/O. The first type of I/O, implemented in functions `readElem` and `writeElem`, involves items that have the same data type. The second type of I/O, implemented in functions `readArray` and `writeArray`, involves items that have different data types.

The function main in lines 90 through 147 performs the following relevant tasks:

☐ Declares in line 96 three instances of class Array, namely, arr1, arr2, and arr3 (the first two instances have the same dynamic array size, specified by the constant SIZE1, whereas instance arr3 has a larger size, specified by the constant SIZE2)

☐ Declares in line 97 the file stream f and opens it (using a stream constructor) to access file ARR1.DAT in binary output mode

☐ Uses the for loops in lines 100 and 104 to assign arbitrary values to the instances arr1 and arr3, respectively

☐ Displays the elements of instance arr1 using the for loop in line 108

☐ Writes the elements of instance arr1 to the output file stream f, using the for loop in line 113 to send the writeElem message to instance arr1 and to supply the message with the output file stream f and the loop control variable i

☐ Closes the output file stream by sending the close message to the output file stream f

☐ Opens, in line 118, the file stream f to access the data file ARR1.DAT (this time, the message open specifies a binary input mode)

☐ Reads the elements of instance arr2 (which has not yet been assigned any values) from the input file stream f, using the for loop in line 120 to send the message readElem to instance arr2 and supply the message with the arguments f, the file stream, and i, the loop control variable

☐ Closes the input file stream, in line 122, by sending the message close to the input file stream f

☐ Displays the elements of instance arr2 using the for loop in line 126 (these elements match those of instance arr1)

☐ Displays the elements of instance arr3 by using the for loop in line 132

☐ Writes the entire instance arr3 by sending the message writeArray to instance arr3 (the message writeArray has the filename argument of ARR3.DAT)

☐ Reads the array in file ARR3.DAT into instance arr1, sending the message readArray to instance arr1 and supplying the message with the filename argument of ARR3.DAT

☐ Displays the new elements of instance arr1 using the for loop in line 143

Random-Access File Stream I/O

Random-access file stream operations also use the stream functions `read` and `write` presented in the last section. The stream library offers a number of stream-seeking functions to enable you to move the stream pointer to any valid location. The function `seekg` is one of these functions.

Syntax

The *seekg* Function

The prototype for the overloaded function `seekg` is

```
istream& seekg(long pos);
istream& seekg(long pos, seek_dir dir);
```

The parameter *pos* in the first version specifies the absolute byte position in the stream. In the second version, the parameter *pos* specifies a relative offset based on the argument for parameter *dir*. Here are the arguments for the *dir* parameter:

Argument	Offset
ios::beg	From the beginning of the file
ios::cur	From the current position of the file
ios::end	From the end of the file

Example:

```
const BLOCK_SIZE = 80;
char buff[BLOCK_SIZE] = "Hello World!";
fstream f("CALC.DAT", ios::in | ios::out);
f.seekg(3 * BLOCK_SIZE); // seek block # 4
f.read((const unsigned char*)buff, BLOCK_SIZE);
cout << buff <<< "\n";
f.close();
```

12

 NEW TERM A *virtual array* is a disk-based array that stores fixed-size strings on disk.

Let's look at an example that uses random-access file stream I/O. Listing 12.3 shows the source code for the IO3.CP program and implements a virtual array. The program performs the following tasks:

☐ Uses an internal list of names to create a virtual array object

☐ Displays the elements in the unordered virtual array object

□ Prompts you to enter a character and press the Return key

□ Sorts the elements of the virtual array object (this process requires random-access I/O)

□ Displays the elements in the sorted virtual array object

 Listing 12.3. Source code for the IO3.CP program.

```
 1: /*
 2:    C++ program that demonstrates random-access binary file I/O
 3: */
 4:
 5: #include <iostream.h>
 6: #include <fstream.h>
 7: #include <stdlib.h>
 8: #include <string.h>
 9:
10: const unsigned MIN_SIZE = 5;
11: const unsigned STR_SIZE = 31;
12: const double BAD_VALUE = -1.0e+30;
13: enum boolean { false, true };
14:
15: class VmArray
16: {
17:    protected:
18:      fstream f;
19:      unsigned size;
20:      double badIndex;
21:
22:    public:
23:      VmArray(unsigned Size, const char* filename);
24:      ~VmArray()
25:        { f.close(); }
26:      unsigned getSize() const
27:        { return size; }
28:      boolean writeElem(const char* str, unsigned index);
29:      boolean readElem(char* str, unsigned index);
30:      void Combsort();
31: };
32:
33: VmArray::VmArray(unsigned Size, const char* filename)
34: {
35:    char s[STR_SIZE+1];
36:    size = (Size < MIN_SIZE) ? MIN_SIZE : Size;
37:    badIndex = BAD_VALUE;
38:    f.open(filename, ios::in | ios::out);
39:    if (f.good()) {
40:      // fill the file stream with empty strings
41:      strcpy(s, "");;
42:      f.seekg(0);
43:      for (unsigned i = 0; i < size; i++)
44:        f.write((unsigned char*)s, sizeof(s));
45:    }
```

```
46: }
47:
48: boolean VmArray::writeElem(const char* str, unsigned index)
49: {
50:    if (index < size) {
51:      f.seekg(index * (STR_SIZE+1));
52:      f.write((unsigned char*)str, (STR_SIZE+1));
53:      return (f.good()) ? true : false;
54:    }
55:    else
56:      return false;
57: }
58:
59: boolean VmArray::readElem(char* str, unsigned index)
60: {
61:    if (index < size) {
62:      f.seekg(index * (STR_SIZE+1));
63:      f.read((unsigned char*)str, (STR_SIZE+1));
64:      return (f.good()) ? true : false;
65:    }
66:    else
67:      return false;
68: }
69:
70: void VmArray::Combsort()
71: {
72:    unsigned i, j, gap = size;
73:    boolean inOrder;
74:    char strI[STR_SIZE+1], strJ[STR_SIZE+1];
75:
76:    do {
77:      gap = (gap * 8) / 11;
78:      if (gap < 1)
79:        gap = 1;
80:      inOrder = true;
81:      for (i = 0, j = gap; i < (size - gap); i++, j++) {
82:        readElem(strI, i);
83:        readElem(strJ, j);
84:        if (strcmp(strI, strJ) > 0) {
85:          inOrder = false;
86:          writeElem(strI, j);
87:          writeElem(strJ, i);
88:        }
89:      }
90:    } while (!(inOrder && gap == 1));
91: }
92:
93: main()
94: {
95:    char* data[] = { "Michigan", "California", "Virginia", "Maine",
96:                     "New York", "Florida", "Nevada", "Alaska",
97:                     "Ohio", "Maryland" };
98:    VmArray arr(10, "arr.dat");
```

continues

12

Listing 12.3. continued

```
 99:    char str[STR_SIZE+1];
100:    char c;
101:
102:    // assign values to array arr
103:    for (unsigned i = 0; i < arr.getSize(); i++) {
104:      strcpy(str, data[i]);
105:      arr.writeElem(str, i);
106:    }
107:    // display unordered array
108:    cout << "Unsorted array is:\n";
109:    for (i = 0; i < arr.getSize(); i++) {
110:      arr.readElem(str, i);
111:      cout << str << "\n";
112:    }
113:    // pause
114:    cout << "\nPress any key and then Return to sort the array...";
115:    cin >> c;
116:    // sort the array
117:    arr.Combsort();
118:    // display sorted array
119:    cout << "Sorted array is:\n";
120:    for (i = 0; i < arr.getSize(); i++) {
121:      arr.readElem(str, i);
122:      cout << str << "\n";
123:    }
124:    return 0;
125: }
```

Here is a sample session with the program in Listing 12.3:

```
Unsorted array is:
Michigan
California
Virginia
Maine
New York
Florida
Nevada
Alaska
Ohio
Maryland

Press any key and then Return to sort the array...d
Sorted array is:
Alaska
California
Florida
Maine
Maryland
Michigan
```

```
Nevada
New York
Ohio
Virginia
```

 The program in Listing 12.3 declares the class VmArray. This class models a disk-based dynamic array that stores all its elements in a random-access binary file. Notice that the class declares an instance of class fstream and that there is no pointer to a dynamic array. The class declares a constructor, a destructor, and a number of member functions.

The class constructor, defined in lines 33 through 46, has two parameters, Size and filename. The parameter Size specifies the size of the virtual array. The parameter filename names the binary file that stores the elements of a class instance. The constructor opens the stream f using the stream function open and supplies it the argument of parameter filename and the I/O mode expression ios::in ¦ ios::out. This expression specifies that the stream is opened for binary input and output mode (that is, random-access mode). If the constructor successfully opens the file stream, it proceeds to fill the file with zeros. The class destructor performs the simple task of closing the file stream f.

The functions writeElem and readElem support the random access of array elements. These functions, defined in lines 48 through 68, use the stream function seekg to position the stream pointer at the appropriate array element. The writeElem then calls the stream function write to store an array element (supplied by the parameter str). By contrast, the function readElem calls the stream function read to retrieve an array element (returned by the parameter str). Both functions return Boolean results that indicate the success of the I/O operation.

The VmArray class also declares the Combsort function to sort the elements of the virtual array. This function, defined in lines 70 through 91, uses the readElem and writeElem member functions to access and swap the array elements.

The function main, defined in lines 93 through 125, performs the following relevant tasks:

☐ Declares the instance arr, of class VmArray (this instance stores 10 strings in the binary file ARR.DAT)

☐ Assigns random values to the elements of instance arr, using the for loop in lines 103 through 106 to assign strings accessed by data[i] to the variable str, then to write the value in str to the instance arr by sending it the message writeElem (the arguments for the message writeElem are the string variable, str, and the loop control variable, i)

☐ Displays the unsorted elements of instance arr using the for loop in line 109 (the statement in line 110 sends the message readElem to the instance arr to obtain an element in the virtual array)

☐ Sorts the array by sending the message Combsort to the instance arr

☐ Displays the sorted elements of instance arr using the for loop in line 120 (the statement in line 121 sends the message readElem to the instance arr to obtain an element in the virtual array)

Summary

Today's lesson gave you a brief introduction to the C++ stream I/O library and discussed the following topics:

☐ Common stream functions include open, close, good, fail, and the operator !. The function open opens a file for stream I/O and supports alternate and multiple I/O modes. The function close shuts down a file stream. The functions good and fail indicate the success or failure, respectively, of a stream I/O operation.

☐ C++ enables you to perform sequential stream I/O for text with the operators << and >> as well as the stream function getline. The operator << can write characters and strings (as well as the other predefined data types). The operator >> is suitable for obtaining characters. The function getline enables your applications to read strings from the keyboard or from a text file.

☐ Sequential stream I/O for binary data uses the stream functions write and read to write and read data from any kind of variable.

☐ Random-access stream I/O for binary data uses the seekg function in conjunction with the functions read and write. The seekg function enables you to move the stream pointer to either absolute or relative byte locations in the stream.

Q&A

Q How can I emulate the random access of lines in a text file?

A First read the lines in the file as text, obtain the length of the lines (plus the two characters for the end of each line), and store the cumulative length in a special array; call it lineIndex. This array stores the byte location where each line starts.

The last array element should store the sizeof the file. To access line number i, use the seek or seekg function to locate the offset value in lineIndex[i]. The size of line number i is equal to lineIndex[i+1]-lineIndex[i].

Q How do I write a general-purpose routine to copy between an input and an output file stream?

A You need to use the stream function gcount() to obtain the number of bytes actually read in the last unformatted stream of input. Here is the function copyStream:

```
void copyStream(fstream& fin, fstream& fout,
                unsigned char* buffer, int buffSize)
{
  int n;
  while (fin.read(buffer, buffSize)) {
    n = fin.gcount();
    fout.write(buffer, n);
  }
}
```

Workshop

The Workshop provides quiz questions to help you solidify your understanding of the material covered and exercises to provide you with experience in using what you've learned. Try to understand the quiz and exercise answers before continuing on to the next day's lesson. Answers are provided in Appendix B, "Answers."

12

Quiz

1. True or false? The stream I/O functions read and write are able to correctly read and write any data type.

2. True or false? The stream I/O functions read and write are able to correctly read and write any data type, as long as the type has no pointer members.

3. True or false? The seek and seekg functions expand the file when you supply them an index that is one byte beyond the current end of file.

4. True or false? The arguments of the functions seek and seekg require no range checking.

Exercise

Create program IO4.CP by modifying program IO3.CP. The class VmArray in IO4.CP should have the function binSearch that conducts a binary search on the members of the sorted array. Add a loop at the end of function main to search in the array arr, using the unordered data of the initializing list. (The members of this list are accessed using the pointer data.)

13

Programming the Mac GUI Using the TCL

Today you begin to learn about programming the Macintosh graphical user interface (GUI) using the THINK Class Library (TCL). This lesson offers mostly background information on the classes in the TCL and discusses the Macintosh messages. You learn about the following topics:

☐ Common data types

☐ Overview of the TCL hierarchy

☐ The Macintosh messages

☐ Defining commands

☐ Responding to commands

Note: Today's lesson is shorter than most of the other lessons in this book because I want to give you ample time to browse through the .h and .cp files that support the relevant TCL classes.

Common Data Types

Every operating system and environment uses numerous data types that support different operational aspects. The Macintosh GUI is no exception. Apple Computer, Inc., built the first Macintosh GUI using Object Pascal, a version of the Pascal programming language with object-oriented extensions. The Macintosh Toolbox represents a library of routines that supports programming the Macintosh. Table 13.1 shows a list of data types that are relevant for this book.

Table 13.1. A selection of common data types.

Data Type	Description
Boolean	A Boolean value
Cell	A cell defined with row and column indices
ControlHandle	A handle to a standard Macintosh control
Handle	A pointer to a pointer

Data Type	Description
Point	A point with vertical and horizontal coordinates
Str255	A Pascal string that stores up to 255 characters
StrPtr	A pointer to a Str255-type string

The Str255 type supports the Pascal string. This kind of string stores up to 255 characters and stores the string size at index 0. Thus, if you declare MyStr as a Str255, and assign it the text "123", then character number 0 contains 3, the size of the string, and character indices 1 to 3 contain the ASCII codes for the digits 1, 2, and 3. Many Macintosh Toolbox routines use Str255-type parameters. To pass a literal string as an argument for a Pascal string, you must include the escape character \p right after the opening double-quote. For example, "\pHello World" is a literal string that can be an argument for a Pascal string—without getting fussed at by the compiler!

Overview of the TCL Hierarchy

The THINK Class Library contains numerous classes that fall into several categories. These categories include classes that handle common data structures, events, applications, the desktop, windows, and controls. The next four sections introduce you to some of the categories of classes in the THINK Class Library. I focus on the classes that are related to the application, windows, and controls because they are relevant to building the graphical user interface.

DO   DON'T

DO study the TCL hierarchy chart that comes with Symantec C++ to view how the various classes are derived—sometimes from multiple parent classes.

DON'T forget that the next sections give an overview of only the relevant classes. I do not include the full list.

13

The Event and Task Classes

This category of classes supports events and tasks. The event and task classes are as follows:

Class	Description
CAppleEvent	Supports objects that contain an Apple event as well as its reply. Apple events include Open Application, Open Documents, Print Documents, and Quit Application.
CAppleEventObject	Supports the operations needed by the Apple event class.
CAppleEventSender	Enables you to create and emit Apple events to other applications and to receive and interpret replies to Apple events.
CTask	An abstract class that supports nonundo-able (that is, irreversible) tasks.
CTextStyleTask	Supports the Undo operation for the style commands in an object whose class is a descendant of class CAbstractText.
CStyleTEStyleTask	Supports the Undo and Redo operations for the style commands in a CStyleText object.
CTextEditTask	Supports the Undo operation for typing in and editing an object whose class is a descendant of CAbstractText.
CStyleTEEditTask	Supports the Undo and Redo operations for typing in and editing CStyleText controls.
CMouseTask	An abstract class that supports tracking the mouse.
CTableDragger	Manages tracking the mouse for the class CTable (which supports a two-dimensional data table).

The Application Classes

This category of classes supports running and managing the Macintosh applications. The application classes are as follows; the first two are also the ancestor classes for the window and control classes:

Class	Description
CCollaborator	An abstract class that enables its descendants to rely on one another by announcing changes to each other.

Class	Description
CBureaucrat	An abstract class that supports a link in the chain of commands. This class enables the instances of its descendants to respond to menu commands, mouse clicks, and control-generated commands.
CDirectorOwner	An abstract class for objects that possess directors. A director is an object that manages the intercommunication between an application and a window.
CApplication	The parent of all your application classes. The runtime system creates only one instance of the application class.
x_CApp	The low-level application class generated by the Visual Architect utility (more about this utility in tomorrow's lesson).
CApp	The high-level application class generated by the Visual Architect utility. This class is a descendant of class x_CApp.
CDirector	The base class for a subhierarchy that manages windows which handle commands. Directors stand between the application's data that appears in a window and the panes in that window.
CDialogDirector	The base class for a director that manages modal and modeless dialog boxes (Day 21 discusses modal and modeless dialog boxes in more detail).
CDLOGDirector	Supports the director that creates dialog boxes from predefined resources (see Appendix A, "Resources").
CDocument	Supports furnishing and manipulating the application's data.
CSaver<CCollaborator>	Supports the standard Open, Close, Save, and Revert operations. The class works with object I/O to store and recall objects in files.
x_CMain	The low-level class that supports the main window in your application. The Visual Architect utility generates this class by customizing a template file.
CMain	The high-level class that supports the main window in your application. The Visual Architect utility generates this class by customizing a template file. The CMain class is a descendant of x_CMain.

13

The Views Classes

This category of classes supports various windows and panes. The views classes are as follows:

Class	Description
CView	An abstract class that supports visual objects.
CPane	An abstract class that defines a drawing area inside a window or within another pane.
CPanorama	Supports panes that display items which are larger than the frame of the pane. Thus, the pane becomes the scrollable viewport that shows part of the items.
CPopupPane	An abstract class that supports pop-up menu panes. A pop-up menu pane is a pane that has a CPopupMenu instance, which pops up a menu when you click the pane.
CWindow	Enables TCL-based programs to manipulate Macintosh windows.
CDialog	An abstract class that supports modal and modeless dialog boxes.
CDLOGDialog	Builds dialog boxes using predefined dialog resources (see Appendix A, "Resources").
CDesktop	Supports the desktop view that contains all other windows. An application has one instance of this class.
Bartender	An independent class that manages the menu bar, menus, and menu items.

The Control Classes

This category of classes supports the various kinds of controls. The control classes are as follows:

Class	Description
CControl	An abstract class that supports buttons, scroll bars, check boxes, and radio controls.
CButton	Supports the standard Macintosh button control.
CRadioControl	Supports the standard Macintosh radio control.
CCheckBox	Supports the standard Macintosh check box.

Class	Description
CScrollBar	Supports the standard Macintosh scroll bar.
CAbstractText	An abstract class that supports the edit text box control.
CEditText	Supports a pane that displays and edits text.
CStaticText	Supports static text that cannot be edited.
CStyleText	Supports a pane that displays text using one or more text styles.
CDialogText	Supports an edit box that is in a dialog box.
CIntegerText	Supports an edit box that specializes in the input of integers. The class also supports input validation.
CTable	Supports a data table control that displays information in rows and columns.
CArrayPane	Supports a list box control that displays a single column of data.
CStdPopupPane	Supports the standard pop-up menu pane.
CArrowPopupPane	Supports the arrow pop-up pane control, which appears as a downward-pointing arrow. When you click on this control, you view the associated menu.
CSwissArmyButton	The base class for the next six classes (CShapeButton, CRoundRectButton, CRectOvalButton, CPolyButton, CPictureButton, and CLine).
CShapeButton	The base class for the rectangle, oval, and round-rectangle buttons.
CRoundRectButton	Supports a rounded rectangle button.
CRectOvalButton	Supports a button that has a rectangle or oval shape.
CPolyButton	Supports a polygon-shaped button.
CPictureButton	Supports a multiple-state button that is drawn using a set of pictures.
CLine	Draws a line between two points.
CIconPane	Supports a simple icon button.
CIconButton	Supports a multi-state icon button.

The GUI Events and Messages

The Macintosh operating system is event-driven, enabling it to respond to multiple kinds of events that provide input. Examples of these events include clicking the mouse button,

typing text in an edit box, and inserting a disk. The Macintosh operating system also allows its components (both visual and non-visual) to generate events. Thus, the Macintosh operating system supports the object model.

The object model views the applications and their components as objects that communicate with each other and with the outside world. When you click the mouse button, you generate an event that is handled by the currently active application. Where you click the mouse determines which part of the application responds to your mouse click. If you click, for example, on a button, then that button (and not any one of its sibling controls) responds to the mouse-click event. The beauty of the Macintosh operating system is that it enables events to be handled in a hierarchical way. For example, the button you click may offer no response (or a limited response), and then pass the event to its supervisor object (the object one level up in the object's hierarchy). This object may not respond to the event either and pass the event to *its* supervisor. The application object is the ultimate supervisor that decides what to do with the event in a program.

The Macintosh Toolbox defines the structure `EventRecord` to package an event:

```
struct EventRecord {
    short what;
    long message;
    long when;
    Point where;
    short modifiers;
};
```

The member `what` is the event type code. Table 13.2 shows the predefined constants for the event type codes. The member message represents the event message. The values for this member range from character codes to addresses. The member `when` indicates the time in ticks (a tick is 1/60 second) when the event was posted. The member `where` contains the coordinates of the event. The member `modifiers` contains the states of the Command key, Shift key, Option key, and mouse button. Table 13.3 shows the predefined constants for the `modifiers` member. Table 13.4 shows the bitmap for the `modifiers` member.

Table 13.2. The predefined constants for the event type codes.

Constant	Value	Meaning
nullEvent	0	No event pending
mouseDown	1	Mouse button pressed
mouseUp	2	Mouse button released
keyDown	3	Key pressed

Constant	Value	Meaning
KeyUp	4	Key released
autoKey	5	Key held down
updateEvt	6	Window requires updating
diskEvt	7	Disk is inserted
activateEvt	8	Activate or deactivate window
osEvt	15	Operating system event
kHighLevelEvent	23	High-level event

Table 13.3. The predefined constants for the modifiers member.

Constant	Value	Meaning
activeFlag	1	Window being activated, or mouse-button-down event caused foreground switch
btnState	128	Mouse button up
cmdKey	256	Command key down
shiftKey	512	Shift key down
alphaLock	1024	Caps Lock key down
optionKey	2048	Option key down
controlKey	4096	Control key down

13

Table 13.4. The bitmap for the modifiers member.

Bit Number	Meaning
0	Window being deactivated or mouse-button-down event caused foreground switch
1	Unused
2	Unused

continues

Table 13.4. continued

Bit Number	Meaning
3	Unused
4	Unused
5	Unused
6	Unused
7	Mouse button up (1) or down (0)
8	Command key up (1) or down (0)
9	Shift key up (1) or down (0)
10	Caps Lock key up (1) or down (0)
11	Options key up (1) or down (0)
12	Control key up (1) or down (0)
13	Right Shift key up (1) or down (0)
14	Right Option key up (1) or down (0)
15	Right Control key up (1) or down (0)

The Visual Architect utility, which I present in tomorrow's lesson, uses the TCL classes to translate various kinds of events into commands. Thus, for example, selecting a menu command, clicking a button, and double-clicking a list box item all are events that generate commands. Dealing with commands enables the Macintosh operating system to streamline handling events. This means that you can have a menu item and a button generate the same command. Consequently, the function that handles a command doesn't need to be concerned about who generated the event behind that command.

Defining Commands

The Visual Architect utility enables you to define your own commands. Once you define these *custom* commands, you then can associate them with controls (Day 14 shows you how to carry out both of these tasks). Defining and associating a command involves using dialog boxes. The typical style for naming commands uses the letters *cmd* as the first three characters of the name followed by a descriptive name. For example, `cmdCalcValue` is a custom command whose name suggests that it is used to calculate a certain value.

Responding to Commands

The remainder of the lessons in this book focus on responding to commands generated by various events. The Visual Architect utility generates the member function x_CMain::DoCommand, which is responsible for handling various commands that you define. Here is a sample function listing:

```
void x_CMain::DoCommand(long theCommand)

{
    switch (theCommand)
    {
        case cmdAppendString:
            DoCmdAppendString();
            break;
        case cmdGetSelection:
            DoCmdGetSelection();
            break;
        case cmdInsertString:
            DoCmdInsertString();
            break;
        default:
            CDocument::DoCommand(theCommand);
    }
}
```

The member function DoCommand has the parameter theCommand which specifies the command to be handled. The function has a switch statement with case labels to handle the custom commands you create for your application. The above sample comes from a program that has the custom commands cmdAppendString, cmdGetSelection, and cmdInsertString. Each case label calls a DoCmd*XXXX* function that also is generated by the Visual Architect utility. Because the DoCmd*XXXX* functions implement the responses you wish to see in the application, you need to manually insert the code in these functions.

Summary

Today's lesson introduced you to the world of programming Macintosh applications and covered the following topics:

- [ ] You learned about the common data types, such as Boolean, Point, and Str255, used by the Macintosh Toolbox.

- [ ] An overview of the THINK Class Library hierarchy introduced you to the categories of TCL classes. You also learned some details about the categories of classes that are relevant to this book; they support events, tasks, applications, views, and controls.

13

☐ You learned the basics of messages in Macintosh applications. Macintosh applications and their components are event-driven and communicate with each other using messages. The Visual Architect utility creates source code (and uses the TCL classes) which converts events into commands.

☐ You can use the Visual Architect utility to define your own custom commands to support particular operations in your programs.

☐ The member function `DoCommand` responds to various commands. In the case of your custom commands, they are handled by the member function `x_CMain::DoCommand`.

Q&A

Q Do the various application classes handle commands using the function `DoCommand`?

A Yes. Each application-related class in your program has its own version of member function `DoCommand` to handle specific commands.

Q Can I extend the control classes to support particular operations?

A Yes. In fact, the Visual Architect utility supports this feature. Days 19, 20, and 21 offer examples for extending TCL classes that support controls and dialog boxes.

Q Where do I get more information about the Macintosh Toolbox that offers the low-level routines for Macintosh programs?

A Apple Computer has written a set of *Inside Macintosh* books that discuss various aspects of the Macintosh Toolbox.

Workshop

The Workshop provides quiz questions to help you solidify your understanding of the material covered and exercises to provide you with experience in using what you've learned. Try to understand the quiz and exercise answers before continuing on to the next day's lesson. Answers are provided in Appendix B, "Answers."

Quiz

1. True or false? Your applications are instances of class CApplication.

2. True or false? The class CControl supports the button, scroll bar, check box, and radio controls.

3. What class supports the integer edit box?

4. What class supports the icon button?

5. True or false? The class CCollaborator is the parent of the views, application, and control classes.

6. True or false? The function DoCommand handles both commands and events.

7. True or false? The class CListBox supports the list box control.

8. What TCL classes are generated by the Visual Architect utility?

Exercise

Using the standard Macintosh text editor, browse through the following header files (move to the THINK Class Library 2.0 folder, which is located in the Development folder's Symantec C++ folder):

1. File CButton.h in the Control Classes folder

2. File CStaticText.h in the Control Classes folder

3. File CEditBox.h in the Control Classes folder

4. File CDialogText.h in the Dialog Classes folder

5. File CRadioControl.h in the Control Classes folder

6. File CCheckBox.h in the Control Classes folder

7. File CArrayPane.h in the Table Classes folder

8. File CScrollBar.h in the Control Classes folder

9. File CStdPopupPane.h in the Control Classes folder

13

Using the Visual Architect Utility

The Visual Architect utility is a versatile tool that greatly simplifies the process of creating Macintosh GUI programs using the TCL classes. The remaining chapters in this book present various aspects of creating Macintosh GUI programs using the Visual Architect utility. In today's lesson you learn about the following topics:

- ☐ Creating views
- ☐ Editing views
- ☐ Editing commands
- ☐ Editing menus
- ☐ Editing classes
- ☐ Generating the code

Note: This chapter discusses, in general, the steps involved with using the parts of the Visual Architect utility that are relevant to this book. The remaining chapters in the book show these steps as they are applied to specific program projects. So, if the general steps seem too general for you, fret not. My aim is to *prepare you* for what the Visual Architect utility can do.

An Overview

The Visual Architect utility is a visual programming tool that uses menus and dialog boxes to assist you in creating, editing, and updating program projects. The Visual Architect is armed with many template files that it uses to create custom code for you. It also provides you with a tools palette for selecting the various controls you want to draw on windows and dialog boxes. Using menu commands and dialog boxes, you specify how to customize the code for these views.

When you create a new project, the THINK Project Manager brings up the New Project dialog box, shown in Figure 14.1, and offers you a choice of project type. To create a project that involves the Visual Architect utility, select the Visual Architect Project option. The THINK Project Manager then creates such a project and displays a long list of files in the project window. To invoke the Visual Architect utility, double-click on the file Visual Architect.rsrc, which is located in the top part of the files list.

Figure 14.1. *The New Project dialog box.*

Creating Views

The Visual Architect creates projects with a default main window. To create additional views (that is, windows, dialog boxes, and so on) invoke the View | New View... command. This command brings up the New View dialog box, shown in Figure 14.2. The dialog box contains the following controls:

☐ The Name edit box in which you type the name of the view. The Visual Architect uses this name to construct the names of classes that support the view. For example, if you enter the name `Sample Dialog`, the Visual Architect creates the view-supporting classes `CSample_Dialog` and `x_CSample_Dialog`.

☐ The View Kind pop-up menu pane, which enables you to specify the kind of view. You can select from Dialog (the default), Floating Window, Main Window, Modal Dialog, New... Dialog, Splash Screen, SubView, Tearoff Menu, and Window.

☐ The OK and Cancel buttons.

Figure 14.2. *The New View dialog box.*

When you create a new view, the Visual Architect presents you with an empty window such as the one shown in Figure 14.3. You can then draw controls on that view by selecting a control from the Tools palette, shown in Figure 14.4.

14

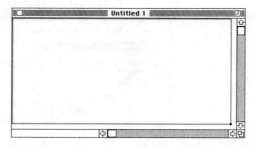

Figure 14.3. *The empty new window.*

Figure 14.4. *The Tools palette.*

Figure 14.5 shows the palette's tools with labels. You select a control tool by clicking on the tool, and then you draw that control in the new view.

Select	Picture	Rectangle
Static text	Scroll bar	Rounded rectangle
Edit box	Icon button	Uncontrained line
Button	Picture button	Oval
Radio control	List/Table	Polygon
Check Box	Subview	
Popup Menu	Panorama	
Icon	Straight line	

Figure 14.5. *The labeled tools in the Tool palette.*

The process of drawing the controls is simple:

1. Position the mouse where you want the control's upper-left corner or left side to appear.

2. Hold the mouse button down to start drawing the control.

3. Drag the mouse to the right and downward to create the rectangular area for the control.

4. Release the mouse button to end drawing the control.

The static text requires that you type in the control's title and then click outside the control to define it. I say more about the static text control in Day 16.

The following several subsections describe each of the control tools in the Tool Palette.

The Static Text Tool

The **Static text** tool draws fixed text that you cannot edit by clicking on it with the mouse. Static text controls typically label other controls that do not have their own captions or titles, such as edit boxes. A program can alter the characters of a static text control to update its message or comment.

The Edit Box Tool

The **Edit box** (also called the "edit text box" or "text box") tool creates a control that displays editable text in a rectangular box. Edit boxes enable programs to accept user input that is not part of a predefined list.

The Button Tool

The **Button** tool creates a pushbutton control, which is a rectangle with rounded edges and a caption inside it. You click on this control with the mouse to perform a specific action, such as closing a window, processing a file, and so on.

The Radio Control Tool

The **Radio control** tool creates a radio button control, which is a small round button that works as a toggle switch to enable and disable options. When you click the radio control, you toggle the small, thick dot that appears inside the circular border. When the dot is present, the control is enabled.

14

The Check Box Tool

The **Check Box** tool creates a control that appears as a button with a square border. When you click a check box control, you toggle the × which appears inside the control's border. When the × mark is present, the control is enabled.

The Scroll Bar Tool

The **Scroll bar** tool creates a control that enables you to select an integer from a range of values. The scroll bar contains the thumb box, which is the control's moving part. Scroll bars frequently are incorporated within other controls, such as list boxes and scrolling windows (that is, panoramas).

The Popup Menu Tool

The **Popup Menu** tool creates a pop-up menu pane control that pops up a predefined or custom menu. You can think of such a menu as a list of items.

The Icon and Picture Tools

The **Icon** and **Picture** tools create standard TCL icon and picture controls, respectively, which appear in either color or black-and-white.

The Icon Button and Picture Button Tools

The **Icon button** and **Picture button** tools create button controls represented by icons and pictures, respectively (instead of the generic button shapes).

The List/Table Tool

The **List/Table** tool creates a control that supports a list box or a table (two-dimensional spreadsheet). These controls support lists of text, icons, and pictures.

The Subview Tool

The **Subview** tool creates panes that are subviews placed inside other panes. A subview is an independent pane that you edit separately.

The Panorama Tool

The **Panorama** tool creates a generic scrollable panorama that contains text or graphics.

The Geometric Shape Tools

The **Straight line**, **Rectangle**, **Rounded rectangle**, **Unconstrained line**, **Oval**, and **Polygon** tools support basic geometric shapes that you can include in a view.

Editing Views and Controls

The Visual Architect creates the various controls and views using default values. These values are the best general-purpose values. You can customize the views and controls to fine-tune the default values.

Editing a View

To edit the currently selected view, invoke the View | View Info... command. The Visual Architect displays the Dialog Info dialog box shown in Figure 14.6. This dialog box enables you to select the kind of view you want to use at runtime. You also can edit the view's name, title, and associated window class. The Visual Architect uses other dialog boxes for editing the Float window and the Subview. Because I do not cover these views in this book, I won't discuss their related dialog boxes.

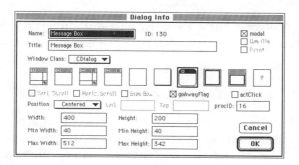

Figure 14.6. *The Dialog Info dialog box.*

14

Editing Controls

To edit a control after you have finished defining it, you need to double-click on it. The Visual Architect brings up a dialog box whose title is the control's identifier. Figure 14.7 shows a sample dialog box for the button control.

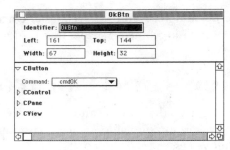

Figure 14.7. *The button control dialog box.*

The dialog box has two parts: a fixed pane that contains edit boxes you use to specify the control's identifier, upper-left corner coordinates, width, and height. The second pane is a scrollable pane which shows the classes that support the control. Each class has the down-arrow symbol located to the left of the class name. When you click this symbol, you view the class's attributes that contribute to the control's characteristics and operations. For example, if you click the down-arrow symbol associated with the class CButton, you view the Command pop-up menu pane. This pane enables you to associate a command with the button currently being edited.

In the case of other controls, the dialog boxes for editing their attributes are very similar. You will become familiar with these dialog boxes in the next chapters.

Editing Commands

Commands represent an essential part of *animating* a program, so to speak. The Macintosh runtime system uses commands to invoke various kinds of response functions. The Visual Architect has a rich set of predefined commands, and it also enables you to add your own custom commands. These custom commands support operations that are particular to your program.

To define new commands, the Visual Architect provides the Edit | Commands command. This command brings up the Commands dialog box, as shown in Figure 14.8. The dialog box contains the following controls:

☐ A scrollable list box (on the left side of the dialog box) that shows the currently defined commands. The list contains both the predefined commands and any custom commands you have defined so far.

☐ The edit box, which contains the name of the currently selected command. This control appears under the title of the dialog box.

☐ The Number static text, which shows the ID number of the currently selected command.

☐ The In Class pop-up menu pane, which shows the class associated with the command. As you'll see in the remaining chapters, you need to associate a custom command with a window or dialog box class. Typically, this book's program projects associate custom commands with the class CMain. The Visual Architect enables you also to associate a command with the application class CApp, and any other custom class you already have defined.

☐ The Do pop-up menu pane, which offers the choices of doing nothing with the command, calling a member function in the class specified by the In Class pop-up menu pane, or opening a new view.

☐ The View pop-up menu pane, which enables you to specify the view to open when you select the Open command in the Do pop-up menu pane.

☐ The OK and Cancel buttons.

Figure 14.8. *The Commands dialog box.*

To define a new command, you first need to have the Commands dialog box visible and active. You then perform the following steps:

1. Invoke the Edit | New Command (or use the ⌘K shortcut) to add a new command. This action puts the Commands dialog box into the new command definition mode.

2. Type the name of the new command in the edit box. Your custom commands should start with the letters cmd and include at least one more letter or digit. The Visual Architect automatically assigns an ID number for your custom command.

3. Select an item from the In Class pop-up menu pane. In most cases, select the class CMain.

4. Select the associated type of action from the Do pop-up menu pane. In most cases, select the item Call.

5. Click the OK button to accept your new custom command.

Deleting a command is very easy. You bring up the Commands dialog box, select the command you want to delete by clicking on it in the list box, and then press the Delete key. That's all!

Editing Menus

The Visual Architect creates applications with a default menu bar that contains the Apple menu along with the File and Edit menus. In addition to these visible menus, the Visual Architect possesses other predefined menus that are not visible by default. These menus include the Font, Size, and Style menus. You can make these menus visible if you need them in your own application.

Editing the Menu List

The Visual Architect enables you to view, add, delete, and edit menus in the pool of available menus (which includes both visible and invisible menus). To view this pool of available menus, invoke the Edit | Menus command. The Visual Architect brings up the Menus dialog box, as shown in Figure 14.9. The Menus dialog box contains the following controls:

☐ The scrollable list box, which shows the available menus.

☐ The edit box, which displays the name of the currently selected menu.

☐ The Apple Menu radio control.

☐ The Edit Menu Items button. When you click this button, the Visual Architect displays the Menu Items dialog box (more about this dialog box later in this section).

☐ The MENU ID edit box, which displays the ID of the menu resource.

☐ The MDEF ID edit box, which contains the custom menu definition procedure. The default value is 0.

☐ The OK and Cancel buttons.

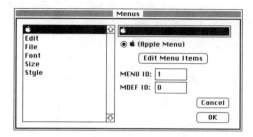

Figure 14.9. *The Menus dialog box.*

To add a new menu, you first need to have the Menus dialog box visible and active. You then perform the following steps:

1. Invoke the Edit | New Menu command (or use the ⌘K shortcut).

2. Type the name of the new menu in the edit box.

3. Click the Edit Menu Items button to prepare to define (and edit) the menu items in the new menu.

Editing Menu Items

After you click the Edit Menu Items button, you see a dialog box that resembles the one in Figure 14.10. This dialog box has the following controls:

☐ The static text control at the left of the dialog box pane. This control contains the name of the currently selected menu, in this case the Edit menu.

☐ The scrollable list box, which contains the current list of menu items.

☐ The Command pop-up menu pane, which shows the name of the cmd*xxxx* command associated with the currently selected menu item.

☐ The edit box, which contains the name of the currently selected menu item.

☐ The Has Submenu check box, which indicates whether or not the currently selected menu item has a submenu.

☐ The Submenu ID pop-up menu pane, which shows the ID of the submenu.

☐ The Cmd-key edit box, which shows the hot-key character.

☐ The Icon control, which shows the icon associated with the currently selected menu item.

☐ The Mark pop-up menu pane, which shows the initial mark associated with the currently selected menu item.

☐ The OK and Cancel buttons.

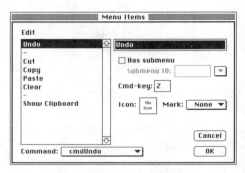

Figure 14.10. *The Menu Items dialog box.*

To add a new menu item, the Menu Items dialog box must be visible and active. You then perform the following steps:

1. Invoke the Edit | New Menu Item command (or use the ⌘K shortcut).

2. Type the name of the new menu item in the edit box.

3. Click on the Commands pop-up menu pane to associate a command with the new menu item.

4. Click on the Cmd-key edit box and enter the hot-key character, if you wish to use one.

5. Click on the Mark pop-up menu pane if you wish to select an initial mark for the new menu item.

6. Click the OK button to close the Menu Items dialog box.

Editing the Menu Bar

The Visual Architect defines a default menu bar that you can view and edit by invoking the Edit | Menu Bar command. This command invokes the Menu Bar dialog box, shown in Figure 14.11. This dialog box is similar to the Menus dialog box except that it has the Add Menu pop-up menu pane. You use this control to add menus to the menu bar from the list of existing menus.

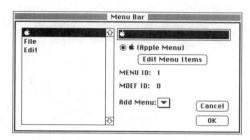

Figure 14.11. *The Menu Bar dialog box.*

Editing Classes

Often you need to customize the operations of a control by extending its associated TCL class. This customization task requires you to create a descendant class that has new data members and new member functions, some of which override inherited member functions. The Visual Architect enables you to define new classes by invoking the Edit | Classes command. This command brings up the Classes dialog box, shown in Figure 14.12. This dialog box contains the following controls:

- ☐ The scrollable list box, which contains the current list of classes in the current project.

- ☐ The edit box, which contains the name of the currently selected class.

- ☐ The Base Class pop-up menu pane, which enables you to select the parent of the new class.

- ☐ The Define Data Members button, which enables you to define data members that have predefined data types.

☐ The Library Class edit box, which enables you to specify the name of one of your custom libraries. This library provides the parent class for the new class you are defining.

☐ The OK and Cancel buttons.

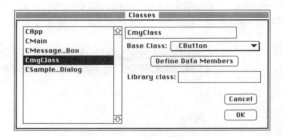

Figure 14.12. *The Classes dialog box.*

To add a new class, the Classes dialog box must be visible and active. You then perform the following commands:

1. Invoke the Edit | New Class command (or use the ⌘K shortcut).

2. Type the name of the new class in the edit box.

3. Click on the Base Class pop-up menu pane to select the parent class.

4. Click the Define Data Members button if you wish to define data members with predefined data types.

5. Click the OK button to close the Classes dialog box.

When you click the Define Data Members button, the Visual Architect brings up the Define Data Members dialog box, shown in Figure 14.13. This dialog box enables you to define new data members and select their predefined data types from the Type pop-up menu pane. If you need to define data members with user-defined types and classes, you need to insert them manually after you generate the code.

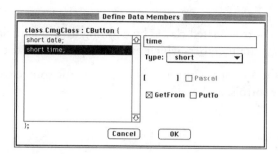

Figure 14.13. *The Define Data Members dialog box.*

Generating the Code

After you create your views, define new commands, draw the controls, and fine-tune the menus, you can generate the source code. Invoke the Generate All.. command from the THINK Project Manager icon menu in the Visual Architect menu bar. This command generates a set of files that reflect your design (more about these files in tomorrow's lesson).

Summary

This chapter presented the relevant aspects of using the Visual Architect utility to create Macintosh applications that use the THINK Class Library. You learned how to:

☐ Create new views that enable you to add dialog boxes, for example, to your applications, and how to draw controls by using the control tools in the Tool palette.

☐ Edit views to select their window style, name, title, and associated class.

☐ Add new commands to the rich set of predefined commands. You can associate the existing commands with various controls that you draw in the view.

☐ Edit menus, menu items, and the menu bar. The Visual Architect utility supports a pool of menus, some of which may not be visible in the default menu bar. You also learned how to add new menus and new menu items to the menu bar as well as how to edit the menu bar.

☐ Follow the basic steps for editing classes. The Visual Architect enables you to extend control-related classes by defining descendant classes. It also supports defining data members which have only predefined data types.

☐ Make the Visual Architect utility generate the source code for your custom views, controls, and menus.

Q&A

Q Is deleting menus, menus items, and classes similar to deleting commands?

A Yes, the Visual Architect uses a similar set of steps. In each case, the associated dialog box must be active, and then you select the item to delete and press the Delete key.

Q What happens to the code generated by the Visual Architect if I go back to the Visual Architect resource and edit it?

A The new set of files overwrites the old set of files.

Q Is there a null command?

A Yes, the command `cmdNull` represents a null command, which performs no task.

Workshop

The Workshop provides quiz questions to help you solidify your understanding of the material covered and exercises to provide you with experience in using what you've learned. Try to understand the quiz and exercise answers before continuing on to the next day's lesson. Answers are provided in Appendix B, "Answers."

Quiz

1. True or false? You can insert a new command directly without first invoking the Commands dialog box.

2. True or false? The Define Data Members dialog box enables you to define data members of any predefined type or previously user-defined type.

3. True or false? You can select specific menus from the pool of menus to display in the menu bar.

4. True or false? You can change the type of view for the main window.

5. True or false? You are responsible for keeping track of the unique numeric IDs for your custom commands.

Exercises

1. Invoke the Commands dialog box, and examine the list of commands.

2. Invoke the Menus dialog box, and examine the menu items in the various menus.

14

To review your second week of learning about programming with Symantec C++, let's look at an enhanced version of the number-guessing game. Listing R2.1 shows the source code for the GAME2.CP program. Although this version interacts with you the same way GAME1.CP does, it uses a class and an enumerated type.

Type

Listing R2.1. Source code for program GAME2.CP.

```
 1:  #include <stdlib.h>
 2:  #include <iostream.h>
 3:  #include <time.h>
 4:
 5:  enum boolean { false, true };
 6:
 7:  class game
 8:  {
 9:    protected:
10:      int n;
11:      int m;
12:      int MaxIter;
```

continues

Listing R2.1. continued

```
13:        int iter;
14:        boolean ok;
15:        void prompt();
16:        void examineInput();
17:
18:     public:
19:        game();
20:        void play();
21:  };
22:
23:  game::game()
24:  {
25:     MaxIter = 11;
26:     iter = 0;
27:     ok = true;
28:
29:     // reseed random-number generator
30:     srand((unsigned int)clock());
31:      n = rand() % 1001;
32:     m = -1;
33:  }
34:
35:  void game::prompt()
36:  {
37:     cout << "Enter a number between 0 and 1000 : ";
38:     cin >> m;
39:     ok = (m < 0) ? false : true;
40:  }
41:
42:  void game::examineInput()
43:  {
44:     // is the user's guess higher?
45:     if (m > n)
46:       cout << "Enter a lower guess\n\n";
47:     else if (m < n)
48:       cout << "Enter a higher guess\n\n";
49:     else
50:       cout << "You guessed it! Congratulations.";
51:  }
52:
53:  void game::play()
54:  {
55:     // loop to obtain the other guesses
56:     while (m != n && iter < MaxIter && ok) {
57:       prompt();
58:       iter++;
59:       examineInput();
60:     }
61:     // did the user guess the secret number
62:     if (iter >= MaxIter || ok == 0)
63:       cout << "The secret number is " << n << "\n";
64:  }
65:
```

```
66:  main()
67:  {
68:    game g;
69:
70:    g.play();
71:    return 0;
72:  }
```

Here is a sample session with the program in Listing R2.1:

```
Enter a number between 0 and 1000 : 500
Enter a lower guess

Enter a number between 0 and 1000 : 250
Enter a higher guess

Enter a number between 0 and 1000 : -1
Enter a higher guess

The secret number is 324
```

The program in Listing R2.1 declares the enumerated type `boolean` to model Boolean values. The program also declares the class `game`, which models the number-guessing game. The class has a number of data members, including the Boolean variable `ok`. In addition, the class declares the protected member functions `prompt` and `examineInput` as well as the public constructor and member function `play`.

The constructor initializes the data members and reseeds the random-number generator. The member function `prompt`, defined in lines 35 through 40, prompts you for input, obtains your input, and based on that input it assigns a true or false value to the variable `ok`.

The function `examineInput`, defined in lines 42 through 51, compares your guess (stored in the data member `m`) with the secret number (stored in the data member `n`) and displays the appropriate message.

The member function `play`, defined in lines 53 through 64, contains the `while` loop that plays the game. The loop statements invoke the member functions `prompt` and `examineInput`, and they also increment the data member `iter`. In addition, the function contains the `if` statement, which displays the secret number if you fail to guess it or if you quit the game.

The function `main` declares the instance `g` of class `game` and sends the message `play` to that instance.

3

WEEK

AT A GLANCE

15

16

17

18

19

20

21

This final week launches you into programming the Macintosh interface. Day 15 starts by showing you how to use the Visual Architect utility to create simple Macintosh applications. Day 16 presents the static text control, and Day 17 presents the edit box and button controls. Day 18 discusses the grouped controls, namely, the check box and radio controls. Day 19 presents the list box control, and Day 20 presents the scroll bar and pop-up menu pane controls. Day 21 shows you how to create and use dialog boxes.

Creating Basic TCL Applications

Today's lesson covers the writing of simple TCL applications using the Visual Architect utility. In addition to becoming familiar with how the Visual Architect uses the TCL classes to build these applications, you learn about the following topics:

☐ Creating a minimal TCL program

☐ Extending the window operations

☐ Responding to menu selections

Creating a Minimal TCL Program

To introduce you to the operations that are supported by the TCL, I present a minimal TCL program. This program also shows you the files generated by the Visual Architect utility. To build the minimal TCL program, perform the following tasks:

1. Create a new project by selecting the Visual Architect Project type from the New Project dialog box.

2. Use MinTCL as the project name, and select the MAC21DAY folder as the parent folder to the new project's folder.

3. When the THINK Project Manager displays the project files (a rather long list of files), click on the file Visual Architect.rsrc. This action brings up the Visual Architect utility (you'll see the THINK Project Manager icon in the menu bar), which displays a window that lists the current project windows. The list has the single item, Main.

4. Click on the item Main to display the main window. This window, by default, has a picture and a static text control.

5. Click on the picture control to select it, and then delete it by pressing the Backspace key.

6. Click on the static text to select it, and then delete it by pressing the Backspace key. Now you have an empty main window.

7. Select the THINK Project Manager icon from the menu bar and invoke the Generate All... command. This command generates the customized source files from a set of template files. The Visual Architect utility places these files in the folder named Source located inside the project's folder.

8. Select the THINK Project Manager icon from the menu bar and invoke the Run command. This command results in the compilation of the project's large number of files (about 150). This is a good time to take a coffee break!

When the compiler finishes building the minimal TCL program, it runs that program. You'll see an empty scrollable window (with the title Main 1) accompanied by a menu bar containing the File and Edit menus. A good number of these menus' commands are disabled. If you invoke the File | New... command, you create another window with the title Main 2. Invoke the File | Quit command to close the windows and end the application. Figure 15.1 shows a sample session with the minimal TCL program.

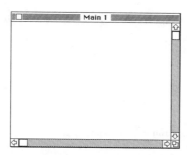

Figure 15.1. *A sample session with the minimal TCL program.*

The Minimal TCL Program Listings

The Visual Architect utility generates a set of source code files to support the minimal TCL program. In this section I present the relevant header and implementation files.

Note: I have edited the listings generated by the Visual Architect utility in this book for the sake of publication.

Listing 15.1 shows the source code for the main.cp implementation file.

Note: Notice the new icon next to the listing head. This icon indicates that the listing contains code generated automatically by the Visual Architect utility; you don't have to type any code yourself.

Listing 15.1. The source code for the main.cp implementation file.

```
1:   /********************************************************
2:   main.c
3:
4:                   Main Program
5:
6:      Copyright (c) 1994 My Software Inc. All rights reserved.
7:
8:    Generated by Visual Architect(TM) 9:28 PM Tue, Jun 7, 1994
9:
10:   ********************************************************/
11:
12:
13:   #include "CApp.h"
14:
15:   void main()
16:
17:   {
18:       CApp    *application = new CApp;
19:
20:       application->ICApp();
21:       application->Run();
22:       application->Exit();
23:   }
```

Analysis Lines 15 to 23 in Listing 15.1 define the function main, which is the starting point for the program. This function performs the following tasks, which indicate that function main performs few but very vital tasks:

☐ Creates a dynamic instance of class CApp and assigns the instance's address to the local pointer application.

☐ Initializes the application instance by sending it the C++ message ICApp.

☐ Runs the program by sending the C++ message Run to the application instance.

☐ Exits the application by sending the C++ message Exit to the application instance.

Note: The Visual Architect inserts the name of the generated program on line 2. You'll notice that the Visual Architect shows the filename extension as .c in the listing, but the created file's actual extension is .cp.

15

Let's look at the header and implementation files for class CApp. Listings 15.2 and 15.3 show the source code for the CApp.h header file and the CApp.cp implementation file, respectively.

Listing 15.2. The source code for the CApp.h header file.

```
 1:  /*************************************************************
 2:   CApp.h
 3:
 4:              Header File For CApp Application Class
 5:
 6:      Copyright (c) 1994 My Software Inc. All rights reserved.
 7:
 8:  Generated by Visual Architect(TM) 9:27 PM Tue, Jun 7, 1994
 9:
10:  This file is only generated once. You can modify it by
11:  redefining in the placeholder definitions and adding any
12:  new methods and data members you wish.
13:
14:  If you change the name of the application, a fresh version
15:  of this file will be generated. If you have made any
16:  changes to the file with the old name, you will have to
17:  copy those changes to the new file by hand.
18:
19:  *************************************************************/
20:
21:  #pragma once
22:
23:  #include "x_CApp.h"
24:
25:  #include <CDialog.h>
26:
27:  class CApp : public x_CApp
28:  {
29:  public:
30:
31:              TCL_DECLARE_CLASS
32:
33:              void    ICApp(void);
34:
35:      virtual   void    ForceClassReferences(void);
36:      virtual   void    DoCommand(long theCommand);
37:
38:              // Remove this function if you do not have
39:              // multiple document types
40:
41:      virtual OSType GetDocTypeFromDialog(CDialogDirector *dialog);
42:  };
43:
44:  //    File Types
45:  //
46:  //    Change the #defines below to reflect the file types
```

continues

Listing 15.2. continued

```
47:  //    your application actually creates or opens
48:
49:  #define kNumFileTypes    1
50:  #define kFileType1       'TEXT'
51:  #define kFileType2       'TEXT'
52:  #define kFileType3       'TEXT'
53:  #define kFileType4       'TEXT'
```

Listing 15.2 declares the class CApp as a descendant of class x_CApp. The class contains declarations for member functions that initialize the class, force class references, manage commands, and obtain the document type. The listing also defines a set of constants which specify default file types.

VArc

Listing 15.3. The source code for the CApp.cp implementation file.

```
1:   /*****************************************************************
2:    CApp.c
3:
4:                    My Application Class
5:
6:      Copyright (c) 1994 My Software Inc. All rights reserved.
7:
8:   Generated by Visual Architect(TM) 9:27 PM Tue, Jun 7, 1994
9:
10:  This file is only generated once. You can modify it by filling
11:  in the placeholder methods and adding any new methods you wish.
12:
13:  If you change the name of the application, a fresh version of
14:  this file will be generated. If you have made any changes to the
15:  file with the old name, you will have to copy those changes to
16:  the new file by hand.
17:
18:  *****************************************************************/
19:
20:  #include "CApp.h"
21:
22:  #include <CDialog.h>
23:  #include <TCLForceReferences.h>
24:
25:  TCL_DEFINE_CLASS_M1(CApp, x_CApp);
26:
27:  /**** C O N S T R U C T I O N / D E S T R U C T I O N
28:                                        M E T H O D S ****/
29:
30:
31:  /*****************************************************************
32:   ICApp
33:
34:  Initialize an Application.
```

```
35:
36:  *****************************************************************/
37:
38:  void     CApp::ICApp()
39:
40:  {
41:  // The values below are:
42:  //
43:  //      extraMasters       - The number of additional master
44:  //                           pointer blocks to be allocated.
45:  //      aRainyDayFund      - The total amount of reserved
46:  //                           memory. When allocation digs into
47:  //                           the rainy day fund, the user is
48:  //                           notified that memory is low. Set
49:  //                           this value to the sum of
50:  //                           aCriticalBalance plus
51:  //                           aToolboxBalance plus a fudge for
52:  //                           user warning.
53:  //      aCriticalBalance   - The part of the rainy day fund
54:  //                           reserved for critical operations,
55:  //                           like Save or Quit. Set this value
56:  //                           to the memory needed for the
57:  //                           largest possible Save plus
58:  //                           aToolboxBalance. This memory will
59:  //                           only be used if
60:  //                           SetCriticalOperation() is set TRUE
61:  //                           or if
62:  //                           RequestMemory()/SetAllocation() is
63:  //                           set FALSE (kAllocCantFail).
64:  //      aToolboxBalance    - The part of the rainy day fund
65:  //                           reserved for ToolBox bozos that
66:  //                           bomb if a memory request fails.
67:  //                           This memory is used unless
68:  //                           RequestMemory()/SetAllocation() is
69:  //                           set TRUE (kAllocCanFail).
70:  //                           Almost all TCL memory allocation
71:  //                           is done with kAllocCanFail, and
72:  //                           yours should be, too. The default
73:  //                           2K is probably enough.
74:
75:      Ix_CApp(4, 24000L, 20480L, 2048L);
76:
77:          // Initialize your own application data here.
78:
79:  }
80:
81:
82:  /****************************************************************
83:   ForceClassReferences      {OVERRIDE}
84:
85:  Reference classes that do object I/O or are created only
86:  by new_by_name.
87:  ****************************************************************/
88:
```

continues

Listing 15.3. continued

```
89:   void CApp::ForceClassReferences(void)
90:
91:   {
92:       x_CApp::ForceClassReferences();
93:
94:           // Insert your own class references here
95:           // by calling TCL_FORCE_REFERENCE for each class
96:           // See x_CApp.cp
97:   }
98:
99:
100:  /**** C O M M A N D   M E T H O D S ****/
101:
102:
103:  /*****************************************************************
104:   DoCommand      {OVERRIDE}
105:
106:  Handle application commands
107:  *****************************************************************/
108:
109:  void CApp::DoCommand(long theCommand)
110:
111:  {
112:      switch (theCommand)
113:      {
114:
115:              // Insert your command cases here
116:
117:          default:
118:              x_CApp::DoCommand(theCommand);
119:              break;
120:      }
121:  }
122:
123:
124:  /*****************************************************************
125:   GetDocTypeFromDialog
126:
127:  Get the document type from the dialog. If you have multiple
128:  document types, you must override this function to extract
129:  the type from the dialog state. (The dialog has been executed
130:  and OK'd by the user.) If you do not have multiple document
131:  types, you can remove this function.
132:  *****************************************************************/
133:
134:  OSType CApp::GetDocTypeFromDialog(CDialogDirector *dialog)
135:
136:  {
137:      return 0;
138:  }
```

 Listing 15.3 contains the definitions of the member functions of class CApp. These functions, which are generated by the Visual Architect utility, offer minimal responses. For example, the member function ICApp (defined in the mostly commented lines 38 to 79) merely invokes the inherited initializing member function Ix_CApp. Another example is member function DoCommand (defined in lines 109 to 121), which responds to the default command by invoking the member function x_CApp::DoCommand.

Let's look at the header and implementation files for class x_CApp. Listings 15.4 and 15.5 show the source code for the x_CApp.h header file and the x_CApp.cp implementation file, respectively.

 Listing 15.4. The source code for the x_CApp.h header file.

```
 1:  /*****************************************************************
 2:   x_CApp.h
 3:
 4:            Header File For CApp "Lower-Layer" Application Class
 5:
 6:      Copyright (c) 1994 My Software Inc. All rights reserved.
 7:
 8:  Generated by Visual Architect(TM) 9:28 PM Tue, Jun 7, 1994
 9:
10:  This file is rewritten each time you generate code. You should not
11:  make changes to this file; changes should go in the CApp.h
12:  file, instead.
13:
14:  If you want to change how Visual Architect generates this file,
15:  you can change the template for this file. It is "_App.h" in
16:  the Visual Architect Templates folder.
17:
18:  *****************************************************************/
19:
20:  #pragma once
21:
22:  #include <CApplication.h>
23:
24:  class CFile;
25:  class CDialogDirector;
26:  class CDocument;
27:
28:  class x_CApp : public CApplication
29:  {
30:  public:
31:
32:      TCL_DECLARE_CLASS
33:
34:      void            Ix_CApp(short extraMasters,
35:                          Size aRainyDayFund,
36:                          Size aCriticalBalance,
```

continues

Listing 15.4. continued

```
37:                                Size aToolboxBalance);
38:      virtual    void    SetUpFileParameters(void);
39:      virtual    void    SetUpMenus(void);
40:      virtual    void    ForceClassReferences(void);
41:
42:      virtual    void    DoCommand(long theCommand);
43:
44:      virtual    void    CreateDocument(void);
45:      virtual    void    OpenDocument(SFReply *macSFReply);
46:
47:
48:      virtual Boolean    FileAlreadyOpen(CFile *aFile);
49:  };
```

Listing 15.4 contains the declaration of class x_CApp, which is a low-level application class. This class is a descendant of the TCL class CApplication and is the parent of the application class CApp. The class declaration specifies a set of member functions that initialize the class instances, set up file parameters, set up menus, force class references, manage commands, create documents, and open documents. The class x_CApp declares no data members.

Listing 15.5. The source code for the x_CApp.cp implementation file.

```
1:  /****************************************************************
2:  x_CApp.c
3:
4:              CApp "Lower-Layer" Application Class
5:
6:      Copyright (c) 1994 My Software Inc. All rights reserved.
7:
8:  Generated by Visual Architect(TM) 9:28 PM Tue, Jun 7, 1994
9:
10: This file is rewritten each time you generate code. You should not
11: make changes to this file; changes should go in the CApp.c
12: file, instead.
13:
14: If you want to change how Visual Architect generates this file,
15: you can change the template for this file. It is "_App_cp" in
16: the Visual Architect Templates folder.
17:
18: ****************************************************************/
19:
20: #include "x_CApp.h"
21:
22: #include "CApp.h"
23:
24: #include "References.h"
25: #include "CMain.h"
```

```
26:    #include <CBartender.h>
27:    #include <Commands.h>
28:    #include <CDesktop.h>
29:    #include <CFile.h>
30:    #include <CFWDesktop.h>
31:    #include <CList.h>
32:    #include <Packages.h>
33:    #include <TBUtilities.h>
34:    #include <TCLForceReferences.h>
35:
36:    #include "CMain.h"
37:
38:    extern OSType          gSignature;    /* Creator for Application's
39:                                             files     */
40:    extern CBartender     *gBartender;    /* Manages all menus */
41:    extern CDesktop       *gDesktop;      /* The visible Desktop */
42:
43:    #define ALRTabout 500
44:
45:
46:    TCL_DEFINE_CLASS_M1(x_CApp, CApplication);
47:
48:    /**** C O N S T R U C T I O N / D E S T R U C T I O N
49:                                        M E T H O D S ****/
50:
51:
52:    /****************************************************************
53:     Ix_CApp
54:
55:            Initialize an Application.
56:    ****************************************************************/
57:
58:    void x_CApp::Ix_CApp(short extraMasters,
59:                          Size aRainyDayFund,
60:                          Size aCriticalBalance,
61:                          Size aToolboxBalance)
62:
63:    {
64:        IApplication(extraMasters, aRainyDayFund, aCriticalBalance,
65:                    aToolboxBalance);
66:    }
67:
68:
69:    /****************************************************************
70:     SetUpFileParameters      {OVERRIDE}
71:
72:        Specify the kinds of files your application opens
73:    ****************************************************************/
74:
75:    void x_CApp::SetUpFileParameters()
76:    {
77:        CApplication::SetUpFileParameters();
78:
79:            // File types as defined in CApp.h
80:
```

continues

Listing 15.5. continued

```
81:        sfNumTypes = kNumFileTypes;
82:        sfFileTypes[0] = kFileType1;
83:        sfFileTypes[1] = kFileType2;
84:        sfFileTypes[2] = kFileType3;
85:        sfFileTypes[3] = kFileType4;
86:        gSignature = 'cApp';
87:    }
88:
89:
90:    /*****************************************************************
91:      SetUpMenus {OVERRIDE}
92:
93:    Set up the menus after first creating any floating/tearoff
94:    windows. The latter must be done before the bartender inits.
95:    *****************************************************************/
96:
97:    void x_CApp::SetUpMenus()
98:    {
99:
100:       CApplication::SetUpMenus();
101:   }
102:
103:
104:   /*****************************************************************
105:     ForceClassReferences     {OVERRIDE}
106:
107:       Reference classes that might do object I/O.
108:   *****************************************************************/
109:
110:   void x_CApp::ForceClassReferences(void)
111:
112:   {
113:       CApplication::ForceClassReferences();
114:
115:                              /* From References.c */
116:       ReferenceStdClasses();  /* See template file Ref */
117:
118:   }
119:
120:
121:   /**** C O M M A N D   M E T H O D S ****/
122:
123:
124:   /*****************************************************************
125:     DoCommand     {OVERRIDE}
126:
127:       Handle application commands
128:   *****************************************************************/
129:
130:   void x_CApp::DoCommand(long theCommand)
131:
132:   {
133:       switch (theCommand)
134:       {
135:           case cmdAbout:
```

```
136:
137:                        // Simple About alert. Subclasses will probably
138:                        // trap this command to do something sexier.
139:
140:                PositionDialog('ALRT', ALRTabout);
141:                InitCursor();
142:                ParamText("\pCApp", "\pMy Software Inc", "\p", "\p");
143:                Alert(ALRTabout, NULL);
144:                break;
145:
146:            default:
147:                CApplication::DoCommand(theCommand);
148:                break;
149:        }
150: }
151:
152:
153: /**** D O C U M E N T   M E T H O D S ****/
154:
155:
156: /****************************************************************
157:   CreateDocument      {OVERRIDE}
158:
159: Make a new document when user chooses New from file menu.
160: This method is entirely generic except for the document class.
161: ****************************************************************/
162:
163: void x_CApp::CreateDocument()
164:
165: {
166:     CDocument       *theDocument = NULL;
167:
168:     theDocument = new CMain;
169:     TRY
170:     {
171:         ((CMain*) theDocument)->ICMain();
172:         theDocument->NewFile();
173:     }
174:     CATCH
175:     {
176:         ForgetObject(theDocument);
177:     }
178:     ENDTRY
179: }
180:
181:
182: /****************************************************************
183:   OpenDocument      {OVERRIDE}
184:
185: Open a document when user chooses Open from file menu.
186: For multiple document types, this method assumes that each
187: document is associated with a single file type.
188: ****************************************************************/
189:
```

continues

Listing 15.5. continued

```
190:  void x_CApp::OpenDocument(SFReply *macSFReply)
191:
192:  {
193:      CDocument    *theDocument = NULL;
194:
195:      theDocument = new CMain;
196:      TRY
197:      {
198:          ((CMain*) theDocument)->ICMain();
199:          theDocument->OpenFile(macSFReply);
200:      }
201:      CATCH
202:      {
203:          ForgetObject(theDocument);
204:      }
205:      ENDTRY
206:  }
207:
208:
209:
210:
211:  /****************************************************************
212:   FileAlreadyOpen
213:
214:  If file already in use return TRUE and bring owning document's
215:  window to the foreground.  Sent from document before opening.
216:  ****************************************************************/
217:
218:      static Boolean EqualFile(CDirector *obj, long param)
219:      {
220:          FSSpec        theFileSpec;
221:          CFile      *theFile;
222:          FSSpec       *theParam = (FSSpec*) param;
223:
224:          if (member(obj, CDocument))
225:          {
226:              theFile = ((CDocument*)obj)->itsFile;
227:              if (theFile == NULL)
228:                  return FALSE;
229:              theFile->GetFSSpec(&theFileSpec);
230:              return theFileSpec.vRefNum == theParam->vRefNum
231:                  && theFileSpec.parID == theParam->parID
232:                  && !IUEqualString(theFileSpec.name,
233:                                        theParam->name);
234:          }
235:          return FALSE;
236:      }
237:
238:  Boolean x_CApp::FileAlreadyOpen(
239:      CFile       *aFile)
240:
241:  {
242:      FSSpec        fileSpec;
243:      CDirector    *theDirector = NULL;
244:
```

```
245:        aFile->GetFSSpec(&fileSpec);
246:        if (itsDirectors) /* Search for matching file */
247:            theDirector = (CDirector*)
248:              itsDirectors->FindItem1(EqualFile, (long) &fileSpec);
249:        if (theDirector) /* If find one, bring to front */
250:            theDirector->GetWindow()->Select();
251:        return theDirector != NULL; /* Tell caller */
252: }
```

Listing 15.5 defines the member function of class x_CApp. The next five subsections discuss the relevant member functions of that class.

The Function *Ix_CApp*

The member function Ix_CApp (defined in lines 58 to 66) initializes the instances of class x_CApp. The function Ix_CApp invokes the inherited function CApplication::IApplication.

The Function *SetUpFileParameters*

The member function SetUpFileParameters (defined in lines 75 to 87) establishes the kinds of files the minimal application works on. The function first invokes the inherited function CApplication::SetUpFileParameters and then assigns the constants kNumFileTypes and kFileType1 through kFileType3 to the inherited data members sfNumTypes and sfFileTypes[0] through sfFileTypes[3], respectively. The function also assigns the signature string to the global variable gSignature.

The Function *DoCommand*

The member function DoCommand (defined in lines 130 to 150) responds to two commands: the cmAbout command and the default command. The function responds to the cmAbout command (generated when you invoke the About Application... command in the Apple menu) by displaying the dialog box shown in Figure 15.2.

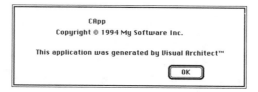

Figure 15.2. *The About dialog box for the minimal TCL program.*

409

The Function *CreateDocument*

The member function CreateDocument (defined in lines 163 to 179) generates a new document by creating and initializing a dynamic instance of class CMain. The function initializes the document instance and sends it the C++ message NewFile inside a TRY-CATCH block, which helps to detect and handle any run time error.

The Function *OpenDocument*

The member function OpenDocument (defined in lines 190 to 206) is similar to function CreateDocument. The main difference is that function OpenDocument sends the C++ message OpenFile to the document object.

Let's look at the header and implementation files for class CMain. Listings 15.6 and 15.7 show the source code for the CMain.h header file and the CMain.cp implementation file, respectively.

Listing 15.6. The source code for the CMain.h header file.

```
1:   /****************************************************************
2:   CMain.h
3:
4:               Header File For CMain Document Class
5:
6:       Copyright (c) 1994 My Software Inc. All rights reserved.
7:
8:   Generated by Visual Architect(TM) 9:27 PM Tue, Jun 7, 1994
9:
10:  This file is only generated once. You can modify it by extending
11:  the placeholder definitions and adding any new methods and
12:  data members you wish.
13:
14:  If you change the name of the document class, a fresh version of
15:  this file will be generated. If you have made any changes to the
16:  file with the old name, you will have to copy those changes to
17:  the new file by hand.
18:
19:  ****************************************************************/
20:
21:  #pragma once
22:
23:  #include "x_CMain.h"
24:
25:  class CMain : public x_CMain
26:
27:  {
28:  public:
29:
30:      TCL_DECLARE_CLASS
```

```
31:
32:
33:        void      ICMain(void);
34:
35:        virtual   void      MakeNewContents(void);
36:        virtual   void      ContentsToWindow(void);
37:        virtual   void      WindowToContents(void);
38:  };
39:
40:        // If you have multiple document classes, you must change
41:        // the file type below to the appropriate type for this class.
42:        // If not, this #define is not used.
43:
44:  #define CMainFType 'TEXT'
```

Listing 15.6 contains the declaration of the document class CMain as a descendant of class x_CMain. The class declares member functions that initialize the class instances and manage the data associated with the document. Managing the document data includes transferring the data between the window and the underlying data objects.

Listing 15.7. The source code for the CMain.cp implementation file.

```
1:  /*******************************************************************
2:   CMain.c
3:
4:                    CMain Document Class
5:
6:      Copyright (c) 1994 My Software Inc. All rights reserved.
7:
8:  Generated by Visual Architect(TM) 9:27 PM Tue, Jun 7, 1994
9:
10: This file is only generated once. You can modify it by filling
11: in the placeholder functions and adding any new functions you
12: wish.
13:
14: If you change the name of the document class, a fresh version of
15: this file will be generated. If you have made any changes to the
16: file with the old name, you will have to copy those changes to
17: the new file by hand.
18:
19: *******************************************************************/
20:
21: #include "CMain.h"
22: //#include "AppCommands.h"    // Remove comments if
23:                              // DoCommand overridden
24:
25: #include <CApplication.h>
26:
27:
```

continues

Listing 15.7. continued

```
28:   TCL_DEFINE_CLASS_M1(CMain, x_CMain);
29:
30:   /**** C O N S T R U C T I O N / D E S T R U C T I O N
31:                                       M E T H O D S ****/
32:
33:
34:   /**************************************************************
35:    ICMain
36:
37:   Initialize the document
38:
39:   **************************************************************/
40:
41:   void CMain::ICMain()
42:
43:   {
44:       Ix_CMain();
45:
46:           // Initialize data members here
47:   }
48:
49:
50:   /**************************************************************
51:    MakeNewContents
52:
53:   Create "blank" document contents. MakeNewContents is called
54:   after itsWindow is created and before it is first selected,
55:   whether or not the document uses a file.
56:   **************************************************************/
57:
58:   void CMain::MakeNewContents()
59:
60:   {
61:           // Initialize document contents and itsWindow here
62:   }
63:
64:
65:   /**************************************************************
66:    ContentsToWindow
67:
68:   Make window reflect document's contents.  If the document does
69:   not use a file, this function is never called and may be deleted.
70:   **************************************************************/
71:
72:   void CMain::ContentsToWindow()
73:
74:   {
75:           // Transfer data from itsContents to itsWindow.
76:           // See Chapter 11, Using Object I/O
77:   }
78:
79:
80:   /**************************************************************
81:    WindowToContents
82:
```

```
83:    Make document's contents reflect window's contents (if they
84:    don't already).  If the document does not use a file, this
85:    function is never called and may be deleted.
86:    ****************************************************************/
87:
88:    void CMain::WindowToContents()
89:
90:    {
91:            // Transfer data from itsWindow to itsContents
92:    }
```

 Listing 15.7 shows the definitions of the member functions in class CMain. Some of these definitions are minimal, whereas others contain no statements—something to be expected from a minimal program that displays no data.

Let's look at the header and implementation files for class x_CMain. Listings 15.8 and 15.9 show the source code for the x_CMain.h header file and the x_CMain.cp implementation file, respectively.

 **Note:** Please pay close attention to Listings 15.8 and 15.9 because most of the programs in the rest of the book generate customized declarations and source code for the class x_CMain. Familiarize yourself with the default output of the Visual Architect utility.

 Listing 15.8. The source code for the x_CMain.h header file.

```
1:    /****************************************************************
2:    x_CMain.h
3:
4:            Header File For CMain Lower-Layer Document Class
5:
6:        Copyright (c) 1994 My Software Inc. All rights reserved.
7:
8:        Generated by Visual Architect(TM)
9:
10:   This file is rewritten each time you generate code. You should not
11:   make changes to this file; changes should go in the My.h
12:   file, instead.
13:
14:   If you want to change how Visual Architect generates this file, you
15:   can change the template for this file. It is "_Doc.h" in the Visual
16:   Architect Templates folder.
```

continues

Listing 15.8. continued

```
17:
18:    **********************************************************************/
19:
20:    #pragma once
21:
22:    #include "CSaver.h"
23:
24:    #include "ItsContentsClass.h"
25:
26:    #define x_CMain_super    CSaver<ITSCONTENTSCLASS>
27:
28:    class CFile;
29:
30:    class x_CMain : public x_CMain_super
31:
32:    {
33:    public:
34:
35:        TCL_DECLARE_CLASS
36:
37:
38:        void      Ix_CMain(void);
39:
40:
41:    protected:
42:        virtual void MakeNewWindow(void);
43:
44:        virtual void FailOpen(CFile *aFile);
45:        virtual void PositionWindow(void);
46:
47:    };
48:
49:    #define   CVueCMain 128
```

Listing 15.8 declares class x_CMain as a descendant of class x_CMain_super and as an alias (which is defined using the #define statement in line 26) to class CSaver<ITSCONTENTSCLASS>. The class declares the member functions that initialize the class instances, create a new window, handle an already opened file, and position the window associated with the document. The class x_CMain declares no data members.

Listing 15.9. The source code for the x_CMain.cp implementation file.

```
1:    /****************************************************************
2:    x_CMain.c
3:
4:                        CMain Document Class
5:
6:        Copyright (c) 1994 My Software Inc. All rights reserved.
7:
```

```
 8:   Generated by Visual Architect(TM) 9:28 PM Tue, Jun 7, 1994
 9:
10:   This file is rewritten each time you generate code. You should not
11:   make changes to this file; changes should go in the My.c
12:   file, instead.
13:
14:   If you want to change how Visual Architect generates this file,
15:   you can change the template for this file. It is "_Doc_cp" in
16:   the Visual Architect Templates folder.
17:
18:   ****************************************************************/
19:
20:   #include "x_CMain.h"
21:
22:   #include "CMain.h"
23:
24:   #include "MainItems.h"
25:
26:   #include "ViewUtilities.h"
27:   #include "CApp.h"
28:
29:   #include <CApplication.h>
30:   #include <CBartender.h>
31:   #include <Commands.h>
32:   #include <Constants.h>
33:   #include <CDecorator.h>
34:   #include <CDesktop.h>
35:   #include <CFile.h>
36:   #include <TBUtilities.h>
37:   #include <CWindow.h>
38:
39:   extern CApplication *gApplication;  /* The application     */
40:   extern CDecorator  *gDecorator; /* Decorator for
41:                                      arranging windows */
42:   extern CDesktop *gDesktop;  /* The visible Desktop */
43:   extern CBartender  *gBartender; /* Manages all menus */
44:
45:
46:   // Define symbols for commands handled by this class
47:   // Prevents a recompile every time any command changed.
48:
49:
50:
51:   TCL_DEFINE_CLASS_M1(x_CMain, x_CMain_super);
52:
53:   /**** C O N S T R U C T I O N / D E S T R U C T I O N
54:                                       M E T H O D S ****/
55:
56:
57:   /****************************************************************
58:    Ix_CMain
59:
60:       Initialize the document
61:   ****************************************************************/
```

continues

Listing 15.9. continued

```
62:
63:  void x_CMain::Ix_CMain()
64:
65:  {
66:      IDocument(gApplication, TRUE);
67:
68:              // Initialize data members below.
69:  }
70:
71:
72:  /****************************************************************
73:   MakeNewWindow
74:
75:  Create a new, empty window.  Subclass may override to populate
76:  the new window.
77:   ****************************************************************/
78:
79:  void x_CMain::MakeNewWindow(void)
80:
81:  {
82:      itsWindow = TCLGetNamedWindow("\pMain", this);
83:
84:      itsMainPane = (CPane*) TCLGetItemPointer(itsWindow, 0);
85:
86:          // Initialize pointers to the subpanes in the window
87:
88:  }
89:
90:
91:  /****************************************************************
92:   FailOpen {OVERRIDE}
93:
94:  Fail if file already open in this application.
95:
96:  This function calls the application's FileAlreadyOpen function
97:  and fails quietly if the file is open.
98:
99:  Note that open may also fail if the file is open in
100: another application. This will cause a failure in open,
101: but you may wish to override this function to detect this
102: case and provide a more meaningful error message than -49.
103:  ****************************************************************/
104:
105: void x_CMain::FailOpen(CFile *aFile)
106:
107: {
108:     /* Only the application knows          */
109:     if (((CApp*)gApplication)->FileAlreadyOpen(aFile))
110:         Failure(kSilentErr, 0);
111: }
112:
113:
114: /****************************************************************
115:  PositionWindow
116:
```

```
117:    The default method in CSaver calls the the decorator, which
118:    staggers and resizes the window. Since the window has already
119:    been positioned when it is initialized from the view resource,
120:    we don't want to do this twice.
121:    **********************************************************/
122:
123:    void x_CMain::PositionWindow()
124:
125:    {
126:    }
```

 Listing 15.9 contains the definitions of the member functions in class x_CMain. The next three subsections discuss the relevant member functions of the x_CMain class.

The Function *Ix_CMain*

The member function Ix_CMain (defined in lines 63 to 69) initializes the class instances by invoking the inherited member function IDocument.

The Function *MakeNewWindow*

The member function MakeNewWindow (defined in lines 79 to 88) creates a new window by performing two tasks. The function first stores the address of the parent window in pointer itsWindow, and then stores the address of the main pane in pointer itsMainPane.

The Function *FailOpen*

The member function FailOpen (defined in lines 105 to 111) determines whether a file is already opened by sending the C++ message FileAlreadyOpen to the application object. If this message returns a non-zero value, the function FailOpen invokes the function Failure.

Extending the Main Window Operations

The minimal TCL program serves to introduce you to the default minimal code generated by the Visual Architect utility. Other than that, the minimum TCL program is a real bore! In this section I present a simple TCL program that displays a

general-purpose alert dialog box when you click on a button. Figure 15.3 shows a sample session with the second TCL program. The figure shows the button titled Message in the main window and also shows the resulting alert dialog box. The second TCL program illustrates, albeit in a simple way, how to customize the response of TCL programs.

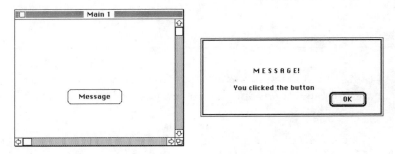

Figure 15.3. *A sample session with the second TCL program.*

Creating the second TCL application involves several steps:

1. Prepare the minimal main window.
2. Draw a button control.
3. Define a new command.
4. Customize the button.
5. Generate and customize the source code.
6. Compile and run the program.

The following subsections describe each stage of crafting the second program.

Preparing the Minimal Main Window

The first stage is identical to the steps of the minimal TCL program, which yield an empty main window.

Drawing a Button Control

In the second stage, you draw a new button in the main window by performing the following steps:

1. Click on the Main item in the Visual Architect.rsrc window.

2. Select the Tools menu to bring up the tools palette. Click on the button tool.

3. Draw a button in the Main window. Hold the mouse button down and move the mouse to define the rectangular area containing the button. Release the mouse button to end drawing the control. The button has the default caption of OK and responds to the predefined command cmdOK.

Defining a New Command

To customize the response of the new button, you need to define a new command by performing the following steps:

1. Select Edit | Commands to bring up the Commands dialog box.

2. Select Edit | New Command to put the Commands dialog box into a mode where you can define a new command.

3. Type cmdShowMsg in the top-most edit box. The Visual Architect utility automatically assigns this command a number.

4. Select class CMain in the In Class pop-up menu.

5. Select item Call in the Do pop-up menu.

6. Click the OK button to close the Commands dialog box.

These steps define a new command that is associated with the class CMain (actually, its parent class x_CMain). The command calls a member function in the associated class.

Customizing the Button

Now you're ready to customize the OK button by altering its control name, title, and associated command. Perform the following steps:

1. Double-click the OK button to open the button's data dialog box.

2. Type MsgBtn in the Identifier edit box. The Visual Architect utility also changes the caption of the dialog box to MsgBtn.

3. Click on the down-arrow symbol to the left of CButton to view the command associated with the button. The current command is cmdOK. Select the command cmdShowMsg from the pop-up menu. Click the same arrow symbol to hide the details of class CButton.

4. Click on the right arrow symbol near CControl to view the control's caption. The current caption is OK. Type Message in the contrlTitle edit box. Click the same right arrow symbol to hide the details of class CControl.

5. Close the MsgBtn dialog box.

Generating and Customizing the Source Code

To generate the source code for the second application, invoke the Generate All... command in the THINK Project Manager icon menu. This command emits various files in the Source folder (nested inside the second program's folder). Most of these files resemble those of the minimal TCL program. Therefore, I present only those files that are relevant to the second program. I also discuss customizing the emitted code to provide the desired operations.

Listing 15.10 shows the source code for the x_CMain.h header file for the second TCL program. The bold lines show the ones that I manually inserted.

Note: Notice the new icon next to the listing head. This icon indicates that the listing contains code generated automatically by the Visual Architect utility *and* code you must add yourself. Code you must add is in **bold** type.

VArc Type

Listing 15.10. The source code for the x_CMain.h header file for the second TCL program.

```
 1:  /****************************************************************
 2:   x_CMain.h
 3:
 4:            Header File For CMain Lower-Layer Document Class
 5:
 6:      Copyright (c) 1994 My Software Inc. All rights reserved.
 7:
 8:  Generated by Visual Architect(TM)
 9:
10:  This file is rewritten each time you generate code. You should
11:  not make changes to this file; changes should go in the My.h
12:  file, instead.
13:
14:  If you want to change how Visual Architect generates this file,
15:  you can change the template for this file. It is "_Doc.h" in the
16:  Visual Architect Templates folder.
```

```
17:
18:    ******************************************************************/
19:
20:    #pragma once
21:
22:    #include "CSaver.h"
23:    class CButton;
24:
25:    #include "ItsContentsClass.h"
26:
27:    #define x_CMain_super    CSaver<ITSCONTENTSCLASS>
28:
29:    class CFile;
30:
31:    class x_CMain : public x_CMain_super
32:
33:    {
34:    public:
35:
36:        TCL_DECLARE_CLASS
37:
38:        // Pointers to panes in window
39:        CButton    *fMain_MsgBtn;
40:
41:        void    Ix_CMain(void);
42:
43:        virtual void    DoCommand(long theCommand);
44:        virtual void    UpdateMenus(void);
45:
46:    protected:
47:        virtual void    MakeNewWindow(void);
48:
49:        virtual void    FailOpen(CFile *aFile);
50:        virtual void    PositionWindow(void);
51:
52:        virtual void    DoCmdShowMsg(void);
53:    };
54:
55:    #define    CVueCMain    128
```

Listing 15.10 declares the class x_CMain. Although this declaration is similar to that of the minimal program, notice the following new members:

☐ Line 39 defines data member fMain_MsgBtn, which is the pointer to class CButton. This member is the pointer to the Message button.

☐ Line 52 contains an additional member function: DoCmdShowMsg. This member function derives its name by appending the word *Do* with the name of the handled command cmdShowMsg (the Visual Architect utility also converts the letter *c* in *cmd* into uppercase).

Listing 15.11 shows the source code for the x_CMain.cp implementation file for the second TCL program. The bold lines indicate the ones that I manually inserted.

VArc Type

Listing 15.11. The source code for the x_CMain.cp implementation file for the second TCL program.

```
 1:   /*******************************************************************
 2:    x_CMain.c
 3:
 4:                   CMain Document Class
 5:
 6:       Copyright (c) 1994 My Software Inc. All rights reserved.
 7:
 8:   Generated by Visual Architect(TM) 2:24 PM Wed, Jun 8, 1994
 9:
10:   This file is rewritten each time you generate code. You should not
11:   make changes to this file; changes should go in the My.c
12:   file, instead.
13:
14:   If you want to change how Visual Architect generates this file,
15:   you can change the template for this file. It is "_Doc_cp" in
16:   the Visual Architect Templates folder.
17:
18:   *******************************************************************/
19:
20:   #include "x_CMain.h"
21:
22:   #include "CMain.h"
23:
24:   #include "MainItems.h"
25:
26:   #include "ViewUtilities.h"
27:   #include "CApp.h"
28:
29:   #include <CApplication.h>
30:   #include <CBartender.h>
31:   #include <Commands.h>
32:   #include <Constants.h>
33:   #include <CDecorator.h>
34:   #include <CDesktop.h>
35:   #include <CFile.h>
36:   #include <TBUtilities.h>
37:   #include <CWindow.h>
38:
39:   extern CApplication *gApplication; /* The application */
40:   extern CDecorator *gDecorator; /* Decorator for arranging
41:                                       windows   */
42:   extern CDesktop *gDesktop; /* The visible Desktop */
43:   extern CBartender *gBartender; /* Manages all menus */
44:
45:   #include "CButton.h"
46:
47:       // Define symbols for commands handled by this class
48:       // Prevents a recompile every time any command changed.
```

```
 49:
 50: #define cmdShowMsg 513
 51: #define ALRTgeneral 128
 52:
 53: TCL_DEFINE_CLASS_M1(x_CMain, x_CMain_super);
 54:
 55: /**** C O N S T R U C T I O N / D E S T R U C T I O N
 56:                                       M E T H O D S ****/
 57:
 58:
 59: /*****************************************************************
 60:   Ix_CMain
 61:
 62: Initialize the document
 63: *****************************************************************/
 64:
 65: void x_CMain::Ix_CMain()
 66:
 67: {
 68:     IDocument(gApplication, TRUE);
 69:
 70:         // Initialize data members below.
 71: }
 72:
 73:
 74: /*****************************************************************
 75:   MakeNewWindow
 76:
 77: Create a new, empty window.  Subclass may override to populate
 78: the new window.
 79: *****************************************************************/
 80:
 81: void x_CMain::MakeNewWindow(void)
 82:
 83: {
 84:     itsWindow = TCLGetNamedWindow("\pMain", this);
 85:
 86:     itsMainPane = (CPane*) TCLGetItemPointer(itsWindow, 0);
 87:
 88:         // Initialize pointers to the subpanes in the window
 89:
 90:   fMain_MsgBtn = (CButton*)
 91:                 itsWindow->FindViewByID(kMain_MsgBtnID);
 92:   ASSERT(member(fMain_MsgBtn, CButton));
 93:
 94: }
 95:
 96:
 97: /*****************************************************************
 98:   FailOpen {OVERRIDE}
 99:
100: Fail if file already open in this application.
101:
102: This function calls the application's FileAlreadyOpen function
```

continues

423

Listing 15.11. continued

```
103:    and fails quietly if the file is open.
104:
105:    Note that open may also fail if the file is open in
106:    another application. This will cause a failure in open,
107:    but you may wish to override this function to detect this
108:    case and provide a more meaningful error message than -49.
109:    ******************************************************************/
110:
111:    void x_CMain::FailOpen(CFile *aFile)
112:
113:    {
114:        /* Only the application knows          */
115:        if (((CApp*)gApplication)->FileAlreadyOpen(aFile))
116:            Failure(kSilentErr, 0);
117:    }
118:
119:
120:    /******************************************************************
121:     PositionWindow
122:
123:    The default method in CSaver calls the the decorator, which
124:    staggers and resizes the window. Since the window has already
125:    been positioned when it is initialized from the view resource,
126:    we don't want to do this twice.
127:    ******************************************************************/
128:
129:    void     x_CMain::PositionWindow()
130:
131:    {
132:    }
133:
134:
135:
136:
137:    /******************************************************************
138:     DoCommand {OVERRIDE}
139:
140:    Dispatch Visual Architect-specified actions.
141:    ******************************************************************/
142:
143:    void x_CMain::DoCommand(long theCommand)
144:
145:    {
146:        switch (theCommand)
147:        {
148:            case cmdShowMsg:
149:                DoCmdShowMsg();
150:                break;
151:            default:
152:                CDocument::DoCommand(theCommand);
153:        }
154:    }
155:
156:
157:    /******************************************************************
```

```
158:    UpdateMenus {OVERRIDE}
159:
160:    Enable menus which generate commands handled by this class.
161:    ****************************************************************/
162:
163:    void x_CMain::UpdateMenus()
164:
165:    {
166:        CDocument::UpdateMenus();
167:        gBartender->EnableCmd(cmdShowMsg);
168:    }
169:
170:
171:    /****************************************************************
172:     DoCmdShowMsg
173:
174:    Respond to cmdShowMsg command.
175:    ****************************************************************/
176:
177:    void x_CMain::DoCmdShowMsg()
178:
179:    {
180:            // Subclass must override this function to
181:            // handle the command
182:            PositionDialog('ALRT', ALRTgeneral);
183:            InitCursor();
184:            ParamText(
185:              "\p          M E S S A G E!\r\rYou clicked the button",
186:              "\p", "\p", "\p");
187:            Alert(ALRTgeneral, NULL);
188:
189:    }
```

Analysis

Listing 15.11 shows the definitions of the member functions in class x_CMain. The output of the Visual Architect utility did not include line 51 and lines 182 to 187. I added these lines manually to support the response of the program.

Lines 50 and 51 define the constants for the command cmdShowMsg and for ALRTgeneral, the predefined resource ID for the general alert (a general-purpose message dialog box). The next four subsections discuss the relevant member functions.

Syntax

The Function *MakeNewWindow*

The member function MakeNewWindow (defined in lines 81 to 94) stores the pointers to the window and pane in the variable itsWindow and itsMainPane, respectively. It also stores the address of the Message button in the data member fMain_MsgBtn. The function obtains this address by sending the C++ message FindViewByID to the window object. The argument for this message is the constant kMain_MsgBtnID, which is defined in line 31 of Listing 15.13.

The Function *DoCommand*

The member function DoCommand (defined in lines 143 to 154) has a case label in the switch statement to respond to the command cmdShowMsg. The first statement after case cmdShowMsg invokes the member function DoCmdShowMsg.

The Function *UpdateMenus*

The member function UpdateMenus (defined in lines 163 to 168) enables the custom command cmdShowMsg by sending the C++ message EnableCmd to the bartender object (which manages the menu bar and its items). The argument for the message is the constant cmdShowMsg.

The Function *DoCmdShowMsg*

The member function DoCmdShowMsg (defined in lines 177 to 189) handles the cmdShowMsg command by displaying an alert dialog box. The calls to functions PositionDialog and InitCursor initialize the general alert box. The function PositionDialog uses the ALRT resource name and the constant ALRTgeneral to specify the general kind of resource and the specific kind of alert, respectively. The call to the function ParamText specifies the strings to be passed to the general alert box. This kind of box uses only the first string argument in the call to function ParamText. To display the alert box itself, the function ParamText calls function Alert and supplies that call with the arguments ALRTgeneral (the ID of the specific alert box) and NULL (the pointer to the function that supports non-default responses to keyboard input).

DO   DON'T

DO use the special escape character \p as the first character in a literal string that is an argument to a Pascal string.

DON'T forget that Pascal strings are limited to 255 characters.

Listing 15.12 shows the source code for the AppCommands.h header file for the second TCL program. This listing defines the constant cmdShowMsg, in line 16, which supports the custom command.

> **Note:** The Visual Architect inserts the name of the generated program on line 2. You'll notice that the Visual Architect shows the filename as MyCommands.h, but the created file's actual name is AppCommands.h.

Listing 15.12. The source code for the AppCommands.h header file for the second TCL program.

```
 1: /****************************************************************
 2: MyCommands.h
 3:
 4:             Header File For Command Symbols
 5:
 6:     Copyright (c) 1994 My Software Inc. All rights reserved.
 7:
 8: Generated by Visual Architect(TM)
 9:
10: This file is regenerated each time.
11:
12: ****************************************************************/
13:
14: #pragma once
15:
16: #define cmdShowMsg     513
```

Listing 15.13 shows the source code for the MainItems.h header file for the second TCL program. The listing defines an untagged enumerated type which defines the identifiers kMain_MsgBtn and kMain_MsgBtnID.

Listing 15.13. The source code for the MainItems.h header file for the second TCL program.

```
 1: /****************************************************************
 2: MainItems.h
 3:
 4:                 Main Item Constants
 5:
 6:     Copyright (c) 1994 My Software Inc. All rights reserved.
 7:
 8: Generated by Visual Architect(TM)
 9:
10: This file is rewritten each time you generate code. You should
11: not make changes to this file.
12:
13: If you want to change how Visual Architect generates this file,
14: you can change the template for this file. It is "Items.h" in
15: the Visual Architect Templates folder.
```

continues

427

Listing 15.13. continued

```
16:
17:    *********************************************************************/
18:
19:    #pragma once
20:
21:
22:        //    Item numbers for each item.
23:        //
24:        //    Use TCLGetItemPointer (ViewUtilities) to convert these
25:        //    item numbers to a pointer to the named item.
26:
27:    enum
28:    {
29:        Main_Begin_,
30:        kMain_MsgBtn = 1,
31:        kMain_MsgBtnID = 1L,
32:        Main_End_
33:    };
```

Compiling and Running the Program

Invoke the Run command from the THINK Project Manager icon menu. This command causes the compiler to process the set of source code files that contribute to the program. Figure 15.4 shows a sample session with the second TCL program, including the resulting alert box.

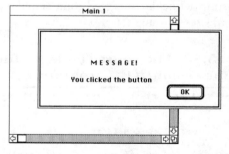

Figure 15.4. *A sample session with the second TCL program showing the alert box.*

Responding to Menu Selections

Commands are generated by buttons and menus. In this section I present a program that responds to several custom commands generated by buttons and menus. I also seize the opportunity to show you how to customize the alert box and how to use a different window style for the main window.

The next program project, which I call Menu1, has two buttons in the main window (see Figure 15.5):

☐ The Message 1 button, which displays the message `You clicked button Message 1` when you click the button.

☐ The Message 2 button, which displays the message `You clicked button Message 2 or menu Message 2` when you click the button.

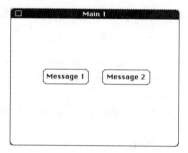

Figure 15.5. *A sample session with the Menu1 program.*

The program has the following additional commands in the Edit menu:

☐ The command Message 2, which displays the message `You clicked button Message 2 or menu Message 2` when you invoke the command.

☐ The command Message 3, which displays the message `You clicked menu Message 3` when you invoke the command.

The program illustrates how a button and a menu command trigger the same message. The program also shows you how a button and a menu command can generate different messages.

Creating the Empty Main Window

The first stage of creating the Menu1 program is to create a new Visual Architect project called Menu1. As before, double-click on the Visual Architect.rsrc file to invoke the list of windows. Delete the predefined controls from the main window. You are now ready for the second stage.

Creating the Custom Alert

The Alert function displays a general alert box with no icons or pictures. You can use the NoteAlert function to display an alert box with the predefined talking-head icon. However, if you use the NoteAlert function with the general alert box, the text of the message overlays the icon's image. Thus, you need to create a copy of the general alert box and customize that copy to properly work with the NoteAlert function.

To customize the alert box in this stage, carry out the following steps:

1. Use the Finder to open the Menu1 f folder.

2. Double-click on the Menu1.π.rsrc file to open the file under the control of the resource editor. Figure 15.6 shows the Menu1.π.rsrc dialog box.

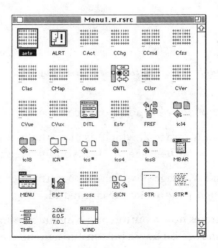

Figure 15.6. *The Menu1.π.rsrc dialog box.*

3. Double-click the ALRT icon to bring up the list of ALRT resources.

4. The first item in the list is the General alert with an ID of 128. This is also the item selected by default. If it is not the selected item in your system, select it.

5. Invoke the Edit | Copy command to copy the General alert.

6. Invoke the Edit | Paste command to insert a copy of the General alert in the list. Naturally, this task would create a duplicate in a list of unique items. Consequently, the resource editor displays an alert box asking you to resolve the problem. Click the Unique ID button to create a copy of the General alert under a different ID. The resource editor selects the next available ID number, which is 130.

7. Double-click the new alert resource. The resource editor shows a dialog box that contains a scaled-down image of the alert box and some related data.

8. Double-click on the image of the alert box. The resource editor displays the template for the actual alert box. The box contains the OK button and the ^0 text control, as shown in Figure 15.7.

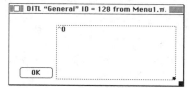

Figure 15.7. *The customized General alert dialog box.*

9. Move the OK button from the lower-right side of the alert box to the lower-left side. To move the button, click on it to select it, and then drag it to the targeted location.

10. Move the ^0 text control to the right and resize it (as you move the control, the resource editor shows the rectangular outline of the control), making its rectangular area narrower and higher. To resize a control, click on it to select it, and then drag the thumbtacks (the small black squares) with the mouse to change the size.

11. Close the alert box.

12. Close the alert information dialog box.

13. Close the alert list dialog box.

14. Close the Menu1.π.rsrc dialog box. The resource editor prompts you to save the changes you just made. Click the Yes button.

15. Exit the resource editor by selecting the File | Quit command.

Customizing the Main Window

The default main window is scrollable—a feature that is not needed when the program displays only buttons. In this section I discuss changing the main window into the kind shown in Figure 15.8.

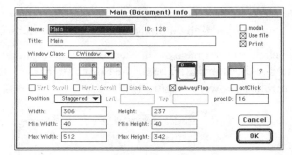

Figure 15.8. *The Main (Document) Info dialog box.*

To change the type of the main window perform the following tasks:

1. Invoke the THINK Project Manager.

2. Select the View | View Info... command. The THINK Project Manager displays the Main (Document) Info dialog box, shown in Figure 15.8.

3. In the row of window icons in the middle of the dialog, click on the fourth icon to the right.

4. Click the OK button to close the dialog box.

It's important to point out that the main window retains its original style in the design stage. In other words, you'll see the new window kind only at runtime.

Creating New Commands

To customize the responses of the new buttons and menus, you need to define three new commands: cmdShowMsg1, cmdShowMsg2, and cmdShowMsg3. First, select the Edit | Commands command to bring up the Commands dialog box. Then perform the following steps for each command:

1. Select the Edit | New Command command to put the Commands dialog box into a mode where you can define a new command.

2. Type cmdShowMsgX in the top-most edit box. The Visual Architect utility automatically assigns this command a number.

3. Select item CMain in the In Class pop-up menu.

4. Select item Call in the Do pop-up menu.

5. Click the OK button to close the Commands dialog box.

These steps define new commands that are associated with the class CMain (actually, its parent class x_CMain). They call various member functions in the associated class.

Creating and Customizing New Buttons

In this stage, you create the two buttons labeled Message 1 and Message 2 by performing these steps:

1. Select the Tools menu to bring up the tools palette. Click on the button tool.

2. Draw the first button in the Main window. This button has the default caption of OK and responds to the predefined command cmdOK.

3. Draw the second button in the Main window. This button has the default caption of Cancel and responds to the predefined command cmdCancel.

4. Double-click the OK button to open the button's data dialog box.

5. Type Msg1Btn in the Identifier edit box. The Visual Architect utility also changes the caption of the dialog box to Msg1Btn.

6. Click on the right arrow symbol near CButton to view the command associated with the button. The current command is cmdOK. Select the command cmdShowMsg1 from the pop-up menu. Click the same right arrow symbol to hide the details of class CButton.

7. Click on the right arrow symbol near CControl to view the control's caption. The current caption is OK. Type Message 1 in the contrlTitle edit box. Click the same right arrow symbol to hide the details of class CControl.

8. Close the Msg1Btn dialog box.

9. Click the Cancel button to open the button's data dialog box.

10. Type Msg2Btn in the Identifier edit box. The Visual Architect utility also changes the caption of the dialog box to Msg2Btn.

11. Click on the right arrow symbol near CButton to view the command associated with the button. The current command is cmdCancel. Select the command cmdShowMsg2 from the pop-up menu. Click the same right arrow symbol to hide the details of class CButton.

12. Click on the right arrow symbol near CControl to view the control's caption. The current caption is Cancel. Type Message 2 in the contrlTitle edit box. Click the same right arrow symbol to hide the details of class CControl.

13. Close the Msg2Btn dialog box.

Creating New Menu Commands

In this stage you add the commands Message 2 and Message 3 to the Edit menu by performing these steps:

1. Select the Edit | Menus command to bring up the Menus dialog box, shown in Figure 15.9.

2. In the list of menus at the left of the dialog, click on Edit to select that menu.

3. Click the Edit Menu Items button to edit the commands associated with the Edit menu. The Visual Architect utility displays the Menu Items dialog box, shown in Figure 15.10.

4. In the list box, click below the Show Clipboard command to switch the dialog box into input mode.

5. Type a hyphen character (-) in the menu item edit box to insert a menu separator.

6. In the list box, click below the last hyphen command to switch the dialog box into input mode.

7. Type Message 2 in the menu item edit box.

8. Select the cmdShowMsg2 item from the Command list box.

9. In the list box, click below the Message 1 command to switch the dialog box into input mode.

10. Type Message 2 in the menu item edit box.

11. Select the cmdShowMsg3 item from the Command list box.

12. Click the OK button in the Menu Items dialog box.

13. Click the OK button in the Menus dialog box.

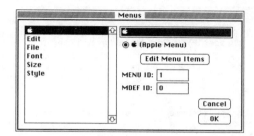

Figure 15.9. *The Menus dialog box.*

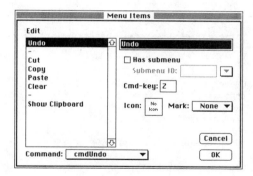

Figure 15.10. *The Menu Items dialog box.*

Generating and Customizing the Source Code

To generate the source code for the second application, invoke the Generate All... command in the THINK Project Manager icon menu. This command emits various files in the Source folder (nested inside this program's folder). Most of these files resemble those of the minimal TCL program. Therefore, I present only those files that are relevant to this program. I also discuss customizing the emitted code to provide the desired operations.

Listing 15.14 shows the source code for the x_CMain.h header file for the second TCL program. The bold lines indicate those that I manually inserted.

VArc Type

Listing 15.14. The source code for the x_CMain.h header file for the Menu1 program.

```
1:  /*****************************************************************
2:   x_CMain.h
3:
4:              Header File For CMain Lower-Layer Document Class
5:
6:      Copyright (c) 1994 My Software Inc. All rights reserved.
7:
8:  Generated by Visual Architect(TM)
9:
10: This file is rewritten each time you generate code. You should
11: not make changes to this file; changes should go in the My.h
12: file, instead.
13:
14: If you want to change how Visual Architect generates this file,
15: you can change the template for this file. It is "_Doc.h" in
16: the Visual Architect Templates folder.
17:
18: *****************************************************************/
19:
20: #pragma once
21:
22: #include "CSaver.h"
23: class CButton;
24:
25: #include "ItsContentsClass.h"
26:
27: #define x_CMain_super    CSaver<ITSCONTENTSCLASS>
28:
29: class CFile;
30:
31: class x_CMain : public x_CMain_super
32:
33: {
34: public:
35:
36:     TCL_DECLARE_CLASS
37:
38:     // Pointers to panes in window
39:     CButton    *fMain_Msg1Btn;
40:     CButton    *fMain_Msg2Btn;
41:
42:     void    Ix_CMain(void);
```

```
43:
44:     virtual    void    DoCommand(long theCommand);
45:     virtual    void    UpdateMenus(void);
46:
47: protected:
48:     virtual    void    MakeNewWindow(void);
49:
50:     virtual    void    FailOpen(CFile *aFile);
51:     virtual void      PositionWindow(void);
52:
53:     virtual void      DoCmdShowMsg1(void);
54:     virtual void      DoCmdShowMsg2(void);
55:     virtual void      DoCmdShowMsg3(void);
56: };
57:
58: #define    CVueCMain    128
```

Listing 15.14 declares the class x_CMain. Although this declaration is similar to that of the minimal program, notice the following new members:

☐ Lines 39 and 40 define the data members fMain_Msg1Btn and fMain_Msg2Btn, which are the pointers to class CButton. These members are pointers to the Message 1 and Message 2 buttons, respectively.

☐ Lines 53 to 55 contain additional member functions: DoCmdShowMsg1, DoCmdShowMsg2, and DoCmdShowMsg3. These functions respond to the commands cmdShowMsg1, cmdShowMsg2, and cmdShowMsg3.

Listing 15.15 shows the source code for the x_CMain.cp implementation file for the third TCL program. The bold lines indicate the ones that I manually inserted.

Listing 15.15. The source code for the x_CMain.cp implementation file for the Menu1 program.

```
1:  /**************************************************************
2:   x_CMain.c
3:
4:                CMain Document Class
5:
6:      Copyright (c) 1994 My Software Inc. All rights reserved.
7:
8:  Generated by Visual Architect(TM) 8:44 PM Wed, Jun 8, 1994
9:
10: This file is rewritten each time you generate code. You should
11: not make changes to this file; changes should go in the My.c
12: file, instead.
13:
14: If you want to change how Visual Architect generates this file,
```

continues

Listing 15.15. continued

```
15:  you can change the template for this file. It is "_Doc_cp" in
16:  the Visual Architect Templates folder.
17:
18:  *****************************************************************/
19:
20:  #include "x_CMain.h"
21:
22:  #include "CMain.h"
23:
24:  #include "MainItems.h"
25:
26:  #include "ViewUtilities.h"
27:  #include "CApp.h"
28:
29:  #include <CApplication.h>
30:  #include <CBartender.h>
31:  #include <Commands.h>
32:  #include <Constants.h>
33:  #include <CDecorator.h>
34:  #include <CDesktop.h>
35:  #include <CFile.h>
36:  #include <TBUtilities.h>
37:  #include <CWindow.h>
38:
39:  extern CApplication *gApplication; /* The application */
40:  extern CDecorator *gDecorator; /* Decorator for arranging
41:                                       windows */
42:  extern CDesktop *gDesktop; /* The visible Desktop */
43:  extern CBartender *gBartender; /* Manages all menus */
44:
45:  #include "CButton.h"
46:
47:  // Define symbols for commands handled by this class
48:  // Prevents a recompile every time any command changed.
49:
50:  #define cmdShowMsg1 512
51:  #define cmdShowMsg2 513
52:  #define cmdShowMsg3 514
53:  #define ALRTnote 130
54:
55:  TCL_DEFINE_CLASS_M1(x_CMain, x_CMain_super);
56:
57:  /**** C O N S T R U C T I O N / D E S T R U C T I O N
58:                                          M E T H O D S ****/
59:
60:
61:  /*****************************************************************
62:   Ix_CMain
63:
64:  Initialize the document
65:  *****************************************************************/
66:
67:  void x_CMain::Ix_CMain()
68:
```

```
 69:  {
 70:      IDocument(gApplication, TRUE);
 71:
 72:      // Initialize data members below.
 73:  }
 74:
 75:
 76:  /*****************************************************************
 77:   MakeNewWindow
 78:
 79:  Create a new, empty window.  Subclass may override to populate
 80:  the new window.
 81:  *****************************************************************/
 82:
 83:  void x_CMain::MakeNewWindow(void)
 84:
 85:  {
 86:     itsWindow = TCLGetNamedWindow("\pMain", this);
 87:
 88:     itsMainPane = (CPane*) TCLGetItemPointer(itsWindow, 0);
 89:
 90:     // Initialize pointers to the subpanes in the window
 91:
 92:     fMain_Msg1Btn = (CButton*)
 93:                        itsWindow->FindViewByID(kMain_Msg1BtnID);
 94:     ASSERT(member(fMain_Msg1Btn, CButton));
 95:
 96:     fMain_Msg2Btn = (CButton*)
 97:                        itsWindow->FindViewByID(kMain_Msg2BtnID);
 98:     ASSERT(member(fMain_Msg2Btn, CButton));
 99:
100:  }
101:
102:
103:  /*****************************************************************
104:   FailOpen {OVERRIDE}
105:
106:  Fail if file already open in this application.
107:
108:  This function calls the application's FileAlreadyOpen function
109:  and fails quietly if the file is open.
110:
111:  Note that open may also fail if the file is open in
112:  another application. This will cause a failure in open,
113:  but you may wish to override this function to detect this
114:  case and provide a more meaningful error message than -49.
115:  *****************************************************************/
116:
117:  void    x_CMain::FailOpen(CFile    *aFile)
118:
119:  {
120:      /* Only the application knows        */
121:      if (((CApp*)gApplication)->FileAlreadyOpen(aFile))
122:          Failure(kSilentErr, 0);
```

continues

439

Listing 15.15. continued

```
123:  }
124:
125:
126:  /****************************************************************
127:   PositionWindow
128:
129:  The default method in CSaver calls the the decorator, which
130:  staggers and resizes the window. Since the window has already
131:  been positioned when it is initialized from the view resource,
132:  we don't want to do this twice.
133:  ****************************************************************/
134:
135:  void    x_CMain::PositionWindow()
136:
137:  {
138:  }
139:
140:
141:
142:
143:  /****************************************************************
144:   DoCommand {OVERRIDE}
145:
146:  Dispatch Visual Architect-specified actions.
147:  ****************************************************************/
148:
149:  void x_CMain::DoCommand(long theCommand)
150:
151:  {
152:      switch (theCommand)
153:      {
154:          case cmdShowMsg1:
155:              DoCmdShowMsg1();
156:              break;
157:          case cmdShowMsg2:
158:              DoCmdShowMsg2();
159:              break;
160:          case cmdShowMsg3:
161:              DoCmdShowMsg3();
162:              break;
163:          default:
164:              CDocument::DoCommand(theCommand);
165:      }
166:  }
167:
168:
169:  /****************************************************************
170:   UpdateMenus {OVERRIDE}
171:
172:  Enable menus which generate commands handled by this class.
173:  ****************************************************************/
174:
175:  void x_CMain::UpdateMenus()
176:
```

```
177:    {
178:        CDocument::UpdateMenus();
179:        gBartender->EnableCmd(cmdShowMsg1);
180:        gBartender->EnableCmd(cmdShowMsg2);
181:        gBartender->EnableCmd(cmdShowMsg3);
182:    }
183:
184:
185:    /*****************************************************************
186:      DoCmdShowMsg1
187:
188:    Respond to cmdShowMsg1 command.
189:    *****************************************************************/
190:
191:    void x_CMain::DoCmdShowMsg1()
192:
193:    {
194:        // Subclass must override this function to
195:        // handle the command
196:        PositionDialog('ALRT', ALRTnote);
197:        InitCursor();
198:        ParamText(
199:          "\p          M E S S A G E\r\rYou clicked button Message 1",
200:          "\p", "\p", "\p");
201:        NoteAlert(ALRTnote, NULL);
202:
203:    }
204:
205:
206:    /*****************************************************************
207:      DoCmdShowMsg2
208:
209:    Respond to cmdShowMsg2 command.
210:    *****************************************************************/
211:
212:    void x_CMain::DoCmdShowMsg2()
213:
214:    {
215:        // Subclass must override this function to
216:        // handle the command
217:        PositionDialog('ALRT', ALRTnote);
218:        InitCursor();
219:        ParamText(
220:          "\p          M E S S A G E\r\rYou clicked button Message 2 or menu
➥ Message 2",
221:          "\p", "\p", "\p");
222:        NoteAlert(ALRTnote, NULL);
223:    }
224:
225:
226:    /*****************************************************************
227:      DoCmdShowMsg3
228:
229:    Respond to cmdShowMsg3 command.
```

continues

Listing 15.15. continued

```
230:    *********************************************************************/
231:
232:    void x_CMain::DoCmdShowMsg3()
233:
234:    {
235:       // Subclass must override this function to
236:       // handle the command
237:       PositionDialog('ALRT', ALRTnote);
238:       InitCursor();
239:       ParamText(
240:          "\p         M E S S A G E\r\rYou clicked menu Message 3",
241:          "\p", "\p", "\p");
242:       NoteAlert(ALRTnote, NULL);
243:    }
```

Listing 15.15 shows the definitions of the member functions in class x_CMain. The output of the Visual Architect utility excludes line 53, lines 196 to 201, lines 217 to 222, and lines 237 to 242. I added these lines manually to support the responses of the Menu1 program.

Lines 50 to 52 define the constants for the commands cmdShowMsg1, cmdShowMsg2, and cmdShowMsg3, respectively. I inserted the definition of constant ALRTgeneral in line 53 to select the resource ID for the customized general alert. The next four subsections discuss the relevant member functions.

The Function *MakeNewWindow*

The member function MakeNewWindow (defined in lines 83 to 100) stores the pointers to the window and pane in the variables itsWindow and itsMainPane, respectively. It also stores the addresses of the buttons in the data members fMain_MsgBtn1 and fMain_MsgBtn2. The MakeNewWindow function obtains these addresses by sending the C++ message FindViewByID to the window object. The arguments for these messages are the constants kMain_Msg1BtnID and kMain_Msg2BtnID, which are defined in lines 31 and 33, respectively, of Listing 15.17.

The Function *DoCommand*

The member function DoCommand (defined in lines 149 to 166) has case labels in the switch statement to respond to the commands cmdShowMsg1, cmdShowMsg2, and cmdShowMsg3. The first statement after each case statement invokes a corresponding member function: case cmdShowMsg1 invokes DoCmdShowMsg1, case cmdShowMsg2 invokes DoCmdShowMsg2, and case cmdShowMsg3 invokes DoCmdShowMsg3.

The Function *UpdateMenus*

The member function UpdateMenus (defined in lines 175 to 182) enables the custom commands by sending the C++ message EnableCmd, for each command, to the bartender object. The arguments for the sequence of EnableCmd messages are the constants cmdShowMsg1, cmdShowMsg2, and cmdShowMsg3.

The Function *DoCmdShowMsg1*

The member function DoCmdShowMsg1 (defined in lines 191 to 203) handles the cmdShowMsg1 command by displaying a note alert box. The calls to functions PositionDialog and InitCursor position and initialize the general alert box, respectively. The function PositionDialog uses the ALRT resource name and the constant ALRTnote to specify the general kind of resource and the specific kind of alert, respectively. The call to the function ParamText specifies the strings to be passed to the general alert box. To display the note alert box itself, the function ParamText calls function NoteAlert and supplies that call with the arguments ALRTnote (the ID of the specific alert box) and NULL.

The member functions DoCmdShowMsg2 and DoCmdShowMsg3 are very similar to the function DoCmdShowMsg1. These functions differ only in the message displayed by the note alert box.

Listing 15.16 shows the source code for the AppCommands.h header file for the third TCL program. This listing defines in lines 16 to 18 the constants cmdShowMsg1, cmdShowMsg2, and cmdShowMsg3, which support the custom commands.

Listing 15.16. The source code for the AppCommands.h header file for the Menu1 program.

```
1:  /*******************************************************************
2:  MyCommands.h
3:
4:              Header File For Command Symbols
5:
6:      Copyright (c) 1994 My Software Inc. All rights reserved.
7:
8:  Generated by Visual Architect(TM)
9:
10: This file is regenerated each time.
11:
12: *******************************************************************/
13:
14: #pragma once
15:
16: #define cmdShowMsg1    512
17: #define cmdShowMsg2    513
18: #define cmdShowMsg3    514
```

Listing 15.17 shows the source code for the MainItems.h header file for the third TCL program. The listing defines an untagged enumerated type, which defines the identifiers kMain_Msg1Btn, kMain_Msg1BtnID, kMain_Msg2Btn, and kMain_Msg2BtnID.

Listing 15.17. The source code for the MainItems.h header file for the Menu1 program.

```
 1:  /****************************************************************
 2:  MainItems.h
 3:
 4:                  Main Item Constants
 5:
 6:      Copyright (c) 1994 My Software Inc. All rights reserved.
 7:
 8:  Generated by Visual Architect(TM)
 9:
10:  This file is rewritten each time you generate code. You should
11:  not make changes to this file.
12:
13:  If you want to change how Visual Architect generates this file,
14:  you can change the template for this file. It is "Items.h" in
15:  the Visual Architect Templates folder.
16:
17:  ****************************************************************/
18:
19:  #pragma once
20:
21:
22:      //    Item numbers for each item.
23:      //
24:      //    Use TCLGetItemPointer (ViewUtilities) to convert these
25:      //    item numbers to a pointer to the named item.
26:
27:  enum
28:  {
29:      Main_Begin_,
30:      kMain_Msg1Btn = 1,
31:      kMain_Msg1BtnID = 1L,
32:      kMain_Msg2Btn = 2,
33:      kMain_Msg2BtnID = 2L,
34:      Main_End_
35:  };
```

Compiling and Running the Program

Invoke the Run command from the THINK Project Manager icon menu. This command causes the compiler to process the set of source code files that contribute to the program. Figures 15.11 through 15.13 show the alert boxes created by the three custom messages.

Figure 15.11. *A sample session with the Menu1 program showing the alert box generated by message* cmdShowMsg1.

Figure 15.12. *A sample session with the Menu1 program showing the alert box generated by message* cmdShowMsg2.

Figure 15.13. *A sample session with the Menu1 program showing the alert box generated by message* cmdShowMsg3.

DO   **DON'T**

DO use the Remove Objects and Close and Compact commands to save the bare essential files in a project.

DON'T forget that when the Visual Architect utility generates a set of files, it overwrites existing files that have the same names. Therefore, make copies of the customized source code files before you use the Visual Architect utility to modify controls, windows, menus, or commands. Using the copies of the files enables you to reinsert the custom code instead of retyping it all in!

Summary

This chapter introduced you to programming Macintosh applications using the TCL classes:

☐ You learned how to create a minimal TCL program, which illustrated the built-in features supported by the TCL classes. By examining the relevant listings presented for this program, you now have a good idea what the code is like.

☐ You learned how to extend the window operations by defining a new command and associating this command to a button control. You also worked through the basic process of drawing a button control.

☐ You learned how to define and respond to custom menu selections. You also learned how to use the Visual Architect utility to add more menu commands, define associated cmdXXXX commands to these menu commands, and how to respond to the cmdXXXX commands.

Q&A

Q Can I create a new project by copying and then modifying the existing files of another project?

A Yes you can. In fact, this approach enables you to inherit the precompiled files from the original project. Consequently, the THINK Project Manager does not recompile all the files from scratch—a process that does take a while!

Q If I regenerate a new batch of files with the Visual Architect utility, do I lose the manually inserted code?

A Yes you do. That's why it's a very good idea to create copies of these files and save them under new names.

Q What happens if I forget to select any item in the In Class and Do pop-up menus when I define a new command?

A The Visual Architect utility does not generate any command-handling code for the CMain or CApp classes. Therefore, such commands will not be handled by the program.

Q Can I use the Visual Architect utility to create new menus and their own commands.

A Yes. The Visual Architect utility enables you to add new menus and define their own sets of commands.

Workshop

The Workshop provides quiz questions to help you solidify your understanding of the material covered and exercises to provide you with experience in using what you've learned. Try to understand the quiz and exercise answers before continuing on to the next day's lesson. Answers are provided in Appendix B, "Answers."

15

Quiz

1. Where is the error in this set of statements:

```
void x_CMain::DoCmdShowMsg3()

{
    // Subclass must override this function to
    // handle the command
    PositionDialog('ALRT', ALRTnote);
    InitCursor();
     ParamText(
     "\p        M E S S A G E\r\rYou clicked menu Message 3",
     "", "", "");
    NoteAlert(ALRTnote, NULL);
}
```

2. By looking at the statements in an x_CMain::DoCommand function, can you tell which command is generated by a button control and which is generated by a menu command?

3. Can more than one button control generate the same cmdXXXX command? Can more than one menu control?

Exercise

Create the program project Menu2, which contains commands in the Edit menu that display the following messages:

☐ Command Message 1, which displays the string This is Message 1 in a general alert box.

☐ Command Message 2, which displays the string This is Message 2 in a general alert box.

☐ Command Message 3, which displays the string This is Message 3 in a general alert box.

Define the new commands cmdShowMsg1, cmdShowMsg2, and cmdShowMsg3 for the above messages.

16

The Static Text Control

Today's lesson examines the simplest type of control, namely, the static text control. This control displays characters that aren't editable by the end user, although the program can change the characters as needed. You learn about the following topics:

☐ The class `CStaticText` which supports the static text control

☐ Using a static text control in a simple read-only window

☐ Using a static text control in a scrollable window

☐ Modifying the text characteristics of a static text control at runtime

The Static Text Control

The static text control displays fixed text that cannot be directly edited by the application's end user. The TCL class `CStaticText` supports the static text control. This class is the descendant of class `CEditText` which supports edit box text. Here is the declaration of class `CStaticText`:

```
class CStaticText : public CEditText { // Class Declaration

public:

    TCL_DECLARE_CLASS


    // Member Functions
    // Construction
    CStaticText();
    CStaticText(CView *anEnclosure, CBureaucrat *aSupervisor,
                short aWidth = 0, short aHeight = 0,
                short aHEncl = 0, short aVEncl = 0,
                SizingOption aHSizing = sizELASTIC,
                SizingOption aVSizing = sizELASTIC,
                short aLineWidth = -1);

                                // Compatibility
    void IStaticText(CView *anEnclosure,
                CBureaucrat *aSupervisor,
                short aWidth, short aHeight,
                short aHEncl, short aVEncl,
                SizingOption aHSizing,
                SizingOption aVSizing,
                short aLineWidth);
};
```

The declaration of class `CStaticText` includes a default constructor, a nondefault constructor, and the initializing member function `IStaticText`. The class inherits its data members and supporting member functions. To give you an idea about the inherited members, I present the declaration of class `CEditText`:

```
class CEditText : public CAbstractText { // Class Declaration

public:

    TCL_DECLARE_CLASS

    // Data Members

    TEHandle macTE;    // Toolbox Text Edit record handle
    long spacingCmd;   // Line spacing command number
    long alignCmd;     // alignment cmd number

    // Member Functions
    // Contruction/Destruction
    CEditText();
    CEditText(CView *anEnclosure,
              CBureaucrat *aSupervisor,
              short aWidth = 0, short aHeight = 0,
              short aHEncl = 0, short aVEncl = 0,
              SizingOption aHSizing = sizELASTIC,
              SizingOption aVSizing = sizELASTIC,
              short aLineWidth = -1,
              Boolean aScrollHoriz = FALSE);
    ~CEditText();

    void IEditText(CView *anEnclosure,
                   CBureaucrat *aSupervisor,
                   short aWidth, short aHeight,
                   short aHEncl, short aVEncl,
                   SizingOption aHSizing,
                   SizingOption aVSizing,
                   short aLineWidth);
    virtual void IViewTemp(CView *anEnclosure,
                           CBureaucrat *aSupervisor,
                           Ptr viewData);
    void IEditTextX();
    virtual void MakeMacTE();

    // Mouse and Keystrokes
    virtual void DoClick(Point hitPt, short modifierKeys,
                         long when);
    virtual void PerformEditCommand(long theCommand);

    // Display
    virtual void Draw(Rect *area);
    virtual void Scroll(long hDelta, long vDelta,
                        Boolean redraw);
    virtual void Activate();
    virtual void Deactivate();
    virtual void SetSelection(long selStart, long selEnd,
                              Boolean fRedraw);
    virtual void HideSelection(Boolean hide,
                               Boolean redraw);  // TCL 1.1.3
                                                 // 11/30/92 BF
    virtual void GetSteps(short *hStep,
                          short *vStep); // TCL 1.1.3 11/30/92 BF

                                        // Text Specification
```

```
virtual void SetTextPtr(Ptr textPtr, long numChars);
virtual Handle GetTextHandle();
virtual Handle CopyTextRange(long start, long end);
virtual void InsertTextPtr(Ptr text,
                           long length,
                           Boolean fRedraw);

virtual void TypeChar(char theChar, short theModifers);

virtual void CheckInsertion(long insertLen, Boolean useSelection);

// Calibrating
virtual void CalcTERects();
virtual void ResizeFrame(Rect *delta);
virtual void AdjustBounds();

virtual long FindLine(long charPos);
virtual long GetLength();

// Text Characteristics
virtual void SetFontNumber(short aFontNumber);
virtual void SetFontStyle(short aStyle);
virtual void SetFontSize(short aSize);
virtual void SetTextMode(short aMode);
virtual void SetAlignment(short anAlignment);
virtual void SetAlignCmd(long alignCmd);
virtual void SetSpacingCmd(long aSpacingCmd);
virtual void GetTEFontInfo(FontInfo *macFontInfo);

virtual long GetHeight(long startLine, long endLine);
virtual long GetCharOffset(LongPt *aPt);
virtual void GetCharPoint(long offset, LongPt *aPt);
virtual void GetTextStyle(short *whichAttributes,
                          TextStyle *aStyle);
virtual void GetCharStyle(long charOffset,
                          TextStyle *theStyle);
virtual long GetSpacingCmd();
virtual long GetAlignCmd();

virtual long GetNumLines();
virtual void GetSelection(long *selStart,
                          long *selEnd);

// Printing
virtual void AboutToPrint(short *firstPage, short *lastPage);
virtual void PrintPage(short pageNum, short pageWidth,
                       short pageHeight, CPrinter *aPRinter);
virtual void DonePrinting();

// Cursor
virtual void Dawdle(long *maxSleep);

// Object I/O
virtual void PutTo(CStream& stream);
virtual void GetFrom(CStream& stream);
```

```
private:
    void CEditTextX();
};

#define  CARRIAGE_RETURN  13 // Character code
#define  kMaxTELength 32000L  // maximum text we allow in
                             // TE record

extern CEditText *gEditText; // the currently active
                            // CEditText, may be NULL
```

In the next six subsections I discuss a selection of the member functions inherited by class CStaticText. These functions affect the appearance of the control's text.

Syntax

The Function *SetFontNumber*

The inherited member function SetFontNumber sets the font of the static text by specifying the font number. The declaration of function SetFontNumber is

```
virtual void SetFontNumber(short aFontNumber);
```

Syntax

The Function *SetFontStyle*

The inherited member function SetFontStyle sets the font style of the static text. The declaration of function SetFontStyle is

```
virtual void SetFontStyle(short aStyle);
```

The arguments for the parameter aStyle specify the font style by using one of the following predefined identifiers or any additive combination: normal, bold, italic, underline, outline, shadow, condense, or extend.

Syntax

The Function *SetFontSize*

The inherited member function SetFontSize sets the font size of the static text. The declaration of function SetFontSize is

```
virtual void SetFontSize(short aSize);
```

Syntax

The Function *SetAlignment*

The inherited member function SetAlignment sets the text alignment for the static text. The declaration of function SetAlignment is

```
virtual void SetAlignment(short anAlignment);
```

The argument for the parameter `anAlignment` can be `teFlushDefault`, `teFlushLeft`, `teCenter`, or `teFlushRight`.

The Function *SetAlignCmd*

The inherited member function `SetAlignCmd` sets the text alignment for the static text using THINK Class Library names for alignment. The function `SetAlignCmd` performs the same task as function `SetAlignment`, but uses a different set of predefined identifiers. The declaration of function `SetAlignCmd` is

```
virtual void SetAlignCmd(long alignCmd);
```

The argument for the parameter `alignCmd` can be `cmdAlignLeft`, `cmdAlignCenter`, or `cmdAlignRight`.

The Function *SetSpacingCmd*

The inherited member function `SetSpacingCmd` sets the text spacing for the static text. The declaration of function `SetSpacingCmd` is

```
virtual void SetSpacingCmd(long aSpacingCmd);
```

The arguments for the parameter `aSpacingCmd` can be `cmdSingleSpace`, `cmd1HalfSpace` (for 1½-line spacing), and `cmdDoubleSpace`.

The Read-Only Window Example

This section shows you how to use static text to provide read-only text in a fixed window. Figure 16.1 shows a sample session with the Main 1 program. The figure shows the fixed window, which includes a set of lines contained in a single static text control.

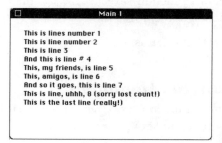

Figure 16.1. *A sample session with the Main 1 program.*

Creating the Main 1 application involves only a few steps:

1. Prepare the minimal main window.

2. Draw the static text control.

3. Customize the main window.

4. Generate and customize the source code.

The following subsections describe each stage of building the Main 1 program.

Preparing the Minimal Main Window

The first stage is identical to the steps you followed in Day 15 (in the section titled "Creating a Minimal TCL Program") to create the minimal TCL program—which yielded an empty main window. Specify Main 1 as the name of the project.

Drawing a Static Text Control

In the second stage, you draw a static text control in the main window by performing the following steps:

1. Click on the Main item in the Visual Architect.rsrc window.

2. Select the Tools menu to bring up the tools palette. Click on the static text tool.

3. Click anywhere inside the Main window and start typing the control's text.

4. When you are done typing, click the mouse outside the static text control to signal that you finished entering the text.

5. Double-click on the control to bring up the control's information dialog box.

6. Replace the current contents of the Identifier edit box with TextLbl, and then close the dialog box.

Customizing the Main Window

The default main window is scrollable, but you need a fixed window for this program. To change from the default style to the fixed window style, perform these tasks:

1. Invoke the THINK Project Manager.

2. Select the View | View Info... command. The THINK Project Manager displays the Main (Document) Info dialog box.

3. In the row of window icons in the middle of the dialog box, click on the fourth icon to the right.

4. Click the OK button to close the dialog box.

Note: It's important to remind you that the main window retains its original style in the design stage. In other words, you'll see the new window style only at runtime.

Generating and Customizing the Source Code

To generate the source code for this application, invoke the Generate All... command in the THINK Project Manager icon menu. This command emits various files in the Source folder (nested inside the program's folder). Most of these files resemble those of the programs in Day 15. I'll present only those files that are relevant to the Main 1 program. I also discuss customizing the emitted code to provide the desired operations.

Listing 16.1 shows the source code for the x_CMain.h header file for the Main 1 program.

 Listing 16.1. The source code for the x_CMain.h header file for the Main 1 program.

```
 1:  /**************************************************************
 2:  x_CMain.h
 3:
 4:            Header File For CMain Lower-Layer Document Class
 5:
 6:       Copyright (c) 1994 My Software Inc. All rights reserved.
 7:
 8:  Generated by Visual Architect(TM)
 9:
10:  This file is rewritten each time you generate code. You should
11:  not make changes to this file; changes should go in the My.h
12:  file, instead.
13:
14:  If you want to change how Visual Architect generates this file,
15:  you can change the template for this file. It is "_Doc.h" in
16:  the Visual Architect Templates folder.
17:
18:  **************************************************************/
19:
20:  #pragma once
```

```
21:
22:    #include "CSaver.h"
23:    class CStaticText;
24:
25:    #include "ItsContentsClass.h"
26:
27:    #define x_CMain_super      CSaver<ITSCONTENTSCLASS>
28:
29:    class CFile;
30:
31:    class x_CMain : public x_CMain_super
32:
33:    {
34:    public:
35:
36:        TCL_DECLARE_CLASS
37:
38:        // Pointers to panes in window
39:        CStaticText    *fMain_TextLbl;
40:
41:        void      Ix_CMain(void);
42:
43:
44:    protected:
45:        virtual void    MakeNewWindow(void);
46:
47:        virtual void    FailOpen(CFile *aFile);
48:        virtual void    PositionWindow(void);
49:
50:    };
51:
52:    #define    CVueCMain     128
```

Listing 16.1 contains the declaration of class x_CMain. This declaration resembles that of the minimal TCL program in Listing 15.8. The main difference is that the class in Listing 16.1 contains the data member fMain_TextLbl, which is a pointer to the static text control.

Listing 16.2 shows the source code for the x_CMain.cp implementation file for the Main 1 program.

Listing 16.2. The source code for the x_CMain.cp implementation file for the Main 1 program.

```
1:    /************************************************************
2:     x_CMain.c
3:
4:                 CMain Document Class
5:
6:        Copyright (c) 1994 My Software Inc. All rights reserved.
7:
```

continues

Listing 16.2. continued

```
 8:   Generated by Visual Architect(TM) 10:30 AM Fri, Jun 10, 1994
 9:
10:   This file is rewritten each time you generate code. You should
11:   not make changes to this file; changes should go in the My.c
12:   file, instead.
13:
14:   If you want to change how Visual Architect generates this file,
15:   you can change the template for this file. It is "_Doc_cp" in
16:   the Visual Architect Templates folder.
17:
18:   ******************************************************************/
19:
20:   #include "x_CMain.h"
21:
22:   #include "CMain.h"
23:
24:   #include "MainItems.h"
25:
26:   #include "ViewUtilities.h"
27:   #include "CApp.h"
28:
29:   #include <CApplication.h>
30:   #include <CBartender.h>
31:   #include <Commands.h>
32:   #include <Constants.h>
33:   #include <CDecorator.h>
34:   #include <CDesktop.h>
35:   #include <CFile.h>
36:   #include <TBUtilities.h>
37:   #include <CWindow.h>
38:
39:   extern CApplication *gApplication; /* The application */
40:   extern CDecorator   *gDecorator;  /* Decorator for
41:                                          arranging windows    */
42:   extern CDesktop     *gDesktop;  /* The visible Desktop */
43:   extern CBartender   *gBartender;  /* Manages all menus */
44:
45:   #include "CStaticText.h"
46:
47:       // Define symbols for commands handled by this class
48:       // Prevents a recompile every time any command changed.
49:
50:
51:
52:   TCL_DEFINE_CLASS_M1(x_CMain, x_CMain_super);
53:
54:   /**** C O N S T R U C T I O N / D E S T R U C T I O N
55:                                          M E T H O D S ****/
56:
57:
58:   /************************************************************
59:    Ix_CMain
60:
61:   Initialize the document
```

```
62:   *****************************************************************/
63:
64:   void x_CMain::Ix_CMain()
65:
66:   {
67:       IDocument(gApplication, TRUE);
68:
69:       // Initialize data members below.
70:   }
71:
72:
73:   /****************************************************************
74:    MakeNewWindow
75:
76:   Create a new, empty window. Subclass may override to populate
77:   the new window.
78:   *****************************************************************/
79:
80:   void x_CMain::MakeNewWindow(void)
81:
82:   {
83:       itsWindow = TCLGetNamedWindow("\pMain", this);
84:
85:       itsMainPane = (CPane*) TCLGetItemPointer(itsWindow, 0);
86:
87:       // Initialize pointers to the subpanes in the window
88:
89:       fMain_TextLbl = (CStaticText*)
90:                       itsWindow->FindViewByID(kMain_TextLblID);
91:       ASSERT(member(fMain_TextLbl, CStaticText));
92:
93:   }
94:
95:
96:   /****************************************************************
97:    FailOpen {OVERRIDE}
98:
99:   Fail if file already open in this application.
100:
101:   This function calls the application's FileAlreadyOpen function
102:   and fails quietly if the file is open.
103:
104:   Note that open may also fail if the file is open in
105:   another application. This will cause a failure in open,
106:   but you may wish to override this function to detect this
107:   case and provide a more meaningful error message than -49.
108:   *****************************************************************/
109:
110:   void x_CMain::FailOpen(CFile *aFile)
111:
112:   {
113:       /* Only the application knows */
114:       if (((CApp*)gApplication)->FileAlreadyOpen(aFile))
115:           Failure(kSilentErr, 0);
116:   }
117:
118:
```

Listing 16.2. continued

```
119:   /***************************************************************
120:     PositionWindow
121:
122:     The default method in CSaver calls the the decorator, which
123:     staggers and resizes the window. Since the window has already
124:     been positioned when it is initialized from the view resource,
125:     we don't want to do this twice.
126:   ***************************************************************/
127:
128:   void    x_CMain::PositionWindow()
129:
130:   {
131:   }
```

Analysis Listing 16.2 contains the definitions for the member functions of class `x_CMain`. These definitions resemble those of the minimal TCL program in Listing 15.9. The main difference is in the function `MakeNewWindow`, which contains the statements in lines 89 to 91 for handling the static text control. The statement spanning lines 89 and 90 stores the address of the static text control in the data member `fMain_TextLbl`. The function `MakeNewWindow` performs this task by sending the C++ message `FindViewByID` to the main window object. The argument for this message is constant `kMain_TextLblID`.

Using Static Text in Scrollable Windows

In a scrollable window, you can have one or more static text controls. A static text control can have a caption consisting of a single line or of multiple lines. The Visual Architect utility by default creates a scrollable window for you. Thus, employing a scrollable window incurs no additional steps. In this section I present the program project Static2, which uses multiple single-line static text controls in a scrollable window. Using multiple single-line static text controls enables the application to use different fonts, font sizes, and font styles for the various controls. Figure 16.2 shows a sample session with the Static2 program. The window contains five static controls whose contents, font, font size, and style are described in Table 16.1. The Static2 program has the following menu commands in the Edit menu:

☐ The `MakeUppercase` menu command writes the text of the static text controls in uppercase.

☐ The `MakeLowercase` menu command writes the text of the static text controls in lowercase.

☐ The MakeMixedcase menu command writes the text of the static text controls in mixed case.

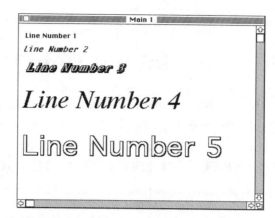

Figure 16.2. *A sample session with the Static2 program.*

Table 16.1. The font, font size, and font styles for the static text controls in the Static2 program.

Control	Text	Font	Size	Style
Line1Lbl	Line Number 1	Chicago	10	Plain Text
Line2Lbl	Line Number 2	Monaco	14	Bold, Italic
Line3Lbl	Line Number 3	New York	18	Shadow, Outline, Italic
Line4Lbl	Line Number 4	Times	48	Italic
Line5Lbl	Line Number 5	Geneva	48	Shadow

Creating the Static2 application involves several stages:

1. Prepare the minimal main window.

2. Define the new commands.

3. Add the new menu commands.

4. Add the static text controls.

5. Generate and customize the source code.

6. Compile and run the program.

The following subsections describe each stage of building the Static2 program.

Preparing the Minimal Main Window

The first stage is identical to the steps you followed in Day 15 (in the section titled "Creating a Minimal TCL Program") to create the minimal TCL program—which yielded an empty main window. Specify the Static2 as the name of the project.

Defining New Programming Commands

To support the Uppercase, Lowercase, and Mixedcase menu commands in the Edit menu, you need to define the programming commands cmdUppercase, cmdLowercase, and cmdMixedcase, respectively. Select the Edit | Commands command to bring up the Commands dialog box. Then perform the following steps to define the three new programming commands:

1. Select the Edit | New Command command to put the Commands dialog box into a mode where you can define a new programming command.

2. Type the name of the new command in the top-most edit box. The Visual Architect utility automatically assigns this command a number.

3. Select item CMain in the In Class pop-up menu.

4. Select item Call in the Do pop-up menu.

5. Repeat steps 1 through 4 for the remaining two commands.

6. When you are done, click the OK button to close the Commands dialog box.

These steps define programming commands that are associated with the class CMain (actually, its parent class x_CMain).

Adding New Menu Commands

To add the new menu commands Uppercase, Lowercase, and Mixedcase to the Edit menu, perform the following steps:

1. Select the Edit | Menus command to bring up the Menus dialog box.

2. Select the Edit menu from the left list box by clicking on it.

3. Click the Edit Menu Items button to edit the commands associated with the Edit menu. The Visual Architect utility displays the Menu Items dialog box (see Figure 15.10).

4. In the list box, click below the Show Clipboard command to switch the dialog box into input mode.

5. Type a hyphen character (-) in the menu item edit box to insert a menu separator.

6. In the list box, click below the last hyphen command to switch the dialog box into input mode.

7. Type Uppercase in the menu item edit box.

8. Select the cmdUppercase item from the Command list box.

9. In the list box, click below the Uppercase command to switch the dialog box into input mode.

10. Type Lowercase in the menu item edit box.

11. Select the cmdLowercase item from the Command list box.

12. In the list box, click below the Lowercase command to switch the dialog box into input mode.

13. Type Mixedcase in the menu item edit box.

14. Select the cmdMixedcase item from the Command list box.

15. Click the OK button in the Menu Items dialog box.

16. Click the OK button in the Menus dialog box.

Adding Static Text Controls

In this stage, you add the five static text controls. The steps involved in this stage are

1. Select the Tools menu to bring up the tools palette. Click on the static text tool (the one with the letter *A*).

2. Click on the main window pane and type Line Number 1.

3. Click in the main window below the control to exit the text input mode.

4. Invoke the Pane | Font command to select the appropriate font for the static text control (see Table 16.1).

5. Invoke the Pane | Size command to choose the appropriate font size for the static text control (see Table 16.1).

6. Invoke the Pane | Style command to choose the appropriate font style(s) for the static text control (see Table 16.1).

7. Double-click on the control to bring up the control's data dialog box. Type in the appropriate control name (see the first column in Table 16.1).

8. Close the data dialog box.

9. Repeat steps 1 through 8 for the other static text controls.

Generating and Customizing the Source Code

To generate the source code for the second application, invoke the Generate All... command in the THINK Project Manager icon menu. This command emits various files in the Source folder (nested inside this program's folder). Most of these files resemble those of the minimal TCL program. Therefore, I present only those files that are relevant to the Static2 program. I also discuss customizing the emitted code to provide the desired operations. Listing 16.3 shows the source code for the x_CMain.h header file for the Static2 program.

Listing 16.3. The source code for the x_CMain.h header file for the Static2 program.

```
 1:  /*************************************************************
 2:   x_CMain.h
 3:
 4:            Header File For CMain Lower-Layer Document Class
 5:
 6:      Copyright (c) 1994 My Software Inc. All rights reserved.
 7:
 8:  Generated by Visual Architect(TM)
 9:
10:  This file is rewritten each time you generate code. You should
11:  not make changes to this file; changes should go in the My.h
12:  file, instead.
13:
14:  If you want to change how Visual Architect generates this file,
15:  you can change the template for this file. It is "_Doc.h" in
16:  the Visual Architect Templates folder.
17:
18:  *************************************************************/
19:
20:  #pragma once
```

```
21:
22:    #include "CSaver.h"
23:    class CStaticText;
24:
25:    #include "ItsContentsClass.h"
26:
27:    #define x_CMain_super       CSaver<ITSCONTENTSCLASS>
28:
29:    class CFile;
30:
31:    class x_CMain : public x_CMain_super
32:
33:    {
34:    public:
35:
36:         TCL_DECLARE_CLASS
37:
38:         // Pointers to panes in window
39:         CStaticText     *fMain_Line1Lbl;
40:         CStaticText     *fMain_Line2Lbl;
41:         CStaticText     *fMain_Line3Lbl;
42:         CStaticText     *fMain_Line4Lbl;
43:         CStaticText     *fMain_Line5Lbl;
44:
45:         void       Ix_CMain(void);
46:
47:         virtual    void     DoCommand(long theCommand);
48:         virtual    void     UpdateMenus(void);
49:
50:    protected:
51:         virtual    void     MakeNewWindow(void);
52:
53:         virtual    void     FailOpen(CFile *aFile);
54:         virtual void        PositionWindow(void);
55:
56:         virtual void        DoCmdLowercase(void);
57:         virtual void        DoCmdUppercase(void);
58:         virtual void        DoCmdMixedcase(void);
59:    };
60:
61:    #define    CVueCMain    128
```

Listing 16.3 declares the class x_CMain. Although this declaration is similar to that of the minimal program, notice the following new members:

☐ Lines 39 and 43 define the data members fMain_Line1Lbl through fMain_Line5Lbl which are the pointers to class CStaticText. These members are pointers to the static text controls.

☐ Lines 56 to 58 contain additional member functions: DoCmdLowercase, DoCmdUppercase, and DoCmdMixedcase.

Listing 16.4 shows the source code for the x_CMain.cp implementation file for the Static2 program. The bold lines indicate ones that I manually inserted.

Listing 16.4. The source code for the x_CMain.cp implementation file for the Static2 program.

```
 1:  /************************************************************
 2:  x_CMain.c
 3:
 4:                    CMain Document Class
 5:
 6:     Copyright (c) 1994 My Software Inc. All rights reserved.
 7:
 8:  Generated by Visual Architect(TM) 12:23 PM Fri, Jun 10, 1994
 9:
10:  This file is rewritten each time you generate code. You should
11:  not make changes to this file; changes should go in the My.c
12:  file, instead.
13:
14:  If you want to change how Visual Architect generates this file,
15:  you can change the template for this file. It is "_Doc_cp" in
16:  the Visual Architect Templates folder.
17:
18:  ************************************************************/
19:
20:  #include "x_CMain.h"
21:
22:  #include "CMain.h"
23:
24:  #include "MainItems.h"
25:
26:  #include "ViewUtilities.h"
27:  #include "CApp.h"
28:
29:  #include <CApplication.h>
30:  #include <CBartender.h>
31:  #include <Commands.h>
32:  #include <Constants.h>
33:  #include <CDecorator.h>
34:  #include <CDesktop.h>
35:  #include <CFile.h>
36:  #include <TBUtilities.h>
37:  #include <CWindow.h>
38:
39:  extern CApplication *gApplication; /* The application */
40:  extern CDecorator *gDecorator;  /* Decorator for arranging
41:                                       windows */
42:  extern CDesktop *gDesktop; /* The visible Desktop */
43:  extern CBartender *gBartender;  /* Manages all menus */
44:
45:  #include "CStaticText.h"
46:
47:      // Define symbols for commands handled by this class
48:      // Prevents a recompile every time any command changed.
```

```
 49:
 50:    #define cmdLowercase 515
 51:    #define cmdUppercase 514
 52:    #define cmdMixedcase 516
 53:
 54:
 55:    TCL_DEFINE_CLASS_M1(x_CMain, x_CMain_super);
 56:
 57:    /**** C O N S T R U C T I O N / D E S T R U C T I O N
 58:                                          M E T H O D S ****/
 59:
 60:
 61:    /************************************************************
 62:     Ix_CMain
 63:
 64:    Initialize the document
 65:    ************************************************************/
 66:
 67:    void x_CMain::Ix_CMain()
 68:
 69:    {
 70:        IDocument(gApplication, TRUE);
 71:
 72:            // Initialize data members below.
 73:    }
 74:
 75:
 76:    /************************************************************
 77:     MakeNewWindow
 78:
 79:    Create a new, empty window. Subclass may override to populate
 80:    the new window.
 81:    ************************************************************/
 82:
 83:    void x_CMain::MakeNewWindow(void)
 84:
 85:    {
 86:        itsWindow = TCLGetNamedWindow("\pMain", this);
 87:
 88:        itsMainPane = (CPane*) TCLGetItemPointer(itsWindow, 0);
 89:
 90:        // Initialize pointers to the subpanes in the window
 91:
 92:        fMain_Line1Lbl = (CStaticText*)
 93:                    itsWindow->FindViewByID(kMain_Line1LblID);
 94:        ASSERT(member(fMain_Line1Lbl, CStaticText));
 95:
 96:        fMain_Line2Lbl = (CStaticText*)
 97:                    itsWindow->FindViewByID(kMain_Line2LblID);
 98:        ASSERT(member(fMain_Line2Lbl, CStaticText));
 99:
100:        fMain_Line3Lbl = (CStaticText*)
101:                    itsWindow->FindViewByID(kMain_Line3LblID);
102:        ASSERT(member(fMain_Line3Lbl, CStaticText));
103:
```

continues

467

Listing 16.4. continued

```
104:        fMain_Line4Lbl = (CStaticText*)
105:                        itsWindow->FindViewByID(kMain_Line4LblID);
106:        ASSERT(member(fMain_Line4Lbl, CStaticText));
107:
108:        fMain_Line5Lbl = (CStaticText*)
109:                        itsWindow->FindViewByID(kMain_Line5LblID);
110:        ASSERT(member(fMain_Line5Lbl, CStaticText));
111:
112: }
113:
114:
115: /************************************************************
116:    FailOpen {OVERRIDE}
117:
118: Fail if file already open in this application.
119:
120: This function calls the application's FileAlreadyOpen function
121: and fails quietly if the file is open.
122:
123: Note that open may also fail if the file is open in
124: another application. This will cause a failure in open,
125: but you may wish to override this function to detect this
126: case and provide a more meaningful error message than -49.
127: ************************************************************/
128:
129: void x_CMain::FailOpen(CFile *aFile)
130:
131: {
132:     /* Only the application knows          */
133:     if (((CApp*)gApplication)->FileAlreadyOpen(aFile))
134:         Failure(kSilentErr, 0);
135: }
136:
137:
138: /************************************************************
139:    PositionWindow
140:
141: The default method in CSaver calls the the decorator, which
142: staggers and resizes the window. Since the window has already
143: been positioned when it is initialized from the view resource,
144: we don't want to do this twice.
145: ************************************************************/
146:
147: void     x_CMain::PositionWindow()
148:
149: {
150: }
151:
152:
153:
154:
155: /************************************************************
156:    DoCommand {OVERRIDE}
157:
158: Dispatch Visual Architect-specified actions.
```

```
159:     *****************************************************************/
160:
161:     void x_CMain::DoCommand(long theCommand)
162:
163:     {
164:         switch (theCommand)
165:         {
166:             case cmdLowercase:
167:                 DoCmdLowercase();
168:                 break;
169:             case cmdUppercase:
170:                 DoCmdUppercase();
171:                 break;
172:             case cmdMixedcase:
173:                 DoCmdMixedcase();
174:                 break;
175:             default:
176:                 CDocument::DoCommand(theCommand);
177:         }
178:     }
179:
180:
181:     /***********************************************************
182:       UpdateMenus {OVERRIDE}
183:
184:     Enable menus which generate commands handled by this class.
185:     *****************************************************************/
186:
187:     void x_CMain::UpdateMenus()
188:
189:     {
190:         CDocument::UpdateMenus();
191:         gBartender->EnableCmd(cmdLowercase);
192:         gBartender->EnableCmd(cmdUppercase);
193:         gBartender->EnableCmd(cmdMixedcase);
194:     }
195:
196:
197:     /***********************************************************
198:       DoCmdLowercase
199:
200:     Respond to cmdLowercase command.
201:     *****************************************************************/
202:
203:     void x_CMain::DoCmdLowercase()
204:
205:     {
206:         // Subclass must override this function to
207:         // handle the command
208:         fMain_Line1Lbl->SetTextString("\pline number 1");
209:         fMain_Line2Lbl->SetTextString("\pline number 2");
210:         fMain_Line3Lbl->SetTextString("\pline number 3");
211:         fMain_Line4Lbl->SetTextString("\pline number 4");
212:         fMain_Line5Lbl->SetTextString("\pline number 5");
213:     }
214:
```

continues

Listing 16.4. continued

```
215:
216:    /************************************************************
217:     DoCmdUppercase
218:
219:    Respond to cmdUppercase command.
220:    ****************************************************************/
221:
222:    void x_CMain::DoCmdUppercase()
223:
224:    {
225:         // Subclass must override this function to
226:         // handle the command
227:         fMain_Line1Lbl->SetTextString("\pLINE NUMBER 1");
228:         fMain_Line2Lbl->SetTextString("\pLINE NUMBER 2");
229:         fMain_Line3Lbl->SetTextString("\pLINE NUMBER 3");
230:         fMain_Line4Lbl->SetTextString("\pLINE NUMBER 4");
231:         fMain_Line5Lbl->SetTextString("\pLINE NUMBER 5");
232:    }
233:
234:
235:    /************************************************************
236:     DoCmdMixedcase
237:
238:    Respond to cmdMixedcase command.
239:    ****************************************************************/
240:
241:    void x_CMain::DoCmdMixedcase()
242:
243:    {
244:         // Subclass must override this function to
245:         // handle the command
246:         fMain_Line1Lbl->SetTextString("\pLine Number 1");
247:         fMain_Line2Lbl->SetTextString("\pLine Number 2");
248:         fMain_Line3Lbl->SetTextString("\pLine Number 3");
249:         fMain_Line4Lbl->SetTextString("\pLine Number 4");
250:         fMain_Line5Lbl->SetTextString("\pLine Number 5");
251:    }
```

Listing 16.4 shows the definitions of the member functions in class x_CMain. The output of the Visual Architect utility excludes lines 208 to 212, lines 227 to 231, and lines 246 to 250. I added these lines manually to support the responses of the Static2 program.

Lines 50 to 53 define the constants for the commands cmdLowercase, cmdUppercase, and cmdMixedcase, respectively. The next four subsections discuss the relevant member functions.

The Function *MakeNewWindow*

The member function MakeNewWindow (defined in lines 83 to 112) stores the pointers to the window and the pane in the variables itsWindow and itsMainPane, respectively. It also stores the addresses of the static text controls in the data members fMain_Line1Lbl through fMain_Line5Lbl. The function obtains these addresses by sending the C++ message FindViewByID to the window object. The arguments for these messages are the constants kMain_Line1LblID through kMain_Line5LblID, which are defined in Listing 16.5 in lines 31, 33, 35, 37, 39, and 41, respectively.

The Function *DoCommand*

The member function DoCommand (defined in lines 161 to 178) has case labels in the switch statement to respond to the commands cmdLowercase, cmdUppercase, and cmdMixedcase. The first statement after case cmdLowercase invokes the member function DoCmdLowercase. The first statement after case cmdUppercase invokes the member function DoCmdUppercase. The first statement after case cmdMixedcase invokes the member function DoCmdMixedcase.

The Function *UpdateMenus*

The member function UpdateMenus (defined in lines 187 to 194) enables the custom commands by sending the C++ message EnableCmd, for each command, to the bartender object. The arguments for the sequence of the EnableCmd message are the constants cmdLowercase, cmdUppercase, and cmdMixedcase.

The Functions *DoCmdLowercase*, *DoCmdUppercase*, and *DoCmdMixedcase*

The member function DoCmdLowercase (defined in lines 203 to 213) handles the cmdLowercase command by displaying the text of the static text controls in lowercase. The function sends the C++ message SetTextString to each static text control. The argument for each message is a lowercase string literal.

The member functions DoCmdUppercase and DoCmdMixedcase are very similar to the function DoCmdLowercase. These functions differ in the message displayed by the note alert box.

Listing 16.5 shows the source code for the MainItems.h header file for the Static2 program. The listing defines an untagged enumerated type that defines the identifiers `kMain_Line1Lbl` through `kMain_Line5Lbl`, and `kMain_Line1LblID` through `kMain_Line5LblID`.

Listing 16.5. The source code for the MainItems.h header file for the Static2 program.

```
1:  /*************************************************************
2:  MainItems.h
3:
4:                    Main Item Constants
5:
6:      Copyright (c) 1994 My Software Inc. All rights reserved.
7:
8:  Generated by Visual Architect(TM)
9:
10: This file is rewritten each time you generate code. You should
11: not make changes to this file.
12:
13: If you want to change how Visual Architect generates this file,
14: you can change the template for this file. It is "Items.h" in
15: the Visual Architect Templates folder.
16:
17: *************************************************************/
18:
19: #pragma once
20:
21:
22:      //    Item numbers for each item.
23:      //
24:      //    Use TCLGetItemPointer (ViewUtilities) to convert these
25:      //    item numbers to a pointer to the named item.
26:
27: enum
28: {
29:     Main_Begin_,
30:     kMain_Line1Lbl = 1,
31:     kMain_Line1LblID = 1L,
32:     kMain_Line2Lbl = 2,
33:     kMain_Line2LblID = 2L,
34:     kMain_Line3Lbl = 3,
35:     kMain_Line3LblID = 3L,
36:     kMain_Line4Lbl = 4,
37:     kMain_Line4LblID = 4L,
38:     kMain_Line5Lbl = 5,
39:     kMain_Line5LblID = 5L,
40:     Main_End_
41: };
```

Listing 16.6 shows the source code for the AppCommands.h header file for the Static2 program. This listing defines the constants `cmdLowercase`, `cmdUppercase`, and `cmdMixedcase`, in lines 16 to 18, which support the custom commands.

Listing 16.6. The source code for the AppCommands.h header file for the Static2 program.

```
 1:  /*************************************************************
 2:   MyCommands.h
 3:
 4:              Header File For Command Symbols
 5:
 6:      Copyright (c) 1994 My Software Inc. All rights reserved.
 7:
 8:  Generated by Visual Architect(TM)
 9:
10:  This file is regenerated each time.
11:
12:  *************************************************************/
13:
14:  #pragma once
15:
16:  #define cmdLowercase     515
17:  #define cmdMixedcase     516
18:  #define cmdUppercase     514
```

16

Compiling and Running the Program

Invoke the Run command from the THINK Project Manager icon menu. This command causes the compiler to process the set of source code files that contribute to the program. Figures 16.3 and 16.4 show the static text in uppercase and in lowercase, respectively.

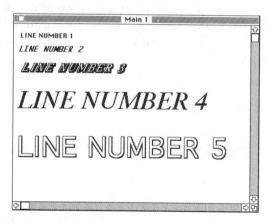

Figure 16.3. *A sample session with the Static2 program showing the text of the static text controls in uppercase characters.*

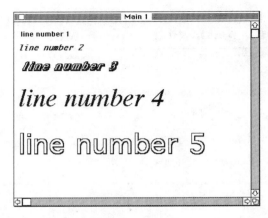

Figure 16.4. *A sample session with the Static2 program showing the text of the static text controls in lowercase characters.*

Runtime Manipulation of Static Text

Let's look at a program that alters the text of a static text control at runtime. The next program project, Static3, enables you to alter the size, spacing, alignment, and style (albeit in a limited way) of the characters in a multiline single static text control. Figure 16.5 shows the initial window, which contains the multiline static text control. There are 20 lines in this control. Table 16.2 shows the custom Font Manipulation menu commands, their associated custom cmd*XXXX* commands, and the operations performed by the menu commands.

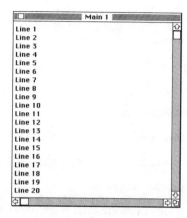

Figure 16.5. *A sample session with the Static3 program showing the initial window.*

Table 16.2. The custom Font Manipulation menu commands, cmdXXXX commands, and their operations for program Static3.

Menu Command	cmdXXXX Command	Operation
Double Spacing	cmdSetSpacingDouble	Set double spacing
Single Spacing	cmdSetSpacingSingle	Set single spacing
1Half Spacing	cmdSpacingHalf	Set 1½-line spacing
-		Separator
Align Left	cmdSetAlignLeft	Align text to the left
Align Center	cmdSetAlignCenter	Center text
Align Right	cmdSetAlignRight	Align text to the right
-		Separator
Bold	cmdSetBold	Set bold style
Italic	cmdSetItalic	Set italic style
Normal	cmdSetNormal	Set normal style

Creating the Static3 application involves several stages:

1. Prepare the minimal main window.

2. Define the new commands.

3. Add the new menu.

4. Add the new menu commands.

5. Add the static text controls.

6. Generate and customize the source code.

7. Compile and run the program.

The following subsections describe each stage of building the Static3 program.

Preparing the Minimal Main Window

The first stage is identical to the steps you followed in Day 15 (in the section titled "Creating a Minimal TCL Program") to create the minimal TCL program—which yielded an empty main window. Specify the Static3 as the name of the project.

Defining New Commands

To support the nine commands listed in Table 16.2, you need to define these commands. Select the Edit | Commands command to bring up the Commands dialog box, and then perform the following steps to define the new commands:

1. Select the Edit | New Command command to put the Commands dialog box into a mode where you can define a new command.

2. Type the name of the new command in the top-most edit box. The Visual Architect utility automatically assigns this command a number.

3. Select item CMain in the In Class pop-up menu.

4. Select item Call in the Do pop-up menu.

5. Repeat steps 1 through 4 for the remaining commands.

6. When you are done, click the OK button to close the Commands dialog box.

These steps define commands that are associated with the class CMain.

Adding a New Menu

To add the Font Manipulation menu to the list of menus, perform the following steps:

1. Select the Edit | Menus command to bring up the Menus dialog box.

2. In the list box, click below the Edit menu to shift into the menu input state.

3. Type Font Manipulation as the name of the new menu.

Adding New Menu Commands

In this stage, you add the Font Manipulation menu commands listed in Table 16.2. Perform the following steps:

1. Make sure that the new menu is currently selected (it should be from the previous stage). Click the Edit Menu Items button to edit the commands associated with the Font Manipulation menu. The Visual Architect utility displays the Menu Items dialog box.

2. Use the ⊞K shortcut to switch the dialog box into input mode.

3. In the menu item edit box, either type a hyphen character (-) to insert a menu separator, or type a menu command (see Table 16.2 for the sequence of separators and menu commands).

4. Select the corresponding item, when appropriate, from the Command list box.

5. Repeat steps 2 through 4 to build the list of commands and separators for the Font Manipulation menu.

6. Click the OK button in the Menu Items dialog box.

7. Click the OK button in the Menus dialog box.

Adding Static Text Controls

To add the five static text controls, perform the following steps:

1. Select the Tools menu to bring up the tools palette. Click on the static text tool (the one with the letter *A*).

2. Click on the main window pane, and type Line Number 1 through Line Number 20, separating each line by pressing Enter.

3. Click the mouse outside the control to end the text input mode.

4. Double-click on the control to bring up the control's data dialog box. Type `TextLbl` in the Identifier edit box.

5. Close the data dialog box.

6. Repeat steps 1 through 5 for the other static text controls.

Generating and Customizing the Source Code

To generate the source code for this third application, invoke the Generate All... command in the THINK Project Manager icon menu. This command emits various files in the Source folder (nested inside this program's folder). Most of these files resemble those of the minimal TCL program. Therefore, I present only those files that are relevant to the Static3 program. I also discuss customizing the emitted code to provide the desired operations.

Listing 16.7 shows the source code for the x_CMain.h header file for the Static3 program.

DO	DON'T

DO use a single multiline static text control to display and manipulate (in the same manner) multiple lines of text.

DON'T use an array of single-line static text controls as a substitute for a single multiline static text control. This approach wastes memory resources in maintaining the array of static text controls.

Listing 16.7. The source code for the x_CMain.h header file for the Static3 program.

```
1:  /**************************************************************
2:   x_CMain.h
3:
4:          Header File For CMain Lower-Layer Document Class
5:
6:      Copyright (c) 1994 My Software Inc. All rights reserved.
7:
8:  Generated by Visual Architect(TM)
9:
```

```
10:    This file is rewritten each time you generate code. You should
11:    not make changes to this file; changes should go in the My.h
12:    file, instead.
13:
14:    If you want to change how Visual Architect generates this file,
15:    you can change the template for this file. It is "_Doc.h" in
16:    the Visual Architect Templates folder.
17:
18:    ****************************************************************/
19:
20:    #pragma once
21:
22:    #include "CSaver.h"
23:    class CStaticText;
24:
25:    #include "ItsContentsClass.h"
26:
27:    #define x_CMain_super     CSaver<ITSCONTENTSCLASS>
28:
29:    class CFile;
30:
31:    class x_CMain : public x_CMain_super
32:
33:    {
34:    public:
35:
36:        TCL_DECLARE_CLASS
37:
38:        // Pointers to panes in window
39:        CStaticText    *fMain_TextLbl;
40:
41:        void      Ix_CMain(void);
42:
43:        virtual   void    DoCommand(long theCommand);
44:        virtual   void    UpdateMenus(void);
45:
46:    protected:
47:        virtual void    MakeNewWindow(void);
48:
49:        virtual void    FailOpen(CFile *aFile);
50:        virtual void    PositionWindow(void);
51:
52:        virtual void    DoCmdSetFont10(void);
53:        virtual void    DoCmdSetFont12(void);
54:        virtual void    DoCmdSetFont14(void);
55:        virtual void    DoCmdSetSpacingDouble(void);
56:        virtual void    DoCmdSetSpacingHalf(void);
57:        virtual void    DoCmdSetSpacingSingle(void);
58:        virtual void    DoCmdSetAlignLeft(void);
59:        virtual void    DoCmdSetAlignRight(void);
60:        virtual void    DoCmdSetAlignCenter(void);
61:        virtual void    DoCmdSetBold(void);
62:        virtual void    DoCmdSetItalic(void);
63:        virtual void    DoCmdSetNormal(void);
64:    };
65:
66:    #define   CVueCMain    128
```

Analysis Listing 16.7 declares the class x_CMain. Although this declaration is similar to that of the minimal program, notice the following new members:

☐ Line 39 defines the data member fMain_TextLbl which is the pointer to class CStaticText. This member accesses the program's static text control.

☐ Lines 52 to 63 contain the definitions of the additional member functions DoCmdSet*XXXX*, which respond to the commands of the Font Manipulation menu.

Listing 16.8 shows the source code for the x_CMain.cp implementation file for the Static3 program. The bold lines show the lines that I manually inserted.

Listing 16.8. The source code for the x_CMain.cp implementation file for the Static3 program.

```
1:  /****************************************************************
2:   x_CMain.c
3:
4:                  CMain Document Class
5:
6:      Copyright (c) 1994 My Software Inc. All rights reserved.
7:
8:  Generated by Visual Architect(TM) 3:54 PM Fri, Jun 10, 1994
9:
10: This file is rewritten each time you generate code. You should
11: not make changes to this file; changes should go in the My.h
12: file, instead.
13:
14: If you want to change how Visual Architect generates this file,
15: you can change the template for this file. It is "_Doc.h" in
16: the Visual Architect Templates folder.
17: ****************************************************************/
18:
19: #include "x_CMain.h"
20:
21: #include "CMain.h"
22:
23: #include "MainItems.h"
24:
25: #include "ViewUtilities.h"
26: #include "CApp.h"
27:
28: #include <CApplication.h>
29: #include <CBartender.h>
30: #include <Commands.h>
31: #include <Constants.h>
32: #include <CDecorator.h>
33: #include <CDesktop.h>
34: #include <CFile.h>
35: #include <TBUtilities.h>
36: #include <CWindow.h>
```

```
37:
38:    extern CApplication *gApplication; /* The application  */
39:    extern CDecorator *gDecorator; /* Decorator for arranging
40:                                     windows */
41:    extern CDesktop *gDesktop; /* The visible Desktop */
42:    extern CBartender *gBartender; /* Manages all menus */
43:
44:    #include "CStaticText.h"
45:
46:        // Define symbols for commands handled by this class
47:        // Prevents a recompile every time any command changed.
48:
49:    #define cmdSetFont10          512
50:    #define cmdSetFont12          513
51:    #define cmdSetFont14          514
52:    #define cmdSetSpacingDouble   517
53:    #define cmdSetSpacingHalf     516
54:    #define cmdSetSpacingSingle   515
55:    #define cmdSetAlignLeft       519
56:    #define cmdSetAlignRight      520
57:    #define cmdSetAlignCenter     522
58:    #define cmdSetBold            523
59:    #define cmdSetItalic          524
60:    #define cmdSetNormal          525
61:
62:
63:    TCL_DEFINE_CLASS_M1(x_CMain, x_CMain_super);
64:
65:    /**** C O N S T R U C T I O N / D E S T R U C T I O N
66:                                             M E T H O D S ****/
67:
68:
69:    /****************************************************************
70:      Ix_CMain
71:
72:    Initialize the document
73:    ****************************************************************/
74:
75:    void x_CMain::Ix_CMain()
76:
77:    {
78:        IDocument(gApplication, TRUE);
79:
80:            // Initialize data members below.
81:    }
82:
83:
84:    /****************************************************************
85:      MakeNewWindow
86:
87:    Create a new, empty window. Subclass may override to populate
88:    the new window.
89:    ****************************************************************/
90:
91:    void x_CMain::MakeNewWindow(void)
92:
```

continues

Listing 16.8. continued

```
93:    {
94:        itsWindow = TCLGetNamedWindow("\pMain", this);
95:
96:        itsMainPane = (CPane*) TCLGetItemPointer(itsWindow, 0);
97:
98:        // Initialize pointers to the subpanes in the window
99:
100:       fMain_TextLbl = (CStaticText*)
101:                       itsWindow->FindViewByID(kMain_TextLblID);
102:       ASSERT(member(fMain_TextLbl, CStaticText));
103:
104:   }
105:
106:
107:   /****************************************************************
108:    FailOpen {OVERRIDE}
109:
110:   Fail if file already open in this application.
111:
112:   This function calls the application's FileAlreadyOpen function
113:   and fails quietly if the file is open.
114:
115:   Note that open may also fail if the file is open in
116:   another application. This will cause a failure in open,
117:   but you may wish to override this function to detect this
118:   case and provide a more meaningful error message than -49.
119:   ****************************************************************/
120:
121:   void x_CMain::FailOpen(CFile *aFile)
122:
123:   {
124:       /* Only the application knows   */
125:       if (((CApp*)gApplication)->FileAlreadyOpen(aFile))
126:           Failure(kSilentErr, 0);
127:   }
128:
129:
130:   /****************************************************************
131:    PositionWindow
132:
133:   The default method in CSaver calls the decorator, which
134:   staggers and resizes the window. Since the window has already
135:   been positioned when it is initialized from the view resource,
136:   we don't want to do this twice.
137:   ****************************************************************/
138:
139:   void    x_CMain::PositionWindow()
140:
141:   {
142:   }
143:
144:
145:
146:
```

```
147:    /****************************************************************
148:      DoCommand {OVERRIDE}
149:
150:    Dispatch Visual Architect-specified actions.
151:    ****************************************************************/
152:
153:    void x_CMain::DoCommand(long theCommand)
154:
155:    {
156:        switch (theCommand)
157:        {
158:            case cmdSetFont10:
159:                DoCmdSetFont10();
160:                break;
161:            case cmdSetFont12:
162:                DoCmdSetFont12();
163:                break;
164:            case cmdSetFont14:
165:                DoCmdSetFont14();
166:                break;
167:            case cmdSetSpacingDouble:
168:                DoCmdSetSpacingDouble();
169:                break;
170:            case cmdSetSpacingHalf:
171:                DoCmdSetSpacingHalf();
172:                break;
173:            case cmdSetSpacingSingle:
174:                DoCmdSetSpacingSingle();
175:                break;
176:            case cmdSetAlignLeft:
177:                DoCmdSetAlignLeft();
178:                break;
179:            case cmdSetAlignRight:
180:                DoCmdSetAlignRight();
181:                break;
182:            case cmdSetAlignCenter:
183:                DoCmdSetAlignCenter();
184:                break;
185:            case cmdSetBold:
186:                DoCmdSetBold();
187:                break;
188:            case cmdSetItalic:
189:                DoCmdSetItalic();
190:                break;
191:            case cmdSetNormal:
192:                DoCmdSetNormal();
193:                break;
194:            default:
195:                CDocument::DoCommand(theCommand);
196:        }
197:    }
198:
199:
200:    /****************************************************************
201:      UpdateMenus {OVERRIDE}
202:
```

continues

Listing 16.8. continued

```
203:    Enable menus which generate commands handled by this class.
204:    ******************************************************************/
205:
206:    void x_CMain::UpdateMenus()
207:
208:    {
209:        CDocument::UpdateMenus();
210:        gBartender->EnableCmd(cmdSetFont10);
211:        gBartender->EnableCmd(cmdSetFont12);
212:        gBartender->EnableCmd(cmdSetFont14);
213:        gBartender->EnableCmd(cmdSetSpacingDouble);
214:        gBartender->EnableCmd(cmdSetSpacingHalf);
215:        gBartender->EnableCmd(cmdSetSpacingSingle);
216:        gBartender->EnableCmd(cmdSetAlignLeft);
217:        gBartender->EnableCmd(cmdSetAlignRight);
218:        gBartender->EnableCmd(cmdSetAlignCenter);
219:        gBartender->EnableCmd(cmdSetBold);
220:        gBartender->EnableCmd(cmdSetItalic);
221:        gBartender->EnableCmd(cmdSetNormal);
222:    }
223:
224:
225:    /******************************************************************
226:     DoCmdSetFont10
227:
228:    Respond to cmdSetFont10 command.
229:    ******************************************************************/
230:
231:    void x_CMain::DoCmdSetFont10()
232:
233:    {
234:            // Subclass must override this function to
235:            // handle the command
236:            fMain_TextLbl->SetFontSize(10);
237:    }
238:
239:
240:    /******************************************************************
241:     DoCmdSetFont12
242:
243:    Respond to cmdSetFont12 command.
244:    ******************************************************************/
245:
246:    void x_CMain::DoCmdSetFont12()
247:
248:    {
249:            // Subclass must override this function to
250:            // handle the command
251:            fMain_TextLbl->SetFontSize(12);
252:    }
253:
254:
255:    /******************************************************************
256:     DoCmdSetFont14
```

```
257:
258:    Respond to cmdSetFont14 command.
259:    ****************************************************************/
260:
261:    void x_CMain::DoCmdSetFont14()
262:
263:    {
264:                // Subclass must override this function to
265:                // handle the command
266:                fMain_TextLbl->SetFontSize(14);
267:    }
268:
269:
270:    /****************************************************************
271:      DoCmdSetSpacingDouble
272:
273:    Respond to cmdSetSpacingDouble command.
274:    ****************************************************************/
275:
276:    void x_CMain::DoCmdSetSpacingDouble()
277:
278:    {
279:                // Subclass must override this function to
280:                // handle the command
281:                fMain_TextLbl->SetSpacingCmd(cmdDoubleSpace);
282:    }
283:
284:
285:    /****************************************************************
286:      DoCmdSetSpacingHalf
287:
288:            Respond to cmdSetSpacingHalf command.
289:    ****************************************************************/
290:
291:    void x_CMain::DoCmdSetSpacingHalf()
292:
293:    {
294:                // Subclass must override this function to
295:                // handle the command
296:                fMain_TextLbl->SetSpacingCmd(cmd1HalfSpace);
297:    }
298:
299:
300:    /****************************************************************
301:      DoCmdSetSpacingSingle
302:
303:    Respond to cmdSetSpacingSingle command.
304:    ****************************************************************/
305:
306:    void x_CMain::DoCmdSetSpacingSingle()
307:
308:    {
309:                // Subclass must override this function to
310:                // handle the command
311:                fMain_TextLbl->SetSpacingCmd(cmdSingleSpace);
312:    }
```

continues

485

Listing 16.8. continued

```
313:
314:
315:    /*****************************************************************
316:     DoCmdSetAlignLeft
317:
318:    Respond to cmdSetAlignLeft command.
319:    *****************************************************************/
320:
321:    void x_CMain::DoCmdSetAlignLeft()
322:
323:    {
324:            // Subclass must override this function to
325:            // handle the command
326:            fMain_TextLbl->SetAlignCmd(cmdAlignLeft);
327:    }
328:
329:
330:    /*****************************************************************
331:     DoCmdSetAlignRight
332:
333:    Respond to cmdSetAlignRight command.
334:    *****************************************************************/
335:
336:    void x_CMain::DoCmdSetAlignRight()
337:
338:    {
339:            // Subclass must override this function to
340:            // handle the command
341:            fMain_TextLbl->SetAlignCmd(cmdAlignRight);
342:    }
343:
344:
345:    /*****************************************************************
346:     DoCmdSetAlignCenter
347:
348:            Respond to cmdSetAlignCenter command.
349:    *****************************************************************/
350:
351:    void x_CMain::DoCmdSetAlignCenter()
352:
353:    {
354:            // Subclass must override this function to
355:            // handle the command
356:            fMain_TextLbl->SetAlignCmd(cmdAlignCenter);
357:    }
358:
359:
360:    /*****************************************************************
361:     DoCmdSetBold
362:
363:    Respond to cmdSetBold command.
364:    *****************************************************************/
365:
366:    void x_CMain::DoCmdSetBold()
```

```
367:
368:    {
369:            // Subclass must override this function to
370:            // handle the command
371:            fMain_TextLbl->SetFontStyle(bold);
372:    }
373:
374:
375:    /****************************************************************
376:     DoCmdSetItalic
377:
378:    Respond to cmdSetItalic command.
379:    ****************************************************************/
380:
381:    void x_CMain::DoCmdSetItalic()
382:
383:    {
384:            // Subclass must override this function to
385:            // handle the command
386:            fMain_TextLbl->SetFontStyle(italic);
387:    }
388:
389:
390:    /****************************************************************
391:     DoCmdSetNormal
392:
393:    Respond to cmdSetNormal command.
394:    ****************************************************************/
395:
396:    void x_CMain::DoCmdSetNormal()
397:
398:    {
399:            // Subclass must override this function to
400:            // handle the command
401:            fMain_TextLbl->SetFontStyle(normal);
402:    }
```

 Listing 16.8 shows the definitions of the member functions in class x_CMain. The output of the Visual Architect utility excludes the executable statements inside the DoCmdSet*XXXX* member functions. I added these lines manually to support the responses of the Static3 program.

Lines 49 to 60 define the constants for the commands of the Font Manipulation menu. The next seven subsections discuss the relevant member functions.

The Function *MakeNewWindow*

The member function MakeNewWindow (defined in lines 91 to 104) stores the pointers to the window and the pane in the variables itsWindow and itsMainPane, respectively. It also stores the address of the static text control in the data member fMain_TextLbl. The

487

function obtains this address by sending the C++ message `FindViewByID` to the window object. The argument for these messages is the constant `kMain_TextLblID`, which is defined in Listing 16.9.

The Function *DoCommand*

The member function `DoCommand` (defined in lines 153 to 197) has case labels in the `switch` statement to respond to the `cmdSetXXXX` commands. Each statement after a case `cmdSetXXXX` invokes its corresponding member function `DoCmdSetXXXX`.

The Function *UpdateMenus*

The member function `UpdateMenus` (defined in lines 206 to 222) enables the custom commands by sending the C++ message `EnableCmd`, for each command, to the bartender object. The arguments for the sequence of `EnableCmd` messages are the constants `cmdSetXXXX`.

The Functions *DoCmdSetFontXX*

The member functions `DoCmdSetFontXX` handle the commands that alter the font size of the text in the static text control. These functions send the C++ message `SetFontSize` to the static text control. Each function supplies the message with a different numeric font size argument.

The Functions *DoCmdSetSpacingXXXX*

The member functions `DoCmdSetSpacingXXXX` handle the commands that alter the spacing of the text in the static text control. These functions send the C++ message `SetSpacingCmd` to the static text control. Each function supplies the message with a different argument (`cmdSingleSpace`, `cmd1HalfSpace`, or `cmdDoubleSpace`).

The Functions *DoCmdSetAlignXXXX*

The member functions `DoCmdSetAlignXXXX` handle the commands that alter the alignment of the text in the static text control. These function send the C++ message `SetAlignCmd` to the static text control. Each function supplies the message with a different argument (`cmdAlignLeft`, `cmdAlignCenter`, or `cmdAlignRight`).

The Function *DoCmdSetXXXX*

The last four `DoCmdSetXXXX` member functions handle the commands that alter the font style of the text in the static text control. These functions send the C++ message `SetFontStyle` to the static text control. Each function supplies the message with a different argument (`bold`, `italic`, or `normal`).

Listing 16.9 shows the source code for the MainItems.h header file for the Static3 program. The listing defines an untagged enumerated type which defines the identifiers `kMain_TextLbl` and `kMain_TextLblID`.

Listing 16.9. The source code for the MainItems.h header file for the Static3 program.

```
 1:   /**************************************************************
 2:   MainItems.h
 3:
 4:                  Main Item Constants
 5:
 6:       Copyright (c) 1994 My Software Inc. All rights reserved.
 7:
 8:   Generated by Visual Architect(TM)
 9:
10:   This file is rewritten each time you generate code. You should
11:   not make changes to this file; changes should go in the My.h
12:   file, instead.
13:
14:   If you want to change how Visual Architect generates this file,
15:   you can change the template for this file. It is "_Doc.h" in
16:   the Visual Architect Templates folder.
17:   **************************************************************/
18:
19:   #pragma once
20:
21:
22:       //    Item numbers for each item.
23:       //
24:       //    Use TCLGetItemPointer (ViewUtilities) to convert these
25:       //    item numbers to a pointer to the named item.
26:
27:   enum
28:   {
29:       Main_Begin_,
30:       kMain_TextLbl = 1,
31:       kMain_TextLblID = 1L,
32:       Main_End_
33:   };
```

489

Listing 16.10 shows the source code for the AppCommands.h header file for the Static3 program. This listing defines the constants cmdSet*XXXX* that support the commands of the Font Manipulation menu.

Listing 16.10. The source code for the AppCommands.h header file for the Static3 program.

```
 1:  /****************************************************************
 2:   MyCommands.h
 3:
 4:              Header File For Command Symbols
 5:
 6:      Copyright (c) 1994 My Software Inc. All rights reserved.
 7:
 8:  Generated by Visual Architect(TM)
 9:
10:  This file is regenerated each time.
11:
12:  ****************************************************************/
13:
14:  #pragma once
15:
16:  #define cmdSetAlignCenter    522
17:  #define cmdSetAlignLeft      519
18:  #define cmdSetAlignRight     520
19:  #define cmdSetBold           523
20:  #define cmdSetFont10         512
21:  #define cmdSetFont12         513
22:  #define cmdSetFont14         514
23:  #define cmdSetItalic         524
24:  #define cmdSetNormal         525
25:  #define cmdSetSpacingDouble  517
26:  #define cmdSetSpacingHalf    516
27:  #define cmdSetSpacingSingle  515
```

Compiling and Running the Program

Invoke the Run command from the THINK Project Manager icon menu. This command causes the compiler to process the set of source code files that contribute to the program. Figures 16.6 and 16.7 show samples of two different font configurations for static text.

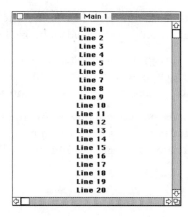

Figure 16.6. *A sample session with the Static3 program showing centered text.*

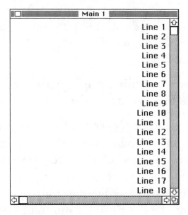

Figure 16.7. *A sample session with the Static3 program showing right-aligned text.*

Summary

This chapter introduced you to programming Macintosh applications using the TCL classes:

☐ You learned about the declarations for class CStaticText and its parent class CEditText, as well as the member functions of these classes that affect the appearance of text in a static text control.

☐ In the first, simple example you learned how to use static text in a fixed window. The program presented a read-only fixed window with some text.

☐ The next, more involved example presented a window with multiple static text controls, each showing text in different font, font style, and font size. The characteristics of the text in the static text controls are fixed at design time.

☐ The final example showed you how to manipulate the font style, font size, and alignment at runtime. The menu-driven program contained member functions that sent font-related messages, at runtime, to the targeted static text control.

Q&A

Q **What are some examples for changing the text of a static text control at runtime?**

A The examples include displaying error messages, the names of currently selected folders, the names of currently opened files, the current date and time, and so on.

Q **When do I use a multiline single static text control, and how do I use an array of single-line static text controls.**

A A multiline single static text control enables you to alter, in one swoop, the font style, font size, and text alignment. By contrast, an array of single-line static text controls requires you to send a C++ font-related message to each control to perform the same task. On the other hand, such an array enables you to display multiple lines of text using different font styles, sizes, and alignment—something that cannot be done using a multiline single static text control.

Q **Can I hide the characters of a static text control?**

A Yes. You can toggle the visibility of a static text control by sending it the C++ messages Hide and Show to hide it and show it, respectively.

Workshop

The Workshop provides quiz questions to help you solidify your understanding of the material covered and exercises to provide you with experience in using what you've learned. Try to understand the quiz and exercise answers before continuing on to the next day's lesson. Answers are provided in Appendix B, "Answers."

Quiz

1. How can you set the font style of a static text control to be both bold and italic?

2. True or false? You can set a font style to small caps.

3. True or false? The function SetAlignCmd supports the vertical display of the characters in a static text control.

4. True or false? The function SetSpacingCmd supports displaying the characters of a static text control in single spacing, 1½-line spacing, and double spacing.

Exercise

Write the program project Static4, which writes the same text using a sequence of different styles, sizes, and alignment. Table 16.3 shows the sequence indices and their associated font styles, sizes, and alignments. The program should cycle among the above five states.

Table 16.3. The sequence indices and their associated font styles, sizes, and alignments for program project Static4.

Sequence Number	Font Style	Font Size	Alignment
0	Normal	10	Left
1	Bold	10	Left
2	Italic	10	Left
3	Normal	14	Left
4	Normal	10	Right

17

The Edit Box and Button Controls

The edit box and button controls are among the most commonly used controls in Macintosh applications, as well as in other GUI environments. This chapter discusses the TCL classes that support these controls and presents examples of using them. You learn about the following topics today:

- ☐ The classes that support the edit box control
- ☐ The relevant member functions of class CEditText
- ☐ The class CDialogText and its relevant member functions
- ☐ The class CIntegerText and its relevant member functions
- ☐ The edit box manipulation example
- ☐ The class CButton that supports the button control
- ☐ The relevant member functions of class CButton
- ☐ The button-manipulation example

The Edit Control Classes

The class CEditText and its ancestor classes support the operations of an edit text control. Among these operations are the cut, copy, paste, text selection, and text scrolling features, to name a few. Here is the declaration of class CEditText:

```
class CEditText : public CAbstractText { // Class Declaration

public:

    TCL_DECLARE_CLASS

    // Data Members

    TEHandle macTE;   // Toolbox Text Edit record handle
    long spacingCmd; // Line spacing command number
    long alignCmd;    // alignment cmd number

    // Member Functions
    // Contruction/Destruction
    CEditText();
    CEditText(CView *anEnclosure,
            CBureaucrat *aSupervisor,
            short aWidth = 0, short aHeight = 0,
            short aHEncl = 0, short aVEncl = 0,
            SizingOption aHSizing = sizELASTIC,
            SizingOption aVSizing = sizELASTIC,
            short aLineWidth = -1,
            Boolean aScrollHoriz = FALSE);
    ~CEditText();
```

```
        void IEditText(CView *anEnclosure,
                    CBureaucrat *aSupervisor,
                    short aWidth, short aHeight,
                    short aHEncl, short aVEncl,
                    SizingOption aHSizing,
                    SizingOption aVSizing,
                    short aLineWidth);
    virtual void IViewTemp(CView *anEnclosure,
                        CBureaucrat *aSupervisor,
                        Ptr viewData);
        void IEditTextX();
    virtual void MakeMacTE();

    // Mouse and Keystrokes
    virtual void DoClick(Point hitPt, short modifierKeys,
                        long when);
    virtual void PerformEditCommand(long theCommand);

    // Display
    virtual void Draw(Rect *area);
    virtual void Scroll(long hDelta, long vDelta,
                        Boolean redraw);
    virtual void Activate();
    virtual void Deactivate();
    virtual void SetSelection(long selStart, long selEnd,
                            Boolean fRedraw);
    virtual void HideSelection(Boolean hide,
                            Boolean redraw);   // TCL 1.1.3
                                                // 11/30/92 BF
    virtual void GetSteps(short *hStep,
                        short *vStep); // TCL 1.1.3 11/30/92 BF

                                    // Text Specification
    virtual void SetTextPtr(Ptr textPtr, long numChars);
    virtual Handle GetTextHandle();
    virtual Handle CopyTextRange(long start, long end);
    virtual void InsertTextPtr(Ptr text,
                            long length,
                            Boolean fRedraw);

    virtual void TypeChar(char theChar, short theModifers);

    virtual void CheckInsertion(long insertLen, Boolean useSelection);

    // Calibrating
    virtual void CalcTERects();
    virtual void ResizeFrame(Rect *delta);
    virtual void AdjustBounds();

    virtual long FindLine(long charPos);
    virtual long GetLength();

    // Text Characteristics
    virtual void SetFontNumber(short aFontNumber);
    virtual void SetFontStyle(short aStyle);
    virtual void SetFontSize(short aSize);
```

17

```
        virtual void SetTextMode(short aMode);
        virtual void SetAlignment(short anAlignment);
        virtual void SetAlignCmd(long alignCmd);
        virtual void SetSpacingCmd(long aSpacingCmd);
        virtual void GetTEFontInfo(FontInfo *macFontInfo);

        virtual long GetHeight(long startLine, long endLine);
        virtual long GetCharOffset(LongPt *aPt);
        virtual void GetCharPoint(long offset, LongPt *aPt);
        virtual void GetTextStyle(short *whichAttributes,
                                  TextStyle *aStyle);
        virtual void GetCharStyle(long charOffset,
                                  TextStyle *theStyle);
        virtual long GetSpacingCmd();
        virtual long GetAlignCmd();

        virtual long GetNumLines();
        virtual void GetSelection(long *selStart,
                                  long *selEnd);

        // Printing
        virtual void AboutToPrint(short *firstPage, short *lastPage);
        virtual void PrintPage(short pageNum, short pageWidth,
                               short pageHeight, CPrinter *aPRinter);
        virtual void DonePrinting();

        // Cursor
        virtual void Dawdle(long *maxSleep);

        // Object I/O
        virtual void PutTo(CStream& stream);
        virtual void GetFrom(CStream& stream);

private:
    void CEditTextX();
};

#define  CARRIAGE_RETURN  13 // Character code
#define  kMaxTELength 32000L  // maximum text we allow in
                              // TE record

extern CEditText *gEditText; // the currently active
                             // CEditText, may be NULL
```

This declaration indicates that class CEditText is a descendant of class CAbstractText. Here is the declaration of class CAbstractText:

```
class CAbstractText : public CPanorama
{
public:
    TCL_DECLARE_CLASS

    static    short cFirstTaskIndex; // index in Undo STR#
                         // resource of first undo label
                         // see further notes below
    CTextEditTask *itsTypingTask; // active typing task
```

```
CAbstractText();
CAbstractText(CView *anEnclosure,
                CBureaucrat *aSupervisor,
                short aWidth, short aHeight,
                short aHEncl, short aVEncl,
                SizingOption aHSizing,
                SizingOption aVSizing,
                short aLineWidth = -1,
                Boolean aScrollHoriz = FALSE);

voidIAbstractText(CView *anEnclosure,
                CBureaucrat *aSupervisor,
                short aWidth, short aHeight,
                short aHEncl, short aVEncl,
                SizingOption aHSizing,
                SizingOption aVSizing,
                short aLineWidth);

virtual void IViewTemp(CView *anEnclosure,
                        CBureaucrat *aSupervisor,
                        Ptr viewData);

// Text Specification
virtual void SetTextString(Str255 textStr);
virtual void SetTextHandle(Handle textHand);
virtual void SetTextPtr(Ptr textPtr, long numChars) = 0;
virtual Handle GetTextHandle(void) = 0;
virtual Handle CopyTextRange(long start, long end) = 0;
virtual void InsertTextPtr(Ptr text, long length,
                        Boolean fRedraw) = 0;
virtual void InsertTextHandle(Handle text, Boolean fRedraw);

virtual void Specify(Boolean fEditable,
                        Boolean fSelectable,
                        Boolean fStylable);
virtual void GetSpecification(Boolean *fEditable,
                                Boolean *fSelectable,
                                Boolean *fStylable);
virtual void SetFontNumber(short aFontNumber) = 0;
virtual void SetFontName(Str255 aFontName);
virtual void SetFontStyle(short aStyle) = 0;
virtual void SetFontSize(short aSize) = 0;
virtual void SetTextMode(short aMode) = 0;
virtual void SetAlignCmd(long anAlignment) = 0;
virtual long GetAlignCmd(void) = 0;
virtual void SetSpacingCmd(long aSpacingCmd) = 0;
virtual long GetSpacingCmd(void) = 0;
virtual void SetHorizontalScroll(Boolean doHoriz);  // TCL
                                        // 1.1.3 11/30/92 BF

virtual long GetHeight(long startLine, long endLine) = 0;
virtual short Get1Height(long aLineNum);
virtual long GetCharOffset(LongPt *aPt) = 0;
virtual void GetCharPoint(long offset, LongPt *aPt) = 0;
```

```
        virtual void GetCharStyle(long charOffset,
                              TextStyle *theStyle) = 0;
        virtual void GetTextStyle(short *whichAttributes,
                              TextStyle *aStyle) = 0;

        virtual void GetCharBefore(long *aPosition,
                               tCharBuf charBuf);
        virtual void GetCharAfter(long *aPosition,
                              tCharBuf charBuf);


        // Calibrating
        virtual void ResizeFrame(Rect *deltaRect);
        virtual void SetWholeLines(Boolean aWholeLines);
        virtual Boolean GetWholeLines();

        virtual long FindLine(long charPos) = 0;
        virtual long GetLength(void) = 0;
        virtual long GetNumLines(void) = 0;
        virtual void DoCommand(long theCommand);
        virtual void PerformEditCommand(long theCommand) = 0;
        virtual void UpdateMenus();

        // Mouse and Keystrokes
        virtual void DoKeyDown(char theChar,
                           Byte keyCode,
                           EventRecord *macEvent);
        virtual void DoAutoKey(char theChar,
                           Byte keyCode,
                           EventRecord *macEvent);
        virtual void TypeChar(char theChar, short theModifiers) = 0;

        virtual void SelectionChanged();
        virtual void ScrollToSelection();

        virtual Boolean BecomeGopher(Boolean fBecoming);
        virtual void SetSelection(long selStart, long selEnd,
                              Boolean fRedraw) = 0;
        virtual void GetSelection(long *selStart, long *selEnd) = 0;
        virtual void SelectAll(Boolean fRedraw);
        virtual void HideSelection(Boolean hide,
                               Boolean redraw) = 0;   // TCL
                                       // 1.1.3 11/30/92 BF

        virtual void Paginate(CPrinter *aPrinter,
                          short pageWidth,
                          short pageHeight);

    // Cursor
    virtual void AdjustCursor(Point where, RgnHandle mouseRgn);

    // Binary streams
    virtual void PutTo(CStream& stream);
    virtual void GetFrom(CStream& stream);

protected:
```

```
      short lineWidth; // Width of a text line in pixels
                    //    if <= 0, width is the same as
                    //    that of the frame
      short lastFontNum;  // last font number
      long lastFontCmd; // last font cmd #
      short lastTextSize; // last seen text size
      long lastSizeCmd;  // last size cmd #
      Boolean fixedLineHeights:1; // TRUE if all lines same height
      Boolean wholeLines:1; // Draw only whole lines? i.e.,
                    //   don't cut off lines vertically
      Boolean editable:1; // TRUE if user can edit text,
                    // FALSE text is read-only
      Boolean stylable:1; // TRUE if user can change
                    // font/size/style
      Boolean scrollHoriz:1; // TRUE if autoscroll horizontally
                    // TCL 1.1.3 11/30/92 BF


      virtual CTextEditTask *MakeEditTask(long editCmd);
      virtual CTextStyleTask *MakeStyleTask(long styleCmd);
      void    CAbstractTextX();
};
```

The class CAbstractText contains, as expected, many declarations of abstract member functions.

17

Note: The Visual Architect utility generates instances of class CEditText when you select the scrollable edit box tool that is located to the right of the subview tool in the Tools palette.

The Relevant *CEditText* Functions

This section presents the relevant member functions declared in the classes CEditText and CAbstractText.

The Function *Activate*

The parameterless member function Activate, as the name might suggest, activates the text pane. This function supports the editing command and either displays the text-insertion caret or highlights the selected text. The declaration of function Activate is

```
void Activate();
```

Syntax

The Function *Deactivate*

The member function Deactivate deactivates the text pane. This function disables the editing command and either hides the text-insertion caret or unhighlights the selected text. The declaration of function Deactivate is

```
void Deactivate();
```

Syntax

The Function *SetSelection*

The member function SetSelection establishes the range of characters that make up the selected text in an edit box control. The declaration of function SetSelection is

```
void SetSelection(long selStart, long selEnd, Boolean fRedraw);
```

The parameters selStart and selEnd are the character indices that define the selected text. The Boolean parameter fRedraw specifies whether or not to redraw the selected text.

Syntax

The Function *GetSelection*

The member function GetSelection obtains the character indices that define the selected text. The declaration of class GetSelection is

```
void GetSelection(long *selStart, long *selEnd);
```

The parameters selStart and selEnd are the pointers to the character indices for the selected text.

Syntax

The Function *HideSelection*

The member function HideSelection shows or hides the selection or insertion caret. The declaration of function HideSelection is

```
void HideSelection(Boolean hide, Boolean redraw);
```

The Boolean parameter hide specifies whether to hide or show the selection (or insertion caret if there is no selection). The parameter redraw is a flag that specifies whether or not to redraw the text.

The Function *FindLine*

The member function FindLine yields the line number that contains the character specified by an index. The declaration of function FindLine is

```
short FindLine(long charPos);
```

The parameter charPos specifies the index of the character containing the queried line number. If the argument of parameter charPos is negative, the function yields 0. By contrast, if the argument of parameter charPos exceeds the end of the text, the function returns the number of the last line.

The Function *GetLength*

The member function GetLength yields the number of bytes in the text pane's text buffer. The declaration of function GetLength is

```
long GetLength();
```

The Function *GetNumLines*

The member function GetNumLines yields the number of lines in the text pane's text buffer. The declaration of function GetNumLines is

```
long GetNumLines();
```

The Function *SetTextPtr*

The member function SetTextPtr copies a specified number of characters to the control's text buffer. The declaration of function SetTextPtr is

```
void SetTextPtr(Ptr textPtr, long numChars);
```

The parameter textPtr is the pointer to the source text. The parameter numChars specifies the number of characters to copy.

> **Note:** The TCL classes that support the various kinds of edit box controls write characters to these controls' text buffers using pointers to characters. By contrast, these same classes read characters from the controls using handles (a handle is pointer-to-character pointer—also called a double-char pointer).

Syntax

The Function *GetTextHandle*

The member function GetTextHandle yields the handle (the pointer to the pointer) of the text in a class instance. The declaration of the function GetTextHandle is

```
Handle GetTextHandle();
```

The function yields the handle to the existing text, not a copy of the text.

Syntax

The Function *CopyTextRange*

The member function CopyTextRange yields a copy of the range of text characters. The declaration of the function CopyTextRange is

```
Handle CopyTextRange(long start, long end);
```

The parameters start and end define the range of characters to copy.

Syntax

The Function *InsertTextPtr*

The member function InsertTextPtr inserts a copy of some given text at the start of the current insertion position. The declaration of the function InsertTextPtr is

```
void InsertTextPtr(Ptr text, long length, Boolean fRedraw);
```

The parameter text is the pointer to the source string. The parameter length specifies the number of characters to copy from the source string. The parameter fRedraw is a Boolean flag that determines whether or not to redraw the pane at the next update event.

Syntax

The Function *Specify*

The inherited member function Specify permits you to specify whether you can edit, select, and style the text in an edit box. The declaration of function Specify is

```
void Specify(Boolean fEditable, Boolean fSelectable,
             Boolean fStylable);
```

The parameter fEditable specifies whether or not you can insert and delete text in the edit box control. The arguments for this parameter are the predefined constants kEditable or kNotEditable. The parameter fSelectable specifies whether or not you can select text for copying to the clipboard. The arguments for this parameter are the predefined constants kSelectable or kNotSelectable. The parameter fStylable determines whether or not you can change the font, font style, and font size of the text in the edit box control. The arguments for this parameter are the predefined constants kStylable or kNotStylable.

Note: If you supply the parameter fSelectable with the argument kNotSelectable, you also disable the editing and styling features, regardless of the arguments for parameters fEditable and fStylable.

The Function *SetFontNumber*

The inherited member function SetFontNumber sets the font of the text by specifying the font number. The declaration of function SetFontNumber is

```
virtual void SetFontNumber(short aFontNumber);
```

The parameter aFontNumber specifies the selected font by number.

The Function *SetFontStyle*

The inherited member function SetFontStyle sets the font style of the text. The declaration of function SetFontStyle is

```
virtual void SetFontStyle(short aStyle);
```

The arguments for the parameter aStyle specify the font style by using one of the following predefined identifiers or any additive combination: normal, bold, italic, underline, outline, shadow, condense, or extend.

The Function *SetFontSize*

The inherited member function SetFontSize sets the font size of the text. The declaration of function SetFontSize is

```
virtual void SetFontSize(short aSize);
```

The parameter aSize specifies the font size.

The Function *SetAlignment*

The inherited member function SetAlignment sets the text alignment for the text. The declaration of function SetAlignment is

```
virtual void SetAlignment(short anAlignment);
```

The arguments for the parameter anAlignment can be the predefined constants teFlushDefault, teFlushLeft, teCenter, and teFlushRight.

17

505

Syntax

The Function *SetAlignCmd*

The inherited member function SetAlignCmd sets the alignment for the text using THINK Class Library names for alignment. The function SetAlignCmd performs the same task as function SetAlignment, but uses a different set of predefined identifiers. The declaration of function SetAlignCmd is

```
virtual void SetAlignCmd(long alignCmd);
```

The arguments for the parameter alignCmd can be the predefined commands cmdAlignLeft, cmdAlignCenter, and cmdAlignRight.

Syntax

The Function *GetAlignCmd*

The inherited member function GetAlignCmd obtains the text alignment for the text using THINK Class Library names for alignment. The declaration of function GetAlignCmd is

```
long GetAlignCmd();
```

The function returns a value that corresponds to one of the following predefined constants: cmdAlignLeft, cmdAlignCenter, or cmdAlignRight.

Syntax

The Function *SetSpacingCmd*

The inherited member function SetSpacingCmd sets the text spacing for the text. The declaration of function SetSpacingCmd is

```
virtual void SetSpacingCmd(long aSpacingCmd);
```

The arguments for the parameter aSpacingCmd can be cmdSingleSpace, cmd1HalfSpace (for 1½-line spacing), or cmdDoubleSpace.

Syntax

The Function *GetSpacingCmd*

The inherited member function GetSpacingCmd obtains the text spacing for the text. The declaration of function GetSpacingCmd is

```
long GetSpacingCmd();
```

The function returns a value that corresponds to one of the predefined constants: cmdSingleSpace, cmd1HalfSpace (for 1½-line spacing), or cmdDoubleSpace.

The next four member functions are inherited from the class CAbstractText.

SAMS
PUBLISHING

The Function *SetTextString*

The member function SetTextString copies the characters in a Pascal string into the edit text pane. The declaration of function SetTextString is

```
void SetTextString(Str255 textStr);
```

The parameter textStr is the Pascal string that supplies the edit control with text. Because Pascal strings are limited to 255 characters, you can use this function only to write strings up to 255 characters long.

The Function *SelectAll*

The member function SelectAll, as the name might suggest, selects all the text in an edit control. The declaration of the function SelectAll is

```
void SelectAll(Boolean fRedraw);
```

The parameter fRedraw is a Boolean flag that specifies whether or not to redraw the control at the next update event.

The Function *SetTextHandle*

The member function SetTextHandle sets the text of an edit text pane to the string accessed by a specified handle. The declaration of function SetTextHandle is

```
void SetTextHandle(Handle textHand);
```

The parameter textHand is the handle of the source text.

The Function *InsertTextHandle*

The member function InsertTextHandle inserts a copy of some text at the current insertion point. The declaration of function InsertTextHandle is

```
void InsertTextHandle(Handle text, Boolean fRedraw);
```

The parameter text is the handle of the inserted text. The parameter fRedraw is a Boolean flag that specifies whether or not to redraw the control at the next update event.

The Class *CDialogText*

The class CDialogText is a descendant of class CEditText, which is used to support text fields in dialog boxes. I present the class here because I am discussing edit box controls. The declaration of class CDialogText is

```
class CDialogText : public CEditText
{
public:
    TCL_DECLARE_CLASS

    CDialogText();
    CDialogText(CView *anEnclosure,
                CView *aSupervisor,
                short aWidth, short aHeight,
                short aHEncl, short aVEncl,
                SizingOption aHSizing = sizFIXEDSTICKY,
                SizingOption aVSizing = sizFIXEDSTICKY,
                short aLineWidth = -1, Boolean aScrollHoriz = 0,
                Boolean aIsRequired = FALSE,
                long aMaxValidLength = MAXLONG,
                Boolean aValidateOnResign = TRUE);
    ~CDialogText();

    void IDialogText(CView *anEnclosure, CView *aSupervisor,
                     short aWidth, short aHeight,
                     short aHEncl, short aVEncl,
                     SizingOption aHSizing, SizingOption aVSizing,
                     short aLineWidth);

    virtual void IViewTemp(CView *anEnclosure,
                           CBureaucrat *aSupervisor,
                           Ptr viewData);
    virtual void SetConstraints(Boolean fRequired,
                                long aMaxChars);

    virtual void SetEnabled(Boolean isEnabled);
    virtual void SetEditable(Boolean isEditable);
    virtual short GetHelpBalloonState();

    virtual void Draw(Rect *area);

    virtual void DoKeyDown(char theChar, Byte keyCode,
                           EventRecord *macEvent);
    virtual void GetTextString(StringPtr aString);
    virtual Boolean Validate();
    virtual Boolean BecomeGopher(Boolean fBecoming);

    virtual void PutTo(CStream& stream);
    virtual void GetFrom(CStream& stream);

protected:
```

```
        Boolean isRequired : 1;   // TRUE if must be non-empty
                                  // to be valid
        Boolean validateOnResign : 1;  // TRUE if validate
                                        // on resigning gopher
        long maxValidLength; // maximum number of chars
                             // for validation

        void IDialogTextX();
        virtual void ReportInvalidText(short strIndex);
        virtual void MakeBorder();
        virtual void SetStatic(Boolean isStatic);
        virtual void DoSetEnabled(Boolean isEnabled);
        virtual void DoSetEditable(Boolean isEditable);
};
```

Note: The Visual Architect utility creates instances of class `CDialogText` when you use the edit box tool in the Tools palette.

17

The following five subsections present the relevant member functions of class `CDialogText`.

The Function *SetConstraints*

The member function `SetConstraints` indicates if and how to validate the contents of a `CDialogText` instance. The declaration of function `SetConstraints` is

```
void SetConstraints(Boolean fRequired, long aMaxChars);
```

The parameter `fRequired` is a Boolean flag that specifies whether or not validation is required. The parameter `aMaxChars` specifies the maximum number of characters in the `CDialogText` instance. When the argument for parameter `fRequired` is TRUE, the argument for the parameter `aMaxChars` must be at least 1.

The Function *GetTextString*

The member function `GetTextString` yields the contents of a dialog edit control using a pointer to a Pascal string. The declaration of function `GetTextString` is

```
void GetTextString(StringPtr aString);
```

The parameter `aString` is the pointer to the Pascal string which receives a copy of the characters in the dialog edit text.

The Function *Validate*

The member function `Validate` yields a `Boolean` value that indicates whether or not the text in the dialog edit text is valid (according to the constraints set by function `SetConstraints`). The declaration of function `Validate` is

```
Boolean Validate();
```

The Function *SetEnabled*

With the member function `SetEnabled`, you can enable or disable a dialog edit text control. The declaration of function `SetEnabled` is

```
void SetEnabled(Boolean isEnabled);
```

The parameter `isEnabled` is a Boolean flag that enables or disables a dialog edit text control. When the argument for this parameter is `FALSE`, the control is uneditable and appears disabled (grayed).

The Function *SetEditable*

The member function `SetEditable` determines whether or not a dialog edit text control is editable. The declaration of function `SetEditable` is

```
void SetEditable(Boolean isEditable);
```

The parameter `isEditable` is a Boolean flag that specifies whether or not a dialog edit text control is editable. When the argument for this parameter is `FALSE`, the control is uneditable and appears as a borderless static text!

DO	DON'T

DO use the member functions `SetTextPtr` and `GetTextHandle` to exchange strings that exceed 255 characters with edit boxes.

DON'T forget that literal strings that are arguments for Pascal string parameters must start with the escape character \p.

The Class *CIntegerText*

The class CIntegerText is a descendant of class CDialogText, which supports numeric fields in dialog boxes. The declaration of class CIntegerText is

```
class CIntegerText : public CDialogText
{
public:

    TCL_DECLARE_CLASS

    CIntegerText() {}
    CIntegerText(CView *anEnclosure,
                 CView *aSupervisor,
                 short aWidth, short aHeight,
                 short aHEncl, short aVEncl,
                 SizingOption aHSizing = sizELASTIC,
                 SizingOption aVSizing = sizELASTIC,
                 short aLineWidth = -1, Boolean aScrollHoriz = 0,
                 Boolean aIsRequired = FALSE,
                 long aMaxValidLength = MAXLONG,
                 long aMinValue = MINLONG,
                 long aMaxValue = MAXLONG,
                 long aDefaultValue = 0,
                 Boolean aShowRangeOnErr = FALSE);

    void IIntegerText(CView *anEnclosure, CView *aSupervisor,
                    short aWidth, short aHeight,
                    short aHEncl, short aVEncl,
                    SizingOption aHSizing,
                    SizingOption aVSizing,
                    short aLineWidth);

    virtual void IViewTemp(CView *anEnclosure,
                        CBureaucrat *aSupervisor,
                        Ptr viewData);
    virtual void SpecifyRange(long aMinimum, long aMaximum);
    virtual void SpecifyDefaultValue(long aDefaultValue);

    virtual void SetIntValue(long aValue);
    virtual long GetIntValue();

    virtual Boolean Validate();

    virtual void PutTo(CStream& stream);
    virtual void GetFrom(CStream& stream);

protected:

    long minValue;          // minimum valid value
    long maxValue;          // maximum valid value
    long defaultValue;      // default value if text empty. If
                            // CDialogText::isRequired is FALSE,
```

17

```
                             // then empty text is considered
                             // valid and default value is
                             // returned by GetIntValue.
        Boolean showRangeOnErr; // If TRUE, validation error
                             // displays allow range of
                             // integers in the alert

        virtual void ConvertToInteger(long *intValue,
                                      Boolean *valid);
};
```

The next five subsections discuss the relevant member functions of class CIntegerText.

The Function *SpecifyRange*

The member function SpecifyRange establishes the range of valid integers for the dialog integer field. The declaration of function SpecifyRange is

```
void SpecifyRange(long aMinimum, long aMaximum);
```

The parameters aMinimum and aMaximum define the range of valid integer values. The function sets the value of the Boolean data member showRangeOnErr. This data member indicates whether or not the specified range appears in an error message. If the arguments for the parameters aMinimum and aMaximum are MINLONG and MAXLONG, the function assigns FALSE to member showRangeOnErr.

The Function *SpecifyDefaultValue*

The member function SpecifyDefaultValue indicates that the targeted integer field is not needed and also specifies the returned value if that field is empty. The declaration of function SpecifyDefaultValue is

```
void SpecifyDefaultValue(long aDefaultValue);
```

The parameter aDefaultValue specifies the default value of a dialog integer field.

The Function *SetIntValue*

The member function SetIntValue sets the value of a dialog integer field. The declaration of function SetIntValue is

```
void SetIntValue(long aValue);
```

The parameter aValue specifies the value for the dialog field.

Syntax

The Function *GetIntValue*

The member function `GetIntValue` gets the value of a dialog integer field. The declaration of function `GetIntValue` is

```
long GetIntValue();
```

Syntax

The Function *Validate*

The member function `Validate` returns a `Boolean` value that indicates whether or not a dialog integer field contains a valid integer. The declaration of function `Validate` is

```
Boolean Validate();
```

The function yields `FALSE` under these conditions: if the field is required and is empty, if the field contains a value outside the valid range, and if the field contains more characters than allowed.

The Edit Box Manipulation Example

Let's look at an example for manipulating text in an edit box. The next program project, Edit1, contains the following controls (see Figure 17.1):

- ☐ The small edit box control, which serves as a text input and output control. I call this control the *input/output box*.

- ☐ The large edit box control, which can show multiple lines of text. I call this control the *multiline box*.

- ☐ The Insert String button, which inserts the string of the input/output box into the current location of the multiline box.

- ☐ The Append String button, which appends the string of the input/output box into the end of the multiline box.

- ☐ The Get Selection button, which overwrites the input/output box with the current selection of the multiline box.

- ☐ The Quit button.

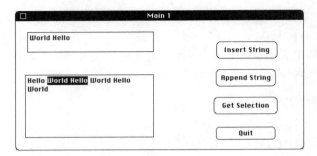

Figure 17.1. *A sample session with the Edit1 program.*

Table 17.1 shows the control names as well as the custom and predefined commands associated with the above controls.

Table 17.1. The control names and commands associated with the controls of project Edit1.

Control	Control Name	Associated Command	Custom?
input/output box	TextBox		
multiline box	MultiLineBox		
Append String	AppendBtn	cmdAppendString	Yes
Insert String	InsertBtn	cmdInsertString	Yes
Get Selection	GetSelBtn	cmdGetSelection	Yes
Quit	QuitBtn	cmdQuit	No

Building the Application

To build the Edit1 program project, perform the following steps:

1. Create a new Visual Architect utility project, and name it Edit1.

2. Delete the default controls in the main window, and select the fixed window style.

3. Expand the width of the main window and its pane.

4. Define the three custom commands specified in Table 17.1. Make sure that these commands are associated with class CMain and result in a Call type of action.

5. Use the Tools menu to select the edit box control tool, and then draw the two edit box controls in the main window.

6. Set the control name, caption, and associated command of each edit box according to the information in Table 17.1.

7. Use the Tools menu to select the button control tool, and then draw the four buttons in the main window.

8. Set the control name, caption, and associated command of each button according to the information in Table 17.1.

9. Generate the custom code by invoking the Generate All... command in the THINK Project Manager icon menu.

Customizing the Source Code

Let's look at the relevant files emitted by the Visual Architect utility and the lines of code that I inserted to support the program's operations. Listing 17.1 shows the source code for the x_CMain.h header file for the Edit1 program project. The bold lines show the ones that I manually inserted.

Listing 17.1. The source code for the x_CMain.h header file for the Edit1 program project.

```
 1:  /*****************************************************************
 2:   x_CMain.h
 3:
 4:              Header File For CMain Lower-Layer Document Class
 5:
 6:       Copyright (c) 1994 My Software Inc. All rights reserved.
 7:
 8:  Generated by Visual Architect(TM)
 9:
10:  This file is rewritten each time you generate code. You should
11:  not make changes to this file; changes should go in the My.h
12:  file, instead.
13:
14:  If you want to change how Visual Architect generates this file,
15:  you can change the template for this file. It is "_Doc.h" in
16:  the Visual Architect Templates folder.
17:
18:  *****************************************************************/
19:
```

Listing 17.1. continued

```
20:  #pragma once
21:
22:  #include "CSaver.h"
23:  class CDialogText;
24:  class CButton;
25:
26:  #include "ItsContentsClass.h"
27:
28:  #define x_CMain_super      CSaver<ITSCONTENTSCLASS>
29:
30:  #define BUF_SIZE 1000
31:
32:  class CFile;
33:
34:  class x_CMain : public x_CMain_super
35:
36:  {
37:  public:
38:
39:      TCL_DECLARE_CLASS
40:
41:      // Pointers to panes in window
42:      CDialogText   *fMain_TextBox;
43:      CDialogText   *fMain_MultiLineBox;
44:      CButton   *fMain_InsertBtn;
45:      CButton   *fMain_AppendBtn;
46:      CButton   *fMain_GetSelBtn;
47:      CButton   *fMain_QuitBtn;
48:      char buff[BUF_SIZE];
49:
50:      void      Ix_CMain(void);
51:
52:      virtual   void   DoCommand(long theCommand);
53:      virtual   void   UpdateMenus(void);
54:
55:  protected:
56:      virtual   void   MakeNewWindow(void);
57:
58:      virtual void   FailOpen(CFile *aFile);
59:      virtual void   PositionWindow(void);
60:
61:      virtual void   DoCmdAppendString(void);
62:      virtual void   DoCmdGetSelection(void);
63:      virtual void   DoCmdInsertString(void);
64:  };
65:
66:  #define   CVueCMain   128
```

Listing 17.1 shows the declaration of class x_CMain. This class contains a number of data members and member functions. The Visual Architect utility generated the data members in lines 42 to 47 which are pointers to the edit box and button

controls. These members are pointers to the classes CDialogText and CButton. I inserted the data member buff in line 48 to provide the class instances with their own text buffer. The member buff is a string that holds 1,000 characters (including the null terminator character). I also inserted the definition of constant BUF_SIZE in line 30. The class x_CMain contains the member functions DoCmdAppendString, DoCmdGetSelection, and DoCmdInsertString which handle the commands cmdAppendString, cmdGetSelection, and cmdInsertString, respectively.

Listing 17.2 shows the source code for the x_CMain.cp implementation file for the Edit1 program project. The bold lines show the ones that I manually inserted.

Listing 17.2. The source code for the x_CMain.cp implementation file for the Edit1 program project.

```
 1:  /**************************************************************
 2:   x_CMain.c
 3:
 4:                   CMain Document Class
 5:
 6:      Copyright (c) 1994 My Software Inc. All rights reserved.
 7:
 8:  Generated by Visual Architect(TM) 7:23 PM Tue, Jun 14, 1994
 9:
10:  This file is rewritten each time you generate code. You should
11:  not make changes to this file; changes should go in the My.c
12:  file, instead.
13:
14:  If you want to change how Visual Architect generates this file,
15:  you can change the template for this file. It is "_Doc_cp" in
16:  the Visual Architect Templates folder.
17:
18:  **************************************************************/
19:
20:  #include "x_CMain.h"
21:
22:  #include "CMain.h"
23:
24:  #include "MainItems.h"
25:
26:  #include "ViewUtilities.h"
27:  #include "CApp.h"
28:
29:  #include <CApplication.h>
30:  #include <CBartender.h>
31:  #include <Commands.h>
32:  #include <Constants.h>
33:  #include <CDecorator.h>
34:  #include <CDesktop.h>
35:  #include <CFile.h>
36:  #include <TBUtilities.h>
37:  #include <CWindow.h>
```

continues

517

Listing 17.2. continued

```
38:
39:  extern CApplication *gApplication; /* The application */
40:  extern CDecorator *gDecorator; /* Decorator for arranging
41:                                    windows */
42:  extern CDesktop *gDesktop; /* The visible Desktop */
43:  extern CBartender *gBartender; /* Manages all menus */
44:
45:  #include "CDialogText.h"
46:  #include "CButton.h"
47:
48:     // Define symbols for commands handled by this class
49:     // Prevents a recompile every time any command changed.
50:
51:  #define cmdAppendString 513
52:  #define cmdGetSelection 514
53:  #define cmdInsertString 515
54:
55:
56:  TCL_DEFINE_CLASS_M1(x_CMain, x_CMain_super);
57:
58:  /**** C O N S T R U C T I O N / D E S T R U C T I O N
59:                                        M E T H O D S ****/
60:
61:
62:  /****************************************************************
63:   Ix_CMain
64:
65:  Initialize the document
66:  ****************************************************************/
67:
68:  void x_CMain::Ix_CMain()
69:
70:  {
71:      IDocument(gApplication, TRUE);
72:
73:          // Initialize data members below.
74:  }
75:
76:
77:  /****************************************************************
78:   MakeNewWindow
79:
80:  Create a new, empty window. Subclass may override to populate
81:  the new window.
82:  ****************************************************************/
83:
84:  void x_CMain::MakeNewWindow(void)
85:
86:  {
87:    itsWindow = TCLGetNamedWindow("\pMain", this);
88:
89:    itsMainPane = (CPane*) TCLGetItemPointer(itsWindow, 0);
90:
91:    // Initialize pointers to the subpanes in the window
```

```
92:
93:     fMain_TextBox = (CDialogText*)
94:                   itsWindow->FindViewByID(kMain_TextBoxID);
95:     ASSERT(member(fMain_TextBox, CDialogText));
96:
97:     fMain_MultiLineBox = (CDialogText*)
98:                     itsWindow->FindViewByID(kMain_MultiLineBoxID);
99:     ASSERT(member(fMain_MultiLineBox, CDialogText));
100:
101:     fMain_InsertBtn = (CButton*)
102:                   itsWindow->FindViewByID(kMain_InsertBtnID);
103:     ASSERT(member(fMain_InsertBtn, CButton));
104:
105:     fMain_AppendBtn = (CButton*)
106:                    itsWindow->FindViewByID(kMain_AppendBtnID);
107:     ASSERT(member(fMain_AppendBtn, CButton));
108:
109:     fMain_GetSelBtn = (CButton*)
110:                    itsWindow->FindViewByID(kMain_GetSelBtnID);
111:     ASSERT(member(fMain_GetSelBtn, CButton));
112:
113:     fMain_QuitBtn = (CButton*)
114:                   itsWindow->FindViewByID(kMain_QuitBtnID);
115:     ASSERT(member(fMain_QuitBtn, CButton));
116:
117: }
118:
119:
120: /***************************************************************
121:   FailOpen {OVERRIDE}
122:
123: Fail if file already open in this application.
124:
125: This function calls the application's FileAlreadyOpen function
126: and fails quietly if the file is open.
127:
128: Note that open may also fail if the file is open in
129: another application. This will cause a failure in open,
130: but you may wish to override this function to detect this
131: case and provide a more meaningful error message than -49.
132: ***************************************************************/
133:
134: void x_CMain::FailOpen(CFile *aFile)
135:
136: {
137:     /* Only the application knows        */
138:     if (((CApp*)gApplication)->FileAlreadyOpen(aFile))
139:         Failure(kSilentErr, 0);
140: }
141:
142:
143: /***************************************************************
144:   PositionWindow
145:
146: The default method in CSaver calls the the decorator, which
147: staggers and resizes the window. Since the window has already
```

continues

Listing 17.2. continued

```
148:    been positioned when it is initialized from the view resource,
149:    we don't want to do this twice.
150:    ****************************************************************/
151:
152:    void      x_CMain::PositionWindow()
153:
154:    {
155:    }
156:
157:
158:
159:
160:    /****************************************************************
161:     DoCommand {OVERRIDE}
162:
163:    Dispatch Visual Architect-specified actions.
164:    ****************************************************************/
165:
166:    void x_CMain::DoCommand(long theCommand)
167:
168:    {
169:        switch (theCommand)
170:        {
171:            case cmdAppendString:
172:                DoCmdAppendString();
173:                break;
174:            case cmdGetSelection:
175:                DoCmdGetSelection();
176:                break;
177:            case cmdInsertString:
178:                DoCmdInsertString();
179:                break;
180:            default:
181:                CDocument::DoCommand(theCommand);
182:        }
183:    }
184:
185:
186:    /****************************************************************
187:     UpdateMenus {OVERRIDE}
188:
189:    Enable menus which generate commands handled by this class.
190:    ****************************************************************/
191:
192:    void x_CMain::UpdateMenus()
193:
194:    {
195:        CDocument::UpdateMenus();
196:        gBartender->EnableCmd(cmdAppendString);
197:        gBartender->EnableCmd(cmdGetSelection);
198:        gBartender->EnableCmd(cmdInsertString);
199:    }
200:
201:
202:    /****************************************************************
```

```
203:    DoCmdAppendString
204:
205: Respond to cmdAppendString command.
206: *******************************************************************/
207:
208: void x_CMain::DoCmdAppendString()
209:
210: {
211:   Handle h = (char**) &buff;
212:   long n, m;
213:
214:   h = fMain_TextBox->GetTextHandle();
215:   n = fMain_TextBox->GetLength();
216:
217:   strncpy(buff, *h, n);
218:   buff[n] = '\0';
219:   m = fMain_MultiLineBox->GetLength();
220:   fMain_MultiLineBox->SetSelection(m , m, FALSE);
221:   fMain_MultiLineBox->InsertTextPtr(buff, n, TRUE);
222: }
223:
224:
225: /*****************************************************************
226:    DoCmdGetSelection
227:
228: Respond to cmdGetSelection command.
229: *******************************************************************/
230:
231: void x_CMain::DoCmdGetSelection()
232:
233: {
234:   Handle h = (char**) &buff;
235:   long n;
236:   long selStart, selEnd;
237:
238:   fMain_MultiLineBox->GetSelection(&selStart, &selEnd);
239:   if (selStart == selEnd)
240:     return;
241:
242:   h = fMain_MultiLineBox->CopyTextRange(selStart, selEnd);
243:   n = selEnd - selStart;
244:   strncpy(buff, *h, n);
245:   buff[n] = '\0';
246:   fMain_TextBox->SetTextPtr(buff, strlen(buff));
247: }
248:
249:
250: /*****************************************************************
251:    DoCmdInsertString
252:
253: Respond to cmdInsertString command.
254: *******************************************************************/
255:
256: void x_CMain::DoCmdInsertString()
257:
258: {
259:   Handle h = (char**) &buff;
```

Listing 17.2. continued

```
260:      long n;
261:
262:      h = fMain_TextBox->GetTextHandle();
263:      n = fMain_TextBox->GetLength();
264:
265:      strncpy(buff, *h, n);
266:      buff[n] = '\0';
267:      fMain_MultiLineBox->InsertTextPtr(buff, n, TRUE);
268:  }
```

Analysis

Listing 17.2 shows the definitions of the member functions of class x_CMain. Lines 51 to 53 define the constants for the commands cmdAppendString, cmdGetSelection, and cmdInsertString, respectively. The next four subsections discuss the relevant member functions.

Syntax

The Function *MakeNewWindow*

The member function MakeNewWindow (defined in lines 84 to 117) stores the pointers to the window and the pane in the variables itsWindow and itsMainPane, respectively. The function also stores the addresses of the edit box and button controls in their respective data members. The function obtains these addresses by sending the C++ message FindViewByID to the window object. The arguments for these messages are the constants kMain_XXXXID, which are defined in Listing 17.4.

Syntax

The Function *DoCommand*

The member function DoCommand (defined in lines 166 to 183) has case labels in the switch statement to respond to the commands cmdAppendString, cmdGetSelection, and cmdInsertString. The first statement after case cmdAppendString invokes the member function DoCmdAppendString. The first statement after case cmdGetSelection invokes the member function DoCmdGetSelection. The first statement after case cmdInsertString invokes the member function DoCmdInsertString.

Note: The Visual Architect utility does not include custom source code lines to handle the predefined cmdQuit, which is emitted by clicking the Quit button. Why? Responding to the cmdQuit button already is built into the TCL classes, so there is no need to generate redundant code. That's why the class x_CMain lacks the member function DoCmdQuit.

The Function *UpdateMenus*

The member function UpdateMenus (defined in lines 192 to 199) enables the custom commands by sending the C++ message EnableCmd, for each command, to the bartender object. The arguments for the sequence of EnableCmd messages are the constants cmdAppendString, cmdGetSelection, and cmdInsertString.

The Function *DoCmdAppendString*

The member function DoCmdAppendString (defined in lines 208 to 222) appends the string of the input/output box to the multiline box. Line 211 declares the handle h as a pointer to the pointer of member buff. The statement in line 215 obtains the handle of the text in the input/output box by sending it the C++ message GetTextHandle. The statement assigns the result of the message to the handle h. Line 215 obtains the number of characters in the input/output box by sending it the C++ message GetLength. This statement assigns the result of the message to the local variable n. To copy the characters from the input/output box into the buffer, line 217 uses the function strncpy. The arguments for this function call are buff, *h, and n. Line 218 stores the null character at index n of the data member buff. The statement in line 219 obtains the number of characters in the multiline box by sending it the C++ message GetLength. The statement assigns the result of this message to the local variable m.

The statement in line 220 moves the insertion cursor to the end of the multiline box by sending the C++ message SetSelection. The arguments for this message are m, m, and TRUE. The last statement, in line 221, inserts the text in member buff into the multiline box by sending the C++ message InsertTextPtr. The arguments for this message are buff, n, and TRUE.

The Function *DoCmdGetSelection*

The member function DoCmdGetSelection (defined in lines 231 to 247) copies the selected text of the multiline box into the input/output box. The function declares the handle h, in line 234, as a pointer to the char pointer to the characters of the data member buff. The statement in line 238 obtains the character indices which define the range of selected text. This statement sends the C++ message GetSelection to the multiline box. The arguments for this messages are the addresses of the local variables selStart and selEnd. The if statement in line 239 determines whether or not there is selected text by comparing the values in variables selStart and selEnd. If these two variables contain the same value, the function exits because there is no selected text.

The statement in line 242 stores the handle of the selected text in the multiline box by sending it the C++ message CopyTextRange. The arguments for this message are selStart and selEnd. The statement assigns the result of the message to handle h. Line 243 calculates the number of characters in the selected text and stores that number in the variable n. Line 244 copies the selected text into the data member buff by calling the function strncpy. The arguments for the function strncpy are buff, *h, and n. The statement in line 245 stores the null character in the character index n of the member buff. The last statement in the function, located in line 246, copies the characters from member buff to the input/output box. This statement sends the C++ message SetTextPtr to the input/output box. The arguments for this message are buff and strlen(buff).

Syntax

The Function *DoCmdInsertString*

The member function DoCmdInsertString (defined in lines 256 to 268) inserts the string of the input/output box into the multiline box. The function declares the handle h, in line 259, as a double-char pointer to the characters in the data member buff. Line 262 stores the handle of the text of the input/output box text in the variable h. This statement sends the C++ message GetTextHandle to the input/output box. The statement in line 263 obtains the number of characters in the input/output box by sending it the C++ message GetLength. The statement stores the result of the message in variable n. Next, the function copies the characters from the input/output box into the member buff by using the statement in line 265. This statement calls function strncpy and supplies this function with the arguments buff, *h, and n. The statement in line 266 stores the null character at index n of the member buff. The last statement, in line 267, inserts the character of member buff into the multiline box by sending the C++ message InsertTextPtr. The arguments for this message are buff, n, and TRUE.

Note: Listing 17.2 shows how the DoCmd*XXXX* member functions manage text without using Pascal strings, which can handle only up to 255 characters.

Listing 17.3 shows the source code for the AppCommands.h header file for the Edit1 program project. In lines 16 to 18, this listing defines the constants cmdAppendString, cmdGetSelection, and cmdInsertString, which support the custom commands.

Listing 17.3. The source code for the AppCommands.h header file for the Edit1 program project.

```
 1:  /*****************************************************************
 2:   MyCommands.h
 3:
 4:              Header File For Command Symbols
 5:
 6:      Copyright (c) 1994 My Software Inc. All rights reserved.
 7:
 8:  Generated by Visual Architect(TM)
 9:
10:  This file is regenerated each time.
11:
12:  *****************************************************************/
13:
14:  #pragma once
15:
16:  #define cmdAppendString    513
17:  #define cmdGetSelection    514
18:  #define cmdInsertString    515
```

Listing 17.4 shows the source code for the MainItems.h header file for the Edit1 program project. The listing declares an untagged enumerated type that defines the identifiers kMain_*XXXX* and kMain_*XXXX*ID.

Listing 17.4. The source code for the MainItems.h header file for the Edit1 program project.

```
 1:  /*****************************************************************
 2:   MainItems.h
 3:
 4:                  Main Item Constants
 5:
 6:      Copyright (c) 1994 My Software Inc. All rights reserved.
 7:
 8:  Generated by Visual Architect(TM)
 9:
10:  This file is rewritten each time you generate code. You should
11:  not make changes to this file.
12:
13:  If you want to change how Visual Architect generates this file,
14:  you can change the template for this file. It is "Items.h" in
15:  the Visual Architect Templates folder.
16:
17:  *****************************************************************/
18:
19:  #pragma once
20:
21:
22:      //     Item numbers for each item.
23:      //
```

continues

525

Listing 17.4. continued

```
24:      //    Use TCLGetItemPointer (ViewUtilities) to convert these
25:      //    item numbers to a pointer to the named item.
26:
27:  enum
28:  {
29:      Main_Begin_,
30:      kMain_TextBox = 1,
31:      kMain_TextBoxID = 1L,
32:      kMain_MultiLineBox = 2,
33:      kMain_MultiLineBoxID = 2L,
34:      kMain_InsertBtn = 3,
35:      kMain_InsertBtnID = 3L,
36:      kMain_AppendBtn = 4,
37:      kMain_AppendBtnID = 4L,
38:      kMain_GetSelBtn = 5,
39:      kMain_GetSelBtnID = 5L,
40:      kMain_QuitBtn = 6,
41:      kMain_QuitBtnID = 6L,
42:      Main_End_
43:  };
```

Compiling and Running the Program

Invoke the Run command from the THINK Project Manager icon menu. This command causes the compiler to process the set of source code files that contribute to the program. When the program runs, type text in the input/output box and then click the Insert String or Append String button to insert or append strings, respectively, in the multiline box. Also, select text in the multiline box, and then click the Get Selection button to copy the selected text of the multiline box into the input/output box. To exit the program, click the Quit button. The program displays a confirmation alert box; click the No button.

The Button Control

The button control is conceptually the most important control because we live in a push-button electronic culture. You press a button, and something happens. Moreover, the word *button* is part of phrases such as *pushing the nuclear button*—you don't hear of the *nuclear edit box*, for example. The class CButton supports the popular button control. Here is the declaration of class CButton:

```
class CButton : public CControl { // Class Declaration

public:
    TCL_DECLARE_CLASS
```

```
// Data Members
long clickCmd; // Command to issue when clicked
short procID; // Saved procID

// Member Functions
// Construction
CButton();
CButton(short CNTLid, CView *anEnclosure,
        CBureaucrat *aSupervisor);
CButton(short aWidth, short aHeight,
        short aHEncl, short aVEncl,
        StringPtr title, Boolean fVisible, short procID,
        CView *anEnclosure, CBureaucrat    *aSupervisor);

// Click Handling
virtual void DoGoodClick(short whichPart);
virtual void SetClickCmd(long aClickCmd);
virtual long GetClickCmd();

virtual void SetDefault(Boolean fDefault);
virtual void SimulateClick();

// Object I/O
virtual void PutTo(CStream& stream);
virtual void GetFrom(CStream& stream);

// Compatibility
void IButton(short CNTLid,
             CView *anEnclosure,
             CBureaucrat *aSupervisor);
void INewButton(short aWidth, short aHeight,
                short aHEncl, short aVEncl,
                StringPtr title, Boolean fVisible,
                short procID,
                CView *anEnclosure,
                CBureaucrat   *aSupervisor);

private:
    void CButtonX();
    void IButtonX(short CNTLid);
    void INewButtonX(StringPtr title, Boolean fVisible,
                     short procID);
};
```

The next four subsections present the relevant member functions of class CButton.

The Function *GetClickCmd*

The member function GetClickCmd yields the command emitted by the button's supervisor object when you click that button. The declaration of function GetClickCmd is

```
long GetClickCmd();
```

Syntax

The Function *SetClickCmd*

The member function SetClickCmd sets the command number to be generated when you click a button. The declaration of function SetClickCmd is

```
void SetClickCmd(long aClickCmd);
```

The parameter aClickCmd specifies the command number to be associated with the button.

Syntax

The Function *SetDefault*

The member function SetDefault specifies whether or not a button is the default button. Such a button appears with a three-pixel-thick rounded rectangle as its border. When you press the Enter key, you invoke the default button. The declaration of the function SetDefault is

```
void SetDefault(Boolean fDefault);
```

The Boolean parameter fDefault specifies the default state of the button.

Syntax

The Function *SimulateClick*

The member function SimulateClick, as the name might suggest, simulates a button click. This function is suitable for creating demos. The declaration of function SimulateClick is

```
void SimulateClick();
```

The class CButton is a descendant of class CControl whose declaration is as follows:

```
class CControl : public CPane { // Class Declaration

public:
    TCL_DECLARE_CLASS

    // Data Members
    ControlHandle macControl;// Toolbox control record

    // Member Functions

    // Construction/Destruction
    CControl();
    CControl(CView *anEnclosure, CBureaucrat *aSupervisor,
                    short aWidth = 0, short aHeight = 0,
                    short aHEncl = 0, short aVEncl = 0,
                    SizingOption aHSizing = sizFIXEDSTICKY,
                    SizingOption aVSizing = sizFIXEDSTICKY);
    ~CControl();
```

```
    // Accessing
    virtual void SetValue(short aValue);
    virtual short       GetValue();
    virtual void SetMaxValue(short aMaxValue);
    virtual short       GetMaxValue();
    virtual void SetMinValue(short aMinValue);
    virtual short       GetMinValue();
    virtual void SetTitle(Str255 aTitle);
    virtual void GetTitle(Str255 aTitle);
    virtual void SetActionProc(ControlActionUPP anActionProc);

    // Manipulating
    virtual void Show();
    virtual void Hide();
    virtual void Activate();
    virtual void Deactivate();
    virtual short       GetHelpBalloonState();
    virtual void Offset(long hOffset, long vOffset,
                        Boolean redraw);
    virtual void ChangeSize(Rect *delta, Boolean redraw);

    // Drawing
    virtual void Draw(Rect *area);
    virtual void DrawAll(Rect *area);
    virtual void Prepare();
    virtual void PrepareToPrint(void); // TCL 1.1.1 DLP 9/18/91
    virtual void RefreshLongRect(LongRect *area);

    // Click Response
    virtual void DoClick(Point hitPt, short modifierKeys,
                        long when);
    virtual void DoThumbDragged(short delta);
    virtual void DoGoodClick(short whichPart);

    virtual void PutTo(CStream& stream);
    virtual void GetControl(CStream& stream, short controlDef);
};
```

The next nine subsections discuss the relevant member functions of class CControl.

Syntax

The Function *SetValue*

The function SetValue sets the value of a control. This function works with controls that have a state (like the check box) or an integer value (like the scroll bar). The declaration of function SetValue is

```
void SetValue(short aValue);
```

The parameter aValue provides the value for the control.

Syntax

The Function *GetValue*

The function GetValue gets the value of a control. This function works with controls that have a state (such as the check box) or an integer value (such as the scroll bar). The declaration of function GetValue is

```
short GetValue();
```

Syntax

The Function *SetMaxValue*

The member function SetMaxValue sets the maximum value of a control. This function works with controls that have a range of integer values, such as the scroll bar. The declaration of function SetMaxValue is

```
void SetMaxValue(short aMaxValue);
```

The parameter aMaxValue specifies the maximum value for the control.

Syntax

The Function *GetMaxValue*

The member function GetMaxValue gets the maximum value of a control. This function works with controls that have a range of integer values, such as the scroll bar. The declaration of function GetMaxValue is

```
short GetMaxValue();
```

Syntax

The Function *SetMinValue*

The member function SetMinValue sets the minimum value of a control. This function works with controls that have a range of integer values, such as the scroll bar. The declaration of function SetMinValue is

```
void SetMinValue(short aMinValue);
```

The parameter aMinValue specifies the minimum value for the control.

Syntax

The Function *GetMinValue*

The member function GetMinValue gets the minimum value of a control. This function works with controls that have a range of integer values, such as the scroll bar. The declaration of function GetMinValue is

```
short GetMinValue();
```

The Function *SetTitle*

The member function SetTitle sets the title or caption of a control. The declaration of the function SetTitle is

```
void SetTitle(Str255 aTitle);
```

The parameter aTitle is a Pascal string that specifies the new title or caption of the control.

The Function *Show*

The member function Show makes a control visible. The declaration of the function Show is

```
void Show();
```

The Function *Hide*

The member function Hide makes the control invisible and inactive. The declaration of function Hide is

```
void Hide();
```

Responding to Button Clicks

The Visual Architect utility enables you to associate a button that you draw, in a window or in a dialog box, with a currently defined cmd*XXXX* command. Such a command can be either a predefined command (such as the command cmdQuit) or a custom command that you define for the currently opened program project.

DO	DON'T

DO disable a button when its associated command is not available to the user. Remember to restore a disabled button when its associated command does become available to the user.

DON'T hide a button unless your application decides to make that button unavailable for the rest of the program session. Disable the button when its unavailability is only temporary.

The Button-Manipulation Example

Let's look at a program that toggles the visibility, toggles the enabled state, and alters the caption of a button at runtime. The next project, Button1, performs these tasks. Figure 17.2 shows a sample session with the Button1 program. The figure reveals that the program's main window contains the following controls:

- ☐ The MyBtn1 button, which displays a general alert box when you click this button.

- ☐ The MyBtn2 button, which displays a general alert box when you click this button.

- ☐ The Disable 'MyBtn1' button, which toggles the enabled state of the button MyBtn1. The program toggles the caption of this button between Disable 'MyBtn1' and Enable 'MyBtn1' depending on whether or not button MyBtn1 is enabled.

- ☐ The Hide 'MyBtn2' button, which toggles the visibility of the button MyBtn2. The program toggles the caption of this button between Hide 'MyBtn2' and Show 'MyBtn2' depending on whether or not button MyBtn1 is visible.

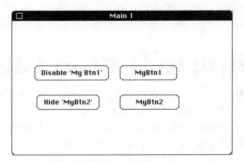

Figure 17.2. *A sample session with the Button1 program.*

Table 17.2 shows the control names as well as the custom and predefined commands associated with these controls.

Table 17.2. The control names and commands associated with the controls of project Button1.

Control Caption	Control Name	Associated Command	Custom?
My Btn1	MyBtn1Btn	cmdShowMsg1	Yes
My Btn2	MyBtn2Btn	cmdShowMsg2	Yes
Disable 'MyBtn1'	EnableBtn	cmdEnableMyBtn1	Yes
Hide 'MyBtn2'	ShowBtn	cmdShowMyBtn2	Yes

Building the Application

To build the Button1 program project, perform the following steps:

1. Create a new Visual Architect utility project, and name it Button1.

2. Delete the default controls in the main window, and select the fixed window style.

3. Expand the width of the main window and its pane.

4. Define the four custom commands specified in Table 17.2. Make sure that these commands are associated with class CMain and result in a Call type of action.

5. Use the Tools menu to select the button control tool, and then draw the button controls in the main window.

6. Set the control name, caption, and associated command of each button according to the information in Table 17.2.

7. Generate the custom code by invoking the Generate All... command in the THINK Project Manager icon menu.

Customizing the Source Code

Let's look at the relevant files emitted by the Visual Architect utility and the lines of code that I inserted to support the program's operations. Listing 17.5 shows the source code for the x_CMain.h header file for the Button1 program project. The bold lines indicate the ones that I manually inserted.

Listing 17.5. The source code for the x_CMain.h header file for project Button1.

```
 1:  /****************************************************************
 2:   x_CMain.h
 3:
 4:              Header File For CMain Lower-Layer Document Class
 5:
 6:       Copyright (c) 1994 My Software Inc. All rights reserved.
 7:
 8:  Generated by Visual Architect(TM)
 9:
10:  This file is rewritten each time you generate code. You should
11:  not make changes to this file; changes should go in the My.h
12:  file, instead.
13:
14:  If you want to change how Visual Architect generates this file,
15:  you can change the template for this file. It is "_Doc.h" in
16:  the Visual Architect Templates folder.
17:
18:  ****************************************************************/
19:
20:  #pragma once
21:
22:  #include "CSaver.h"
23:  class CButton;
24:
25:  #include "ItsContentsClass.h"
26:
27:  #define x_CMain_super    CSaver<ITSCONTENTSCLASS>
28:
29:  class CFile;
30:
31:  class x_CMain : public x_CMain_super
32:
33:  {
34:  public:
35:
36:      TCL_DECLARE_CLASS
37:
38:      // Pointers to panes in window
39:      CButton    *fMain_EnableBtn;
40:      CButton    *fMain_MyBtn1Btn;
41:      CButton    *fMain_ShowBtn;
42:      CButton    *fMain_MyBtn2Btn;
43:      Boolean fShowMyBtn2;
44:      Boolean fEnableMyBtn1;
45:
46:      void    Ix_CMain(void);
47:
48:      virtual    void    DoCommand(long theCommand);
49:      virtual    void    UpdateMenus(void);
50:
51:  protected:
52:      virtual void    MakeNewWindow(void);
53:
```

```
54:      virtual void     FailOpen(CFile *aFile);
55:      virtual void     PositionWindow(void);
56:
57:      virtual void     DoCmdShowMsg1(void);
58:      virtual void     DoCmdShowMsg2(void);
59:      virtual void     DoCmdEnableMyBtn1(void);
60:      virtual void     DoCmdShowMyBtn2(void);
61: };
62:
63: #define    CVueCMain    128
```

Listing 17.5 shows the declaration of class x_CMain. This class contains a number of data members and member functions. The Visual Architect utility generated data members in lines 39 to 42 that are pointers to the various button controls. These members are pointers to the CButton class. I inserted the data members fShowMyBtn2 and fEnableMyBtn1 in lines 43 and 44. These members are flags for the visibility of button MyBtn2 and the enabled state of button MyBtn1, respectively. The class x_CMain contains the member functions DoCmdShowMsg1, DoCmdShowMsg2, DoCmdEnableMyBtn1, and DoCmdShowMyBtn2, which handle the commands cmdShowMsg1, cmdShowMsg2, cmdEnableMyBtn1, and cmdShowMyBtn2, respectively.

Listing 17.6 shows the source code for the x_CMain.cp implementation file for the Button1 program project. The bold lines show the ones that I manually inserted.

Listing 17.6. The source code for the x_CMain.cp implementation file for project Button1.

```
1:  /*******************************************************************
2:   x_CMain.c
3:
4:               CMain Document Class
5:
6:     Copyright (c) 1994 My Software Inc. All rights reserved.
7:
8:  Generated by Visual Architect(TM) 1:13 PM Mon, Jun 13, 1994
9:
10: This file is rewritten each time you generate code. You should
11: not make changes to this file; changes should go in the My.c
12: file, instead.
13:
14: If you want to change how Visual Architect generates this file,
15: you can change the template for this file. It is "_Doc_cp" in
16: the Visual Architect Templates folder.
17:
18: *******************************************************************/
19:
20: #include "x_CMain.h"
21:
22: #include "CMain.h"
```

continues

Listing 17.6. continued

```
23:
24:  #include "MainItems.h"
25:
26:  #include "ViewUtilities.h"
27:  #include "CApp.h"
28:
29:  #include <CApplication.h>
30:  #include <CBartender.h>
31:  #include <Commands.h>
32:  #include <Constants.h>
33:  #include <CDecorator.h>
34:  #include <CDesktop.h>
35:  #include <CFile.h>
36:  #include <TBUtilities.h>
37:  #include <CWindow.h>
38:
39:  extern CApplication *gApplication; /* The application */
40:  extern CDecorator *gDecorator; /* Decorator for arranging
41:                    windows */
42:  extern CDesktop *gDesktop; /* The visible Desktop */
43:  extern CBartender *gBartender; /* Manages all menus   */
44:
45:  #include "CButton.h"
46:
47:      // Define symbols for commands handled by this class
48:      // Prevents a recompile every time any command changed.
49:
50:  #define cmdShowMsg1 512
51:  #define cmdShowMsg2 513
52:  #define cmdEnableMyBtn1 514
53:  #define cmdShowMyBtn2 515
54:  #define ALRTgeneral 128
55:
56:  TCL_DEFINE_CLASS_M1(x_CMain, x_CMain_super);
57:
58:  /**** C O N S T R U C T I O N / D E S T R U C T I O N
59:                                    M E T H O D S ****/
60:
61:
62:  /****************************************************************
63:   Ix_CMain
64:
65:  Initialize the document
66:  ****************************************************************/
67:
68:  void x_CMain::Ix_CMain()
69:
70:  {
71:      IDocument(gApplication, TRUE);
72:
73:      // Initialize data members below.
74:      fEnableMyBtn1 = TRUE;
75:      fShowMyBtn2 = TRUE;
76:
```

```
77:    }
78:
79:
80:    /****************************************************************
81:     MakeNewWindow
82:
83:    Create a new, empty window. Subclass may override to populate
84:    the new window.
85:    ****************************************************************/
86:
87:    void x_CMain::MakeNewWindow(void)
88:
89:    {
90:      itsWindow = TCLGetNamedWindow("\pMain", this);
91:
92:      itsMainPane = (CPane*) TCLGetItemPointer(itsWindow, 0);
93:
94:      // Initialize pointers to the subpanes in the window
95:
96:      fMain_EnableBtn = (CButton*)
97:                        itsWindow->FindViewByID(kMain_EnableBtnID);
98:      ASSERT(member(fMain_EnableBtn, CButton));
99:
100:     fMain_MyBtn1Btn = (CButton*)
101:                       itsWindow->FindViewByID(kMain_MyBtn1BtnID);
102:     ASSERT(member(fMain_MyBtn1Btn, CButton));
103:
104:     fMain_ShowBtn = (CButton*)
105:                     itsWindow->FindViewByID(kMain_ShowBtnID);
106:     ASSERT(member(fMain_ShowBtn, CButton));
107:
108:     fMain_MyBtn2Btn = (CButton*)
109:                       itsWindow->FindViewByID(kMain_MyBtn2BtnID);
110:     ASSERT(member(fMain_MyBtn2Btn, CButton));
111:
112:   }
113:
114:
115:   /****************************************************************
116:    FailOpen {OVERRIDE}
117:
118:   Fail if file already open in this application.
119:
120:   This function calls the application's FileAlreadyOpen function
121:   and fails quietly if the file is open.
122:
123:   Note that open may also fail if the file is open in
124:   another application. This will cause a failure in open,
125:   but you may wish to override this function to detect this
126:   case and provide a more meaningful error message than -49.
127:   ****************************************************************/
128:
129:   void x_CMain::FailOpen(CFile *aFile)
130:
131:   {
132:       /* Only the application knows          */
```

continues

Listing 17.6. continued

```
133:        if (((CApp*)gApplication)->FileAlreadyOpen(aFile))
134:            Failure(kSilentErr, 0);
135:  }
136:
137:
138:  /**************************************************************
139:   PositionWindow
140:
141:  The default method in CSaver calls the the decorator, which
142:  staggers and resizes the window. Since the window has already
143:  been positioned when it is initialized from the view resource,
144:  we don't want to do this twice.
145:  **************************************************************/
146:
147:  void    x_CMain::PositionWindow()
148:
149:  {
150:  }
151:
152:
153:
154:
155:  /**************************************************************
156:   DoCommand {OVERRIDE}
157:
158:  Dispatch Visual Architect-specified actions.
159:  **************************************************************/
160:
161:  void x_CMain::DoCommand(long theCommand)
162:
163:  {
164:      switch (theCommand)
165:      {
166:          case cmdShowMsg1:
167:              DoCmdShowMsg1();
168:              break;
169:          case cmdShowMsg2:
170:              DoCmdShowMsg2();
171:              break;
172:          case cmdEnableMyBtn1:
173:              DoCmdEnableMyBtn1();
174:              break;
175:          case cmdShowMyBtn2:
176:              DoCmdShowMyBtn2();
177:              break;
178:          default:
179:              CDocument::DoCommand(theCommand);
180:      }
181:  }
182:
183:
184:  /**************************************************************
185:   UpdateMenus {OVERRIDE}
186:
```

```
187:    Enable menus which generate commands handled by this class.
188:    ****************************************************************/
189:
190:    void x_CMain::UpdateMenus()
191:
192:    {
193:        CDocument::UpdateMenus();
194:        gBartender->EnableCmd(cmdShowMsg1);
195:        gBartender->EnableCmd(cmdShowMsg2);
196:        gBartender->EnableCmd(cmdEnableMyBtn1);
197:        gBartender->EnableCmd(cmdShowMyBtn2);
198:    }
199:
200:
201:    /****************************************************************
202:      DoCmdShowMsg1
203:
204:    Respond to cmdShowMsg1 command.
205:    ****************************************************************/
206:
207:    void x_CMain::DoCmdShowMsg1()
208:
209:    {
210:      // Subclass must override this function to
211:      // handle the command
212:      PositionDialog('ALRT', ALRTgeneral);
213:      InitCursor();
214:      ParamText(
215:          "\p          M E S S A G E!\r\rYou clicked 'My Btn1'",
216:          "\p", "\p", "\p");
217:      Alert(ALRTgeneral, NULL);
218:    }
219:
220:
221:    /****************************************************************
222:      DoCmdShowMsg2
223:
224:    Respond to cmdShowMsg2 command.
225:    ****************************************************************/
226:
227:    void x_CMain::DoCmdShowMsg2()
228:
229:    {
230:      // Subclass must override this function to
231:      // handle the command
232:      PositionDialog('ALRT', ALRTgeneral);
233:      InitCursor();
234:      ParamText(
235:          "\p          M E S S A G E!\r\rYou clicked 'My Btn2'",
236:          "\p", "\p", "\p");
237:      Alert(ALRTgeneral, NULL);
238:
239:    }
240:
241:
242:    /****************************************************************
```

17

continues

Listing 17.6. continued

```
243:   DoCmdEnableMyBtn1
244:
245:   Respond to cmdEnableMyBtn1 command.
246:   *************************************************************/
247:
248:   void x_CMain::DoCmdEnableMyBtn1()
249:
250:   {
251:     // Subclass must override this function to
252:     // handle the command
253:     fEnableMyBtn1 = (fEnableMyBtn1) ? FALSE : TRUE;
254:     if (fEnableMyBtn1) {
255:       fMain_MyBtn1Btn->Activate();
256:       fMain_EnableBtn->SetTitle("\pDisable 'My Btn1'");
257:     }
258:     else {
259:       fMain_MyBtn1Btn->Deactivate();
260:       fMain_EnableBtn->SetTitle("\pEnable 'My Btn1'");
261:     }
262:   }
263:
264:
265:   /*************************************************************
266:    DoCmdShowMyBtn2
267:
268:   Respond to cmdShowMyBtn2 command.
269:   *************************************************************/
270:
271:   void x_CMain::DoCmdShowMyBtn2()
272:
273:   {
274:     // Subclass must override this function to
275:     // handle the command
276:     fShowMyBtn2 = (fShowMyBtn2) ? FALSE : TRUE;
277:     if (fShowMyBtn2) {
278:       fMain_MyBtn2Btn->Show();
279:       fMain_ShowBtn->SetTitle("\pHide 'My Btn2'");
280:     }
281:     else {
282:       fMain_MyBtn2Btn->Hide();
283:       fMain_ShowBtn->SetTitle("\pShow 'My Btn2'");
284:     }
285:   }
```

Analysis Listing 17.6 shows the definitions of the member functions of class x_CMain. Lines 50 to 53 define the constants for the commands cmdShowMsg1, cmdShowMsg2, cmdEnableMyBtn1, and cmdShowMyBtn2, respectively. I inserted the definition of constant ALRTgeneral in line 54. The next eight subsections discuss the relevant member functions.

The Function *Ix_CMain*

The member function Ix_CMain (defined in lines 68 to 77) initializes the main window's document. I inserted the statements in lines 74 and 75 to initialize the Boolean data members fEnableMyBtn1 and fShowMyBtn2 with the value TRUE.

The Function *MakeNewWindow*

The member function MakeNewWindow (defined in lines 87 to 112) stores the pointers to the window and the pane in the variables itsWindow and itsMainPane, respectively. It also stores the addresses of the button controls in their respective data members. The function obtains these addresses by sending the C++ message FindViewByID to the window object. The arguments for these messages are the constants kMain_XXXXBtnID, which are defined in Listing 17.8.

The Function *DoCommand*

The member function DoCommand (defined in lines 161 to 180) has case labels in the switch statement to respond to the four commands cmdShowMsg1, cmdShowMsg2, cmdEnableMyBtn1, and cmdShowMyBtn2 by invoking their corresponding member functions. The first statement after case cmdShowMsg1 invokes the member function DoCmdShowMsg1. The first statement after case cmdShowMsg2 invokes the member function DoCmdShowMsg2. The first statement after case cmdEnableMyBtn1 invokes the member function DoCmdEnableMyBtn1. The first statement after case cmdShowMyBtn2 invokes the member function DoCmdShowMyBtn2.

The Function *UpdateMenus*

The member function UpdateMenus (defined in lines 190 to 198) enables the custom commands by sending the C++ message EnableCmd, for each command, to the bartender object. The arguments for the sequence of EnableCmd messages are the constants cmdShowMsg1, cmdShowMsg2, cmdEnableMyBtn2, and cmdShowMyBtn2.

The Function *DoCmdShowMsg1*

The member function DoCmdShowMsg1 (defined in lines 207 to 218) displays a general alert box. This box shows the message You clicked 'My Btn1'.

Syntax

The Function *DoCmdShowMsg2*

The member function DoCmdShowMsg2 (defined in lines 248 to 262) displays a general alert box. This box shows the message You clicked 'My Btn2'.

Syntax

The Function *DoCmdEnableMyBtn1*

The member function DoCmdEnableMyBtn1 (defined in lines 248 to 262) toggles the enabled state of button MyBtn1. The function first toggles the Boolean value of member fEnabledMyBtn1 using the statement in line 253. The if-else statement, which begins at line 254, examines the value of member fEnabledMyBtn1. If this member contains a nonzero value, the function executes the statements in lines 255 and 256. Otherwise, the function executes the statements in lines 259 and 260.

The statement in lines 255 activates the button MyBtn1 by sending it the C++ message Activate. The statement in line 256 updates the caption of the button you clicked by setting that caption to Disable 'MyBtn1'. This task involves sending the C++ message SetTitle to the button you clicked.

The statement in lines 259 deactivates the button MyBtn1 by sending it the C++ message Deactivate. The statement in line 260 updates the caption of the button you clicked by setting that caption to Enable 'MyBtn1'. This task involves sending the C++ message SetTitle to the button you clicked.

Syntax

The Function *DoCmdShowMyBtn2*

The member function DoCmdShowMyBtn2 (defined in lines 271 to 285) toggles the visibility of button MyBtn2. The function first toggles the Boolean value of member fShowMyBtn2 using the statement in line 276. The if-else statement, which begins at line 277, examines the value of member fShowMyBtn2. If this member contains a nonzero value, the function executes the statements in lines 278 and 279. Otherwise, the function executes the statements in lines 282 and 283.

The statement in lines 278 displays the button MyBtn1 by sending it the C++ message Show. The statement in line 278 updates the caption of the button you clicked by setting that caption to Hide 'MyBtn2'. This task involves sending the C++ message SetTitle to the button you clicked.

The statement in lines 282 hides the button MyBtn1 by sending it the C++ message Hide. The statement in line 283 updates the caption of the button you clicked by setting that caption to Show 'MyBtn2'. This task involves sending the C++ message SetTitle to the button you clicked.

Listing 17.7 shows the source code for the AppCommands.h header file for the Button1 program project. In lines 16 to 19, this listing defines the constants cmdShowMsg1, cmdShowMsg2, cmsEnableMyBtn1, and cmdShowMyBtn2, which support the custom commands.

Listing 17.7. The source code for the AppCommands.h header file for project Button1.

```
1:   /****************************************************************
2:   MyCommands.h
3:
4:            Header File For Command Symbols
5:
6:      Copyright (c) 1994 My Software Inc. All rights reserved.
7:
8:      Generated by Visual Architect(TM)
9:
10:     This file is regenerated each time.
11:
12:   ****************************************************************/
13:
14:   #pragma once
15:
16:   #define cmdEnableMyBtn1    514
17:   #define cmdShowMsg1        512
18:   #define cmdShowMsg2        513
19:   #define cmdShowMyBtn2      515
```

Listing 17.8 shows the source code for the MainItems.h header file for the Button1 program project. The listing declares an untagged enumerated type that defines the identifiers kMain_XXXXBtn and kMain_XXXXBtnID.

Listing 17.8. The source code for the MainItems.h header file for project Button1.

```
1:   /****************************************************************
2:   MainItems.h
3:
4:                Main Item Constants
5:
6:      Copyright (c) 1994 My Software Inc. All rights reserved.
7:
8:   Generated by Visual Architect(TM)
9:
10:  This file is rewritten each time you generate code. You should
11:  not make changes to this file.
12:
13:  If you want to change how Visual Architect generates this file,
14:  you can change the template for this file. It is "Items.h" in
15:  the Visual Architect Templates folder.
```

Listing 17.8. continued

```
16:
17:    ****************************************************************/
18:
19:    #pragma once
20:
21:
22:        //      Item numbers for each item.
23:        //
24:        //      Use TCLGetItemPointer (ViewUtilities) to convert these
25:        //      item numbers to a pointer to the named item.
26:
27:    enum
28:    {
29:        Main_Begin_,
30:        kMain_EnableBtn = 1,
31:        kMain_EnableBtnID = 1L,
32:        kMain_MyBtn1Btn = 2,
33:        kMain_MyBtn1BtnID = 2L,
34:        kMain_ShowBtn = 3,
35:        kMain_ShowBtnID = 3L,
36:        kMain_MyBtn2Btn = 4,
37:        kMain_MyBtn2BtnID = 4L,
38:        Main_End_
39:    };
```

Compiling and Running the Program

Invoke the Run command from the THINK Project Manager icon menu. This command causes the compiler to process the set of source code files that contribute to the program. When the program runs, click the Disable 'My Btn1' button to disable button MyBtn1 (see the result of this click in Figure 17.3). Also click the button Hide 'MyBtn2' to hide the button MyBtn2 (see the result of this click in Figure 17.4).

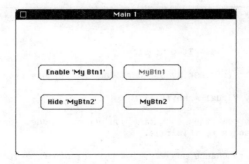

Figure 17.3. *A sample session with program Button1 showing the result of clicking the button titled Disable 'My Btn1'.*

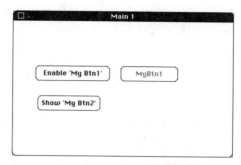

Figure 17.4. *A sample session with program Button1 showing the result of clicking the button titled Hide 'My Btn2'.*

17

Summary

This chapter discussed the edit box and button controls, as supported by the TCL classes:

☐ You learned about the TCL classes CAbstractText and CEditText, which support the edit box control. These controls support basic operations, such as writing text, reading text, copying a text range, setting the selected text, querying the selected text, hiding the selected text, showing the selected text, accessing the font type, accessing the font style, and accessing the text spacing.

☐ You learned about the class CDialogText and its relevant member functions. This class supports edit controls for dialog boxes, and it also is used by the Visual Architect utility to draw edit boxes in main windows.

☐ You learned about the class CIntegerText and its relevant member functions. This control enables you to manage edit boxes that accept integer input and to validate that input.

☐ From the edit box manipulation example, you learned how to append and insert text from an edit box. The program also showed you how to obtain selected text from an edit box.

☐ You learned about the classes CButton and CControl, which support the button control. The text discussed the relevant member functions of these classes. These functions support the click command, select a default button, enable a button, disable a button, and set the caption of a button.

☐ From the button-manipulation example, you learned how to enable and disable a button, how to show and hide a button, and how to alter a button's caption at runtime.

Q&A

Q Can I perform an edit command, such as cut and paste, on the text of an edit box?

A Yes. The member function `CEditText::PerformEditCommand` supports such an edit operation. This function takes one argument which is a long integer that represents the value of an edit command.

Q How can I toggle the selected text between the highlighted state and the unhighlighted state?

A Use the member function `CEditText::HideSelection`.

Workshop

The Workshop provides quiz questions to help you solidify your understanding of the material covered and exercises to provide you with experience in using what you've learned. Try to understand the quiz and exercise answers before continuing on to the next day's lesson. Answers are provided in Appendix B, "Answers."

Quiz

1. True or false? Clicking on an invisible button still generates the command associated with that button.

2. True or false? To access the text of an edit box, use the member function `GetTextPtr`.

3. How are the functions that support reading text in an edit box control different from member functions that write the text?

Exercise

Create the program project Button2, which implements a command-line-oriented calculator. This program supports integer calculations. Figure 17.5 shows a sample session with the program.

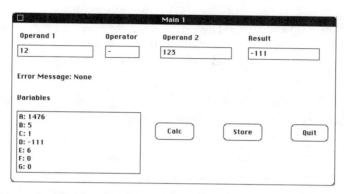

Figure 17.5. *A sample session with the Button2 program.*

The main window of this project contains the following controls:

- ☐ The Operand 1 edit box. This edit box accepts either an integer input or the name of a single-letter variable A to Z.

- ☐ The Operator edit box. This control accepts a character that represents a valid mathematical operation. The program supports +, -, *, /, and ^ (raising to powers).

- ☐ The Operand 2 edit box. This edit box accepts either an integer input or the name of a single-letter variable A to Z.

- ☐ The Result edit box. This control displays the result of the most recent mathematical operation.

- ☐ The Error Message static text. This control displays the error associated with the most recent mathematical operation.

- ☐ The Variables edit box. This multiline edit box displays the names and values associated with 27 single-letter variables, named A to Z.

- ☐ The Calc button. This button performs the requested mathematical operation using the values or single-letter variables in the Operand 1 and Operand 2 edit boxes.

- ☐ The Store button. This button stores the current value of the Result box in the Variables edit box. The program selects the variable whose line contains the current insertion point in the Variables edit box.

☐ The Quit button. This button exits the application.

☐ The static text controls that label the various edit boxes.

The Button2 program supports the following features:

☐ The operations +, -, *, /, and ^. You are responsible to make sure that these operations do not lead to an integer overflow. The program works with long integers.

☐ If the requested operation fails, the program deactivates the Store button. By contrast, if the requested operation succeeds, the program activates the Store button.

☐ The Error Message static control displays the error status for the most recent mathematical operation. The program deals with errors related to invalid operators, division by zero, and raising an integer to a negative power.

☐ The Operand 1 and Operand 2 edit boxes accept the names of the single-letter variables in either lowercase or uppercase. The program uses the value associated with these single-letter variables in performing the requested operations.

Table 17.3 shows the control names as well as the custom and predefined commands associated with the main window's controls.

Table 17.3. The control names and commands associated with the controls of project Button2.

Control Caption	Control Name	Type	Associated Command
Operand 1	Operand1Lbl	Static text	
Operator	OperatorLbl	Static text	
Operand 2	Operand2Lbl	Static text	
Result	ResultLbl	Static text	
Error Message: None	ErrMsgLbl	Static text	
Variables	VariableBox	Static text	
	Operand1Box	Edit box	
	OperatorBox	Edit box	
	Operand2Box	Edit box	
	ResultBox	Edit box	
	VarsBox	Edit box	

Control Caption	Control Name	Type	Associated Command
Calc	CalcBtn	Button	cmdCalc
Store	StoreBtn	Button	cmdStore
Quit	QuitBtn	Button	cmdQuit*

* This command is predefined.

To build the Button2 program project, perform the following steps:

1. Create a new Visual Architect utility project, and name it Button1.

2. Delete the default controls in the main window, and select the fixed window style.

3. Expand the width of the main window and its pane.

4. Define the two associated commands specified in Table 17.3. Make sure that these commands are associated with class CMain and result in a Call type of action.

5. Use the Tools menu to select the text control tool, and then draw the static text controls in the main window.

6. Set the control name, caption, and associated command of each static text control according to the information in Table 17.3.

7. Use the Tools menu to select the edit box control tool, and then draw the edit box controls in the main window.

8. Set the control name, caption, and associated command of each edit box according to the information in Table 17.3.

9. Use the Tools menu to select the button control tool, and then draw the button controls in the main window.

10. Set the control name, caption, and associated command of each button according to the information in Table 17.3.

11. Generate the custom code by invoking the Generate All... command in the THINK Project Manager icon menu.

12. Customize the code to support the mathematical operations and data storage features.

Appendix B, "Answers," discusses the relevant listings generated by the Visual Architect utility for this program.

Grouped Controls

The grouped controls consist of the check box and radio controls. These controls are special buttons which toggle states that help fine-tune the various operations of a program. Today you learn about the following topics:

☐ The class CCheckBox and its relevant member functions

☐ The class CRadioControl and its relevant member functions

☐ The class CGroupButton and its relevant member functions

☐ How to use the check box and radio control (via an example)

☐ How to use multiple groups of radio controls (via an example)

The Class *CCheckBox*

The check box appears as a button with a square border. When you click a check box control, you toggle the × mark which appears inside the control's border. Check boxes, which are mutually nonexclusive, are used either individually or in groups. In other words, each check box represents a specific Boolean state that you can logically AND together. Checking on or off a check box typically does not affect other check boxes. If you have an application where a set of *slave* check boxes depends on the state of a *master* check box, then the slave check boxes should be deactivated if the master check box is not checked.

The class CCheckBox supports the check box control and is a descendant of classes CButton and CGroupButton. Multiple inheritance empowers class CCheckBox to tap into the attributes and operations of both parent classes. Here is the declaration for the class CCheckBox:

```
class CCheckBox : public CButton, public CGroupButton {

public:
    TCL_DECLARE_CLASS

    // Data Members
        // None

    // Member Functions
    // Construction/destruction
    CCheckBox();
    CCheckBox(short CNTLid, CView *anEnclosure,
            CBureaucrat *aSupervisor);
    CCheckBox(short aWidth, short aHeight,
            short aHEncl, short aVEncl,
            StringPtr title, Boolean fVisible, short procID,
            CView *anEnclosure,    CBureaucrat    *aSupervisor);
```

```
        // Checking
        virtual void DoGoodClick(short whichPart);
        virtual Boolean IsChecked();

        // ButtonGroup
        virtual void TurnOff();
        virtual void SetValue(short aValue);

        // Object I/O
        virtual void PutTo(CStream& stream);
        virtual void GetFrom(CStream& stream);

        // Compatibility
        void ICheckBox(short CNTLid, CView *anEnclosure,
                       CBureaucrat *aSupervisor);
        void INewCheckBox(short aWidth, short aHeight,
                          short aHEncl, short aVEncl,
                          StringPtr title, Boolean fVisible,
                          CView *anEnclosure, CBureaucrat *aSupervisor);
};
```

The next three subsections present the relevant member functions of class CCheckBox.

The Function *IsChecked*

The member function IsChecked returns a Boolean value that reflects the check state of a check box. The declaration of function IsChecked is

```
Boolean IsChecked();
```

The Function *TurnOff*

The member function TurnOff clears the check mark in the check box control. The declaration of function TurnOff is

```
void TurnOff();
```

The Function *SetValue*

The member function SetValue empowers you to set or clear the check mark in a check box control. The declaration of function SetValue is

```
void SetValue(short aValue);
```

The parameter aValue specifies the integer code for the check state. You can use the predefined constants BUTTON_ON or BUTTON_OFF as arguments to parameter aValue.

18

The *CRadioControl* Class

The radio control (sometimes called "radio button") is a button with a small circular border. When you click the radio control, you toggle the small thick dot that appears inside the circular border. Unlike check boxes, radio controls are mutually exclusive (within a group). When you click a radio control, the runtime system deselects the other radio controls in the same group. Thus, radio controls represent states that are logically ORed—only one is true at a time, within a group.

The class CRadioControl supports the radio control and is a descendant of the classes CButton and CGroupButton. Here is the declaration of class CRadioControl:

```
class CRadioControl : public CButton, public CGroupButton
{
public:

    TCL_DECLARE_CLASS

    CRadioControl();
    CRadioControl(short CNTLid, CView *anEnclosure,
                CBureaucrat *aSupervisor);
    CRadioControl(short aWidth, short aHeight,
                short aHEncl, short aVEncl,
                StringPtr title, Boolean fVisible, short procID,
                CView *anEnclosure, CBureaucrat *aSupervisor);
    ~CRadioControl();

    void IRadioControl(short CNTLid, CView *anEnclosure,
                CBureaucrat *aSupervisor);

    void INewRadioControl(short aWidth, short aHeight,
                short aHEncl, short aVEncl,
                StringPtr title, Boolean fVisible,
                CView *anEnclosure, CBureaucrat *aSupervisor);

    virtual void DoGoodClick(short whichPart);

    void TurnOff();
    void SetValue(short aValue);
    Boolean IsRadioButton();

    // Object I/O
    virtual void PutTo(CStream& stream);
    virtual void GetFrom(CStream& stream);
};
```

The next three subsections present the relevant member functions of class CRadioControl.

The Function *IsRadioButton*

The member function IsRadioButton returns TRUE. The declaration of function IsRadioButton is

```
Boolean IsRadioButton();
```

The Function *TurnOff*

The member function TurnOff deselects the radio control. The declaration of function TurnOff is

```
void TurnOff();
```

The Function *SetValue*

The member function SetValue empowers you to select or deselect the radio control. The declaration of function SetValue is

```
void SetValue(short aValue);
```

The parameter aValue specifies the integer code for the button selection state. You can use the predefined constants BUTTON_ON or BUTTON_OFF as arguments to parameter aValue.

The *CGroupButton* Class

The class CGroupButton is the parent class, together with class CButton, of the CCheckBox and CRadioControl classes. Here is the declaration of class CGroupButton:

```
class CGroupButton
{
public:

    TCL_DECLARE_CLASS

    // Construction/Destruction
    CGroupButton(CView *anEnclosure = NULL, short aGroupID = 0);
    virtual ~CGroupButton();
    void IGroupButton(CView *anEnclosure);

    // Accessing
    void SetGroupID(short id) { groupID = id; }
    short GetGroupID() { return groupID; }

    // Turning on and off
    virtual void TurningOn(CGroupButton *button);
```

```
     // Object I/O
     virtual void        PutTo(CStream& stream);
     virtual void        GetFrom(CStream& stream);

#ifdef TCL_USE_DISPOSE
     // Disposing (for CPtrArray)
     virtual void        Dispose();
#endif

protected:
     unsigned short groupID;        // The button group ID
     CGroupButtonEnclosure *itsGroupEnclosure;      // The group enclosure

     virtual void TellTurningOn();
     virtual void TurnOff() = 0;
     virtual Boolean IsRadioButton() { return FALSE; }
};
```

The next two subsections present the relevant member functions of class CGroupButton.

Syntax

The Function *SetGroupID*

The member function SetGroupID plays a main role in grouping controls (especially radio controls and check boxes that are supported by descendants of this class). The declaration of function SetGroupID is

```
void SetGroupID(short id);
```

The parameter id represents the ID number of a group used to logically group check boxes or radio buttons.

Syntax

The Function *GetGroupID*

The member function GetGroupID obtains the group ID of a control. The declaration of function GetGroupID is

```
short GetGroupID();
```

Use this function to implement your own system of accessing and manipulating radio controls and check boxes that are part of the same group.

Responding to Control Clicks

The Visual Architect utility enables you to associate a check box or radio control that you draw, in a window or in a dialog box, with a currently defined cmdXXXX command. Such a command can be either a predefined command or a custom command that you define for the currently opened program project.

DO	DON'T

DO use the inherited member functions `CButton::Activate` and `CButton::Deactivate` to enable and disable, respectively, a radio control or a check box.

DON'T forget that drawing a rectangle around a set of radio controls does not logically group these controls. You need to use the member function `SetGroupID` to group the radio controls.

The Unsigned Integer Example

Let's look at an example that uses a set of radio controls and a set of check boxes. The next program, which I call Group1, uses these controls to manipulate and display an 8-bit unsigned integer. Figure 18.1 shows a sample session with the Group1 program project, which has the following controls:

☐ An edit box which displays the unsigned integer.

☐ A rectangle which contains the next three radio controls.

☐ The Decimal radio control. When you select this button, you display the unsigned integer as a decimal number.

☐ The Hexadecimal radio control. When you select this button, you display the unsigned integer as a hexadecimal number. The hexadecimal mode represents integers using the digits 0 to 9 and the letters A to F. For example, the decimal integers 10 to 15 are equivalent to the hexadecimal integers A to F, respectively. The decimal 16 is equivalent to the hexadecimal 10.

☐ The Octal radio control. When you select this button, you display the unsigned integer as an octal number. The octal mode represents integers using the digits 0 to 7. For example, the decimal integers 8 and 9 are equivalent to the octal integers 10 to 11, respectively.

☐ The set of check boxes with the captions Bit 0 through Bit 7. Each check box toggles a specific bit in the simulated unsigned integer. When you click a check box, the program alters the value of the displayed integer to reflect the update in the check states of the eight check boxes.

18

☐ The Quit button.

☐ The static text controls which label the edit box and the radio controls.

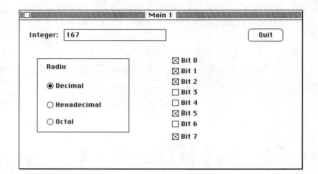

Figure 18.1. *A sample session with the Group1 program.*

Table 18.1 shows the control names as well as the custom and predefined commands associated with these controls.

Table 18.1. The control names and commands associated with the controls of project Group1.

Control Caption	Control Name	Control Type	Associated Command
Integer	IntLbl0	Static text	
	IntBox	Edit box	
Quit	QuitBtn	Button	cmdQuit
	RadixRect	Rectangle	
Radix	RadixLbl	Static text	
Decimal	DecRbt	Radio control	cmdDecRadix
Hexadecimal	HexRbt	Radio control	cmdHexRadix
Octal	OctRbt	Radio control	cmdOctalRadix
Bit 0	Bit0Chk	Check box	cmdBit0
Bit 1	Bit1Chk	Check box	cmdBit1
Bit 2	Bit2Chk	Check box	cmdBit2

Control Caption	Control Name	Control Type	Associated Command
Bit 3	Bit3Chk	Check box	cmdBit3
Bit 4	Bit4Chk	Check box	cmdBit4
Bit 5	Bit5Chk	Check box	cmdBit5
Bit 6	Bit6Chk	Check box	cmdBit6
Bit 7	Bit7Chk	Check box	cmdBit7

Building the Application

To build the Group1 program project, perform the following steps:

1. Create a new Visual Architect utility project, and name it Group1.

2. Delete the default controls in the main window.

3. Expand the width of the main window and its pane.

4. Define the non-predefined associated commands specified in Table 18.1. Make sure that these commands are associated with class CMain and result in a Call type of action.

5. Use the Tools menu to select the edit box control tool, and then draw the edit box control in the main window.

6. Set the control name of the edit box according to the information in Table 18.1.

7. Use the Tools menu to select the static text control, draw the static text control associated with the edit box.

8. Set the static text control's name and caption according to the information in Table 18.1.

9. Use the Tools menu to select the rectangle control tool, and then draw the rectangle that visually includes the radio controls.

10. Set the control name of the rectangle to RadixRect.

11. Draw the static text controls inside (and visually on top of) the rectangle.

12. Set the static text control's name and caption according to the information in Table 18.1.

18

13. Use the Tools menu to select the radio control tool, and then draw the radio controls inside the rectangle.

14. Set the control name, caption, and associated command of each radio control according to the information in Table 18.1.

15. Use the Tools menu to select the check box control tool, and then draw the eight check boxes.

16. Set the control name, caption, and associated command of each check box according to the information in Table 18.1.

17. Generate the custom code by invoking the Generate All... command in the THINK Project Manager icon menu.

Customizing the Source Code

Let's look at the relevant files emitted by the Visual Architect utility and the lines of code that I inserted to support the program's operations.

Listing 18.1 shows the source code for the x_CMain.h header file for the Group1 program project. The bold lines show the ones that I manually inserted.

Listing 18.1. The source code for the x_CMain.h header file for the Group1 program project.

```
 1:  /***************************************************************
 2:   x_CMain.h
 3:
 4:            Header File For CMain Lower-Layer Document Class
 5:
 6:      Copyright (c) 1994 My Software Inc. All rights reserved.
 7:
 8:  Generated by Visual Architect(TM)
 9:
10:  This file is rewritten each time you generate code. You should
11:  not make changes to this file; changes should go in the My.h
12:  file, instead.
13:
14:  If you want to change how Visual Architect generates this file,
15:  you can change the template for this file. It is "_Doc.h" in
16:  the Visual Architect Templates folder.
17:
18:  ***************************************************************/
19:
20:  #pragma once
21:
22:  #include "CSaver.h"
23:  class CStaticText;
```

```
24:    class CDialogText;
25:    class CButton;
26:    class CRectOvalButton;
27:    class CRadioControl;
28:    class CCheckBox;
29:
30:    #include "ItsContentsClass.h"
31:
32:    #define x_CMain_super       CSaver<ITSCONTENTSCLASS>
33:    #define NUM_BITS 8
34:    #define MaxEditLen 10
35:
36:    class CFile;
37:
38:    class x_CMain : public x_CMain_super
39:
40:    {
41:    public:
42:
43:        TCL_DECLARE_CLASS
44:
45:        enum radixMode { decRadix, hexRadix, octalRadix};
46:
47:        // Pointers to panes in window
48:        CStaticText        *fMain_IntLbl;
49:        CDialogText        *fMain_IntBox;
50:        CButton            *fMain_QuitBtn;
51:        CRectOvalButton    *fMain_RadixRect;
52:        CStaticText        *fMain_RadixLbl;
53:        CRadioControl      *fMain_DecRbt;
54:        CRadioControl      *fMain_HexRbt;
55:        CRadioControl      *fMain_OctRbt;
56:        CCheckBox          *fMain_Bit0Chk;
57:        CCheckBox          *fMain_Bit1Chk;
58:        CCheckBox          *fMain_Bit2Chk;
59:        CCheckBox          *fMain_Bit3Chk;
60:        CCheckBox          *fMain_Bit4Chk;
61:        CCheckBox          *fMain_Bit5Chk;
62:        CCheckBox          *fMain_Bit6Chk;
63:        CCheckBox          *fMain_Bit7Chk;
64:
65:        short fBits[NUM_BITS];
66:        radixMode fRadix;
67:        int fIntVal;
68:
69:        void       Ix_CMain(void);
70:
71:        virtual    void    DoCommand(long theCommand);
72:        virtual    void    UpdateMenus(void);
73:
74:    protected:
75:        virtual void       MakeNewWindow(void);
76:
77:        virtual void       FailOpen(CFile *aFile);
78:        virtual void       PositionWindow(void);
```

continues

Listing 18.1. continued

```
79:
80:      virtual void    DoCmdBit0(void);
81:      virtual void    DoCmdBit1(void);
82:      virtual void    DoCmdBit2(void);
83:      virtual void    DoCmdBit3(void);
84:      virtual void    DoCmdBit4(void);
85:      virtual void    DoCmdBit5(void);
86:      virtual void    DoCmdBit6(void);
87:      virtual void    DoCmdBit7(void);
88:      virtual void    DoCmdDecRadix(void);
89:      virtual void    DoCmdHexRadix(void);
90:      virtual void    DoCmdOctalRadix(void);
91:
92:      void toggleBit(int bitNum);
93:  };
94:
95:  #define    CVueCMain    128
```

Listing 18.1 shows the declaration of class x_CMain. This class contains a number of data members and member functions, as well as a nested enumerated type that I inserted. Line 45 defines the enumerated type radixMode which supports the three radix modes used in the program. These modes are represented by the enumerated types decRadix, hexRadix, and octalRadix. The Visual Architect utility generated the data members, in lines 48 to 63, which are pointers to the various controls. These members are pointers to the classes CCheckBox, CRadioControl, CDialogText, and CButton. I inserted the data members in lines 65 to 67. Line 65 defines the member fBits, which is an eight-element array of short. This member stores the zeros and ones in the simulated bits. Line 66 contains the definition of the data member fRadix, which stores the currently used radix. Line 67 declares the data member fIntVal which stores the value of the integer displayed in the edit box. I also inserted the definition of constant NUM_BITS in line 33. The class x_CMain contains the sets of member functions DoCmdBit*X* and DoCmd*XXXX*Radix. I inserted the declaration of member function toggleBit in line 92. This function manages toggling the check boxes.

Listing 18.2 shows the source code for the x_CMain.cp implementation file for the Group1 program project. The bold lines show the ones that I manually inserted.

VAre
Type

Listing 18.2. The source code for the x_CMain.cp implementation file for the Group1 program project.

```
1:   /*******************************************************
2:   x_CMain.c
3:
4:              CMain Document Class
```

```
5:
6:         Copyright (c) 1994 My Software Inc. All rights reserved.
7:
8: Generated by Visual Architect(TM) 3:42 PM Fri, Jun 17, 1994
9:
10: This file is rewritten each time you generate code. You should
11: not make changes to this file; changes should go in the My.h
12: file, instead.
13:
14: If you want to change how Visual Architect generates this file,
15: you can change the template for this file. It is "_Doc.h" in
16: the Visual Architect Templates folder.
17: **********************************************************/
18:
19: #include "x_CMain.h"
20:
21: #include "CMain.h"
22:
23: #include "MainItems.h"
24:
25: #include "ViewUtilities.h"
26: #include "CApp.h"
27:
28: #include <CApplication.h>
29: #include <CBartender.h>
30: #include <Commands.h>
31: #include <Constants.h>
32: #include <CDecorator.h>
33: #include <CDesktop.h>
34: #include <CFile.h>
35: #include <TBUtilities.h>
36: #include <CWindow.h>
37:
38: extern CApplication *gApplication; /* The application */
39: extern CDecorator    *gDecorator;  /* Decorator for arranging
40:                                       windows */
41: extern CDesktop       *gDesktop;   /* The visible Desktop */
42: extern CBartender    *gBartender;  /* Manages all menus */
43:
44: #include "CStaticText.h"
45: #include "CDialogText.h"
46: #include "CButton.h"
47: #include "CRectOvalButton.h"
48: #include "CRadioControl.h"
49: #include "CCheckBox.h"
50:
51:     // Define symbols for commands handled by this class
52:     // Prevents a recompile every time any command changed.
53:
54: #define cmdBit0 518
55: #define cmdBit1 519
56: #define cmdBit2 520
57: #define cmdBit3 521
58: #define cmdBit4 522
59: #define cmdBit5 523
```

continues

Listing 18.2. continued

```
60:  #define cmdBit6 524
61:  #define cmdBit7 525
62:  #define cmdDecRadix 515
63:  #define cmdHexRadix 516
64:  #define cmdOctalRadix 517
65:
66:
67:  TCL_DEFINE_CLASS_M1(x_CMain, x_CMain_super);
68:
69:  /**** C O N S T R U C T I O N / D E S T R U C T I O N
70:                                        M E T H O D S ****/
71:
72:
73:  /****************************************************************
74:   Ix_CMain
75:
76:      Initialize the document
77:  ****************************************************************/
78:
79:  void x_CMain::Ix_CMain()
80:
81:  {
82:      IDocument(gApplication, TRUE);
83:
84:      // Initialize data members below.
85:      for (int i = 0; i < NUM_BITS; i++)
86:        fBits[i] = 0;
87:      fRadix = decRadix; // set the initial radix mode
88:  }
89:
90:
91:  /****************************************************************
92:   MakeNewWindow
93:
94:  Create a new, empty window. Subclass may override to populate
95:  the new window.
96:  ****************************************************************/
97:
98:  void x_CMain::MakeNewWindow(void)
99:
100: {
101:   itsWindow = TCLGetNamedWindow("\pMain", this);
102:
103:   itsMainPane = (CPane*) TCLGetItemPointer(itsWindow, 0);
104:
105:   // Initialize pointers to the subpanes in the window
106:
107:   fMain_IntLbl = (CStaticText*)
108:               itsWindow->FindViewByID(kMain_IntLblID);
109:   ASSERT(member(fMain_IntLbl, CStaticText));
110:
111:   fMain_IntBox = (CDialogText*)
112:               itsWindow->FindViewByID(kMain_IntBoxID);
113:   ASSERT(member(fMain_IntBox, CDialogText));
114:
```

```
115:      fMain_QuitBtn = (CButton*)
116:                    itsWindow->FindViewByID(kMain_QuitBtnID);
117:      ASSERT(member(fMain_QuitBtn, CButton));
118:
119:      fMain_RadixRect = (CRectOvalButton*)
120:                    itsWindow->FindViewByID(kMain_RadixRectID);
121:      ASSERT(member(fMain_RadixRect, CRectOvalButton));
122:
123:      fMain_RadixLbl = (CStaticText*)
124:                    itsWindow->FindViewByID(kMain_RadixLblID);
125:      ASSERT(member(fMain_RadixLbl, CStaticText));
126:
127:      fMain_DecRbt = (CRadioControl*)
128:                    itsWindow->FindViewByID(kMain_DecRbtID);
129:      ASSERT(member(fMain_DecRbt, CRadioControl));
130:
131:      fMain_HexRbt = (CRadioControl*)
132:                    itsWindow->FindViewByID(kMain_HexRbtID);
133:      ASSERT(member(fMain_HexRbt, CRadioControl));
134:
135:      fMain_OctRbt = (CRadioControl*)
136:                    itsWindow->FindViewByID(kMain_OctRbtID);
137:      ASSERT(member(fMain_OctRbt, CRadioControl));
138:
139:      fMain_Bit0Chk = (CCheckBox*)
140:                    itsWindow->FindViewByID(kMain_Bit0ChkID);
141:      ASSERT(member(fMain_Bit0Chk, CCheckBox));
142:
143:      fMain_Bit1Chk = (CCheckBox*)
144:                    itsWindow->FindViewByID(kMain_Bit1ChkID);
145:      ASSERT(member(fMain_Bit1Chk, CCheckBox));
146:
147:      fMain_Bit2Chk = (CCheckBox*)
148:                    itsWindow->FindViewByID(kMain_Bit2ChkID);
149:      ASSERT(member(fMain_Bit2Chk, CCheckBox));
150:
151:      fMain_Bit3Chk = (CCheckBox*)
152:                    itsWindow->FindViewByID(kMain_Bit3ChkID);
153:      ASSERT(member(fMain_Bit3Chk, CCheckBox));
154:
155:      fMain_Bit4Chk = (CCheckBox*)
156:                    itsWindow->FindViewByID(kMain_Bit4ChkID);
157:      ASSERT(member(fMain_Bit4Chk, CCheckBox));
158:
159:      fMain_Bit5Chk = (CCheckBox*)
160:                    itsWindow->FindViewByID(kMain_Bit5ChkID);
161:      ASSERT(member(fMain_Bit5Chk, CCheckBox));
162:
163:      fMain_Bit6Chk = (CCheckBox*)
164:                    itsWindow->FindViewByID(kMain_Bit6ChkID);
165:      ASSERT(member(fMain_Bit6Chk, CCheckBox));
166:
167:      fMain_Bit7Chk = (CCheckBox*)
168:                    itsWindow->FindViewByID(kMain_Bit7ChkID);
169:      ASSERT(member(fMain_Bit7Chk, CCheckBox));
```

18

continues

Listing 18.2. continued

```
170:
171:      fMain_IntBox->SetTextString("\p0");
172:      fMain_DecRbt->SetValue(BUTTON_ON);
173:      fIntVal = 0;
174:  }
175:
176:
177:  /****************************************************************
178:   FailOpen {OVERRIDE}
179:
180:  Fail if file already open in this application.
181:
182:  This function calls the application's FileAlreadyOpen function
183:  and fails quietly if the file is open.
184:
185:  Note that open may also fail if the file is open in
186:  another application. This will cause a failure in open,
187:  but you may wish to override this function to detect this
188:  case and provide a more meaningful error message than -49.
189:  ****************************************************************/
190:
191:  void x_CMain::FailOpen(CFile *aFile)
192:
193:  {
194:      /* Only the application knows          */
195:      if (((CApp*)gApplication)->FileAlreadyOpen(aFile))
196:          Failure(kSilentErr, 0);
197:  }
198:
199:
200:  /****************************************************************
201:   PositionWindow
202:
203:  The default method in CSaver calls the the decorator, which
204:  staggers and resizes the window. Since the window has already
205:  been positioned when it is initialized from the view resource,
206:  we don't want to do this twice.
207:  ****************************************************************/
208:
209:  void      x_CMain::PositionWindow()
210:
211:  {
212:  }
213:
214:
215:
216:
217:  /****************************************************************
218:   DoCommand {OVERRIDE}
219:
220:  Dispatch Visual Architect-specified actions.
221:  ****************************************************************/
222:
223:  void x_CMain::DoCommand(long theCommand)
```

```
224:
225:    {
226:        switch (theCommand)
227:        {
228:            case cmdBit0:
229:                DoCmdBit0();
230:                break;
231:            case cmdBit1:
232:                DoCmdBit1();
233:                break;
234:            case cmdBit2:
235:                DoCmdBit2();
236:                break;
237:            case cmdBit3:
238:                DoCmdBit3();
239:                break;
240:            case cmdBit4:
241:                DoCmdBit4();
242:                break;
243:            case cmdBit5:
244:                DoCmdBit5();
245:                break;
246:            case cmdBit6:
247:                DoCmdBit6();
248:                break;
249:            case cmdDecRadix:
250:                DoCmdDecRadix();
251:                break;
252:            case cmdHexRadix:
253:                DoCmdHexRadix();
254:                break;
255:            case cmdOctalRadix:
256:                DoCmdOctalRadix();
257:                break;
258:            case cmdBit7:
259:                DoCmdBit7();
260:                break;
261:            default:
262:                CDocument::DoCommand(theCommand);
263:        }
264:    }
265:
266:
267:    /****************************************************************
268:      UpdateMenus {OVERRIDE}
269:
270:    Enable menus which generate commands handled by this class.
271:    ****************************************************************/
272:
273:    void x_CMain::UpdateMenus()
274:
275:    {
276:        CDocument::UpdateMenus();
277:        gBartender->EnableCmd(cmdBit0);
278:        gBartender->EnableCmd(cmdBit1);
```

continues

Listing 18.2. continued

```
279:        gBartender->EnableCmd(cmdBit2);
280:        gBartender->EnableCmd(cmdBit3);
281:        gBartender->EnableCmd(cmdBit4);
282:        gBartender->EnableCmd(cmdBit5);
283:        gBartender->EnableCmd(cmdBit6);
284:        gBartender->EnableCmd(cmdDecRadix);
285:        gBartender->EnableCmd(cmdHexRadix);
286:        gBartender->EnableCmd(cmdOctalRadix);
287:        gBartender->EnableCmd(cmdBit7);
288: }
289:
290: /*************************************************************
291:  DoCmdBit0
292:
293: Respond to cmdBit0 command.
294: *************************************************************/
295:
296: void x_CMain::DoCmdBit0()
297:
298: {
299:    // Subclass must override this function to
300:    // handle the command
301:    toggleBit(0);
302: }
303:
304:
305: /*************************************************************
306:  DoCmdBit1
307:
308: Respond to cmdBit1 command.
309: *************************************************************/
310:
311: void x_CMain::DoCmdBit1()
312:
313: {
314:    // Subclass must override this function to
315:    // handle the command
316:    toggleBit(1);
317: }
318:
319:
320: /*************************************************************
321:  DoCmdBit2
322:
323: Respond to cmdBit2 command.
324: *************************************************************/
325:
326: void x_CMain::DoCmdBit2()
327:
328: {
329:    // Subclass must override this function to
330:    // handle the command
331:    toggleBit(2);
332: }
```

```
333:
334:
335:    /****************************************************************
336:     DoCmdBit3
337:
338:    Respond to cmdBit3 command.
339:    ****************************************************************/
340:
341:    void x_CMain::DoCmdBit3()
342:
343:    {
344:      // Subclass must override this function to
345:      // handle the command
346:      toggleBit(3);
347:    }
348:
349:
350:    /****************************************************************
351:     DoCmdBit4
352:
353:    Respond to cmdBit4 command.
354:    ****************************************************************/
355:
356:    void x_CMain::DoCmdBit4()
357:
358:    {
359:      // Subclass must override this function to
360:      // handle the command
361:      toggleBit(4);
362:    }
363:
364:
365:    /****************************************************************
366:     DoCmdBit5
367:
368:    Respond to cmdBit5 command.
369:    ****************************************************************/
370:
371:    void x_CMain::DoCmdBit5()
372:
373:    {
374:      // Subclass must override this function to
375:      // handle the command
376:      toggleBit(5);
377:    }
378:
379:
380:    /****************************************************************
381:     DoCmdBit6
382:
383:    Respond to cmdBit6 command.
384:    ****************************************************************/
385:
386:    void x_CMain::DoCmdBit6()
```

18

continues

Listing 18.2. continued

```
387:
388:  {
389:    // Subclass must override this function to
390:    // handle the command
391:    toggleBit(6);
392:  }
393:
394:  /****************************************************************
395:   DoCmdBit7
396:
397:  Respond to cmdBit7 command.
398:  ****************************************************************/
399:
400:  void x_CMain::DoCmdBit7()
401:
402:  {
403:    // Subclass must override this function to
404:    // handle the command
405:    toggleBit(7);
406:  }
407:
408:  /****************************************************************
409:   DoCmdDecRadix
410:
411:  Respond to cmdDecRadix command.
412:  ****************************************************************/
413:
414:  void x_CMain::DoCmdDecRadix()
415:
416:  {
417:    char s[MaxEditLen+1];
418:    // Subclass must override this function to
419:    // handle the command
420:    sprintf(s, "%d", fIntVal);
421:    fMain_IntBox->SetTextPtr(s, strlen(s));
422:    fRadix = decRadix;
423:  }
424:
425:
426:  /****************************************************************
427:   DoCmdHexRadix
428:
429:  Respond to cmdHexRadix command.
430:  ****************************************************************/
431:
432:  void x_CMain::DoCmdHexRadix()
433:
434:  {
435:    char s[MaxEditLen+1];
436:    // Subclass must override this function to
437:    // handle the command
438:    sprintf(s, "%X", fIntVal);
439:    fMain_IntBox->SetTextPtr(s, strlen(s));
440:    fRadix = hexRadix;
441:  }
```

```
442:
443:
444:    /****************************************************************
445:      DoCmdOctalRadix
446:
447:    Respond to cmdOctalRadix command.
448:    ****************************************************************/
449:
450:    void x_CMain::DoCmdOctalRadix()
451:
452:    {
453:      char s[MaxEditLen+1];
454:      // Subclass must override this function to
455:      // handle the command
456:      sprintf(s, "%o", fIntVal);
457:      fMain_IntBox->SetTextPtr(s, strlen(s));
458:      fRadix = octalRadix;
459:    }
460:
461:    /****************************************************************
462:      toggleBit
463:
464:    Toggle a bit.
465:    ****************************************************************/
466:
467:    void x_CMain::toggleBit(int bitNum)
468:    {
469:      int pwr = 1;
470:      char s[MaxEditLen+1];
471:
472:      // toggle value of targeted bit
473:      fBits[bitNum] = 1 - fBits[bitNum];
474:      // calculate the new integer value
475:      fIntVal = 0;
476:      for (int i = 0; i < NUM_BITS; i++) {
477:        fIntVal += pwr * fBits[i];
478:        pwr *= 2;
479:      }
480:
481:      // create string image of integer
482:      switch (fRadix) {
483:        case decRadix:
484:          sprintf(s, "%d", fIntVal);
485:          break;
486:
487:        case hexRadix:
488:          sprintf(s, "%X", fIntVal);
489:          break;
490:
491:        case octalRadix:
492:          sprintf(s, "%o", fIntVal);
493:          break;
494:      }
495:      // write string image to the edit box
496:      fMain_IntBox->SetTextPtr(s, strlen(s));
497:    }
```

18

Analysis

Listing 18.2 shows the definitions of the member functions of class x_CMain. Lines 54 to 61 define the constants for the commands cmdBit0 to cmdBit7. Lines 62 to 64 define the commands cmdDecRadix, cmdHexRadix, and cmdOctalRadix, respectively. The next nine subsections discuss the relevant member functions.

The Function *Ix_CMain*

The member function Ix_CMain (defined in lines 79 to 88) initializes the data members fBits and fRadix. The for loop statement, in lines 85 and 86, assigns 0 to each element of member fBits. The statement in line 87 assigns the enumerated value decRadix to the data member fRadix.

The Function *MakeNewWindow*

The member function MakeNewWindow (defined in lines 98 to 174) stores the pointers to the window and the pane in the variables itsWindow and itsMainPane, respectively. It also stores the addresses of the various controls in their respective data members. The function obtains these addresses by sending the C++ message FindViewByID to the window object. The arguments for these messages are the constants kMain_*XXXX*ID, which are defined in Listing 18.4.

I inserted the statements in lines 171 to 173 to perform additional control initialization. The statement in line 171 writes the string "0" to the edit box by sending the C++ message SetTextString to that control. The argument for this message is the literal string "\p0" (I inserted the \p because the argument for this message must be a Pascal string). The statement in line 172 selects the Decimal radio control by sending it the C++ message SetValue. The argument for this message is the predefined constant BUTTON_ON. The statement in line 173 initializes the data member fIntVal to 0.

The Function *DoCommand*

The member function DoCommand (defined in lines 223 to 264) has case labels in the switch statement to respond to the commands cmdBit*X* and cmd*XXX*Radix. The first statement in each case label invokes the corresponding member function DoCmd*XXXX*.

The Function *UpdateMenus*

The member function UpdateMenus (defined in lines 273 to 288) enables the custom commands by sending the C++ message EnableCmd, for each command, to the bartender object. The arguments for the sequence of EnableCmd messages are the sets of constants cmdBit*X* and cmd*XXXX*Radix.

The Functions *DoCmdBitX*

The member functions DoCmdBit0 through DoCmdBit7 toggle the bits associated with their respective check boxes. Each DoCmdBit*X* function invokes the member function toggleBit and supplies that function with a bit number.

The Function *toggleBit*

The member function toggleBit (defined in lines 467 to 497) updates the value of the simulated unsigned 8-bit integer and displays the new value. The function first toggles the element of member fBits, which is specified by the parameter bitNum. This element simulates the bit toggled by clicking the corresponding check box. The statement in line 475 initializes the integer value. The for loop in lines 476 to 479 calculates the new integer value using the values in the member fBits. The function uses the switch statement, in lines 482 to 494, to convert the integer value into a string image that has the proper radix mode. Each case label calls the sprintf function to convert the integer value into a string image. The statement in line 496 writes the string image to the edit box. The function performs this task by sending the C++ message SeTexPtr to the edit box. The arguments for this message are the variable s and the expression strlen(s).

18

The Function *DoCmdDecRadix*

The member function DoCmdDecRadix (defined in lines 414 to 423) displays the current value of the simulated unsigned 8-bit integer in decimal mode. The function creates the string image of member fIntVal (which stores the current integer value) into a string image of a decimal number. This task involves calling the function sprintf. The function DoCmdDecRadix then writes that string image to the edit box by sending it the C++ message SetTextPtr. The arguments for this message are the variable s and the expression strlen(s). The statement in line 422 stores the enumerated value decRadix in the data member fRadix.

Syntax

The Function *DoCmdHexRadix*

The member function DoCmdHexRadix (defined in lines 432 to 441) displays the current value of the simulated unsigned 8-bit integer in hexadecimal mode. The function creates the string image of member fIntVal into a string image of a hexadecimal number. This task involves calling the function sprintf. The function DoCmdHexRadix then writes that string image to the edit box by sending it the C++ message SetTextPtr. The arguments for this message are the variable s and the expression strlen(s). The statement in line 440 stores the enumerated value hexRadix in the data member fRadix.

Syntax

The Function *DoCmdOctalRadix*

The member function DoCmdOctalRadix (defined in lines 450 to 459) displays the current value of the simulated unsigned 8-bit integer in octal mode. The function creates the string image of member fIntVal into a string image of an octal number. This task involves calling the function sprintf. The function DoCmdOctalRadix then writes that string image to the edit box by sending it the C++ message SetTextPtr. The arguments for this message are the variable s and the expression strlen(s). The statement in line 458 stores the enumerated value octalRadix in the data member fRadix.

Listing 18.3 shows the source code for the AppCommands.h header file for the Group1 program project. In lines 16 to 26, this listing defines the sets of constants cmdBitX and cmdXXXXRadix, which support the custom commands.

Listing 18.3. The source code for the AppCommands.h header file for the Group1 program project.

```
 1:  /****************************************************************
 2:  MyCommands.h
 3:
 4:          Header File For Command Symbols
 5:
 6:      Copyright (c) 1994 My Software Inc. All rights reserved.
 7:
 8:      Generated by Visual Architect(TM)
 9:
10:      This file is regenerated each time.
11:
12:  ****************************************************************/
13:
14:  #pragma once
15:
16:  #define cmdBit0     518
17:  #define cmdBit1     519
18:  #define cmdBit2     520
```

```
19:    #define cmdBit3       521
20:    #define cmdBit4       522
21:    #define cmdBit5       523
22:    #define cmdBit6       524
23:    #define cmdBit7       525
24:    #define cmdDecRadix     515
25:    #define cmdHexRadix     516
26:    #define cmdOctalRadix    517
```

Listing 18.4 shows the source code for the MainItems.h header file for the Group1 program project. The listing declares an untagged enumerated type which defines the identifiers kMain_*XXXX* and kMain_*XXXX*ID.

Listing 18.4. The source code for the MainItems.h header file for the Group1 program project.

```
1:    /*****************************************************************
2:    MainItems.h
3:
4:                    Main Item Constants
5:
6:        Copyright (c) 1994 My Software Inc. All rights reserved.
7:
8:    Generated by Visual Architect(TM)
9:
10:    This file is rewritten each time you generate code. You should
11:    not make changes to this file; changes should go in the My.h
12:    file, instead.
13:
14:    If you want to change how Visual Architect generates this file,
15:    you can change the template for this file. It is "_Doc.h" in
16:    the Visual Architect Templates folder.
17:    *****************************************************************/
18:
19:    #pragma once
20:
21:
22:        //    Item numbers for each item.
23:        //
24:        //    Use TCLGetItemPointer (ViewUtilities) to convert these
25:        //    item numbers to a pointer to the named item.
26:
27:    enum
28:    {
29:        Main_Begin_,
30:        kMain_IntLbl = 1,
31:        kMain_IntLblID = 1L,
32:        kMain_IntBox = 2,
33:        kMain_IntBoxID = 2L,
34:        kMain_QuitBtn = 3,
35:        kMain_QuitBtnID = 3L,
```

continues

Listing 18.4. continued

```
36:        kMain_RadixRect = 4,
37:        kMain_RadixRectID = -2147483644L,
38:        kMain_RadixLbl = 5,
39:        kMain_RadixLblID = 5L,
40:        kMain_DecRbt = 6,
41:        kMain_DecRbtID = 1075838982L,
42:        kMain_HexRbt = 7,
43:        kMain_HexRbtID = 1075838983L,
44:        kMain_OctRbt = 8,
45:        kMain_OctRbtID = 1075838984L,
46:        kMain_Bit0Chk = 9,
47:        kMain_Bit0ChkID = 536870921L,
48:        kMain_Bit1Chk = 10,
49:        kMain_Bit1ChkID = 536870922L,
50:        kMain_Bit2Chk = 11,
51:        kMain_Bit2ChkID = 536870923L,
52:        kMain_Bit3Chk = 12,
53:        kMain_Bit3ChkID = 536870924L,
54:        kMain_Bit4Chk = 13,
55:        kMain_Bit4ChkID = 536870925L,
56:        kMain_Bit5Chk = 14,
57:        kMain_Bit5ChkID = 536870926L,
58:        kMain_Bit6Chk = 15,
59:        kMain_Bit6ChkID = 536870927L,
60:        kMain_Bit7Chk = 16,
61:        kMain_Bit7ChkID = 536870928L,
62:        Main_End_
63:  };
```

Compiling and Running the Program

Invoke the Run command from the THINK Project Manager icon menu. This command causes the compiler to process the set of source code files that contribute to the program. When the program runs, click the various check boxes to view automatically the resulting unsigned integer. Click the Hexadecimal radio control to view the equivalent integer in hexadecimal radix mode. Click the Octal radio control to view the equivalent integer in octal radix mode. In any one of the three radix modes, click various check boxes to view how the integer value changes in the current radix mode. When you are finished experimenting, click the Quit button to close the main window and end the program.

The Current Date Example

The example in project Group1 has only one set of radio controls. Consequently there was no need to explicitly group these radio controls—the default grouping of these controls works fine for the example. Let's look at a simple example that illustrates the use of multiple groups of radio controls. The next program project, which I call Group2, enables you to obtain the current date and time in various formats. Figure 18.2 shows a sample session with the Group2 program. The program's main window contains the following controls:

☐ The edit box, which displays the current date and time.

☐ The button Now, which displays the current date and time using the format specified by the radio controls mentioned in the next two bullet items.

☐ The Date rectangle, which contains the radio controls with the captions mm/dd/yyyy, dd/mm/yyyy, and yyyy/mm/dd. Each radio control specifies a date format indicated by its caption.

☐ The Time rectangle, which contains the radio controls with the captions AM/PM and 24 Hour. Each radio control specifies the time format indicated by its caption.

☐ The Quit button.

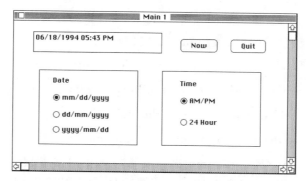

Figure 18.2. *A sample session with the Group2 program.*

Table 18.2 shows the control names as well as the custom and predefined commands associated with the above controls.

Table 18.2. The control names and commands associated with the controls of project Group2.

Control Caption	Control Name	Control Type	Associated Command
	DateBox	Edit box	
Now	NowBtn	Button	cmdNow
Quit	QuitBtn	Button	cmdQuit
	DateRect	Rectangle	
	TimeRect	Rectangle	
Date	DateLbl	Static text	
Time	TimeLbl	Static text	
mm/dd/yyyy	mdyRbt	Radio control	cmdNull
dd/mm/yyyy	dmyRbt	Radio control	cmdNull
yyyy/mm/dd	ymdRbt	Radio control	cmdNull
AM/PM	AmPmRbt	Radio control	cmdNull
24 Hour	Hour24Rbt	Radio control	cmdNull

Building the Application

To build the Group2 program project, perform the following steps:

1. Create a new Visual Architect utility project, and name it Group2.

2. Delete the default controls in the main window.

3. Expand the width of the main window and its pane.

4. Define the custom command cmdNow specified in Table 18.2. Make sure that the command is associated with class CMain and results in a Call type of action.

5. Use the Tools menu to select the edit box control tool, and then draw the edit box control in the main window.

6. Set the control name of the edit box according to the information in Table 18.2.

7. Use the Tools menu to select the rectangle control tool, and then draw the rectangles that visually include the radio controls.

8. Set the control name of each rectangle using the information in Table 18.2.

9. Draw the static text controls inside (and visually on top of) each rectangle.

10. Set the control name and caption of each static control according to the information in Table 18.2.

11. Use the Tools menu to select the radio control tool, and then draw the radio controls inside the rectangles.

12. Set the control name and caption of each radio control according to the information in Table 18.2.

13. Use the Tools menu to select the button control tool, and then draw the Now and Quit buttons.

14. Set the control name and caption of each button according to the information in Table 18.2.

15. Generate the custom code by invoking the Generate All... command in the THINK Project Manager icon menu.

Customizing the Source Code

Let's look at the relevant files emitted by the Visual Architect utility and the lines of code that I inserted to support the program's operations.

Listing 18.5 shows the source code for the x_CMain.h header file for the Group2 program project.

Listing 18.5. The source code for the x_CMain.h header file for the Group2 program project.

```
 1:  /****************************************************************
 2:  x_CMain.h
 3:
 4:              Header File For CMain Lower-Layer Document Class
 5:
 6:      Copyright (c) 1994 My Software Inc. All rights reserved.
 7:
 8:  Generated by Visual Architect(TM)
 9:
10:  This file is rewritten each time you generate code. You should
```

continues

Listing 18.5. continued

```
11:  not make changes to this file; changes should go in the My.h
12:  file, instead.
13:
14:  If you want to change how Visual Architect generates this file,
15:  you can change the template for this file. It is "_Doc.h" in
16:  the Visual Architect Templates folder.
17:  *****************************************************************/
18:
19:  #pragma once
20:
21:  #include "CSaver.h"
22:  class CButton;
23:  class CRectOvalButton;
24:  class CStaticText;
25:  class CDialogText;
26:  class CRadioControl;
27:
28:  #include "ItsContentsClass.h"
29:
30:  #define x_CMain_super       CSaver<ITSCONTENTSCLASS>
31:
32:  class CFile;
33:
34:  class x_CMain : public x_CMain_super
35:
36:  {
37:  public:
38:
39:      TCL_DECLARE_CLASS
40:
41:      // Pointers to panes in window
42:      CButton             *fMain_QuitBtn;
43:      CRectOvalButton     *fMain_TimeRect;
44:      CRectOvalButton     *fMain_DateRect;
45:      CStaticText         *fMain_TimeLbl;
46:      CStaticText         *fMain_DateLbl;
47:      CDialogText         *fMain_DateBox;
48:      CButton             *fMain_NowBtn;
49:      CRadioControl       *fMain_mdyRbt;
50:      CRadioControl       *fMain_dmyRbt;
51:      CRadioControl       *fMain_ymdRbt;
52:      CRadioControl       *fMain_AmPmRbt;
53:      CRadioControl       *fMain_Hour24Rbt;
54:
55:      void      Ix_CMain(void);
56:
57:      virtual   void    DoCommand(long theCommand);
58:      virtual   void    UpdateMenus(void);
59:
60:  protected:
61:      virtual void      MakeNewWindow(void);
62:
63:      virtual void      FailOpen(CFile *aFile);
64:      virtual void      PositionWindow(void);
```

```
65:
66:     virtual void      DoCmdNow(void);
67:  };
68:
69:  #define    CVueCMain    128
```

Listing 18.5 shows the declaration of class x_CMain. This class contains a number of data members and member functions. The Visual Architect utility generated the data members, in lines 42 to 53, which are pointers to various controls. The class x_CMain also contains the member function DoCmdNow which handles the command cmdNow.

Listing 18.6 shows the source code for the x_CMain.cp implementation file for the Group2 program project. The bold lines show the ones that I manually inserted.

VArc Type

Listing 18.6. The source code for the x_CMain.cp implementation file for the Group2 program project.

18

```
1:  /****************************************************************
2:  x_CMain.c
3:
4:                CMain Document Class
5:
6:      Copyright (c) 1994 My Software Inc. All rights reserved.
7:
8:  Generated by Visual Architect(TM) 4:49 PM Fri, Jun 17, 1994
9:
10: This file is rewritten each time you generate code. You should
11: not make changes to this file; changes should go in the My.h
12: file, instead.
13:
14: If you want to change how Visual Architect generates this file,
15: you can change the template for this file. It is "_Doc.h" in
16: the Visual Architect Templates folder.
17: ****************************************************************/
18:
19: #include "x_CMain.h"
20:
21: #include "CMain.h"
22:
23: #include "MainItems.h"
24:
25: #include "ViewUtilities.h"
26: #include "CApp.h"
27:
28: #include <CApplication.h>
29: #include <CBartender.h>
30: #include <Commands.h>
31: #include <Constants.h>
```

continues

Listing 18.6. continued

```
32:   #include <CDecorator.h>
33:   #include <CDesktop.h>
34:   #include <CFile.h>
35:   #include <TBUtilities.h>
36:   #include <CWindow.h>
37:
38:   extern CApplication *gApplication; /* The application  */
39:   extern CDecorator    *gDecorator;  /* Decorator for arranging
40:                                          windows      */
41:   extern CDesktop         *gDesktop;  /* The visible Desktop */
42:   extern CBartender    *gBartender;  /* Manages all menus */
43:
44:   #include "CButton.h"
45:   #include "CRectOvalButton.h"
46:   #include "CStaticText.h"
47:   #include "CDialogText.h"
48:   #include "CRadioControl.h"
49:
50:       // Define symbols for commands handled by this class
51:       // Prevents a recompile every time any command changed.
52:
53:   #include <stdlib.h>
54:   #include <time.h>
55:
56:   #define cmdNow 527
57:   #define DATE_GROUP 101
58:   #define TIME_GROUP 102
59:
60:   TCL_DEFINE_CLASS_M1(x_CMain, x_CMain_super);
61:
62:   /**** C O N S T R U C T I O N / D E S T R U C T I O N
63:                                       M E T H O D S ****/
64:
65:
66:   /****************************************************************
67:    Ix_CMain
68:
69:   Initialize the document
70:   ****************************************************************/
71:
72:   void x_CMain::Ix_CMain()
73:
74:   {
75:       IDocument(gApplication, TRUE);
76:
77:       // Initialize data members below.
78:   }
79:
80:
81:   /****************************************************************
82:    MakeNewWindow
83:
84:       Create a new, empty window. Subclass may override to populate
85:       the new window.
```

```
86:    ****************************************************************/
87:
88:    void x_CMain::MakeNewWindow(void)
89:
90:    {
91:        itsWindow = TCLGetNamedWindow("\pMain", this);
92:
93:        itsMainPane = (CPane*) TCLGetItemPointer(itsWindow, 0);
94:
95:        // Initialize pointers to the subpanes in the window
96:
97:        fMain_QuitBtn = (CButton*)
98:                    itsWindow->FindViewByID(kMain_QuitBtnID);
99:        ASSERT(member(fMain_QuitBtn, CButton));
100:
101:        fMain_TimeRect = (CRectOvalButton*)
102:                    itsWindow->FindViewByID(kMain_TimeRectID);
103:        ASSERT(member(fMain_TimeRect, CRectOvalButton));
104:
105:        fMain_DateRect = (CRectOvalButton*)
106:                    itsWindow->FindViewByID(kMain_DateRectID);
107:        ASSERT(member(fMain_DateRect, CRectOvalButton));
108:
109:        fMain_TimeLbl = (CStaticText*)
110:                    itsWindow->FindViewByID(kMain_TimeLblID);
111:        ASSERT(member(fMain_TimeLbl, CStaticText));
112:
113:        fMain_DateLbl = (CStaticText*)
114:                    itsWindow->FindViewByID(kMain_DateLblID);
115:        ASSERT(member(fMain_DateLbl, CStaticText));
116:
117:        fMain_DateBox = (CDialogText*)
118:                    itsWindow->FindViewByID(kMain_DateBoxID);
119:        ASSERT(member(fMain_DateBox, CDialogText));
120:
121:        fMain_NowBtn = (CButton*)
122:                    itsWindow->FindViewByID(kMain_NowBtnID);
123:        ASSERT(member(fMain_NowBtn, CButton));
124:
125:        fMain_mdyRbt = (CRadioControl*)
126:                    itsWindow->FindViewByID(kMain_mdyRbtID);
127:        ASSERT(member(fMain_mdyRbt, CRadioControl));
128:
129:        fMain_dmyRbt = (CRadioControl*)
130:                    itsWindow->FindViewByID(kMain_dmyRbtID);
131:        ASSERT(member(fMain_dmyRbt, CRadioControl));
132:
133:        fMain_ymdRbt = (CRadioControl*)
134:                    itsWindow->FindViewByID(kMain_ymdRbtID);
135:        ASSERT(member(fMain_ymdRbt, CRadioControl));
136:
137:        fMain_AmPmRbt = (CRadioControl*)
138:                    itsWindow->FindViewByID(kMain_AmPmRbtID);
139:        ASSERT(member(fMain_AmPmRbt, CRadioControl));
140:
```

18

continues

Listing 18.6. continued

```
141:      fMain_Hour24Rbt = (CRadioControl*)
142:                  itsWindow->FindViewByID(kMain_Hour24RbtID);
143:      ASSERT(member(fMain_Hour24Rbt, CRadioControl));
144:
145:      // group the radio controls in the Date box
146:      fMain_mdyRbt->SetGroupID(DATE_GROUP);
147:      fMain_dmyRbt->SetGroupID(DATE_GROUP);
148:      fMain_ymdRbt->SetGroupID(DATE_GROUP);
149:
150:      // group the radio controls in the Time box
151:      fMain_AmPmRbt->SetGroupID(TIME_GROUP);
152:      fMain_Hour24Rbt->SetGroupID(TIME_GROUP);
153:
154:      // select initial radio controls
155:      fMain_mdyRbt->SetValue(BUTTON_ON);
156:      fMain_AmPmRbt->SetValue(BUTTON_ON);
157:  }
158:
159:
160:  /****************************************************************
161:   FailOpen {OVERRIDE}
162:
163:  Fail if file already open in this application.
164:
165:  This function calls the application's FileAlreadyOpen function
166:  and fails quietly if the file is open.
167:
168:  Note that open may also fail if the file is open in
169:  another application. This will cause a failure in open,
170:  but you may wish to override this function to detect this
171:  case and provide a more meaningful error message than -49.
172:  ****************************************************************/
173:
174:  void x_CMain::FailOpen(CFile *aFile)
175:
176:  {
177:      /* Only the application knows        */
178:      if (((CApp*)gApplication)->FileAlreadyOpen(aFile))
179:          Failure(kSilentErr, 0);
180:  }
181:
182:
183:  /****************************************************************
184:   PositionWindow
185:
186:  The default method in CSaver calls the the decorator, which
187:  staggers and resizes the window. Since the window has already
188:  been positioned when it is initialized from the view resource,
189:  we don't want to do this twice.
190:  ****************************************************************/
191:
192:  void     x_CMain::PositionWindow()
193:
194:  {
```

```
195:    }
196:
197:
198:
199:
200:    /***************************************************************
201:      DoCommand {OVERRIDE}
202:
203:    Dispatch Visual Architect-specified actions.
204:    ***************************************************************/
205:
206:    void x_CMain::DoCommand(long theCommand)
207:
208:    {
209:        switch (theCommand)
210:        {
211:            case cmdNow:
212:                DoCmdNow();
213:                break;
214:            default:
215:                CDocument::DoCommand(theCommand);
216:        }
217:    }
218:
219:
220:    /***************************************************************
221:      UpdateMenus {OVERRIDE}
222:
223:    Enable menus which generate commands handled by this class.
224:    ***************************************************************/
225:
226:    void x_CMain::UpdateMenus()
227:
228:    {
229:        CDocument::UpdateMenus();
230:        gBartender->EnableCmd(cmdNow);
231:    }
232:
233:
234:    /***************************************************************
235:      DoCmdNow
236:
237:            Respond to cmdNow command.
238:    ***************************************************************/
239:
240:    void x_CMain::DoCmdNow()
241:
242:    {
243:      time_t now;
244:      struct tm *date;
245:      char s[80];
246:      Boolean isAmPm = (fMain_AmPmRbt->GetValue() == BUTTON_ON) ?
247:                                              TRUE : FALSE;
248:
249:      now = time(NULL);
```

continues

Listing 18.6. continued

```
250:    date = localtime(&now);
251:
252:    if (fMain_mdyRbt->GetValue() == BUTTON_ON) {
253:      if (isAmPm)
254:        strftime(s, 80, "%m/%d/%Y %I:%M %p", date);
255:      else
256:        strftime(s, 80, "%m/%d/%Y %H:%M", date);
257:    }
258:    else if (fMain_dmyRbt->GetValue() == BUTTON_ON) {
259:      if (isAmPm)
260:        strftime(s, 80, "%d/%m/%Y %I:%M %p", date);
261:      else
262:        strftime(s, 80, "%d/%m/%Y %H:%M", date);
263:    }
264:    else if (fMain_ymdRbt->GetValue() == BUTTON_ON) {
265:      if (isAmPm)
266:        strftime(s, 80, "%Y/%m/%d %I:%M %p", date);
267:      else
268:        strftime(s, 80, "%Y/%m/%d %H:%M", date);
269:    }
270:    fMain_DateBox->SetTextPtr(s, strlen(s));
271:  }
```

 Listing 18.6 shows the definitions of the member functions of class x_CMain. Line 56 defines the constant cmdNow for the command cmdNow. I inserted the declarations of constants DATE_GROUP and TIME_GROUP in lines 57 and 58, respectively. The next seven subsections discuss the relevant member functions.

The Function *MakeNewWindow*

The member function MakeNewWindow (defined in lines 88 to 157) stores the pointers to the window and the pane in the variables itsWindow and itsMainPane, respectively. It also stores the addresses of the various controls in their respective data members. The function obtains these addresses by sending the C++ message FindViewByID to the window object. The arguments for these messages are the constants kMain_XXXXID, which are defined in Listing 18.8.

I inserted the statements in lines 145 to 156. Lines 146 to 148 contain statements that logically group the date-related radio controls. The function performs this task by sending the C++ message SetGroupID to each of the date-related radio controls. The argument for each message is DATE_GROUP. Lines 150 and 151 contain statements that logically group the time-related radio controls. The function performs this task by sending the C++ message SetGroupID to each of the time-related radio controls. The argument for each message is TIME_GROUP. The statement in line 155 selects the mm/dd/yyyy radio control by sending it the C++ message SetValue. The argument for this value is the predefined constant BUTTON_ON. The statement in line 156 selects the AM/PM radio control by sending it the C++ message SetValue. The argument for this value is the predefined constant BUTTON_ON.

The Function *DoCommand*

Syntax

The member function DoCommand (defined in lines 206 to 217) has case labels in the switch statement to respond to the command cmdNow. The first statement after case cmdNow invokes the member function DoCmdNow.

The Function *UpdateMenus*

Syntax

The member function UpdateMenus (defined in lines 226 to 231) enables the custom command by sending the C++ message EnableCmd, for the command cmdNow, to the bartender object. The argument for the EnableCmd message is the constant cmdNow.

The Function *DoCmdNow*

Syntax

18

The member function DoCmdNow (defined in lines 240 to 271) displays the current date and time in the edit box. The function declares the local variables now and date to access the date and time. The function declares the Boolean flag isAmPm and initializes it with a conditional expression that involves sending the message GetValue to the AM/PM radio control. The statements in lines 249 and 250 obtain the date and time, respectively. The function uses a multiple-alternative if statement in lines 252 to 269 to create a date/time string image based on the currently selected date and time formats. The if statement sends GetValue messages to the date-related radio controls to determine which radio control is selected. Each if and else if clause contains a nested if statement that examines the Boolean value of the variable isAmPm. Each nested if statement invokes the function strftime to obtain the properly formatted string image of the date and time. The function stores that image in the local string variable s. The statement in line 270 writes the string image to the edit box by sending that control the C++ message SetTexPtr. The arguments for this message are the variable s and the expression strlen(s).

Listing 18.7 shows the source code for the AppCommands.h header file for the Group2 program project. This listing defines the constant cmdNow, in line 16, which supports the program's custom command.

Listing 18.7. The source code for the AppCommands.h header file for the Group2 program project.

```
 1:  /****************************************************************
 2:  MyCommands.h
 3:
 4:              Header File For Command Symbols
 5:
 6:      Copyright (c) 1994 My Software Inc. All rights reserved.
 7:
 8:  Generated by Visual Architect(TM)
 9:
10:  This file is regenerated each time.
11:
12:  ****************************************************************/
13:
14:  #pragma once
15:
16:  #define cmdNow    527
```

Listing 18.8 shows the source code for the MainItems.h header file for the Group2 program project. The listing declares an untagged enumerated type which defines the identifiers kMain_XXXX and kMain_XXXXID.

Listing 18.8. The source code for the MainItems.h header file for the Group2 program project.

```
 1:  /****************************************************************
 2:  MainItems.h
 3:
 4:                   Main Item Constants
 5:
 6:      Copyright (c) 1994 My Software Inc. All rights reserved.
 7:
 8:  Generated by Visual Architect(TM)
 9:
10:  This file is rewritten each time you generate code. You should
11:  not make changes to this file; changes should go in the My.h
12:  file, instead.
13:
14:  If you want to change how Visual Architect generates this file,
15:  you can change the template for this file. It is "_Doc.h" in
16:  the Visual Architect Templates folder.************************/
17:
18:  #pragma once
19:
20:
21:      //    Item numbers for each item.
22:      //
```

```
23:      //   Use TCLGetItemPointer (ViewUtilities) to convert these
24:      //   item numbers to a pointer to the named item.
25:
26:   enum
27:   {
28:       Main_Begin_,
29:       kMain_QuitBtn = 1,
30:       kMain_QuitBtnID = 1L,
31:       kMain_TimeRect = 2,
32:       kMain_TimeRectID = -2147483646L,
33:       kMain_DateRect = 3,
34:       kMain_DateRectID = -2147483645L,
35:       kMain_TimeLbl = 4,
36:       kMain_TimeLblID = 4L,
37:       kMain_DateLbl = 5,
38:       kMain_DateLblID = 5L,
39:       kMain_DateBox = 6,
40:       kMain_DateBoxID = 6L,
41:       kMain_NowBtn = 7,
42:       kMain_NowBtnID = 7L,
43:       kMain_mdyRbt = 8,
44:       kMain_mdyRbtID = 1075838984L,
45:       kMain_dmyRbt = 9,
46:       kMain_dmyRbtID = 1075838985L,
47:       kMain_ymdRbt = 10,
48:       kMain_ymdRbtID = 1075838986L,
49:       kMain_AmPmRbt = 11,
50:       kMain_AmPmRbtID = 1075838987L,
51:       kMain_Hour24Rbt = 12,
52:       kMain_Hour24RbtID = 1075838988L,
53:       Main_End_
54:   };
```

Compiling and Running the Program

Invoke the Run command from the THINK Project Manager icon menu. This command causes the compiler to process the set of source code files that contribute to the program. When the program runs, click the Now button to view the current date and time using the default date and time formats. For each different date and time format combination, select the date and time formats, and then click the Now button to view the results in the edit box. When you are finished experimenting with the program, click the Quit button. Figure 18.3 shows the date and time with the dd/mm/yyyy and 24-hour formats, respectively. Figure 18.4 shows the date and time with the yyyy/mm/dd and AM/PM formats, respectively.

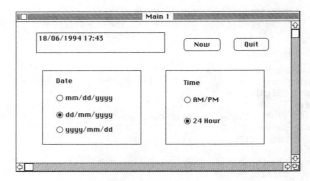

Figure 18.3. *A sample session with the Group2 program showing the date and time with the dd/mm/yyyy and 24-hour formats.*

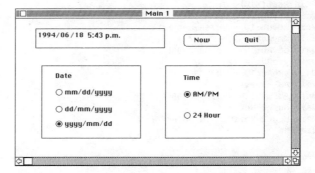

Figure 18.4. *A sample session with the Group2 program showing the date and time with the yyyy/mm/dd and AM/PM formats.*

Summary

This chapter discussed the check box and radio controls that manipulate various states in a program. In addition, you can logically group these controls, especially the radio controls. The following topics were covered:

☐ You learned about the class CCheckBox and its relevant member functions. This class supports the check box controls and offers operations that query and manipulate the state of a check box control.

☐ You learned about the class CRadioControl and its relevant member functions. This class supports the radio controls and offers operations that query and manipulate the state of a radio control.

☐ You learned about the class CGroupButton, which is the co-parent class (together with class CButton) of the CCheckBox and CRadioControl classes. You also learned about the relevant member functions of class CGroupButton that query and set the group ID of check boxes and radio controls.

☐ From the first example program, you learned how to use the check box and radio control. The program uses the check box controls to manipulate the simulated bits of an 8-bit unsigned integer. It also uses the radio controls to select between displaying the integer in decimal, hexadecimal, and octal numbers.

☐ From the second example program, you learned how to use multiple groups of radio controls. The program displays the current date and time and uses two sets of radio buttons: one to specify the date format, the other to specify the time format. The program shows you how to logically group multiple sets of radio controls.

18

Q&A

Q When is it better to use a pair of radio controls instead of a single check box to offer the same choice to the application user?

A There are two criteria to consider for using pairs of radio controls to replace single check boxes. First, use a pair of radio controls when you have relatively few options to choose from. Second, use a pair of radio controls when they really offer clearer choices to the application user.

Q Do the TCL classes have a control which can visually contain radio controls or check boxes and also logically group them?

A No. The grouping of radio controls and check boxes is performed only by using the member function SetGroupID.

Q Does the logical grouping of check boxes help the operations of a program?

A No, because check boxes are mutually nonexclusive. Grouping these controls offers no operational advantage.

Workshop

The Workshop provides quiz questions to help you solidify your understanding of the material covered and exercises to provide you with experience in using what you've learned. Try to understand the quiz and exercise answers before continuing on to the next day's lesson. Answers are provided in Appendix B, "Answers."

Quiz

1. True or false? A check box can replace any two radio controls in the same logical group.

2. True or false? You should explicitly assign a group ID to radio controls in a group when you have three or more options.

3. True or false? A set of check boxes parallels the bits in a byte or word.

4. True or false? Radio controls, in the same logical group, are mutually nonexclusive.

5. True or false? You must assign a group ID number to a set of radio controls even if these controls are part of only one logical group.

Exercise

Modify the program in project Group1 to create project Group3. The new program version does not update the simulated unsigned integer automatically when you click the check boxes. Instead, it uses an Update button to perform this task. Figure 18.5 shows a sample session with the Group3 program project, which has the following controls:

☐ An edit box which displays the unsigned integer.

☐ A rectangle which contains the three radio controls described in the next three bullet items.

☐ The Decimal radio control. When you select this button, you display the unsigned integer as a decimal number.

☐ The Hexadecimal radio control. When you select this button, you display the unsigned integer as a hexadecimal number.

☐ The Octal radio control. When you select this button, you display the unsigned integer as an octal number.

☐ The set of check boxes with the captions Bit 0 through Bit 7. When you click a check box, the program merely toggles the check mark in that control.

☐ The Quit button.

☐ The Update button. When you click this button, the program displays the value of the simulated unsigned 8-bit integer using the current states of the check boxes.

☐ The static text controls that label the edit box and the radio controls.

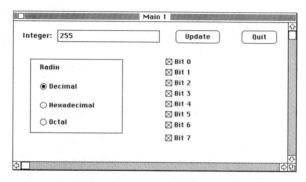

Figure 18.5. *A sample session with the Group3 program.*

Table 18.3 shows the control names as well as the custom and predefined commands associated with the above controls.

Table 18.3. The control names and commands associated with the controls of project Group3.

Control Caption	Control Name	Control Type	Associated Command
Integer	IntLbl	Static text	
	IntBox	Edit box	
Quit	QuitBtn	Button	cmdQuit
Update	UpdateBtn	Button	cmdUpdateInt

continues

Table 18.3. continued

Control Caption	Control Name	Control Type	Associated Command
	RadixRect	Rectangle	
Radix	RadixLbl	Static text	
Decimal	DecRbt	Radio control	cmdDecRadix
Hexadecimal	HexRbt	Radio control	cmdHexRadix
Octal	OctRbt	Radio control	cmdOctalRadix
Bit 0	Bit0Chk	Check box	cmdNull
Bit 1	Bit1Chk	Check box	cmdNull
Bit 2	Bit2Chk	Check box	cmdNull
Bit 3	Bit3Chk	Check box	cmdNull
Bit 4	Bit4Chk	Check box	cmdNull
Bit 5	Bit5Chk	Check box	cmdNull
Bit 6	Bit6Chk	Check box	cmdNull
Bit 7	Bit7Chk	Check box	cmdNull

The List Box Control

The list box is a versatile control because it enables your applications to offer scrolling lists of items to select from. These kinds of lists absolve you from having to remember the names of the items in the lists, let alone their exact spelling! Today you learn about the following topics:

- ☐ The class `CArrayPane` and its relevant member functions
- ☐ The class `CTable` and its relevant member functions
- ☐ The class `CArray` and its relevant member functions
- ☐ An example of using the list box control

The Class *CArrayPane*

The class `CArrayPane`, a descendant of class `CTable`, supports the list box control. Here is the declaration of class `CArrayPane`:

```
class CArrayPane : public CTable
{
public:
    TCL_DECLARE_CLASS

    CArrayPane();
    CArrayPane(CView *anEnclosure, CBureaucrat *aSupervisor,
              short aWidth, short aHeight,
              short aHEncl, short aVEncl,
              SizingOption aHSizing = sizELASTIC,
              SizingOption aVSizing = sizELASTIC);
    ~CArrayPane();

    void IArrayPane(CView *anEnclosure,
                CBureaucrat *aSupervisor,
                short aWidth, short aHeight,
                short aHEncl, short aVEncl,
                SizingOption aHSizing,
                SizingOption aVSizing);

    virtual void IViewTemp(CView *anEnclosure,
                        CBureaucrat *aSupervisor,
                        Ptr viewData);

    void SetArray(CArray *anArray, Boolean fOwnership);
    virtual CArray *GetArray();
    virtual void ChangeSize(Rect *delta, Boolean redraw);

    virtual void        PutTo(CStream& stream);
    virtual void        GetFrom(CStream& stream);

protected:
```

```
CArray    *itsArray; // array being displayed
Boolean   ownsArray; // TRUE if Dispose should
                     // dispose of itsArray


virtual void ProviderChanged(CCollaborator *aProvider,
                             long reason, void* info);
};
```

The next two subsections discuss the relevant member functions of class CArrayPane.

Syntax

The Function *SetArray*

The member function SetArray sets the array that appears in the list box. The declaration of function SetArray is

```
void SetArray(CArray* anArray, Boolean fOwnership);
```

The parameter anArray is the pointer to a CArray instance. Such an instance represents a dynamic array. The parameter fOwnership is a Boolean flag that determines whether or not the list box owns the array. When the argument for this parameter is TRUE, the list box owns the array and deletes the array when the list box is destroyed. By contrast, when the argument for parameter fOwnership is FALSE, the list box does not own the array and therefore does not delete it.

Syntax

The Function *GetArray*

The member function GetArray returns a pointer to the array displayed in the list box. The declaration of function GetArray is

```
CArray *GetArray();
```

The *CTable* Class

The class CTable is the parent of class CArrayPane. The latter class inherits many operations defined in class CTable. The class CTable supports a table that typically displays a spreadsheet. The CTable displays multiple columns and rows of data (in *cells*), whereas the CArrayPane displays information in a single column. Here is the declaration of class CTable:

```
class CTable : public CPanorama
{
public:

    TCL_DECLARE_CLASS
```

```
CTable();
CTable(CView *anEnclosure, CBureaucrat *aSupervisor,
       short aWidth, short aHeight,
       short aHEncl, short aVEncl,
       SizingOption aHSizing = sizELASTIC,
       SizingOption aVSizing = sizELASTIC);
~CTable();

void ITable(CView *anEnclosure, CBureaucrat *aSupervisor,
            short aWidth, short aHeight,
            short aHEncl, short aVEncl,
            SizingOption aHSizing, SizingOption aVSizing);

virtual void IViewTemp(CView *anEnclosure,
                       CBureaucrat *aSupervisor,
                       Ptr viewData);

virtual void SetDefaults(short colWidth, short rowHeight);
virtual void SetDrawOrder(tTblDrawOrder aDrawOrder);
virtual void SetScrollPane(CScrollPane *aScrollPane);

// change size

virtual void AddRow(short numRows, short afterRow);
virtual void AddCol(short numCols, short afterCols);

virtual void DeleteRow(short numRows, short startRow);
virtual void DeleteCol(short numCols, short startCol);

virtual void SetRowHeight(short rowNum, short newHeight);
virtual void SetColWidth(short colNum, short newWidth);

// query

virtual void GetTableBounds(Rect *aTableBounds);
virtual short GetRowCount();
virtual short GetColCount();
virtual short GetRowHeight(short rowNum);
virtual short GetColWidth(short colNum);
virtual long  GetRowStart(short rowNum);
virtual long  GetColStart(short colNum);

virtual RgnHandle GetSelection();
virtual long GetSelectionFlags();

virtual void GetCellRect(Cell theCell,
                         LongRect *cellRect);
virtual Boolean IsSelected(Cell aCell);
virtual Boolean NextCell(Boolean hNext, Boolean vNext,
                         Cell *theCell);
virtual Boolean GetSelect(Boolean next, Cell *theCell);

virtual short FindRow(long vLoc);
virtual short FindCol(long hLoc);
virtual Boolean PixelsToCells(LongRect *pixelsRect,
                              Rect *cellsRect);
```

```
        virtual Boolean CellsToPixels(Rect *cellsRect,
                                LongRect *pixelsRect);

    // clicks

    virtual void DoClick(Point hitPt,
                        short modifierKeys,
                        long when);
    virtual void DoDblClick(Cell hitCell,
                        short modifierKeys,
                        long when);

    virtual Boolean HitSamePart(Point pointA, Point pointB);
    virtual void FindHitCell(LongPt *hitPt, Cell *hitCell);

    virtual void SetDblClickCmd(long aCmd);

    virtual void Draw(Rect *area);

    virtual void RefreshCell(Cell aCell);
    virtual void RefreshCellRect(Rect *cells);

    virtual void SetDrawActiveBorder(Boolean fDrawActiveBorder);
    virtual void SetRowBorders(short thickness, short penMode,
                        ConstPatternParam penPat);
    virtual void SetColBorders(short thickness, short penMode,
                        ConstPatternParam penPat);

    virtual void Paginate(CPrinter *aPrinter,
                        short pageWidth, short pageHeight);

    virtual void Activate();
    virtual void Deactivate();

    // typing

    virtual void DoKeyDown(char theChar, Byte keyCode,
                        EventRecord *macEvent);
    virtual void DoAutoKey(char theChar, Byte keyCode,
                        EventRecord *macEvent);

    // commands

    virtual void DoCommand(long aCmd);
    virtual void UpdateMenus();

    virtual Boolean BecomeGopher(Boolean fBecoming);

    // selecting

    virtual void SetSelectionFlags(long selFlags);
    virtual void SelectCell(Cell aCell, Boolean keepPrevious,
                        Boolean reDraw);
    virtual void SelectRect(Rect *selectRect,
                        Boolean keepPrevious,
                        Boolean reDraw);
    virtual void DeselectCell(Cell aCell, Boolean redraw);
```

```
        virtual void DeselectRect(Rect *deselectRect,
                                     Boolean redraw);
        virtual void DeselectAll(Boolean redraw);

        virtual void ScrollToSelection();

        // binary streams

        virtual void PutTo(CStream& stream);
        virtual void GetFrom(CStream& stream);

protected:

        Rect tableBounds; // defines table size in cells
        Point topLeftIndent; // top and left indent of entire table
        RgnHandle itsSelection; // maintains the selection

        CRunArray *itsRows; // runs of row heights
        CRunArray *itsCols; // runs of column widths

        tTblDrawOrder drawOrder; // defines CTable draws
                                 // in row or column order
        short defRowHeight, defColWidth;  // default size of new
                                          // rows and cols
        long selectionFlags; // flags for selection behavior

        FontInfo fontInfo; // for text tables
        Point indent; // used by derived classes for cell drawing

        long dblClickCmd; // command sent for cell double click
        Boolean drawActiveBorder;
        Boolean clipToCells;
        Rect qdClip;

        CPaneBorder *saveBorder; // border before gopher

        tTableBorder rowBorders;
        tTableBorder colBorders;

        static RgnHandle cDeselection, cNewSelection, cCurrHilite;


        void ITableX();
        virtual void CreateTextEnvironment();

        virtual void AdjustBounds();

        virtual CMouseTask *MakeMouseTask(short modifiers);
        virtual void ClickOutsideBounds(Point hitPt,
                                          short modifierKeys,
                                          long when);


        // drawing
```

```
virtual void DrawRow(short rowNum, short firstCol,
                     short lastCol, Boolean doHilite);
virtual void DrawCol(short colNum, short firstRow,
                     short lastRow, Boolean doHilite);
virtual void DrawCell(Cell theCell, Rect *cellRect);

virtual void DrawBorders(Rect *theCells);
virtual void Hilite(Rect *cells, Boolean hiliteFlag);
virtual void HiliteCellRegion(RgnHandle cellRgn, Boolean fHilite);

// text tables only

virtual void GetCellText(Cell aCell,
                         short availableWidth,
                         StringPtr itsText);
private:
    void          CTableX();
};
```

The following subsections discuss the member functions of class CTable that support the operations of class CArrayPane. Keep in mind that the reference to a cell in class CTable is equivalent to a list item in class CArrayPane. The type Cell has two integer data members, v and h.

The Function *SetSelectionFlags*

The member function SetSelectionFlags enables you to specify how you can choose cells in a table. The declaration of function SetSelectionFlags is

```
void SetSelectionFlags(long selFlags);
```

The parameter selFlags specifies the cell selection scheme. The argument for this parameter can be selOnlyOne (to select only one cell), selNoDisjoint (disjoint selection is not allowed), selExtendDrag (extend the selection by adding cells that are dragged, not by extending the table's rectangles), or selDragRects (dragging always selects rectangle). The last two arguments are particular to tabulated data.

The Function *GetSelectionFlags*

The member function GetSelectionFlags returns the value for the selection flags. The declaration of function GetSelectionFlags is

```
long GetSelectionFlags();
```

19

Syntax

The Function *IsSelected*

The member function `IsSelected` returns a Boolean value that indicates whether or not the queried cell is selected. The declaration of function `IsSelected` is

```
Boolean IsSelected(Cell aCell);
```

The parameter `aCell` specifies the queried cell.

Syntax

The Function *GetRowCount*

The member function `GetRowCount` returns the number of rows in a table. The function, as inherited by class `CArrayPane`, returns the number of items in the list box. The declaration of function `GetRowCount` is

```
short GetRowCount();
```

Syntax

The Function *RefreshCell*

The member function `RefreshCell` redraws a cell. The declaration of function `RefreshCell` is

```
void RefreshCell(Cell aCell);
```

The parameter `aCell` specifies the targeted cell.

Syntax

The Function *Activate*

The member function `Activate`, as the name might suggest, activates the instance of class `CTable` (and its descendants). The declaration of function `Activate` is

```
void Activate();
```

Syntax

The Function *Deactivate*

The member function `Deactivate`, as the name might suggest, deactivates the instance of class `CTable` (and its descendants). The declaration of function `Deactivate` is

```
void Deactivate();
```

Syntax

The Function *SelectCell*

The member function `SelectCell` selects a cell, with the option of keeping the previously selected cells. The declaration of function `SelectCell` is

```
void SelectCell(Cell aCell, Boolean keepPrevious,
                Boolean redraw);
```

The parameter `aCell` specifies the targeted cell. The parameter `keepPrevious` is a Boolean flag that determines whether or not to keep the previous selection. The parameter `redraw` determines whether or not to redraw the instance of `CTable` (or its descendants).

Syntax

The Function *DeselectCell*

The member function `DeselectCell` deselects a cell. The declaration of function `DeselectCell` is

```
void DeselectCell(Cell aCell, Boolean redraw);
```

The parameter `aCell` specifies the targeted cell. The parameter `redraw` determines whether or not to redraw the instance of `CTable` (or its descendants).

Syntax

The Function *DeselectAll*

The member function `DeselectAll` deselects all the cells. The declaration of function `DeselectAll` is

```
void DeselectAll(Boolean redraw);
```

The parameter `redraw` determines whether or not to redraw the instance of `CTable` (or its descendants).

19

Syntax

The Function *GetCellText*

The member function `GetCellText` has the vital role of associating the cells of a table (and the items in a list box) with the table's data (or the data of the list box, in the case of class `CArrayPane`). The declaration of function `GetCellText` is

```
void GetCellText(Cell aCell, short availableWidth,
                StringPtr itsText);
```

The parameter `aCell` specifies the targeted cell. The parameter `availableWidth` specifies the width of the cell. The parameter `itsText` is the string associated with the targeted cell. The function generates strings that have the format `"rr, cc"` where *rr* and *cc* are the row and column indices of the targeted cell, respectively.

DO   **DON'T**

DO remember that class CTable provides many operations for the list box controls.

DON'T forget class CArrayPane itself cannot manage any list of strings. To manage such a list, you must derive a class from CArrayPane and override member function GetCellText.

The *CArray* Class

The class CArray supports dynamic homogenous arrays. This kind of array can store various kinds of data—each class instance stores a consistent kind of information. In addition, the size of the instance of CArray can grow or shrink at runtime. The class CArray supports the CArrayPane by offering a container for the data of the descendant's of CArrayPane. Here is the declaration of class CArray:

```
class CArray : public CCollection
{
public:
    TCL_DECLARE_CLASS

    short blockSize; // Number of slots to allocate when
                     //   more space is needed
    long slots; // Total number of slots allocated
    Handle hItems; // Items in the array

    long elementSize; // size of each element in bytes
    Boolean lockChanges;  // can't insert or delete if locked
    Boolean usingTemporary; // TRUE if temporary element storage
                            // buffer is in use

    CArray(long elementSize = 0, short blockSize = 3);
    CArray(CArray& source);
    virtual ~CArray();

    virtual void *Copy() { return new CArray(*this); }
    void    IArray(long elementSize);

    virtual void    SetBlockSize(short aBlockSize);
    virtual void    InsertAtIndex(void *itemPtr, long index);
    virtual void    Add(void *itemPtr);
    virtual void    DeleteItem(long index);
    virtual void    MoveItemToIndex(long currentIndex,
                                    long newIndex);
    virtual void    SetArrayItem(void *itemPtr, long index);
    virtual void    GetArrayItem(void *itemPtr, long index);
```

```
        // Apple's universal headers invade the name space with
        // hundreds of new macros, like SetItem/GetItem below!!!

#if !defined(TCL_UNIVERSAL_HEADERS) || !OLDROUTINENAMES
    virtual void      SetItem(void *itemPtr, long index)
                          { SetArrayItem(itemPtr, index); }
    virtual void      GetItem(void *itemPtr, long index)
                          { GetArrayItem(itemPtr, index); }
#endif

    virtual void      Swap(long index1, long index2);
    virtual long      Search(void *itemPtr, CompareFunc compare);
    virtual Boolean   SetLockChanges(Boolean fLockChanges);

    virtual void      Resize(long numSlots);
    virtual void      MoreSlots();
    virtual void      Store(void *itemPtr, long index);
    virtual void      Retrieve(void *itemPtr, long index);
    virtual void      CopyToTemporary(long index);
    virtual void      CopyFromTemporary(long index);
    virtual long      ItemOffset(long itemIndex);

    virtual void      PutTo(CStream& stream);
    virtual void      GetFrom(CStream& stream);

protected:
    virtual void      PutItems(CStream& stream);
    virtual void      GetItems(CStream& stream);
    virtual void      InsertItem(long index);
};
```

The following subsections discuss the member functions of class `CArray` that are relevant in supporting the class `CArrayPane` and its descendants. It's important to point out that the class `CArray` has its first element at index 1 and not 0. I encourage you to learn about the other member functions of class `CArray` because this class offers a versatile support for dynamic arrays.

DO	DON'T
DO remember that you must store consistent data in each instance of class `CArray`.	**DON'T** forget that the first element in a `CArray` instance has the index of 1 and not 0.

Syntax

The Function *InsertAtIndex*

The member function InsertAtIndex inserts a new element at the specified position, moving the elements in the specified index and then ones at the higher indices. The declaration of function InsertAtIndex is

```
void InsertAtIndex(void *itemPtr, long index);
```

The parameter itemPtr is the pointer to the inserted element. The parameter index specifies the insertion index. If the argument for this parameter exceeds the last array index, the function allocates more space to the class instance.

Syntax

The Function *DeleteItem*

The member function DeleteItem deletes an element at a specified index. The declaration of function DeleteItem is

```
void DeleteItem(long index);
```

The parameter index specifies the index of the element to delete.

Syntax

The Function *Add*

The member function Add appends a new element in the array, increasing the array's size if needed. The declaration of function Add is

```
void Add(void *itemPtr);
```

The parameter itemPtr is the pointer to the inserted element.

Syntax

The Function *SetArrayItem*

The member function SetArrayItem assigns new data to an existing array element. The declaration of member function SetArrayItem is

```
void SetArrayItem(void *itemPtr, long index);
```

The parameter itemPtr is the pointer to the new data. The parameter index specifies the index of the targeted array element.

The Function *GetArrayItem*

The member function GetArrayItem retrieves data from an existing array element. The declaration of member function GetArrayItem is

```
void GetArrayItem(void *itemPtr, long index);
```

The parameter itemPtr is the pointer to a variable receiving the data from the array. The parameter index specifies the index of the targeted array element.

The Function *Resize*

The member function Resize alters the size of the array. The declaration of function Resize is

```
void Resize(long numSlots);
```

The parameter numSlots specifies the new number of elements in the array. Use this function to expand or shrink the size of a CArray instance.

Note: The member functions SetItem and GetItem invoke the functions SetArrayItem and GetArrayItem, respectively. The functions SetItem and GetItem support backward compatibility with earlier versions of Symantec C++.

19

Responding to Double-Clicking an Item

The Visual Architect utility enables you to associate double-clicking a list box item with a currently defined cmd*XXXX* command. Such a command is typically a custom command that you define to process the selected list box.

The List Box Example

Let's look at an example of a list box that manipulates a list of names. The next program, which I call List1, uses the list box, edit box, and button controls to manipulate a list of names. Figure 19.1 shows a sample session with the List1 program project, which has the following controls:

☐ The In/Out edit box in which you type names and obtain the name of a double-clicked item.

☐ The Index edit box in which you type the index of an item to delete. The control also displays the index of a list box item that matches a search string.

☐ The Insert button, which inserts the string of the In/Out edit box at the index of the current list box selection. If there is no selected item in the list box, the button appends the new name.

☐ The Delete button, which deletes the list box item whose index appears in the Index edit box.

☐ The Find button, which searches the list box items for the string that appears in the In/Out edit box. If the program finds a match, it displays the index of the matching item in the Index edit box. Otherwise, the program displays an alert box telling you that the search failed.

☐ The Quit button.

☐ The list box that displays the names.

☐ The static text controls that label the edit boxes.

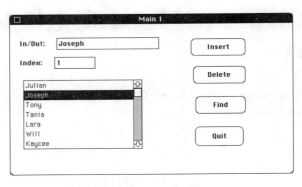

Figure 19.1. *A sample session with the List1 program.*

Table 19.1 shows the control names as well as the custom and predefined commands associated with the above controls.

Table 19.1. The control names and commands associated with the controls of project Group1.

Control Caption	Control Name	Control Type	Associated Command
In/Out	InOutLbl	Static text	
Index	IndexLbl	StaticText	
	InOutBox	Edit box	
	IndexBox	Edit box	
	StringLst	List box	cmdSelectStr
Insert	InsertBtn	Button	cmdInsertStr
Delete	DeleteBtn	Button	cmdDeleteStr
Find	FindBtn	Button	cmdFindStr
Quit	QuitBtn	Button	cmdQuit

Preparing the Application

Building the List1 program project is a bit more elaborate than building the programs in the last few chapters. The process involves several stages. In the first stage, you prepare the core part of the application by performing the following steps:

1. Create a new Visual Architect utility project, and name it Group1.

2. Delete the default controls in the main window.

3. Select a fixed window style for the main window.

4. Define the custom commands specified in Table 19.1. Make sure that these commands are associated with class CMain and result in a Call type of action.

Declaring the New Class *CListBox*

In the second stage, you must declare the class CListBox as a descendant of class CArrayPane. The Visual Architect utility offers a menu command that supports this stage. Perform the following steps:

1. Invoke the Edit | Classes command to invoke the Classes dialog box.

2. In the list box, click below the CMain class to shift the dialog box into input mode.

3. Enter CListBox in the input box.

4. Use the Base Class pop-up menu to set class CArrayPane as the parent of class CListBox.

5. Click the OK button to close the Classes dialog box.

Drawing the Controls

This stage involves drawing the controls in Figure 19.1. Perform the following steps:

1. Use the Tools menu to select the static text control tool, and then draw the static text controls associated with the edit boxes.

2. Set the names and captions of each static control according to the information in Table 19.1.

3. Use the Tools menu to select the edit box control tool, and then draw the edit box controls.

4. Set the name of each edit box control according to the information in Table 19.1.

5. Use the Tools menu to select the button control tool, and then draw the button controls.

6. Set the names and captions of each button control according to the information in Table 19.1.

7. Use the Tools menu to select the list control tool, and then draw the list box control.

8. Set the control name of the list box to StringLst.

9. Click the black arrow symbol to the left of CTable.

10. Click the selOnlyOne check box to make the list box select only one item at a time.

11. Click the Command pop-up menu to associate the list box with the command cmdSelectStr.

12. Close the dialog box of the list box control.

Associating *CListBox* with the List Box

This stage associates the class CListBox with the list box control. Without this association the program regards the list box as an instance of class CArrayPane. To associate the class with the control, follow these steps:

1. Select the list box control.

2. Invoke the Pane | Class command. This command brings up a floating menu that contains the names of classes CArrayPane and CListBox.

3. Select the CListBox class to associate this class with the list box control.

Generating and Customizing the Source Code

To generate the custom source code for this application, invoke the Generate All... command in the THINK Project Manager icon menu.

Now let's look at the relevant files emitted by the Visual Architect utility and the lines of code that I inserted to support the program's operations. Because I declare the class CListBox, the Visual Architect utility generates files for this class.

Listing 19.1 shows the source code for the CListBox.h header file for the List1 program project.

Listing 19.1. The source code for the CListBox.h header file for project List1.

```
1:  /*******************************************************************
2:  CListBox.h
3:
4:              Header for CListBox ArrayPane Class
5:
6:      Copyright (c) 1994 My Software Inc. All rights reserved.
7:
8:  Generated by Visual Architect(TM) 1:37 PM Wed, Jun 22, 1994
```

continues

611

Listing 19.1. continued

```
 9:
10:  This file is only generated once. You can modify it by filling
11:  in the placeholder functions and adding any new functions you
12:  wish.
13:
14:  If you change the name of the document class, a fresh version of
15:  this file will be generated. If you have made any changes to the
16:  file with the old name, you will have to copy those changes to
17:  the new file by hand.
18:
19:  ****************************************************************/
20:
21:  #pragma once
22:
23:  #include "x_CListBox.h"
24:
25:  class CListBox : public x_CListBox
26:  {
27:  public:
28:
29:      TCL_DECLARE_CLASS
30:
31:      /** Object I/O **/
32:      virtual void        PutTo(CStream &aStream);
33:      virtual void        GetFrom(CStream &aStream);
34:  };
```

 Listing 19.1 shows that class CListBox is a descendant of x_CListBox. The class CListBox declares only stream-related member functions.

Listing 19.2 shows the source code for the CListBox.cp implementation file for project List1.

 ### Listing 19.2. The source code for the CListBox.cp implementation file for project List1.

```
 1:  /****************************************************************
 2:   CListBox.c
 3:
 4:                  CListBox ArrayPane Class
 5:
 6:      Copyright (c) 1994 My Software Inc. All rights reserved.
 7:
 8:  Generated by Visual Architect(TM) 1:37 PM Wed, Jun 22, 1994
 9:
10:  This file is only generated once. You can modify it by filling
11:  in the placeholder functions and adding any new functions you wish.
12:
13:  If you change the name of the document class, a fresh version of
14:  this file will be generated. If you have made any changes to the
```

```
15:  file with the old name, you will have to copy those changes to the
16:  new file by hand.
17:
18:  ***************************************************************/
19:
20:  #include "CListBox.h"
21:
22:
23:  TCL_DEFINE_CLASS_D1(CListBox, x_CListBox);
24:
25:  /**** C O N S T R U C T I O N / D E S T R U C T I O N
26:                                          M E T H O D S ****/
27:
28:
29:  /***************************************************************
30:   PutTo
31:
32:          Put the contents of this object to the stream
33:  ***************************************************************/
34:
35:  void    CListBox::PutTo(
36:      CStream      &aStream)
37:  {
38:      // Put any additional data members for this class
39:      // before calling the superclass PutTo.
40:
41:      // If you have no additional data members, the
42:      // PutTo and GetFrom functions can be eliminated.
43:
44:      x_CListBox::PutTo(aStream); /* Let superclass save */
45:
46:      // By convention, any subordinate objects are put
47:      // after the superclass has had a chance to write
48:      // its instance variables.
49:  }
50:
51:
52:  /***************************************************************
53:   GetFrom
54:
55:          Get the contents of this object from the stream and
56:          initialize the object
57:  ***************************************************************/
58:
59:  void CListBox::GetFrom(CStream &aStream)
60:  {
61:      // Get any additional data members for this class
62:      // before calling the superclass GetFrom
63:
64:
65:      /* Let superclass restore */
66:      x_CListBox::GetFrom(aStream);
67:
68:      // Restore any subordinate objects below
69:  }
```

19

 Listing 19.2 contains the implementations of member functions `PutTo` and `GetFrom`. The statements in these functions invoke the corresponding member functions of the parent class.

Listing 19.3 shows the source code for the x_CListBox.h header file for project List1. The bold lines show the ones that I manually added.

 Listing 19.3. The source code for the x_CListBox.h header file for project List1.

```
1:  /****************************************************************
2:   x_CListBox.h
3:
4:           Header File For CListBox Lower-Layer ArrayPane Class
5:
6:       Copyright (c) 1994 My Software Inc. All rights reserved.
7:
8:  Generated by Visual Architect(TM)
9:
10: This file is rewritten each time you generate code. You should
11: not make changes to this file; changes should go in the
12: CListBox.h file, instead.
13:
14: If you want to change how Visual Architect generates this file,
15: you can change the template for this file. It is "_Table.h" in
16: the Visual Architect Templates folder.
17:
18: ****************************************************************/
19:
20: #pragma once
21:
22: #include "CArrayPane.h"
23:
24: class CDirectorOwner;
25:
26: class x_CListBox : public CArrayPane
27: {
28: public:
29:
30:     TCL_DECLARE_CLASS
31:
32:
33:     /** Object I/O **/
34:     virtual void        PutTo(CStream &aStream);
35:     virtual void        GetFrom(CStream &aStream);
36:
37:     virtual void GetCellText(Cell aCell, short availableWidth,
38:                             StringPtr itsText);
39:
40:     CArray *fArr;
41:
42: };
```

Analysis

Listing 19.3 declares the class x_CListBox. The Visual Architect utility generated the declarations of member functions PutTo and GetFrom in lines 34 and 35, respectively. I inserted the member function GetCellText in lines 37 and 38. I also inserted the data member fArr in line 40. This member accesses a dynamic instance of class CArray which stores the list of names.

Listing 19.4 shows the source code for the x_CListBox.cp implementation file for project List1. The bold lines show the ones that I manually added.

Listing 19.4. The source code for the x_CListBox.cp implementation file for project List1.

```
1:  /***************************************************************
2:  x_CListBox.c
3:
4:                    CListBox ArrayPane Class
5:
6:     Copyright (c) 1994 My Software Inc. All rights reserved.
7:
8:  Generated by Visual Architect(TM)
9:
10: This file is rewritten each time you generate code. You should
11: not make changes to this file; changes should go in the
12: CListBox.c file, instead.
13:
14: If you want to change how Visual Architect generates this file,
15: you can change the template for this file. It is "_Table_cp"
16: in the Visual Architect Templates folder.
17:
18: ***************************************************************/
19:
20: #include "x_CListBox.h"
21:
22: #include "ViewUtilities.h"
23:
24:
25: TCL_DEFINE_CLASS_M1(x_CListBox, CArrayPane);
26:
27: /**** C O N S T R U C T I O N / D E S T R U C T I O N
28:                                      M E T H O D S ****/
29:
30:
31: /***************************************************************
32:  PutTo
33:
34: Put the contents of this object to the stream
35: ***************************************************************/
36:
37: void x_CListBox::PutTo(
38:                 CStream& aStream) // changed ptr arg to ref
39: {
40:     // Put data members for this class
```

continues

Listing 19.4. continued

```
41:
42:
43:      CArrayPane::PutTo(aStream);    // let base class save
44:  }
45:
46:
47:  /****************************************************************
48:   GetFrom
49:
50:  Get the contents of this object from the stream and
51:  initialize the object
52:  ****************************************************************/
53:
54:  void x_CListBox::GetFrom(CStream &aStream)
55:  {
56:      // Get data members for this class
57:
58:
59:      // let base class restore
60:      CArrayPane::GetFrom(aStream);
61:  }
62:
63:  /****************************************************************
64:   GetCellText
65:
66:  Writes the text in a list box item.
67:  ****************************************************************/
68:
69:  void x_CListBox::GetCellText(Cell aCell, short availableWidth,
70:                               StringPtr itsText)
71:  {
72:    fArr->GetArrayItem(itsText, aCell.v + 1);
73:  }
```

The most relevant member function of class x_CListBox is GetCellText. Lines 69 to 73 define this member function, which contains a single statement. This statement sends the C++ message GetArrayItem to the dynamic array (accessed by data member fArr). The arguments for this message are the parameter itsText and the expression aCell.v + 1.

Listing 19.5 contains the source code for the x_CMain.h header file for project List1.

Listing 19.5. The source code for the x_CMain.h header file for project List1.

```
1:  /****************************************************************
2:   x_CMain.h
3:
4:            Header File For CMain Lower-Layer Document Class
```

```
 5:
 6:        Copyright (c) 1994 My Software Inc. All rights reserved.
 7:
 8:    Generated by Visual Architect(TM)
 9:
10:    Generated by Visual Architect(TM)
11:
12:    This file is rewritten each time you generate code. You should
13:    not make changes to this file.
14:
15:    If you want to change how Visual Architect generates this file,
16:    you can change the template for this file. It is "Items.h" in
17:    the Visual Architect Templates folder.
18:
19:    **************************************************************/
20:
21:    #pragma once
22:
23:    #include "CSaver.h"
24:    class CListBox;
25:    class CDialogText;
26:    class CStaticText;
27:    class CButton;
28:
29:    #include "ItsContentsClass.h"
30:
31:    #define x_CMain_super      CSaver<ITSCONTENTSCLASS>
32:
33:    class CFile;
34:
35:    class x_CMain : public x_CMain_super
36:
37:    {
38:    public:
39:
40:        TCL_DECLARE_CLASS
41:
42:        // Pointers to panes in window
43:        CListBox    *fMain_StringLst;
44:        CDialogText    *fMain_InOutBox;
45:        CStaticText    *fMain_InOutLbl;
46:        CStaticText    *fMain_IndexLbl;
47:        CDialogText    *fMain_IndexBox;
48:        CButton    *fMain_InsertBtn;
49:        CButton    *fMain_DeleteBtn;
50:        CButton    *fMain_FindBtn;
51:        CButton    *fMain_QuitBtn;
52:
53:        void    Ix_CMain(void);
54:
55:        virtual    void    DoCommand(long theCommand);
56:        virtual    void    UpdateMenus(void);
57:
58:    protected:
59:        virtual    void    MakeNewWindow(void);
60:
```

19

continues

Listing 19.5. continued

```
61:     virtual    void      FailOpen(CFile *aFile);
62:     virtual void      PositionWindow(void);
63:
64:     virtual void      DoCmdInsertStr(void);
65:     virtual void      DoCmdDeleteStr(void);
66:     virtual void      DoCmdFindStr(void);
67:     virtual void      DoCmdSelectStr(void);
68: };
69:
70: #define    CVueCMain    128
```

 Listing 19.5 shows the declaration of class x_CMain. This class contains a number of data members and member functions, all emitted by the Visual Architect utility. Lines 43 to 51 define the various data members that are pointers to the different controls. These members are pointers to the classes CListBox, CStaticText, CDialogText, and CButton. The class x_CMain contains the set of member functions DoCmdXXXX which respond to the custom commands that appear in Table 19.1.

Listing 19.6 shows the source code for the x_CMain.cp implementation file for project List1. The bold lines show the ones that I inserted manually.

 ## Listing 19.6. The source code for the x_CMain.cp implementation file for project List1.

```
1:  /*************************************************************
2:   x_CMain.c
3:
4:                CMain Document Class
5:
6:      Copyright (c) 1994 My Software Inc. All rights reserved.
7:
8:  Generated by Visual Architect(TM) 1:37 PM Wed, Jun 22, 1994
9:
10: This file is rewritten each time you generate code. You should
11: not make changes to this file.
12:
13: If you want to change how Visual Architect generates this file,
14: you can change the template for this file. It is "Items.h" in
15: the Visual Architect Templates folder.
16:
17: *************************************************************/
18:
19: #include "x_CMain.h"
20:
21: #include "CMain.h"
22:
23: #include "MainItems.h"
24:
```

```
25:    #include "ViewUtilities.h"
26:    #include "CApp.h"
27:
28:    #include <CApplication.h>
29:    #include <CBartender.h>
30:    #include <Commands.h>
31:    #include <Constants.h>
32:    #include <CDecorator.h>
33:    #include <CDesktop.h>
34:    #include <CFile.h>
35:    #include <TBUtilities.h>
36:    #include <CWindow.h>
37:
38:    extern CApplication *gApplication;   /* The application  */
39:    extern CDecorator    *gDecorator;    /* Decorator for arranging
40:                                            windows */
41:    extern CDesktop         *gDesktop;   /* The visible Desktop */
42:    extern CBartender    *gBartender;    /* Manages all menus */
43:
44:    #include "CListBox.h"
45:    #include "CDialogText.h"
46:    #include "CStaticText.h"
47:    #include "CButton.h"
48:
49:    #include <stdlib.h>
50:        // Define symbols for commands handled by this class
51:        // Prevents a recompile every time any command changed.
52:
53:    #define cmdInsertStr 527
54:    #define cmdDeleteStr 528
55:    #define cmdFindStr 529
56:    #define cmdSelectStr 530
57:    #define ALRTgeneral 128
58:
59:    TCL_DEFINE_CLASS_M1(x_CMain, x_CMain_super);
60:
61:
62:    /**** C O N S T R U C T I O N / D E S T R U C T I O N
63:                                            M E T H O D S ****/
64:
65:
66:    /***************************************************************
67:     Ix_CMain
68:
69:    Initialize the document
70:    ***************************************************************/
71:
72:    void x_CMain::Ix_CMain()
73:
74:    {
75:        IDocument(gApplication, TRUE);
76:
77:        // Initialize data members below.
78:    }
79:
80:
```

continues

Listing 19.6. continued

```
81:   /****************************************************************
82:    MakeNewWindow
83:
84:   Create a new, empty window. Subclass may override to populate
85:   the new window.
86:   ****************************************************************/
87:
88:   void x_CMain::MakeNewWindow(void)
89:
90:   {
91:       const maxNames = 12;
92:       Str255 s255;
93:       char *names[maxNames] = { "Julian", "Joseph", "Tony",
94:                                 "Tania", "Lara", "Will",
95:                                 "Kaycee", "Ann", "Bitsy",
96:                                 "Carter", "Barkley", "Whitney" };
97:
98:       itsWindow = TCLGetNamedWindow("\pMain", this);
99:
100:      itsMainPane = (CPane*) TCLGetItemPointer(itsWindow, 0);
101:
102:      // Initialize pointers to the subpanes in the window
103:
104:      fMain_StringLst = (CListBox*)
105:                     itsWindow->FindViewByID(kMain_StringLstID);
106:      ASSERT(member(fMain_StringLst, CListBox));
107:
108:      fMain_InOutBox = (CDialogText*)
109:                     itsWindow->FindViewByID(kMain_InOutBoxID);
110:      ASSERT(member(fMain_InOutBox, CDialogText));
111:
112:      fMain_InOutLbl = (CStaticText*)
113:                     itsWindow->FindViewByID(kMain_InOutLblID);
114:      ASSERT(member(fMain_InOutLbl, CStaticText));
115:
116:      fMain_IndexLbl = (CStaticText*)
117:                     itsWindow->FindViewByID(kMain_IndexLblID);
118:      ASSERT(member(fMain_IndexLbl, CStaticText));
119:
120:      fMain_IndexBox = (CDialogText*)
121:                     itsWindow->FindViewByID(kMain_IndexBoxID);
122:      ASSERT(member(fMain_IndexBox, CDialogText));
123:
124:      fMain_InsertBtn = (CButton*)
125:                     itsWindow->FindViewByID(kMain_InsertBtnID);
126:      ASSERT(member(fMain_InsertBtn, CButton));
127:
128:      fMain_DeleteBtn = (CButton*)
129:                     itsWindow->FindViewByID(kMain_DeleteBtnID);
130:      ASSERT(member(fMain_DeleteBtn, CButton));
131:
132:      fMain_FindBtn = (CButton*)
133:                     itsWindow->FindViewByID(kMain_FindBtnID);
134:      ASSERT(member(fMain_FindBtn, CButton));
```

```
135:
136:     fMain_QuitBtn = (CButton*)
137:                    itsWindow->FindViewByID(kMain_QuitBtnID);
138:     ASSERT(member(fMain_QuitBtn, CButton));
139:
140:     // create a dynamic array
141:     fMain_StringLst->fArr = new CArray(sizeof(Str255));
142:
143:     // insert the set fo names in the dynamic array
144:     for (int i = 0; i < maxNames; i++) {
145:       strcpy((char*)s255 + 1, names[i]);
146:       s255[0] = strlen(names[i]);
147:       fMain_StringLst->fArr->Add(s255);
148:     }
149:     // insert the data of the dynamic array in the list box
150:     fMain_StringLst->SetArray(fMain_StringLst->fArr, FALSE);
151:  }
152:
153:
154:  /***************************************************************
155:   FailOpen {OVERRIDE}
156:
157:  Fail if file already open in this application.
158:
159:  This function calls the application's FileAlreadyOpen function
160:  and fails quietly if the file is open.
161:
162:  Note that open may also fail if the file is open in
163:  another application. This will cause a failure in open,
164:  but you may wish to override this function to detect this
165:  case and provide a more meaningful error message than -49.
166:  ***************************************************************/
167:
168:  void x_CMain::FailOpen(CFile *aFile)
169:
170:  {
171:      /* Only the application knows        */
172:      if (((CApp*)gApplication)->FileAlreadyOpen(aFile))
173:          Failure(kSilentErr, 0);
174:  }
175:
176:
177:  /***************************************************************
178:   PositionWindow
179:
180:  The default method in CSaver calls the the decorator, which
181:  staggers and resizes the window. Since the window has already
182:  been positioned when it is initialized from the view resource,
183:  we don't want to do this twice.
184:  ***************************************************************/
185:
186:  void x_CMain::PositionWindow()
187:
188:  {
189:  }
190:
```

continues

Listing 19.6. continued

```
191:
192:
193:
194:    /****************************************************************
195:     DoCommand {OVERRIDE}
196:
197:    Dispatch Visual Architect-specified actions.
198:    ****************************************************************/
199:
200:    void x_CMain::DoCommand(long theCommand)
201:
202:    {
203:        switch (theCommand)
204:        {
205:            case cmdInsertStr:
206:                DoCmdInsertStr();
207:                break;
208:            case cmdDeleteStr:
209:                DoCmdDeleteStr();
210:                break;
211:            case cmdFindStr:
212:                DoCmdFindStr();
213:                break;
214:            case cmdSelectStr:
215:                DoCmdSelectStr();
216:                break;
217:            default:
218:                CDocument::DoCommand(theCommand);
219:        }
220:    }
221:
222:
223:    /****************************************************************
224:     UpdateMenus {OVERRIDE}
225:
226:    Enable menus which generate commands handled by this class.
227:    ****************************************************************/
228:
229:    void x_CMain::UpdateMenus()
230:
231:    {
232:        CDocument::UpdateMenus();
233:        gBartender->EnableCmd(cmdInsertStr);
234:        gBartender->EnableCmd(cmdDeleteStr);
235:        gBartender->EnableCmd(cmdFindStr);
236:        gBartender->EnableCmd(cmdSelectStr);
237:    }
238:
239:
240:    /****************************************************************
241:     DoCmdInsertStr
242:
243:    Respond to cmdInsertStr command.
244:    ****************************************************************/
```

```
245:
246:    void x_CMain::DoCmdInsertStr()
247:
248:    {
249:        Str255 s255;
250:        char s[11];
251:        Boolean notFound = TRUE;
252:        Cell aCell = { 0, 0 };
253:
254:        // get the string to insert from the In/Out box
255:        fMain_InOutBox->GetTextString(s255);
256:
257:        // find the selected item
258:        while (aCell.v < fMain_StringLst->GetRowCount() && notFound) {
259:            if (!fMain_StringLst->IsSelected(aCell))
260:                aCell.v++;
261:            else
262:                notFound = FALSE;
263:        }
264:
265:        // is there a selected item?
266:        if (!notFound)
267:            // insert string
268:            fMain_StringLst->fArr->InsertAtIndex(s255, aCell.v + 1);
269:        else
270:            // append string
271:            fMain_StringLst->fArr->Add(s255);
272:        // update the list box
273:        fMain_StringLst->SetArray(fMain_StringLst->fArr, FALSE);
274:    }
275:
276:
277:    /****************************************************************
278:      DoCmdDeleteStr
279:
280:    Respond to cmdDeleteStr command.
281:    ****************************************************************/
282:
283:    void x_CMain::DoCmdDeleteStr()
284:
285:    {
286:        Str255 s255;
287:        char s[256];
288:        long index;
289:        int numItems = fMain_StringLst->GetRowCount();
290:
291:        if (numItems <= 0) {
292:            PositionDialog('ALRT', ALRTgeneral);
293:            InitCursor();
294:            ParamText(
295:                "\p          ERROR MESSAGE!\r\rList box is empty",
296:                "\p", "\p", "\p");
297:            Alert(ALRTgeneral, NULL);
298:            return;
299:        }
300:
```

19

continues

Listing 19.6. continued

```
301:      // get the index image from the Index box
302:      fMain_IndexBox->GetTextString(s255);
303:      strncpy(s, (char*)s255 + 1, s255[0]);
304:      s[s255[0]] = '\0';
305:      // check if string s does NOT start with a digit?
306:      if (s[0] < '0' || s[0] > '9') {
307:        PositionDialog('ALRT', ALRTgeneral);
308:        InitCursor();
309:        ParamText(
310:          "\p          ERROR MESSAGE!\r\rIndex Box is empty or contains text",
311:          "\p", "\p", "\p");
312:        Alert(ALRTgeneral, NULL);
313:        return;
314:      }
315:      // convert the string image into a long integer
316:      index = atol(s);
317:      // is the index valid?
318:      if (index > -1 && index < numItems) {
319:        // delete the targeted item
320:        fMain_StringLst->fArr->DeleteItem(index + 1);
321:        // update the list box
322:        fMain_StringLst->SetArray(fMain_StringLst->fArr, FALSE);
323:      }
324:      else {
325:        PositionDialog('ALRT', ALRTgeneral);
326:        InitCursor();
327:        ParamText(
328:          "\p          ERROR MESSAGE!\r\rIndex is out of range'",
329:          "\p", "\p", "\p");
330:        Alert(ALRTgeneral, NULL);
331:      }
332:    }
333:
334:
335:    /****************************************************************
336:      DoCmdFindStr
337:
338:    Respond to cmdFindStr command.
339:    ****************************************************************/
340:
341:    void x_CMain::DoCmdFindStr()
342:
343:    {
344:      Str255 s255;
345:      char s[256];
346:      char findStr[256];
347:      Boolean notFound = TRUE;
348:      int numItems = fMain_StringLst->GetRowCount();
349:      int n;
350:      Cell aCell = { 0, 0 };
351:
352:      if (numItems <= 0) {
353:        PositionDialog('ALRT', ALRTgeneral);
354:        InitCursor();
```

624

```
355:      ParamText(
356:        "\p            ERROR MESSAGE!\r\rList box is empty",
357:        "\p", "\p", "\p");
358:      Alert(ALRTgeneral, NULL);
359:      return;
360:    }
361:
362:    // get the search string from the In/Out box
363:    fMain_InOutBox->GetTextString(s255);
364:    n = s255[0];
365:    strncpy(findStr, (char*)s255 + 1, n);
366:    findStr[n] = '\0';
367:
368:    while (aCell.v < numItems && notFound) {
369:      // get the array item
370:      fMain_StringLst->fArr->GetArrayItem(s255, aCell.v + 1);
371:      n = s255[0];
372:      strncpy(s, (char*)s255 + 1, n);
373:      s[n] = '\0';
374:      if (strcmp(s, findStr) != 0)
375:        aCell.v++;
376:      else
377:        notFound = FALSE;
378:    }
379:
380:    if (!notFound) {
381:      sprintf(s, "%ld", aCell.v);
382:      fMain_IndexBox->SetTextPtr(s, strlen(s));
383:    }
384:    else {
385:      PositionDialog('ALRT', ALRTgeneral);
386:      InitCursor();
387:      ParamText(
388:        "\p            MESSAGE!\r\rNo match found",
389:        "\p", "\p", "\p");
390:      Alert(ALRTgeneral, NULL);
391:    }
392:  }
393:
394:
395:
396:
397: /*************************************************************
398:  DoCmdSelectStr
399:
400:  Respond to cmdSelectStr command.
401:  *************************************************************/
402:
403: void x_CMain::DoCmdSelectStr()
404:
405: {
406:    Str255 s255;
407:    char s[11];
408:    Boolean notFound = TRUE;
409:    Cell aCell = { 0, 0 };
410:
```

continues

Listing 19.6. continued

```
411:    // search for the selected cell
412:    while (aCell.v < fMain_StringLst->GetRowCount() && notFound) {
413:      if (!fMain_StringLst->IsSelected(aCell))
414:        aCell.v++;
415:      else
416:        notFound = FALSE;
417:    }
418:    // recall the selected item
419:    fMain_StringLst->fArr->GetArrayItem(s255, aCell.v + 1);
420:    // copy selected item to In/Out box
421:    fMain_InOutBox->SetTextString(s255);
422:    // create string image of the selection's index
423:    sprintf(s, "%ld", aCell.v);
424:    // write string image to the Index box
425:    fMain_IndexBox->SetTextPtr(s, strlen(s));
426:  }
```

 Listing 19.6 defines the member functions of class x_CMain. The next seven subsections discuss the relevant member functions of that class.

The Function *MakeNewWindow*

The member function MakeNewWindow (defined in lines 88 to 151) stores the pointers to the window and the pane in the variables itsWindow and itsMainPane, respectively. It also stores the addresses of the various controls in their respective data members. The function obtains these addresses by sending the C++ message FindViewByID to the window object. The arguments for these messages are the constants kMain_XXXXID, which are defined in Listing 19.8.

I inserted the declarations in lines 91 to 96. The array names is an array of strings that contains an initial list of names. The statements in lines 140 to 150 insert and display these names in the list box. The statement in line 141 creates a dynamic instance of class CArray and stores its address in the data member fArr. The for loop in lines 144 to 148 inserts the set of strings, accessed by the variable names, in the dynamic array. The statement in line 147 sends the C++ message Add to the dynamic array. The argument for this message is the Pascal-string variable s255. The statement in line 150 associates the data of the dynamic array with the list box control. The function performs this task by sending the C++ message SetArray to the list box control. The arguments for this message are the data member fArr and the Boolean value FALSE.

The Function *DoCommand*

The member function DoCommand (defined in lines 200 to 220) has case labels in the switch statement to respond to the custom commands cmd*XXXX*. The first statement after each case label invokes the corresponding member function DoCmd*XXXX*.

The Function *UpdateMenus*

The member function UpdateMenus (defined in lines 229 to 237) enables the custom commands by sending the C++ message EnableCmd, for each command, to the bartender object. The arguments for the sequence of EnableCmd messages are the constants cmd*XXXX*.

The Function *DoCmdInsertStr*

The member function DoCmdInsertStr (defined in lines 246 to 274) inserts or appends the string of the In/Out edit box in the list box control. Line 251 initializes the not-found search flag (stored in variable notFound) to TRUE. Line 252 initializes the Cell-type variable aCell to access the first list box item. The statement in line 255 obtains the string of the In/Out edit box, and stores that string in the Pascal-string variable s255. The function uses the while statement in lines 258 to 264 to search for the selected item. The loop's condition involves sending the C++ message GetRowCount to the list box in order to obtain the number of list box items. Line 259 contains an if statement whose condition sends the C++ message IsSelected. This message, whose argument is variable aCell, determines whether or not variable aCell refers to the selected list box item. If the message returns FALSE, the loop increments the member v of variable aCell. Otherwise, the loop assigns FALSE to variable notFound to stop iterating.

Line 266 contains an if statement that determines whether or not the while loop did find a selected item. If it did, the function inserts the characters of variable s255 by sending the C++ message InsertAtIndex to the dynamic array. The arguments for this message are the variable s255 and the expression aCell.v + 1. Otherwise, the function appends the characters of variable s255 by sending the C++ message Add to the dynamic array. Line 273 updates the list box with the new data in the dynamic array. The function performs this update by sending the C++ message SetArray to the list box. The arguments for this message are fMain_StringLst->fArr and FALSE.

19

The Function *DoCmdDeleteStr*

The member function DoCmdDeleteStr (defined in lines 283 to 299) deletes a list box item using the index specified in the Index edit box. If the list box is empty, the function displays an alert box and exits (see the statements in lines 291 to 299).

Line 302 obtains the string in the Index edit box. Lines 303 and 304 convert the Pascal-string in variable s255 to a null-terminated string that is stored in variable s. The statements in lines 306 to 314 determine whether or not the first character in variable s is a digit. If this condition is true, the function displays an alert box and then exits.

The statement in line 316 converts the characters in variable s into a long integer. The function stores that integer in the local variable index. The function verifies the value in variable index using the if statement in line 318. If the tested condition is true, the function deletes the targeted list box item. This task involves sending the C++ message DeleteItem to the dynamic array. The argument for this message is the expression index + 1. The function then updates the list box by sending it the C++ message SetArray. The arguments for this message are member fMain_StringLst->fArr and the Boolean value FALSE. When the condition of the if statement in line 318 is false, the function displays an alert message box stating that the index you supplied is out of range.

The Function *DoCmdFindStr*

The member function DoCmdFindStr (defined in lines 341 to 392) searches the list box for a string that matches the one in the In/Out edit box. If the list box is empty, the function displays an alert box and exits (see the statements in lines 352 to 360).

The statement in line 363 obtains the characters of the In/Out edit box and stores them in the Pascal-string variable s255. Lines 364 to 366 convert the Pascal string into a null-terminator string that is stored in variable findStr—the search string.

The function uses the while loop statements, in lines 368 to 378, to search for a matching string. The if statement in line 380 acts on the search outcome. If the search is successful, the function displays the index of the matching list box item in the Index edit box. Otherwise, the function displays an alert box telling you that the search found no matching string.

The Function *DoCmdSelectStr*

The member function DoCmdSelectStr (defined in lines 403 to 426) responds to the command cmdSelectStr generated by double-clicking a list box item. The function uses the while loop statements, in lines 412 to 417, to search for the selected item. The search examines the current list box item (accessed by variable aCell). The function performs this examination by sending the C++ message IsSelected to the list box. The argument for this message is variable aCell.

The statement in line 419 obtains the selected item by sending the C++ message GetArrayItem to the dynamic array. The arguments for this message are the Pascal-string variable s255 and the expression aCell.v + 1. Line 421 copies the characters of variable s255 to the In/Out edit box. Lines 423 to 425 create a string image for the selection's index and write that string to the Index edit box.

Listing 19.7 shows the source code for the AppCommands.h header file for the Group1 program project. This listing defines the set of constants cmdXXXX, in lines 16 to 19, that support the custom commands.

Listing 19.7. The source code for the AppCommands.h header file for project List1.

```
 1:   /*****************************************************************
 2:   MyCommands.h
 3:
 4:              Header File For Command Symbols
 5:
 6:       Copyright (c) 1994 My Software Inc. All rights reserved.
 7:
 8:   Generated by Visual Architect(TM)
 9:
10:   This file is regenerated each time.
11:
12:   *****************************************************************/
13:
14:   #pragma once
15:
16:   #define cmdDeleteStr    528
17:   #define cmdFindStr      529
18:   #define cmdInsertStr    527
19:   #define cmdSelectStr    530
```

Listing 19.8 shows the source code for the MainItems.h header file for the List1 program project. The listing declares an untagged enumerated type which defines the identifiers kMain_XXXX and kMain_XXXXID.

19

Listing 19.8. The source code for the MainItems.h header file for project List1.

```
 1: /****************************************************************
 2:  MainItems.h
 3:
 4:                  Main Item Constants
 5:
 6:     Copyright (c) 1994 My Software Inc. All rights reserved.
 7:
 8: Generated by Visual Architect(TM)
 9:
10: This file is rewritten each time you generate code. You should
11: not make changes to this file.
12:
13: If you want to change how Visual Architect generates this file,
14: you can change the template for this file. It is "Items.h" in
15: the Visual Architect Templates folder.
16:
17: ****************************************************************/
18:
19: #pragma once
20:
21:
22:        //     Item numbers for each item.
23:        //
24:        //     Use TCLGetItemPointer (ViewUtilities) to convert these
25:        //     item numbers to a pointer to the named item.
26:
27: enum
28: {
29:        Main_Begin_,
30:        kMain_StringLst = 1,
31:        kMain_StringLstID = 1L,
32:        kMain_InOutBox = 2,
33:        kMain_InOutBoxID = 2L,
34:        kMain_InOutLbl = 3,
35:        kMain_InOutLblID = 3L,
36:        kMain_IndexLbl = 4,
37:        kMain_IndexLblID = 4L,
38:        kMain_IndexBox = 5,
39:        kMain_IndexBoxID = 5L,
40:        kMain_InsertBtn = 6,
41:        kMain_InsertBtnID = 6L,
42:        kMain_DeleteBtn = 7,
43:        kMain_DeleteBtnID = 7L,
44:        kMain_FindBtn = 8,
45:        kMain_FindBtnID = 8L,
46:        kMain_QuitBtn = 9,
47:        kMain_QuitBtnID = 9L,
48:        Main_End_
49: };
```

Compiling and Running the Program

Invoke the Run command from the THINK Project Manager icon menu. This command causes the compiler to process the set of source code files that contribute to the program. When the program runs, double-click a list box item. The program displays that item and its index in the In/Out and Index edit boxes, respectively. Click the Delete button to delete the item whose index appears in the Index box (which also happens to be the selected item). Type a new name, and then click the Insert button. This button inserts the new name you typed at the location of the selection. Click the Find button to search for the name you just inserted. The program finds a match and displays its index in the Index edit box. When you are finished experimenting, click the Quit button to close the main window and end the program.

Summary

This chapter presented the list box, which is a control that enables you to present the application's users with a list of items to select from. The following topics were covered:

☐ The class CArrayPane is a descendant of class CTable. The class CArrayPane supports the list box control as a single-column table. You learned about the relevant member functions declared in class CArrayPane.

☐ The class CTable provides list boxes with many operations. You learned about its relevant member functions that enable you to manage list boxes. The most relevant member function in class CTable is GetCellText, which specifies how a list box displays its data.

☐ The class CArray stores the data for a list box. You learned about the member functions of class CArray that are most relevant to list boxes.

☐ From a sample program, you learned how to use the list box control. The program enables you to insert, delete, and find a string in a list box control. The program also shows you how to respond to double-clicking a list box item.

Q&A

Q Can I change, at runtime, the command associated with double-clicking a list box item?

A Yes. You can perform this task using the member function `SetDblClickCmd`, which is declared as follows:

```
void SetDblClickCmd(long aCmd);
```

The parameter `aCmd` represents the new command that is generated when you double-click a list box item.

Q How can I gain better control over clicking and double-clicking on list box items?

A Derive a descendant of class `CArrayPane` that declares its own member functions `DoClick` and `DoDblClick`.

Q Can a list box easily toggle between several lists of strings?

A Yes it can. Typically, such a list uses a class with multiple data members that are pointers to different `CArray` instances—each instance stores a set of names. In addition, the class has a list-selection data member. The member function `GetCellText` uses the latter data member to determine which list to display.

Workshop

The Workshop provides quiz questions to help you solidify your understanding of the material covered and exercises to provide you with experience in using what you've learned. Try to understand the quiz and exercise answers before continuing on to the next day's lesson. Answers are provided in Appendix B, "Answers."

Quiz

1. True or false? The list box control only support single-item selections.

2. How do you select a cell from within the program code?

3. Can you deselect a cell from within the program code?

4. How do you obtain the current number of list box items?

5. What does the member function `CTable::GetCellText` perform as a default task?

6. What happens if you leave out the member function `GetCellText` from class `CListBox` in program project List1?

Exercise

Modify the program project List1 to create a new version that maintains the list of names in ascending order. The new program project, call it List2, needs a member function `CListBox::Sort(long numElems)` to sort the list of strings. Invoke the function `Sort` in the member functions `MakeNewWindow` and `DoCmdInsertStr`.

19

20

The Scroll Bar and Pop-up Menu Controls

Day 19 presented the list box control, which permits you to scroll through and select from a list of data items. Today's lesson looks at two other controls, the scroll bar and the pop-up menu pane, which also permit you to scroll through and select from a list of values. The scroll bar control enables you to scroll through a range of integer values. The pop-up menu pane control enables you to scroll through menu commands. Today you learn about the following topics:

- ☐ The class CScrollBar and its relevant member functions

- ☐ A sample program illustrates how to use the scroll bar control

- ☐ The class CStdPopupPane and its relevant member functions

- ☐ A sample program illustrates how to use the pop-up menu pane control

The Class *CScrollBar*

The scroll bar control is a sophisticated control compared to other controls such as buttons, radio controls, and check boxes. The scroll bar has a range of integers to scroll through and is made up of the following components:

- ☐ The mobile *thumb box* (also called simply the *thumb*). This is the moving part of the scroll bar that you can drag with the mouse. The position of the thumb box specifies the current value of the scroll bar.

- ☐ The *up arrow button*, which, when clicked, decreases the value of the scroll bar by one line. This decrease also moves the thumb up by one line.

- ☐ The *down arrow button*, which, when clicked, increases the value of the scroll bar by one line. This increase also moves the thumb down by one line.

- ☐ The *page up area*, which is the gray part of the scroll bar that resides above the thumb box. When you click on this area, you decrease the value of the control by a page size and move the thumb up.

- ☐ The *page down area*, which is the gray part of the scroll bar that resides below the thumb box. When you click on this area, you increase the value of the control by a page size and move the thumb down.

These controls describe a vertical scroll bar. In the case of a horizontal scroll bar, the up and down directions become the left and right directions, respectively. Your application

is responsible for defining the minimum value, maximum value, line size, and page size for the application's scroll bars.

The class CScrollBar, a descendant of class CControl, supports the scroll bar control. Here is the declaration of class CScrollBar:

```
class CScrollBar : public CControl { // Class Declaration

public:

    TCL_DECLARE_CLASS
    // Data Members
    Orientation theOrientation; // Horizontal or Vertical
    ThumbFuncType theThumbFunc; // Function to call for thumb
                                // drag

    // Member Functions
    // Contruction/Destruction
    CScrollBar();
    CScrollBar(CView *anEnclosure, CBureaucrat *aSupervisor,
                Orientation anOrientation, short aLength,
                short aHEncl, short aVEncl);
    void IScrollBar(CView *anEnclosure, CBureaucrat *aSupervisor,
                    Orientation anOrientation, short aLength,
                    short aHEncl, short aVEncl);
    void IScrollBarX(Orientation anOrientation, short aLength);

    // Accessing
    virtual void SetThumbFunc(ThumbFuncType aThumbFunc);

    // Drawing
    virtual void Draw(Rect *area);
    virtual void Activate();
    virtual void Deactivate();

    // Click Response
    virtual void DoClick(Point hitPt, short modifierKeys,
                        long when);
    virtual void DoThumbDragged(short delta);

    // Manipulating TCL 1.1.3 BF
    virtual void Offset(long hOffset, long vOffset,
                        Boolean redraw);

    virtual void PutTo(CStream& stream);
    virtual void GetFrom(CStream& stream);
};
```

The remainder of this section discusses the relevant member functions of class CScrollBar, as well as the relevant member function inherited from class CControl.

20

> **Note:** Because the scroll bar control is made up of several components, your application needs to define two functions that specify the responses to dragging the thumb box and to clicking the nonmoving parts of the scroll bar. These functions are arguments to the member functions `CScrollBar::SetThumbFunc` and `CControl:SetActionProc`. I say more about these member functions and their arguments in the following subsections.

The Function *SetValue*

The function `SetValue` sets the value of a scroll bar and moves the thumb box to reflect the new value. The declaration of function `SetValue` is

```
void SetValue(short aValue);
```

The parameter `aValue` provides the value for the control.

The Function *GetValue*

The function `GetValue` gets the value of a scroll bar. The declaration of function `GetValue` is

```
short GetValue();
```

The Function *SetMaxValue*

The member function `SetMaxValue` sets the maximum value of a scroll bar. The declaration of function `SetMaxValue` is

```
void SetMaxValue(short aMaxValue);
```

The parameter `aMaxValue` specifies the maximum value for the control.

The Function *GetMaxValue*

The member function `GetMaxValue` gets the maximum value of a scroll bar. The declaration of function `GetMaxValue` is

```
short GetMaxValue();
```

Syntax

The Function *SetMinValue*

The member function `SetMinValue` sets the minimum value of a scroll bar. The declaration of function `SetMinValue` is

```
void SetMinValue(short aMinValue);
```

The parameter `aMinValue` specifies the minimum value for the control.

Syntax

The Function *GetMinValue*

The member function `GetMinValue` gets the minimum value of a scroll bar. The declaration of function `GetMinValue` is

```
short GetMinValue();
```

Syntax

The Function *SetThumbFunc*

The member function `SetThumbFunc` assigns a function-pointer to the data member `theThumbFunc`. This member provides the response for dragging the thumb box. The declaration of function `SetThumbFunc` is

```
void SetThumbFunc(ThumbFuncType aThumbFunc);
```

The parameter `aThumbFunc` is the function that specifies how to update the control when you draw the thumb box. Here is the general form for the thumb-dragging function:

```
void MyThumbFunc(CControl *theControl, short delta);
```

The parameter `theControl` is the pointer to the scroll bar control. The parameter `delta` specifies the amount of change in the value of the scroll bar due to dragging the thumb box. Here is an example of a simple `MyThumbFunc`:

```
void MyThumbFunc(CScrollBar *theControl, short delta)
{
  long newVal = theControl->GetValue()  + delta;
  theControl->SetValue(newVal);
}
```

20

Syntax

The Function *SetActionProc*

The inherited member function `SetActionProc` sets the action function for the scroll bar. The action function specifies how to respond to clicking on the nonmoving parts of the scroll bar. The declaration of function `SetActionProc` is

```
void SetActionProc(ActionProcPtr anActionProc);
```

The parameter anActionProc is the pointer to the action function. Here is the general form for declaring your action function:

```
void pascal MyAction(ControlHandle macControl, short whichPart);
```

The parameter macControl is the handle (that is, pointer to a pointer) to the scroll bar control. The parameter whichPart specifies the part that you clicked. Your version of the action function should use a switch statement to examine the different arguments for parameter whichPart. These arguments are inUpButton (the up arrow button), inDownButton (the down arrow button), inPageUp (the page up area), and inPageDown (the page down area). Here is an example of function MyAction:

```
#define MAX_SB_VALUE 100
#define MIN_SB_VALUE 0
#define SB_PAGE_SIZE 10

void pascal MyAction(ControlHandle macControl, short whichPart)
{
  short delta;
  long newVal;

  switch (whichPart) {
    case inUpButton:
      delta = -1;
      break;

    case inDownButton:
      delta = 1;
      break;

    case inPageUp:
     delta = -(MAX_SB_VALUE - MIN_SB_VALUE) / SB_PAGE_SIZE;
     break;

    case inPageDown:
     delta = (MAX_SB_VALUE - MIN_SB_VALUE) / SB_PAGE_SIZE;
     break;
  }
  // get the control's current value
  newVal = GetControlValue(macControl) + delta;
  // check the value with the control's limits
  newVal = (newVal > MAX_SB_VALUE) ? MAX_SB_VALUE : newVal;
  newVal = (newVal < MIN_SB_VALUE) ? MIN_SB_VALUE : newVal;
  // set the control's new value
  SetControlValue(macControl, newVal);
}
```

Syntax

The Function *Activate*

The member function `Activate`, as the name might suggest, activates the scroll bar. The declaration of function `Activate` is

```
void Activate();
```

Syntax

The Function *Deactivate*

The member function `Deactivate` deactivates the scroll bar. The declaration of function `Deactivate` is

```
void Deactivate();
```

Syntax

The Function *DoClick*

The member function `DoClick` manages a click in the scroll bar control. The declaration of function `DoClick` is

```
void DoClick(Point hitPtr, short modifierKeys, long when);
```

The parameter `hitPtr` specifies the coordinates of the mouse click. The parameter `modifierKeys` specifies the status of the modifier keys (the Option, Alt, and Shift keys). The parameter `when` specifies the time of the click.

> **Note:** Override the member function `DoClick` to customize clicking on the scroll bar.

20

The Scroll Bar Example

Let's look at an example of a scroll bar that triggers a simple timer. This program, which I call ScrollBar1, uses a scroll bar to trigger a timer that runs up to 60 seconds. Figure 20.1 shows a sample session with the ScrollBar1 program project, which has the following controls:

☐ The vertical scroll bar, which helps you to specify the duration. The program moves the thumb of the scroll bar when the timer is active.

☐ The edit box in which you type the timer's duration. The program also displays the current scroll bar value when you click on the control or move its thumb box.

☐ The Start button, which triggers the timer. When you click this button, the program starts a timer loop and moves the thumb of the scroll bar after each second interval.

☐ The Quit button.

☐ The static text controls that label the limits of the scroll bar.

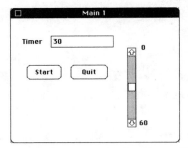

Figure 20.1. *A sample session with the ScrollBar1 program.*

Table 20.1 shows the control names as well as the custom and predefined commands associated with the main window's controls.

Table 20.1. The control names and commands associated with the controls of project ScrollBar1.

Control Caption	Control Name	Control Type	Associated Command
0	MinLbl	Static text	
60	MaxLbl	Static text	
	TimerScr	Scroll bar	
Timer	TimerLbl	Static text	
	TimerBox	Edit box	
Start	StartBtn	Button	cmdStartTimer
Quit	QuitBtn	Button	cmdQuit

Preparing the Application

Building the ScrollBar1 program project is a bit elaborate, because I need to derive a new class from CScrollBar. The new class, CMyScrollBar, provides the special feature of echoing the scroll bar value in the edit box when the timer is not running. The process of building the ScrollBar1 program involves several stages. In the first stage, you prepare the core part of the application by performing the following steps:

1. Create a new Visual Architect utility project, and name it ScrollBar1.

2. Delete the default controls in the main window.

3. Define the custom command cmdStartTimer as specified in Table 20.1. Make sure that this command is associated with class CMain and results in a Call type of action.

Declaring the New Class *CMyScrollBar*

In the second stage you must declare the class CMyScrollBar as a descendant of class CScrollBar. The Visual Architect utility offers a menu command that supports this stage. Perform the following steps:

1. Invoke the Edit | Classes command to invoke the Classes dialog box.

2. In the list box, click below the CMain class to put the dialog box in input mode.

3. Type CMyScrollBar in the input box.

4. Use the Base Class pop-up menu to set class CScrollBar as the parent of class CMyScrollBar.

5. Click the OK button to close the Classes dialog box.

Drawing the Controls

In this stage, you draw the controls shown in Figure 20.1. Perform the following steps:

1. Use the Tools menu to select this kind of control, and then draw the scroll bar control.

2. Set the scroll bar's control name according to the information in Table 20.1.

3. Use the Tools menu to select the static text control, and then draw the static text controls associated with the scroll bar.

20

4. Set the names and captions of each static control according to the information in Table 20.1.

5. Use the Tools menu to select the edit box control, and then draw the edit box control.

6. Set the name of the edit box control according to the information in Table 20.1.

7. Use the Tools menu to select the button control, and then draw the button controls.

8. Set the names and captions of each button control according to the information in Table 20.1.

Associating *CMyScrollBar* with the Scroll Bar

In this stage, you associate the class CMyScrollBar with the list box control. Without this association, the program regards the scroll bar as an instance of class CScrollBar. To perform the needed association, follow these steps:

1. Select the list box control.

2. Invoke the Pane | Class command. This command brings up a floating menu that contains the names of classes CScrollBar and CMyScrollBar.

3. Select the CMyScrollBar class to associate this class with the list box control.

Generating and Customizing the Source Code

To generate the custom code for this application, invoke the Generate All... command in the THINK Project Manager icon menu.

Now let's look at the relevant files emitted by the Visual Architect utility and the lines of code that I inserted to support the program's operations. Because I declare the class CMyScrollBar, the Visual Architect utility generates files for this class.

Listing 20.1 shows the source code for the CMyScrollBar.h header file for the ScrollBar1 program project.

Listing 20.1. The source code for the CMyScrollbar.h header file for project ScrollBar1.

```
 1:  /************************************************************
 2:  CMyScrollBar.h
 3:
 4:                Header for CMyScrollBar ScrollBar Class
 5:
 6:      Copyright (c) 1994 My Software Inc. All rights reserved.
 7:
 8:  Generated by Visual Architect(TM) 3:04 PM Thu, Jun 23, 1994
 9:
10:  This file is only generated once. You can modify it by filling
11:  in the placeholder functions and adding any new functions you
12:  wish.
13:
14:  If you change the name of the document class, a fresh version of
15:  this file will be generated. If you have made any changes to the
16:  file with the old name, you will have to copy those changes to
17:  the new file by hand.
18:
19:  ************************************************************/
20:
21:  #pragma once
22:
23:  #include "x_CMyScrollBar.h"
24:
25:  class CMyScrollBar : public x_CMyScrollBar
26:  {
27:  public:
28:
29:      TCL_DECLARE_CLASS
30:
31:                                  /** Object I/O **/
32:      virtual void      PutTo(CStream &aStream);
33:      virtual void      GetFrom(CStream &aStream);
34:  };
```

Listing 20.1 shows that class `CMyScrollBar` is a descendant of `x_CMyScrollBar`. The class `CMyScrollBar` declares stream-related member functions.

Listing 20.2 shows the source code for the CMyScrollBar.cp implementation file for project ScrollBar1.

Listing 20.2. The source code for the CMyScrollBar.cp implementation file for project ScrollBar1.

```
 1:  /************************************************************
 2:  CMyScrollBar.c
 3:
 4:                CMyScrollBar ScrollBar Class
```

continues

20

Listing 20.2. continued

```
 5:
 6:      Copyright (c) 1994 My Software Inc. All rights reserved.
 7:
 8: Generated by Visual Architect(TM) 3:04 PM Thu, Jun 23, 1994
 9:
10: This file is only generated once. You can modify it by filling
11: in the placeholder functions and adding any new functions you
12: wish.
13:
14: If you change the name of the document class, a fresh version of
15: this file will be generated. If you have made any changes to the
16: file with the old name, you will have to copy those changes to
17: the new file by hand.
18:
19: **************************************************************/
20:
21: #include "CMyScrollBar.h"
22:
23:
24: TCL_DEFINE_CLASS_D1(CMyScrollBar, x_CMyScrollBar);
25:
26: /**** C O N S T R U C T I O N / D E S T R U C T I O N
27:                                        M E T H O D S ****/
28:
29:
30: /*************************************************************
31:   PutTo
32:
33: Put the contents of this object to the stream
34: **************************************************************/
35:
36: void CMyScrollBar::PutTo(CStream &aStream)
37: {
38:     // Put any additional data members for this class
39:     // before calling the superclass PutTo.
40:
41:     // If you have no additional data members, the
42:     // PutTo and GetFrom functions can be eliminated.
43:
44:     x_CMyScrollBar::PutTo(aStream); /* Let superclass save */
45:
46:     // By convention, any subordinate objects are put
47:     // after the superclass has had a chance to write
48:     // its instance variables.
49: }
50:
51:
52: /*************************************************************
53:   GetFrom
54:
55: Get the contents of this object from the stream and
56: initialize the object
57: **************************************************************/
58:
```

```
59:   void CMyScrollBar::GetFrom(CStream &aStream)
60:   {
61:       // Get any additional data members for this class
62:       // before calling the superclass GetFrom
63:
64:
65:       /* Let superclass restore          */
66:       x_CMyScrollBar::GetFrom(aStream);
67:
68:       // Restore any subordinate objects below
69:   }
```

Listing 20.2 contains the implementations of member functions PutTo and GetFrom. The statements in these functions invoke the corresponding member functions of the parent class.

Listing 20.3 shows the source code for the x_CMyScrollBar.h header file for project ScrollBar1. The bold lines show the ones that I manually added.

Listing 20.3. The source code for the x_CMyScrollBar.h header file for project ScrollBar1.

```
1:    /****************************************************************
2:     x_CMyScrollBar.h
3:
4:               Header File For CMyScrollBar Lower-Layer ScrollBar Class
5:
6:        Copyright (c) 1994 My Software Inc. All rights reserved.
7:
8:    Generated by Visual Architect(TM)
9:
10:   This file is rewritten each time you generate code. You should
11:   not make changes to this file; changes should go in the My.h
12:   file, instead.
13:
14:   If you want to change how Visual Architect generates this file,
15:   you can change the template for this file. It is "_Bar.h" in
16:   the Visual Architect Templates folder.
17:
18:   ****************************************************************/
19:
20:   #pragma once
21:
22:   #include "CScrollBar.h"
23:   #include "CDialogText.h"
24:
25:   class CDirectorOwner;
26:
27:   class x_CMyScrollBar : public CScrollBar
28:   {
29:   public:
```

continues

647

Listing 20.3. continued

```
30:
31:        TCL_DECLARE_CLASS
32:
33:
34:        /** Object I/O **/
35:        virtual void      PutTo(CStream &aStream);
36:        virtual void      GetFrom(CStream &aStream);
37:
38:        void DoClick(Point hitPt, short modifierKeys, long when);
39:
40:        CDialogText* fTimerBox;
41: };
```

Listing 20.3 declares the class x_CMyScrollBar. The Visual Architect utility generated the declarations of member functions PutTo and GetFrom in lines 35 and 36,
respectively. I inserted the declaration of member function DoClick in line 38. I
also inserted the declaration of data member fTimerBox in line 40. This member accesses
the main window's edit box, which displays the scroll bar value.

Listing 20.4 shows the source code for the x_CMyScrollBar.cp implementation file for
project ScrollBar1. The bold lines show the ones that I manually added.

**VArc
Type**

Listing 20.4. The source code for the x_CMyScrollBar.cp implementation file for project ScrollBar1.

```
1: /*****************************************************************
2:  x_CMyScrollBar.c
3:
4:              CMyScrollBar ScrollBar Class
5:
6:      Copyright (c) 1994 My Software Inc. All rights reserved.
7:
8: Generated by Visual Architect(TM)
9:
10: This file is rewritten each time you generate code. You should
11: not make changes to this file; changes should go in the My.c
12: file, instead.
13:
14: If you want to change how Visual Architect generates this file,
15: you can change the template for this file. It is "_Bar_cp" in
16: the Visual Architect Templates folder.
17:
18: *****************************************************************/
19:
20: #include "x_CMyScrollBar.h"
21:
22: #include "ViewUtilities.h"
```

```
23:
24:
25:    TCL_DEFINE_CLASS_M1(x_CMyScrollBar, CScrollBar);
26:
27:    /***************************************************************
28:     PutTo
29:
30:    Put the contents of this object to the stream
31:    ***************************************************************/
32:
33:    void x_CMyScrollBar::PutTo(CStream &aStream)
34:    {
35:        // Put data members for this class
36:
37:
38:        CScrollBar::PutTo(aStream); /* Let superclass save */
39:    }
40:
41:
42:    /***************************************************************
43:     GetFrom
44:
45:    Get the contents of this object from the stream and
46:    initialize the object
47:    ***************************************************************/
48:
49:    void x_CMyScrollBar::GetFrom(CStream &aStream)
50:    {
51:        // Get data members for this class
52:
53:
54:        /* Let superclass restore              */
55:        CScrollBar::GetFrom(aStream);
56:    }
57:
58:    /***************************************************************
59:     DoClick {OVERRIDE}
60:
61:    Handle a click inside a scroll bar. Let the inherited method to
62:    do all the work, then tack on.
63:    ***************************************************************/
64:
65:    void x_CMyScrollBar::DoClick(
66:        Point           hitPt,
67:        short           modifierKeys,
68:        long            when)
69:    {
70:        char s[11];
71:
72:        CScrollBar::DoClick(hitPt, modifierKeys, when);
73:        sprintf(s, "%ld", GetValue());
74:        fTimerBox->SetTextPtr(s, strlen(s));
75:    }
```

20

The most relevant member function of class x_CMyScrollBar is DoClick. Lines 65 to 75 define this member function, which updates the edit box with the value of the scroll bar. The statement in line 72 calls the inherited function DoClick to perform the inherited operations. Line 73 converts the value of the scroll bar into a string image. This task involves the member function GetValue and stores the image in variable s. Line 74 stores the string image of variable s in the edit box. The function performs this task by sending the C++ message SetTextPtr to the edit box (accessed by data member fTimerBox).

Listing 20.5 contains the source code for the x_CMain.h header file for project ScrollBar1. The bold lines indicate the ones that I manually inserted.

Listing 20.5. The source code for the x_CMain.h header file for project ScrollBar1.

```
 1:  /****************************************************************
 2:   x_CMain.h
 3:
 4:              Header File For CMain Lower-Layer Document Class
 5:
 6:      Copyright (c) 1994 My Software Inc. All rights reserved.
 7:
 8:  Generated by Visual Architect(TM)
 9:
10:  This file is rewritten each time you generate code. You should
11:  not make changes to this file.
12:
13:  If you want to change how Visual Architect generates this file,
14:  you can change the template for this file. It is "Items.h" in
15:  the Visual Architect Templates folder.
16:
17:  ****************************************************************/
18:
19:  #pragma once
20:
21:  #include "CSaver.h"
22:  class CStaticText;
23:  class CDialogText;
24:  class CButton;
25:  class CMyScrollBar;
26:
27:  #include "ItsContentsClass.h"
28:
29:  #define x_CMain_super     CSaver<ITSCONTENTSCLASS>
30:
31:  #define MIN_TIMER 0
32:  #define MAX_TIMER 60
33:  #define TIMER_PAGE_SIZE 6
34:
35:  class CFile;
```

```
36:
37:    class x_CMain : public x_CMain_super
38:
39:    {
40:    public:
41:
42:        TCL_DECLARE_CLASS
43:
44:        // Pointers to panes in window
45:        CStaticText    *fMain_TimerLbl;
46:        CDialogText    *fMain_TimerBox;
47:        CButton    *fMain_StartBtn;
48:        CButton    *fMain_QuitBtn;
49:        CMyScrollBar    *fMain_TimerScr;
50:        CStaticText    *fMain_MinLbl;
51:        CStaticText    *fMain_MaxLbl;
52:
53:        void    Ix_CMain(void);
54:
55:        virtual    void    DoCommand(long theCommand);
56:        virtual    void    UpdateMenus(void);
57:
58:    protected:
59:        virtual    void    MakeNewWindow(void);
60:
61:        virtual    void    FailOpen(CFile *aFile);
62:        virtual void    PositionWindow(void);
63:
64:        virtual void    DoCmdStartTimer(void);
65:
66:        void SetLabelTitle(CStaticText *aText, long n);
67:    };
68:
69:    #define    CVueCMain    128
```

Analysis Listing 20.5 shows the declaration of class x_CMain. I inserted the lines 31 to 33 to
define the constants for the scroll bar value range and page size. The class x_CMain
contains a number of data members and member functions, all emitted by the
Visual Architect utility. Lines 45 to 51 define the various data members that are pointers
to the different controls. These members are pointers to the classes CMyScrollBar,
CStaticText, CDialogText, and CButton. The class x_CMain contains the member
function DoCmdStartTimer which responds to the custom command cmdStartTimer. I
also inserted the declaration of member function SetLabelTitle in line 66. This function
converts a value into text and makes that text the new title of a static text control.

Listing 20.6 shows the source code for the x_CMain.cp implementation file for project
ScrollBar1. The bold lines show the ones that I manually inserted.

20

Listing 20.6. The source code for the x_CMain.cp implementation file for project ScrollBar1.

```
1:  /****************************************************************
2:  x_CMain.c
3:
4:                  CMain Document Class
5:
6:      Copyright (c) 1994 My Software Inc. All rights reserved.
7:
8:  Generated by Visual Architect(TM) 3:04 PM Thu, Jun 23, 1994
9:
10: This file is rewritten each time you generate code. You should
11: not make changes to this file; changes should go in the My.c
12: file, instead.
13:
14: If you want to change how Visual Architect generates this file,
15: you can change the template for this file. It is "_Doc_cp" in
16: the Visual Architect Templates folder.
17:
18: ****************************************************************/
19:
20: #include "x_CMain.h"
21:
22: #include "CMain.h"
23:
24: #include "MainItems.h"
25:
26: #include "ViewUtilities.h"
27: #include "CApp.h"
28:
29: #include <CApplication.h>
30: #include <CBartender.h>
31: #include <Commands.h>
32: #include <Constants.h>
33: #include <CDecorator.h>
34: #include <CDesktop.h>
35: #include <CFile.h>
36: #include <TBUtilities.h>
37: #include <CWindow.h>
38:
39: extern CApplication *gApplication; /* The application */
40: extern CDecorator    *gDecorator;  /* Decorator for arranging
41:                                       windows */
42: extern CDesktop       *gDesktop;   /* The visible Desktop */
43: extern CBartender    *gBartender;  /* Manages all menus */
44:
45: #include "CStaticText.h"
46: #include "CDialogText.h"
47: #include "CButton.h"
48: #include "CMyScrollBar.h"
49:
50: #include <stdlib.h>
51:
52:     // Define symbols for commands handled by this class
53:     // Prevents a recompile every time any command changed.
```

```
54:
55:    #define cmdStartTimer 512
56:
57:
58:    TCL_DEFINE_CLASS_M1(x_CMain, x_CMain_super);
59:
60:    /****************************************************************
61:      MyThumbFunc
62:
63:    Respond to moving the thumb box.
64:    ****************************************************************/
65:
66:    void MyThumbFunc(CScrollBar *theControl, short delta)
67:    {
68:      char s[11];
69:      long newVal = theControl->GetValue() + delta;
70:
71:      // check the value with the control's limits
72:      newVal = (newVal > MAX_TIMER) ? MAX_TIMER : newVal;
73:      newVal = (newVal < MIN_TIMER) ? MIN_TIMER : newVal;
74:      theControl->SetValue(newVal);
75:    }
76:
77:    /****************************************************************
78:      MyAction
79:
80:    Respond to clicking the non-moving parts of the scroll bar.
81:    ****************************************************************/
82:
83:    void pascal MyAction(ControlHandle macControl, short whichPart)
84:    {
85:      short delta;
86:      long newVal;
87:
88:      switch (whichPart) {
89:        case inUpButton:
90:          delta = -1;
91:          break;
92:
93:        case inDownButton:
94:          delta = 1;
95:          break;
96:
97:        case inPageUp:
98:          delta = -(MAX_TIMER - MIN_TIMER) / TIMER_PAGE_SIZE;
99:          break;
100:
101:        case inPageDown:
102:          delta = (MAX_TIMER - MIN_TIMER) / TIMER_PAGE_SIZE;
103:          break;
104:      }
105:      // get the control's current value
106:      newVal = GetControlValue(macControl) + delta;
107:      // check the value with the control's limits
108:      newVal = (newVal > MAX_TIMER) ? MAX_TIMER : newVal;
109:      newVal = (newVal < MIN_TIMER) ? MIN_TIMER : newVal;
```

20

continues

Listing 20.6. continued

```
110:     // set the control's new value
111:     SetControlValue(macControl, newVal);
112: }
113:
114:
115: /**** C O N S T R U C T I O N / D E S T R U C T I O N
116:                                       M E T H O D S ****/
117:
118:
119: /*****************************************************************
120:  Ix_CMain
121:
122: Initialize the document
123: *****************************************************************/
124:
125: void x_CMain::Ix_CMain()
126:
127: {
128:     IDocument(gApplication, TRUE);
129:
130:     // Initialize data members below.
131: }
132:
133:
134: /*****************************************************************
135:  MakeNewWindow
136:
137: Create a new, empty window. Subclass may override to populate
138: the new window.
139: *****************************************************************/
140:
141: void x_CMain::MakeNewWindow(void)
142:
143: {
144:     itsWindow = TCLGetNamedWindow("\pMain", this);
145:
146:     itsMainPane = (CPane*) TCLGetItemPointer(itsWindow, 0);
147:
148:     // Initialize pointers to the subpanes in the window
149:
150:     fMain_TimerLbl = (CStaticText*)
151:                     itsWindow->FindViewByID(kMain_TimerLblID);
152:     ASSERT(member(fMain_TimerLbl, CStaticText));
153:
154:     fMain_TimerBox = (CDialogText*)
155:                     itsWindow->FindViewByID(kMain_TimerBoxID);
156:     ASSERT(member(fMain_TimerBox, CDialogText));
157:
158:     fMain_StartBtn = (CButton*)
159:                     itsWindow->FindViewByID(kMain_StartBtnID);
160:     ASSERT(member(fMain_StartBtn, CButton));
161:
162:     fMain_QuitBtn = (CButton*)
163:                     itsWindow->FindViewByID(kMain_QuitBtnID);
164:     ASSERT(member(fMain_QuitBtn, CButton));
```

```
165:
166:    fMain_TimerScr = (CMyScrollBar*)
167:                    itsWindow->FindViewByID(kMain_TimerScrID);
168:    ASSERT(member(fMain_TimerScr, CMyScrollBar));
169:
170:    fMain_MinLbl = (CStaticText*)
171:                    itsWindow->FindViewByID(kMain_MinLblID);
172:    ASSERT(member(fMain_MinLbl, CStaticText));
173:
174:    fMain_MaxLbl = (CStaticText*)
175:                    itsWindow->FindViewByID(kMain_MaxLblID);
176:    ASSERT(member(fMain_MaxLbl, CStaticText));
177:
178:    fMain_TimerScr->fTimerBox = fMain_TimerBox;
179:    fMain_TimerScr->SetMinValue(MIN_TIMER);
180:    fMain_TimerScr->SetMaxValue(MAX_TIMER);
181:    fMain_TimerScr->SetThumbFunc(MyThumbFunc);
182:    fMain_TimerScr->SetActionProc(MyAction);
183:    SetLabelTitle(fMain_MinLbl, MIN_TIMER);
184:    SetLabelTitle(fMain_MaxLbl, MAX_TIMER);
185: }
186:
187:
188: /****************************************************************
189:  FailOpen {OVERRIDE}
190:
191:  Fail if file already open in this application.
192:
193:  This function calls the application's FileAlreadyOpen function
194:  and fails quietly if the file is open.
195:
196:  Note that open may also fail if the file is open in
197:  another application. This will cause a failure in open,
198:  but you may wish to override this function to detect this
199:  case and provide a more meaningful error message than -49.
200:  ****************************************************************/
201:
202: void x_CMain::FailOpen(CFile *aFile)
203:
204: {
205:     /* Only the application knows          */
206:     if (((CApp*)gApplication)->FileAlreadyOpen(aFile))
207:         Failure(kSilentErr, 0);
208: }
209:
210:
211: /****************************************************************
212:  PositionWindow
213:
214:  The default method in CSaver calls the the decorator, which
215:  staggers and resizes the window. Since the window has already
216:  been positioned when it is initialized from the view resource,
217:  we don't want to do this twice.
218:  ****************************************************************/
219:
```

20

continues

Listing 20.6. continued

```
220:  void      x_CMain::PositionWindow()
221:
222:  {
223:  }
224:
225:
226:
227:
228:  /*****************************************************************
229:   DoCommand {OVERRIDE}
230:
231:  Dispatch Visual Architect-specified actions.
232:  *****************************************************************/
233:
234:  void x_CMain::DoCommand(long theCommand)
235:
236:  {
237:      switch (theCommand)
238:      {
239:          case cmdStartTimer:
240:              DoCmdStartTimer();
241:              break;
242:          default:
243:              CDocument::DoCommand(theCommand);
244:      }
245:  }
246:
247:
248:  /*****************************************************************
249:   UpdateMenus {OVERRIDE}
250:
251:  Enable menus which generate commands handled by this class.
252:  *****************************************************************/
253:
254:  void x_CMain::UpdateMenus()
255:
256:  {
257:      CDocument::UpdateMenus();
258:      gBartender->EnableCmd(cmdStartTimer);
259:  }
260:
261:
262:  /*****************************************************************
263:   DoCmdStartTimer
264:
265:  Respond to cmdStartTimer command.
266:  *****************************************************************/
267:
268:  void x_CMain::DoCmdStartTimer()
269:
270:  {
```

```
271:      Str255 s255;
272:      char s[11];
273:      long start, duration, delta, lastDelta;
274:
275:      // Subclass must override this function to
276:      // handle the command
277:      // get the string in the edit box
278:      fMain_TimerBox->GetTextString(s255);
279:      strncpy(s, (char*)s255+1, s255[0]);
280:      s[s255[0]] = '\0';
281:      // convert string to a numeric duration
282:      duration = atol(s);
283:      // validate the duration
284:      duration = (duration <= MIN_TIMER) ? 15 : duration;
285:      duration = (duration > MAX_TIMER) ? MAX_TIMER : duration;
286:      // set the new maximum scroll value
287:      fMain_TimerScr->SetMaxValue(duration);
288:      fMain_TimerScr->SetValue(MIN_TIMER);
289:      // store the initial tick count
290:      start = TickCount();
291:      delta = (TickCount() - start) / 60;
292:      // loop for the duration
293:      while (delta < duration) {
294:        lastDelta = delta;
295:        delta = (TickCount() - start) / 60;
296:        if (delta != lastDelta)
297:          fMain_TimerScr->SetValue(delta);
298:      }
299:      fMain_TimerScr->SetMaxValue(MAX_TIMER);
300:      fMain_TimerScr->SetValue(duration);
301: }
302:
303: /****************************************************************
304:    SetLabelTitle
305:
306: Assigns a new numeric title to a static text control.
307: ****************************************************************/
308:
309: void x_CMain::SetLabelTitle(CStaticText *aText, long n)
310: {
311:    char s[11];
312:
313:    sprintf(s, "%ld", n);
314:    aText->SetTextPtr(s, strlen(s));
315:    aText->Refresh();
316: }
```

Listing 20.6 defines the functions MyThumbFunc and MyAction as well as the member functions of class x_CMain. The next five subsections discuss the functions MyThumbFunc and MyAction along with the relevant member functions of class x_CMain.

The Function *MyThumbFunc*

The function MyThumbFunc (defined in lines 66 to 75) specifies how to update the value of the scroll bar control when you drag the thumb box. Line 69 declares the local variable newVal and assigns it the new scroll bar value. This assignment involves sending the C++ message GetValue to the scroll bar and then adding the message's result to the parameter delta. The statements in lines 72 and 73 ensure that the value in variable newVal stays in the valid range defined by the constants MIN_TIMER and MAX_TIMER. Line 74 assigns the new control value to the scroll bar by sending it the C++ message SetValue. The argument for this message is the variable newVal.

The Function *MyAction*

The function MyAction (defined in lines 83 to 112) handles updating the scroll bar value when you click on a nonmoving part of that control. The function uses a switch statement (in lines 88 to 104) to assign a value to variable delta (which stores the change in the scroll bar value). The four case labels handle clicking the up arrow box, down arrow box, page up area, and page down area. Line 106 obtains the new scroll bar value by adding the old control value to variable delta. The function obtains the old control value by invoking the Macintosh toolbox function GetControlValue. The argument for this function call is the parameter macControl. The function MyAction stores the new control value in variable newVal. The statements in lines 108 and 109 ensure that the value in variable newVal stays in the valid range defined by constants MIN_TIMER and MAX_TIMER. Line 111 stores the value of variable newVal in the scroll bar control. This task involves calling the Macintosh toolbox function SetControlValue. The arguments for this function call are the parameter macControl and the local variable newVal.

The Function *MakeNewWindow*

The member function MakeNewWindow (defined in lines 141 to 185) stores the pointers to the window and the pane in the variables itsWindow and itsMainPane, respectively. It also stores the addresses of the various controls in their respective data members. The function obtains these addresses by sending the C++ message FindViewByID to the window object. The arguments for these messages are the constants kMain_*XXXX*ID, which are defined in Listing 20.8.

I inserted the statement in lines 178 to 184. Line 178 copies the address of the edit box to the scroll bar's data member fTimerBox. Line 179 assigns the minimum value for the scroll bar by sending the C++ message SetMinVal to that control. The argument for this message is `MIN_TIMER`. Line 180 assigns the maximum value for the scroll bar by sending the C++ message `SetMaxVal` to that control. The argument for this message is `MAX_TIMER`. Line 181 sets the thumb function of the scroll bar by sending the C++ message `SetThumbFunc` to that control. The argument for this message is the name of the function `MyThumbFunc`. Line 182 sets the action function of the scroll bar by sending the C++ message `SetActionProc` to that control. The argument for this message is the name of the function `MyAction`. Lines 183 and 184 set the titles of the static text controls to the string images of `MIN_TIMER` and `MAX_TIMER`. Each statement in these lines invokes the member function `SetLabelTitle`.

Syntax

The Function *DoCommand*

The member function `DoCommand` (defined in lines 234 to 245) has a `case` label in the `switch` statement to respond to the custom command `cmdStartTimer`. The first statement after `case cmdStartTimer` invokes the member function `DoCmdStartTimer`.

Syntax

The Function *UpdateMenus*

The member function `UpdateMenus` (defined in lines 254 to 259) enables the custom command by sending the C++ message `EnableCmd` to the bartender object. The argument for the message is the constant `cmdStartTimer`.

Syntax

The Function *DoCmdStartTimer*

The member function `DoCmdStartTimer` (defined in lines 268 to 301) starts and runs the timer. Line 278 copies the characters of the edit box into the Pascal-string variable `s255`. Lines 279 and 280 convert the string in variable `s255` to the null-terminated string and store this string in variable `s`. Line 282 converts the characters of variable `s` into a long integer and stores this integer in variable `duration`. Line 284 assigns 15 to the variable `duration` if that variable contains a value that is equal to or less than the value of `MIN_TIMER`. Line 285 assigns `MAX_TIMER` to variable `duration` if that variable exceeds the value of `MAX_TIMER`.

The statement in line 287 sets the maximum scroll bar value to match the integer in variable `duration`. The function performs this assignment by sending the C++ message `SetMaxValue` to the scroll bar. The statement in line 288 resets the current scroll bar value to the minimum value. The function performs this assignment by sending the C++ message `SetValue` to the scroll bar. Line 290 stores the current tick value (a tick is about one-sixtieth of a second) in variable `start`. This line invokes the Macintosh toolbox

20

function `TickCount`. Line 291 calculates the initial timer lapse (in seconds) and stores it in variable `delta`.

The `while` loop in lines 293 to 298 is the timing loop. The loop iterates as long as the value in variable `delta` is less than that in variable `duration`. The statement in line 294 copies the value of variable `delta` into variable `lastDelta`. The statement in line 295 calculates a new value for variable `delta`. The `if` statement in line 296 compares the values in variables `delta` and `lastDelta`. If these values differ (that is, the timer has reached the next second), the loop updates the scroll bar value by sending it the C++ message `SetValue`. The argument for this message is the variable `delta`.

When the timing loop stops iterating, the function restores the maximum and original scroll bar values using the statements in lines 299 and 300.

Listing 20.7 shows the source code for the AppCommands.h header file for the ScrollBar1 program project. This listing defines the constant `cmdStartTimer`, in line 16, which supports the custom command.

Listing 20.7. The source code for the AppCommands.h header file for project ScrollBar1.

```
 1: /****************************************************************
 2:   MyCommands.h
 3:
 4:              Header File For Command Symbols
 5:
 6:      Copyright (c) 1994 My Software Inc. All rights reserved.
 7:
 8: Generated by Visual Architect(TM)
 9:
10: This file is regenerated each time.
11:
12: ****************************************************************/
13:
14: #pragma once
15:
16: #define cmdStartTimer     512
```

Listing 20.8 shows the source code for the MainItems.h header file for the ScrollBar1 program project. The listing declares an untagged enumerated type which defines the identifiers `kMain_XXXX` and `kMain_XXXXID`.

Listing 20.8. The source code for the MainItems.h header file for project ScrollBar1.

```
1:  /****************************************************************
2:    MainItems.h
3:
4:                    Main Item Constants
5:
6:      Copyright (c) 1994 My Software Inc. All rights reserved.
7:
8:  Generated by Visual Architect(TM)
9:
10: This file is rewritten each time you generate code. You should
11: not make changes to this file.
12:
13: If you want to change how Visual Architect generates this file,
14: you can change the template for this file. It is "Items.h" in
15: the Visual Architect Templates folder.
16:
17: ****************************************************************/
18:
19: #pragma once
20:
21:
22:      //    Item numbers for each item.
23:      //
24:      //    Use TCLGetItemPointer (ViewUtilities) to convert these
25:      //    item numbers to a pointer to the named item.
26:
27: enum
28: {
29:      Main_Begin_,
30:      kMain_TimerLbl = 1,
31:      kMain_TimerLblID = 1L,
32:      kMain_TimerBox = 2,
33:      kMain_TimerBoxID = 2L,
34:      kMain_StartBtn = 3,
35:      kMain_StartBtnID = 3L,
36:      kMain_QuitBtn = 4,
37:      kMain_QuitBtnID = 4L,
38:      kMain_TimerScr = 5,
39:      kMain_TimerScrID = 5L,
40:      kMain_MinLbl = 6,
41:      kMain_MinLblID = 6L,
42:      kMain_MaxLbl = 7,
43:      kMain_MaxLblID = 7L,
44:      Main_End_
45: };
```

20

Compiling and Running the Program

Invoke the Run command from the THINK Project Manager icon menu. This command causes the compiler to process the set of source code files that contribute to the program. When the program runs, drag the scroll bar thumb and watch the program display the current scroll bar in the edit box. Also, click on the nonmoving parts of the scroll bar and watch the program update the current scroll bar in the edit box. Click the Start button to trigger the timer. Watch the scroll bar thumb move down by a page size after each second. When you are finished experimenting, click the Quit button to close the main window and end the program.

The Class *CStdPopupPane*

The pop-up menu pane is a control that is associated with a menu. The control typically displays a preselected menu item. When you click on the control's menu pane, the control displays a scrollable list of items. Many dialog boxes in the Visual Architect utility use pop-up menu panes. The class CStdPopupPane, a descendant of class CPopupPane, supports the standard pop-up pane control. Here is the declaration of class CStdPopupPane:

```
class CStdPopupPane : public CPopupPane
{
public:

    TCL_DECLARE_CLASS

    // Construction/destruction
    CStdPopupPane();
    CStdPopupPane(short menuID,
                CView *anEnclosure, CBureaucrat *aSupervisor,
                short aWidth, short aHeight,
                short aHEncl, short aVEncl,
                Boolean fAutoSelect = FALSE,
                Boolean fMultiSelect = FALSE,
                Boolean fRadioStyle = TRUE);

    // Compatibility
    void IStdPopupPane(short menuID,
                CView *anEnclosure, CBureaucrat *aSupervisor,
                short aWidth, short aHeight,
                short aHEncl, short aVEncl,
                Boolean fAutoSelect = TRUE,
                Boolean fMultiSelect = FALSE,
                Boolean fRadioStyle = FALSE);

    virtual void IViewTemp(CView *anEnclosure,
                        CBureaucrat *aSupervisor,
                        Ptr    viewData);
```

```
        virtual void NewMenuSelection(short itemSelected);
        virtual void DoClick(Point hitPt, short modifierKeys,
                             long when);
        virtual void DoKeyDown(char theChar, Byte keyCode,
                               EventRecord *macEvent);

        virtual void Prepare();
        virtual void Draw(Rect *area);
        virtual void Activate();
        virtual void Deactivate();

        virtual void CalcPopupBox(); // TCL 1.1.3 12/7/92 BF
        static void PreloadStdPopup(short menuID); // TCL 1.1.3
                                                   // 12/7/92 BF

        virtual void PutTo(CStream& stream);
        virtual void GetFrom(CStream& stream);

    protected:

        short    textFont;
        short    textSize;

        short    titleWidth;
        short    fontAscent;
        CPane    *itsPopupBox;
        Point    popupPt;
        Point    sicnPt;
        Rect     hiliteRect;

        void IStdPopupPaneX(Boolean fFirstInstall);
        virtual void InstallHook();
        static void HookMenu(MenuHandle menu); // TCL 1.1.3
                                               // 12/7/92 BF
        virtual void CalcDimensions();
        virtual void MakePopupBox();
        virtual void InvertTitle();
        virtual void SetTextFont(short aFont, short aSize);

    private:

        void CStdPopupPaneX();
    };
```

The next five subsections discuss the relevant member functions of class CStdPopupPane.

Syntax

The Function *NewMenuSelection*

The function NewMenuSelection places the new item's text in the menu. The declaration of function NewMenuSelection is

```
void NewMenuSelection(short itemSelected);
```

The parameter `itemSelected` specifies the index of the selected menu item.

> **Note:** Override the member function `NewMenuSelection` in a descendant of class `CStdPopupPane` if you need to respond to new selections in a special way.

The Function *GetMenu*

The function `GetMenu` returns a pointer to a `CPopupMenu` instance associated with an instance of class `CStdPopupPane`. The declaration of function `GetMenu` is

```
CPopupMenu *GetMenu();
```

The Function *SetMenu*

The member function `SetMenu` sets the menu associated with an instance of class `CStdPopupPane`. The declaration of function `SetMenu` is

```
void SetMenu(CPopupMenu *aMenu);
```

The parameter `aMenu` specifies the new menu associated with the standard menu pop-up pane. The function deletes the old instance of class `CPopupMenu` that was associated with the control.

The Function *Activate*

The member function `Activate` activates the pop-up menu pane. The declaration of function `Activate` is

```
void Activate();
```

The Function *Deactivate*

The member function `Deactivate` deactivates the pop-up menu pane. The declaration of function `Deactivate` is

```
void Deactivate();
```

The Pop-up Menu Example

Let's look at an example of a list box that uses a pop-up menu pane control. The next program, which I call PopupMenu1, uses a pop-up menu pane, an edit box, and a button control to select items from the pop-up menu pane and to respond to them. Figure 20.2 shows a sample session with the PopupMenu1 program project, which has the following controls:

☐ The MyMenu pop-up menu pane, which shows the items of a custom menu. The menu items are Text 1, Text 2, Text 3, and Text 4.

☐ The edit box, which echoes text that results from selecting an item in the pop-up menu pane control.

☐ The Quit button.

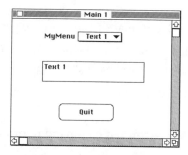

Figure 20.2. *A sample session with the PopupMenu1 program.*

Table 20.2 shows the control names as well as the custom and predefined commands associated with these controls.

Table 20.2. The control names and commands associated with the controls of project PopupMenu1.

Control Caption	Control Name	Control Type	Associated Command
	MyMenuPop	Popup pane	
	TextBox	Edit box	
Quit	QuitBtn	Button	cmdQuit

Preparing the Application

Building the PopupMenu1 program project is somewhat elaborate, because it involves extending the class CStdPopupPane to override member function NewMenuSelection. The process of creating the PopupMenu1 program involves several stages. In this first stage, you prepare the core part of the application by performing the following steps:

1. Create a new Visual Architect utility project, and name it PopupMenu1.

2. Delete the default controls in the main window.

Defining the New Menu

In this stage, you define the new commands cmdText1, cmdText2, cmdText3, and cmdText4, as well as a new menu that invokes these commands. Perform the following steps:

1. Invoke the Edit | Commands command to bring up the Commands dialog box.

2. Press the ⌘K keys to define the new command cmdText1. Do not associate this command with any class at this stage.

3. Repeat steps 1 and 2 to create the commands cmdText2, cmdText3, and cmdText4.

4. Invoke the Edit | Menu Bar command to bring up the Menu Bar dialog box.

5. Press ⌘K to define the new menu MyMenu.

6. Click the Edit Menu Items button to define the commands for the new menu.

7. Press ⌘K to define the new menu item Text 1. Click on the Command pop-up menu pane to associate the command cmdText1 with the menu item Text 1.

8. Repeat steps 4 through 7 to define the menu commands Text 2 through Text 4 and to associate them with the commands cmdText2 through cmdText4, respectively.

Declaring the New Class *CMyMenu*

For this stage, you must declare the class CMyMenu as a descendant of class CStdPopupPane. The Visual Architect utility offers a menu command that supports this stage. Perform the following steps:

1. Invoke the Edit | Classes command to invoke the Classes dialog box.

2. In the text box, click below the CMain class to shift the dialog box into input mode.

3. Type CMyMenu in the input box.

4. Use the Base Class pop-up menu pane to set class CStdPopupPane as the parent of class CMyMenu.

5. Click the OK button to close the Classes dialog box.

Drawing the Controls

In this stage, you draw the controls shown in Figure 20.1. Perform the following steps:

1. Use the Tools menu to select the pop-up menu pane control, and then draw the pop-up menu pane control.

2. Set the names of the pop-up menu pane control according to the information in Table 20.2. Associate this control with the MyMenu menu.

3. Use the Tools menu to select the edit box control, and then draw the edit box control.

4. Set the name of the edit box control according to the information in Table 20.2.

5. Use the Tools menu to select the button control, and then draw the Quit button control.

6. Set the name and caption of the button control according to the information in Table 20.2.

Associating *CMyPopupMenu* with the Pop-up Menu

In this stage, you associate the class CMyMenu with the pop-up menu pane control. Without this association, the program regards the pop-up menu pane as an instance of class CStdPopupPane. To perform the needed association, follow these steps:

1. Select the list box control.

2. Invoke the Pane | Class command. This command brings up a floating menu that contains the names of the classes CStdPopupPane and CMyMenu.

3. Select the CMyMenu class to associate this class with the pop-up menu pane control.

Generating and Customizing the Source Code

To generate the custom code for this application, invoke the Generate All... command in the THINK Project Manager icon menu.

Now let's look at the relevant files emitted by the Visual Architect utility and the lines of code that I inserted to support the program's operations. Because I declare the class CMyMenu, the Visual Architect utility generates files for this class.

Listing 20.9 shows the source code for the CMyMenu.h header file for the PopupMenu1 program project.

Listing 20.9. The source code for the CMyMenu.h header file for project PopupMenu1.

```
1:   /**************************************************************
2:   CMyMenu.h
3:
4:                    Header for CMyMenu ScrollBar Class
5:
6:       Copyright (c) 1994 My Software Inc. All rights reserved.
7:
8:   Generated by Visual Architect(TM) 5:17 PM Thu, Jun 23, 1994
9:
10:  This file is only generated once. You can modify it by filling
11:  in the placeholder functions and adding any new functions you
12:  wish.
13:
14:  If you change the name of the document class, a fresh version
15:  of this file will be generated. If you have made any changes
16:  to the file with the old name, you will have to copy those
17:  changes to the new file by hand.
18:
19:  **************************************************************/
20:
21:  #pragma once
22:
23:  #include "x_CMyMenu.h"
24:
25:  class CMyMenu : public x_CMyMenu
26:  {
27:  public:
28:
29:      TCL_DECLARE_CLASS
30:
```

```
31:       /** Object I/O **/
32:       virtual void        PutTo(CStream &aStream);
33:       virtual void        GetFrom(CStream &aStream);
34:    };
```

Listing 20.9 shows that class CMyMenu is a descendant of x_CMyScrollBar. The class CMyMenu declares only stream-related member functions.

Listing 20.10 shows the source code for the CMyMenu.cp implementation file for project PopupMenu1.

Listing 20.10. The source code for the CMyMenu.cp implementation file for project PopupMenu1.

```
1:  /*****************************************************************
2:  CMyMenu.c
3:
4:              CMyMenu StdPopupPane Class
5:
6:      Copyright (c) 1994 My Software Inc. All rights reserved.
7:
8:  Generated by Visual Architect(TM) 5:17 PM Thu, Jun 23, 1994
9:
10: This file is only generated once. You can modify it by filling
11: in the placeholder functions and adding any new functions you
12: wish.
13:
14: If you change the name of the document class, a fresh version
15: of this file will be generated. If you have made any changes
16: to the file with the old name, you will have to copy those
17: changes to the new file by hand.
18:
19: *****************************************************************/
20:
21: #include "CMyMenu.h"
22:
23:
24: TCL_DEFINE_CLASS_D1(CMyMenu, x_CMyMenu);
25:
26: /**** C O N S T R U C T I O N / D E S T R U C T I O N
27:                                       M E T H O D S ****/
28:
29:
30: /*****************************************************************
31:   PutTo
32:
33: Put the contents of this object to the stream
34: *****************************************************************/
35:
36: void CMyMenu::PutTo(CStream &aStream)
37: {
```

continues

Listing 20.10. continued

```
38:      // Put any additional data members for this class
39:      // before calling the superclass PutTo.
40:
41:      // If you have no additional data members, the
42:      // PutTo and GetFrom functions can be eliminated.
43:
44:      x_CMyMenu::PutTo(aStream);  /* Let superclass save */
45:
46:      // By convention, any subordinate objects are put
47:      // after the superclass has had a chance to write
48:      // its instance variables.
49: }
50:
51:
52: /*****************************************************************
53:   GetFrom
54:
55: Get the contents of this object from the stream and
56: initialize the object
57: *****************************************************************/
58:
59: void CMyMenu::GetFrom(CStream &aStream)
60: {
61:      // Get any additional data members for this class
62:      // before calling the superclass GetFrom
63:
64:
65:      /* Let superclass restore */
66:      x_CMyMenu::GetFrom(aStream);
67:
68:      // Restore any subordinate objects below
69: }
```

Listing 20.10 contains the implementations of member functions PutTo and GetFrom. The statements in these functions invoke the corresponding member functions of the parent class.

Listing 20.11 shows the source code for the x_CMyMenu.h header file for project PopupMenu1. The bold lines show the ones that I manually added.

Listing 20.11. The source code for the x_CMyMenu.h header file for project PopupMenu1.

```
1: /*****************************************************************
2:   x_CMyMenu.h
3:
4:            Header File For CMyMenu Lower-Layer Popup Class
```

```
 5:
 6:      Copyright (c) 1994 My Software Inc. All rights reserved.
 7:
 8:  Generated by Visual Architect(TM)
 9:
10:  This file is rewritten each time you generate code. You should
11:  not make changes to this file; changes should go in the
12:  CMyMenu.h file, instead.
13:
14:  If you want to change how Visual Architect generates this file,
15:  you can change the template for this file. It is "_Std.h" in
16:  the Visual Architect Templates folder.
17:
18:  **************************************************************/
19:
20:  #pragma once
21:
22:  #include "CStdPopupPane.h"
23:
24:  #define Text1Sel 1
25:  #define Text2Sel 2
26:  #define Text3Sel 3
27:  #define Text4Sel 4
28:
29:
30:  class x_CMyMenu : public CStdPopupPane
31:  {
32:  public:
33:
34:      TCL_DECLARE_CLASS
35:
36:
37:      /** Object I/O **/
38:      virtual void        PutTo(CStream &aStream);
39:      virtual void        GetFrom(CStream &aStream);
40:
41:      virtual void NewMenuSelection(short itemSelected);
42:
43:      CDialogText *fTextBox;
44:  };
```

Analysis Listing 20.11 declares the class x_CMyMenu. The Visual Architect utility generated the declarations of member functions PutTo and GetFrom in lines 38 and 39, respectively. I inserted the member function NewMenuSelection in line 41. I also inserted the data member fTextBox. This member accesses the edit box in the main window.

Listing 20.12 shows the source code for the x_CMyMenu.cp implementation file for project PopupMenu1. The bold lines show the ones that I manually added.

VArc Type

Listing 20.12. The source code for the x_CMyMenu.cp implementation file for project PopupMenu1.

```
 1:  /****************************************************************
 2:   x_CMyMenu.c
 3:
 4:                    CMyMenu ScrollBar Class
 5:
 6:      Copyright (c) 1994 My Software Inc. All rights reserved.
 7:
 8:  Generated by Visual Architect(TM)
 9:
10:  This file is rewritten each time you generate code. You should
11:  not make changes to this file; changes should go in the
12:  CMyMenu.c file, instead.
13:
14:  If you want to change how Visual Architect generates this file,
15:  you can change the template for this file. It is "_Std_cp" in
16:  the Visual Architect Templates folder.
17:
18:  ****************************************************************/
19:
20:  #include "x_CMyMenu.h"
21:
22:  #include "ViewUtilities.h"
23:
24:
25:  TCL_DEFINE_CLASS_M1(x_CMyMenu, CStdPopupPane);
26:
27:  /**** C O N S T R U C T I O N / D E S T R U C T I O N
28:                                          M E T H O D S ****/
29:
30:
31:  /****************************************************************
32:   PutTo
33:
34:  Put the contents of this object to the stream
35:  ****************************************************************/
36:
37:  void x_CMyMenu::PutTo(CStream &aStream)
38:  {
39:      // Put data members for this class
40:
41:
42:      CStdPopupPane::PutTo(aStream);   /* Let superclass save */
43:  }
44:
45:
46:  /****************************************************************
47:   GetFrom
48:
49:  Get the contents of this object from the stream and
50:  initialize the object
51:  ****************************************************************/
52:
53:  void x_CMyMenu::GetFrom(CStream &aStream)
```

```
54:  {
55:      // Get data members for this class
56:
57:
58:      /* Let superclass restore  */
59:      CStdPopupPane::GetFrom(aStream);
60:  }
61:
62:
63:  /*****************************************************************
64:   NewMenuSelection
65:
66:  Respond to selecting a new popup menu pane item
67:  *****************************************************************/
68:
69:  void x_CMyMenu::NewMenuSelection(short itemSelected)
70:  {
71:    char s[81];
72:
73:    // call inherited member function
74:    CStdPopupPane::NewMenuSelection(itemSelected);
75:
76:    switch(itemSelected) {
77:      case Text1Sel:
78:        strcpy(s, "Text 1");
79:        break;
80:
81:      case Text2Sel:
82:        strcpy(s, "Text 2");
83:        break;
84:
85:      case Text3Sel:
86:        strcpy(s, "Text 3");
87:        break;
88:
89:      case Text4Sel:
90:        strcpy(s, "Text 4");
91:        break;
92:    }
93:    fTextBox->SetTextPtr(s, strlen(s));
94:  }
```

20

Analysis The most relevant member function of class x_CMyMenu is NewMenuSelection. Lines 69 to 94 define this member function. This statement first invokes the inherited function to update the selected item. Then, the function uses a switch statement to respond to the selected item. Each case label in the switch statement copies a specific string to the variable s. Line 93 writes the characters of variable s in the edit box. The function performs this task by sending the C++ message SetTextPtr to the data member fTextBox. The arguments for this message are the variable s and the expression strlen(s).

Listing 20.13 contains the source code for the x_CMain.h header file for project PopupMenu1.

Listing 20.13. The source code for the x_CMain.h header file for project PopupMenu1.

```
1:  /****************************************************************
2:  x_CMain.h
3:
4:              Header File For CMain Lower-Layer Document Class
5:
6:      Copyright (c) 1994 My Software Inc. All rights reserved.
7:
8:  Generated by Visual Architect(TM)
9:
10: This file is rewritten each time you generate code. You should
11: not make changes to this file; changes should go in the My.h
12: file, instead.
13:
14: If you want to change how Visual Architect generates this file,
15: you can change the template for this file. It is "_Doc.h" in the
16: Visual Architect Templates folder.
17:
18: ****************************************************************/
19:
20: #pragma once
21:
22: #include "CSaver.h"
23: class CDialogText;
24: class CButton;
25: class CMyMenu;
26:
27: #include "ItsContentsClass.h"
28:
29: #define x_CMain_super      CSaver<ITSCONTENTSCLASS>
30:
31: class CFile;
32:
33: class x_CMain : public x_CMain_super
34:
35: {
36: public:
37:
38:     TCL_DECLARE_CLASS
39:
40:     // Pointers to panes in window
41:     CDialogText    *fMain_TextBox;
42:     CButton     *fMain_QuitBtn;
43:     CMyMenu     *fMain_MyMenuPop;
44:
45:     void     Ix_CMain(void);
46:
47:
48: protected:
```

```
49:      virtual void    MakeNewWindow(void);
50:
51:      virtual void    FailOpen(CFile *aFile);
52:      virtual void    PositionWindow(void);
53:
54:  };
55:
56:  #define    CVueCMain    128
```

Listing 20.13 shows the declaration of class x_CMain. This class contains a number
of data members and member functions, all emitted by the Visual Architect utility.
Lines 41 to 43 define the various data members that are pointers to the different
controls. These members are pointers to the classes CMyMenu, CDialogText, and CButton.

Listing 20.14 shows the source code for the x_CMain.cp implementation file for project
PopupMenu1. The bold lines show the ones that I manually inserted.

**VArc
Type**

Listing 20.14. The source code for the x_CMain.cp implementation file for project PopupMenu1.

```
1:   /*******************************************************
2:    x_CMain.c
3:
4:               CMain Document Class
5:
6:     Copyright (c) 1994 My Software Inc. All rights reserved.
7:
8:  Generated by Visual Architect(TM) 7:01 PM Thu, Jun 23, 1994
9:
10:  This file is rewritten each time you generate code. You should
11:  not make changes to this file; changes should go in the My.c
12:  file, instead.
13:
14:  If you want to change how Visual Architect generates this file,
15:  you can change the template for this file. It is "_Doc_cp" in
16:  the Visual Architect Templates folder.
17:
18:  *******************************************************/
19:
20:  #include "x_CMain.h"
21:
22:  #include "CMain.h"
23:
24:  #include "MainItems.h"
25:
26:  #include "ViewUtilities.h"
27:  #include "CApp.h"
28:
29:  #include <CApplication.h>
30:  #include <CBartender.h>
```

continues

Listing 20.14. continued

```
31:  #include <Commands.h>
32:  #include <Constants.h>
33:  #include <CDecorator.h>
34:  #include <CDesktop.h>
35:  #include <CFile.h>
36:  #include <TBUtilities.h>
37:  #include <CWindow.h>
38:
39:  extern CApplication *gApplication; /* The application */
40:  extern CDecorator     *gDecorator;  /* Decorator for arranging
41:                                          windows */
42:  extern CDesktop        *gDesktop;   /* The visible Desktop */
43:  extern CBartender     *gBartender;  /* Manages all menus */
44:
45:  #include "CDialogText.h"
46:  #include "CButton.h"
47:  #include "CMyMenu.h"
48:
49:      // Define symbols for commands handled by this class
50:      // Prevents a recompile every time any command changed.
51:
52:
53:
54:  TCL_DEFINE_CLASS_M1(x_CMain, x_CMain_super);
55:
56:  /**** C O N S T R U C T I O N / D E S T R U C T I O N
57:                                          M E T H O D S ****/
58:
59:
60:  /****************************************************************
61:   Ix_CMain
62:
63:  Initialize the document
64:  ****************************************************************/
65:
66:  void x_CMain::Ix_CMain()
67:
68:  {
69:      IDocument(gApplication, TRUE);
70:
71:      // Initialize data members below.
72:  }
73:
74:
75:  /****************************************************************
76:   MakeNewWindow
77:
78:  Create a new, empty window. Subclass may override to populate
79:  the new window.
80:  ****************************************************************/
81:
82:  void x_CMain::MakeNewWindow(void)
83:
84:  {
```

```
85:      itsWindow = TCLGetNamedWindow("\pMain", this);
86:
87:      itsMainPane = (CPane*) TCLGetItemPointer(itsWindow, 0);
88:
89:      // Initialize pointers to the subpanes in the window
90:
91:      fMain_TextBox = (CDialogText*)
92:                      itsWindow->FindViewByID(kMain_TextBoxID);
93:      ASSERT(member(fMain_TextBox, CDialogText));
94:
95:      fMain_QuitBtn = (CButton*)
96:                      itsWindow->FindViewByID(kMain_QuitBtnID);
97:      ASSERT(member(fMain_QuitBtn, CButton));
98:
99:      fMain_MyMenuPop = (CMyMenu*)
100:                     itsWindow->FindViewByID(kMain_MyMenuPopID);
101:     ASSERT(member(fMain_MyMenuPop, CMyMenu));
102:
103:     fMain_MyMenuPop->fTextBox = fMain_TextBox;
104:
105: }
106:
107:
108: /****************************************************************
109:   FailOpen {OVERRIDE}
110:
111: Fail if file already open in this application.
112:
113: This function calls the application's FileAlreadyOpen function
114: and fails quietly if the file is open.
115:
116: Note that open may also fail if the file is open in
117: another application. This will cause a failure in open,
118: but you may wish to override this function to detect this
119: case and provide a more meaningful error message than -49.
120: ****************************************************************/
121:
122: void x_CMain::FailOpen(CFile *aFile)
123:
124: {
125:      /* Only the application knows        */
126:      if (((CApp*)gApplication)->FileAlreadyOpen(aFile))
127:          Failure(kSilentErr, 0);
128: }
129:
130:
131: /****************************************************************
132:   PositionWindow
133:
134: The default method in CSaver calls the the decorator, which
135: staggers and resizes the window. Since the window has already
136: been positioned when it is initialized from the view resource,
137: we don't want to do this twice.
138: ****************************************************************/
139:
```

continues

Listing 20.14. continued

```
140:  void    x_CMain::PositionWindow()
141:
142:  {
143:  }
```

Listing 20.14 defines the member functions of class x_CMain. These functions resemble those generated in the minimal TCL program in Day 15. I inserted the statement in line 103 to copy the address of the edit box control to the pop-up menu pane's fTextBox data member. This assignment allows the pop-up menu pane to write text to the edit box that echoes the currently selected pop-up menu pane item.

Listing 20.15 shows the source code for the AppCommands.h header file for the PopupMenu1 program project. This listing defines the set of constants cmdTextX, in lines 16 to 19, that support the custom commands.

Listing 20.15. The source code for the AppCommands.h header file for project Pop-upMenu1.

```
1:   /*******************************************************************
2:   MyCommands.h
3:
4:              Header File For Command Symbols
5:
6:      Copyright (c) 1994 My Software Inc. All rights reserved.
7:
8:   Generated by Visual Architect(TM)
9:
10:  This file is regenerated each time.
11:
12:  *******************************************************************/
13:
14:  #pragma once
15:
16:  #define cmdText1     513
17:  #define cmdText2     514
18:  #define cmdText3     515
19:  #define cmdText4     516
```

Listing 20.16 shows the source code for the MainItems.h header file for the PopupMenu1 program project. The listing declares an untagged enumerated type which defines the identifiers kMain_XXXX and kMain_XXXXID.

Listing 20.16. The source code for the MainItems.h header file for project PopupMenu1.

```
 1:   /****************************************************************
 2:   MainItems.h
 3:
 4:                    Main Item Constants
 5:
 6:       Copyright (c) 1994 My Software Inc. All rights reserved.
 7:
 8:   Generated by Visual Architect(TM)
 9:
10:   This file is rewritten each time you generate code. You should
11:   not make changes to this file.
12:
13:   If you want to change how Visual Architect generates this file,
14:   you can change the template for this file. It is "Items.h" in
15:   the Visual Architect Templates folder.
16:
17:   ****************************************************************/
18:
19:   #pragma once
20:
21:
22:       //     Item numbers for each item.
23:       //
24:       //     Use TCLGetItemPointer (ViewUtilities) to convert these
25:       //     item numbers to a pointer to the named item.
26:
27:   enum
28:   {
29:       Main_Begin_,
30:       kMain_TextBox = 1,
31:       kMain_TextBoxID = 1L,
32:       kMain_QuitBtn = 2,
33:       kMain_QuitBtnID = 2L,
34:       kMain_MyMenuPop = 3,
35:       kMain_MyMenuPopID = 3L,
36:       Main_End_
37:   };
```

Compiling and Running the Program

Invoke the Run command from the THINK Project Manager icon menu. This command causes the compiler to process the set of source code files that contribute to the program. When the program runs, select the item Text3 in the pop-up menu pane control. When you release the button, the program writes the string Text 3 in the edit box. Select another pop-up menu pane item and watch the program echo your selection in a similar way. When you are finished experimenting, click the Quit button to close the main window and end the program.

Summary

This chapter presented the scroll bar and pop-up menu pane controls. The scroll bar control enables you to scroll through a range of integers. The pop-up menu pane control enables you to select from a set of menu items. The following topics were covered:

☐ You learned about the class CScrollBar and its relevant member functions. This class supports operations that define the range of scroll bar values, query the range of scroll bar values, assign the current scroll bar value, and query the current dialog box value.

☐ From a sample program, you learned how to implement the scroll bar control. The program uses a scroll bar control to implement a simple timer. While the timer is running, the program moves the scroll bar thumb to reflect the timer's progress. The program also illustrated how to update other controls when you either drag the scroll bar thumb or click on its nonmoving parts.

☐ You learned about the class CStdPopupPane and its relevant member functions. This class supports the standard pop-up menu pane control. You also learned how to respond to selecting items in the pop-up menu pane control.

☐ You also learned from another program example, which illustrates using the pop-up menu pane control to select from a custom menu. The program also demonstrates how to respond to selecting a new item from the pop-up menu pane.

Q&A

Q Must the menu associated with a pop-up menu pane be visible in the menu bar?

A No.

Q What is the nature of the menus associated with pop-up menu panes?

A Such menus merely contain a list of items to select from. Therefore, think of them as lists more than menu commands.

Q What happens if I omit line 74 (shown below) from Listing 20.12?

```
74:     CStdPopupPane::NewMenuSelection(itemSelected);
```

A If you omit line 74, you end up not calling the inherited member function `NewMenuSelection`. Consequently, the pop-up menu pane also shows the initial selection (Text 1) when you do not click on it.

Workshop

The Workshop provides quiz questions to help you solidify your understanding of the material covered and exercises to provide you with experience in using what you've learned. Try to understand the quiz and exercise answers before continuing on to the next day's lesson. Answers are provided in Appendix B, "Answers."

Quiz

1. True or false? The menu items in a pop-up menu pane must also be accessible through a menu in the menu bar.

2. True or false? You cannot change the range of values of a scroll bar at runtime.

3. True or false? You can alter the scroll bar value using member function `SetValue` in such a way that you do not move the position of the scroll bar thumb.

4. True or false? You can associate only predefined menus with a pop-up menu pane.

Exercise

Extend the custom menu in project PopupMenu1 to include other items. Make some of the new items alter the case, font size, and alignment of the string `"Any Text"`. I leave the final design to your discretion.

The Dialog Box

Dialog boxes are special windows that enable an application to interact with the end user by displaying data and obtaining input. The THINK Project Manager and Visual Architect utility (and just about every other Macintosh application) use dialog boxes to fine-tune their operations. In this chapter you learn about the following topics:

☐ The basics of dialog boxes

☐ The class CDialog and its relevant member functions

☐ The class CDLOGDialog and its relevant member functions

☐ The class CDialogDirector and its relevant member functions

☐ The class CDLOGDirector and its relevant member functions

☐ Implementing dialog boxes (via a programming example)

Overview

Dialog boxes are special windows that enable applications to interact with you. There are two basic kinds of dialog boxes: modal and modeless.

A *modal* dialog box requires that you close it before you can access any other window or dialog box in the same application. The reason for this mode of operation is that a modal dialog box handles critical data needed for the program to proceed.

A *modeless* dialog box enables you to select other windows and dialog boxes in the same application without having to close the dialog box because it does not handle critical data.

If you have the chance to talk to a veteran Macintosh programmer, you'll learn that programming Macintosh applications using the Apple MPW (Macintosh Programmer's Workshop) often involves working with resources that define dialog boxes. Appendix A, "Resources," gives a brief overview of resources. Resources are specifications that define windows, controls, icons, dialog boxes, strings, string lists, menus, and so on. The good news is that the Visual Architect utility is sophisticated enough to handle creating and compiling the dialog box resources for you so you don't have to work with resources directly.

This chapter shows you how to create and work with dialog boxes using the Visual Architect utility. The Visual Architect does an excellent job of supporting dialog boxes.

The Class *CDialog*

The class CDialog, a descendant of class CWindow, is an abstract class that supports modal and modeless dialog boxes. Here is the declaration of class CDialog:

```
class CDialog : public CWindow
{
public:
    TCL_DECLARE_CLASS

    CDialog();
    CDialog(short WINDid, CDirector *aSupervisor);
    CDialog(Rect *bounds, Boolean fVisible,
            short procID, Boolean fHasGoAway,
            CDirector *aSupervisor);

    void IDialog(short WINDid, CDesktop *anEnclosure,
                CDirector *aSupervisor);
    void INewDialog(Rect *bounds, Boolean fVisible,
                short procID, Boolean fHasGoAway,
                CDesktop *anEnclosure,
                CDirector *aSupervisor);

    virtual void DoKeyDown(char theChar, Byte keyCode,
                        EventRecord *macEvent);
    virtual void DoTab(Boolean fForward);

    virtual void FindGophers(tGopherInfo *gopherInfo);
    virtual CButton *FindButton(long aCmd);

    virtual void SetCmdEnable(long aCmd, Boolean fEnable);
    virtual void SetDefaultCmd(long aCmd);
    virtual void SetDefaultButton(CButton *aButton);

    virtual void ScrollToPane(CPane *aPane);

    virtual void Close();
    virtual Boolean Validate();

    virtual void ProviderChanged(CCollaborator *aProvider,
                        long reason, void* info);

    virtual void PutTo(CStream& stream);
    virtual void GetFrom(CStream& stream);

protected:

    CButton *defaultBtn;      // current default button
    CPanorama *itsPanorama;   // panorama that encloses all
                              // dialog items
    Boolean scrollable;       // TRUE if autoscrolling is enabled.
                              // This is the case when itsPanorama
                              // is enclosed in a scroll pane.
```

21

```
virtual void MakePanorama(Boolean fHasHScroll,
                          Boolean fHasVScroll,
                          Boolean fHasSizeBox);

private:

    void CDialogX();
};
```

The following six subsections describe the relevant member functions of class CDialog.

The Function *Close*

The member function Close, as the name might suggest, closes the dialog box. The declaration of function Close is

```
void Close();
```

The Function *Validate*

The member function Validate returns a Boolean value to indicate whether or not *all* the controls in the dialog box contain valid data. The declaration of function Validate is

```
Boolean Validate();
```

The Function *FindButton*

The member function FindButton returns the pointer to the button associated with a specific cmd*XXXX* command. The declaration of function FindButton is

```
CButton *FindButton(long aCmd);
```

The parameter aCmd is the queried command.

The Function *SetDefaultCmd*

The member function SetDefaultCmd sets the default cmd*XXXX* command for the dialog box. This is the command that is invoked when you press Enter. The declaration of function SetDefaultCmd is

```
void SetDefaultCmd(long aCmd);
```

The parameter aCmd is the default command.

Syntax

The Function *SetDefaultButton*

The member function `SetDefaultButton` sets the default button in the dialog box. This is the button that is invoked when you press Enter. The declaration of function `SetDefaultButton` is

```
void SetDefaultButton(CButton *aButton);
```

The parameter `aButton` is the pointer to the default button.

Syntax

The Function *SetCmdEnable*

The member function `SetCmdEnable` toggles the enabled state of a button in the dialog box. The declaration of function `SetCmdEnable` is

```
void SetCmdEnable(long aCmd, Boolean fEnable);
```

The parameter `aCmd` is the command of the targeted button. The `Boolean` parameter `fEnable` specifies whether to enable or disable the control associated with the command `aCmd`.

The *CDLOGDialog* Class

The class `CDLOGDialog`, a descendant of class `CDialog`, creates a dialog box from the resources `DLOG` and `DITL`. Here is the declaration of class `CDLOGDialog`:

```
class CDLOGDialog : public CDialog
{
public:

    TCL_DECLARE_CLASS

    // Construction
    CDLOGDialog();
    CDLOGDialog(short DLOGid, CDirector *aSupervisor);

                                // Compatibility
    void IDLOGDialog(short DLOGid, CDesktop *anEnclosure,
                CDirector *aSupervisor);

protected:

    short    staticTextFont;    // default font to use for
                                // static text items
    short    staticTextSize;    // default size to use for
                                // static text items
    short    editTextFont;      // default font for edit
                                // text items
```

21

```
short     editTextSize;      // default size for edit
                             // text items
short     defaultBorderPen;  // default border thickness for
                             // user items and RadioGroupPanes

virtual void AddDITLItems(short DITLid, long baseID);

virtual CView *FindEnclosingView(Rect *boundsRect);

virtual CPane *AddDITLPushBtn(short aWidth, short aHeight,
                short hEncl, short vEncl,
                CView *enclosure, tDITLItem *ditlItem);
virtual CPane *AddDITLRadioBtn(short aWidth, short aHeight,
                short hEncl, short vEncl,
                CView *enclosure, tDITLItem *ditlItem,
                long anID);
virtual CPane *AddDITLCheckBox(short aWidth, short aHeight,
                short hEncl, short vEncl,
                CView *enclosure, tDITLItem *ditlItem);
virtual CPane *AddDITLResControl(short aWidth, short aHeight,
                short hEncl, short vEncl,
                CView *enclosure, tDITLItem *ditlItem);
virtual CPane *AddDITLStatText(short aWidth, short aHeight,
                short hEncl, short vEncl,
                CView *enclosure, tDITLItem *ditlItem);
virtual CPane *AddDITLEditText(short aWidth, short aHeight,
                short hEncl, short vEncl,
                CView *enclosure, tDITLItem *ditlItem);
virtual CPane *AddDITLIcon(short aWidth, short aHeight,
                short hEncl, short vEncl,
                CView *enclosure, tDITLItem *ditlItem);
virtual CPane *AddDITLPicture(short aWidth, short aHeight,
                short hEncl, short vEncl,
                CView *enclosure, tDITLItem *ditlItem);
virtual CPane *AddDITLUserItem(short aWidth, short aHeight,
                short hEncl, short vEncl,
                CView *enclosure, tDITLItem *ditlItem);
virtual CPane *AddOverloadedItem(StringPtr itemText,
                short aWidth, short aHeight,
                short hEncl, short vEncl,
                CView *enclosure, tDITLItem *ditlItem);

private:

void      CDLOGDialogX();
void      IDLOGDialogX(short DLOGid,
                CDirector *aSupervisor);
};
```

This declaration of class CDLOGDialog reveals that the class has a set of member functions AddDITLXXXX which handle various kinds of controls. Table 21.1 lists the AddDITLXXXX member functions and the controls they add.

Table 21.1. The list of AddDITLXXXX member functions in class CDLOGDialog.

Member Function	Added Control
AddDITLPushBtn	Pushbutton
AddDITLRadioBtn	Radio control
AddDITLCheckBox	Check box
AddDITLResControl	Resource control
AddDITLStatText	Static text
AddDITLEditText	Edit text
AddDITLIcon	Icon
AddDITLPicture	Picture
AddDITLUserItem	User item

The *CDialogDirector* Class

The class CDialogDirector is the base class for a director object that manages a dialog box. Here is the declaration of class CDialogDirector:

```
class CDialogDirector : public CDirector
{
public:

    CDialogDirector(CDirectorOwner *aSupervisor = 0);

    void IDialogDirector(CDirectorOwner *aSupervisor);
    virtual void DoCommand(long aCmd);
    virtual long DoModalDialog(long defaultCmd);
    virtual long DoChangeableModalDialog(long defaultCmd,
                                    Boolean changeDoc);
    virtual Boolean Validate();
    virtual void BeginModalDialog(); // TCL 1.1.3 11/30/92 BF
    virtual void BeginDialog();
    virtual Boolean Close(Boolean fQuitting);
    virtual Boolean EndDialog(long withCmd, Boolean fValidate);

protected:

    long dismissCmd; // command that dismissed the dialog
    long barState;   // previous state of disabled menu bar
                     // TCL 1.1.3 11/30/92 BF
```

21

```
    virtual void DisableTheMenus();
    virtual void EnableTheMenus();
};
```

The following six subsections describe the member functions of class `CDialogDirector`.

Syntax

The Function *DoCommand*

The member function `DoCommand` manages the response to the standard OK and Cancel commands. The declaration of function `DoCommand` is

```
void DoCommand(long aCmd);
```

The parameter `aCmd` is the handled command. In the case of the OK command, the director closes the dialog box if the function `Validate` returns `TRUE`. In the case of the Cancel command, the director always closes the dialog box.

Syntax

The Function *Close*

The member function `Close` handles the Close command. The declaration of function `Close` is

```
void Close(Boolean fQuitting);
```

The function closes the dialog box if the function `Validate` returns `TRUE`. The function `Close` returns `TRUE` if it closed the dialog box. Otherwise, the function yields `FALSE`.

Syntax

The Function *BeginDialog*

The member function `BeginDialog` brings up the dialog box. The function selects the dialog box window and activates the first dialog item that receives input. If that item is an edit box, the function selects the text in that control. The declaration of function `BeginDialog` is

```
void BeginDialog();
```

Note: Call the member function `BeginDialog` only with modeless dialog boxes.

Syntax

The Function *DoModalDialog*

The member function DoModalDialog brings up the modal dialog box. The declaration of function DoModalDialog is

```
long DoModalDialog(long defaultCmd);
```

The parameter defaultCmd specifies the default command for the modal dialog box. The function returns the command that closes the dialog box. Typically, the cmdOK or cmdCancel commands close the dialog box.

Syntax

The Function *EndDialog*

The member function EndDialog attempts to stop using the dialog box but does not close it. The declaration of function EndDialog is

```
void EndDialog(long withCmd, Boolean fValidate);
```

The parameter fValidate is a flag that tells the function whether or not to validate the data in the controls of the dialog box. When the argument for this parameter is TRUE, the function EndDialog calls function Validate. If the function Validate returns TRUE, or if the argument for parameter fValidate is FALSE, the function EndDialog sets member dismissCmd to the argument of parameter withCmd.

Syntax

The Function *Validate*

The member function Validate returns a Boolean value to indicate whether *all* the controls in the director's dialog box contain valid data. The declaration of function Validate is

```
Boolean Validate();
```

21

The *CDLOGDirector*

The class CDLOGDirector, a descendant of class CDialogDirector, supports the directors for dialog boxes created from the DLOG and DITL resources. The declaration of class CDLOGDirector is

```
class CDLOGDirector : public CDialogDirector
{
public:

    // Constructor
    CDLOGDirector();
    CDLOGDirector(short DLOGid, CDirectorOwner *aSupervisor);

    // Compatibility
    void IDLOGDirector(short DLOGid,
                       CDirectorOwner *aSupervisor);

private:
    void IDLOGDirectorX(short DLOGid);
};
```

The class CDLOGDirector inherits most of its operations from its parent class. The specialization of class CDLOGDirector is determined by its constructors and initializing member function.

The Dialog Boxes Example

Let's look at program that creates and uses two dialog boxes. One of the dialog boxes is similar to an alert box, whereas the other is somewhat similar to the Find dialog box used in the THINK Project Manager. The next program, which I call Dialog1, illustrates how to use the first dialog box as a custom alert box and how to use the second dialog box to interact with the user. Figure 21.1 shows the main window in a sample session with the Dialog1 program project. The figure shows that the main window has the following controls:

☐ The Message button, which invokes the Message Box dialog box

☐ The Test Dialog button, which invokes the Sample Dialog dialog box

☐ The Quit button

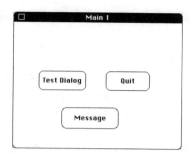

Figure 21.1. *The main window in a sample session with the Dialog1 program.*

Table 21.2 shows the control names as well as the custom and predefined commands associated with the main window's controls.

Table 21.2. The control names and commands associated with the controls in the main window of project Dialog1.

Control Caption	Control Name	Control Type	Associated Command
Test Dialog	TestDlgBtn	Button	cmdTestDlg
Message	MessageBtn	Button	cmdShowMsgDlg
Quit	QuitBtn	Button	cmdQuit

Figure 21.2 shows the Message Box dialog box, which contains the following controls:

☐ The Static text control, which shows a greeting message. The text has a non-default font and font size.

☐ The set of lines and oval shapes making up the smiling face (okay, so now you know why I write books and not paint for a living!).

☐ The OK button.

21

Figure 21.2. *The Message Box dialog box in a sample session with the Dialog1 program.*

Table 21.3 lists the non-shape control names as well as the custom and predefined commands associated with the Message Box's controls.

Table 21.3. The control names and commands associated with the non-shape controls in the Message Box dialog box of project Dialog1.

Control Caption	Control Name	Control Type	Associated Command
Greetings..	Stat1	Static text	
OK	OKBtn	Button	cmdOK

Figure 21.3 shows the Sample Dialog dialog box, which contains the following controls:

- ☐ The Find edit box, which contains the initial text `find me`
- ☐ The Replace edit box, which contains the initial text `replace me`
- ☐ The rectangular-shaped control, which contains the following three radio controls:
  - ☐ The Forward radio control, which initially is selected
  - ☐ The Backward radio control
  - ☐ The Entire radio control

☐ The Whole Word check box, which initially is checked

☐ The Case Sensitive check box, which is initially checked

☐ The static text controls that label the edit boxes

☐ The Cancel button

☐ The OK button

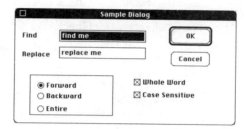

Figure 21.3. *The Sample Dialog dialog box in a sample session with the Dialog1 program.*

Table 21.4 shows the control names as well as the custom and predefined commands associated with the Sample Dialog dialog box controls.

Table 21.4. The control names and commands associated with the controls in the Sample Dialog dialog box of project Dialog1.

Control Caption	Control Name	Control Type	Associated Command
Find	FindLbl	Static text	
Replace	ReplaceLbl	Static text	
Find me	FindBox	Edit box	
Replace me	ReplaceBox	Edit box	
	Rect5	Rectangle control	

continues

21

Table 21.4. continued

Control Caption	Control Name	Control Type	Associated Command
Forward*	ForwardRbt	Radio control	
Backward	BackwardRbt	Radio control	
Entire	EntireRbt	Radio control	
Whole Word*	WholeWordChk	Check box	
Case Sensitive*	CaseSenseChk	Check box	
OK	OKBtn	Button	cmdOK
Cancel	CancelBtn	Button	cmdCancel

*This control is initially selected or checked.

Preparing the Application

Building the Dialog1 program project is more elaborate than building the programs in the last few chapters because it involves creating two dialog boxes. The process involves the several stages you should be familiar with by now. In the first stage, you prepare the core part of the application by performing the following steps:

1. Create a new Visual Architect utility project, and name it Group1.

2. Delete the default controls from the main window.

3. Select a fixed window style for the main window.

4. Define the custom commands specified in Table 21.2. Make sure that these commands are associated with class CMain and result in a Call type of action.

Drawing the Message Box

In the second stage, you draw the Message Box dialog box. Perform the following steps:

1. Invoke the View | New View... command to invoke the dialog box for naming the Message Box dialog, as shown in Figure 21.4.

2. Enter `Message Box` in the edit box.

3. Click the OK button to close the dialog box.

4. The Visual Architect utility displays a blank view.

5. Draw the smiling face by selecting the various geometric shape controls from the Toolbar.

6. Draw the static text control that displays the greeting text. Select a non-default font and font size at your discretion.

7. Draw the OK button. The Visual Architect utility automatically displays the first button in a view as the OK button. Set the button's control name to `OkBtn`.

8. Invoke the View | View Info command and select the fixed window as the window style for this dialog box. Also click on the modal check box.

9. Close the View Info dialog box.

10. Close the Message Box window.

Figure 21.4. *The New View dialog box.*

Drawing the Sample Dialog

This stage involves drawing the Sample Dialog dialog box. Perform the following steps:

1. Invoke the View | New View... command to invoke the dialog box for naming the Message Box dialog.

2. Enter `Sample Dialog` in the edit box.

3. Click the OK button to close the dialog box.

4. The Visual Architect utility displays a blank view.

5. Draw the various controls for this dialog box based on the information in Table 21.3.

6. Set the control names, captions, and initial values as indicated by Table 21.3.

7. Invoke the View | View Info command and select the fixed window as the window style for this dialog box. Also click on the modal check box.

8. Close the View Info dialog box.

9. Close the Sample Dialog window.

Now you can generate the custom code by invoking the Generate All... command in the THINK Project Manager icon menu.

Generating and Customizing the Source Code

To generate the custom code for this application, invoke the Generate All... command in the THINK Project Manager icon menu.

Now let's look at the relevant files emitted by the Visual Architect utility and the lines of code that I inserted to support the program's operations. Because I created two dialog boxes, the Visual Architect utility generates two sets of classes for each dialog box.

Listing 21.1 shows the source code for the CMessage_Box.h header file for the Dialog1 program project.

Listing 21.1. The source code for the CMessage_Box.h header file for project Dialog1.

```
1:  /*****************************************************************
2:  CMessage_Box.h
3:
4:                  CMessage_Box Dialog Director Class
5:
6:      Copyright (c) 1994 My Software Inc. All rights reserved.
7:
8:  Generated by Visual Architect(TM) 9:21 PM Thu, Jun 23, 1994
9:
10: This file is only generated once. You can modify it by filling
11: in the placeholder functions and adding any new functions you
12: wish.
13:
14: If you change the name of the dialog class, a fresh version of
15: this file will be generated. If you have made any changes to
16: the file with the old name, you will have to copy those changes
17: to the new file by hand.
18:
19: *****************************************************************/
20:
21: #pragma once
22:
23: #include "x_CMessage_Box.h"
24:
25:
26: class CDirectorOwner;
27:
28: class CMessage_Box : public x_CMessage_Box
29: {
30: public:
31:
32:     TCL_DECLARE_CLASS
33:
34:     // Insert your own public data members here
35:
36:     void ICMessage_Box(CDirectorOwner *aSupervisor);
37:
38:     virtual void ProviderChanged(CCollaborator *aProvider,
39:                                  long reason, void* info);
40:     virtual void DoCommand(long theCommand);
41:
42: protected:
43:
44:     virtual void BeginData(CMessage_BoxData *initial);
45:     virtual void UpdateData(CMessage_BoxUpdate *update,
46:                             long itemNo);
47:     virtual void EndData(CMessage_BoxData *final);
48: };
```

21

 Listing 21.1 shows that class CMessage_Box is a descendant of x_CMessage_Box. The class CMessage_Box declares the member functions ICMessage_Box, ProviderChanged, DoCommand, BeginData, UpdateData, and EndData. The last three functions handle the data-exchange mechanism between the class instances and the dialog box. In the case of the Message Box, there is no actual data exchange because the dialog box offers read-only text.

Listing 21.2 shows the source code for the CMessage_Box.cp implementation file for project Dialog1.

 Listing 21.2. The source code for the CMessage_Box.cp implementation file for project Dialog1.

```
 1:   /****************************************************************
 2:   CMessage_Box.c
 3:
 4:                   CMessage_Box Dialog Director Class
 5:
 6:      Copyright (c) 1994 My Software Inc. All rights reserved.
 7:
 8:   Generated by Visual Architect(TM) 9:21 PM Thu, Jun 23, 1994
 9:
10:   This file is only generated once. You can modify it by filling
11:   in the placeholder functions and adding any new functions you
12:   wish.
13:
14:   If you change the name of the dialog class, a fresh version of
15:   this file will be generated. If you have made any changes to
16:   the file with the old name, you will have to copy those changes
17:   to the new file by hand.
18:
19:   ****************************************************************/
20:
21:   #include "CMessage_Box.h"
22:
23:   #include "Message_BoxItems.h"
24:   //#include "AppCommands.h" // Remove comments if
25:                             // DoCommand overridden
26:
27:   #include <CIntegerText.h>
28:   #include <CControl.h>
29:   #include <CPopupMenu.h>
30:   #include <CPopupPane.h>
31:   #include <CArrayPane.h>
32:   #include <CIconButton.h>
33:   #include <CPictureButton.h>
34:   #include <CSwissArmyButton.h>
35:
36:   #include <CApplication.h>
37:   #include <Constants.h>
38:   #include <CDecorator.h>
39:   #include <CDesktop.h>
```

```
40:    #include <CDirectorOwner.h>
41:    #include <CFile.h>
42:    #include <TBUtilities.h>
43:    #include <CWindow.h>
44:
45:    extern CApplication *gApplication; /* The application */
46:    extern CDecorator    *gDecorator;  /* Decorator for arranging
47:                                          windows */
48:    extern CDesktop         *gDesktop; /* The visible Desktop */
49:
50:
51:    TCL_DEFINE_CLASS_M1(CMessage_Box, x_CMessage_Box);
52:
53:    /**** C O N S T R U C T I O N / D E S T R U C T I O N
54:                                        M E T H O D S ****/
55:
56:
57:    /*****************************************************************
58:      ICMessage_Box
59:
60:      Initialize the dialog
61:
62:    *****************************************************************/
63:
64:    void CMessage_Box::ICMessage_Box(CDirectorOwner *aSupervisor)
65:
66:    {
67:        // Initialize data members that must be set up before
68:        // BeginData is called here
69:
70:        x_CMessage_Box::Ix_CMessage_Box(aSupervisor);
71:
72:        // Initialize any other data members here
73:
74:    }
75:
76:
77:    /*****************************************************************
78:      BeginData
79:
80:    Set up initial pane values
81:    *****************************************************************/
82:
83:    void CMessage_Box::BeginData(CMessage_BoxData *initial)
84:
85:    {
86:    //   Base class calls BeginData once after the window is created
87:    //   to gather the initial values for the dialog panes. Note that
88:    //   BeginData is called *before* Ix_CMessage_Box returns. The
89:    //   initial struct is cleared to zeros.
90:
91:    //   Calling CollectPaneValues copies the initial values you set
92:    //   in Visual Architect from the panes. This lets you
93:    //   use these values as the starting point every time the dialog
94:    //   is run. If you want to use values determined by your program
95:    //   instead, omit this call.
```

continues

Listing 21.2. continued

```
 96:
 97:        CollectPaneValues(*initial);
 98:
 99: //     Add code to replace some or all of the initial pane values
100: //     below.
101:
102: }
103:
104:
105: /****************************************************************
106:    UpdateData
107:
108: React to changes by the user (or the program)
109: ****************************************************************/
110:
111: void CMessage_Box::UpdateData(CMessage_BoxUpdate *update,
112:                                    long itemNo)
113:
114: {
115: //     UpdateData is called every time the user or the program
116: //     changes the value of a dialog pane. (Changes you make to
117: //     panes during a call to UpdateData do not result in
118: //     recursive calls to UpdateData.)
119:
120: //     Override to dynamically update other program objects.
121: //     Note that *only* the value corresponding to itemNo is
122: //     present in the update record. If you need the values of
123: //     other panes, you must ask the panes for them.
124: }
125:
126:
127: /****************************************************************
128:    EndData
129:
130: Receive final values from the dialog
131: ****************************************************************/
132:
133: void CMessage_Box::EndData(CMessage_BoxData *final)
134:
135: {
136: //     The values of all panes are returned by this function,
137: //     which is called just before Close for a modeless dialog,
138: //     or just before returning from DoModalDialog.
139:
140: //     If DoModalDialog returns cmdCancel, EndData is called
141: //     with the values initially supplied to BeginData, allowing
142: //     you to back out any intermediate changes made in response
143: //     to UpdateData. If you do not use UpdateData, you can
144: //     test the value of dismissCmd to see whether to respond
145: //     to EndData.
146: }
147:
148:
149: /****************************************************************
```

```
150:    ProviderChanged      {OVERRIDE}
151:
152:    A pane changed value
153:    ****************************************************************/
154:
155:    void CMessage_Box::ProviderChanged(CCollaborator *aProvider,
156:                                           long reason, void* info)
157:
158:    {
159:    //    Override this function if you need to respond more directly
160:    //    to changes in pane values. See the superclass's
161:    //    ProviderChanged function for an example of how to check for
162:    //    changes.
163:
164:    //    Note that there is a lot of traffic through this function
165:    //    in addition to change notices. Do not forget to call the
166:    //    superclass for all changes you do not handle completely.
167:
168:        x_CMessage_Box::ProviderChanged(aProvider, reason, info);
169:    }
170:
171:
172:    /****************************************************************
173:     DoCommand {OVERRIDE}
174:
175:    Dispatch commands
176:    ****************************************************************/
177:
178:    void CMessage_Box::DoCommand(long theCommand)
179:
180:    {
181:        switch (theCommand)
182:        {
183:            // Insert your command handler cases here, e.g.,
184:            //
185:            //    case cmdMine:
186:            //        DoMyCmd();
187:            //        break;
188:
189:            default:
190:                x_CMessage_Box::DoCommand(theCommand);
191:        }
192:    }
```

Listing 21.2 contains the implementations of the member functions of class CMessage_Box. These functions have minimal code or no code at all.

Listing 21.3 shows the source code for the x_CMessage_Box.h header file for project Dialog1.

Listing 21.3. The source code for the x_CMessage_Box.h header file for project Dialog1.

```
 1: /****************************************************************
 2:  x_CMessage_Box.h
 3:
 4:              Header File For CMessage_Box Lower-Layer Dialog Class
 5:
 6:      Copyright (c) 1994 My Software Inc. All rights reserved.
 7:
 8: Generated by Visual Architect(TM)
 9:
10: This file is rewritten each time you generate code. You should
11: not make changes to this file; changes should go in the My.h
12: file, instead.
13:
14: If you want to change how Visual Architect generates this file,
15: you can change the template for this file. It is "_Dialog.h" in
16: the Visual Architect Templates folder.
17:
18: ****************************************************************/
19:
20: #pragma once
21:
22: #include "CDialogDirector.h"
23:
24: class CStaticText;
25: class CButton;
26: class CRectOvalButton;
27: class CPolyButton;
28: class CLine;
29:
30:     // Data struct for initializing dialog items
31:     // and receiving changed values
32:
33: typedef struct
34: {
35:      short fMessage_Box_Rect4;
36:      short fMessage_Box_Rect5;
37:      short fMessage_Box_Rect7;
38:      short fMessage_Box_Poly10;
39:      short fMessage_Box_Line11;
40:      short fMessage_Box_Line12;
41: } CMessage_BoxData;
42:
43:     // We define a separate struct for UpdateData() which
44:     // eliminates duplicate data types
45:
46: typedef struct
47: {
48:      Str255 stringvalue; // CDialogText
49:      long   longvalue;   // CIntegerText
50:      short  value;       // All other controls and buttons
51:      Point  selection;   // CArrayPane
52: } CMessage_BoxUpdate;
53:
```

704

```
54:   class CDirectorOwner;
55:   class CPanorama;
56:   class CPane;
57:
58:   class x_CMessage_Box : public CDialogDirector
59:   {
60:   public:
61:
62:       TCL_DECLARE_CLASS
63:
64:       // Pointers to panes in window
65:       CStaticText   *fMessage_Box_Stat1;
66:       CButton   *fMessage_Box_OkBtn;
67:       CRectOvalButton   *fMessage_Box_Rect4;
68:       CRectOvalButton   *fMessage_Box_Rect5;
69:       CRectOvalButton   *fMessage_Box_Rect7;
70:       CPolyButton   *fMessage_Box_Poly10;
71:       CLine   *fMessage_Box_Line11;
72:       CLine   *fMessage_Box_Line12;
73:
74:
75:       void Ix_CMessage_Box(CDirectorOwner *aSupervisor);
76:
77:       virtual long DoModalDialog(long defaultCmd);
78:       virtual Boolean Close(Boolean quitting);
79:       virtual void ProviderChanged(CCollaborator *aProvider,
80:                                    long reason, void* info);
81:
82:   protected:
83:       Boolean ignore;
84:       CMessage_BoxData saveData;
85:
86:       virtual void MakeNewWindow(void);
87:       virtual void BeginData(CMessage_BoxData *initial);
88:       virtual void UpdateData(CMessage_BoxUpdate *update,
89:                               long itemNo);
90:       virtual void EndData(CMessage_BoxData *final);
91:
92:       virtual void CollectPaneValues(CMessage_BoxData& data);
93:
94:
95:       CPane *FindPane(long ID);
96:
97:   private:
98:       virtual void DoBeginData(void);
99:       virtual void DoEndData(long theCommand);
100:  };
101:
102:  #define   CVueCMessage_Box   130
```

Listing 21.3 declares the class x_CMessage_Box. The Visual Architect utility generated the declarations of the structure CMessage_BoxData in lines 33 to 41. This structure contains a member that in principle should help the Message Box to

exchange data. In reality, the structure is neither needed nor used by the code. The Visual Architect utility also declared the structure CMessage_BoxUpdate in lines 46 to 52. This structure is supposed to help in updating the class instances with the data from the controls of the dialog box. The Visual Architect also generated the data members of class x_CMessage_Box in lines 65 to 72. These members are pointers to the various controls of the Message Box dialog box. In addition, the Visual Architect inserted the declarations of the Boolean data member ignore and the CMessage_BoxData structure saveData. The class also contains the declarations of member functions that invoke the modal dialog box, close the dialog box, and exchange data between the dialog box controls and the class instance.

Listing 21.4 shows the source code for the x_CMessage_Box.cp implementation file for project Dialog1.

Listing 21.4. The source code for the x_CMessage_Box.cp implementation file for project Dialog1.

```
 1:  /***************************************************************
 2:   x_CMessage_Box.c
 3:
 4:                  CMessage_Box Dialog Director Class
 5:
 6:      Copyright (c) 1994 My Software Inc. All rights reserved.
 7:
 8:  Generated by Visual Architect(TM)
 9:
10:  This file is rewritten each time you generate code. You should
11:  not make changes to this file; changes should go in the
12:  CMessage_Box.c file, instead.
13:
14:  If you want to change how Visual Architect generates this file,
15:  you can change the template for this file. It is "_Dialog_cp"
16:  in the Visual Architect Templates folder.
17:
18:  ***************************************************************/
19:
20:  #include "x_CMessage_Box.h"
21:
22:  #include "Message_BoxItems.h"
23:
24:  #include "ViewUtilities.h"
25:
26:  #include <CIntegerText.h>
27:  #include <Commands.h>
28:  #include <CControl.h>
29:  #include <CPopupMenu.h>
30:  #include <CPopupPane.h>
31:  #include <CArrayPane.h>
32:  #include <CIconButton.h>
33:  #include <CPictureButton.h>
```

```
34:    #include <CSwissArmyButton.h>
35:
36:    #include "CStaticText.h"
37:    #include "CButton.h"
38:    #include "CRectOvalButton.h"
39:    #include "CPolyButton.h"
40:    #include "CLine.h"
41:
42:
43:    #include <CApplication.h>
44:    #include <CBartender.h>
45:    #include <Commands.h>
46:    #include <Constants.h>
47:    #include <CDecorator.h>
48:    #include <CDesktop.h>
49:    #include <CDirectorOwner.h>
50:    #include <CFile.h>
51:    #include <CList.h>
52:    #include <CPanorama.h>
53:    #include <TBUtilities.h>
54:    #include <CWindow.h>
55:
56:    extern CApplication *gApplication; /* The application */
57:    extern CDecorator    *gDecorator;  /* Decorator for arranging
58:                                          windows */
59:    extern CDesktop        *gDesktop;  /* The visible Desktop */
60:    extern CBartender    *gBartender;  /* Manages all menus */
61:
62:        // Define symbols for commands handled by this class
63:        // Prevents a recompile every time any command changed.
64:
65:
66:    TCL_DEFINE_CLASS_M1(x_CMessage_Box, CDialogDirector);
67:
68:    /**** C O N S T R U C T I O N / D E S T R U C T I O N
69:                                        M E T H O D S ****/
70:
71:
72:    /*****************************************************************
73:     Ix_CMessage_Box
74:
75:    Initialize the dialog
76:    *****************************************************************/
77:
78:    void x_CMessage_Box::Ix_CMessage_Box(CDirectorOwner *aSupervisor)
79:
80:    {
81:        IDialogDirector(aSupervisor);
82:
83:        // There are several circumstances where we don't want
84:        // ProviderChanged to be called. During initialization,
85:        // during calls to UpdateData, etc. The ignore flag
86:        // heads these off.
87:
88:        ignore = TRUE;  /* Don't call UpdateData now  */
```

continues

Listing 21.4. continued

```
 89:
 90:      MakeNewWindow(); /* Create the dialog's window  */
 91:
 92:      DoBeginData();    /* Gather initial values */
 93:
 94:      ignore = FALSE;
 95: }
 96:
 97:
 98: /****************************************************************
 99:  MakeNewWindow
100:
101: Create a window by reading a view resource
102: ****************************************************************/
103:
104: void x_CMessage_Box::MakeNewWindow(void)
105:
106: {
107:   itsWindow = TCLGetNamedWindow("\pMessage Box", this);
108:
109:   // Initialize pointers to the subpanes in the window
110:
111:   fMessage_Box_Stat1 = (CStaticText*)
112:                    FindPane(kMessage_Box_Stat1ID);
113:   ASSERT(member(fMessage_Box_Stat1, CStaticText));
114:
115:   fMessage_Box_OkBtn = (CButton*)
116:                    FindPane(kMessage_Box_OkBtnID);
117:   ASSERT(member(fMessage_Box_OkBtn, CButton));
118:
119:   fMessage_Box_Rect4 = (CRectOvalButton*)
120:                    FindPane(kMessage_Box_Rect4ID);
121:   ASSERT(member(fMessage_Box_Rect4, CRectOvalButton));
122:
123:   fMessage_Box_Rect5 = (CRectOvalButton*)
124:                    FindPane(kMessage_Box_Rect5ID);
125:   ASSERT(member(fMessage_Box_Rect5, CRectOvalButton));
126:
127:   fMessage_Box_Rect7 = (CRectOvalButton*)
128:                    FindPane(kMessage_Box_Rect7ID);
129:   ASSERT(member(fMessage_Box_Rect7, CRectOvalButton));
130:
131:   fMessage_Box_Poly10 = (CPolyButton*)
132:                     FindPane(kMessage_Box_Poly10ID);
133:   ASSERT(member(fMessage_Box_Poly10, CPolyButton));
134:
135:   fMessage_Box_Line11 = (CLine*)
136:                     FindPane(kMessage_Box_Line11ID);
137:   ASSERT(member(fMessage_Box_Line11, CLine));
138:
139:   fMessage_Box_Line12 = (CLine*)
140:                     FindPane(kMessage_Box_Line12ID);
141:   ASSERT(member(fMessage_Box_Line12, CLine));
142:
```

```
143:    }
144:
145:
146:    /*****************************************************************
147:      FindPane
148:
149:    Locate a subpane of this window by ID. Note that Visual
150:    Architect-generated IDs are unique within a project, so
151:    this function will find panes within subviews, even if
152:    dynamically loaded.
153:    *****************************************************************/
154:
155:    CPane *x_CMessage_Box::FindPane(long ID)
156:
157:    {
158:        return (CPane*) itsWindow->FindViewByID(ID);
159:    }
160:
161:
162:    /*****************************************************************
163:      DoBeginData
164:
165:    Collect initial values from subclass and initialize panes
166:    *****************************************************************/
167:
168:    void x_CMessage_Box::DoBeginData()
169:
170:    {
171:        CMessage_BoxData data = {0}; /* The initial value record */
172:
173:        BeginData(&data); /* Ask subclass for initial values */
174:
175:        // Initialize the panes based on the values supplied.
176:        // The ASSERT statements ensure that the generated
177:        // code is in synch with the view resource.
178:
179:        // Save the initial values in case user cancels
180:
181:        saveData = data;
182:    }
183:
184:
185:    /*****************************************************************
186:      DoEndData
187:
188:    Collect final values from panes and tell subclass
189:    *****************************************************************/
190:
191:    void x_CMessage_Box::DoEndData(long theCommand)
192:
193:    {
194:        CMessage_BoxData data; /* The initial value record */
195:        RgnHandle rgn; /* Selection region  */
196:
197:        /* If user canceled the dialog,  */
```

21

continues

Listing 21.4. continued

```
198:      /*     return the initial values   */
199:      if (theCommand == cmdCancel)
200:      {
201:          data = saveData;
202:          EndData(&data);
203:          return;
204:      }
205:
206:      CollectPaneValues(data); // Get current pane values
207:
208:      EndData(&data); // Tell the derived class
209: }
210:
211:
212: /****************************************************************
213:   CollectPaneValues
214:
215: Collect final values from panes and tell subclass
216: ****************************************************************/
217:
218: void x_CMessage_Box::CollectPaneValues(CMessage_BoxData& data)
219:
220: {
221:      RgnHandle rgn; /* Selection region  */
222:
223:      /* Collect values from panes  */
224: }
225:
226:
227: /****************************************************************
228:   BeginData
229:
230: Collect initial values from subclass and initialize panes.
231: The default function does nothing.
232: ****************************************************************/
233:
234: void x_CMessage_Box::BeginData(CMessage_BoxData *initial)
235:
236: {
237: }
238:
239:
240: /****************************************************************
241:   UpdateData
242:
243: Tell subclass when panes change
244: ****************************************************************/
245:
246: void x_CMessage_Box::UpdateData(CMessage_BoxUpdate *update,
247:                                     long itemNo)
248:
249: {
250: }
251:
```

```
252:
253:   /***************************************************************
254:    EndData
255:
256:   Tell subclass the final values. For a canceled modal dialog,
257:        these are the same as the initial values.
258:   ***************************************************************/
259:
260:   void x_CMessage_Box::EndData(CMessage_BoxData *final)
261:
262:   {
263:   }
264:
265:
266:   /***************************************************************
267:    DoModalDialog     {OVERRIDE}
268:
269:        Override to call EndData
270:   ***************************************************************/
271:
272:   long x_CMessage_Box::DoModalDialog(long defaultCmd)
273:
274:   {
275:        long result = CDialogDirector::DoModalDialog(defaultCmd);
276:
277:        DoEndData(result);
278:        return result;
279:   }
280:
281:
282:   /***************************************************************
283:    Close {OVERRIDE}
284:
285:   Override to call EndData
286:   ***************************************************************/
287:
288:   Boolean x_CMessage_Box::Close(Boolean quitting)
289:
290:   {
291:        if (itsWindow && !itsWindow->active)
292:            itsWindow->Select();
293:
294:        if (EndDialog(cmdOK, TRUE))
295:        {
296:            /* For a modal dialog, exit through */
297:            if (itsWindow->IsModal()) /* DoModalDialog  */
298:            {
299:                dismissCmd = cmdClose;
300:                return TRUE;
301:            }
302:            else
303:            {
304:                                    /* Collect final values and call */
305:                DoEndData(cmdOK); /*     EndData */
306:                                    /* Do the Close */
```

continues

711

Listing 21.4. continued

```
307:                    return CDialogDirector::Close(quitting);
308:             }
309:         }
310:     else
311:         return FALSE;
312: }
313:
314:
315: /****************************************************************
316:   ProviderChanged     {OVERRIDE}
317:
318: User did something. Note that the TCL
319: does not currently report changes to plain CEditText items.
320: ****************************************************************/
321:
322: void x_CMessage_Box::ProviderChanged(CCollaborator *aProvider,
323:                                     long reason, void* info)
324:
325: {
326:     CMessage_BoxUpdate data; /* The update value record */
327:     Str255 str;
328:     Boolean saveIgnore = ignore;
329:
330:     if (ignore) /* Don't be a chatterbox */
331:         return;
332:     ignore = TRUE;
333:
334:     TRY
335:     {
336:         if (FALSE) {}
337:         else
338:             CDialogDirector::ProviderChanged(aProvider, reason,
339:                                             info);
340:     }
341:     CATCH
342:         ignore = saveIgnore;
343:     ENDTRY
344:
345:     ignore = saveIgnore; /* ProviderChanged() can't Close()! */
346: }
```

Listing 21.4 shows the implementation for the member functions of class x_CMessage_Box. Because the code for these functions is very similar to those of the more interesting Sample Dialog dialog box, I discuss only the implementation of the Sample Dialog dialog box here.

Listing 21.5 shows the source code for the CSample_DialogBox.h header file for the Dialog1 program project.

Listing 21.5. The source code for the CSample_Dialog.h header file for project Dialog1.

```
1:  /****************************************************************
2:  CSample_Dialog.h
3:
4:                  CSample_Dialog Dialog Director Class
5:
6:      Copyright (c) 1994 My Software Inc. All rights reserved.
7:
8:  Generated by Visual Architect(TM) 9:21 PM Thu, Jun 23, 1994
9:
10: This file is only generated once. You can modify it by filling
11: in the placeholder functions and adding any new functions you
12: wish.
13:
14: If you change the name of the dialog class, a fresh version of
15: this file will be generated. If you have made any changes to
16: the file with the old name, you will have to copy those changes
17: to the new file by hand.
18:
19: ****************************************************************/
20:
21: #pragma once
22:
23: #include "x_CSample_Dialog.h"
24:
25:
26: class CDirectorOwner;
27:
28: class CSample_Dialog : public x_CSample_Dialog
29: {
30: public:
31:
32:     TCL_DECLARE_CLASS
33:
34:     // Insert your own public data members here
35:
36:     void ICSample_Dialog(CDirectorOwner *aSupervisor);
37:
38:     virtual void ProviderChanged(CCollaborator *aProvider,
39:                                   long reason, void* info);
40:     virtual void DoCommand(long theCommand);
41:
42: protected:
43:
44:     virtual void BeginData(CSample_DialogData *initial);
45:     virtual void UpdateData(CSample_DialogUpdate *update,
46:                              long itemNo);
47:     virtual void EndData(CSample_DialogData *final);
48: };
```

21

Listing 21.5 shows that class `CSampleDialog` is a descendant of `x_CSampleDialog`. The class `CSampleDialog` declares the member functions `ICSample_Dialog`, `ProviderChanged`, `DoCommand`, `BeginData`, `UpdateData`, and `EndData`. The last three functions handle the data-exchange mechanism between the class instances and the dialog box.

Listing 21.6 shows the source code for the CSample_Dialog.cp implementation file for project Dialog1. The bold lines indicate the ones that I manually inserted to customize the program.

Listing 21.6. The source code for the CSample_Dialog.cp implementation file for project Dialog1.

```
 1:  /****************************************************************
 2:   CSample_Dialog.c
 3:
 4:                  CSample_Dialog Dialog Director Class
 5:
 6:      Copyright (c) 1994 My Software Inc. All rights reserved.
 7:
 8:  Generated by Visual Architect(TM) 9:21 PM Thu, Jun 23, 1994
 9:
10:  This file is only generated once. You can modify it by filling
11:  in the placeholder functions and adding any new functions you
12:  wish.
13:
14:  If you change the name of the dialog class, a fresh version of
15:  this file will be generated. If you have made any changes to the
16:  file with the old name, you will have to copy those changes to
17:  the new file by hand.
18:
19:  ****************************************************************/
20:
21:  #include "CSample_Dialog.h"
22:
23:  #include "Sample_DialogItems.h"
24:  //#include "AppCommands.h"  // Remove comments if
25:                             // DoCommand overridden
26:
27:  #include <CIntegerText.h>
28:  #include <CControl.h>
29:  #include <CPopupMenu.h>
30:  #include <CPopupPane.h>
31:  #include <CArrayPane.h>
32:  #include <CIconButton.h>
33:  #include <CPictureButton.h>
34:  #include <CSwissArmyButton.h>
35:
36:  #include <CApplication.h>
37:  #include <Constants.h>
38:  #include <CDecorator.h>
39:  #include <CDesktop.h>
```

```
40:    #include <CDirectorOwner.h>
41:    #include <CFile.h>
42:    #include <TBUtilities.h>
43:    #include <CWindow.h>
44:
45:    extern CApplication *gApplication;   /* The application */
46:    extern CDecorator    *gDecorator;    /* Decorator for arranging
47:                                            windows*/
48:    extern CDesktop         *gDesktop;   /* The visible Desktop */
49:
50:
51:    TCL_DEFINE_CLASS_M1(CSample_Dialog, x_CSample_Dialog);
52:
53:    /**** C O N S T R U C T I O N / D E S T R U C T I O N
54:                                        M E T H O D S ****/
55:
56:
57:    /****************************************************************
58:     ICSample_Dialog
59:
60:    Initialize the dialog
61:
62:    ****************************************************************/
63:
64:    void CSample_Dialog::ICSample_Dialog(CDirectorOwner *aSupervisor)
65:
66:    {
67:        // Initialize data members that must be set up before
68:        // BeginData is called here
69:
70:        x_CSample_Dialog::Ix_CSample_Dialog(aSupervisor);
71:
72:        // Initialize any other data members here
73:
74:    }
75:
76:
77:    /****************************************************************
78:     BeginData
79:
80:    Set up initial pane values
81:    ****************************************************************/
82:
83:    void CSample_Dialog::BeginData(CSample_DialogData *initial)
84:
85:    {
86:    //    Base class calls BeginData once after the window is created
87:    //    to gather the initial values for the dialog panes. Note that
88:    //    BeginData is called *before* Ix_CSample_Dialog returns. The
89:    //    initial struct is cleared to zeros.
90:
91:    //    Calling CollectPaneValues copies the initial values you set
92:    //    in Visual Architect from the panes. This lets you
93:    //    use these values as the starting point every time the dialog
94:    //    is run. If you want to use values determined by your program
```

continues

715

Listing 21.6. continued

```
95:  //     instead, omit this call.
96:
97:      if (firstTime) {
98:        CollectPaneValues(*initial);
99:        saveData = *initial;
100:     }
101:
102: //     Add code to replace some or all of the initial pane values
103: //     below.
104:      else {
105:        *initial = saveData;
106:      }
107:      firstTime = FALSE;
108: }
109:
110:
111: /****************************************************************
112:   UpdateData
113:
114:       React to changes by the user (or the program)
115: ****************************************************************/
116:
117: void CSample_Dialog::UpdateData(CSample_DialogUpdate *update,
118:                                 long itemNo)
119: {
120: //     UpdateData is called every time the user or the program
121: //     changes the value of a dialog pane. (Changes you make to
122: //     panes during a call to UpdateData do not result in
123: //     recursive calls to UpdateData.)
124:
125: //     Override to dynamically update other program objects.
126: //     Note that *only* the value corresponding to itemNo is
127: //     present in the update record. If you need the values of
128: //     other panes, you must ask the panes for them.
129: }
130:
131:
132: /****************************************************************
133:   EndData
134:
135:       Receive final values from the dialog
136: ****************************************************************/
137:
138: void CSample_Dialog::EndData(CSample_DialogData *final)
139:
140: {
141: //     The values of all panes are returned by this function,
142: //     which is called just before Close for a modeless dialog,
143: //     or just before returning from DoModalDialog.
144:
145: //     If DoModalDialog returns cmdCancel, EndData is called
146: //     with the values initially supplied to BeginData, allowing
147: //     you to back out any intermediate changes made in response
148: //     to UpdateData. If you do not use UpdateData, you can
```

```
149:  //    test the value of dismissCmd to see whether to respond
150:  //    to EndData.
151:          saveData = *final;
152:  }
153:
154:
155:  /****************************************************************
156:   ProviderChanged      {OVERRIDE}
157:
158:      A pane changed value
159:  ****************************************************************
160:
161:  void CSample_Dialog::ProviderChanged(CCollaborator *aProvider,
162:                                       long reason, void* info)
163:
164:  {
165:  //    Override this function if you need to respond more directly
166:  //    to changes in pane values. See the superclass's
167:  //    ProviderChanged function for an example of how to check for
168:  //    changes.
169:
170:  //    Note that there is a lot of traffic through this function
171:  //    in addition to change notices. Do not forget to call the
172:  //    superclass for all changes you do not handle completely.
173:
174:      x_CSample_Dialog::ProviderChanged(aProvider, reason, info);
175:  }
176:
177:
178:  /****************************************************************
179:   DoCommand {OVERRIDE}
180:
181:  Dispatch commands
182:  ****************************************************************/
183:
184:  void CSample_Dialog::DoCommand(long theCommand)
185:
186:  {
187:      switch (theCommand)
188:      {
189:          // Insert your command handler cases here, e.g.,
190:          //
191:          //    case cmdMine:
192:          //        DoMyCmd();
193:          //        break;
194:
195:          default:
196:              x_CSample_Dialog::DoCommand(theCommand);
197:      }
198:  }
```

Listing 21.6 contains the implementations of the member functions of class
CMessage_Box. The next two subsections discuss the relevant member functions.

The Function *BeginData*

The member function BeginData (defined in lines 83 to 100) gathers the initial values from the controls. The Visual Architect utility generated a version of function BeginData that simply invokes the function CollectPaneValue to obtain the same initial values from the controls. This kind of default response prevents the dialog box from displaying the latest values in subsequent invocations. Instead, the dialog box displays the same initial values.

I customized the code for function BeginData to enable the dialog box to remember the most recent data. The if statement in line 97 examines the value in the inherited static Boolean data member firstTime. If this member contains a non-zero value, the function executes the statements in lines 98 and 99. The statement in line 98 collects the initial data from the controls in the dialog box. Line 99 saves that data in the inherited static data member saveData. The function executes the else clause in line 104 when the member firstTime is zero. Line 105 copies the data from the static data member saveData to the data accessed by pointer initial. Line 107 assigns FALSE to the data member firstTime.

The Function *EndData*

The member function EndData stores the values of the dialog box controls in the inherited static data member saveData. The function simply copies the data accessed by parameter final into member saveData.

Listing 21.7 shows the source code for the x_CSample_Dialog.h header file for project Dialog1. The bold lines indicate the ones that I either manually inserted or modified.

Listing 21.7. The source code for the x_CSample_Dialog.h header file for project Dialog1.

```
 1:  /************************************************************
 2:  x_CSample_Dialog.h
 3:
 4:            Header File For CSample_Dialog Lower-Layer Dialog Class
 5:
 6:      Copyright (c) 1994 My Software Inc. All rights reserved.
 7:
 8:  Generated by Visual Architect(TM)
 9:
10:  This file is rewritten each time you generate code. You should
11:  not make changes to this file; changes should go in the My.h
12:  file, instead.
13:
```

```
14:   If you want to change how Visual Architect generates this file,
15:   you can change the template for this file. It is "_Dialog.h" in
16:   the Visual Architect Templates folder.
17:
18:   ****************************************************************/
19:
20:   #pragma once
21:
22:   #include "CDialogDirector.h"
23:
24:   class CStaticText;
25:   class CDialogText;
26:   class CRectOvalButton;
27:   class CRadioControl;
28:   class CCheckBox;
29:   class CButton;
30:
31:       // Data struct for initializing dialog items
32:       // and receiving changed values
33:
34:   typedef struct
35:   {
36:       /* Dialog text */
37:       Str255 fSample_Dialog_FindBox;
38:       /* Dialog text */
39:       Str255 fSample_Dialog_ReplaceBox;
40:       short fSample_Dialog_Rect5;
41:       /* Control (radio or checkbox) */
42:       short fSample_Dialog_ForwardRbt;
43:       /* Control (radio or checkbox) */
44:       short fSample_Dialog_BackwardRbt;
45:       /* Control (radio or checkbox) */
46:       short fSample_Dialog_EntireRbt;
47:       /* Control (radio or checkbox) */
48:       short fSample_Dialog_WholeWordChk;
49:       /* Control (radio or checkbox) */
50:       short fSample_Dialog_CaseSenseChk;
51:   } CSample_DialogData;
52:
53:       // We define a separate struct for UpdateData() which
54:       // eliminates duplicate data types
55:
56:   typedef struct
57:   {
58:       Str255 stringvalue; // CDialogText
59:       long longvalue;     // CIntegerText
60:       short value;        // All other controls and buttons
61:       Point selection;    // CArrayPane
62:   } CSample_DialogUpdate;
63:
64:   class CDirectorOwner;
65:   class CPanorama;
66:   class CPane;
67:
68:   class x_CSample_Dialog : public CDialogDirector
```

21

continues

719

Listing 21.7. continued

```
 69:    {
 70:    public:
 71:
 72:            TCL_DECLARE_CLASS
 73:
 74:            // Pointers to panes in window
 75:            CStaticText      *fSample_Dialog_FindLbl;
 76:            CStaticText      *fSample_Dialog_ReplaceLbl;
 77:            CDialogText      *fSample_Dialog_FindBox;
 78:            CDialogText      *fSample_Dialog_ReplaceBox;
 79:            CRectOvalButton     *fSample_Dialog_Rect5;
 80:            CRadioControl     *fSample_Dialog_ForwardRbt;
 81:            CRadioControl     *fSample_Dialog_BackwardRbt;
 82:            CRadioControl     *fSample_Dialog_EntireRbt;
 83:            CCheckBox      *fSample_Dialog_WholeWordChk;
 84:            CCheckBox      *fSample_Dialog_CaseSenseChk;
 85:            CButton      *fSample_Dialog_OkBtn;
 86:            CButton      *fSample_Dialog_CancelBtn;
 87:
 88:
 89:            void      Ix_CSample_Dialog(CDirectorOwner *aSupervisor);
 90:
 91:            virtual long DoModalDialog(long defaultCmd);
 92:            virtual Boolean Close(Boolean quitting);
 93:            virtual void ProviderChanged(CCollaborator *aProvider,
 94:                                              long reason, void* info);
 95:
 96:    protected:
 97:            Boolean ignore;
 98:            static CSample_DialogData saveData;
 99:            static Boolean firstTime;
100:
101:            virtual void MakeNewWindow(void);
102:            virtual void BeginData(CSample_DialogData *initial);
103:            virtual void UpdateData(CSample_DialogUpdate *update,
104:                                       long itemNo);
105:            virtual void EndData(CSample_DialogData *final);
106:
107:            virtual void CollectPaneValues(CSample_DialogData& data);
108:
109:
110:            CPane *FindPane(long ID);
111:
112:    private:
113:            virtual void DoBeginData(void);
114:            virtual void DoEndData(long theCommand);
115:    };
116:
117:    #define    CVueCSample_Dialog    129
```

 Listing 21.7 declares the class `x_CSample_dialog`. The Visual Architect utility generated the declarations of the structure `CSample_DialogData` in lines 34 to 51. This structure contains a member that enables the dialog box to exchange data with the class instance. The names of the members in this structure match the names of their corresponding dialog box controls. The Visual Architect declared the structure `CSample_DialogUpdate` in lines 56 to 62. This structure helps in updating the class instances with the data from the controls of the dialog box. The Visual Architect also generated the data members of class `x_CSample_Dialog` in lines 75 to 86. These members are pointers to the various controls of the dialog box. In addition, the Visual Architect inserted the declarations of the `Boolean` data member `ignore` in line 97 and the `CSample_DialogData` structure `saveData` in line 98.

I added the `static` keyword to the data member `saveData` to enable the class to retain the controls' data after you close the dialog box. The class also contains the declarations of member functions that invoke the modal dialog box, close the dialog box, and exchange data between the dialog box controls and the class instance.

Listing 21.8 shows the source code for the x_CSample_Dialog.cp implementation file for project Dialog1.

 Listing 21.8. The source code for the x_CSample_Dialog.cp implementation file for project Dialog1.

```
1:   /*****************************************************************
2:   x_CSample_Dialog.c
3:
4:                  CSample_Dialog Dialog Director Class
5:
6:       Copyright (c) 1994 My Software Inc. All rights reserved.
7:
8:   Generated by Visual Architect(TM)
9:
10:  This file is rewritten each time you generate code. You should
11:  not make changes to this file; changes should go in the
12:  CSample_Dialog.c file, instead.
13:
14:  If you want to change how Visual Architect generates this file,
15:  you can change the template for this file. It is "_Dialog_cp"
16:  in the Visual Architect Templates folder.
17:
18:  *****************************************************************/
19:
20:  #include "x_CSample_Dialog.h"
21:
22:  #include "Sample_DialogItems.h"
23:
24:  #include "ViewUtilities.h"
```

21

continues

Listing 21.8. continued

```
25:
26:  #include <CIntegerText.h>
27:  #include <Commands.h>
28:  #include <CControl.h>
29:  #include <CPopupMenu.h>
30:  #include <CPopupPane.h>
31:  #include <CArrayPane.h>
32:  #include <CIconButton.h>
33:  #include <CPictureButton.h>
34:  #include <CSwissArmyButton.h>
35:
36:  #include "CStaticText.h"
37:  #include "CDialogText.h"
38:  #include "CRectOvalButton.h"
39:  #include "CRadioControl.h"
40:  #include "CCheckBox.h"
41:  #include "CButton.h"
42:
43:
44:  #include <CApplication.h>
45:  #include <CBartender.h>
46:  #include <Commands.h>
47:  #include <Constants.h>
48:  #include <CDecorator.h>
49:  #include <CDesktop.h>
50:  #include <CDirectorOwner.h>
51:  #include <CFile.h>
52:  #include <CList.h>
53:  #include <CPanorama.h>
54:  #include <TBUtilities.h>
55:  #include <CWindow.h>
56:
57:  extern CApplication *gApplication; /* The application */
58:  extern CDecorator    *gDecorator; /* Decorator for arranging
59:                                         windows */
60:  extern CDesktop        *gDesktop; /* The visible Desktop */
61:  extern CBartender    *gBartender; /* Manages all menus */
62:
63:      // Define symbols for commands handled by this class
64:      // Prevents a recompile every time any command changed.
65:
66:  Boolean x_CSample_Dialog::firstTime = TRUE;
67:  CSample_DialogData x_CSample_Dialog::saveData = { 0 };
68:
69:  TCL_DEFINE_CLASS_M1(x_CSample_Dialog, CDialogDirector);
70:
71:  /**** C O N S T R U C T I O N / D E S T R U C T I O N
72:                                      M E T H O D S ****/
73:
74:
75:  /****************************************************************
76:   Ix_CSample_Dialog
77:
```

```
78:    Initialize the dialog
79:    ***********************************************************/
80:
81:    void x_CSample_Dialog::Ix_CSample_Dialog(
82:                            CDirectorOwner *aSupervisor)
83:
84:    {
85:        IDialogDirector(aSupervisor);
86:
87:        // There are several circumstances where we don't want
88:        // ProviderChanged to be called. During initialization,
89:        // during calls to UpdateData, etc. The ignore flag
90:        // heads these off.
91:
92:        ignore = TRUE; /* Don't call UpdateData now */
93:
94:        MakeNewWindow(); /* Create the dialog's window */
95:
96:        DoBeginData();   /* Gather initial values */
97:
98:        ignore = FALSE;
99:    }
100:
101:
102:    /***********************************************************
103:     MakeNewWindow
104:
105:    Create a window by reading a view resource
106:    ***********************************************************/
107:
108:    void x_CSample_Dialog::MakeNewWindow(void)
109:
110:    {
111:        itsWindow = TCLGetNamedWindow("\pSample Dialog", this);
112:
113:        // Initialize pointers to the subpanes in the window
114:
115:        fSample_Dialog_FindLbl = (CStaticText*)
116:                            FindPane(kSample_Dialog_FindLblID);
117:        ASSERT(member(fSample_Dialog_FindLbl, CStaticText));
118:
119:        fSample_Dialog_ReplaceLbl = (CStaticText*)
120:                            FindPane(kSample_Dialog_ReplaceLblID);
121:        ASSERT(member(fSample_Dialog_ReplaceLbl, CStaticText));
122:
123:        fSample_Dialog_FindBox = (CDialogText*)
124:                            FindPane(kSample_Dialog_FindBoxID);
125:        ASSERT(member(fSample_Dialog_FindBox, CDialogText));
126:
127:        fSample_Dialog_ReplaceBox = (CDialogText*)
128:                            FindPane(kSample_Dialog_ReplaceBoxID);
129:        ASSERT(member(fSample_Dialog_ReplaceBox, CDialogText));
130:
131:        fSample_Dialog_Rect5 = (CRectOvalButton*)
132:                            FindPane(kSample_Dialog_Rect5ID);
```

21

continues

Listing 21.8. continued

```
133:     ASSERT(member(fSample_Dialog_Rect5, CRectOvalButton));
134:
135:     fSample_Dialog_ForwardRbt = (CRadioControl*)
136:                          FindPane(kSample_Dialog_ForwardRbtID);
137:     ASSERT(member(fSample_Dialog_ForwardRbt, CRadioControl));
138:
139:     fSample_Dialog_BackwardRbt = (CRadioControl*)
140:                          FindPane(kSample_Dialog_BackwardRbtID);
141:     ASSERT(member(fSample_Dialog_BackwardRbt, CRadioControl));
142:
143:     fSample_Dialog_EntireRbt = (CRadioControl*)
144:                          FindPane(kSample_Dialog_EntireRbtID);
145:     ASSERT(member(fSample_Dialog_EntireRbt, CRadioControl));
146:
147:     fSample_Dialog_WholeWordChk = (CCheckBox*)
148:                          FindPane(kSample_Dialog_WholeWordChkID);
149:     ASSERT(member(fSample_Dialog_WholeWordChk, CCheckBox));
150:
151:     fSample_Dialog_CaseSenseChk = (CCheckBox*)
152:                          FindPane(kSample_Dialog_CaseSenseChkID);
153:     ASSERT(member(fSample_Dialog_CaseSenseChk, CCheckBox));
154:
155:     fSample_Dialog_OkBtn = (CButton*)
156:                          FindPane(kSample_Dialog_OkBtnID);
157:     ASSERT(member(fSample_Dialog_OkBtn, CButton));
158:
159:     fSample_Dialog_CancelBtn = (CButton*)
160:                          FindPane(kSample_Dialog_CancelBtnID);
161:     ASSERT(member(fSample_Dialog_CancelBtn, CButton));
162:
163: }
164:
165:
166: /*****************************************************************
167:    FindPane
168:
169: Locate a subpane of this window by ID. Note that Visual
170: Architect-generated IDs are unique within a project, so this
171: function will find panes within subviews, even if dynamically
172: loaded.
173: *****************************************************************/
174:
175: CPane *x_CSample_Dialog::FindPane(long ID)
176:
177: {
178:     return (CPane*) itsWindow->FindViewByID(ID);
179: }
180:
181:
182: /*****************************************************************
183:    DoBeginData
184:
185: Collect initial values from subclass and initialize panes
186: *****************************************************************/
```

```
187:
188:    void x_CSample_Dialog::DoBeginData()
189:
190:    {
191:        CSample_DialogData  data = {0}; /* The initial value
192:                                        record */
193:
194:        BeginData(&data); /* Ask subclass for initial values */
195:
196:        // Initialize the panes based on the values supplied.
197:        // The ASSERT statements ensure that the generated
198:        // code is in synch with the view resource.
199:
200:        fSample_Dialog_FindBox->SetTextString(
201:                                data.fSample_Dialog_FindBox);
202:
203:        fSample_Dialog_ReplaceBox->SetTextString(
204:                                data.fSample_Dialog_ReplaceBox);
205:
206:        fSample_Dialog_ForwardRbt->SetValue(
207:                                data.fSample_Dialog_ForwardRbt);
208:
209:        fSample_Dialog_BackwardRbt->SetValue(
210:                                data.fSample_Dialog_BackwardRbt);
211:
212:        fSample_Dialog_EntireRbt->SetValue(
213:                                data.fSample_Dialog_EntireRbt);
214:
215:        fSample_Dialog_WholeWordChk->SetValue(
216:                                data.fSample_Dialog_WholeWordChk);
217:
218:        fSample_Dialog_CaseSenseChk->SetValue(
219:                                data.fSample_Dialog_CaseSenseChk);
220:
221:        // Save the initial values in case user cancels
222:
223:        saveData = data;
224:    }
225:
226:
227:    /***************************************************************
228:     DoEndData
229:
230:    Collect final values from panes and tell subclass
231:    ***************************************************************/
232:
233:    void x_CSample_Dialog::DoEndData(long theCommand)
234:
235:    {
236:        CSample_DialogData data;      /* The initial value record */
237:        RgnHandle rgn; /* Selection region */
238:
239:        /* If user canceled the dialog, return the initial values */
240:        if (theCommand == cmdCancel)
241:        {
```

continues

Listing 21.8. continued

```
242:            data = saveData;
243:            EndData(&data);
244:            return;
245:        }
246:
247:        CollectPaneValues(data); // Get current pane values
248:
249:        EndData(&data); // Tell the derived class
250: }
251:
252:
253: /****************************************************************
254:   CollectPaneValues
255:
256: Collect final values from panes and tell subclass
257: ****************************************************************/
258:
259: void x_CSample_Dialog::CollectPaneValues(
260:                        CSample_DialogData& data)
261:
262: {
263:     RgnHandle rgn; /* Selection region */
264:
265:     /* Collect values from panes*/
266:     fSample_Dialog_FindBox->GetTextString(
267:                        data.fSample_Dialog_FindBox);
268:
269:     fSample_Dialog_ReplaceBox->GetTextString(
270:                        data.fSample_Dialog_ReplaceBox);
271:
272:     data.fSample_Dialog_ForwardRbt =
273:                        fSample_Dialog_ForwardRbt->GetValue();
274:
275:     data.fSample_Dialog_BackwardRbt =
276:                        fSample_Dialog_BackwardRbt->GetValue();
277:
278:     data.fSample_Dialog_EntireRbt =
279:                        fSample_Dialog_EntireRbt->GetValue();
280:
281:     data.fSample_Dialog_WholeWordChk =
282:                        fSample_Dialog_WholeWordChk->GetValue();
283:
284:     data.fSample_Dialog_CaseSenseChk =
285:                        fSample_Dialog_CaseSenseChk->GetValue();
286:
287: }
288:
289:
290: /****************************************************************
291:   BeginData
292:
293: Collect initial values from subclass and initialize panes.
294: The default function does nothing.
295: ****************************************************************/
```

```
296:
297:    void x_CSample_Dialog::BeginData(CSample_DialogData *initial)
298:
299:    {
300:    }
301:
302:
303:    /*****************************************************************
304:      UpdateData
305:
306:          Tell subclass when panes change
307:    *****************************************************************/
308:
309:    void x_CSample_Dialog::UpdateData(CSample_DialogUpdate *update,
310:                                      long itemNo)
311:
312:    {
313:    }
314:
315:
316:    /*****************************************************************
317:      EndData
318:
319:    Tell subclass the final values. For a canceled modal dialog,
320:    these are the same as the initial values.
321:    *****************************************************************/
322:
323:    void x_CSample_Dialog::EndData(CSample_DialogData *final)
324:
325:    {
326:    }
327:
328:
329:    /*****************************************************************
330:      DoModalDialog     {OVERRIDE}
331:
332:    Override to call EndData
333:    *****************************************************************/
334:
335:    long x_CSample_Dialog::DoModalDialog(long defaultCmd)
336:
337:    {
338:        long result = CDialogDirector::DoModalDialog(defaultCmd);
339:
340:        DoEndData(result);
341:        return result;
342:    }
343:
344:
345:    /*****************************************************************
346:      Close {OVERRIDE}
347:
348:    Override to call EndData
349:    *****************************************************************/
350:
```

continues

21

Listing 21.8. continued

```
351:  Boolean x_CSample_Dialog::Close(Boolean quitting)
352:
353:  {
354:      if (itsWindow && !itsWindow->active)
355:          itsWindow->Select();
356:
357:      if (EndDialog(cmdOK, TRUE))
358:      {
359:          /* For a modal dialog, exit through DoModalDialog */
360:          if (itsWindow->IsModal())
361:          {
362:              dismissCmd = cmdClose;
363:              return TRUE;
364:          }
365:          else
366:          {
367:                                     /* Collect final values and call */
368:              DoEndData(cmdOK);   /*     EndData */
369:                                     /* Do the Close */
370:              return CDialogDirector::Close(quitting);
371:          }
372:      }
373:      else
374:          return FALSE;
375:  }
376:
377:
378:  /****************************************************************
379:   ProviderChanged      {OVERRIDE}
380:
381:  User did something. Note that the TCL
382:  does not currently report changes to plain CEditText items.
383:  ****************************************************************/
384:
385:  void x_CSample_Dialog::ProviderChanged(CCollaborator *aProvider,
386:                                          long reason, void* info)
387:
388:  {
389:      CSample_DialogUpdate data;    /* The update value record */
390:      Str255 str;
391:      Boolean saveIgnore = ignore;
392:
393:      if (ignore) /* Don't be a chatterbox */
394:          return;
395:      ignore = TRUE;
396:
397:      TRY
398:      {
399:          if (FALSE) {}
400:          else if (reason == dialogTextChanged
401:                  && aProvider == fSample_Dialog_FindBox)
402:          {
403:              ((CDialogText*) aProvider)->GetTextString(
404:                                          data.stringvalue);
```

```
405:                    UpdateData(&data, kSample_Dialog_FindBoxID);
406:                }
407:            else if (reason == dialogTextChanged
408:                    && aProvider == fSample_Dialog_ReplaceBox)
409:                {
410:                    ((CDialogText*) aProvider)->GetTextString(
411:                                            data.stringvalue);
412:                    UpdateData(&data, kSample_Dialog_ReplaceBoxID);
413:                }
414:            else if (reason == controlValueChanged
415:                    && aProvider == fSample_Dialog_ForwardRbt)
416:                {
417:                    data.value = *(short*) info;
418:                    UpdateData(&data, kSample_Dialog_ForwardRbtID);
419:                }
420:            else if (reason == controlValueChanged
421:                    && aProvider == fSample_Dialog_BackwardRbt)
422:                {
423:                    data.value = *(short*) info;
424:                    UpdateData(&data, kSample_Dialog_BackwardRbtID);
425:                }
426:            else if (reason == controlValueChanged
427:                    && aProvider == fSample_Dialog_EntireRbt)
428:                {
429:                    data.value = *(short*) info;
430:                    UpdateData(&data, kSample_Dialog_EntireRbtID);
431:                }
432:            else if (reason == controlValueChanged
433:                    && aProvider == fSample_Dialog_WholeWordChk)
434:                {
435:                    data.value = *(short*) info;
436:                    UpdateData(&data, kSample_Dialog_WholeWordChkID);
437:                }
438:            else if (reason == controlValueChanged
439:                    && aProvider == fSample_Dialog_CaseSenseChk)
440:                {
441:                    data.value = *(short*) info;
442:                    UpdateData(&data, kSample_Dialog_CaseSenseChkID);
443:                }
444:            else
445:                CDialogDirector::ProviderChanged(aProvider, reason,
446:                                            info);
447:        }
448:    CATCH
449:        ignore = saveIgnore;
450:    ENDTRY
451:
452:    ignore = saveIgnore; /* ProviderChanged() can't Close()! */
453: }
```

21

Analysis

Listing 21.8 shows the implementation for the member functions of class x_CSample_Dialog. The next five subsections discuss the relevant member functions of this class.

The Function *Ix_CSample_Dialog*

The member function Ix_CSample_Dialog initializes the instances of class CSample_Dialog. Line 85 invokes function IDialogDirector to initialize the dialog director. Line 92 assigns TRUE to data member ignore to prevent calling member function UpdateData. Line 94 creates the dialog box window by calling function MakeNewWindow. Line 96 calls function DoBeginData to collect the initial values from the controls. Line 98 assigns FALSE to data member ignore.

The Function *MakeNewWindow*

The member function MakeNewWindow (defined in lines 108 to 163) creates the dialog box window. It assigns the address of the dialog box window to member itsWindow, and then assigns the address of the controls to their respective data members. Each assignment involves calling the function FindPane.

The Function *DoBeginData*

The member function DoBeginData starts by copying data to the controls. Line 191 declares the local CSample_DialogData structure data and initializes it with zeros. Line 194 requests the data by calling function BeginData. The argument for this call is the address of variable data. The function then assigns the strings to the edit box by sending the SetTextString messages to these controls. The arguments for these messages are the members of variable data that store the values for the edit boxes. The function also sets the values of the check boxes and radio controls by sending the C++ message SetValue to these controls. The arguments for these messages are the members of variable data that store the states of these controls. Line 223 copies the values in variable data into the static data member saveData.

The Function *DoEndData*

The member function DoEndData copies data from the dialog box controls to the data member saveData. The if statement in line 240 determines whether or not you clicked the Cancel button. If this condition is true, the function throws away the updated control data by copying the contents of member saveData to the local structured variable data. The function DoEndData then invokes function EndData and passes it the address of variable data as the argument. Finally, the function exits.

On the other hand, when the condition of the `if` statement is false, the function `DoEndData` invokes the function `CollectPaneValues` to get the current control values. The argument for this function call is the structured variable `data`. The function `DoEndData` then calls function `EndData` with the address of structured variable `data` as the argument.

The Function *CollectPaneValues*

The member function `CollectPaneValues` (defined in lines 259 to 287) copies the data from the controls to the members of the parameter `data` (which is a `CSample_DialogData` structure). The function copies the text in the edit boxes by sending the C++ message `GetTextString` to these controls. The function then copies the states of the check boxes and radio controls by sending these functions the C++ message `GetValue`.

Listing 21.9 contains the source code for the x_CMain.h header file for project Dialog1.

Listing 21.9. The source code for the x_CMain.h header file for project Dialog1.

```
 1:  /*****************************************************************
 2:  x_CMain.h
 3:
 4:              Header File For CMain Lower-Layer Document Class
 5:
 6:      Copyright (c) 1994 My Software Inc. All rights reserved.
 7:
 8:  Generated by Visual Architect(TM)
 9:
10:  This file is rewritten each time you generate code. You should
11:  not make changes to this file; changes should go in the My.h
12:  file, instead.
13:
14:  If you want to change how Visual Architect generates this file,
15:  you can change the template for this file. It is "_Doc.h" in the
16:  Visual Architect Templates folder.
17:
18:  *****************************************************************/
19:
20:  #pragma once
21:
22:  #include "CSaver.h"
23:  class CButton;
24:
25:  #include "ItsContentsClass.h"
26:
27:  #define x_CMain_super       CSaver<ITSCONTENTSCLASS>
28:
29:  class CFile;
```

continues

Listing 21.9. continued

```
30:
31:    class x_CMain : public x_CMain_super
32:
33:    {
34:    public:
35:
36:        TCL_DECLARE_CLASS
37:
38:        // Pointers to panes in window
39:        CButton    *fMain_TestDlgBtn;
40:        CButton    *fMain_QuitBtn;
41:        CButton    *fMain_MessageBtn;
42:
43:        void       Ix_CMain(void);
44:
45:        virtual    void    DoCommand(long theCommand);
46:        virtual    void    UpdateMenus(void);
47:
48:    protected:
49:        virtual void    MakeNewWindow(void);
50:
51:        virtual void    FailOpen(CFile *aFile);
52:        virtual void    PositionWindow(void);
53:
54:        virtual void    DoCmdTestDialog(void);
55:        virtual void    DoCmdShowMsgDlg(void);
56:    };
57:
58:    #define    CVueCMain    128
```

 Listing 21.9 shows the declaration of class x_CMain. This class contains a number of data members and member functions, all emitted by the Visual Architect utility. Lines 39 to 41 define the various data members which are pointers to the different buttons. These members are pointers to the class CButton. The class x_CMain contains the sets of member functions DoCmdTestDialog and DoCmdShowMsgDlg, which respond to the custom commands cmdTestDialog and cmdShowMsgDlg, respectively.

Listing 21.10 shows the source code for the x_CMain.cp implementation file for project Dialog1.

Listing 21.10. The source code for the x_CMain.cp implementation file for project Dialog1.

```
1:    /*************************************************************
2:    x_CMain.c
3:
4:                CMain Document Class
5:
```

```
 6:        Copyright (c) 1994 My Software Inc. All rights reserved.
 7:
 8:   Generated by Visual Architect(TM) 10:14 PM Thu, Jun 23, 1994
 9:
10:   This file is rewritten each time you generate code. You should
11:   not make changes to this file; changes should go in the My.c
12:   file, instead.
13:
14:   If you want to change how Visual Architect generates this file,
15:   you can change the template for this file. It is "_Doc_cp" in
16:   the Visual Architect Templates folder.
17:
18:   *****************************************************************/
19:
20:   #include "x_CMain.h"
21:
22:   #include "CMain.h"
23:
24:   #include "MainItems.h"
25:
26:   #include "ViewUtilities.h"
27:   #include "CSample_Dialog.h"
28:   #include "CMessage_Box.h"
29:   #include "CApp.h"
30:
31:   #include <CApplication.h>
32:   #include <CBartender.h>
33:   #include <Commands.h>
34:   #include <Constants.h>
35:   #include <CDecorator.h>
36:   #include <CDesktop.h>
37:   #include <CFile.h>
38:   #include <TBUtilities.h>
39:   #include <CWindow.h>
40:
41:   extern CApplication *gApplication; /* The application */
42:   extern CDecorator    *gDecorator;  /* Decorator for arranging
43:                                         windows */
44:   extern CDesktop       *gDesktop;   /* The visible Desktop */
45:   extern CBartender    *gBartender;  /* Manages all menus */
46:
47:   #include "CButton.h"
48:
49:       // Define symbols for commands handled by this class
50:       // Prevents a recompile every time any command changed.
51:
52:   #define cmdTestDialog 512
53:   #define cmdShowMsgDlg 513
54:
55:
56:   TCL_DEFINE_CLASS_M1(x_CMain, x_CMain_super);
57:
58:   /**** C O N S T R U C T I O N / D E S T R U C T I O N
59:                                       M E T H O D S ****/
60:
```

continues

Listing 21.10. continued

```
61:
62:  /*****************************************************************
63:   Ix_CMain
64:
65:  Initialize the document
66:  *****************************************************************/
67:
68:  void x_CMain::Ix_CMain()
69:
70:  {
71:      IDocument(gApplication, TRUE);
72:
73:          // Initialize data members below.
74:  }
75:
76:
77:  /*****************************************************************
78:   MakeNewWindow
79:
80:  Create a new, empty window.  Subclass may override to populate
81:  the new window.
82:  *****************************************************************/
83:
84:  void x_CMain::MakeNewWindow(void)
85:
86:  {
87:    itsWindow = TCLGetNamedWindow("\pMain", this);
88:
89:    itsMainPane = (CPane*) TCLGetItemPointer(itsWindow, 0);
90:
91:    // Initialize pointers to the subpanes in the window
92:
93:    fMain_TestDlgBtn = (CButton*)
94:                          itsWindow->FindViewByID(kMain_TestDlgBtnID);
95:    ASSERT(member(fMain_TestDlgBtn, CButton));
96:
97:    fMain_QuitBtn = (CButton*)
98:                          itsWindow->FindViewByID(kMain_QuitBtnID);
99:    ASSERT(member(fMain_QuitBtn, CButton));
100:
101:    fMain_MessageBtn = (CButton*)
102:                          itsWindow->FindViewByID(kMain_MessageBtnID);
103:    ASSERT(member(fMain_MessageBtn, CButton));
104:
105:  }
106:
107:
108:  /*****************************************************************
109:   FailOpen {OVERRIDE}
110:
111:  Fail if file already open in this application.
112:
113:  This function calls the application's FileAlreadyOpen function
114:  and fails quietly if the file is open.
```

734

```
115:
116:    Note that open may also fail if the file is open in
117:    another application. This will cause a failure in open,
118:    but you may wish to override this function to detect this
119:    case and provide a more meaningful error message than -49.
120:    ************************************************************/
121:
122:    void x_CMain::FailOpen(CFile *aFile)
123:
124:    {
125:        /* Only the application knows*/
126:        if (((CApp*)gApplication)->FileAlreadyOpen(aFile))
127:            Failure(kSilentErr, 0);
128:    }
129:
130:
131:    /************************************************************
132:      PositionWindow
133:
134:    The default method in CSaver calls the the decorator, which
135:    staggers and resizes the window. Since the window has already
136:    been positioned when it is initialized from the view resource,
137:    we don't want to do this twice.
138:    ************************************************************/
139:
140:    void x_CMain::PositionWindow()
141:
142:    {
143:    }
144:
145:
146:
147:
148:    /************************************************************
149:      DoCommand {OVERRIDE}
150:
151:    Dispatch Visual Architect-specified actions.
152:    ************************************************************/
153:
154:    void x_CMain::DoCommand(long theCommand)
155:
156:    {
157:        switch (theCommand)
158:        {
159:            case cmdTestDialog:
160:                DoCmdTestDialog();
161:                break;
162:            case cmdShowMsgDlg:
163:                DoCmdShowMsgDlg();
164:                break;
165:            default:
166:                CDocument::DoCommand(theCommand);
167:        }
168:    }
169:
```

continues

Listing 21.10. continued

```
170:
171:  /****************************************************************
172:   UpdateMenus {OVERRIDE}
173:
174:  Enable menus which generate commands handled by this class.
175:  ****************************************************************/
176:
177:  void x_CMain::UpdateMenus()
178:
179:  {
180:      CDocument::UpdateMenus();
181:      gBartender->EnableCmd(cmdTestDialog);
182:      gBartender->EnableCmd(cmdShowMsgDlg);
183:  }
184:
185:
186:  /****************************************************************
187:   DoCmdTestDialog
188:
189:  Respond to cmdTestDialog command.
190:  ****************************************************************/
191:
192:  void x_CMain::DoCmdTestDialog()
193:
194:  {
195:      CSample_Dialog *dialog;
196:
197:      // Respond to command by opening a dialog
198:
199:      dialog = new CSample_Dialog;
200:      dialog->ICSample_Dialog(this);
201:      dialog->BeginDialog();
202:
203:
204:      dialog->DoModalDialog(cmdNull); /* cmdNull because
205:                                         dialog already knows */
206:      ForgetObject(dialog);
207:  }
208:
209:
210:  /****************************************************************
211:   DoCmdShowMsgDlg
212:
213:  Respond to cmdShowMsgDlg command.
214:  ****************************************************************/
215:
216:  void x_CMain::DoCmdShowMsgDlg()
217:
218:  {
219:      CMessage_Box *dialog;
220:
221:      // Respond to command by opening a dialog
222:
223:      dialog = new CMessage_Box;
```

```
224:        dialog->ICMessage_Box(this);
225:        dialog->BeginDialog();
226:
227:
228:        dialog->DoModalDialog(cmdNull);  /* cmdNull because dialog
229:                                            already knows */
230:        ForgetObject(dialog);
231:  }
```

Listing 21.10 defines the member functions of class x_CMain. The next four subsections discuss the relevant member functions of that class.

The Function *MakeNewWindow*

The member function MakeNewWindow (defined in lines 84 to 105) stores the pointers to the window and the pane in the variables itsWindow and itsMainPane, respectively. It also stores the addresses of the various controls in their respective data members. The function obtains these addresses by sending the C++ message FindViewByID to the window object. The arguments for these messages are the constants kMain_*XXXX*ID, which are defined in Listing 21.11.

The Function *DoCommand*

The member function DoCommand (defined in lines 154 to 168) has case labels in the switch statement to respond to the custom commands cmd*XXXX*. The first statement in each case label invokes the corresponding member function DoCmd*XXXX*.

The Function *UpdateMenus*

The member function UpdateMenus (defined in lines 177 to 183) enables the custom commands by sending the C++ message EnableCmd, for each command, to the bartender object. The arguments for the sequence of EnableCmd messages are the constants cmd*XXXX*.

The Function *DoCmdtestDialog*

The member function DoCmdtestDialog (defined in lines 192 to 207) brings up the Sample Dialog dialog box. Line 195 declares the pointer dialog to the CSample_Dialog class. Line 199 creates a new dynamic instance of class CSample_Dialog and stores its address in pointer dialog. Line 200 initializes the dialog box. Line 201 starts using the dialog box by sending the C++ message BeginDialog to the dialog box. Line 204 invokes the modal dialog box by sending it the C++ message DoModalDialog. The statement in

21

line 206 disposes of the dynamic instance of the dialog box by calling function `ForgetObject`.

The member function `DoCmdShowMsgDlg` (defined in lines 216 to 231) invokes the Message Box dialog box. This function is very similar to the member function `DoCmdTestDialog`; it differs only in the dialog box class associated with the local pointer `dialog`.

Listing 21.11 shows the source code for the AppCommands.h header file for the Dialog1 program project. In lines 16 to 19, this listing defines the set of constants cmd*XXXX* that support the custom commands.

Listing 21.11. The source code for the AppCommands.h header file for project Dialog1.

```
 1:   /****************************************************************
 2:   MyCommands.h
 3:
 4:                Header File For Command Symbols
 5:
 6:       Copyright (c) 1994 My Software Inc. All rights reserved.
 7:
 8:   Generated by Visual Architect(TM)
 9:
10:   This file is regenerated each time.
11:
12:   ****************************************************************/
13:
14:   #pragma once
15:
16:   #define cmdDeleteStr    528
17:   #define cmdFindStr      529
18:   #define cmdInsertStr    527
19:   #define cmdSelectStr    530
```

Listing 21.12 shows the source code for the MainItems.h header file for the Dialog1 program project. The listing declares an untagged enumerated type that defines the identifiers kMain_*XXXX* and kMain_*XXXX*ID.

Listing 21.12. The source code for the MainItems.h header file for project Dialog1.

```
 1:   /****************************************************************
 2:   MainItems.h
 3:
 4:                    Main Item Constants
 5:
 6:       Copyright (c) 1994 My Software Inc. All rights reserved.
```

```
7:
8:      Generated by Visual Architect(TM)
9:
10:     This file is rewritten each time you generate code. You should
11:     not make changes to this file.
12:
13:     If you want to change how Visual Architect generates this file,
14:     you can change the template for this file. It is "Items.h" in
15:     the Visual Architect Templates folder.
16:
17:     ****************************************************************/
18:
19:     #pragma once
20:
21:
22:         //      Item numbers for each item.
23:         //
24:         //      Use TCLGetItemPointer (ViewUtilities) to convert these
25:         //      item numbers to a pointer to the named item.
26:
27:     enum
28:     {
29:         Main_Begin_,
30:         kMain_StringLst = 1,
31:         kMain_StringLstID = 1L,
32:         kMain_InOutBox = 2,
33:         kMain_InOutBoxID = 2L,
34:         kMain_InOutLbl = 3,
35:         kMain_InOutLblID = 3L,
36:         kMain_IndexLbl = 4,
37:         kMain_IndexLblID = 4L,
38:         kMain_IndexBox = 5,
39:         kMain_IndexBoxID = 5L,
40:         kMain_InsertBtn = 6,
41:         kMain_InsertBtnID = 6L,
42:         kMain_DeleteBtn = 7,
43:         kMain_DeleteBtnID = 7L,
44:         kMain_FindBtn = 8,
45:         kMain_FindBtnID = 8L,
46:         kMain_QuitBtn = 9,
47:         kMain_QuitBtnID = 9L,
48:         Main_End_
49:     };
```

Compiling and Running the Program

Invoke the Run command from the THINK Project Manager icon menu. This command causes the compiler to process the set of source code files that contribute to the program. When the program runs, click the Message button to view the Message Box. Close this dialog box, and then click the Test Dialog button to bring up the Sample Dialog dialog box.

First you need to test that the dialog box retains the data you entered the last time you invoked the dialog box. Type different text in the edit boxes, and alter the state of the radio controls and check boxes. Click the OK button to close the dialog box. Click one more time on the Test Dialog button in the main window. When the Sample Dialog dialog box appears, it should contain your most recent input from the last invocation.

Now test that the dialog box does not retain data when you click Cancel. Type different text in the edit boxes and alter the state of the radio controls and check boxes. Click the Cancel button to close the dialog box. Reinvoke the same dialog box to determine whether the changes you made most recently were lost because you clicked the Cancel button.

When you finish experimenting with the dialog boxes, click the Quit button in the main window.

Summary

This final chapter presented dialog boxes and showed you how to create and use them by employing the Visual Architect utility. The following topics were covered:

- [ ] An overview of dialog boxes explained the difference between a modal and modeless dialog box. You also learned about the role of resources in creating dialog boxes and how the Visual Architect utility handles resources in a manner that is transparent to you.

- [ ] The class `CDialog` is an abstract class that supports modal and modeless dialog boxes. You also learned about the member functions `Close`, `Validate`, `FindButton`, `SetDefaultCmd`, `SetDefaultButton`, and `SetCmdEnable`.

- [ ] The class `CDLOGDialog` is a descendant of class `CDialog` that creates a dialog box from the resources `DLOG` and `DITL`.

- [ ] The class `CDialogDirector` is the base class for a director object that manages a dialog box. You learned about the member functions `DoCommand`, `Close`, `BeginDialog`, `DoModalDialog`, `EndDialog`, and `Validate`.

- [ ] The class `CDLOGDirector` supports the directors for dialog boxes created from the `DLOG` and `DITL` resources.

- [ ] From a programming example that implements two dialog boxes, you learned what steps are involved in creating dialog boxes using the Visual Architect utility. You also learned about all the relevant listings generated by the Visual Architect utility to support the dialog box classes.

Q&A

Q Can an active modal dialog box display another modal dialog box?

A Yes.

Q Can I make the main window modal?

A Yes, by invoking the Main Window dialog box and clicking the modal check box.

Q How does the static data member saveData store the dialog box controls' data?

A Because the member is static, it really belongs to the class and not to any particular instance. Therefore, the static member retains its data regardless of how many class instances there are. This persistence enables the dialog box class to update the next dialog box invocation with the data from the previous one (assuming that the previous dialog box invocation was closed by clicking the OK button).

Workshop

The Workshop provides quiz questions to help you solidify your understanding of the material covered and exercises to provide you with experience in using what you've learned. Answers are provided in Appendix B, "Answers."

Quiz

1. True or false? The member function CDialog::FindButton returns the address of a button in a dialog box.

2. True or false? The member function CDialogDirector::EndDialog closes a dialog box.

3. Which CDLOGDialog member function adds a radio control?

4. True or false? You need to explicitly associate a dialog box view with its supporting class.

21

Exercise

Create the program project Dialog1b that has the same main window and the same two dialog boxes as project Dialog1. Do not customize the code for this project the way you did for Dialog1. Instead, maintain the source code generated by the Visual Architect utility. Compile and run this program to get a feel for the different behavior of the Sample Dialog.

3

To review your third week of learning about programming with Symantec C++, let's look at yet another enhanced version of the number-guessing game. This version uses the static text edit box and some button controls. Figure R3.1 shows a sample session with the GAME3.CP program project, which I created using the Visual Architect utility. As you can see from the figure, the main window has the following controls:

- ☐ The Static text control, which displays a message
- ☐ The edit box, which accepts your input
- ☐ The Guess button
- ☐ The Quit button

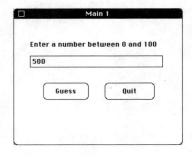

Figure R3.1. *A sample session with the GAME3 program project.*

Table R3.1 shows the captions, names, types, and associated commands for the four controls.

Table R3.1. The caption, name, type, and associated command for each control in the GAME3 program project.

Control Caption	Control Name	Control Type	Associated Command
Enter...	MsgLbl	Static text	
	TextBox	Edit box	
Guess	GuessBtn	Button	cmdGuess
Quit	QuitBtn	Button	cmdQuit

I created the controls of the main window using the steps you should be familiar with by now, especially because this Macintosh program has a rather simple interface. The GAME3 program project requires that you add the files time.c and rand.c to the list of project files. These additional files are part of the standard C library. Listing R3.1 shows the source code for the x_CMain.h header file. The bold lines indicate the ones that I manually inserted.

Listing R3.1. The source code for the x_CMain.h header file.

```
1:  /**********************************************************
2:  x_CMain.h
3:
4:  Header File For CMain Lower-Layer Document Class
5:
```

```
 6:    Copyright (c) 1994 My Software Inc. All rights reserved.
 7:
 8:    Generated by Visual Architect(TM)
 9:
10:    This file is rewritten each time you generate code. You should not
11:    make changes to this file; changes should go in the My.h
12:    file, instead.
13:
14:    If you want to change how Visual Architect generates this file, you can
15:    change the template for this file. It is "_Doc.h" in the Visual Architect
16:    Templates folder.
17:
18:    ***********************************************************/
19:
20:    #pragma once
21:
22:    #include "CSaver.h"
23:    class CStaticText;
24:    class CDialogText;
25:    class CButton;
26:
27:    #include "ItsContentsClass.h"
28:
29:    #define x_CMain_super      CSaver<ITSCONTENTSCLASS>
30:
31:    class CFile;
32:
33:    class x_CMain : public x_CMain_super
34:
35:    {
36:    public:
37:
38:         TCL_DECLARE_CLASS
39:
40:         // Pointers to panes in window
41:         CStaticText     *fMain_MsgLbl;
42:         CDialogText     *fMain_GuessBox;
43:         CButton         *fMain_GuessBtn;
44:         CButton         *fMain_QuitBtn;
45:
46:         void      Ix_CMain(void);
47:
48:         virtual   void DoCommand(long theCommand);
49:         virtual   void UpdateMenus(void);
50:
51:    protected:
52:         virtual   void MakeNewWindow(void);
53:
54:         virtual   void FailOpen(CFile *aFile);
55:         virtual void   PositionWindow(void);
56:
57:         virtual void   DoCmdGuess(void);
58:
59:         int fIter;
60:         int fMaxIter;
```

continues

Listing R3.1. continued

```
61:        int fSecretNum;
62:        Boolean foundGuess;
63:
64: };
65:
66: #define    CVueCMain 128
```

 I inserted the data members in lines 59 through 62. The member fIter stores the current iteration number. The member fMaxIter stores the maximum number of iterations. The member fSecretNum stores the secret number that the program generates using random numbers. The Boolean member foundGuess stores the found-guess status.

Listing R3.2 shows the source code for the x_CMain.cp implementation file. The bold lines indicate the ones that I inserted.

VArc Type Listing R3.2. The source code for the x_CMain.cp implementation file.

```
 1: /****************************************************************
 2:   x_CMain.c
 3:
 4:                    CMain Document Class
 5:
 6:      Copyright (c) 1994 My Software Inc. All rights reserved.
 7:
 8: Generated by Visual Architect(TM) 8:35 PM Mon, Jun 27, 1994
 9:
10: This file is rewritten each time you generate code. You should not
11: make changes to this file; changes should go in the My.c
12: file, instead.
13:
14: If you want to change how Visual Architect generates this file, you can
15: change the template for this file. It is "_Doc_cp" in the Visual Architect
16: Templates folder.
17:
18:    ******************************************************/
19:
20: #include "x_CMain.h"
21:
22: #include "CMain.h"
23:
24: #include "MainItems.h"
25:
26: #include "ViewUtilities.h"
27: #include "CApp.h"
28:
29: #include <CApplication.h>
30: #include <CBartender.h>
31: #include <Commands.h>
```

```
32:   #include <Constants.h>
33:   #include <CDecorator.h>
34:   #include <CDesktop.h>
35:   #include <CFile.h>
36:   #include <TBUtilities.h>
37:   #include <CWindow.h>
38:
39:   extern CApplication *gApplication; /* The application */
40:   extern CDecorator    *gDecorator; /* Decorator for arranging windows */
41:   extern CDesktop *gDesktop; /* The visible Desktop */
42:   extern CBartender *gBartender;    /* Manages all menus */
43:
44:   #include "CStaticText.h"
45:   #include "CDialogText.h"
46:   #include "CButton.h"
47:
48:   #include <stdlib.h>
49:   #include <time.h>
50:
51:        // Define symbols for commands handled by this class
52:        // Prevents a recompile every time any command changed.
53:
54:   #define cmdGuess 512
55:
56:
57:   TCL_DEFINE_CLASS_M1(x_CMain, x_CMain_super);
58:
59:   /**** C O N S T R U C T I O N / D E S T R U C T I O N
60:                                      M E T H O D S ****/
61:
62:   /***************************************************************
63:     Ix_CMain
64:
65:   Initialize the document
66:   ***************************************************************/
67:
68:   void x_CMain::Ix_CMain()
69:
70:   {
71:        IDocument(gApplication, TRUE);
72:
73:             // Initialize data members below.
74:        fIter = 0;
75:        fMaxIter = 11;
76:        srand((unsigned int)clock());
77:        fSecretNum =  rand() % 1001;
78:        foundGuess = FALSE;
79:   }
80:
81:
82:   /***************************************************************
83:     MakeNewWindow
84:
85:   Create a new, empty window.  Subclass may override to populate
86:   the new window.
87:   ***************************************************************/
```

continues

Listing R3.2. continued

```
88:
89:   void x_CMain::MakeNewWindow(void)
90:
91:   {
92:       itsWindow = TCLGetNamedWindow("\pMain", this);
93:
94:       itsMainPane = (CPane*) TCLGetItemPointer(itsWindow, 0);
95:
96:           // Initialize pointers to the subpanes in the window
97:
98:     fMain_MsgLbl = (CStaticText*) itsWindow->FindViewByID(kMain_MsgLblID);
99:     ASSERT(member(fMain_MsgLbl, CStaticText));
100:
101:     fMain_GuessBox = (CDialogText*)
102:                     itsWindow->FindViewByID(kMain_GuessBoxID);
103: ASSERT(member(fMain_GuessBox, CDialogText));
104:     fMain_GuessBtn = (CButton*) itsWindow->FindViewByID(kMain_GuessBtnID);
105:     ASSERT(member(fMain_GuessBtn, CButton));
106:
107:     fMain_QuitBtn = (CButton*) itsWindow->FindViewByID(kMain_QuitBtnID);
108:     ASSERT(member(fMain_QuitBtn, CButton));
109:
110:   }
111:
112:
113:   /**********************************************************
114:    FailOpen {OVERRIDE}
115:
116:   Fail if file already open in this application.
117:
118:   This function calls the application's FileAlreadyOpen function
119:   and fails quietly if the file is open.
120:
121:   Note that open may also fail if the file is open in
122:   another application. This will cause a failure in open,
123:   but you may wish to override this function to detect this
124:   case and provide a more meaningful error message than -49.
125:   **********************************************************/
126:
127:   void x_CMain::FailOpen(CFile *aFile)
128:
129:   {
130:       /* Only the application knows      */
131:       if (((CApp*)gApplication)->FileAlreadyOpen(aFile))
132:           Failure(kSilentErr, 0);
133:   }
134:
135:
136:   /**********************************************************
137:    PositionWindow
138:
139:   The default method in CSaver calls the the decorator, which
140:   staggers and resizes the window. Since the window has already
141:   been positioned when it is initialized from the view resource,
142:   we don't want to do this twice.
143:   **********************************************************/
```

```
144:
145:    void      x_CMain::PositionWindow()
146:
147:    {
148:    }
149:
150:
151:
152:
153:    /************************************************************
154:      DoCommand {OVERRIDE}
155:
156:    Dispatch Visual Architect-specified actions.
157:    ************************************************************/
158:
159:    void x_CMain::DoCommand(long theCommand)
160:
161:    {
162:        switch (theCommand)
163:        {
164:            case cmdGuess:
165:                    DoCmdGuess();
166:                    break;
167:            default:
168:                    CDocument::DoCommand(theCommand);
169:        }
170:    }
171:
172:
173:    /************************************************************
174:      UpdateMenus {OVERRIDE}
175:
176:    Enable menus which generate commands handled by this class.
177:    ************************************************************/
178:
179:    void x_CMain::UpdateMenus()
180:
181:    {
182:        CDocument::UpdateMenus();
183:        gBartender->EnableCmd(cmdGuess);
184:    }
185:
186:
187:    /************************************************************
188:      DoCmdGuess
189:
190:    Respond to cmdGuess command.
191:    ************************************************************/
192:
193:    void x_CMain::DoCmdGuess()
194:
195:    {
196:      char s[81];
197:      Str255 s255;
198:      int n;
199:
```

continues

Listing R3.2. continued

```
200:    if (foundGuess)
201:      return;
202:
203:    if (fIter++ >= fMaxIter) {
204:      fMain_GuessBtn->Deactivate();
205:      sprintf(s, "Secret number is %d", fSecretNum);
206:      fMain_MsgLbl->SetTextPtr(s, strlen(s));
207:      return;
208:    }
209:
210:    fMain_GuessBox->GetTextString(s255);
211:    strncpy(s, (char*)s255 + 1, s255[0]);
212:    s[ s255[0] ] = '\0';
213:    n = atoi(s);
214:
215:    if (n == fSecretNum) {
216:      foundGuess = TRUE;
217:      fMain_GuessBox->SetTextString("\pYou guessed it!");
218:    }
219:    else if (n > fSecretNum)
220:      fMain_MsgLbl->SetTextString("\pGuess is high");
221:    else
222:      fMain_MsgLbl->SetTextString("\pGuess is low");
223:  }
```

Analysis

In Listing R3.2 I inserted the `#include` directives in lines 48 and 49. I also inserted the statements in lines 74 through 78 to initialize the data members of class `x_CMain`. Finally, I inserted the statements in lines 196 to 222 to support the response for the command `cmdGuess`.

The `if` statement in line 200 examines the value in member `foundGuess` and exits if that member contains a non-zero value.

The `if` statement in line 203 handles the case when you have run out of iterations. The function deactivates the Guess button and displays the secret number in the static text control.

The statements in lines 210 to 213 obtain the string from the edit box and convert it into an integer. Line 213 stores that integer in the local variable n. The multi-alternative `if` statement in lines 215 to 222 compares the value in variable n with that in member `fSecretNum`. If the two values match, the function displays a congratulatory message in the static text control. Otherwise, the function displays a hint to help you with the next guess.

Notice that this version of the number-guessing game does not have a `while` loop in the function `DoCmdGuess`. The reason is that clicking the Guess button constitutes a single iteration (or trial, if you prefer) in guessing the secret number.

Resources

Resources are basic elements of every Macintosh program. The process of defining the specifications of windows, dialog boxes, menus, controls, sounds, fonts, and icons simplifies the creation and management of these program components. This appendix introduces you to the following topics:

☐ An overview of resources

☐ Menu resources

☐ Window resources

☐ Control resources

☐ Dialog box resources

Resources: An Overview

Macintosh applications do not rely entirely on a high-level programming language to create every program component. Instead, Macintosh programs use resources defined separately (in separate files) and compiled by resource compilers. Resources define the visual interface of a window, dialog box, control, menu, and icon. In addition, resources define strings and string lists. Using resources to define strings and string lists provides a special advantage in porting Macintosh applications to different human languages without recompiling your applications.

This book shows you how to use the Visual Architect utility to create Macintosh applications. This utility simplifies the creation of applications and shields you from having to deal with resources directly. Yet, you have come across resources and resource files in several instances in Day 15 through Day 21.

Resources have types and unique numeric IDs. Table A.1 shows a sample list of resources. The resource names are four-character strings, whereas the resource IDs are integers that range from 128 to 32767.

Table A.1. Sample resources.

Resource Type	Description
'ALRT'	Alert box
'CNTL'	Control
'CURS'	Cursor
'CODE'	Application code segment

Resource Type	Description
'DITL'	Item list in a dialog box or in an alert box
'DLOG'	Dialog box
'ICN#'	Large black-and-white icon with mask
'ICON'	Large black-and-white icon without mask
'INIT'	System extension
'MBAR'	Menu bar
'MDEF'	Menu definition procedure
'MENU'	Menu
'NFNT'	Bitmapped font
'STR '	String
'STR#'	String list
'WIND'	Window
'movv'	QuickTime movie
'snd '	Sound

Note: To learn more about resources and other lower-level aspects of Macintosh programming, I recommend that you obtain a copy of the different *Inside Macintosh* volumes. You at least should obtain the *Macintosh Toolbox Essentials* and *More Macintosh Toolbox*. All *Inside Macintosh* volumes are published by Addison-Wesley and are written by Apple Computer.

Menu Resources

Menu resources include the menu bar resource and the menu items resources.

Syntax

The Menu Bar Resource

The general syntax for the menu bar resource is

```
resource 'MBAR' (menuBarID, preload) {
    { <list of menus in this menu bar> };
};
```

Example:

```
resource 'MBAR' (myMenuBar, preload) {
    { mApple, mFile, mEdit };
};
```

In this example, the menu bar resource defines a menu bar with the Apple, File, and Edit menus.

Syntax

The Menu Resource

The general syntax for the menu resource is

```
resource 'MENU' (resourceID, preload) {
    menuID,
    menuDefProc, /* menu definition procedure */
    enableFlag, /* enable/disable flag */
    enabled, /* enabled title */
    "menuTitleText", /* text for menu title */
    {
        menuItem1, noicon, keyCode, markCode, plain;
        <other menu items>
    }
};
```

The *keyCode* parameter represents the hot key character. The *markCode* parameter represents the marking character.

Example:

```
resource 'MENU' (mEdit, preload) {
    mEdit,
    textMenuProc, /* menu definition procedure */
    0b000000000000000000000010010000000, /* enable/disable
                                    flag */
    enabled, /* enabled title */
    "Edit", /* text for menu title */
    {
        "Undo", noicon, "Z", nomark, plain;
        "-", noicon, nokey, normak, plain;
        "Cut", noicon, "X", nomark, plain;
        "Copy"", noicon, "C", nomark, plain;
        "Paste", noicon, "V", nomark, plain;
        "Clear", noicon, nokey, nomark, plain
    }
```

```
};
```

In this example, the menu resource defines an Edit menu with the items Undo, Cut, Copy, Paste, and Clear.

Window Resources

Window resources define non-dialog windows.

Syntax

The Window Resource

The general syntax for the window resource is

```
resource 'WIND' (windowResID, preload, purgeable) {
    { Xulc, Yulc, Xlrc, Ylrc }, /* coordinates for upper left
                                    and lower right corners */
    windowProc, /* window definition procedure */
    visibleFlag,
    goAwayFlag,
    0x0, /* reference constant for your own use */
    "windowTitle",
    positionSpecs,
};
```

Example:

```
resource 'WIND' (mywindowRes, preload, purgeable) {
    { 50, 60, 150, 200 },
    rDocProc, /* rounded-corner window */
    visible,
    goAway,
    0x0,
    "View",
    staggerParentWindowScreen
};
resource 'WIND' (mywindowRes, preload, purgeable) {
    { 50, 60, 250, 300 },
    rZoomDocProc, /* rounded-corner window */
    invisible,
    noGoAway,
    0x0,
    "Peek",
    centerParentWindowScreen
};
```

Control Resources

The control resources define various kinds of controls including buttons, radio controls, check boxes, scroll bars, pop-up menu panes, and so on.

The Control Resource

The general syntax for the control resource is

```
resource 'CNTL' (controlResID, preload, purgeable) {
    { Xulc, Yulc, Xlrc, Ylrc }, /* coordinates for upper left
                                       and lower right corners */
    initialSetting,
    visibleFlag,
    maximumSetting,
    minimumSetting,
    controlDefinitionID,
    referenceValue,
    "controlTitle"
};
```

Examples:

```
/* button */
resource 'CNTL' (myCalcBtn, preload, purgeable) {
    { 50, 60, 60, 70 },
    0,
    visible,
    1,
    0,
    pushButProc,
    0,
    "Calc"
};

/* check box */
resource 'CNTL' (wordChkBox, preload, purgeable) {
    { 50, 60, 60, 70 },
    1, /* check box initially checked */
    visible,
    1,
    0,
    radioButProc,
    0,
    "Whole Word"
};

/* scroll bar */
resource 'CNTL' (timerScrollbar, preload, purgeable) {
    { 50, 60, 150, 70 },
    0,
    visible,
    100,
    0,
    scrollBarProc,
    0,
    ""
};
```

Dialog Resources

The DLOG dialog resource defines the basic dialog box, whereas the DITL resource defines a dialog box and also specifies the controls in that dialog box.

The *DLOG* Dialog Resource

The general syntax for the DLOG dialog resource is

```
resource 'DLOG' (dialogResID, preload, purgeable) {
    { Xulc, Yulc, Xlrc, Ylrc }, /* coordinates for upper left
                                    and lower right corners */
    dlgBoxProc, /* dialog box definition procedure
                    for modal dialog */
    visibleFlag,
    goAwayFlag,
    0x0, /* reference constant for your own use */
    listItemResourceID,
    "dialogTitle",
    positionSpecs,
};
```

Example:

```
resource 'DLOG' (myCalcDlg, preload, purgeable) {
    { 50, 60, 350, 400 },
    dBoxProc,
    visible,
    noGoAway,
    0x0,
    kCalcDITL,
    "Calculator",
    alertPsotionParentWindow
};
```

The *DITL* Dialog Resource

The general syntax for the DITL dialog resource is

```
resource 'DITL' (dialogResID, preload, purgeable) {
    {
    /* control # 1 */
        { Xulc, Yulc, Xlrc, Ylrc }, /* coordinates for upper
                                left and lower right corners */
        control1Type {
            <list of control data>
        },
    /* control # 2 */
        { Xulc, Yulc, Xlrc, Ylrc }, /* coordinates for upper
                                left and lower right corners */
        control2Type {
            <list of control data>
```

```
        },
    /* control # 3 */
        { Xulc, Yulc, Xlrc, Ylrc }, /* coordinates for upper
                            left and lower right corners */
        control3Type {
            <list of control data>
        },
    <other controls >
};
```

Example:

```
resource 'DITL' (myCalcDlg, preload, purgeable) {
    {
        { 50, 50, 100, 100 },
        Button {
                enabled,
                "OK"
        },

        { 10, 10, 40, 40 },
        Icon {
            disabled,
            kMyIconID
        },

        StatiText {
            disabled,
            "Error Message: None",
        },
    }
};
```

Answers

> **Note:** Due to space limitations, not every Exercise is answered.

Answers to Day 1, "Getting Started"

Quiz

1. The program generates the string C++ in 21 Days?.

2. The program generates no output because the cout statement appears inside a comment! The function main simply returns 0.

3. The cout statement is missing the semicolon.

Exercise

```
// Exercise program

#include <iostream.h>

main()
{
  cout << "I am a C++ Programmer";
  return 0;
}
```

Answers to Day 2, "C++ Program Components"

Quiz

1. The following table indicates which identifiers are valid, which are not, and why:

Identifiers	Valid?	Reason (if invalid)
numFiles	Yes	
n0Distance_02_Line	Yes	
0Weight	No	Starts with a digit
Bin Number	No	Contains a space
static	No	Reserved keyword
Static	Yes	

2. The output of the program is

    ```
    a = 10 and b = 3
    ```

    The function swap fails to swap the arguments a and b because it swaps only a copy of their values.

3. The output of the program is

    ```
    a = 3 and b = 10
    ```

    The function swap succeeds in swapping the arguments a and b because it uses reference parameters. Consequently, the changes in the values of parameters i and j go beyond the scope of the function itself.

4. The second version of function inc has a default argument that, when used, hinders the compiler from determining which version of inc to call. The compiler flags a compile-time error for such functions.

5. Because the second parameter has a default argument, the third one also must have a default argument. Here is one version of the correct definition of function volume:

    ```
    double volume(double length, double width = 1, double height = 1)
    {
      return length * width * height
    }
    ```

6. The parameter i is a lowercase letter. However, the function uses the uppercase I in the assignment statement. The compiler complains that the identifier I is not defined.

7. The function main requires a prototype of function sqr. The correct version of the program is

    ```
    #include <iostream.h>
    ```

```
      // declare prototype of function sqr
      double sqr(double);

      main()
      {
        double x = 5.2;

        cout << x << "^2 = " << sqr(x);
        return 0;
      }


      double sqr(double x)
      { return x * x ; }
```

Exercise

Here is my version of program OVERLOD2.CP:

```
// C++ program illustrates function overloading
// and default arguments

#include <iostream.h>

// inc version for int types
void inc(int& i, int diff = 1)
{
  i = i + diff;
}

// inc version for double types
void inc(double& x, double diff = 1)
{
  x = x + diff;
}

// inc version for char types
void inc(char& c, int diff = 1)
{
  c = c + diff;
}

main()
{
  char c = 'A';
  int i = 10;
  double x = 10.2;

  // display initial values
  cout << "c = " << c << "\n"
```

```
        << "i = " << i << "\n"
        << "x = " << x << "\n";
   // invoke the inc functions using default arguments
   inc(c);
   inc(i);
   inc(x);
   // display updated values
   cout << "After using the overloaded inc function\n";
   cout << "c = " << c << "\n"
        << "i = " << i << "\n"
        << "x = " << x << "\n";
     return 0;
}
```

Answers to Day 3, "Operators and Expressions"

Quiz

1. The output is

   12
   8
   2
   3.64851
   150.5

2. The output is

   12
   8
   2

3. The output is

   12
   27

4. The output is

   TRUE
   TRUE
   TRUE
   FALSE

Exercises

1. Here is my version of the function `max`:

```
int max(int i, int j)
{
   return (i > j) ? i : j;
}
```

2. Here is my version of the function `min`:

```
int min(int i, int j)
{
   return (i < j) ? i : j;
}
```

3. Here is my version of the function `abs`:

```
int abs(int i)
{
   return (i > 0) ? i : -i;
}
```

4. Here is my version of the function `isOdd`:

```
int isOdd(int i)
{
   return (i % 2 != 0) ? 1 : 0;
}
```

Answers to Day 4, "Managing I/O"

Quiz

1. The output statement cannot contain the inserter operator `>>`. The statement can be corrected as follows:

```
count << "Enter a number ";
cin >> x;
```

2. Because the variable x appears in the first and last items, the last number overwrites the first number.

Exercises

1. Here is my version of program OUT3.CP:

```
// C++ program uses the printf function for formatted output

#include <stdio.h>
#include <math.h>

main()
{
  double x;

  // display table heading
  printf("     X            Sqrt(X)\n");
  printf("-----------------------\n");
  x = 2;
  printf("     %3.0lf          %3.4lf\n", x, sqrt(x));
  x++;
  printf("     %3.0lf          %3.4lf\n", x, sqrt(x));
  x++;
  printf("     %3.0lf          %3.4lf\n", x, sqrt(x));
  x++;
  printf("     %3.0lf          %3.4lf\n", x, sqrt(x));
  x++;
  printf("     %3.0lf          %3.4lf\n", x, sqrt(x));
  x++;
  printf("     %3.0lf          %3.4lf\n", x, sqrt(x));
  x++;
  printf("     %3.0lf          %3.4lf\n", x, sqrt(x));
  x++;
  printf("     %3.0lf          %3.4lf\n", x, sqrt(x));
  x++;
  printf("     %3.0lf          %3.4lf\n", x, sqrt(x));
  return 0;
}
```

2. Here is my version of program OUT4.CP:

```
// C++ program which displays octal and hexadecimal integers
```

```
#include <iostream.h>
#include <stdio.h>

main()
{
  long i;
  cout << "Enter an integer : ";
  cin >> i;

  printf("%ld = %lX (hex) = %lo (octal)\n", i, i, i);
  return 0;
}
```

Answers to Day 5, "Decision-Making Constructs"

Quiz

1. The simpler version is

    ```
    if (i > 0 && i < 10)
      cout << "i = " << i << "\n";
    ```

2. The simpler version is

    ```
    if (i > 0) {
      j = i * i;
      cout << "j = " << j << "\n";
    }
    else if (i < 0) {
      j = 4 * i;
      cout << "j = " << j << "\n";
    }
    else {
      j = 10 + i;
      cout << "j = " << j << "\n";
    }
    ```

3. False. When the variable i stores values between −10 and −1, the statements in the clauses of the two if statements execute. In this case, all the assignment statements are executed. By contrast, it's impossible to execute the statements in both the if and else clauses of the supposedly equivalent if-else statement.

4. The simplified version is

```
if (i > 0 && i < 100)
    j = i * i;
else if (i >= 100)
    j = i;
else
    j = 1;
```

Notice that I eliminate the original first else if clause because the tested condition is a subset of the first tested condition. Consequently, the condition in the first else if never gets examined, and the associated assign statement never gets executed. This is an example of what is called *dead code*.

5. The tested condition is always false. Consequently, the statements in the clause are never executed. This is another example of dead code.

Exercises

1. Here is my version of program IF5.CP:

```
// C++ program to solve quadratic equation

#include <iostream.h>
#include <math.h>

main()
{
  double A, B, C, discrim, root1, root2, twoA;

  cout << "Enter coefficients for equation A*X^2 + B*X + C\n";
  cout << "Enter A: ";
  cin >> A;
  cout << "Enter B: ";
  cin >> B;
  cout << "Enter C: ";
  cin >> C;
```

```
       if (A != 0) {
          twoA = 2 * A;
          discrim = B * B - 4 * A * C;
          if (discrim > 0) {
             root1 = (-B + sqrt(discrim)) / twoA;
             root2 = (-B - sqrt(discrim)) / twoA;
             cout << "root1 = " << root1 << "\n";
             cout << "root2 = " << root2 << "\n";
          }
          else if (discrim < 0) {

             discrim = -discrim;
             cout << "root1 = (" << -B/twoA
                  << ") + i (" << sqrt(discrim) / twoA <<")\n";
             cout << "root2 = (" << -B/twoA
                  << ") - i (" << sqrt(discrim) / twoA << ")\n";
          }
          else {
             root1 = -B / 2 / A;
             root2 = root1;
             cout << "root1 = " << root1 << "\n";
             cout << "root2 = " << root2 << "\n";
          }
       }
       else
          cout << "root = " << (-C / B) << "\n";


       return 0;
    }
```

2. Here is my version of program SWITCH2.CP:

```
// C++ program which uses the switch statement to implement
// a simple four-function calculator program

#include <iostream.h>

const int TRUE = 1;
const int FALSE = 0;
```

```
main()
{
  double x, y, z;
  char op;
  int error = FALSE;

  cout << "Enter the first operand: ";
  cin >> x;
  cout << "Enter the operator: ";
  cin >> op;
  cout << "Enter the second operand: ";
  cin >> y;

  switch (op) {
    case '+':
      z = x + y;
      break;
    case '-':
      z = x - y;
      break;
    case '*':
      z = x * y;
      break;
    case '/':
      if (y != 0)
        z = x / y;
      else
        error = TRUE;
      break;
    default:
      error = TRUE;
  }

  if (!error)
    cout << x << " " << op << " " << y << " = " << z << "\n";
  else
    cout << "Bad operator or division-by-zero error\n";

  return 0;
}
```

Answers to Day 6, "Loops"

Quiz

1. The statements inside the loop fail to alter the value of I. Consequently, the tested condition is always true, and the loop iterates endlessly.

2. The output of the program consists of the numbers 3, 5, and 7.

3. The output of the program is an endless sequence of lines that display the value 3. The reason for the indefinite looping is that the loop control variable is not incremented.

4. The nested for loops use the same loop control variable. This program will not run.

5. Both for loops declare the variable i as their loop control variable. The compiler generates an error for this duplication.

6. The condition of the while loop is always true. Therefore, the loop iterates endlessly.

7. The program lacks a statement that explicitly initializes the variable factorial to 1. Without this statement, the program automatically initializes the variable factorial to 0—the wrong value. Consequently, the for loop ends up assigning 0 to the variable factorial in every iteration. Here is the correct version of the code:

```
int n;
double factorial = 1;
cout << "Enter positive integer : ";
cin >> n;
for (int i = 1; i <= n; i++)
  factorial *= i;
cout << n << "!= " << factorial;
```

Exercises

1. Here is my version of program FOR5.CP:

```
// Program calculates a sum of odd integers in
// the range of 11 to 121
```

```cpp
#include <iostream.h>

const int FIRST = 11;
const int LAST = 121;

main()
{
    double sum = 0;
    for (int i = FIRST; i <= LAST; i += 2)
      sum += (double)i;

    cout << "Sum of odd integers from "
         << FIRST << " to " << LAST << " = "
         << sum << "\n";
    return 0;
}
```

2. Here is my version of program WHILE2.CP:

```cpp
// Program calculates a sum of squared odd integers in
// the range of 11 to 121

#include <iostream.h>

const int FIRST = 11;
const int LAST = 121;

main()
{
    double sum = 0;
    int i = FIRST;
    while (i <= LAST) {
      sum += double(i * i++);
    }
    cout << "Sum of squared odd integers from "
         << FIRST << " to " << LAST << " = "
         << sum << "\n";
    return 0;
}
```

3. Here is my version of program DOWHILE2.CP:

```
// Program calculates a sum of squared odd integers in
// the range of 11 to 121

#include <iostream.h>

const int FIRST = 11;
const int LAST = 121;

main()
{
    double sum = 0;
    int i = FIRST;
    do {
      sum += double(i * i++);
    } while (i <= LAST);
    cout << "Sum of squared odd integers from "
        << FIRST << " to " << LAST << " = "
        << sum << "\n";
    return 0;
}
```

Answers to Day 7, "Arrays"

Quiz

1. The program displays the factorials for the numbers 0 to 4:

```
x[0] = 1
x[1] = 1
x[2] = 2
x[3] = 6
x[4] = 24
```

2. The program displays the square roots for the numbers 0 to 4:

```
x[0] = 0
x[1] = 1
x[2] = 1.41421
```

```
        x[3] = 1.73205
        x[4] = 2
```

3. The first `for` loop should iterate between 1 and `MAX-1`, not between 0 and `MAX-1`. The first loop iteration uses an out-of-range index.

Exercise

Here is my version of program ARRAY7.CP:

```cpp
// C++ program that sorts arrays using the Comb sort method
#include <iostream.h>

const int MAX = 10;
const int TRUE = 1;
const int FALSE = 0;

int obtainNumData()
{
  int m;
  do { // obtain number of data points
    cout << "Enter number of data points [2 to "
        << MAX << "] : ";
    cin >> m;
    cout << "\n";
  } while (m < 2 || m > MAX);
  return m;
}

void inputArray(int intArr[], int n)
{
  // prompt user for data
  for (int i = 0; i < n; i++) {
    cout << "arr[" << i << "] : ";
    cin >> intArr[i];
  }
}

void showArray(int intArr[], int n)
{
  for (int i = 0; i < n; i++) {
    cout.width(5);
    cout << intArr[i] << " ";
  }
  cout << "\n";
}

void sortArray(int intArr[], int n)
{
  int offset, temp, inOrder;

  offset = n;
  while (offset > 1) {
```

```
      offset /= 2;
      do {
        inOrder = TRUE;
        for (int i = 0, j = offset; i < (n - offset); i++, ++) {
          if (intArr[i] > intArr[j]) {
            inOrder = FALSE;
            temp = intArr[i];
            intArr[i] = intArr[j];
            intArr[j] = temp;
          }
        }
      } while (!inOrder);
  }
}

main()
{
  int arr[MAX];
  int n;

  n = obtainNumData();
  inputArray(arr, n);
  cout << "Unordered array is:\n";
  showArray(arr, n);
  sortArray(arr, n);
  cout << "\nSorted array is:\n";
  showArray(arr, n);
  return 0;
}
```

Answers to Day 8, "User-Defined Types and Pointers"

Quiz

1. The enumerated values on and off appear in two different enumerated types. Here is a correct version of these statements:

   ```
   enum Boolean { false, true };
   enum State { state_on, state_off };
   enum YesNo { yes, no };
   enum DiskDriveStatus { drive_on , drive_off };
   ```

2. False. The enumerated type YesNo is correctly declared.

3. The program lacks a delete statement before the return statement. Here is the correct version:

```
#include <iostream.h>
main()
{
  int *p = new int;
  cout << "Enter a number : ";
  cin >> *p;
  cout << "The square of " << *p << " = " << (*p * *p);
  delete p;
  return 0;
}
```

Exercise

1. Here is my version of PTR6.CP:

```
/* C++ program that demonstrates pointers to structured types */

#include <iostream.h>
#include <stdio.h>
#include <math.h>

const MAX_RECT = 4;
const TRUE = 1;
const FALSE = -1;

struct point {
  double x;
  double y;
};

struct rect {
  point ulc; // upper left corner
  point lrc; // lower right corner
  double area;
  int id;
};

typedef rect rectArr[MAX_RECT];
```

```
main()
{
  rectArr r;
  rect temp;
  rect* pr = r;
  rect* pr2;
  double length, width;
  int offset;
  int inOrder;

  for (int i = 0; i < MAX_RECT; i++, pr++) {
    cout << "Enter (X,Y) coord. for ULC of rect. # "
         << i << " : ";
    cin >> pr->ulc.x >> pr->ulc.y;
    cout << "Enter (X,Y) coord. for LRC of rect. # "
         << i << " : ";
    cin >> pr->lrc.x >> pr->lrc.y;
    pr->id = i;
    length = fabs(pr->ulc.x - pr->lrc.x);
    width = fabs(pr->ulc.y - pr->lrc.y);
    pr->area = length * width;
  }

  // sort the rectangles by areas
  offset = MAX_RECT;
  do {
    offset = (8 * offset) / 11;
    offset = (offset == 0) ? 1 : offset;
    inOrder = TRUE;
    pr = r;
    pr2 = r + offset;
    for (int i = 0;
         i < MAX_RECT - offset;
         i++, pr++, pr2++)
      if (pr->area > pr2->area) {
        inOrder = FALSE;
        temp = *pr;
        *pr = *pr2;
        *pr2 = temp;
```

```
      }
    } while (!(offset == 1 && inOrder));

    pr = r; // reset pointer
    // display rectangles sorted by area
    for (i = 0; i < MAX_RECT; i++, pr++)
      printf("Rect # %d has area %5.4lf\n", pr->id, pr->area);
    return 0;
}
```

2. Here is my version of structure intArrStruct:

```
struct intArrStruct {
  int* dataPtr;
  unsigned size;
};
```

3. Here is my version of structure matStruct:

```
struct matStruct {
  double* dataPtr;
  unsigned rows;
  unsigned columns;
};
```

Answers to Day 9, "Strings"

Quiz

1. The string s1 is smaller than string s2. Consequently, the call to function strcpy causes a program bug.

2. Using the function strncpy to include the constant MAX as the third argument ensures that string s1 receives MAX characters (excluding the null terminator) from string s1:

```
#include <iostream.h>
#include <string.h>
const in MAX = 10;
main()
{
```

```
    char s1[MAX+1];
    char s2[] = "12345678901234567890";
    strncpy(s1, s2, MAX);
    cout << "String 1 is " << s1
        << "\nString 2 is " << s2;
    return 0;
}
```

3. Because the string in variable s1 is greater than that in variable s2, the statement assigns a positive number (1, to be exact) in variable i.

4. The call to function strcmp compares the substring "C++" with "Pascal" because the arguments include an offset value. Because "C++" is greater than "Pascal", the statement assigns a positive number (1, to be exact) in variable i.

5. False! Although the basic idea for the function is sound, dimensioning the local variable requires a constant. One solution is to use the same constant, call it MAX_STRING_SIZE, to size up the arguments of parameter s:

```
int hasNoLowerCase(const char* s)
{
  char s2[MAX_STRING_SIZE+1];
  strcpy(s2, s);
  strupr(s2);
  return (strcmp(s1, s2) == 0) ? 1 : 0);
}
```

The other solution uses dynamic allocation to create a dynamic local string that stores a copy of the arguments of parameter s. This solution works with all arguments of parameter s:

```
int hasNoLowerCase(const char* s)
{
  char *s2 = new char[strlen(s)+1];
  int i;
  strcpy(s2, s);
  strupr(s2);
  // store result in variable i
  i = (strcmp(s1, s2) == 0) ? 1 : 0);
  delete [] s2; // first delete local dynamic string
  return i; // then return the result of the function
}
```

Exercises

1. Here is my version of function `strlen`:

```
int strlen(const char* s)
{
  int i = 0;
  while (s[i] != '\0')
    i++;
  return i;
}
```

2. Here is the other version of function `strlen`:

```
int strlen(const char* s)
{
  char *p = s;
  while (p++ != '\0')
    /* do nothing */;
  return p - s;
}
```

3. Here is my version of program STRING5.CP:

```
#include <stdio.h>
#include <string.h>

main()
{
    char str[] = "2*(X+Y)/(X+Z) - (X+10)/(Y-5)";
    char strCopy[41];
    char* tkn[3] = { "+-*/ ()", "( )", "+-*/ " };
    char* ptr;

    strcpy(strCopy, str); // copy str into strCopy
    printf("%s\n", str);
    printf("Using token string %s\n", tkn[0]);
    // the first call
    ptr = strtok(str, tkn[0]);
    printf("String is broken into: %s",ptr);
    while (ptr) {
      printf("  ,%s", ptr);
```

```
    // must make first argument a NULL character
    ptr = strtok(NULL, tkn[0]);
}

strcpy(str, strCopy); // restore str
printf("\nUsing token string %s\n", tkn[1]);
// the first call
ptr = strtok(str, tkn[1]);
printf("String is broken into: %s",ptr);
while (ptr) {
    printf("   ,%s", ptr);
    // must make first argument a NULL character
    ptr = strtok(NULL, tkn[1]);
}

strcpy(str, strCopy); // restore str
printf("\nUsing token string %s\n", tkn[2]);
// the first call
ptr = strtok(str, tkn[2]);
printf("String is broken into: %s",ptr);
while (ptr) {
    printf("   ,%s", ptr);
    // must make first argument a NULL character
    ptr = strtok(NULL, tkn[2]);
}
printf("\n\n");
return 0;
}
```

Answers to Day 10, "Advanced Parameters of Functions"

Quiz

1. The function is

```
double factorial(int i)
{ return (i > 1) ? double(i) * factorial(i-1) : 1; }
```

2. At first glance, the function may seem correct, although somewhat unusual. The case labels offer quick results for arguments of 0 to 4. However, the catch-all default clause traps arguments that are greater than 4 *and* are negative values! The latter kind of argument causes the recursion to overflow the memory resources. Here is a corrected version that returns a very large negative number when the argument is a negative number:

```
double factorial(int i)
{
  if (i > -1)
    switch (i) {
        case 0:
        case 1:
            return 1;
            break;
        case 2:
            return 2;
            break;
        case 3:
            return 6;
            break;
        case 4:
            return 24;
            break;
        default:
            return double(i) * factorial(i-1);
    }
  else
    return -1.0e+30; // numeric code for a bad argument
}
```

3. The nonrecursive version of function Fibonacci is

```
double Fibonacci(int n)
{
  double Fib0 = 0;
  double Fib1 = 1;
  double Fib2;

  if (n == 0)
    return 0;
```

```
        else if (n == 1 || n == 2)
          return 1;
        else
          for (int i = 0; i <= n; i++) {
            Fib2 = Fib0 + Fib1;
            Fib0 = Fib1;
            Fib1 = Fib2;
          }
          return Fib2;
      }
```

4. True. The first function uses a formal reference parameter, whereas the second parameter uses a pointer parameter.

Exercise

Here is my version of program ADVFUN9.CP:

```
/*
   C++ program that uses pointers to functions to implement a
   a linear regression program that supports temporary
   mathematical transformations.
*/

#include <iostream.h>
#include <math.h>

const unsigned MAX_SIZE = 100;

typedef double vector[MAX_SIZE];

struct regression {
   double Rsqr;
   double slope;
   double intercept;
};

// declare array of function pointers
double (*f[2])(double);

// declare function prototypes
void initArray(double*, double*, unsigned);
double linear(double);
double _sqrt(double);
double _log(double);
double sqr(double);
double reciprocal(double);
void calcRegression(double*, double*, unsigned, regression&,
                    double (*f[2])(double));
```

```
int select_transf(const char*);

main()
{
    char ans;
    unsigned count;
    vector x, y;
    regression stat;
    int trnsfx, trnsfy;

    do {
        cout << "Enter array size [2.."
            << MAX_SIZE << "] : ";
        cin >> count;
    } while (count <= 1 || count > MAX_SIZE);

    // initialize array
    initArray(x, y, count);
    // transform data
    do {
      // set the transformation functions
      trnsfx = select_transf("X");
      trnsfy = select_transf("Y");
      // set function pointer f[0]
      switch (trnsfx) {
       case 0 :
          f[0] = linear;
          break;
       case 1 :
          f[0] = _log;
          break;
       case 2 :
          f[0] = _sqrt;
          break;
       case 3 :
          f[0] = sqr;
          break;
       case 4 :
          f[0] = reciprocal;
          break;
       default :
          f[0] = linear;
          break;
      }
      // set function pointer f[1]
      switch (trnsfy) {
       case 0 :
          f[1] = linear;
          break;
       case 1 :
          f[1] = _log;
          break;
       case 2 :
          f[1] = _sqrt;
          break;
       case 3 :
```

```
                f[1] = sqr;
                break;
            case 4 :
                f[1] = reciprocal;
                break;
            default :
                f[1] = linear;
                break;
        }

        calcRegression(x, y, count, stat, f);

        cout << "\n\n\n\n"
             << "R-square = " << stat.Rsqr << "\n"
             << "Slope = " << stat.slope << "\n"
             << "Intercept = " << stat.intercept << "\n\n\n";
        cout << "Want to use other transformations? (Y/N) ";
        cin >> ans;
    } while (ans == 'Y' || ans == 'y');
    return 0;
}

void initArray(double* x, double* y, unsigned count)
// read data for array from the keyboard
{
    for (unsigned i = 0; i < count; i++, x++, y++) {
        cout << "X[" << i << "] : ";
        cin >> *x;
        cout << "Y[" << i << "] : ";
        cin >> *y;
    }
}

int select_transf(const char* var_name)
// select choice of transformation
{

    int choice = -1;
    cout << "\n\n\n";
    cout << "select transformation for variable " << var_name
         << "\n\n\n"
         << "0) No transformation\n"
         << "1) Logarithmic transformation\n"
         << "2) Square root transformation\n"
         << "3) Square   transformation\n"
         << "4) Reciprocal transformation\n";
    while (choice < 0 || choice > 4) {
        cout << "\nSelect choice by number : ";
        cin >> choice;
    }
    return choice;
}

double linear(double x)
{ return x; }

double _sqrt(double x)
{ return sqrt(x); }
```

```
double _log(double x)
{ return log(x); }

double sqr(double x)
{ return x * x; }

double reciprocal(double x)
{ return 1.0 / x; }

void calcRegression(double* x,
                    double* y,
                    unsigned count,
                    regression &stat,
                    double (*f[2])(double))

{
    double meanx, meany, sdevx, sdevy;
    double sum = (double) count, sumx = 0, sumy = 0;
    double sumxx = 0, sumyy = 0, sumxy = 0;
    double xdata, ydata;

    for (unsigned i = 0; i < count; i++) {
        xdata = (*f[0])(*(x+i));
        ydata = (*f[1])(*(y+i));
        sumx += xdata;
        sumy += ydata;
        sumxx += sqr(xdata);
        sumyy += sqr(ydata);
        sumxy += xdata * ydata;
    }

    meanx = sumx / sum;
    meany = sumy / sum;
    sdevx = sqrt((sumxx - sqr(sumx) / sum)/(sum-1.0));
    sdevy = sqrt((sumyy - sqr(sumy) / sum)/(sum-1.0));
    stat.slope = (sumxy - meanx * meany * sum) /
                 sqr(sdevx)/(sum-1);
    stat.intercept = meany - stat.slope * meanx;
    stat.Rsqr = sqr(sdevx / sdevy * stat.slope);
}
```

Answers to Day 11, "Object-Oriented Programming and C++ Classes"

Quiz

1. By default, the members of a class are protected. Therefore, the class declaration has no public member and cannot be used to create instances.

2. The third constructor has a default argument, which makes it redundant with the fourth constructor. The C++ compiler detects such an error.

3. True. `String("Hello Symantec C++")` creates a temporary instance of class `String` and then assigns it to the instance `s`.

4. Yes. The new statements are valid.

Exercise

Here is the implementation of function `main` in my version of program CLASS7.CP:

```
main()
{

  Complex c[5];
  c[1].assign(3, 5);
  c[2].assign(7, 5);
  c[4].assign(2, 3);

  c[3] = c[1] + c[2];
  cout << c[1] << " + " << c[2] << " = " << c[3] << "\n";
  cout << c[3] << " + " << c[4] << " = ";
  c[3] += c[4];
  cout << c[3] << "\n";
  return 0;
}
```

Answers to Day 12, "Basic Stream File I/O"

Quiz

1. False. The `read` and `write` functions cannot store and recall the dynamic data, which is accessed by a pointer member of a structure or a class.

2. True.

3. True.

4. False.

Exercise

Here is the code for member function `binSearch` and the updated function `main` in program IO4.CP (the output also shows the new global constant `NOT_FOUND` and the updated class declaration):

```
const unsigned NOT_FOUND = 0xffff;

class VmArray
{
   protected:
     fstream f;
     unsigned size;
     double badIndex;

   public:
     VmArray(unsigned Size, const char* filename);
     ~VmArray()
       { f.close(); }
     unsigned getSize() const
       { return size; }
     boolean writeElem(const char* str, unsigned index);
     boolean readElem(char* str, unsigned index);
     void Combsort();
     unsigned binSearch(const char* search);
};

unsigned VmArray::binSearch(const char* search)
{
  unsigned low = 0;
  unsigned high = size - 1;
  unsigned median;
  char str[STR_SIZE+1];
  int result;

  do {
    median = (low + high) / 2;
    readElem(str, median);
    result = strcmp(search, str);
    if (result > 0)
      low = median + 1;
    else
      high = median - 1;
  } while (result != 0 && low <= high);
  return (result == 0) ? median : NOT_FOUND;
}

main()
{
  const unsigned NUM_ELEMS = 10;
  char* data[] = { "Michigan", "California", "Virginia", "Maine",
                   "New York", "Florida", "Nevada", "Alaska",
                   "Ohio", "Maryland" };
  VmArray arr(NUM_ELEMS, "arr.dat");
  char str[STR_SIZE+1];
```

```
char c;
unsigned index;

// assign values to array arr
for (unsigned i = 0; i < arr.getSize(); i++) {
  strcpy(str, data[i]);
  arr.writeElem(str, i);
}
// display unordered array
cout << "Unsorted arrays is:\n";
for (i = 0; i < arr.getSize(); i++) {
  arr.readElem(str, i);
  cout << str << "\n";
}
// pause
cout << "\nPress any key and then Return to sort the array...";
cin >> c;
// sort the array
arr.Combsort();
// display sorted array
cout << "Sorted arrays is:\n";
for (i = 0; i < arr.getSize(); i++) {
  arr.readElem(str, i);
  cout << str << "\n"
}
// pause
cout << "\nPress any key and then Return to search the array...";
cin >> c;
// search for array elements using the pointer data
for (i = 0; i < NUM_ELEMS; i++) {
  index = arr.binSearch(data[i]);
  if (index != NOT_FOUND)
    cout << "Found " << data[i]
         << " at index " << index << "\n";
  else
    cout << "No match for " << data[i] << "\n";
}
return 0;
```

Answers to Day 13, "Programming the Mac GUI Using the TCL"

Quiz

1. False. Your applications are instances of the *descendants* of class CApplication.

2. True.

3. The class CIntegerText.

4. The class `CIconButton`.

5. True.

6. False. The function `DoCommands` handles only commands.

7. False. The TCL classes have no class `CListBox`. The class `CArrayPane` supports the list box.

8. The Visual Architect utility generates the classes `CApp`, `x_CApp`, `CMain`, and `x_CMain`.

Answers to Day 14, "Using the Visual Architect Utility"

Quiz

1. False. You must invoke the Commands dialog box before you can add or delete commands.

2. False. The Define Data Members dialog box allows you to define only data members that have predefined data types.

3. True.

4. True.

5. False. The Visual Architect utility performs this task for you.

Answers to Day 15, "Creating Basic TCL Applications"

Quiz

1. The last three arguments of function `ParamText` are empty literal strings. Each one of these parameters should be `"\p"`, since it is an argument to a Pascal string.

2. No, the code in function `DoCommand` does not reveal this information.

3. They certainly can. In fact, this feature enables your programs to have menu commands and buttons that generate the same command to perform the same task.

Exercise

Here is my version of file x_CMain.h for the Menu2 program project:

```
 1:  /****************************************************************
 2:   x_CMain.h
 3:
 4:              Header File For CMain Lower-Layer Document Class
 5:
 6:      Copyright (c) 1994 My Software Inc. All rights reserved.
 7:
 8:  Generated by Visual Architect(TM)
 9:
10:  This file is rewritten each time you generate code. You should
11:  not make changes to this file; changes should go in the My.h
12:  file, instead.
13:
14:  If you want to change how Visual Architect generates this file,
15:  you can change the template for this file. It is "_Doc.h" in
16:  the Visual Architect Templates folder.
17:
18:  ****************************************************************/
19:
20:  #pragma once
21:
22:  #include "CSaver.h"
23:
24:  #include "ItsContentsClass.h"
25:
26:  #define x_CMain_super      CSaver<ITSCONTENTSCLASS>
27:
28:  class CFile;
29:
30:  class x_CMain : public x_CMain_super
31:
32:  {
33:  public:
34:
35:      TCL_DECLARE_CLASS
36:
37:
38:      void      Ix_CMain(void);
39:
40:      virtual   void    DoCommand(long theCommand);
41:      virtual   void    UpdateMenus(void);
42:
43:  protected:
44:      virtual   void    MakeNewWindow(void);
45:
```

```
46:      virtual   void    FailOpen(CFile *aFile);
47:      virtual void    PositionWindow(void);
48:
49:      virtual void    DoCmdShowMsg1(void);
50:      virtual void    DoCmdShowMsg2(void);
51:      virtual void    DoCmdShowMsg3(void);
52:   };
53:
54:   #define    CVueCMain    128
```

Here is my version of file x_CMain.cp for the Menu2 program project (the bold lines indicate the ones that I manually inserted):

```
1:    /****************************************************************
2:     x_CMain.c
3:
4:                    CMain Document Class
5:
6:        Copyright (c) 1994 My Software Inc. All rights reserved.
7:
8:    Generated by Visual Architect(TM) 10:14 PM Sun, Jun 12, 1994
9:
10:   This file is rewritten each time you generate code. You should
11:   not make changes to this file; changes should go in the My.h
12:   file, instead.
13:
14:   If you want to change how Visual Architect generates this file,
15:   you can change the template for this file. It is "_Doc.h" in
16:   the Visual Architect Templates folder.
17:   ****************************************************************/
18:
19:   #include "x_CMain.h"
20:
21:   #include "CMain.h"
22:
23:   #include "MainItems.h"
24:
25:   #include "ViewUtilities.h"
26:   #include "CApp.h"
27:
28:   #include <CApplication.h>
29:   #include <CBartender.h>
30:   #include <Commands.h>
31:   #include <Constants.h>
32:   #include <CDecorator.h>
33:   #include <CDesktop.h>
34:   #include <CFile.h>
35:   #include <TBUtilities.h>
36:   #include <CWindow.h>
37:
38:   extern CApplication *gApplication; /* The application */
39:   extern CDecorator *gDecorator; /* Decorator for arranging
40:                                        windows */
41:   extern CDesktop *gDesktop;  /* The visible Desktop */
42:   extern CBartender *gBartender; /* Manages all menus */
43:
```

```
44:
45:       // Define symbols for commands handled by this class
46:       // Prevents a recompile every time any command changed.
47:
48:  #define cmdShowMsg1 512
49:  #define cmdShowMsg2 513
50:  #define cmdShowMsg3 514
51:  #define ALRTgeneral 128
52:
53:  TCL_DEFINE_CLASS_M1(x_CMain, x_CMain_super);
54:
55:  /**** C O N S T R U C T I O N / D E S T R U C T I O N
56:                                        M E T H O D S ****/
57:
58:
59:  /****************************************************************
60:    Ix_CMain
61:
62:       Initialize the document
63:  ****************************************************************/
64:
65:  void x_CMain::Ix_CMain()
66:
67:  {
68:       IDocument(gApplication, TRUE);
69:
70:           // Initialize data members below.
71:  }
72:
73:
74:  /****************************************************************
75:    MakeNewWindow
76:
77:  Create a new, empty window. Subclass may override to populate
78:  the new window.
79:  ****************************************************************/
80:
81:  void x_CMain::MakeNewWindow(void)
82:
83:  {
84:       itsWindow = TCLGetNamedWindow("\pMain", this);
85:
86:       itsMainPane = (CPane*) TCLGetItemPointer(itsWindow, 0);
87:
88:       // Initialize pointers to the subpanes in the window
89:
90:  }
91:
92:
93:  /****************************************************************
94:    FailOpen {OVERRIDE}
95:
96:  Fail if file already open in this application.
97:
98:  This function calls the application's FileAlreadyOpen function
99:  and fails quietly if the file is open.
```

```
100:
101:    Note that open may also fail if the file is open in
102:    another application. This will cause a failure in open,
103:    but you may wish to override this function to detect this
104:    case and provide a more meaningful error message than -49.
105:    *****************************************************************/
106:
107:    void x_CMain::FailOpen(CFile *aFile)
108:
109:    {
110:        /* Only the application knows          */
111:        if ((((CApp*)gApplication)->FileAlreadyOpen(aFile))
112:            Failure(kSilentErr, 0);
113:    }
114:
115:
116:    /*****************************************************************
117:     PositionWindow
118:
119:    The default method in CSaver calls the the decorator, which
120:    staggers and resizes the window. Since the window has already
121:    been positioned when it is initialized from the view resource,
122:    we don't want to do this twice.
123:    *****************************************************************/
124:
125:    void      x_CMain::PositionWindow()
126:
127:    {
128:    }
129:
130:
131:
132:
133:    /*****************************************************************
134:     DoCommand {OVERRIDE}
135:
136:    Dispatch Visual Architect-specified actions.
137:    *****************************************************************/
138:
139:    void x_CMain::DoCommand(long theCommand)
140:
141:    {
142:        switch (theCommand)
143:        {
144:            case cmdShowMsg1:
145:                DoCmdShowMsg1();
146:                break;
147:            case cmdShowMsg2:
148:                DoCmdShowMsg2();
149:                break;
150:            case cmdShowMsg3:
151:                DoCmdShowMsg3();
152:                break;
153:            default:
154:                CDocument::DoCommand(theCommand);
155:        }
```

```
156:   }
157:
158:
159:   /****************************************************************
160:    UpdateMenus {OVERRIDE}
161:
162:   Enable menus which generate commands handled by this class.
163:   ****************************************************************/
164:
165:   void x_CMain::UpdateMenus()
166:
167:   {
168:       CDocument::UpdateMenus();
169:       gBartender->EnableCmd(cmdShowMsg1);
170:       gBartender->EnableCmd(cmdShowMsg2);
171:       gBartender->EnableCmd(cmdShowMsg3);
172:   }
173:
174:
175:   /****************************************************************
176:    DoCmdShowMsg1
177:
178:   Respond to cmdShowMsg1 command.
179:   ****************************************************************/
180:
181:   void x_CMain::DoCmdShowMsg1()
182:
183:   {
184:           // Subclass must override this function to
185:           // handle the command
186:           PositionDialog('ALRT', ALRTgeneral);
187:           InitCursor();
188:           ParamText(
189:            "\p           M E S S A G E\r\rThis is Message 3",
190:            "\p", "\p", "\p");
191:           Alert(ALRTgeneral, NULL);
192:   }
193:
194:
195:   /****************************************************************
196:    DoCmdShowMsg2
197:
198:   Respond to cmdShowMsg2 command.
199:   ****************************************************************/
200:
201:   void x_CMain::DoCmdShowMsg2()
202:
203:   {
204:           // Subclass must override this function to
205:           // handle the command
206:           PositionDialog('ALRT', ALRTgeneral);
207:           InitCursor();
208:           ParamText(
209:            "\p           M E S S A G E\r\rThis is Message 3",
210:            "\p", "\p", "\p");
211:           Alert(ALRTgeneral, NULL);
212:   }
```

```
213:
214:
215:    /*****************************************************************
216:      DoCmdShowMsg3
217:
218:    Respond to cmdShowMsg3 command.
219:    *****************************************************************/
220:
221:    void x_CMain::DoCmdShowMsg3()
222:
223:    {
224:            // Subclass must override this function to
225:            // handle the command
226:            PositionDialog('ALRT', ALRTgeneral);
227:            InitCursor();
228:            ParamText(
229:              "\p            M E S S A G E\r\rThis is Message 3",
230:              "\p", "\p", "\p");
231:            Alert(ALRTgeneral, NULL);
232:    }
```

Here is my version of file MainItems.h for the Menu2 program project:

```
1:    /*****************************************************************
2:      MainItems.h
3:
4:                    Main Item Constants
5:
6:        Copyright (c) 1994 My Software Inc. All rights reserved.
7:
8:    Generated by Visual Architect(TM)
9:
10:   This file is rewritten each time you generate code. You should
11:   not make changes to this file; changes should go in the My.h
12:   file, instead.
13:
14:   If you want to change how Visual Architect generates this file,
15:   you can change the template for this file. It is "_Doc.h" in
16:   the Visual Architect Templates folder.
17:   *****************************************************************/
18:
19:   #pragma once
20:
21:
22:       //    Item numbers for each item.
23:       //
24:       //    Use TCLGetItemPointer (ViewUtilities) to convert these
25:       //    item numbers to a pointer to the named item.
26:
27:   enum
28:   {
29:       Main_Begin_,
30:       Main_End_
31:   };
```

Here is my version of file AppCommands.cp for the Menu2 program project:

```
1:   /**************************************************************
2:   MyCommands.h
3:
4:               Header File For Command Symbols
5:
6:       Copyright (c) 1994 My Software Inc. All rights reserved.
7:
8:   Generated by Visual Architect(TM)
9:
10:  This file is regenerated each time.
11:
12:  **************************************************************/
13:
14:  #pragma once
15:
16:  #define cmdShowMsg1      512
17:  #define cmdShowMsg2      513
18:  #define cmdShowMsg3      514
```

Answers to Day 16, "The Static Text Control"

Quiz

1. To set font style of a static text control to be both bold and italic, send that control the C++ message SetFontStyle. Supply that message with the argument bold + italic.

2. False. The small caps style is not supported by the TCL classes.

3. False. You can display the multiple characters of a static text only horizontally.

4. True.

Exercise

Here is my version of file x_CMain.h for the Static4 program project:

```
1:   /**************************************************************
2:   x_CMain.h
3:
4:               Header File For CMain Lower-Layer Document Class
5:
6:       Copyright (c) 1994 My Software Inc. All rights reserved.
7:
```

```
 8:   Generated by Visual Architect(TM)
 9:
10:   This file is rewritten each time you generate code. You should
11:   not make changes to this file; changes should go in the My.h
12:   file, instead.
13:
14:   If you want to change how Visual Architect generates this file,
15:   you can change the template for this file. It is "_Doc.h" in
16:   the Visual Architect Templates folder.
17:   *****************************************************************/
18:
19:   #pragma once
20:
21:   #include "CSaver.h"
22:   class CStaticText;
23:
24:   #include "ItsContentsClass.h"
25:
26:   #define x_CMain_super       CSaver<ITSCONTENTSCLASS>
27:
28:   class CFile;
29:
30:   class x_CMain : public x_CMain_super
31:
32:   {
33:   public:
34:
35:       TCL_DECLARE_CLASS
36:
37:       // Pointers to panes in window
38:       CStaticText     *fMain_TextLbl;
39:       int fontState;
40:
41:       void      Ix_CMain(void);
42:
43:       virtual     void    DoCommand(long theCommand);
44:       virtual     void    UpdateMenus(void);
45:
46:   protected:
47:       virtual void    MakeNewWindow(void);
48:
49:       virtual void    FailOpen(CFile *aFile);
50:       virtual void    PositionWindow(void);
51:
52:       virtual void    DoCmdSetText(void);
53:   };
54:
55:   #define     CVueCMain     128
```

Here is my version of file x_CMain.cp for the Static4 program project:

```
1:   /*****************************************************************
2:    x_CMain.c
3:
4:                CMain Document Class
5:
```

```
 6:      Copyright (c) 1994 My Software Inc. All rights reserved.
 7:
 8: Generated by Visual Architect(TM) 10:25 PM Sun, Jun 12, 1994
 9:
10: This file is rewritten each time you generate code. You should
11: not make changes to this file; changes should go in the My.h
12: file, instead.
13:
14: If you want to change how Visual Architect generates this file,
15: you can change the template for this file. It is "_Doc.h" in
16: the Visual Architect Templates folder.
17: **************************************************************/
18:
19: #include "x_CMain.h"
20:
21: #include "CMain.h"
22:
23: #include "MainItems.h"
24:
25: #include "ViewUtilities.h"
26: #include "CApp.h"
27:
28: #include <CApplication.h>
29: #include <CBartender.h>
30: #include <Commands.h>
31: #include <Constants.h>
32: #include <CDecorator.h>
33: #include <CDesktop.h>
34: #include <CFile.h>
35: #include <TBUtilities.h>
36: #include <CWindow.h>
37:
38: extern CApplication *gApplication; /* The application */
39: extern CDecorator *gDecorator; /* Decorator for arranging
40:                                      windows */
41: extern CDesktop *gDesktop;   /* The visible Desktop */
42: extern CBartender *gBartender; /* Manages all menus */
43:
44: #include "CStaticText.h"
45:
46:     // Define symbols for commands handled by this class
47:     // Prevents a recompile every time any command changed.
48:
49: #define cmdSetText 512
50:
51:
52: TCL_DEFINE_CLASS_M1(x_CMain, x_CMain_super);
53:
54: /**** C O N S T R U C T I O N / D E S T R U C T I O N
55:                                        M E T H O D S ****/
56:
57:
58: /*************************************************************
59:   Ix_CMain
60:
61: Initialize the document
```

```
 62:    *****************************************************************/
 63:
 64:    void x_CMain::Ix_CMain()
 65:
 66:    {
 67:        IDocument(gApplication, TRUE);
 68:
 69:        // Initialize data members below.
 70:        fontState = 0;
 71:    }
 72:
 73:
 74:    /****************************************************************
 75:     MakeNewWindow
 76:
 77:    Create a new, empty window. Subclass may override to populate
 78:    the new window.
 79:    *****************************************************************/
 80:
 81:    void x_CMain::MakeNewWindow(void)
 82:
 83:    {
 84:      itsWindow = TCLGetNamedWindow("\pMain", this);
 85:
 86:      itsMainPane = (CPane*) TCLGetItemPointer(itsWindow, 0);
 87:
 88:      // Initialize pointers to the subpanes in the window
 89:
 90:      fMain_TextLbl = (CStaticText*)
 91:                    itsWindow->FindViewByID(kMain_TextLblID);
 92:      ASSERT(member(fMain_TextLbl, CStaticText));
 93:
 94:    }
 95:
 96:
 97:    /****************************************************************
 98:     FailOpen {OVERRIDE}
 99:
100:    Fail if file already open in this application.
101:
102:    This function calls the application's FileAlreadyOpen function
103:    and fails quietly if the file is open.
104:
105:    Note that open may also fail if the file is open in
106:    another application. This will cause a failure in open,
107:    but you may wish to override this function to detect this
108:    case and provide a more meaningful error message than -49.
109:    *****************************************************************/
110:
111:    void x_CMain::FailOpen(CFile *aFile)
112:
113:    {
114:        /* Only the application knows        */
115:        if (((CApp*)gApplication)->FileAlreadyOpen(aFile))
116:            Failure(kSilentErr, 0);
117:    }
```

B

```
118:
119:
120:    /***************************************************************
121:      PositionWindow
122:
123:    The default method in CSaver calls the the decorator, which
124:    staggers and resizes the window. Since the window has already
125:    been positioned when it is initialized from the view resource,
126:    we don't want to do this twice.
127:    ***************************************************************/
128:
129:    void      x_CMain::PositionWindow()
130:
131:    {
132:    }
133:
134:
135:
136:
137:    /***************************************************************
138:      DoCommand {OVERRIDE}
139:
140:    Dispatch Visual Architect-specified actions.
141:    ***************************************************************/
142:
143:    void x_CMain::DoCommand(long theCommand)
144:
145:    {
146:        switch (theCommand)
147:        {
148:            case cmdSetText:
149:                DoCmdSetText();
150:                break;
151:            default:
152:                CDocument::DoCommand(theCommand);
153:        }
154:    }
155:
156:
157:    /***************************************************************
158:      UpdateMenus {OVERRIDE}
159:
160:    Enable menus which generate commands handled by this class.
161:    ***************************************************************/
162:
163:    void x_CMain::UpdateMenus()
164:
165:    {
166:        CDocument::UpdateMenus();
167:        gBartender->EnableCmd(cmdSetText);
168:    }
169:
170:
171:    /***************************************************************
172:      DoCmdSetText
173:
```

```
174:     Respond to cmdSetText command.
175:     **************************************************************/
176:
177:     void x_CMain::DoCmdSetText()
178:
179:     {
180:         const MAX_STATE = 5;
181:         // Subclass must override this function to
182:         // handle the command
183:         switch (fontState) {
184:           case 0:
185:             fMain_TextLbl->SetFontStyle(normal);
186:             fMain_TextLbl->SetFontSize(10);
187:             fMain_TextLbl->SetAlignCmd(cmdAlignLeft);
188:             break;
189:
190:           case 1:
191:             fMain_TextLbl->SetFontStyle(bold);
192:             break;
193:
194:           case 2:
195:             fMain_TextLbl->SetFontStyle(italic);
196:             break;
197:
198:           case 3:
199:             fMain_TextLbl->SetFontStyle(normal);
200:             fMain_TextLbl->SetFontSize(14);
201:             break;
202:
203:           case 4:
204:             fMain_TextLbl->SetFontSize(10);
205:             fMain_TextLbl->SetAlignCmd(cmdAlignRight);
206:             break;
207:         }
208:         fontState = (fontState + 1) % MAX_STATE;
209:     }
```

Here is my version of file MainItems.h for the Static4 program project:

```
1:    /***************************************************************
2:     MainItems.h
3:
4:                    Main Item Constants
5:
6:         Copyright (c) 1994 My Software Inc. All rights reserved.
7:
8:    Generated by Visual Architect(TM)
9:
10:   This file is rewritten each time you generate code. You should
11:   not make changes to this file; changes should go in the My.h
12:   file, instead.
13:
14:   If you want to change how Visual Architect generates this file,
15:   you can change the template for this file. It is "_Doc.h" in
16:   the Visual Architect Templates folder.
17:   ***************************************************************/
```

```
18:
19:    #pragma once
20:
21:
22:        //     Item numbers for each item.
23:        //
24:        //     Use TCLGetItemPointer (ViewUtilities) to convert these
25:        //     item numbers to a pointer to the named item.
26:
27:    enum
28:    {
29:        Main_Begin_,
30:        kMain_Stat4 = 1,
31:        kMain_Stat4ID = 1L,
32:        kMain_TextLbl = 2,
33:        kMain_TextLblID = 2L,
34:        Main_End_
35:    };
```

Here is my version of file AppCommands.h for the Static4 program project:

```
1:    /****************************************************************
2:    MyCommands.h
3:
4:                    Header File For Command Symbols
5:
6:        Copyright (c) 1994 My Software Inc. All rights reserved.
7:
8:    Generated by Visual Architect(TM)
9:
10:    This file is regenerated each time.
11:
12:    ****************************************************************/
13:
14:    #pragma once
15:
16:    #define cmdSetText     512
```

Answers to Day 17, "The Edit Box and Button Controls"

Quiz

1. False. An invisible button is a disabled button.

2. False. There is no member function GetTextPtr. Instead, use the member function GetTextHandle.

3. The functions that write text use the char pointer to the source string. By contrast, the functions that read the text from an edit box use a handle, which is a double char pointer.

Exercise

The following listing shows the source code for the x_CMain.h header file for the Button2 program project. The bold lines indicate the ones that I manually inserted to customize the program.

B

```
 1:   /*****************************************************************
 2:   x_CMain.h
 3:
 4:              Header File For CMain Lower-Layer Document Class
 5:
 6:       Copyright (c) 1994 My Software Inc. All rights reserved.
 7:
 8:   Generated by Visual Architect(TM)
 9:
10:   This file is rewritten each time you generate code. You should
11:   not make changes to this file; changes should go in the My.h
12:   file, instead.
13:
14:   If you want to change how Visual Architect generates this file,
15:   you can change the template for this file. It is "_Doc.h" in
16:   the Visual Architect Templates folder.
17:
18:   *****************************************************************/
19:
20:   #pragma once
21:
22:   #include "CSaver.h"
23:   class CStaticText;
24:   class CDialogText;
25:   class CButton;
26:
27:   #include "ItsContentsClass.h"
28:
29:   #define x_CMain_super     CSaver<ITSCONTENTSCLASS>
30:
31:   #define BUF_SIZE 1000
32:   #define MAX_MEMREG 26
33:
34:   class CFile;
35:
36:   class x_CMain : public x_CMain_super
37:
38:   {
39:   public:
40:
41:        TCL_DECLARE_CLASS
42:
```

```
43:      // Pointers to panes in window
44:      CStaticText    *fMain_Operand1Lbl;
45:      CStaticText    *fMain_OperatorLbl;
46:      CStaticText    *fMain_Operand2Lbl;
47:      CStaticText    *fMain_ResutLbl;
48:      CDialogText    *fMain_Operand1Box;
49:      CDialogText    *fMain_OperatorBox;
50:      CDialogText    *fMain_Operand2Box;
51:      CDialogText    *fMain_ResultBox;
52:      CStaticText    *fMain_ErrMsgLbl;
53:      CDialogText    *fMain_VarsBox;
54:      CStaticText    *fMain_VarLbl;
55:      CButton    *fMain_CalcBtn;
56:      CButton    *fMain_StoreBtn;
57:      CButton    *fMain_QuitBtn;
58:
59:      char buff[BUF_SIZE];
60:      long var[MAX_MEMREG];
61:
62:      void    Ix_CMain(void);
63:
64:      virtual    void    DoCommand(long theCommand);
65:      virtual    void    UpdateMenus(void);
66:
67:  protected:
68:      virtual    void    MakeNewWindow(void);
69:
70:      virtual    void    FailOpen(CFile *aFile);
71:      virtual void    PositionWindow(void);
72:
73:      virtual void    DoCmdCalc(void);
74:      virtual void    DoCmdStore(void);
75:
76:      long getVar(long LineNum);
77:      void putVar(long x);
78:  };
79:
80:  #define    CVueCMain    128
```

This listing shows the declaration of class x_CMain, which contains a number of data members and member functions. The Visual Architect utility generated the data members (in lines 44 to 47) which are pointers to the various controls. These members are pointers to the CStaticText, CDialogText, and CButton classes. I inserted the data members buff and var in lines 59 and 60. The data member buff offers a text buffer for the class. The data member var stores the values for the single-letter variables. Although this information also appears in the Variables edit box, using the member var speeds up updating the contents of the Variables edit box. This increase in speed is due to the fact that the program writes only the updated list of values to the Variables edit box. The class x_CMain contains the member functions DoCmdShowMsg1, DoCmdCalc, and DoCmdStore, which handle the commands cmdShowMsg1, cmdCalc, and cmdStore, respectively. I manually inserted the declarations of member functions getVar and putVar to read and write data to the Variables edit box, respectively.

The following listing shows the source code for the x_CMain.cp implementation file for the Button2 program project. The bold lines show the ones that I manually inserted.

```
1:  /****************************************************************
2:   x_CMain.c
3:
4:                  CMain Document Class
5:
6:      Copyright (c) 1994 My Software Inc. All rights reserved.
7:
8:  Generated by Visual Architect(TM) 3:25 PM Mon, Jun 13, 1994
9:
10: This file is rewritten each time you generate code. You should
11: not make changes to this file; changes should go in the My.c
12: file, instead.
13:
14: If you want to change how Visual Architect generates this file,
15: you can change the template for this file. It is "_Doc_cp" in
16: the Visual Architect Templates folder.
17:
18: ****************************************************************/
19:
20: // my own include directives
21: #include <ctype.h>
22: #include <stdlib.h>
23: #include <stdio.h>
24: #include <string.h>
25: #include <math.h>
26:
27: #include "x_CMain.h"
28:
29: #include "CMain.h"
30:
31: #include "MainItems.h"
32:
33: #include "ViewUtilities.h"
34: #include "CApp.h"
35:
36: #include <CApplication.h>
37: #include <CBartender.h>
38: #include <Commands.h>
39: #include <Constants.h>
40: #include <CDecorator.h>
41: #include <CDesktop.h>
42: #include <CFile.h>
43: #include <TBUtilities.h>
44: #include <CWindow.h>
45:
46: extern CApplication *gApplication;  /* The application  */
47: extern CDecorator *gDecorator;  /* Decorator for arranging
48:                                    windows */
49: extern CDesktop  *gDesktop;   /* The visible Desktop */
50: extern CBartender *gBartender;  /* Manages all menus */
51:
52: #include "CStaticText.h"
53: #include "CDialogText.h"
```

```
54:   #include "CButton.h"
55:
56:   // Define symbols for commands handled by this class
57:   // Prevents a recompile every time any command changed.
58:
59:   #define cmdCalc 512
60:   #define cmdStore 513
61:   #define MaxEditLen 255
62:
63:   TCL_DEFINE_CLASS_M1(x_CMain, x_CMain_super);
64:
65:   /**** C O N S T R U C T I O N / D E S T R U C T I O N
66:                                        M E T H O D S ****/
67:
68:
69:   /****************************************************************
70:    Ix_CMain
71:
72:   Initialize the document
73:   ****************************************************************/
74:
75:   void x_CMain::Ix_CMain()
76:
77:   {
78:
79:      IDocument(gApplication, TRUE);
80:
81:      // Initialize data members below.
82:      // initialize the data member var
83:      for (int i = 0; i < MAX_MEMREG; i++)
84:        var[i] = 0;
85:   }
86:
87:
88:   /****************************************************************
89:    MakeNewWindow
90:
91:   Create a new, empty window. Subclass may override to populate
92:   the new window.
93:   ****************************************************************/
94:
95:   void x_CMain::MakeNewWindow(void)
96:
97:   {
98:      char s[MaxEditLen+1];
99:
100:     itsWindow = TCLGetNamedWindow("\pMain", this);
101:
102:     itsMainPane = (CPane*) TCLGetItemPointer(itsWindow, 0);
103:
104:     // Initialize pointers to the subpanes in the window
105:
106:     fMain_Operand1Lbl = (CStaticText*)
107:                    itsWindow->FindViewByID(kMain_Operand1LblID);
108:     ASSERT(member(fMain_Operand1Lbl, CStaticText));
109:
```

```
110:      fMain_OperatorLbl = (CStaticText*)
111:                      itsWindow->FindViewByID(kMain_OperatorLblID);
112:      ASSERT(member(fMain_OperatorLbl, CStaticText));
113:
114:      fMain_Operand2Lbl = (CStaticText*)
115:                      itsWindow->FindViewByID(kMain_Operand2LblID);
116:      ASSERT(member(fMain_Operand2Lbl, CStaticText));
117:
118:      fMain_ResutLbl = (CStaticText*)
119:                      itsWindow->FindViewByID(kMain_ResutLblID);
120:      ASSERT(member(fMain_ResutLbl, CStaticText));
121:
122:      fMain_Operand1Box = (CDialogText*)
123:                      itsWindow->FindViewByID(kMain_Operand1BoxID);
124:      ASSERT(member(fMain_Operand1Box, CDialogText));
125:
126:      fMain_OperatorBox = (CDialogText*)
127:                      itsWindow->FindViewByID(kMain_OperatorBoxID);
128:      ASSERT(member(fMain_OperatorBox, CDialogText));
129:
130:      fMain_Operand2Box = (CDialogText*)
131:                      itsWindow->FindViewByID(kMain_Operand2BoxID);
132:      ASSERT(member(fMain_Operand2Box, CDialogText));
133:
134:      fMain_ResultBox = (CDialogText*)
135:                      itsWindow->FindViewByID(kMain_ResultBoxID);
136:      ASSERT(member(fMain_ResultBox, CDialogText));
137:
138:      fMain_ErrMsgLbl = (CStaticText*)
139:                      itsWindow->FindViewByID(kMain_ErrMsgLblID);
140:      ASSERT(member(fMain_ErrMsgLbl, CStaticText));
141:
142:      fMain_VarsBox = (CDialogText*)
143:                      itsWindow->FindViewByID(kMain_VarsBoxID);
144:      ASSERT(member(fMain_VarsBox, CDialogText));
145:
146:      fMain_VarLbl = (CStaticText*)
147:                      itsWindow->FindViewByID(kMain_VarLblID);
148:      ASSERT(member(fMain_VarLbl, CStaticText));
149:
150:      fMain_CalcBtn = (CButton*)
151:                      itsWindow->FindViewByID(kMain_CalcBtnID);
152:      ASSERT(member(fMain_CalcBtn, CButton));
153:
154:      fMain_StoreBtn = (CButton*)
155:                      itsWindow->FindViewByID(kMain_StoreBtnID);
156:      ASSERT(member(fMain_StoreBtn, CButton));
157:
158:      fMain_QuitBtn = (CButton*)
159:                      itsWindow->FindViewByID(kMain_QuitBtnID);
160:      ASSERT(member(fMain_QuitBtn, CButton));
161:
162:      // insert single-letter variables in Variables box
163:      for (char c = 'A'; c <= 'Z'; c++) {
164:        sprintf(s, "%c: %ld\r", c, var[c - 'A']);
165:        fMain_VarsBox->InsertTextPtr(s, strlen(s), TRUE);
166:      }
```

```
167:  }
168:
169:
170:  /***************************************************************
171:   FailOpen {OVERRIDE}
172:
173:  Fail if file already open in this application.
174:
175:  This function calls the application's FileAlreadyOpen function
176:  and fails quietly if the file is open.
177:
178:  Note that open may also fail if the file is open in
179:  another application. This will cause a failure in open,
180:  but you may wish to override this function to detect this
181:  case and provide a more meaningful error message than -49.
182:  ***************************************************************/
183:
184:  void x_CMain::FailOpen(CFile *aFile)
185:
186:  {
187:    /* Only the application knows   */
188:    if (((CApp*)gApplication)->FileAlreadyOpen(aFile))
189:      Failure(kSilentErr, 0);
190:  }
191:
192:
193:  /***************************************************************
194:   PositionWindow
195:
196:  The default method in CSaver calls the the decorator, which
197:  staggers and resizes the window. Since the window has already
198:  been positioned when it is initialized from the view resource,
199:  we don't want to do this twice.
200:  ***************************************************************/
201:
202:  void x_CMain::PositionWindow()
203:
204:  {
205:  }
206:
207:
208:
209:
210:  /***************************************************************
211:   DoCommand {OVERRIDE}
212:
213:  Dispatch Visual Architect-specified actions.
214:  ***************************************************************/
215:
216:  void x_CMain::DoCommand(long theCommand)
217:
218:  {
219:    switch (theCommand)
220:    {
221:      case cmdCalc:
```

```
222:        DoCmdCalc();
223:          break;
224:      case cmdStore:
225:        DoCmdStore();
226:          break;
227:      default:
228:        CDocument::DoCommand(theCommand);
229:    }
230:  }
231:
232:
233:  /****************************************************************
234:    UpdateMenus {OVERRIDE}
235:
236:  Enable menus which generate commands handled by this class.
237:  ****************************************************************/
238:
239:  void x_CMain::UpdateMenus()
240:
241:  {
242:    CDocument::UpdateMenus();
243:    gBartender->EnableCmd(cmdCalc);
244:    gBartender->EnableCmd(cmdStore);
245:  }
246:
247:
248:  /****************************************************************
249:    DoCmdCalc
250:
251:    Respond to cmdCalc command.
252:  ****************************************************************/
253:
254:  void x_CMain::DoCmdCalc()
255:
256:  {
257:    long x, y, z;
258:    Boolean bInError;
259:    char opStr[MaxEditLen+1];
260:    char s[MaxEditLen+1];
261:    Handle h = (char**) &buff;
262:    long n;
263:
264:    // obtain the string in the Operand1 edit box
265:    h = fMain_Operand1Box->GetTextHandle();
266:    n = fMain_Operand1Box->GetLength();
267:    strncpy(s, *h, n);
268:    // does the Operand1Box contain the name
269:    // of a single-letter variable?
270:    if (isalpha(s[0]))
271:      // obtain the value from the Variables edit box
272:      x = getVar(toupper(s[0]) - 'A');
273:    else
274:      // convert string in the edit box into a number
275:      x = atol(s);
276:
277:    // obtain the string in the Operand 2 edit box
```

```
278:    h = fMain_Operand2Box->GetTextHandle();
279:    n = fMain_Operand2Box->GetLength();
280:    strncpy(s, *h, n);
281:    // does the Operand2Box contain the name
282:    // of a single-letter variable?
283:    if (isalpha(s[0]))
284:      // obtain the value from the Variables edit box
285:      y = getVar(toupper(s[0]) - 'A');
286:    else
287:      // convert string in the edit box into a number
288:      y = atol(s);
289:
290:    // obtain the string in the Operator edit box
291:    h = fMain_OperatorBox->GetTextHandle();
292:    n = fMain_OperatorBox->GetLength();
293:    strncpy(opStr, *h, n);
294:
295:    // Reset the error message
296:    fMain_ErrMsgLbl->SetTextString("\pError Message: None");
297:    bInError = FALSE;
298:
299:    // determine the requested operation
300:    if (opStr[0] == '+')
301:      z = x + y;
302:    else if (opStr[0] == '-')
303:      z = x - y;
304:    else if (opStr[0] == '*')
305:      z = x * y;
306:    else if (opStr[0] == '/') {
307:      if (y != 0)
308:        z = x / y;
309:      else {
310:        bInError = TRUE;
311:        fMain_ErrMsgLbl->SetTextString(
312:              "\pError Message: Division by zero");
313:      }
314:    }
315:    else if (opStr[0] == '^') {
316:      z = 1;
317:      if (y >= 0)
318:        for (int i = 1; i <= y; i++)
319:          z *= x;
320:      else {
321:        bInError = TRUE;
322:        fMain_ErrMsgLbl->SetTextString(
323:            "\pError Message: negative exponent");
324:      }
325:    }
326:    else {
327:      bInError = TRUE;
328:      fMain_ErrMsgLbl->SetTextString(
329:            "\pError Message: Invalid operator");
330:    }
331:
332:    // display the result if there is no error
333:    if (!bInError) {
```

```
334:        sprintf(s, "%ld", z);
335:        fMain_ResultBox->SetTextPtr(s, strlen(s));
336:        fMain_StoreBtn->Activate();
337:      }
338:      else
339:        fMain_StoreBtn->Deactivate();
340:    }
341:
342:
343:    /***************************************************************
344:      DoCmdStore
345:
346:    Respond to cmdStore command.
347:    ***************************************************************/
348:
349:    void x_CMain::DoCmdStore()
350:
351:    {
352:      long n;
353:      char s[MaxEditLen+1];
354:      Handle h = (char**) &buff;
355:
356:      h = fMain_ResultBox->GetTextHandle();
357:      n = fMain_ResultBox->GetLength();
358:      strncpy(s, *h, n);
359:      s[n] = '\0';
360:      putVar(atol(s));
361:    }
362:
363:    /***************************************************************
364:      getVar
365:
366:    obtain a variable from the Variables edit box.
367:    ***************************************************************/
368:
369:    long x_CMain::getVar(long LineNum)
370:
371:    {
372:      long lineSize, lineStart, lineEnd;
373:      long n;
374:      char s[MaxEditLen+1];
375:      Handle h = (char**) &buff;
376:
377:      if (LineNum >= MAX_MEMREG || LineNum < 0)
378:        return 0;
379:
380:      h = fMain_VarsBox->GetTextHandle();
381:      n = fMain_VarsBox->GetLength();
382:      strncpy(buff, *h, n);
383:      buff[n] = '\0';
384:      lineStart = 0;
385:      // find the start of the sought line
386:      while (lineStart < n && LineNum > 0) {
387:        if (buff[lineStart] == '\r')
388:          LineNum – ;
389:        lineStart++;
```

```
390:    }
391:    lineEnd = lineStart;
392:    // the end end of the sought line
393:    while (lineEnd < n && buff[lineEnd] != '\r')
394:      lineEnd++;
395:    lineEnd - ;
396:    // skip over first three characters of the line
397:    lineStart += 3;
398:    lineSize = lineEnd - lineStart + 1;
399:    strncpy(s, buff + lineStart, lineSize);
400:    s[n] = '\0';
401:    return atol(s);
402: }
403:
404: /***************************************************************
405:  putVar
406:
407: store a variable in the Variables edit box.
408: ***************************************************************/
409:
410: void x_CMain::putVar(long x)
411:
412: {
413:    long selStart, selEnd;
414:    long lineNum;
415:    long numLines;
416:    char s[MaxEditLen+1];
417:    Handle h = (char**) &buff;
418:
419:    // locate the character position of the cursor
420:    fMain_VarsBox->GetSelection(&selStart, &selEnd);
421:    // turn off the selected text
422:    if (selStart != selEnd)
423:      fMain_VarsBox->SetSelection(selStart, selStart, TRUE);
424:    // get the line number where the cursor is located
425:    lineNum = fMain_VarsBox->FindLine(selStart);
426:    h = fMain_VarsBox->GetTextHandle();
427:    var[lineNum] = x;
428:    *h[0] = '\0';
429:    // insert single-letter variables in Variables box
430:    for (char c = 'A'; c <= 'Z'; c++) {
431:      sprintf(s, "%c: %ld\r", c, var[c - 'A']);
432:      strcat(*h, s);
433:    }
434:    fMain_VarsBox->SetTextHandle(h);
435: }
```

This listing shows the definitions of the member functions of class x_CMain. Lines 59 and 60 define the constants for the commands cmdCalc and cmdStore, respectively. I inserted the definition of constant MaxEditLen in line 61 to specify the limit of local string variables. The next subsections discuss the relevant member functions.

The Function *Ix_CMain*

The member function Ix_CMain (defined in lines 79 to 85) initializes the main window's document. I inserted the for loop statements in lines 83 and 84 to initialize the elements of data member var.

The Function *MakeNewWindow*

The member function MakeNewWindow (defined in lines 95 to 167) stores the pointers to the window and the pane in the variables itsWindow and itsMainPane, respectively. It also stores the addresses of the button controls in their respective data members. The function obtains these addresses by sending the C++ message FindViewByID to the window object. The arguments for these messages are the constants kMain_XXXXID, which are defined in file MainItems.h. I manually inserted the for loop statement in lines 163 to 166. This statement inserted the names and values of the single-letter variables in the Variables edit box. Line 164 uses function sprintf to create the string image of each line and to store that image in the local variable s. Line 165 inserts the character of variable s in the Variables edit box by sending that control the C++ message InsertTextPtr. The arguments for this message are s, strlen(s), and TRUE. This statement inserts the lines of the Variables edit box, one at a time.

The Function *DoCommand*

The member function DoCommand (defined in lines 216 to 230) has case labels in the switch statement to respond to the commands cmdCalc and cmdStore. The first statement after case cmdCalc invokes the member function DoCmdCalc. The first statement after case cmdStore invokes the member function DoCmdStore.

The Function *UpdateMenus*

The member function UpdateMenus (defined in lines 239 to 245) enables the custom commands by sending the C++ message EnableCmd, for each command, to the bartender object. The arguments for the sequence of EnableCmd messages are the constants cmdCalc and cmdStore.

The Function *DoCmdCalc*

The member function DoCmdCalc (defined in lines 254 to 330) performs the requested mathematical operation. The function performs the following tasks:

☐ Copies the string of the Operand 1 edit box into the variable s, using the statements in lines 265 to 267. This task involves using the text handle h and sending the C++ messages GetTextHandle and GetLength to the Operand 1 edit box.

☐ Examines the first character in variable s to determine whether or not it contains a letter. If this condition is true, the function DoCmdCalc uses the member function getVar to obtain the value associated with the single-letter variable. If the first character of variable s is not a letter, the function converts the characters of variable s into a long integer by calling the function atol. The function stores the resulting number (obtained from either member function getVar or function atol) in the local variable x.

☐ Copies the string of the Operand 2 edit box into the variable s, using the statements in lines 278 to 280. This task involves using the text handle h and sending the C++ messages GetTextHandle and GetLength to the Operand 2 edit box.

☐ Examines the first character in variable s to determine whether or not it contains a letter. If this condition is true, the function DoCmdCalc uses the member function getVar to obtain the value associated with the single-letter variable. If the first character of variable s is not a letter, the function converts the characters of variable s into a long integer by calling the function atol. The function stores the resulting number (obtained from either member function getVar or function atol) in the local variable y.

☐ Copies the string of the Operator edit box into the variable opStr, using the statements in lines 291 to 293. This task involves using the text handle h and sending the C++ messages GetTextHandle and GetLength to the Operator edit box.

☐ Resets the text in the error message control by sending it the C++ message SetTextString. This message writes the text Error Message: None to the error message static text control.

☐ Resets the error flag stored in variable bInError.

☐ Performs the requested mathematical operation using the multi-alternative if statement in lines 300 to 330. If the function detects an error, it assigns TRUE to the variable bInError and updates the message of error message static text. If there is no error, the function calculates the result and stores it in variable z.

☐ Determines whether there is no error using the `if` statement in line 333. If this condition is true, the function converts the value of variable z into a string image and writes that image to the Result edit box. This task involves sending the C++ message `SetTextPtr` to the Result edit box. The function also activates the Store button by sending it the C++ message `Activate`. By contrast, if there is an error, the function deactivates the Store button by sending it the C++ message `Deactivate`.

The Function *DoCmdStore*

The member function `DoCmdStore` (defined in lines 349 to 361) stores the current result in the currently selected single-letter variable. You select such a variable by placing the insertion cursor on the line associated with that variable. The function copies the text from the Result edit box into the local string variable s. This task involves using the text handle h and sending the C++ messages `GetTextHandle` and `GetLength` to the Result edit box. Line 360 contains the statement that invokes the member function `putVar` to store the result in the currently selected single-letter variable. The argument for calling function `putVar` is the expression `atol(s)`, which converts the string of variables into a long integer.

The Function *getVar*

The member function `getVar` (defined in lines 369 to 402) obtains the value associated with a variable by accessing the lines in the Variables box. The function first checks whether the argument for the parameter `LineNum` is within range before performing the following tasks:

☐ Copies the text of the Variables box into the data member `buff`. The statements in lines 380 to 383 perform this task.

☐ Locates the beginning of the targeted line. This task uses the statements in lines 384 to 390. These statements scan the characters in the member `buff` until the appropriate carriage return character is located.

☐ Locates the end of the targeted line. This task uses the statements in lines 391 to 395.

☐ Extracts and returns the long integer in the targeted line, using the statements in lines 397 to 401.

The Function *putVar*

The member function putVar (defined in lines 410 to 435) stores the argument for parameter x in the line of the Variables box that contains the current insertion point. The function performs the following tasks:

- ☐ Locates the current insertion point or the current selection. If there is selected text, the function deselects that text. This task uses the statements in lines 420 to 423.

- ☐ Finds the line of the Variables box that contains the current insertion point. This task sends the C++ message FindLine to the Variables box control and stores the result of the message in the variable lineNum.

- ☐ Obtains the handle of the text in the Variables box and stores it in the variable h.

- ☐ Stores the argument of parameter x in the element number lineNum of member var.

- ☐ Rebuilds the lines of the Variables box by using the statements in lines 428 to 432. These statements are contained in the for loop in line 430.

- ☐ Writes the new string image to the Variables box by sending the C++ message SetTextHandle to that control. The argument for this message is the variable h.

The following listing shows the source code for the AppCommands.h header file for the Button2 program project. This listing defines the constants cmdCalc and cmdStore, in lines 16 and 17, that support the custom commands.

```
 1:   /*************************************************************
 2:   MyCommands.h
 3:
 4:               Header File For Command Symbols
 5:
 6:      Copyright (c) 1994 My Software Inc. All rights reserved.
 7:
 8:   Generated by Visual Architect(TM)
 9:
10:   This file is regenerated each time.
11:
12:   *************************************************************/
13:
14:   #pragma once
15:
16:   #define cmdCalc     512
17:   #define cmdStore    513
```

The following listing shows the source code for the MainItems.h header file for the Button2 program project. The listing declares an untagged enumerated type which defines the identifiers kMain_*XXXX*Btn and kMain_*XXXX*BtnID.

```
 1:    /****************************************************************
 2:    MainItems.h
 3:
 4:                    Main Item Constants
 5:
 6:        Copyright (c) 1994 My Software Inc. All rights reserved.
 7:
 8:    Generated by Visual Architect(TM)
 9:
10:    This file is rewritten each time you generate code. You should
11:    not make changes to this file.
12:
13:    If you want to change how Visual Architect generates this file,
14:    you can change the template for this file. It is "Items.h" in
15:    the Visual Architect Templates folder.
16:
17:    ****************************************************************/
18:
19:    #pragma once
20:
21:
22:        //     Item numbers for each item.
23:        //
24:        //     Use TCLGetItemPointer (ViewUtilities) to convert these
25:        //     item numbers to a pointer to the named item.
26:
27:    enum
28:    {
29:        Main_Begin_,
30:        kMain_Operand1Lbl = 1,
31:        kMain_Operand1LblID = 1L,
32:        kMain_OperatorLbl = 2,
33:        kMain_OperatorLblID = 2L,
34:        kMain_Operand2Lbl = 3,
35:        kMain_Operand2LblID = 3L,
36:        kMain_ResutLbl = 4,
37:        kMain_ResutLblID = 4L,
38:        kMain_Operand1Box = 5,
39:        kMain_Operand1BoxID = 5L,
40:        kMain_OperatorBox = 6,
41:        kMain_OperatorBoxID = 6L,
42:        kMain_Operand2Box = 7,
43:        kMain_Operand2BoxID = 7L,
44:        kMain_ResultBox = 8,
45:        kMain_ResultBoxID = 8L,
46:        kMain_ErrMsgLbl = 9,
47:        kMain_ErrMsgLblID = 9L,
48:        kMain_VarsBox = 10,
49:        kMain_VarsBoxID = 10L,
50:        kMain_VarLbl = 11,
51:        kMain_VarLblID = 11L,
```

817

```
52:        kMain_CalcBtn = 12,
53:        kMain_CalcBtnID = 12L,
54:        kMain_StoreBtn = 13,
55:        kMain_StoreBtnID = 13L,
56:        kMain_QuitBtn = 14,
57:        kMain_QuitBtnID = 14L,
58:        Main_End_
59: };
```

Answers to Day 18, "Grouped Controls"

Quiz

1. False. The check box can replace the two radio controls only if these controls offer opposite alternatives.

2. True.

3. True. Each check box can be independently toggled.

4. False. Radio controls in a logical group are mutually exclusive.

5. False. The runtime system assigns a default group ID which is adequate for radio controls in a single group.

Exercise

Here is the source code for the x_CMain.h header file for the Group3 program project. The bold lines indicate the statements that must be manually inserted.

```
1:  /****************************************************************
2:   x_CMain.h
3:
4:              Header File For CMain Lower-Layer Document Class
5:
6:       Copyright (c) 1994 My Software Inc. All rights reserved.
7:
8:  Generated by Visual Architect(TM)
9:
10: This file is rewritten each time you generate code. You should
11: not make changes to this file; changes should go in the My.h
12: file, instead.
13:
14: If you want to change how Visual Architect generates this file,
15: you can change the template for this file. It is "_Doc.h" in
16: the Visual Architect Templates folder.
```

```
17:     *****************************************************************/
18:
19:     #pragma once
20:
21:     #include "CSaver.h"
22:     class CStaticText;
23:     class CDialogText;
24:     class CButton;
25:     class CRectOvalButton;
26:     class CRadioControl;
27:     class CCheckBox;
28:
29:     #include "ItsContentsClass.h"
30:
31:     #define x_CMain_super      CSaver<ITSCONTENTSCLASS>
32:     #define MaxEditLen 10
33:
34:     class CFile;
35:
36:     class x_CMain : public x_CMain_super
37:
38:     {
39:     public:
40:
41:         TCL_DECLARE_CLASS
42:
43:         enum radixMode { decRadix, hexRadix, octalRadix };
44:
45:         // Pointers to panes in window
46:         CStaticText     *fMain_IntLbl;
47:         CDialogText     *fMain_IntBox;
48:         CButton         *fMain_QuitBtn;
49:         CRectOvalButton *fMain_RadixRect;
50:         CStaticText     *fMain_RadixLbl;
51:         CRadioControl   *fMain_DecRbt;
52:         CRadioControl   *fMain_HexRbt;
53:         CRadioControl   *fMain_OctRbt;
54:         CCheckBox       *fMain_Bit0Chk;
55:         CCheckBox       *fMain_Bit1Chk;
56:         CCheckBox       *fMain_Bit2Chk;
57:         CCheckBox       *fMain_Bit3Chk;
58:         CCheckBox       *fMain_Bit4Chk;
59:         CCheckBox       *fMain_Bit5Chk;
60:         CCheckBox       *fMain_Bit6Chk;
61:         CCheckBox       *fMain_Bit7Chk;
62:         CButton         *fMain_UpdateBtn;
63:
64:         radixMode fRadix;
65:
66:         void    Ix_CMain(void);
67:
68:         virtual   void   DoCommand(long theCommand);
69:         virtual   void   UpdateMenus(void);
70:
71:     protected:
72:         virtual void    MakeNewWindow(void);
```

```
73:
74:        virtual void    FailOpen(CFile *aFile);
75:        virtual void    PositionWindow(void);
76:
77:        virtual void    DoCmdDecRadix(void);
78:        virtual void    DoCmdHexRadix(void);
79:        virtual void    DoCmdOctalRadix(void);
80:        virtual void    DoCmdUpdateInt(void);
81:
82:        int calcInt();
83:    };
84:
85:    #define    CVueCMain    128
```

Here is the source code for the x_CMain.cp implementation file for the Group3 program project. The bold lines indicate the statements that must be manually inserted.

```
1:    /****************************************************************
2:    x_CMain.c
3:
4:                    CMain Document Class
5:
6:        Copyright (c) 1994 My Software Inc. All rights reserved.
7:
8:    Generated by Visual Architect(TM) 3:58 PM Fri, Jun 17, 1994
9:
10:   This file is rewritten each time you generate code. You should
11:   not make changes to this file; changes should go in the My.c
12:   file, instead.
13:
14:   If you want to change how Visual Architect generates this file,
15:   you can change the template for this file. It is "_Doc_cp" in
16:   the Visual Architect Templates folder.
17:
18:   ****************************************************************/
19:
20:   #include "x_CMain.h"
21:
22:   #include "CMain.h"
23:
24:   #include "MainItems.h"
25:
26:   #include "ViewUtilities.h"
27:   #include "CApp.h"
28:
29:   #include <CApplication.h>
30:   #include <CBartender.h>
31:   #include <Commands.h>
32:   #include <Constants.h>
33:   #include <CDecorator.h>
34:   #include <CDesktop.h>
35:   #include <CFile.h>
36:   #include <TBUtilities.h>
37:   #include <CWindow.h>
38:
```

```
39:    extern CApplication *gApplication;   /* The application */
40:    extern CDecorator     *gDecorator;   /* Decorator for arranging
41:                                             windows      */
42:    extern CDesktop         *gDesktop;   /* The visible Desktop */
43:    extern CBartender     *gBartender;   /* Manages all menus */
44:
45:    #include "CStaticText.h"
46:    #include "CDialogText.h"
47:    #include "CButton.h"
48:    #include "CRectOvalButton.h"
49:    #include "CRadioControl.h"
50:    #include "CCheckBox.h"
51:
52:        // Define symbols for commands handled by this class
53:        // Prevents a recompile every time any command changed.
54:
55:    #define cmdDecRadix 515
56:    #define cmdHexRadix 516
57:    #define cmdOctalRadix 517
58:    #define cmdUpdateInt 526
59:
60:
61:    TCL_DEFINE_CLASS_M1(x_CMain, x_CMain_super);
62:
63:    /**** C O N S T R U C T I O N / D E S T R U C T I O N
64:                                          M E T H O D S ****/
65:
66:
67:    /*****************************************************************
68:      Ix_CMain
69:
70:    Initialize the document
71:    *****************************************************************/
72:
73:    void x_CMain::Ix_CMain()
74:
75:    {
76:        IDocument(gApplication, TRUE);
77:
78:        // Initialize data members below.
79:        fRadix = decRadix;
80:    }
81:
82:
83:    /*****************************************************************
84:      MakeNewWindow
85:
86:    Create a new, empty window. Subclass may override to populate
87:    the new window.
88:    *****************************************************************/
89:
90:    void x_CMain::MakeNewWindow(void)
91:
92:    {
93:      itsWindow = TCLGetNamedWindow("\pMain", this);
94:
95:      itsMainPane = (CPane*) TCLGetItemPointer(itsWindow, 0);
```

```
96:
97:      // Initialize pointers to the subpanes in the window
98:
99:      fMain_IntLbl = (CStaticText*)
100:               itsWindow->FindViewByID(kMain_IntLblID);
101:     ASSERT(member(fMain_IntLbl, CStaticText));
102:
103:     fMain_IntBox = (CDialogText*)
104:               itsWindow->FindViewByID(kMain_IntBoxID);
105:     ASSERT(member(fMain_IntBox, CDialogText));
106:
107:     fMain_QuitBtn = (CButton*)
108:               itsWindow->FindViewByID(kMain_QuitBtnID);
109:     ASSERT(member(fMain_QuitBtn, CButton));
110:
111:     fMain_RadixRect = (CRectOvalButton*)
112:               itsWindow->FindViewByID(kMain_RadixRectID);
113:     ASSERT(member(fMain_RadixRect, CRectOvalButton));
114:
115:     fMain_RadixLbl = (CStaticText*)
116:               itsWindow->FindViewByID(kMain_RadixLblID);
117:     ASSERT(member(fMain_RadixLbl, CStaticText));
118:
119:     fMain_DecRbt = (CRadioControl*)
120:               itsWindow->FindViewByID(kMain_DecRbtID);
121:     ASSERT(member(fMain_DecRbt, CRadioControl));
122:
123:     fMain_HexRbt = (CRadioControl*)
124:               itsWindow->FindViewByID(kMain_HexRbtID);
125:     ASSERT(member(fMain_HexRbt, CRadioControl));
126:
127:     fMain_OctRbt = (CRadioControl*)
128:               itsWindow->FindViewByID(kMain_OctRbtID);
129:     ASSERT(member(fMain_OctRbt, CRadioControl));
130:
131:     fMain_Bit0Chk = (CCheckBox*)
132:               itsWindow->FindViewByID(kMain_Bit0ChkID);
133:     ASSERT(member(fMain_Bit0Chk, CCheckBox));
134:
135:     fMain_Bit1Chk = (CCheckBox*)
136:               itsWindow->FindViewByID(kMain_Bit1ChkID);
137:     ASSERT(member(fMain_Bit1Chk, CCheckBox));
138:
139:     fMain_Bit2Chk = (CCheckBox*)
140:               itsWindow->FindViewByID(kMain_Bit2ChkID);
141:     ASSERT(member(fMain_Bit2Chk, CCheckBox));
142:
143:     fMain_Bit3Chk = (CCheckBox*)
144:               itsWindow->FindViewByID(kMain_Bit3ChkID);
145:     ASSERT(member(fMain_Bit3Chk, CCheckBox));
146:
147:     fMain_Bit4Chk = (CCheckBox*)
148:               itsWindow->FindViewByID(kMain_Bit4ChkID);
149:     ASSERT(member(fMain_Bit4Chk, CCheckBox));
150:
```

```
151:    fMain_Bit5Chk = (CCheckBox*)
152:                itsWindow->FindViewByID(kMain_Bit5ChkID);
153:    ASSERT(member(fMain_Bit5Chk, CCheckBox));
154:
155:    fMain_Bit6Chk = (CCheckBox*)
156:                itsWindow->FindViewByID(kMain_Bit6ChkID);
157:    ASSERT(member(fMain_Bit6Chk, CCheckBox));
158:
159:    fMain_Bit7Chk = (CCheckBox*)
160:                itsWindow->FindViewByID(kMain_Bit7ChkID);
161:    ASSERT(member(fMain_Bit7Chk, CCheckBox));
162:
163:    fMain_UpdateBtn = (CButton*)
164:                itsWindow->FindViewByID(kMain_UpdateBtnID);
165:    ASSERT(member(fMain_UpdateBtn, CButton));
166:
167:    fMain_DecRbt->SetValue(BUTTON_ON);
168:    fMain_IntBox->SetTextString("\p0");
169:
170:  }
171:
172:
173:  /****************************************************************
174:    FailOpen {OVERRIDE}
175:
176:  Fail if file already open in this application.
177:
178:  This function calls the application's FileAlreadyOpen function
179:  and fails quietly if the file is open.
180:
181:  Note that open may also fail if the file is open in
182:  another application. This will cause a failure in open,
183:  but you may wish to override this function to detect this
184:  case and provide a more meaningful error message than -49.
185:  ****************************************************************/
186:
187:  void x_CMain::FailOpen(CFile *aFile)
188:
189:  {
190:      /* Only the application knows        */
191:      if (((CApp*)gApplication)->FileAlreadyOpen(aFile))
192:          Failure(kSilentErr, 0);
193:  }
194:
195:
196:  /****************************************************************
197:    PositionWindow
198:
199:  The default method in CSaver calls the the decorator, which
200:  staggers and resizes the window. Since the window has already
201:  been positioned when it is initialized from the view resource,
202:  we don't want to do this twice.
203:  ****************************************************************/
204:
205:  void    x_CMain::PositionWindow()
206:
```

```
207:    {
208:    }
209:
210:
211:
212:
213:    /****************************************************************
214:     DoCommand {OVERRIDE}
215:
216:    Dispatch Visual Architect-specified actions.
217:    ****************************************************************/
218:
219:    void x_CMain::DoCommand(long theCommand)
220:
221:    {
222:        switch (theCommand)
223:        {
224:            case cmdDecRadix:
225:                DoCmdDecRadix();
226:                break;
227:            case cmdHexRadix:
228:                DoCmdHexRadix();
229:                break;
230:            case cmdOctalRadix:
231:                DoCmdOctalRadix();
232:                break;
233:            case cmdUpdateInt:
234:                DoCmdUpdateInt();
235:                break;
236:            default:
237:                CDocument::DoCommand(theCommand);
238:        }
239:    }
240:
241:
242:    /****************************************************************
243:     UpdateMenus {OVERRIDE}
244:
245:    Enable menus which generate commands handled by this class.
246:    ****************************************************************/
247:
248:    void x_CMain::UpdateMenus()
249:
250:    {
251:        CDocument::UpdateMenus();
252:        gBartender->EnableCmd(cmdDecRadix);
253:        gBartender->EnableCmd(cmdHexRadix);
254:        gBartender->EnableCmd(cmdOctalRadix);
255:        gBartender->EnableCmd(cmdUpdateInt);
256:    }
257:
258:
259:    /****************************************************************
260:     DoCmdDecRadix
261:
262:    Respond to cmdDecRadix command.
263:    ****************************************************************/
```

```
264:
265:   void x_CMain::DoCmdDecRadix()
266:
267:   {
268:     char s[MaxEditLen+1];
269:     // Subclass must override this function to
270:     // handle the command
271:     sprintf(s, "%d", calcInt());
272:     fMain_IntBox->SetTextPtr(s, strlen(s));
273:     fRadix = decRadix;
274:   }
275:
276:
277:   /****************************************************************
278:    DoCmdHexRadix
279:
280:   Respond to cmdHexRadix command.
281:   ****************************************************************/
282:
283:   void x_CMain::DoCmdHexRadix()
284:
285:   {
286:     char s[MaxEditLen+1];
287:     // Subclass must override this function to
288:     // handle the command
289:     sprintf(s, "%X", calcInt());
290:     fMain_IntBox->SetTextPtr(s, strlen(s));
291:     fRadix = hexRadix;
292:   }
293:
294:
295:   /****************************************************************
296:    DoCmdOctalRadix
297:
298:   Respond to cmdOctalRadix command.
299:   ****************************************************************/
300:
301:   void x_CMain::DoCmdOctalRadix()
302:
303:   {
304:     char s[MaxEditLen+1];
305:     // Subclass must override this function to
306:     // handle the command
307:     sprintf(s, "%o", calcInt());
308:     fMain_IntBox->SetTextPtr(s, strlen(s));
309:     fRadix = octalRadix;
310:   }
311:
312:
313:   /****************************************************************
314:    DoCmdUpdateInt
315:
316:   Respond to cmdUpdateInt command.
317:   ****************************************************************/
318:
319:   void x_CMain::DoCmdUpdateInt()
```

```
320:
321: {
322:   char s[MaxEditLen+1];
323:   int x;
324:   // Subclass must override this function to
325:   // handle the command
326:   x = calcInt();
327:   // create string image of integer
328:   switch (fRadix) {
329:     case decRadix:
330:       sprintf(s, "%d", x);
331:       break;
332:
333:     case hexRadix:
334:       sprintf(s, "%X", x);
335:       break;
336:
337:     case octalRadix:
338:       sprintf(s, "%o", x);
339:       break;
340:   }
341:   // write string image to the edit box
342:   fMain_IntBox->SetTextPtr(s, strlen(s));
343: }
344:
345: /*************************************************************
346:   calcInt
347:
348: Toggle a bit.
349: *************************************************************/
350:
351: int x_CMain::calcInt()
352: {
353:   int x;
354:
355:   // calculate the new integer value
356:   x = 0;
357:   if (fMain_Bit0Chk->IsChecked())
358:     x += 1;
359:   if (fMain_Bit1Chk->IsChecked())
360:     x += 2;
361:   if (fMain_Bit2Chk->IsChecked())
362:     x += 4;
363:   if (fMain_Bit3Chk->IsChecked())
364:     x += 8;
365:   if (fMain_Bit4Chk->IsChecked())
366:     x += 16;
367:   if (fMain_Bit5Chk->IsChecked())
368:     x += 32;
369:   if (fMain_Bit6Chk->IsChecked())
370:     x += 64;
371:   if (fMain_Bit7Chk->IsChecked())
372:     x += 128;
373:
374:   return x;
375: }
```

Here is the source code for the AppCommands.h header file for the Group3 program project:

```
 1:   /*****************************************************************
 2:     MyCommands.h
 3:
 4:                 Header File For Command Symbols
 5:
 6:         Copyright (c) 1994 My Software Inc. All rights reserved.
 7:
 8:     Generated by Visual Architect(TM)
 9:
10:     This file is regenerated each time.
11:
12:     *****************************************************************/
13:
14:     #pragma once
15:
16:     #define cmdDecRadix     515
17:     #define cmdHexRadix     516
18:     #define cmdOctalRadix   517
19:     #define cmdUpdateInt    526
```

Here is the source code for the MainItems.h header file for the Group3 program project:

```
 1:   /*****************************************************************
 2:     MainItems.h
 3:
 4:                     Main Item Constants
 5:
 6:         Copyright (c) 1994 My Software Inc. All rights reserved.
 7:
 8:     Generated by Visual Architect(TM)
 9:
10:     This file is rewritten each time you generate code. You should
11:     not make changes to this file; changes should go in the My.h
12:     file, instead.
13:
14:     If you want to change how Visual Architect generates this file,
15:     you can change the template for this file. It is "_Doc.h" in
16:     the Visual Architect Templates folder.
17:     *****************************************************************/
18:
19:     #pragma once
20:
21:
22:         //      Item numbers for each item.
23:         //
24:         //      Use TCLGetItemPointer (ViewUtilities) to convert these
25:         //      item numbers to a pointer to the named item.
26:
27:     enum
28:     {
29:         Main_Begin_,
30:         kMain_IntLbl = 1,
31:         kMain_IntLblID = 1L,
```

```
32:        kMain_IntBox = 2,
33:        kMain_IntBoxID = 2L,
34:        kMain_QuitBtn = 3,
35:        kMain_QuitBtnID = 3L,
36:        kMain_RadixRect = 4,
37:        kMain_RadixRectID = -2147483644L,
38:        kMain_RadixLbl = 5,
39:        kMain_RadixLblID = 5L,
40:        kMain_DecRbt = 6,
41:        kMain_DecRbtID = 1075838982L,
42:        kMain_HexRbt = 7,
43:        kMain_HexRbtID = 1075838983L,
44:        kMain_OctRbt = 8,
45:        kMain_OctRbtID = 1075838984L,
46:        kMain_Bit0Chk = 9,
47:        kMain_Bit0ChkID = 536870921L,
48:        kMain_Bit1Chk = 10,
49:        kMain_Bit1ChkID = 536870922L,
50:        kMain_Bit2Chk = 11,
51:        kMain_Bit2ChkID = 536870923L,
52:        kMain_Bit3Chk = 12,
53:        kMain_Bit3ChkID = 536870924L,
54:        kMain_Bit4Chk = 13,
55:        kMain_Bit4ChkID = 536870925L,
56:        kMain_Bit5Chk = 14,
57:        kMain_Bit5ChkID = 536870926L,
58:        kMain_Bit6Chk = 15,
59:        kMain_Bit6ChkID = 536870927L,
60:        kMain_Bit7Chk = 16,
61:        kMain_Bit7ChkID = 536870928L,
62:        kMain_UpdateBtn = 17,
63:        kMain_UpdateBtnID = 17L,
64:     Main_End_
65:  };
```

Answers to Day 19, "The List Box Control"

Quiz

1. False. The list box supports multiple-item selections.

2. Use the member function SelectCell to select a cell from within the program code.

3. Yes, using the member function DeselectCell.

4. You obtain the current number of list box items by using the member function GetRowCount.

5. The member function `GetCellText` returns a string in the form `"rr, cc"` where *rr* and *cc* represent the row and column numbers of the cells.

6. The program would display a list of strings with the pattern `"00, 00"`, `"01, 00"`, `"02, 00"` and so on, regardless of the data in the dynamic array (which is accessed by data member `fArr`).

Answers to Day 20, "The Scroll Bar and Pop-up Menu Controls"

Quiz

1. False.

2. False.

3. False. The member function `SetValue` also moves the location of the thumb box.

4. False. You can associate custom menus.

Answers to Day 21, "The Dialog Box"

Quiz

1. True.

2. False.

3. The member function `AddDITLRadioBtn` adds a radio control.

4. False. The Visual Architect utility performs this association for you.

Glossary

address: The location of each memory byte in the computer's memory. The lowest memory address is 0. The highest memory address depends on the amount of memory in a computer.

ancestor class: A class that is one or more levels higher in the class hierarchy than a referenced class.

argument: The value that is passed to a parameter of a function or a procedure.

array: A collection of variables that share the same name and use one or more indices to access an individual member.

ASCII: Acronym for American Standard Code for Information Interchange.

ASCII file: A file that contains readable text. ASCII files also are called *text files*.

backup file: A duplicate copy of a file that protects your work in case you damage the text or data in the main file.

base class: The root of a class hierarchy. A base class has no parent class.

Boolean: Synonymous with logical (true or false). The word *Boolean* comes from the name of the English mathematician George Bool, who studied logical values and created the truth table.

bubblesort: The slowest and simplest method for ordering the elements of an array in ascending or descending order.

buffer: A memory location where transient data flows in and out.

bug: A common name for a logical program error.

.C: The extension of a C file.

class: A category of objects.

clipboard: A special memory area in the Macintosh environment that holds text you either copied or deleted.

Comb sort: A new and efficient method for sorting the elements of an array. This method is an improvement of the bubblesort method.

compiler: A tool that converts the source code of a program file into a binary object code file. The object code must be linked with other object files and library files to generate an executable file.

concatenation: The process of joining two or more strings by chaining their characters.

conditional loop: A loop that iterates until or while a tested condition is true.

constant: Information that remains fixed during the execution of a program.

.CP: The extension of a C++ source file used in THINK C++ projects.

crash: The state in which a computer seems to freeze and does not respond to the keyboard, mouse, or any other input device.

cursor: The blinking underline or block that appears on the screen to indicate where the next character you type will be inserted.

data member: The fields in a class that store data.

data processing: The manipulating and/or managing of information.

data record: A collection of data items that convey meaningful information. Your mailing address, for example, is a data record.

debug: To detect and remove logical errors in the program.

debugger: A tool that assists you in debugging the program. The C++ environment contains a powerful debugger.

default: A preselected action or value that is used when no other action or value is offered.

descendant class: Any child class derived from a parent class.

dialog box: A special pop-up screen that prompts you for input.

display adapter: The board inside a computer that assists in displaying text and graphics.

drag: The act of holding a mouse button down while moving the mouse. This action typically moves an object from one location to another.

element (of an array):   The member of an array that is accessed by specifying one or more indices.

file: The name of a location on a disk that contains a program, text, or other data.

file extension: The letters used by Macintosh files to identify the type of a file.

file I/O: File input and/or output.

filename: The name of a file that contains data or a program.

folder: A section or compartment of a hard, floppy, or electronic disk that contains files.

format: The image or map used to output data.

function: A subprogram that executes one or more statements and returns a single value.

global variable: A variable accessible to all functions and procedures in a program.

.H: The extension of a header file.

header file: A file that contains the declarations of constants, data types, function prototypes, and class declarations.

inheritance: The ability of a class to reuse data members and member functions in a parent class.

input: The data that a program obtains from the keyboard, disk drive, communication port, or any other input device.

I/O: Acronym for Input/Output.

linker: A tool that combines the various files generated by the compiler with the various library files to create the executable file.

local variable: A variable that is declared inside a function or procedure.

loop: A set of statements that are repeatedly executed.

Macintosh Toolbox: A set of simple functions and procedures that support the various operations of the Macintosh applications.

main module: The program section containing the function `main`.

math operator: A symbol that performs a mathematical operation, such as addition, subtraction, multiplication, division, and raising to powers.

matrix: A two-dimensional array. The elements of a matrix are accessed by specifying the row and column indices.

member function: A function that is a member in a class.

menu: A display that offers a set of options to select from.

menu-driven: A program that depends on one or more menus to perform its tasks, as guided by the user.

message: What an object-oriented program does to an object.

method: How an object-oriented program manipulates an object.

modulus: The integer remainder of a division.

multidimensional arrays: Arrays that have multiple subscripts.

nested loop: A loop inside another loop.

null string: An empty string.

numeric functions: A function that returns a numerical value.

object: An instance of a class.

object file: The output of the compiler. The linker combines various object and library files to create the executable file.

object-oriented programming (OOP): Programming techniques that focus on modeling objects and their operations.

open loop: A loop that in principle iterates indefinitely. In practice, most open loops use an exit mechanism located in a statement inside the loop.

order of operators: The priority of executing operations in an expression.

output device: A device that receives output. Common output devices are the screen, the printer, the disk drive, and the communication port. Some output devices also support input, such as the communication port and the disk drive.

palette: A set of possible colors.

parameter: A special variable that appears after the declaration of a function or procedure and that fine-tunes the operations of the function or procedure.

Pascal: A structured programming language that Apple Computer, Inc., used (with object-oriented language extensions) to first program the Macintosh Toolbox.

Pascal string: A string that holds up to 255 characters. The byte at index 0 stores the current length of the Pascal string.

passing by reference: The task of passing an argument to a function or procedure by providing its reference. Consequently, the parameter receiving the reference becomes an alias to the argument. Any changes made to the parameter inside the function or procedure also affect the argument.

passing by value: The task of passing an argument to a function or procedure by providing a copy of its value. Consequently, any changes made to the parameter inside the function or procedure do not affect the argument.

pixel: The short name for *picture element.*

pointer: A special variable that stores the address of another variable or system information.

polymorphism: The feature of object-oriented programming that supports abstract functionality.

precedence of operators: *See* **order of operators**.

procedure: A function that performs a task but returns no value. Procedures are supported formally in languages such as Pascal. In C and C++, a void function is equivalent to a procedure.

program: A collection of executable statements or instructions.

programming language: The high-level human interface for communicating with a machine.

random access file: A file that permits you to access its fixed-length records for input and output by specifying the record number. Random access files are suitable for databases.

.RSRC: The extension of a resource file.

record: A unit of storing information in a data file. Typically, text files have variable-length records. Random access files contain fixed-length records.

relational operators: Symbols that compare two compatible data items and return a logical value.

resource file: A file that defines resources to be used by one or more Macintosh applications. Resource files can be shared by applications written in different programming languages. Resources include strings, keyboard, menu, controls, and dialog box resources.

scientific notation: A special form for representing numbers by specifying the mantissa and the exponent. In a number such as 1.23E+44, the 1.23 is the mantissa and +44 is the exponent (the power of 10). Therefore, 1.23E+44 is a more convenient way to write 1.23×10^{44}.

sequential file: A file that stores readable text using variable-length records.

single-dimensional arrays: An array that requires a single subscript to access its elements.

sorting: The task of arranging the elements of an array in either ascending or descending order. The array is ordered using part or all of the value in each element.

static variable: A variable with a fixed memory location. Usually, static variables are declared in functions and are able to retain their values between function calls.

string: An array of characters that stores text.

string constant: A constant associated with a string literal.

string literal: A set of characters enclosed in a pair of double quotes.

string variable: A variable that stores a string of characters.

structure: A user-defined data type. C++ enables you to define a structure using the TYPE statement.

structured array: An array whose elements have a user-defined data type.

structured variable: A variable whose type is a user-defined data type.

subdirectory: A directory that is connected to a parent directory.

subscript: The index of an array.

syntax error: An error in writing a statement.

system hang: *See* **crash**.

text file: *See* **ASCII file**.

unary operator: Symbols that require only one operand.

user-defined data type: *See* **structure**.

user-defined functions: A function defined by a programmer to conceptually extend the C++ language and serve the host program.

variable: A tagged memory location that stores data.

variable-length record: A record with a varying number of bytes or characters.

variable-length string variables: A string variable that can accommodate a varying number of characters.

variable scope: The visibility of a variable in the different components of a program.

virtual function: A function that, when overridden by a descendant class, must have the same purpose and parameter list as the one in an ancestor class.

word: A unit of data storage that contains 2 bytes or 16 bits.

Index

Symbols

A

F

listings

SAMS
LEARNING
CENTER

SAMS
PUBLISHING

listings

M

X–Y–Z

Add to Your Sams Library Today with the Best Books for Programming, Operating Systems, and New Technologies

The easiest way to order is to pick up the phone and call

1-800-428-5331

between 9:00 a.m. and 5:00 p.m. EST.
For faster service please have your credit card available.

ISBN	Quantity	Description of Item	Unit Cost	Total Cost
0-672-30188-1		Tom Swan's C++ Primer (Book/Disk)	$34.95	
0-56686-155-1		Symantec C++ Programming for Macintosh, 2E (Book/Disk)	$45.00	
0-672-30519-4		Teach Yourself the Internet: Around the World in 21 Days	$24.99	
0-672-30520-8		Your Internet Consultant	$24.99	
0-672-30466-X		Internet Unleashed (Book/Disk)	$39.95	
0-672-30463-5		Becoming a Computer Animator (Book/Disk)	$39.99	
0-672-30513-5		Becoming a Computer Musician (Book/CD-ROM)	$39.99	
❑ 3 ½" Disk		Shipping and Handling: See information below.		
❑ 5 ¼" Disk		TOTAL		

Shipping and Handling: $4.00 for the first book, and $1.75 for each additional book. Floppy disk: add $1.75 for shipping and handling. If you need to have it NOW, we can ship product to you in 24 hours for an additional charge of approximately $18.00, and you will receive your item overnight or in two days. Overseas shipping and handling adds $2.00 per book and $8.00 for up to three disks. Prices subject to change. Call for availability and pricing information on latest editions.

201 W. 103rd Street, Indianapolis, Indiana 46290

1-800-428-5331 — Orders   1-800-835-3202 — FAX   1-800-858-7674 — Customer Service

Book ISBN 0-672-30610-7

Disk Offer

The programs in *Teach Yourself Mac C++ Programming in 21 Days* are available from the author. Fill out this form and enclose a check for $15.00 to receive a copy. Outside the U.S., please enclose a check for $20.00 in U.S. currency, drawn on a U.S. bank. Please make the check payable to Namir C. Shammas. Sorry, no credit card orders. Mail this form to:

Namir C. Shammas
3928 Margate Drive
Richmond, VA 23235

Name _____

Company (for company name) _____

Street_____

City_____

State/Province _____

ZIP or Postal Code _____

Country (outside the USA) _____

Disk format (check one):

5.25-inch _____   3.5-inch _____

GO AHEAD. PLUG YOURSELF INTO
MACMILLAN COMPUTER PUBLISHING.

Introducing the Macmillan Computer Publishing Forum on CompuServe®

Yes, it's true. Now, you can have CompuServe access to the same professional, friendly folks who have made computers easier for years. On the Macmillan Computer Publishing Forum, you'll find additional information on the topics covered by every Macmillan Computer Publishing imprint—including Que, Sams Publishing, New Riders Publishing, Alpha Books, Brady Books, Hayden Books, and Adobe Press. In addition, you'll be able to receive technical support and disk updates for the software produced by Que Software and Paramount Interactive, a division of the Paramount Technology Group. It's a great way to supplement the best information in the business.

WHAT CAN YOU DO ON THE MACMILLAN COMPUTER PUBLISHING FORUM?

Play an important role in the publishing process—and make our books better while you make your work easier:

- Leave messages and ask questions about Macmillan Computer Publishing books and software—you're guaranteed a response within 24 hours
- Download helpful tips and software to help you get the most out of your computer
- Contact authors of your favorite Macmillan Computer Publishing books through electronic mail
- Present your own book ideas
- Keep up to date on all the latest books available from each of Macmillan Computer Publishing's exciting imprints

JOIN NOW AND GET A FREE COMPUSERVE STARTER KIT!

To receive your free CompuServe Introductory Membership, call toll-free, **1-800-848-8199** and ask for representative **#597**. The Starter Kit Includes:

- Personal ID number and password
- $15 credit on the system
- Subscription to CompuServe Magazine

HERE'S HOW TO PLUG INTO MACMILLAN COMPUTER PUBLISHING:

Once on the CompuServe System, type any of these phrases to access the Macmillan Computer Publishing Forum:

GO MACMILLAN   **GO BRADY**
GO QUEBOOKS   **GO HAYDEN**
GO SAMS   **GO QUESOFT**
GO NEWRIDERS   **GO ALPHA**

Once you're on the CompuServe Information Service, be sure to take advantage of all of CompuServe's resources. CompuServe is home to more than 1,700 products and services—plus it has over 1.5 million members worldwide. You'll find valuable online reference materials, travel and investor services, electronic mail, weather updates, leisure-time games and hassle-free shopping (no jam-packed parking lots or crowded stores).

Seek out the hundreds of other forums that populate CompuServe. Covering diverse topics such as pet care, rock music, cooking, and political issues, you're sure to find others with the same concerns as you—and expand your knowledge at the same time.